WORKERS OF ALL COUNTRIES, UNITE!

LENIN

COLLECTED WORKS

31

THE RUSSIAN EDITION WAS PRINTED
IN ACCORDANCE WITH A DECISION
OF THE NINTH CONGRESS OF THE R.C.P.(B.)
AND THE SECOND CONGRESS OF SOVIETS
OF THE U.S.S.R.

ИНСТИТУТ МАРКСИЗМА-ЛЕНИНИЗМА при ЦК КПСС

В. И. ЛЕНИН

СОЧИНЕНИЯ

Издание четвертое

ГОСУДАРСТВЕННОЕ ИЗДАТЕЛЬСТВО
ПОЛИТИЧЕСКОЙ ЛИТЕРАТУРЫ
МОСКВА

V. I. LENIN

COLLECTED WORKS

VOLUME 31

April–December 1920

PROGRESS PUBLISHERS
MOSCOW

TRANSLATED FROM THE RUSSIAN
EDITED BY JULIUS KATZER

First printing 1966
Second printing 1974
Third printing 1977

11-17-78

Л $\frac{10102-066}{014(01)-77}$ 37–76

CONTENTS

ILLUSTRATIONS

PREFACE

Volume 31 contains Lenin's writings of the period between April and December 1920, during the conclusive defeat of the interventionists' basic forces in the war against the White Poles and Wrangel, the Entente's last puppets.

The bulk of the volume is made up of writings dealing with the defence of the Soviet Republic, the tasks of socialist construction, and problems of the international communist movement.

The volume includes *"Left-Wing" Communism—an Infantile Disorder* in which—from the experience of the history of Bolshevism, the three Russian revolutions, and the first years of the Soviet state—Lenin further developed the theory of the proletarian revolution and the dictatorship of the proletariat, set forth the strategy and the tactics of Leninism, and revealed the international significance of the Great October Socialist Revolution and the revolutionary experience of the Bolshevik Party. Lenin showed that international opportunism was the chief enemy within the working-class movement, branded the Second International's leaders as accomplices in the imperialists' banditry, and subjected to an exhaustive criticism the anti-Marxist sectarian tactics of the "Left-wing" Communists in the international working-class movement.

A considerable part of the volume consists of documents pertaining to preparations for the Second Congress of the Communist International, as well as Lenin's reports and speeches to the Congress. Among these are: "Preliminary Draft Theses on the National and the Colonial Questions", "Preliminary Draft Theses on the Agrarian Question",

"Theses on the Fundamental Tasks of the Second Congress of the Communist International", "The Terms of Admission into the Communist International", "Report on the International Situation and the Fundamental Tasks of the Communist International, July 19, 1920" and others. These documents substantiated the programme and the organisational and tactical principles of the world communist movement.

The documents: "Letter to the Austrian Communists", "Letter to the German and the French Workers. Regarding the Discussion on the Second Congress of the Communist International", "On the Struggle Within the Italian Socialist Party" reflect the struggle waged by Lenin for the implementation of the Comintern's fundamental decisions in the world working-class movement.

In speeches on international and home situation delivered at the Ninth All-Russia Conference of the Russian Communist Party (Bolsheviks), the Moscow Gubernia Conference, and trade union congresses, Lenin unmasked the Entente's new plan to strangle Soviet Russia with the aid of bourgeois-landowner Poland and Wrangel, and called upon the working class and the working masses to bend every effort to organise for victory over the interventionists, and summed up the Red Army's successes in smashing the military forces of Wrangel and bourgeois-landowner Poland.

A group of documents, viz., "Report on Concessions Delivered to the R.C.P.(B.) Group at the Eighth Congress of Soviets, December 21, 1920", "Report on the Work of the Council of People's Commissars, December 22, 1920", "Draft Resolution of the Eighth Congress of Soviets on the Report on Electrification" and others deal with questions of state and economic construction and substantiate the part to be played by electrification in the restoration and socialist development of the national economy.

In the draft resolution for the Proletcult Congress, entitled "On Proletarian Culture", and in "Speech Delivered at an All-Russia Conference of Political Education Workers of Gubernia and Uyezd Education Departments, November 3, 1920" Lenin criticised Proletcult's distortion of the Party line in the sphere of culture, showed the role of the

Party and the proletarian state in building up a socialist culture, set forth the Marxist attitude towards the finest achievements of human thought and culture, and defined the tasks confronting art and education in the struggle for the consolidation of the proletariat's dictatorship.

In his speech "The Tasks of the Youth Leagues", delivered at the Third All-Russia Congress of the Russian Young Communist League on October 2, 1920, Lenin named the fundamental task confronting the League—the communist upbringing of the rising generation, revealed the close links between that work and the struggle waged by the proletariat and all working people to build up a communist society, and formulated the principles of communist morality.

This volume contains twenty-one documents first published in the Fourth (Russian) Edition of the *Collected Works*. In his "Speech to Men of the Red Army Leaving for the Polish Front, May 5, 1920", and in his "Speech at an Enlarged Conference of Workers and Red Army Men in Rogozhsko-Simonovsky District of Moscow, May 13, 1920" Lenin called upon the workers and Red Army men to spare no effort to bring about the defeat of the enemy.

The documents, "To the Indian Revolutionary Association", "Reply to a Letter from the Joint Provisional Committee for the Communist Party of Britain", "Article Twenty of the Terms of Admission into the Communist International"—all deal with problems of the world communist movement.

A number of documents: "Speech at a Meeting Dedicated to the Laying of the Foundation Stone of a Monument to Liberated Labour, May 1, 1920", "To the Poor Peasants of the Ukraine", "Telegram to the Soviet Government of the Ukraine and the General Headquarters of the Southern Front", "Speech Delivered at a Meeting of Cells' Secretaries of the Moscow Organisation of the R.C.P.(B.), November 26, 1920", "Concluding Remarks" to the report at a general meeting of Communists of Zamoskvorechye District, November 29, 1920, "Telegram to the Chairman of the Revolutionary Military Committee of Armenia" have as their subject the tasks set by the rehabilitation and development of the national economy.

The following documents were published for the first time in the Fourth (Russian) Edition of the *Collected Works*: "Draft Resolution on 'The Tasks of the Trade Unions, and the Methods of Their Accomplishment'" and "Speech Delivered at the Moscow Gubernia Conference of the R.C.P.(B.) on Elections to the Moscow Committee, November 21, 1920". These deal with problems of Party and trade union work, and the foreign policy of the Soviet Government.

V. I. LENIN
May 1920

"LEFT-WING" COMMUNISM—AN INFANTILE DISORDER*[1]

Written in April-May 1920

Published in pamphlet form, in June 1920

Published according to the text of the pamphlet, as checked against the manuscript

* Revised translation by Julius Katzer.

1

Детская болезнь „левизны" в коммунизме

I. В каком смысле можно говорить о международном значении русской революции?

Первые месяцы после завоевания пролетариатом политической власти в России (25.X–7.XI 1917) могло казаться, что громадные отличия отсталой России от передовых западноевропейских стран сделают революцию пролетариата в этих последних очень мало похожей на нашу. Теперь мы имеем уже перед собой очень порядочный международный опыт, который говорит с полнейшей определённостью, что некоторые основные черты нашей революции имеют не местное, не национально-особенное, не русское только, а международное значение. И я говорю здесь о международном значении не в широком смысле слова: не некоторые, а все основные и многие второстепенные черты нашей революции имеют международное значение в смысле воздействия ее на все страны. Нет, в самом узком смысле слова, т. е. понимая под международным значением международную значимость или историческую неизбежность повторения в международном масштабе того, что было у нас, приходится признать такое значение за некоторыми основными чертами нашей революции.

Конечно, было бы величайшей ошибкой преувеличить эту истину, распространить ее не только на некоторые из основных черт нашей революции. Точно так же было бы ошибочно упустить из виду, что после победы пролетарской революции хотя бы в одной из передовых стран наступит, по всей вероятности, крутой перелом, именно: Россия сделается вскоре после этого не образцовой, а опять отсталой (в „советском" и в социалистическом смысле) страной.

The first page of V. I. Lenin's manuscript
"Left-Wing" Communism—an Infantile Disorder,
April-May 1920

Reduced

I
IN WHAT SENSE WE CAN SPEAK OF THE INTERNATIONAL SIGNIFICANCE OF THE RUSSIAN REVOLUTION

In the first months after the proletariat in Russia had won political power (October 25 [November 7], 1917), it might have seemed that the enormous difference between backward Russia and the advanced countries of Western Europe would lead to the proletarian revolution in the latter countries bearing very little resemblance to ours. We now possess quite considerable international experience, which shows very definitely that certain fundamental features of our revolution have a significance that is not local, or peculiarly national, or Russian alone, but international. I am not speaking here of international significance in the broad sense of the term: not merely several but all the primary features of our revolution, and many of its secondary features, are of international significance in the meaning of its effect on all countries. I am speaking of it in the narrowest sense of the word, taking international significance to mean the international validity or the historical inevitability of a repetition, on an international scale, of what has taken place in our country. It must be admitted that certain fundamental features of our revolution do possess that significance.

It would, of course, be grossly erroneous to exaggerate this truth and to extend it beyond certain fundamental features of our revolution. It would also be erroneous to lose sight of the fact that, soon after the victory of the proletarian revolution in at least one of the advanced countries, a sharp change will probably come about: Russia will cease to be the model and will once again become a backward country (in the "Soviet" and the socialist sense).

At the present moment in history, however, it is the Russian model that reveals to *all* countries something—and something highly significant—of their near and inevitable future. Advanced workers in all lands have long realised this; more often than not, they have grasped it with their revolutionary class instinct rather than realised it. Herein lies the international "significance" (in the narrow sense of the word) of Soviet power, and of the fundamentals of Bolshevik theory and tactics. The "revolutionary" leaders of the Second International, such as Kautsky in Germany and Otto Bauer and Friedrich Adler in Austria, have failed to understand this, which is why they have proved to be reactionaries and advocates of the worst kind of opportunism and social treachery. Incidentally, the anonymous pamphlet entitled *The World Revolution* (*Weltrevolution*), which appeared in Vienna in 1919 (*Sozialistische Bücherei*, Heft 11; Ignaz Brand*), very clearly reveals their entire thinking and their entire range of ideas, or, rather, the full extent of their stupidity, pedantry, baseness and betrayal of working-class interests—and that, moreover, under the guise of "defending" the idea of "world revolution".

We shall, however, deal with this pamphlet in greater detail some other time. We shall here note only one more point: in bygone days, when he was still a Marxist and not a renegade, Kautsky, dealing with the question as an historian, foresaw the possibility of a situation arising in which the revolutionary spirit of the Russian proletariat would provide a model to Western Europe. This was in 1902, when Kautsky wrote an article for the revolutionary *Iskra*,[2] entitled "The Slavs and Revolution". Here is what he wrote in the article:

"At the present time [in contrast with 1848]** it would seem that not only have the Slavs entered the ranks of the revolutionary nations, but that the centre of revolutionary thought and revolutionary action is shifting more and more to the Slavs. The revolutionary centre is shifting from the West to the East. In the first half of the nineteenth

---

* Ignaz Brand, *Socialist Library*, Vol. 11.—*Ed.*

** Interpolations in brackets within quotations are by Lenin, unless otherwise indicated.—*Ed.*

century it was located in France, at times in England. In 1848 Germany too joined the ranks of the revolutionary nations.... The new century has begun with events which suggest the idea that we are approaching a further shift of the revolutionary centre, namely, to Russia.... Russia, which has borrowed so much revolutionary initiative from the West, is now perhaps herself ready to serve the West as a source of revolutionary energy. The Russian revolutionary movement that is now flaring up will perhaps prove to be the most potent means of exorcising the spirit of flabby philistinism and coldly calculating politics that is beginning to spread in our midst, and it may cause the fighting spirit and the passionate devotion to our great ideals to flare up again. To Western Europe, Russia has long ceased to be a bulwark of reaction and absolutism. I think the reverse is true today. Western Europe is becoming Russia's bulwark of reaction and absolutism.... The Russian revolutionaries might perhaps have coped with the tsar long ago had they not been compelled at the same time to fight his ally—European capital. Let us hope that this time they will succeed in coping with both enemies, and that the new 'Holy Alliance' will collapse more rapidly than its predecessors did. However the present struggle in Russia may end, the blood and suffering of the martyrs whom, unfortunately, it will produce in too great numbers, will not have been in vain. They will nourish the shoots of social revolution throughout the civilised world and make them grow more luxuriantly and rapidly. In 1848 the Slavs were a killing frost which blighted the flowers of the people's spring. Perhaps they are now destined to be the storm that will break the ice of reaction and irresistibly bring with it a new and happy spring for the nations" (Karl Kautsky, "The Slavs and Revolution", *Iskra*, Russian Social-Democratic revolutionary newspaper, No. 18, March 10, 1902).

How well Karl Kautsky wrote eighteen years ago!

II

AN ESSENTIAL CONDITION OF THE BOLSHEVIKS' SUCCESS

It is, I think, almost universally realised at present that the Bolsheviks could not have retained power for two and a half months, let alone two and a half years, without the most rigorous and truly iron discipline in our Party, or without the fullest and unreserved support from the entire mass of the working class, that is, from all thinking, honest, devoted and influential elements in it, capable of leading the backward strata or carrying the latter along with them.

The dictatorship of the proletariat means a most determined and most ruthless war waged by the new class against a *more powerful* enemy, the bourgeoisie, whose resistance is increased *tenfold* by their overthrow (even if only in a single country), and whose power lies, not only in the strength of international capital, the strength and durability of their international connections, but also in the *force of habit*, in the strength of *small-scale production*. Unfortunately, small-scale production is still widespread in the world, and small-scale production *engenders* capitalism and the bourgeoisie continuously, daily, hourly, spontaneously, and on a mass scale. All these reasons make the dictatorship of the proletariat necessary, and victory over the bourgeoisie is impossible without a long, stubborn and desperate life-and-death struggle which calls for tenacity, discipline, and a single and inflexible will.

I repeat: the experience of the victorious dictatorship of the proletariat in Russia has clearly shown even to those who are incapable of thinking or have had no occasion to give thought to the matter that absolute centralisation and rigorous discipline of the proletariat are an essential condition of victory over the bourgeoisie.

This is often dwelt on. However, not nearly enough thought is given to what it means, and under what conditions it is possible. Would it not be better if the salutations addressed to the Soviets and the Bolsheviks were *more frequently* accompanied by a *profound analysis* of the reasons *why* the Bolsheviks have been able to build up the discipline needed by the revolutionary proletariat?

As a current of political thought and as a political party, Bolshevism has existed since 1903. Only the history of Bolshevism during the *entire* period of its existence can satisfactorily explain why it has been able to build up and maintain, under most difficult conditions, the iron discipline needed for the victory of the proletariat.

The first questions to arise are: how is the discipline of the proletariat's revolutionary party maintained? How is it tested? How is it reinforced? First, by the class-consciousness of the proletarian vanguard and by its devotion to the revolution, by its tenacity, self-sacrifice and heroism. Second, by its ability to link up, maintain the closest contact, and—if you wish—merge, in certain measure, with the broadest masses of the working people—primarily with the proletariat, *but also with the non-proletarian* masses of working people. Third, by the correctness of the political leadership exercised by this vanguard, by the correctness of its political strategy and tactics, provided the broad masses have seen, *from their own experience*, that they are correct. Without these conditions, discipline in a revolutionary party really capable of being the party of the advanced class, whose mission it is to overthrow the bourgeoisie and transform the whole of society, cannot be achieved. Without these conditions, all attempts to establish discipline inevitably fall flat and end up in phrasemongering and clowning. On the other hand, these conditions cannot emerge at once. They are created only by prolonged effort and hard-won experience. Their creation is facilitated by a correct revolutionary theory, which, in its turn, is not a dogma, but assumes final shape only in close connection with the practical activity of a truly mass and truly revolutionary movement.

The fact that, in 1917-20, Bolshevism was able, under unprecedentedly difficult conditions, to build up and successfully maintain the strictest centralisation and iron discipline was due simply to a number of historical peculiarities of Russia.

On the one hand, Bolshevism arose in 1903 on a very firm foundation of Marxist theory. The correctness of this revolutionary theory, and of it alone, has been proved, not only by world experience throughout the nineteenth century, but especially by the experience of the seekings and vacillations, the errors and disappointments of revolutionary thought in Russia. For about half a century—approximately from the forties to the nineties of the last century—progressive thought in Russia, oppressed by a most brutal and reactionary tsarism, sought eagerly for a correct revolutionary theory, and followed with the utmost diligence and thoroughness each and every "last word" in this sphere in Europe and America. Russia achieved Marxism—the only correct revolutionary theory—through the *agony* she experienced in the course of half a century of unparalleled torment and sacrifice, of unparalleled revolutionary heroism, incredible energy, devoted searching, study, practical trial, disappointment, verification, and comparison with

European experience. Thanks to the political emigration caused by tsarism, revolutionary Russia, in the second half of the nineteenth century, acquired a wealth of international links and excellent information on the forms and theories of the world revolutionary movement, such as no other country possessed.

On the other hand, Bolshevism, which had arisen on this granite foundation of theory, went through fifteen years of practical history (1903-17) unequalled anywhere in the world in its wealth of experience. During those fifteen years, no other country knew anything even approximating to that revolutionary experience, that rapid and varied succession of different forms of the movement—legal and illegal, peaceful and stormy, underground and open, local circles and mass movements, and parliamentary and terrorist forms. In no other country has there been concentrated, in so brief a period, such a wealth of forms, shades, and methods of struggle of *all* classes of modern society, a struggle which, owing to the backwardness of the country and the severity of the tsarist yoke, matured with exceptional rapidity, and assimilated most eagerly and successfully the appropriate "last word" of American and European political experience.

III

THE PRINCIPAL STAGES IN THE HISTORY OF BOLSHEVISM

The years of preparation for revolution (1903-05). The approach of a great storm was sensed everywhere. All classes were in a state of ferment and preparation. Abroad, the press of the political exiles discussed the theoretical aspects of *all* the fundamental problems of the revolution. Representatives of the three main classes, of the three principal political trends—the liberal-bourgeois, the petty-bourgeois-democratic (concealed behind "social-democratic" and "social-revolutionary" labels[3]), and the proletarian-revolutionary—anticipated and prepared the impending open class struggle by waging a most bitter struggle on issues of programme and tactics. *All* the issues on which the masses waged an armed struggle in 1905-07 and 1917-20 can (and should) be studied, in their embryonic form, in the press of the period. Among these three main trends there were, of course, a host of intermediate, transitional or half-hearted forms. It would be more correct to say that those political and ideological trends which were genuinely of a class nature crystallised in the struggle of press organs, parties, factions and groups; the classes were forging the requisite political and ideological weapons for the impending battles.

The years of revolution (1905-07). All classes came out into the open. All programmatical and tactical views were tested by the action of the masses. In its extent and acuteness, the strike struggle had no parallel anywhere in the world. The economic strike developed into a political strike, and the latter into insurrection. The relations between the proletariat, as the leader, and the vacillating and unstable peasantry, as the led, were tested in practice. The Soviet form of organisation came into being in the spontaneous development of the struggle. The controversies of that period over the significance of the Soviets anticipated the great struggle of 1917-20. The alternation of parliamentary and non-parliamentary forms of struggle, of the tactics of boycotting parliament and that of participating in parliament, of legal and illegal forms of struggle, and likewise their interrelations and connections—all this was marked by an extraordinary wealth of content. As for teaching the fundamentals of political science to masses and leaders, to classes and parties alike, each month of this period was equivalent to an entire year of "peaceful" and "constitutional" development. Without the "dress rehearsal" of 1905, the victory of the October Revolution in 1917 would have been impossible.

The years of reaction (1907-10). Tsarism was victorious. All the revolutionary and opposition parties were smashed. Depression, demoralisation, splits, discord, defection, and pornography took the place of politics. There was an ever greater drift towards philosophical idealism; mysticism became the garb of counter-revolutionary sentiments. At the same time, however, it was this great defeat that taught the revolutionary parties and the revolutionary class a real and very useful lesson, a lesson in historical dialectics, a lesson in an understanding of the political struggle, and in the art and science of waging that struggle. It is at moments of need that one learns who one's friends are. Defeated armies learn their lesson.

Victorious tsarism was compelled to speed up the destruction of the remnants of the pre-bourgeois, patriarchal mode of life in Russia. The country's development along bourgeois lines proceeded apace. Illusions that stood outside and above class distinctions, illusions concerning the possibility of avoiding capitalism, were scattered to the winds. The class struggle manifested itself in a quite new and more distinct way.

The revolutionary parties had to complete their education. They were learning how to attack. Now they had to realise that such knowledge must be supplemented with the knowledge of how to retreat in good order. They had to realise—and it is from bitter experience that the revolutionary class learns to realise this—that victory is impossible unless one has learned how to attack and retreat properly. Of all the defeated opposition and revolutionary parties, the Bolsheviks effected the most orderly retreat, with the least loss to their "army", with its core best preserved, with the least significant splits (in point of depth and incurability), with the least demoralisation, and in the best condition to resume work on the broadest scale and in the most correct and energetic manner. The Bolsheviks achieved this only because they ruthlessly exposed and expelled the revolutionary phrase-mongers, those who did not wish to understand that one had to retreat, that one had to know how to retreat, and that one had absolutely to learn how to work legally in the most reactionary of parliaments, in the most reactionary of trade unions, co-operative and insurance societies and similar organisations.

The years of revival (1910-14). At first progress was incredibly slow, then, following the Lena events of 1912, it became somewhat more rapid. Overcoming unprecedented difficulties, the Bolsheviks thrust back the Mensheviks, whose role as bourgeois agents in the working-class movement was clearly realised by the entire bourgeoisie after 1905, and whom the bourgeoisie therefore supported in a thousand ways against the Bolsheviks. But the Bolsheviks would never have succeeded in doing this had they not followed the correct tactics of combining illegal work with the utilisation of "legal opportunities", which they made a point of doing. In the elections to the arch-reactionary Duma, the Bolsheviks won the full support of the worker curia.

The First Imperialist World War (1914-17). Legal parliamentarianism, with an extremely reactionary "parliament", rendered most useful service to the Bolsheviks, the party of the revolutionary proletariat. The Bolshevik deputies were exiled to Siberia.[4] All shades of social-imperialism, social-chauvinism, social-patriotism, inconsistent and consistent internationalism, pacifism, and the revolutionary repudiation of pacifist illusions found full expression in the Russian émigré press. The learned fools and the old women of the Second International, who had arrogantly and contemptuously turned up their noses at the abundance of "factions" in the Russian socialist movement and at the bitter struggle they were waging among themselves, were unable—when the war deprived them of their vaunted "legality" in *all* the advanced countries—to organise anything even approximating such a free (illegal) interchange of views and such a free (illegal) evolution of correct views as the Russian revolutionaries did in Switzerland and in a number of other countries. That was why both the avowed social-patriots and the "Kautskyites" of all countries proved to be the worst traitors to the proletariat. One of the principal reasons why Bolshevism was able to achieve victory in 1917-20 was that, since the end of 1914, it has been ruthlessly exposing the baseness and vileness of social-chauvinism and "Kautskyism" (to which Longuetism[5] in France, the views of the Fabians[6] and the leaders of the Independent Labour Party[7] in Britain, of Turati in Italy, etc., correspond), the masses later becoming more and more convinced, from their own experience, of the correctness of the Bolshevik views.

The second revolution in Russia (February to October 1917). Tsarism's senility and obsoleteness had (with the aid of the blows and hardships of a most agonising war) created an incredibly destructive force directed against it. Within a few days Russia was transformed into a democratic bourgeois republic, freer—in war conditions—than any other country in the world. The leaders of the opposition and revolutionary parties began to set up a government, just as is done in the most "strictly parliamentary" republics; the fact that a man had been a leader of an opposition party in parliament—even in a most reactionary parliament—*facilitated* his subsequent role in the revolution.

In a few weeks the Mensheviks and Socialist-Revolutionaries thoroughly assimilated all the methods and manners, the arguments and sophistries of the European heroes of the Second International, of the ministerialists[8] and other opportunist riff-raff. Everything we now read about the Scheidemanns and Noskes, about Kautsky and Hilferding, Renner and Austerlitz, Otto Bauer and Fritz Adler, Turati and Longuet, about the Fabians and the leaders of the Independent Labour Party of Britain—all this seems to us (and indeed is) a dreary repetition, a reiteration, of an old and familiar refrain. We have already witnessed all this in the instance of the Mensheviks. As history would have it, the opportunists of a backward country became the forerunners of the opportunists in a number of advanced countries.

If the heroes of the Second International have all gone bankrupt and have disgraced themselves over the question of the significance and role of the Soviets and Soviet rule; if the leaders of the three very important parties which have now left the Second International (namely, the German Independent Social-Democratic Party,[9] the French Longuetists and the British Independent Labour Party) have disgraced themselves and become entangled in this question in a most "telling" fashion; if they have all shown themselves slaves to the prejudices of petty-bourgeois democracy (fully in the spirit of the petty-bourgeois of 1848 who called themselves "Social-Democrats")—then we can only say that we have *already* witnessed *all this* in the instance of the Mensheviks. As history would have it, the Soviets came into being in Russia in 1905; from February to October 1917 they were turned to a false use by the Mensheviks, who went bankrupt because of their inability to understand the role and significance of the Soviets; today the idea of Soviet power has emerged *throughout the world* and is spreading among the proletariat of all countries with extraordinary speed. Like our Mensheviks, the old heroes of the Second International are *everywhere* going bankrupt, because they are incapable of understanding the role and significance of the Soviets. Experience has proved that, on certain very important questions of the proletarian revolution, *all* countries will inevitably have to do what Russia has done.

Despite views that are today often to be met with in Europe and America, the Bolsheviks began their victorious struggle against the parliamentary and (in fact) bourgeois republic and against the Mensheviks in a very cautious manner, and the preparations they made for it were by no means simple. At the beginning of the period mentioned, we did *not* call for the overthrow of the government but explained that it was impossible to overthrow it *without* first changing the composition and the temper of the Soviets. We did not proclaim a boycott of the bourgeois parliament, the Constituent Assembly, but said—and following the April (1917) Conference of our Party began to state officially in the name of the Party—that a bourgeois republic with a Constituent Assembly would be better than a bourgeois republic without a Constituent Assembly, but that a "workers' and peasants'" republic, a Soviet republic, would be better than any bourgeois-democratic, parliamentary republic. Without such thorough, circumspect and long preparations, we could not have achieved victory in October 1917, or have consolidated that victory.

IV

THE STRUGGLE AGAINST WHICH ENEMIES WITHIN THE WORKING-CLASS MOVEMENT HELPED BOLSHEVISM DEVELOP, GAIN STRENGTH, AND BECOME STEELED

First and foremost, the struggle against opportunism, which in 1914 definitely developed into social-chauvinism and definitely sided with the bourgeoisie, against the proletariat. Naturally, this was Bolshevism's principal enemy within the working-class movement. It still remains the principal enemy on an international scale. The Bolsheviks have been devoting the greatest attention to this enemy.

This aspect of Bolshevik activities is now fairly well known abroad too.

It was, however, different with Bolshevism's other enemy within the working-class movement. Little is known in other countries of the fact that Bolshevism took shape, developed and became steeled in the long years of struggle against *petty-bourgeois revolutionism*, which smacks of anarchism, or borrows something from the latter and, in all essential matters, does not measure up to the conditions and requirements of a consistently proletarian class struggle. Marxist theory has established—and the experience of all European revolutions and revolutionary movements has fully confirmed—that the petty proprietor, the small master (a social type existing on a very extensive and even mass scale in many European countries), who, under capitalism, always suffers oppression and very frequently a most acute and rapid deterioration in his conditions of life, and even ruin, easily goes to revolutionary extremes, but is incapable of perseverance, organisation, discipline and steadfastness. A petty bourgeois driven to frenzy by the horrors of capitalism is a social phenomenon which, like anarchism, is characteristic of all capitalist countries. The instability of such revolutionism, its barrenness, and its tendency to turn rapidly into submission, apathy, phantasms, and even a frenzied infatuation with one bourgeois fad or another—all this is common knowledge. However, a theoretical or abstract recognition of these truths does not at all rid revolutionary parties of old errors, which always crop up at unexpected occasions, in somewhat new forms, in a hitherto unfamiliar garb or surroundings, in an unusual—a more or less unusual—situation.

Anarchism was not infrequently a kind of penalty for the opportunist sins of the working-class movement. The two monstrosities complemented each other. And if in Russia—despite the more petty-bourgeois composition of her population as compared with the other European countries—anarchism's influence was negligible during the two revolutions (of 1905 and 1917) and the preparations for them, this should no doubt stand partly to the credit of Bolshevism, which has always waged a most ruthless and uncompromising struggle against opportunism. I say "partly", since of still greater importance in weakening anarchism's influence in Russia was the circumstance that in the past (the seventies of the nineteenth century) it was able to develop inordinately and to reveal its absolute erroneousness, its unfitness to serve the revolutionary class as a guiding theory.

When it came into being in 1903, Bolshevism took over the tradition of a ruthless struggle against petty-bourgeois, semi-anarchist (or dilettante-anarchist) revolutionism, a tradition which had always existed in revolutionary Social-Democracy and had become particularly strong in our country during the years 1900-03, when the foundations for a mass party of the revolutionary proletariat were being laid in Russia. Bolshevism took over and carried on the struggle against a party which, more than any other, expressed the tendencies of petty-bourgeois revolutionism, namely, the "Socialist-Revolutionary" Party, and waged that struggle on three main issues. First, that party, which rejected Marxism, stubbornly refused (or, it might be more correct to say: was unable) to understand the need for a strictly objective appraisal of the class forces and their alignment, before taking any political action. Second, this party considered itself particularly "revolutionary", or "Left", because of its recognition of individual terrorism, assassination—something that we Marxists emphatically rejected. It was, of course, only on grounds of expediency that we rejected individual terrorism, whereas people who were capable of condemning "on principle" the terror of the Great French Revolution, or, in general, the terror employed by a victorious revolutionary party which is besieged by the bourgeoisie of the whole world, were ridiculed and laughed to scorn by Plekhanov in 1900-03, when he was a Marxist and a revolutionary. Third, the "Socialist-Revolutionaries" thought it very "Left" to sneer at the comparatively insignificant opportunist sins of the German Social-Democratic Party, while they themselves imitated the extreme opportunists of that party, for example, on the agrarian question, or on the question of the dictatorship of the proletariat.

History, incidentally, has now confirmed on a vast and world-wide scale the opinion we have always advocated, namely, that German *revolutionary* Social-Democracy (note that as far back as 1900-03 Plekhanov demanded Bernstein's expulsion from the Party, and in 1913 the Bolsheviks, always continuing this tradition, exposed Legien's[10] baseness, vileness and treachery) *came closest* to being the party the revolutionary proletariat needs in order to achieve victory. Today, in 1920, after all the ignominious failures and crises of the war period and the early post-war years, it can be plainly seen that, of all the Western parties, the German revolutionary Social-Democrats produced the finest leaders, and recovered and gained new strength more rapidly than the others did. This may be seen in the instances both of the Spartacists[11] and the Left, proletarian wing of the Independent Social-Democratic Party of Germany, which is waging an incessant struggle against the opportunism and spinelessness of the Kautskys, Hilferdings, Ledebours and Crispiens. If we now cast a glance to take in a complete historical period, namely, from the Paris Commune to the first Socialist Soviet Republic, we shall find that Marxism's attitude to anarchism in general stands out most definitely and unmistakably. In the final analysis, Marxism proved to be correct, and although the anarchists rightly pointed to the opportunist views on the state prevalent among most of the socialist parties, it must be said, first, that this opportunism was connected with the distortion, and even deliberate suppression, of Marx's views on the state (in my book, *The State and Revolution*, I pointed out that for thirty-six years, from 1875 to 1911, Bebel withheld a letter by Engels,[12] which very clearly, vividly, bluntly and definitively exposed the opportunism of the current Social-Democratic views on the state); second, that the rectification of these opportunist views, and the recognition of Soviet power and its superiority to bourgeois parliamentary democracy proceeded most rapidly and extensively among those trends in the socialist parties of Europe and America that were most Marxist.

The struggle that Bolshevism waged against "Left" deviations within its own Party assumed particularly large proportions on two occasions: in 1908, on the question of whether or not to participate in a most reactionary "parliament" and in the legal workers' societies, which were being restricted by most reactionary laws; and again in 1918 (the Treaty of Brest-Litovsk[13]), on the question of whether one "compromise" or another was permissible.

In 1908 the "Left" Bolsheviks were expelled from our Party for stubbornly refusing to understand the necessity of participating in a most reactionary "parliament".[14] The "Lefts"—among whom there were many splendid revolutionaries who subsequently were (and still are) commendable members of the Communist Party—based themselves particularly on the successful experience of the 1905 boycott. When, in August 1905, the tsar proclaimed the convocation of a consultative "parliament",[15] the Bolsheviks called for its boycott, in the teeth of all the opposition parties and the Mensheviks, and the "parliament" was in fact swept away by the revolution of October 1905.[16] The boycott proved correct at the time, not because non-participation in reactionary parliaments is correct in general, but because we accurately appraised the objective situation, which was leading to the rapid development of the mass strikes first into a political strike, then into a revolutionary strike, and finally into an uprising. Moreover, the struggle centred at that time on the question of whether the convocation of the first representative assembly should be left to the tsar, or an attempt should be made to wrest its convocation from the old regime. When there was not, and could not be, any certainty that the objective situation was of a similar kind, and when there was no certainty of a similar trend and the same rate of development, the boycott was no longer correct.

The Bolsheviks' boycott of "parliament" in 1905 enriched the revolutionary proletariat with highly valuable political experience and showed that, when legal and illegal, parliamentary and non-parliamentary forms of struggle are combined, it is sometimes useful and even essential to reject parliamentary forms. It would, however, be highly erroneous to apply this experience blindly, imitatively and uncritically to *other* conditions and *other* situations. The Bolsheviks' boycott of the Duma in 1906 was a mistake, although a minor and easily remediable one.* The boycott

* What applies to individuals also applies—with necessary modifications—to politics and parties. It is not he who makes no mistakes

of the Duma in 1907, 1908 and subsequent years was a most serious error and difficult to remedy, because, on the one hand, a very rapid rise of the revolutionary tide and its conversion into an uprising was not to be expected, and, on the other hand, the entire historical situation attendant upon the renovation of the bourgeois monarchy called for legal and illegal activities being combined. Today, when we look back at this fully completed historical period, whose connection with subsequent periods has now become quite clear, it becomes most obvious that in 1908-14 the Bolsheviks *could not have* preserved (let alone strengthened and developed) the core of the revolutionary party of the proletariat, had they not upheld, in a most strenuous struggle, the viewpoint that it was *obligatory* to combine legal and illegal forms of struggle, and that it was *obligatory* to participate even in a most reactionary parliament and in a number of other institutions hemmed in by reactionary laws (sick benefit societies, etc.).

In 1918 things did not reach a split. At that time the "Left" Communists formed only a separate group or "faction" within our Party, and that not for long. In the same year, 1918, the most prominent representatives of 'Left Communism", for example, Comrades Radek and Bukharin, openly acknowledged their error. It had seemed to them that the Treaty of Brest-Litovsk was a compromise with the imperialists, which was inexcusable on principle and harmful to the party of the revolutionary proletariat. It was indeed a compromise with the imperialists, but it was a compromise which, under the circumstances, *had to be made*.

Today, when I hear our tactics in signing the Brest-Litovsk Treaty being attacked by the Socialist-Revolutionaries, for instance, or when I hear Comrade Lansbury say, in a conversation with me, "Our British trade union leaders say that if it was permissible for the Bolsheviks to compromise, it is permissible for them to compromise too", I usually reply by first of all giving a simple and "popular" example:

---

that is intelligent. There are no such men, nor can there be. It is he whose errors are not very grave and who is able to rectify them easily and quickly that is intelligent.

Imagine that your car is held up by armed bandits. You hand them over your money, passport, revolver and car. In return you are rid of the pleasant company of the bandits. That is unquestionably a compromise. "*Do ut des*" (I "give" you money, fire-arms and a car "so that you give" me the opportunity to get away from you with a whole skin). It would, however, be difficult to find a sane man who would declare such a compromise to be "inadmissible on principle", or who would call the compromiser an accomplice of the bandits (even though the bandits might use the car and the fire-arms for further robberies). Our compromise with the bandits of German imperialism was just that kind of compromise.

But when, in 1914-18 and then in 1918-20, the Mensheviks and Socialist-Revolutionaries in Russia, the Scheidemannites (and to a large extent the Kautskyites) in Germany, Otto Bauer and Friedrich Adler (to say nothing of the Renners and Co.) in Austria, the Renaudels and Longuets and Co. in France, the Fabians, the Independents and the Labourites in Britain entered into *compromises* with the bandits of their own bourgeoisie, and sometimes of the "Allied" bourgeoisie, and *against* the revolutionary proletariat of their own countries, all these gentlemen were actually acting as *accomplices in banditry*.

The conclusion is clear: to reject compromises "on principle", to reject the permissibility of compromises in general, no matter of what kind, is childishness, which it is difficult even to consider seriously. A political leader who desires to be useful to the revolutionary proletariat must be able to distinguish *concrete* cases of compromises that are inexcusable and are an expression of opportunism and *treachery*; he must direct all the force of criticism, the full intensity of merciless exposure and relentless war, against *these concrete* compromises, and not allow the past masters of "practical" socialism and the parliamentary Jesuits to dodge and wriggle out of responsibility by means of disquisitions on "compromises in general". It is in this way that the "leaders" of the British trade unions, as well as of the Fabian society and the "Independent" Labour Party, dodge responsibility *for the treachery they have perpetrated*, for having made *a compromise* that is really tantamount to the worst kind of opportunism, treachery and betrayal.

There are different kinds of compromises. One must be able to analyse the situation and the concrete conditions of each compromise, or of each variety of compromise. One must learn to distinguish between a man who has given up his money and fire-arms to bandits so as to lessen the evil they can do and to facilitate their capture and execution, and a man who gives his money and fire-arms to bandits so as to share in the loot. In politics this is by no means always as elementary as it is in this childishly simple example. However, anyone who is out to think up for the workers some kind of recipe that will provide them with cut-and-dried solutions for all contingencies, or promises that the policy of the revolutionary proletariat will never come up against difficult or complex situations, is simply a charlatan.

To leave no room for misinterpretation, I shall attempt to outline, if only very briefly, several fundamental rules for the analysis of concrete compromises.

The party which entered into a compromise with the German imperialists by signing the Treaty of Brest-Litovsk had been evolving its internationalism in practice ever since the end of 1914. It was not afraid to call for the defeat of the tsarist monarchy and to condemn "defence of country" in a war between two imperialist robbers. The parliamentary representatives of this party preferred exile in Siberia to taking a road leading to ministerial portfolios in a bourgeois government. The revolution that overthrew tsarism and established a democratic republic put this party to a new and tremendous test—it did not enter into any agreements with its "own" imperialists, but prepared and brought about their overthrow. When it had assumed political power, this party did not leave a vestige of either landed or capitalist ownership. After making public and repudiating the imperialists' secret treaties, this party proposed peace to *all* nations, and yielded to the violence of the Brest-Litovsk robbers only after the Anglo-French imperialists had torpedoed the conclusion of a peace, and after the Bolsheviks had done everything humanly possible to hasten the revolution in Germany and other countries.

The absolute correctness of this compromise, entered into by such a party in such a situation, is becoming ever clearer and more obvious with every day.

The Mensheviks and the Socialist-Revolutionaries in Russia (like all the leaders of the Second International throughout the world, in 1914-20) began with treachery—by directly or indirectly justifying "defence of country", i.e., the defence of *their own* predatory bourgeoisie. They continued their treachery by entering into a coalition with the bourgeoisie of *their own* country, and fighting, together with *their own* bourgeoisie, against the revolutionary proletariat of their own country. Their bloc, first with Kerensky and the Cadets, and then with Kolchak and Denikin in Russia—like the bloc of their *confrères* abroad with the bourgeoisie of *their* respective countries—was in fact desertion to the side of the bourgeoisie, against the proletariat. From beginning to end, *their* compromise with the bandits of imperialism meant their becoming *accomplices* in imperialist banditry.

V

"LEFT-WING" COMMUNISM IN GERMANY. THE LEADERS, THE PARTY, THE CLASS, THE MASSES

The German Communists we must now speak of call themselves, not "Left-wingers" but, if I am not mistaken, an "opposition on principle".[17] From what follows below it will, however, be seen that they reveal all the symptoms of the "infantile disorder of Leftism".

Published by the "local group in Frankfurt am Main", a pamphlet reflecting the point of view of this opposition, and entitled *The Split in the Communist Party of Germany* (*The Spartacus League*) sets forth the substance of this opposition's views most saliently, and with the utmost clarity and concision. A few quotations will suffice to acquaint the reader with that substance:

"The Communist Party is the party of the most determined class struggle...."

"... Politically, the transitional period [between capitalism and socialism]: is one of the proletarian dictatorship...."

"... The question arises: who is to exercise this dictatorship: *the Communist Party or the proletarian class? ... Fundamentally*, should we strive for a dictatorship of the Communist Party, or for a dictatorship of the proletarian class?..."

(All italics as in the original.)

The author of the pamphlet goes on to accuse the Central Committee of the Communist Party of Germany of seeking ways of achieving a *coalition with the Independent Social-Democratic Party of Germany*, and of raising "*the question of recognising, in principle, all political means*" of struggle, including parliamentarianism, with the sole purpose of concealing its actual and main efforts to form a coalition with the Independents. The pamphlet goes on to say:

"The opposition have chosen another road. They are of the opinion that the question of the rule of the Communist Party and of the dictatorship of the Party is merely one of tactics. In any case, rule by the Communist Party is the ultimate form of any party rule. *Fundamentally*, we must work for the dictatorship of the proletarian class. And all the measures of the Party, its organisations, methods of struggle, strategy and tactics should be directed to that end. Accordingly, all compromise with other parties, all reversion to parliamentary forms of struggle, which have become historically and politically obsolete, and any policy of manoeuvring and compromise must be emphatically rejected." "Specifically proletarian methods of revolutionary struggle must be strongly emphasised. New forms of organisation must be created on the widest basis and with the widest scope in order to enlist the most extensive proletarian circles and strata to take part in the revolutionary struggle under the leadership of the Communist Party. A *Workers' Union*, based on factory organisations, should be the rallying point for all revolutionary elements. This should unite all workers who follow the slogan: 'Get out of the trade unions!' It is here that the militant proletariat musters its ranks for battle. Recognition of the class struggle, of the Soviet system and of the dictatorship should be sufficient for enrolment. All subsequent political education of the fighting masses and their political orientation in the struggle are the task of the Communist Party, which stands outside the Workers' Union....

"... Consequently, two Communist parties are now arrayed against each other:

"*One is a party of leaders*, which is out to organise the revolutionary struggle and to direct it from *above*, accepting compromises and parliamentarianism so as to create a situation enabling it to join a coalition government exercising a dictatorship.

"*The other is a mass party*, which expects an upsurge of the revolutionary struggle from *below*, which knows and applies a single method in this struggle—a method which clearly leads to the goal—

and rejects all parliamentary and opportunist methods. That single method is the unconditional *overthrow of the bourgeoisie*, so as then to set up the proletarian class dictatorship for the accomplishment of socialism....

"... There—the dictatorship of leaders; here—the dictatorship of the masses! That is our slogan."

Such are the main features characterising the views of the opposition in the German Communist Party.

Any Bolshevik who has consciously participated in the development of Bolshevism since 1903 or has closely observed that development will at once say, after reading these arguments, "What old and familiar rubbish! What 'Left-wing' childishness!"

But let us examine these arguments a little more closely.

The mere presentation of the question—"dictatorship of the party *or* dictatorship of the class; dictatorship (party) of the leaders, *or* dictatorship (party) of the masses?"—testifies to most incredibly and hopelessly muddled thinking. These people want to *invent* something quite out of the ordinary, and, in their effort to be clever, make themselves ridiculous. It is common knowledge that the masses are divided into classes; that the masses can be contrasted with classes only by contrasting the vast majority in general, regardless of division according to status in the social system of production, with categories holding a definite status in the social system of production; that as a rule and in most cases—at least in present-day civilised countries—classes are led by political parties; that political parties, as a general rule, are run by more or less stable groups composed of the most authoritative, influential and experienced members, who are elected to the most responsible positions, and are called leaders. All this is elementary. All this is clear and simple. Why replace this with some kind of rigmarole, some new Volapük? On the one hand, these people seem to have got muddled when they found themselves in a predicament, when the party's abrupt transition from legality to illegality upset the customary, normal and simple relations between leaders, parties and classes. In Germany, as in other European countries, people had become too accustomed to legality, to the free and proper election of "leaders" at regular party congresses, to the convenient method of testing the class composition of parties through parliamentary elections, mass meetings, the press, the sentiments of the trade unions and other associations, etc. When, instead of this customary procedure, it became necessary, because of the stormy development of the revolution and the development of the civil war, to go over rapidly from legality to illegality, to combine the two, and to adopt the "inconvenient" and "undemocratic" methods of selecting, or forming, or preserving "groups of leaders"—people lost their bearings and began to think up some unmitigated nonsense. Certain members of the Communist Party of Holland,* who were unlucky enough to be born in a small country with traditions and conditions of highly privileged and highly stable legality, and who had never seen a transition from legality to illegality, probably fell into confusion, lost their heads, and helped create these absurd inventions.

On the other hand, one can see simply a thoughtless and incoherent use of the now "fashionable" terms: "masses" and "leaders". These people have heard and memorised a great many attacks on "leaders", in which the latter have been contrasted with the "masses"; however, they have proved unable to think matters out and gain a clear understanding of what it was all about.

The divergence between "leaders" and "masses" was brought out with particular clarity and sharpness in all countries at the end of the imperialist war and following it. The principal reason for this was explained many times by Marx and Engels between the years 1852 and 1892, from the example of Britain. That country's exclusive position led to the emergence, from the "masses", of a semi-petty-bourgeois, opportunist "labour aristocracy". The leaders of this labour aristocracy were constantly going over to the bourgeoisie, and were directly or indirectly on its pay roll. Marx earned the honour of incurring the hatred of these disreputable persons by openly branding them as traitors. Present-day (twentieth-century) imperialism has given a few advanced countries an exceptionally privileged position, which, everywhere in the Second International, has produced a certain type of traitor, opportunist, and

* See Note No. 41.—*Ed.*

social-chauvinist leaders, who champion the interests of their own craft, their own section of the labour aristocracy. The opportunist parties have become separated from the "masses", i.e., from the broadest strata of the working people, their majority, the lowest-paid workers. The revolutionary proletariat cannot be victorious unless this evil is combated, unless the opportunist, social-traitor leaders are exposed, discredited and expelled. That is the policy the Third International has embarked on.

To go so far, in this connection, as to contrast, *in general*, the dictatorship of the masses with a dictatorship of the leaders is ridiculously absurd, and stupid. What is particularly amusing is that, in fact, instead of the old leaders, who hold generally accepted views on simple matters, *new leaders* are brought forth (under cover of the slogan "Down with the leaders!"), who talk rank stuff and nonsense. Such are Laufenberg, Wolffheim, Horner,[18] Karl Schröder, Friedrich Wendel and Karl Erler,* in Germany. Erler's attempts to give the question more "profundity" and to proclaim that in general political parties are unnecessary and "bourgeois" are so supremely absurd that one can only shrug one's shoulders. It all goes to drive home the truth that a minor error can always assume monstrous proportions if it is persisted in, if profound justifications are sought for it, and if it is carried to its logical conclusion.

Repudiation of the Party principle and of Party discipline—that is what the opposition has *arrived at*. And this is tantamount to completely disarming the proletariat *in*

* Karl Erler, "The Dissolution of the Party", *Kommunistische Arbeiterzeitung*,[19] Hamburg, February 7, 1920, No. 32: "The working class cannot destroy the bourgeois state without destroying bourgeois democracy, and it cannot destroy bourgeois democracy without destroying parties."

The more muddle-headed of the syndicalists and anarchists in the Latin countries may derive "satisfaction" from the fact that solid Germans, who evidently consider themselves Marxists (by their articles in the above-mentioned paper K. Erler and K. Horner have shown most plainly that they consider themselves sound Marxists, but talk incredible nonsense in a most ridiculous manner and reveal their failure to understand the ABC of Marxism), go to the length of making utterly inept statements. Mere acceptance of Marxism does not save one from errors. We Russians know this especially well, because Marxism has been very often the "fashion" in our country.

the interests of the bourgeoisie. It all adds up to that petty-bourgeois diffuseness and instability, that incapacity for sustained effort, unity and organised action, which, if encouraged, must inevitably destroy any proletarian revolutionary movement. From the standpoint of communism, repudiation of the Party principle means attempting to leap from the eve of capitalism's collapse (in Germany), not to the lower or the intermediate phase of communism, but to the higher. We in Russia (in the third year since the overthrow of the bourgeoisie) are making the first steps in the transition from capitalism to socialism or the lower stage of communism. Classes still remain, and will remain everywhere *for years after* the proletariat's conquest of power. Perhaps in Britain, where there is no peasantry (but where petty proprietors exist), this period may be shorter. The abolition of classes means, not merely ousting the landowners and the capitalists—that is something we accomplished with comparative ease; it also means *abolishing the small commodity producers*, and they *cannot be ousted*, or crushed; we *must learn to live* with them. They can (and must) be transformed and re-educated only by means of very prolonged, slow, and cautious organisational work. They surround the proletariat on every side with a petty-bourgeois atmosphere, which permeates and corrupts the proletariat, and constantly causes among the proletariat relapses into petty-bourgeois spinelessness, disunity, individualism, and alternating moods of exaltation and dejection. The strictest centralisation and discipline are required within the political party of the proletariat in order to counteract this, in order that the *organisational* role of the proletariat (and that is its *principal* role) may be exercised correctly, successfully and victoriously. The dictatorship of the proletariat means a persistent struggle—bloody and bloodless, violent and peaceful, military and economic, educational and administrative—against the forces and traditions of the old society. The force of habit in millions and tens of millions is a most formidable force. Without a party of iron that has been tempered in the struggle, a party enjoying the confidence of all honest people in the class in question, a party capable of watching and influencing the mood of the masses, such a struggle cannot be waged successfully. It is a thousand times easier to vanquish the centralised big bourgeoisie than to "vanquish" the millions upon millions of petty proprietors; however, through their ordinary, everyday, imperceptible, elusive and demoralising activities, they produce the *very* results which the bourgeoisie need and which tend to *restore* the bourgeoisie. Whoever brings about even the slightest weakening of the iron discipline of the party of the proletariat (especially during its dictatorship), is actually aiding the bourgeoisie against the proletariat.

Parallel with the question of the leaders—the party—the class—the masses, we must pose the question of the "reactionary" trade unions. But first I shall take the liberty of making a few concluding remarks based on the experience of our Party. There *have always been* attacks on the "dictatorship of leaders" in our Party. The first time I heard such attacks, I recall, was in 1895, when, officially, no party yet existed, but a central group was taking shape in St. Petersburg, which was to assume the leadership of the district groups.[20] At the Ninth Congress of our Party (April 1920)[21] there was a small opposition, which also spoke against the "dictatorship of leaders", against the "oligarchy", and so on. There is therefore nothing surprising, new, or terrible in the "infantile disorder" of "Left-wing communism" among the Germans. The ailment involves no danger, and after it the organism even becomes more robust. In our case, on the other hand, the rapid alternation of legal and illegal work, which made it necessary to keep the general staff—the leaders—under cover and cloak them in the greatest secrecy, sometimes gave rise to extremely dangerous consequences. The worst of these was that in 1912 the *agent provocateur* Malinovsky got into the Bolshevik Central Committee. He betrayed scores and scores of the best and most loyal comrades, caused them to be sentenced to penal servitude, and hastened the death of many of them. That he did not cause still greater harm was due to the correct balance between legal and illegal work. As member of the Party's Central Committee and Duma deputy, Malinovsky was forced, in order to gain our confidence, to help us establish legal daily papers, which even under tsarism were able to wage a struggle against the Menshevik opportunism and to spread the fundamentals of Bolshevism in a suitably disguised form. While, with one hand, Malinovsky sent scores and scores of the finest Bolsheviks to penal servitude and death, he was obliged, with the other, to assist in the education of scores and scores of thousands of new Bolsheviks through the medium of the legal press. Those German (and also British, American, French and Italian) comrades who are faced with the task of learning how to conduct revolutionary work within the reactionary trade unions would do well to give serious thought to this fact.*

In many countries, including the most advanced, the bourgeoisie are undoubtedly sending *agents provocateurs* into the Communist parties and will continue to do so. A skilful combining of illegal and legal work is one of the ways to combat this danger.

VI

SHOULD REVOLUTIONARIES WORK IN REACTIONARY TRADE UNIONS?

The German "Lefts" consider that, as far as they are concerned, the reply to this question is an unqualified negative. In their opinion, declamations and angry outcries (such as uttered by K. Horner in a particularly "solid" and particularly stupid manner) against "reactionary" and "counter-revolutionary" trade unions are sufficient "proof" that it is unnecessary and even inexcusable for revolutionaries and Communists to work in yellow, social-chauvinist, compromising and counter-revolutionary trade unions of the Legien type.

* Malinovsky was a prisoner of war in Germany. On his return to Russia when the Bolsheviks were in power he was instantly put on trial and shot by our workers. The Mensheviks attacked us most bitterly for our mistake—the fact that an *agent provocateur* had become a member of the Central Committee of our Party. But when, under Kerensky, we demanded the arrest and trial of Rodzyanko, the Chairman of the Duma, because he had known, even before the war, that Malinovsky was an *agent provocateur* and *had not informed* the Trudoviks and the workers in the Duma, neither the Mensheviks nor the Socialist-Revolutionaries in the Kerensky government supported our demand, and Rodzyanko remained at large and made off unhindered to join Denikin.

However firmly the German "Lefts" may be convinced of the revolutionism of such tactics, the latter are in fact fundamentally wrong, and contain nothing but empty phrases.

To make this clear, I shall begin with our own experience, in keeping with the general plan of the present pamphlet, which is aimed at applying to Western Europe whatever is universally practicable, significant and relevant in the history and the present-day tactics of Bolshevism.

In Russia today, the connection between leaders, party, class and masses, as well as the attitude of the dictatorship of the proletariat and its party to the trade unions, are concretely as follows: the dictatorship is exercised by the proletariat organised in the Soviets; the proletariat is guided by the Communist Party of Bolsheviks, which, according to the figures of the latest Party Congress (April 1920), has a membership of 611,000. The membership varied greatly both before and after the October Revolution, and used to be much smaller, even in 1918 and 1919.[22] We are apprehensive of an excessive growth of the Party, because careerists and charlatans, who deserve only to be shot, inevitably do all they can to insinuate themselves into the ranks of the ruling party. The last time we opened wide the doors of the Party—to workers and peasants only—was when (in the winter of 1919) Yudenich was within a few versts of Petrograd, and Denikin was in Orel (about 350 versts from Moscow), i.e., when the Soviet Republic was in mortal danger, and when adventurers, careerists, charlatans and unreliable persons generally could not possibly count on making a profitable career (and had more reason to expect the gallows and torture) by joining the Communists.[23] The Party, which holds annual congresses (the most recent on the basis of one delegate per 1,000 members), is directed by a Central Committee of nineteen elected at the Congress, while the current work in Moscow has to be carried on by still smaller bodies, known as the Organising Bureau and the Political Bureau, which are elected at plenary meetings of the Central Committee, five members of the Central Committee to each bureau. This, it would appear, is a full-fledged "oligarchy". No important political or organisational question is decided by any state institution in our republic without the guidance of the Party's Central Committee.

In its work, the Party relies directly on the *trade unions*, which, according to the data of the last congress (April 1920), now have a membership of over four million and are formally *non-Party*. Actually, all the directing bodies of the vast majority of the unions, and primarily, of course, of the all-Russia general trade union centre or bureau (the All-Russia Central Council of Trade Unions), are made up of Communists and carry out all the directives of the Party. Thus, on the whole, we have a formally non-communist, flexible and relatively wide and very powerful proletarian apparatus, by means of which the Party is closely linked up with the *class* and the *masses*, and by means of which, under the leadership of the Party, the *class dictatorship* is exercised. Without close contacts with the trade unions, and without their energetic support and devoted efforts, not only in economic, *but also in military* affairs, it would of course have been impossible for us to govern the country and to maintain the dictatorship for two and a half months, let alone two and a half years. In practice, these very close contacts naturally call for highly complex and diversified work in the form of propaganda, agitation, timely and frequent conferences, not only with the leading trade union workers, but with influential trade union workers generally; they call for a determined struggle against the Mensheviks, who still have a certain though very small following—to whom they teach all kinds of counter-revolutionary machinations, ranging from an ideological defence of (*bourgeois*) democracy and the preaching that the trade unions should be "independent" (independent of proletarian state power!) to sabotage of proletarian discipline, etc., etc.

We consider that contacts with the "masses" through the trade unions are not enough. In the course of our revolution, practical activities have given rise to such institutions as *non-Party workers' and peasants' conferences*, and we strive by every means to support, develop and extend this institution in order to be able to observe the temper of the masses, come closer to them, meet their requirements, promote the best among them to state posts, etc. Under a recent decree on the transformation of the People's Commissariat of State Control into the Workers' and Peasants' Inspection, non-Party conferences of this kind have been empowered to select members of the State Control to carry out various kinds of investigations, etc.

Then, of course, all the work of the Party is carried on through the Soviets, which embrace the working masses, irrespective of occupation. The district congresses of Soviets are *democratic* institutions, the like of which even the best of the democratic republics of the bourgeois world have never known; through these congresses (whose proceedings the Party endeavours to follow with the closest attention), as well as by continually appointing class-conscious workers to various posts in the rural districts, the proletariat exercises its role of leader of the peasantry, gives effect to the dictatorship of the urban proletariat, wages a systematic struggle against the rich, bourgeois, exploiting and profiteering peasantry, etc.

Such is the general mechanism of the proletarian state power viewed "from above", from the standpoint of the practical implementation of the dictatorship. We hope that the reader will understand why the Russian Bolshevik, who has known this mechanism for twenty-five years and has seen it develop out of small, illegal and underground circles, cannot help regarding all this talk about "from above" *or* "from below", about the dictatorship of leaders *or* the dictatorship of the masses, etc., as ridiculous and childish nonsense, something like discussing whether a man's left leg or right arm is of greater use to him.

We cannot but regard as equally ridiculous and childish nonsense the pompous, very learned, and frightfully revolutionary disquisitions of the German Lefts to the effect that Communists cannot and should not work in reactionary trade unions, that it is permissible to turn down such work, that it is necessary to withdraw from the trade unions and create a brand-new and immaculate "Workers' Union" invented by very pleasant (and, probably, for the most part very youthful) Communists, etc., etc.

Capitalism inevitably leaves socialism the legacy, on the one hand, of the old trade and craft distinctions among the workers, distinctions evolved in the course of centuries;

on the other hand, trade unions, which only very slowly, in the course of years and years, can and will develop into broader industrial unions with less of the craft union about them (embracing entire industries, and not only crafts, trades and occupations), and later proceed, through these industrial unions, to eliminate the division of labour among people, to educate and school people, give them *all-round development and an all-round* training, so that they *are able to do everything.* Communism is advancing and must advance towards that goal, and *will reach* it, but only after very many years. To attempt in practice, today, to anticipate this future result of a fully developed, fully stabilised and constituted, fully comprehensive and mature communism would be like trying to teach higher mathematics to a child of four.

We can (and must) begin to build socialism, not with abstract human material, or with human material specially prepared by us, but with the human material bequeathed to us by capitalism. True, that is no easy matter, but no other approach to this task is serious enough to warrant discussion.

The trade unions were a tremendous step forward for the working class in the early days of capitalist development, inasmuch as they marked a transition from the workers' disunity and helplessness to the *rudiments* of class organisation. When the *revolutionary party of the proletariat*, the *highest* form of proletarian class organisation, began to take shape (and the Party will not merit the name until it learns to weld the leaders into one indivisible whole with the class and the masses) the trade unions inevitably began to reveal *certain* reactionary features, a certain craft narrow-mindedness, a certain tendency to be non-political, a certain inertness, etc. However, the development of the proletariat did not, and could not, proceed anywhere in the world otherwise than through the trade unions, through reciprocal action between them and the party of the working class. The proletariat's conquest of political power is a gigantic step forward for the proletariat as a class, and the Party must more than ever and in a new way, not only in the old, educate and guide the trade unions, at the same time bearing in mind that they are and will long remain an indispensable "school of communism" and a preparatory school that trains proletarians to exercise their dictatorship, an indispensable organisation of the workers for the gradual transfer of the management of the whole economic life of the country to the working *class* (and not to the separate trades), and later to all the working people.

In the sense mentioned above, a *certain* "reactionism" in the trade unions is *inevitable* under the dictatorship of the proletariat. Not to understand this means a complete failure to understand the fundamental conditions of the *transition* from capitalism to socialism. It would be egregious folly to fear *this* "reactionism" or to try to *evade* or leap over it, for it would mean fearing that function of the proletarian vanguard which consists in training, educating, enlightening and drawing into the new life the most backward strata and masses of the working class and the peasantry. On the other hand, it would be a still graver error to postpone the achievement of the dictatorship of the proletariat until a time when there will not be a single worker with a narrow-minded craft outlook, or with craft and craft-union prejudices. The art of politics (and the Communist's correct understanding of his tasks) consists in correctly gauging the conditions and the moment when the vanguard of the proletariat can successfully assume power, when it is able—during and after the seizure of power—to win adequate support from sufficiently broad strata of the working class and of the non-proletarian working masses, and when it is able thereafter to maintain, consolidate and extend its rule by educating, training and attracting ever broader masses of the working people.

Further. In countries more advanced than Russia, a certain reactionism in the trade unions has been and was bound to be manifested in a far greater measure than in our country. Our Mensheviks found support in the trade unions (and to some extent still do so in a small number of unions), as a result of the latter's craft narrow-mindedness, craft selfishness and opportunism. The Mensheviks of the West have acquired a much firmer footing in the trade unions; there the *craft-union, narrow-minded, selfish, case-hardened, covetous, and petty-bourgeois "labour aristocracy*", *imperialist-minded*, *and imperialist-corrupted*, has developed into a much stronger section than in our country. That is incontestable. The struggle against the Gompers-ses, and against the Jouhaux, Hendersons, Merrheims, Legiens and Co. in Western Europe is much more difficult than the struggle against our Mensheviks, who are an *absolutely homogeneous* social and political type. This struggle must be waged ruthlessly, and it must unfailingly be brought—as we brought it—to a point when all the incorrigible leaders of opportunism and social-chauvinism are completely discredited and driven out of the trade unions. Political power cannot be captured (and the attempt to capture it should not be made) until the struggle has reached a *certain* stage. This "certain stage" will be *different* in different countries and in different circumstances; it can be correctly gauged only by thoughtful, experienced and knowledgeable political leaders of the proletariat in each particular country. (In Russia the elections to the Constituent Assembly in November 1917, a few days after the proletarian revolution of October 25, 1917, were one of the criteria of the success of this struggle. In these elections the Mensheviks were utterly defeated; they received 700,000 votes—1,400,000 if the vote in Transcaucasia is added—as against 9,000,000 votes polled by the Bolsheviks. See my article, "The Constituent Assembly Elections and the Dictatorship of the Proletariat",[24] in the *Communist International*[25] No. 7-8.)

We are waging a struggle against the "labour aristocracy" in the name of the masses of the workers and in order to win them over to our side; we are waging the struggle against the opportunist and social-chauvinist leaders in order to win the working class over to our side. It would be absurd to forget this most elementary and most self-evident truth. Yet it is this very absurdity that the German "Left" Communists perpetrate when, *because* of the reactionary and counter-revolutionary character of the trade union *top leadership*, they jump to the conclusion that ... we must withdraw from the trade unions, refuse to work in them, and create new and *artificial* forms of labour organisation! This is so unpardonable a blunder that it is tantamount to the greatest service Communists could render the bourgeoisie. Like all the opportunist, social-chauvinist, and Kautskyite trade union leaders, our Mensheviks are nothing but "agents of the bourgeoisie in the working-class movement" (as we have always said the Mensheviks are), or "labour lieutenants of the capitalist class", to use the splendid and profoundly true expression of the followers of Daniel De Leon in America. To refuse to work in the reactionary trade unions means leaving the insufficiently developed or backward masses of workers under the influence of the reactionary leaders, the agents of the bourgeoisie, the labour aristocrats, or "workers who have become completely bourgeois" (cf. Engels's letter to Marx in 1858 about the British workers[26]).

This ridiculous "theory" that Communists should not work in reactionary trade unions reveals with the utmost clarity the frivolous attitude of the "Left" Communists towards the question of influencing the "masses", and their misuse of clamour about the "masses". If you want to help the "masses" and win the sympathy and support of the "masses", you should not fear difficulties, or pinpricks, chicanery, insults and persecution from the "leaders" (who, being opportunists and social-chauvinists, are in most cases directly or indirectly connected with the bourgeoisie and the police), but must absolutely *work wherever the masses are to be found*. You must be capable of any sacrifice, of overcoming the greatest obstacles, in order to carry on agitation and propaganda systematically, perseveringly, persistently and patiently in those institutions, societies and associations—even the most reactionary—in which proletarian or semi-proletarian masses are to be found. The trade unions and the workers' co-operatives (the latter sometimes, at least) are the very organisations in which the masses are to be found. According to figures quoted in the Swedish paper *Folkets Dagblad Politiken* of March 10, 1920, the trade union membership in Great Britain increased from 5,500,000 at the end of 1917 to 6,600,000 at the end of 1918, an increase of 19 per cent. Towards the close of 1919, the membership was estimated at 7,500,000. I have not got the corresponding figures for France and Germany to hand, but absolutely incontestable and generally known facts testify to a rapid rise in the trade union membership in these countries too.

These facts make crystal clear something that is confirmed by thousands of other symptoms, namely, that class-consciousness and the desire for organisation are growing among the proletarian masses, among the rank and file, among the backward elements. Millions of workers in Great Britain, France and Germany are *for the first time* passing from a complete lack of organisation to the elementary, lowest, simplest, and (to those still thoroughly imbued with bourgeois-democratic prejudices) most easily comprehensible form of organisation, namely, the trade unions; yet the revolutionary but imprudent Left Communists stand by, crying out "the masses", "the masses!" but *refusing to work within the trade unions*, on the pretext that they are "reactionary", and invent a brand-new, immaculate little "Workers' Union", which is guiltless of bourgeois-democratic prejudices and innocent of craft or narrow-minded craft-union sins, a union which, they claim, will be (!) a broad organisation. "Recognition of the Soviet system and the dictatorship" will be the *only* (!) condition of membership. (See the passage quoted above.)

It would be hard to imagine any greater ineptitude or greater harm to the revolution than that caused by the "Left" revolutionaries! Why, if we in Russia today, after two and a half years of unprecedented victories over the bourgeoisie of Russia and the Entente, were to make "recognition of the dictatorship" a condition of trade union membership, we would be doing a very foolish thing, damaging our influence among the masses, and helping the Mensheviks. The task devolving on Communists is to *convince* the backward elements, to work *among* them, and not to *fence themselves off* from them with artificial and childishly "Left" slogans.

There can be no doubt that the Gomperses, the Hendersons, the Jouhaux and the Legiens are very grateful to those "Left" revolutionaries who, like the German opposition "on principle" (heaven preserve us from such "principles"!), or like some of the revolutionaries in the American Industrial Workers of the World[27] advocate quitting the reactionary trade unions and refusing to work in them. These men, the "leaders" of opportunism, will no doubt resort to every device of bourgeois diplomacy and to the aid of bourgeois governments, the clergy, the police and the courts, to keep Communists out of the trade unions, oust them by every means, make their work in the trade unions as unpleasant as possible, and insult, bait and persecute them. We must be able to stand up to all this, agree to make any sacrifice, and even—if need be—to resort to various stratagems, artifices and illegal methods, to evasions and subterfuges, as long as we get into the trade unions, remain in them, and carry on communist work within them at all costs. Under tsarism we had no "legal opportunities" whatsoever until 1905. However, when Zubatov, agent of the secret police, organised Black-Hundred workers' assemblies and workingmen's societies for the purpose of trapping revolutionaries and combating them, we sent members of our Party to these assemblies and into these societies (I personally remember one of them, Comrade Babushkin, a leading St. Petersburg factory worker, shot by order of the tsar's generals in 1906). They established contacts with the masses, were able to carry on their agitation, and succeeded in wresting workers from the influence of Zubatov's agents.* Of course, in Western Europe, which is imbued with most deep-rooted legalistic, constitutionalist and bourgeois-democratic prejudices, this is more difficult of achievement. However, it can and must be carried out, and systematically at that.

The Executive Committee of the Third International must, in my opinion, positively condemn, and call upon the next congress of the Communist International to condemn both the policy of refusing to work in reactionary trade unions in general (explaining in detail why such refusal is unwise, and what extreme harm it does to the cause of the proletarian revolution) and, in particular, the line of conduct of some members of the Communist Party of Holland, who—whether directly or indirectly, overtly or covertly, wholly or partly, it does not matter—have supported this erroneous policy. The Third Interna-

---

* The Gomperses, Hendersons, Jouhaux and Legiens are nothing but Zubatovs, differing from our Zubatov only in their European garb and polish, and the civilised, refined and democratically suave manner of conducting their despicable policy.

tional must break with the tactics of the Second International; it must not evade or play down points at issue, but must pose them in a straightforward fashion. The whole truth has been put squarely to the "Independents" (the Independent Social-Democratic Party of Germany); the whole truth must likewise be put squarely to the "Left" Communists.

VII
SHOULD WE PARTICIPATE IN BOURGEOIS PARLIAMENTS?

It is with the utmost contempt—and the utmost levity—that the German "Left" Communists reply to this question in the negative. Their arguments? In the passage quoted above we read:

"... All reversion to parliamentary forms of struggle, which have become historically and politically obsolete, must be emphatically rejected...."

This is said with ridiculous pretentiousness, and is patently wrong. "Reversion" to parliamentarianism, forsooth! Perhaps there is already a Soviet republic in Germany? It does not look like it! How, then, can one speak of "reversion"? Is this not an empty phrase?

Parliamentarianism has become "historically obsolete". That is true in the propaganda sense. However, everybody knows that this is still a far cry from overcoming it in *practice*. Capitalism could have been declared—and with full justice—to be "historically obsolete" many decades ago, but that does not at all remove the need for a very long and very persistent struggle *on the basis* of capitalism. Parliamentarianism is "historically obsolete" from the standpoint of *world history*, i.e., the *era* of bourgeois parliamentarianism is over, and the *era* of the proletarian dictatorship has *begun*. That is incontestable. But world history is counted in decades. Ten or twenty years earlier or later makes no difference when measured with the yardstick of world history; from the standpoint of world history it is a trifle that cannot be considered even approximately. But for that very reason, it is a glaring theoretical error to apply the yardstick of world history to practical politics.

Is parliamentarianism "politically obsolete"? That is quite a different matter. If that were true, the position of the "Lefts" would be a strong one. But it has to be proved by a most searching analysis, and the "Lefts" do not even know how to approach the matter. In the "Theses on Parliamentarianism", published in the *Bulletin of the Provisional Bureau in Amsterdam of the Communist International* No. 1, February 1920, and obviously expressing the Dutch-Left or Left-Dutch strivings, the analysis, as we shall see, is also hopelessly poor.

In the first place, contrary to the opinion of such outstanding political leaders as Rosa Luxemburg and Karl Liebknecht, the German "Lefts", as we know, considered parliamentarianism "politically obsolete" even in January 1919. We know that the "Lefts" were mistaken. This fact alone utterly destroys, at a single stroke, the proposition that parliamentarianism is "politically obsolete". It is for the "Lefts" to prove why their error, indisputable at that time, is no longer an error. They do not and cannot produce even a shred of proof. A political party's attitude towards its own mistakes is one of the most important and surest ways of judging how earnest the party is and how it fulfils *in practice* its obligations towards its *class* and the *working people*. Frankly acknowledging a mistake, ascertaining the reasons for it, analysing the conditions that have led up to it, and thrashing out the means of its rectification—that is the hallmark of a serious party; that is how it should perform its duties, and how it should educate and train its *class*, and then the *masses*. By failing to fulfil this duty and give the utmost attention and consideration to the study of their patent error, the "Lefts" in Germany (and in Holland) have proved that they are not a *party of a class*, but a circle, not a *party of the masses*, but a group of intellectualists and of a few workers who ape the worst features of intellectualism.

Second, in the same pamphlet of the Frankfurt group of "Lefts", which we have already cited in detail, we read:

"... The millions of workers who still follow the policy of the Centre [the Catholic "Centre" Party] are counter-revolutionary. The rural proletarians provide the legions of counter-revolutionary troops." (Page 3 of the pamphlet.)

Everything goes to show that this statement is far too sweeping and exaggerated. But the basic fact set forth here is incontrovertible, and its acknowledgement by the "Lefts" is particularly clear evidence of their mistake. How can one say that "parliamentarianism is politically obsolete", when "millions" and "legions" of *proletarians* are not only still in favour of parliamentarianism in general, but are downright "counter-revolutionary"!? It is obvious that parliamentarianism in Germany is *not yet* politically obsolete. It is obvious that the "Lefts" in Germany have mistaken *their desire*, their politico-ideological attitude, for objective reality. That is a most dangerous mistake for revolutionaries to make. In Russia—where, over a particularly long period and in particularly varied forms, the most brutal and savage yoke of tsarism produced revolutionaries of diverse shades, revolutionaries who displayed amazing devotion, enthusiasm, heroism and will power—in Russia we have observed this mistake of the revolutionaries at very close quarters; we have studied it very attentively and have a first-hand knowledge of it; that is why we can also see it especially clearly in others. Parliamentarianism is of course "politically obsolete" to the Communists in Germany; but—and that is the whole point—we must *not* regard what is obsolete *to us* as something obsolete *to a class, to the masses*. Here again we find that the "Lefts" do not know how to reason, do not know how to act as the party of a *class*, as the party of the *masses*. You must not sink to the level of the masses, to the level of the backward strata of the class. That is incontestable. You must tell them the bitter truth. You are in duty bound to call their bourgeois-democratic and parliamentary prejudices what they are—prejudices. But at the same time you must *soberly* follow the *actual* state of the class-consciousness and preparedness of the entire class (not only of its communist vanguard), and of all the *working people* (not only of their advanced elements).

Even if only a fairly large *minority* of the industrial workers, and not "millions" and "legions", follow the lead of the Catholic clergy—and a similar minority of rural workers follow the landowners and kulaks (Grossbauern)—it *undoubtedly* signifies that parliamentarianism in Germany has *not yet* politically outlived itself, that participation in parliamentary elections and in the struggle on the parliamentary rostrum is *obligatory* on the party of the revolutionary proletariat *specifically* for the purpose of educating the backward strata of *its own class*, and for the purpose of awakening and enlightening the undeveloped, downtrodden and ignorant rural *masses*. Whilst you lack the strength to do away with bourgeois parliaments and every other type of reactionary institution, you *must* work within them because *it is there* that you will still find workers who are duped by the priests and stultified by the conditions of rural life; otherwise you risk turning into nothing but windbags.

Third, the "Left" Communists have a great deal to say in praise of us Bolsheviks. One sometimes feels like telling them to praise us less and to try to get a better knowledge of the Bolsheviks' tactics. We took part in the elections to the Constituent Assembly, the Russian bourgeois parliament, in September-November 1917. Were our tactics correct or not? If not, then this should be clearly stated and proved, for it is necessary in evolving the correct tactics for international communism. If they were correct, then certain conclusions must be drawn. Of course, there can be no question of placing conditions in Russia on a par with conditions in Western Europe. But as regards the particular question of the meaning of the concept that "parliamentarianism has become politically obsolete", due account should be taken of our experience, for unless concrete experience is taken into account such concepts very easily turn into empty phrases. In September-November 1917, did we, the Russian Bolsheviks, not have *more* right than any Western Communists to consider that parliamentarianism was politically obsolete in Russia? Of course we did, for the point is not whether bourgeois parliaments have existed for a long time or a short time, but how far the masses of the working people are *prepared* (ideologically, politically and practically) to accept the Soviet system and to dissolve the bourgeois-democratic parliament (or allow it to be dissolved). It is an absolutely incontestable and fully established historical fact that, in September-November 1917, the urban working class and the soldiers and peasants of Russia were, because of a number of special conditions, exceptionally well prepared to accept the Soviet system and to disband the most democratic of bourgeois parliaments. Nevertheless, the Bolsheviks did *not* boycott the Constituent Assembly, but took part in the elections both before *and after* the proletariat conquered political power. That these elections yielded exceedingly valuable (and to the proletariat, highly useful) political results has, I make bold to hope, been proved by me in the above-mentioned article, which analyses in detail the returns of the elections to the Constituent Assembly in Russia.

The conclusion which follows from this is absolutely incontrovertible: it has been proved that, far from causing harm to the revolutionary proletariat, participation in a bourgeois-democratic parliament, even a few weeks before the victory of a Soviet republic and even *after* such a victory, actually helps that proletariat to *prove* to the backward masses why such parliaments deserve to be done away with; it *facilitates* their successful dissolution, and *helps* to make bourgeois parliamentarianism "politically obsolete". To ignore this experience, while at the same time claiming affiliation to the Communist *International*, which must work out its tactics internationally (not as narrow or exclusively national tactics, but as international tactics), means committing a gross error and actually abandoning internationalism in deed, while recognising it in word.

Now let us examine the "Dutch-Left" arguments in favour of non-participation in parliaments. The following is the text of Thesis No. 4, the most important of the above-mentioned "Dutch" theses:

> "When the capitalist system of production has broken down, and society is in a state of revolution, parliamentary action gradually loses importance as compared with the action of the masses themselves. When, in these conditions, parliament becomes the centre and organ of the counter-revolution, whilst, on the other hand, the labouring class builds up the instruments of its power in the Soviets, it may even prove necessary to abstain from all and any participation in parliamentary action."

The first sentence is obviously wrong, since action by the masses, a big strike, for instance, is more important than parliamentary activity at *all* times, and not only during a revolution or in a revolutionary situation. This obviously untenable and historically and politically incorrect argument merely shows very clearly that the authors completely ignore both the general European experience (the French experience before the revolutions of 1848 and 1870; the German experience of 1878-90, etc.) and the Russian experience (see above) of the importance of *combining* legal and illegal struggle. This question is of immense importance both in general and in particular, because in *all* civilised and advanced countries the time is rapidly approaching when such a combination will more and more become—and has already partly become—mandatory on the party of the revolutionary proletariat, inasmuch as civil war between the proletariat and the bourgeoisie is maturing and is imminent, and because of savage persecution of the Communists by republican governments and bourgeois governments generally, which resort to any violation of legality (the example of America is edifying enough), etc. The Dutch, and the Lefts in general, have utterly failed to understand this highly important question.

The second sentence is, in the first place, historically wrong. We Bolsheviks participated in the most counter-revolutionary parliaments, and experience has shown that this participation was not only useful but indispensable to the party of the revolutionary proletariat, after the first bourgeois revolution in Russia (1905), so as to pave the way for the second bourgeois revolution (February 1917), and then for the socialist revolution (October 1917). In the second place, this sentence is amazingly illogical. If a parliament becomes an organ and a "centre" (in reality it never has been and never can be a "centre", but that is by the way) of counter-revolution, while the workers are building up the instruments of their power in the form of the Soviets, then it follows that the workers must prepare—ideologically, politically and technically—for the struggle of the Soviets against parliament, for the dispersal of parliament by the Soviets. But it does not at all follow that this dispersal is hindered, or is not facilitated, by the presence of a Soviet opposition *within* the counter-revolutionary parliament. In the course of our victorious struggle against Denikin and Kolchak, we never found that the existence of a Soviet and proletarian opposition in their camp was immaterial to our victories. We know perfectly well that the dispersal of the Constituent Assembly on January 5, 1918 was not hampered but was actually facilitated by the fact that, within the counter-revolutionary Constituent Assembly which was about to be dispersed, there was a consistent Bolshevik, as well as an inconsistent, Left Socialist-Revolutionary Soviet opposition. The authors of the theses are engaged in muddled thinking; they have forgotten the experience of many, if not all, revolutions, which shows the great usefulness, during a revolution, of a *combination* of mass action outside a reactionary parliament with an opposition sympathetic to (or, better still, directly supporting) the revolution within it. The Dutch, and the "Lefts" in general, argue in this respect like doctrinaires of the revolution, who have never taken part in a real revolution, have never given thought to the history of revolutions, or have naïvely mistaken subjective "rejection" of a reactionary institution for its actual destruction by the combined operation of a number of objective factors. The surest way of discrediting and damaging a new political (and not only political) idea is to reduce it to absurdity on the plea of defending it. For any truth, if "overdone" (as Dietzgen Senior put it), if exaggerated, or if carried beyond the limits of its actual applicability, can be reduced to an absurdity, and is even bound to become an absurdity under these conditions. That is just the kind of disservice the Dutch and German Lefts are rendering to the new truth of the Soviet form of government being superior to bourgeois-democratic parliaments. Of course, anyone would be in error who voiced the outmoded viewpoint or in general considered it impermissible, in all and any circumstances, to reject participation in bourgeois parliaments. I cannot attempt here to formulate the conditions under which a boycott is useful, since the object of this pamphlet is far more modest, namely, to study Russian experience in connection with certain topical questions of international communist tactics. Russian experience has provided us with one successful and correct instance (1905), and another that was incorrect (1906), of the use of a boycott by the Bolsheviks. Analysing the first case, we see that we succeeded in *preventing* a reactionary government from *convening* a reactionary parliament in a situation in which extra-parliamentary revolutionary mass action (strikes in particular) was developing at great speed, when not a single section of the proletariat and the peasantry could support the reactionary government in any way, and when the revolutionary proletariat was gaining influence over the backward masses through the strike struggle and through the agrarian movement. It is quite obvious that *this* experience is not applicable to present-day European conditions. It is likewise quite obvious—and the foregoing arguments bear this out—that the advocacy, even if with reservations, by the Dutch and the other "Lefts" of refusal to participate in parliaments is fundamentally wrong and detrimental to the cause of the revolutionary proletariat.

In Western Europe and America, parliament has become most odious to the revolutionary vanguard of the working class. That cannot be denied. It can readily be understood, for it is difficult to imagine anything more infamous, vile or treacherous than the behaviour of the vast majority of socialist and Social-Democratic parliamentary deputies during and after the war. It would, however, be not only unreasonable but actually criminal to yield to this mood when deciding *how* this generally recognised evil should be fought. In many countries of Western Europe, the revolutionary mood, we might say, is at present a "novelty", or a "rarity", which has all too long been vainly and impatiently awaited; perhaps that is why people so easily yield to that mood. Certainly, without a revolutionary mood among the masses, and without conditions facilitating the growth of this mood, revolutionary tactics will never develop into action. In Russia, however, lengthy, painful and sanguinary experience has taught us the truth that revolutionary tactics cannot be built on a revolutionary mood alone. Tactics must be based on a sober and strictly objective appraisal of *all* the class forces in a particular state (and of the states that surround it, and of all states the world over) as well as of the experience of revolutionary movements. It is very easy to show one's "revolutionary" temper merely by hurling abuse at parliamentary opportunism, or merely by repudiating participation in parliaments;

its very ease, however, cannot turn this into a solution of a difficult, a very difficult, problem. It is far more difficult to create a really revolutionary parliamentary group in a European parliament than it was in Russia. That stands to reason. But it is only a particular expression of the general truth that it was easy for Russia, in the specific and historically unique situation of 1917, to *start* the socialist revolution, but it will be more difficult for Russia than for the European countries to *continue* the revolution and bring it to its consummation. I had occasion to point this out already at the beginning of 1918, and our experience of the past two years has entirely confirmed the correctness of this view. Certain specific conditions, viz., (1) the possibility of linking up the Soviet revolution with the ending, as a consequence of this revolution, of the imperialist war, which had exhausted the workers and peasants to an incredible degree; (2) the possibility of taking temporary advantage of the mortal conflict between the world's two most powerful groups of imperialist robbers, who were unable to unite against their Soviet enemy; (3) the possibility of enduring a comparatively lengthy civil war, partly owing to the enormous size of the country and to the poor means of communication; (4) the existence of such a profound bourgeois-democratic revolutionary movement among the peasantry that the party of the proletariat was able to adopt the revolutionary demands of the peasant party (the Socialist-Revolutionary Party, the majority of whose members were definitely hostile to Bolshevism) and realise them at once, thanks to the conquest of political power by the proletariat—all these specific conditions do not at present exist in Western Europe, and a repetition of such or similar conditions will not occur so easily. Incidentally, apart from a number of other causes, that is why it is more difficult for Western Europe to *start* a socialist revolution than it was for us. To attempt to "circumvent" this difficulty by "skipping" the arduous job of utilising reactionary parliaments for revolutionary purposes is absolutely childish. You want to create a new society, yet you fear the difficulties involved in forming a good parliamentary group made up of convinced, devoted and heroic Communists, in a reactionary parliament! Is that not childish? If Karl Liebknecht in Germany and Z. Höglund in Sweden were able, even without mass support from below, to set examples of the truly revolutionary utilisation of reactionary parliaments, why should a rapidly growing revolutionary mass party, in the midst of the post-war disillusionment and embitterment of the masses, be unable to *forge* a communist group in the worst of parliaments? It is because, in Western Europe, the backward masses of the workers and—to an even greater degree—of the small peasants are much more imbued with bourgeois-democratic and parliamentary prejudices than they were in Russia; because of that, it is *only* from within such institutions as bourgeois parliaments that Communists can (and must) wage a long and persistent struggle, undaunted by any difficulties, to expose, dispel and overcome these prejudices.

The German "Lefts" complain of bad "leaders" in their party, give way to despair, and even arrive at a ridiculous "negation" of "leaders". But in conditions in which it is often necessary to hide "leaders" underground, the *evolution* of good "leaders", reliable, tested and authoritative, is a very difficult matter; these difficulties *cannot* be successfully overcome without combining legal and illegal work, and *without testing the "leaders", among other ways*, in parliaments. Criticism—the most keen, ruthless and uncompromising criticism—should be directed, not against parliamentarianism or parliamentary activities, but against those leaders who are unable—and still more against those who are *unwilling*—to utilise parliamentary elections and the parliamentary rostrum in a revolutionary and communist manner. Only such criticism—combined, of course, with the dismissal of incapable leaders and their replacement by capable ones—will constitute useful and fruitful revolutionary work that will simultaneously train the "leaders" to be worthy of the working class and of all working people, and train the masses to be able properly to understand the political situation and the often very complicated and intricate tasks that spring from that situation.*

---

* I have had too little opportunity to acquaint myself with "Left-wing" communism in Italy. Comrade Bordiga and his faction of Abstentionist Communists (*Comunista astensionista*) are certainly wrong

VIII
NO COMPROMISES?

In the quotation from the Frankfurt pamphlet, we have seen how emphatically the "Lefts" have advanced this slogan. It is sad to see people who no doubt consider themselves Marxists, and want to be Marxists, forget the fundamental truths of Marxism. This is what Engels—who, like Marx, was one of those rarest of authors whose every sentence in every one of their fundamental works contains a remarkably profound content—wrote in 1874, against the manifesto of the thirty-three Blanquist Communards:

"'We are Communists' [the Blanquist Communards wrote in their manifesto], 'because we want to attain our goal without stopping at intermediate stations, without any compromises, which only postpone the day of victory and prolong the period of slavery.'

"The German Communists are Communists because, through all the intermediate stations and all compromises created, not by them but by the course of historical development, they clearly perceive and constantly pursue the final aim—the abolition of classes and the creation of a society in which there will no longer be private ownership of land

---

in advocating non-participation in parliament. But on one point, it seems to me, Comrade Bordiga is right—as far as can be judged from two issues of his paper, *Il Soviet* (Nos. 3 and 4, January 18 and February 1, 1920), from four issues of Comrade Serrati's excellent periodical, *Comunismo* (Nos. 1-4, October 1-November 30, 1919), and from separate issues of Italian bourgeois papers which I have seen. Comrade Bordiga and his group are right in attacking Turati and his partisans, who remain in a party which has recognised Soviet power and the dictatorship of the proletariat, and yet continue their former pernicious and opportunist policy as members of parliament. Of course, in tolerating this, Comrade Serrati and the entire Italian Socialist Party[28] are making a mistake which threatens to do as much harm and give rise to the same dangers as it did in Hungary, where the Hungarian Turatis sabotaged both the party and the Soviet government[29] from within. Such a mistaken, inconsistent, or spineless attitude towards the opportunist parliamentarians gives rise to "Left-wing" communism, on the one hand, and *to a certain extent* justifies its existence, on the other. Comrade Serrati is obviously wrong when he accuses Deputy Turati of being "inconsistent" (*Comunismo* No. 3), for it is the Italian Socialist Party itself that is inconsistent in tolerating such opportunist parliamentarians as Turati and Co.

or of the means of production. The thirty-three Blanquists are Communists just because they imagine that, merely because *they* want to skip the intermediate stations and compromises, the matter is settled, and if 'it begins' in the next few days—which they take for granted—and they take over power, 'communism will be introduced' the day after tomorrow. If that is not immediately possible, they are not Communists.

"What childish innocence it is to present one's own impatience as a theoretically convincing argument!" (Frederick Engels, "Programme of the Blanquist Communards",[30] from the German Social-Democratic newspaper *Volksstaat*, 1874, No. 73, given in the Russian translation of *Articles, 1871-1875*, Petrograd, 1919, pp. 52-53).

In the same article, Engels expresses his profound esteem for Vaillant, and speaks of the "unquestionable merit" of the latter (who, like Guesde, was one of the most prominent leaders of international socialism until their betrayal of socialism in August 1914). But Engels does not fail to give a detailed analysis of an obvious error. Of course, to very young and inexperienced revolutionaries, as well as to petty-bourgeois revolutionaries of even very respectable age and great experience, it seems extremely "dangerous", incomprehensible and wrong to "permit compromises". Many sophists (being unusually or excessively "experienced" politicians) reason exactly in the same way as the British leaders of opportunism mentioned by Comrade Lansbury: "If the Bolsheviks are permitted a certain compromise, why should we not be permitted any kind of compromise?" However, proletarians schooled in numerous strikes (to take only this manifestation of the class struggle) usually assimilate in admirable fashion the very profound truth (philosophical, historical, political and psychological) expounded by Engels. Every proletarian has been through strikes and has experienced "compromises" with the hated oppressors and exploiters, when the workers have had to return to work either without having achieved anything or else agreeing to only a partial satisfaction of their demands. Every proletarian—as a result of the conditions of the mass struggle and the acute intensification of class antagonisms he lives among—sees the difference between a compromise enforced by objective conditions (such as lack of strike funds, no outside support, starvation and exhaustion)—a compromise which in no way minimises the revolutionary devotion and readiness to carry on the struggle on the part of the workers who have agreed to such a compromise—and, on the other hand, a compromise by traitors who try to ascribe to objective causes their self-interest (strike-breakers also enter into "compromises"!), their cowardice, desire to toady to the capitalists, and readiness to yield to intimidation, sometimes to persuasion, sometimes to sops, and sometimes to flattery from the capitalists. (The history of the British labour movement provides a very large number of instances of such treacherous compromises by British trade union leaders, but, in one form or another, almost all workers in all countries have witnessed the same sort of thing.)

Naturally, there are individual cases of exceptional difficulty and complexity, when the greatest efforts are necessary for a proper assessment of the actual character of this or that "compromise", just as there are cases of homicide when it is by no means easy to establish whether the homicide was fully justified and even necessary (as, for example, legitimate self-defence), or due to unpardonable negligence, or even to a cunningly executed perfidious plan. Of course, in politics, where it is sometimes a matter of extremely complex relations—national and international—between classes and parties, very many cases will arise that will be much more difficult than the question of a legitimate "compromise" in a strike or a treacherous "compromise" by a strike-breaker, treacherous leader, etc. It would be absurd to formulate a recipe or general rule ("No compromises!") to suit all cases. One must use one's own brains and be able to find one's bearings in each particular instance. It is, in fact, one of the functions of a party organisation and of party leaders worthy of the name, to acquire, through the prolonged, persistent, variegated and comprehensive efforts of all thinking representatives of a given class,* the knowledge, experience and—in addition to

* Within every class, even in the conditions prevailing in the most enlightened countries, even within the most advanced class,

knowledge and experience—the political flair necessary for the speedy and correct solution of complex political problems.

Naïve and quite inexperienced people imagine that the permissibility of compromise *in general* is sufficient to obliterate any distinction between opportunism, against which we are waging, and must wage, an unremitting struggle, and revolutionary Marxism, or communism. But if such people do not yet know that in nature and in society *all* distinctions are fluid and up to a certain point conventional, nothing can help them but lengthy training, education, enlightenment, and political and everyday experience. In the practical questions that arise in the politics of any particular or specific historical moment, it is important to single out those which display the principal type of intolerable and treacherous compromises, such as embody an opportunism that is fatal to the revolutionary class, and to exert all efforts to explain them and combat them. During the 1914-18 imperialist war between two groups of equally predatory countries, social-chauvinism was the principal and fundamental type of opportunism, i.e., support of "defence of country", which in *such* a war was really equivalent to defence of the predatory interests of one's "own" bourgeoisie. After the war, defence of the robber League of Nations,[31] defence of direct or indirect alliances with the bourgeoisie of one's own country against the revolutionary proletariat and the "Soviet" movement, and defence of bourgeois democracy and bourgeois parliamentarianism against "Soviet power" became the principal manifestations of those intolerable and treacherous compromises, whose sum total constituted an opportunism fatal to the revolutionary proletariat and its cause.

> "... All compromise with other parties ... any policy of manoeuvring and compromise must be emphatically rejected,"

the German Lefts write in the Frankfurt pamphlet.

---

and even when the circumstances of the moment have aroused all its spiritual forces to an exceptional degree, there always are—and inevitably *will be* as long as classes exist, as long as a classless society has not fully consolidated itself, and has not developed on its own foundations—representatives of the class who do *not* think, and are incapable of thinking, for themselves. Capitalism would not be the oppressor of the masses that it actually is, if things were otherwise.

It is surprising that, with such views, these Lefts do not emphatically condemn Bolshevism! After all, the German Lefts cannot but know that the entire history of Bolshevism, both before and after the October Revolution, is *full* of instances of changes of tack, conciliatory tactics and compromises with other parties, including bourgeois parties!

To carry on a war for the overthrow of the international bourgeoisie, a war which is a hundred times more difficult, protracted and complex than the most stubborn of ordinary wars between states, and to renounce in advance any change of tack, or any utilisation of a conflict of interests (even if temporary) among one's enemies, or any conciliation or compromise with possible allies (even if they are temporary, unstable, vacillating or conditional allies)—is that not ridiculous in the extreme? Is it not like making a difficult ascent of an unexplored and hitherto inaccessible mountain and refusing in advance ever to move in zigzags, ever to retrace one's steps, or ever to abandon a course once selected, and to try others? And yet people so immature and inexperienced (if youth were the explanation, it would not be so bad; young people are preordained to talk such nonsense for a certain period) have met with support—whether direct or indirect, open or covert, whole or partial, it does not matter—from some members of the Communist Party of Holland.

After the first socialist revolution of the proletariat, and the overthrow of the bourgeoisie in some country, the proletariat of that country remains *for a long time weaker* than the bourgeoisie, simply because of the latter's extensive international links, and also because of the spontaneous and continuous restoration and regeneration of capitalism and the bourgeoisie by the small commodity producers of the country which has overthrown the bourgeoisie. The more powerful enemy can be vanquished only by exerting the utmost effort, and by the most thorough, careful, attentive, skilful and *obligatory* use of any, even the smallest, rift between the enemies, any conflict of interests among the bourgeoisie of the various countries and among the various groups or types of bourgeoisie within the various countries, and also by taking advantage of any, even the smallest, opportunity of winning a mass ally, even though this ally is temporary, vacillating, unstable, unreliable and conditional. Those who do not understand this reveal a failure to understand even the smallest grain of Marxism, of modern scientific socialism *in general*. Those who have not proved *in practice*, over a fairly considerable period of time and in fairly varied political situations, their ability to apply this truth in practice have not yet learned to help the revolutionary class in its struggle to emancipate all toiling humanity from the exploiters. And this applies equally to the period *before* and *after* the proletariat has won political power.

Our theory is not a dogma, but a *guide to action*, said Marx and Engels.[32] The greatest blunder, the greatest crime, committed by such "out-and-out" Marxists as Karl Kautsky, Otto Bauer, etc., is that they have not understood this and have been unable to apply it at crucial moments of the proletarian revolution. "Political activity is not like the pavement of Nevsky Prospekt" (the well-kept, broad and level pavement of the perfectly straight principal thoroughfare of St. Petersburg), N. G. Chernyshevsky, the great Russian socialist of the pre-Marxist period, used to say. Since Chernyshevsky's time, disregard or forgetfulness of this truth has cost Russian revolutionaries countless sacrifices. We must strive at all costs to *prevent* the Left Communists and West-European and American revolutionaries that are devoted to the working class from paying *as dearly* as the backward Russians did to learn this truth.

Prior to the downfall of tsarism, the Russian revolutionary Social-Democrats made repeated use of the services of the bourgeois liberals, i.e., they concluded numerous practical compromises with the latter. In 1901-02, even prior to the appearance of Bolshevism, the old editorial board of *Iskra* (consisting of Plekhanov, Axelrod, Zasulich, Martov, Potresov and myself) concluded (not for long, it is true) a formal political alliance with Struve, the political leader of bourgeois liberalism, while at the same time being able to wage an unremitting and most merciless ideological and political struggle against bourgeois liberalism and against the slightest manifestations of its influence in the working-class movement. The Bolsheviks have always adhered to this policy. Since 1905 they have systematically advocated an alliance between the working class and the peasantry, against the liberal bourgeoisie and tsarism, never, however, refusing to support the bourgeoisie against tsarism (for instance, during second rounds of elections, or during second ballots) and never ceasing their relentless ideological and political struggle against the Socialist-Revolutionaries, the bourgeois-revolutionary peasant party, exposing them as petty-bourgeois democrats who have falsely described themselves as socialists. During the Duma elections of 1907, the Bolsheviks entered briefly into a formal political bloc with the Socialist-Revolutionaries. Between 1903 and 1912, there were periods of several years in which we were formally united with the Mensheviks in a single Social-Democratic Party, but we *never stopped* our ideological and political struggle against them as opportunists and vehicles of bourgeois influence on the proletariat. During the war, we concluded certain compromises with the Kautskyites, with the Left Mensheviks (Martov), and with a section of the Socialist-Revolutionaries (Chernov and Natanson); we were together with them at Zimmerwald and Kienthal,[33] and issued joint manifestos. However, we never ceased and never relaxed our ideological and political struggle against the Kautskyites, Martov and Chernov (when Natanson died in 1919, a "Revolutionary-Communist" Narodnik,[34] he was very close to and almost in agreement with us). At the very moment of the October Revolution, we entered into an informal but very important (and very successful) political bloc with the petty-bourgeois peasantry by adopting the *Socialist-Revolutionary* agrarian programme *in its entirety*, without a single alteration—i.e., we effected an undeniable compromise in order to prove to the peasants that we wanted, not to "steam-roller" them but to reach agreement with them. At the same time we proposed (and soon after effected) a formal political bloc, including participation in the government, with the Left Socialist-Revolutionaries, who dissolved this bloc after the conclusion of the Treaty of Brest-Litovsk and then, in July 1918, went to the length of armed rebellion, and subsequently of an armed struggle, against us.

It is therefore understandable why the attacks made by

the German Lefts against the Central Committee of the Communist Party of Germany for entertaining the idea of a bloc with the Independents (the Independent Social-Democratic Party of Germany—the Kautskyites) are absolutely inane, in our opinion, and clear proof that the "Lefts" are in the *wrong*. In Russia, too, there were Right Mensheviks (participants in the Kerensky government), who corresponded to the German Scheidemanns, and Left Mensheviks (Martov), corresponding to the German Kautskyites and standing in opposition to the Right Mensheviks. A gradual shift of the worker masses from the Mensheviks over to the Bolsheviks was to be clearly seen in 1917. At the First All-Russia Congress of Soviets, held in June 1917, we had only 13 per cent of the votes; the Socialist-Revolutionaries and the Mensheviks had a majority. At the Second Congress of Soviets (October 25, 1917, old style) we had 51 per cent of the votes. Why is it that in Germany the *same* and absolutely *identical* shift of the workers from Right to Left did not immediately strengthen the Communists, but first strengthened the midway Independent Party, although the latter never had independent political ideas or an independent policy, but merely wavered between the Scheidemanns and the Communists?

One of the evident reasons was the *erroneous* tactics of the German Communists, who must fearlessly and honestly admit this error and learn to rectify it. The error consisted in their denial of the need to take part in the reactionary bourgeois parliaments and in the reactionary trade unions; the error consisted in numerous manifestations of that "Left-wing" infantile disorder which has now come to the surface and will consequently be cured the more thoroughly, the more rapidly and with greater advantage to the organism.

The German Independent Social-Democratic Party is obviously not a homogeneous body. Alongside the old opportunist leaders (Kautsky, Hilferding and apparently, to a considerable extent, Crispien, Ledebour and others)—these have revealed their inability to understand the significance of Soviet power and the dictatorship of the proletariat, and their inability to lead the proletariat's revolutionary struggle—there has emerged in this party a Left and proletarian wing, which is growing most rapidly. Hundreds of thousands of members of this party (which has, I think, a membership of some three-quarters of a million) are proletarians who are abandoning Scheidemann and are rapidly going over to communism. This proletarian wing has already proposed—at the Leipzig Congress of the Independents (1919)—immediate and unconditional affiliation to the Third International. To fear a "compromise" with this wing of the party is positively ridiculous. On the contrary, it is the *duty* of Communists to seek *and find* a suitable form of compromise with them, a compromise which, on the one hand, will facilitate and accelerate the necessary complete fusion with this wing and, on the other, will in no way hamper the Communists in their ideological and political struggle against the opportunist Right wing of the Independents. It will probably be no easy matter to devise a suitable form of compromise—but only a charlatan could promise the German workers and the German Communists an "easy" road to victory.

Capitalism would not be capitalism if the proletariat *pur sang* were not surrounded by a large number of exceedingly motley types intermediate between the proletarian and the semi-proletarian (who earns his livelihood in part by the sale of his labour-power), between the semi-proletarian and the small peasant (and petty artisan, handicraft worker and small master in general), between the small peasant and the middle peasant, and so on, and if the proletariat itself were not divided into more developed and less developed strata, if it were not divided according to territorial origin, trade, sometimes according to religion, and so on. From all this follows the necessity, the absolute necessity, for the Communist Party, the vanguard of the proletariat, its class-conscious section, to resort to changes of tack, to conciliation and compromises with the various groups of proletarians, with the various parties of the workers and small masters. It is entirely a matter of *knowing how* to apply these tactics in order to *raise*—not lower—the *general* level of proletarian class-consciousness, revolutionary spirit, and ability to fight and win. Incidentally, it should be noted that the Bolsheviks' victory over the Mensheviks called for the application of tactics of changes of tack, conciliation and compromises, not only before *but also after* the

October Revolution of 1917, but the changes of tack and compromises were, of course, such as assisted, boosted and consolidated the Bolsheviks at the expense of the Mensheviks. The petty-bourgeois democrats (including the Mensheviks) inevitably vacillate between the bourgeoisie and the proletariat, between bourgeois democracy and the Soviet system, between reformism and revolutionism, between love for the workers and fear of the proletarian dictatorship, etc. The Communists' proper tactics should consist in *utilising* these vacillations, not ignoring them; utilising them calls for concessions to elements that are turning towards the proletariat—whenever and in the measure that they turn towards the proletariat—in addition to fighting those who turn towards the bourgeoisie. As a result of the application of the correct tactics, Menshevism began to disintegrate, and has been disintegrating more and more in our country; the stubbornly opportunist leaders are being isolated, and the best of the workers and the best elements among the petty-bourgeois democrats are being brought into our camp. This is a lengthy process, and the hasty "decision"—"No compromises, no manoeuvres"—can only prejudice the strengthening of the revolutionary proletariat's influence and the enlargement of its forces.

Lastly, one of the undoubted errors of the German "Lefts" lies in their downright refusal to recognise the Treaty of Versailles. The more "weightily" and "pompously", the more "emphatically" and peremptorily this viewpoint is formulated (by K. Horner, for instance), the less sense it seems to make. It is not enough, under the present conditions of the international proletarian revolution, to repudiate the preposterous absurdities of "National Bolshevism" (Laufenberg and others), which has gone to the length of advocating a bloc with the German bourgeoisie for a war against the Entente. One must realise that it is utterly false tactics to refuse to admit that a Soviet Germany (if a German Soviet republic were soon to arise) would have to recognise the Treaty of Versailles for a time, and to submit to it. From this it does not follow that the Independents—at a time when the Scheidemanns were in the government, when the Soviet government in Hungary had not yet been overthrown, and when it was still possible that a

Soviet revolution in Vienna would support Soviet Hungary—were right, *under the circumstances*, in putting forward the demand that the Treaty of Versailles should be signed. At that time the Independents tacked and manoeuvred very clumsily, for they more or less accepted responsibility for the Scheidemann traitors, and more or less backslid from advocacy of a ruthless (and most calmly conducted) class war against the Scheidemanns, to advocacy of a "classless" or "above-class" standpoint.

In the present situation, however, the German Communists should obviously not deprive themselves of freedom of action by giving a positive and categorical promise to repudiate the Treaty of Versailles in the event of communism's victory. That would be absurd. They should say: the Scheidemanns and the Kautskyites have committed a number of acts of treachery hindering (and in part quite ruining) the chances of an alliance with Soviet Russia and Soviet Hungary. We Communists will do all we can to *facilitate* and *pave the way* for such an alliance. However, we are in no way obligated to repudiate the Treaty of Versailles, come what may, or to do so at once. The possibility of its successful repudiation will depend, not only on the German, but also on the international successes of the Soviet movement. The Scheidemanns and the Kautskyites have hampered this movement; we are helping it. That is the gist of the matter; therein lies the fundamental difference. And if our class enemies, the exploiters and their Scheidemann and Kautskyite lackeys, have missed many an opportunity of strengthening both the German and the international Soviet movement, of strengthening both the German and the international Soviet revolution, the blame lies with them. The Soviet revolution in Germany will strengthen the international Soviet movement, which is the strongest bulwark (and the only reliable, invincible and world-wide bulwark) against the Treaty of Versailles and against international imperialism in general. To give absolute, categorical and immediate precedence to liberation from the Treaty of Versailles and to give it *precedence over the question* of liberating *other* countries oppressed by imperialism, from the yoke of imperialism, is philistine nationalism (worthy of the Kautskys, the Hilferdings, the Otto Bauers and Co.), not of revolutionary internationalism. The overthrow of the bourgeoisie in any of the large European countries, including Germany, would be such a gain for the international revolution that, for its sake, one can, and if necessary should, tolerate a *more prolonged existence of the Treaty of Versailles.* If Russia, standing alone, could endure the Treaty of Brest-Litovsk for several months, to the advantage of the revolution, there is nothing impossible in a Soviet Germany, allied with Soviet Russia, enduring the existence of the Treaty of Versailles for a longer period, to the advantage of the revolution.

The imperialists of France, Britain, etc., are trying to provoke and ensnare the German Communists: "Say that you will not sign the Treaty of Versailles!" they urge. Like babes, the Left Communists fall into the trap laid for them, instead of skilfully manoeuvring against the crafty and, *at present*, stronger enemy, and instead of telling him, "We shall sign the Treaty of Versailles now." It is folly, not revolutionism, to deprive ourselves in advance of any freedom of action, openly to inform an enemy who is at present better armed than we are whether we shall fight him, and when. To accept battle at a time when it is obviously advantageous to the enemy, but not to us, is criminal; political leaders of the revolutionary class are absolutely useless if they are incapable of "changing tack, or offering conciliation and compromise" in order to take evasive action in a patently disadvantageous battle.

IX

"LEFT-WING" COMMUNISM IN GREAT BRITAIN

There is no Communist Party in Great Britain as yet, but there is a fresh, broad, powerful and rapidly growing communist movement among the workers, which justifies the best hopes. There are several political parties and organisations (the British Socialist Party,[35] the Socialist Labour Party, the South Wales Socialist Society, the Workers' Socialist Federation[36]), which desire to form a Communist Party and are already negotiating among themselves to this end. In its issue of February 21, 1920, Vol. VI,

No. 48, *The Workers' Dreadnought*, weekly organ of the last of the organisations mentioned, carried an article by the editor, Comrade Sylvia Pankhurst, entitled "Towards a Communist Party". The article outlines the progress of the negotiations between the four organisations mentioned, for the formation of a united Communist Party, on the basis of affiliation to the Third International, the recognition of the Soviet system instead of parliamentarianism, and the recognition of the dictatorship of the proletariat. It appears that one of the greatest obstacles to the immediate formation of a united Communist Party is presented by the disagreement on the questions of participation in Parliament and on whether the new Communist Party should affiliate to the old, trade-unionist, opportunist and social-chauvinist Labour Party, which is mostly made up of trade unions. The Workers' Socialist Federation and the Socialist Labour Party* are opposed to taking part in parliamentary elections and in Parliament, and they are opposed to affiliation to the Labour Party; in this they disagree with all or with most of the members of the British Socialist Party, which they regard as the "Right wing of the Communist parties" in Great Britain. (Page 5, Sylvia Pankhurst's article.)

Thus, the main division is the same as in Germany, notwithstanding the enormous difference in the forms in which the disagreements manifest themselves (in Germany the form is far closer to the "Russian" than it is in Great Britain), and in a number of other things. Let us examine the arguments of the "Lefts".

On the question of participation in Parliament, Comrade Sylvia Pankhurst refers to an article in the same issue, by Comrade Gallacher, who writes in the name of the Scottish Workers' Council in Glasgow.

> "The above council," he writes, "is definitely anti-parliamentarian, and has behind it the Left wing of the various political bodies. We represent the revolutionary movement in Scotland, striving continually to build up a revolutionary organisation within the industries [in various branches of production], and a Communist Party, based on social committees, throughout the country. For

---

* I believe this party is opposed to affiliation to the Labour Party but not all its members are opposed to participation in Parliament.

a considerable time we have been sparring with the official parliamentarians. We have not considered it necessary to declare open warfare on them, and they are *afraid* to open an attack on us.

"But this state of affairs cannot long continue. We are winning all along the line.

"The rank and file of the I.L.P. in Scotland is becoming more and more disgusted with the thought of Parliament, and the Soviets [the Russian word transliterated into English is used] or Workers' Councils are being supported by almost every branch. This is very serious, of course, for the gentlemen who look to politics for a profession, and they are using any and every means to persuade their members to come back into the parliamentary fold. Revolutionary comrades *must not* [all italics are the author's] give any support to this gang. Our fight here is going to be a difficult one. One of the worst features of it will be the treachery of those whose personal ambition is a more impelling force than their regard for the revolution. Any support given to parliamentarism is simply assisting to put power into the hands of our British Scheidemanns and Noskes. Henderson, Clynes and Co. are hopelessly reactionary. The official I.L.P. is more and more coming under the control of middle-class Liberals, who ... have found their 'spiritual home' in the camp of Messrs. MacDonald, Snowden and Co. The official I.L.P. is bitterly hostile to the Third International, the rank and file is for it. Any support to the parliamentary opportunists is simply playing into the hands of the former. The B.S.P. doesn't count at all here.... What is wanted here is a sound revolutionary industrial organisation, and a Communist Party working along clear, well-defined, scientific lines. If our comrades can assist us in building these, we will take their help gladly; if they cannot, for God's sake let them keep out altogether, lest they betray the revolution by lending their support to the reactionaries, who are so eagerly clamouring for parliamentary 'honours' (?) [the query mark is the author's] and who are so anxious to prove that they *can rule* as effectively as the 'boss' class politicians themselves."

In my opinion, this letter to the editor expresses excellently the temper and point of view of the young Communists, or of rank-and-file workers who are only just beginning to accept communism. This temper is highly gratifying and valuable; we must learn to appreciate and support it for, in its absence, it would be hopeless to expect the victory of the proletarian revolution in Great Britain, or in any other country for that matter. People who can give expression to this temper of the masses, and are able to evoke such a temper (which is very often dormant, unconscious and latent) among the masses, should be appreciated and given every assistance. At the same time, we must tell them openly and frankly that a state of mind is *by itself* insufficient for leadership of the masses in a great revolutionary struggle, and that the cause of the revolution may well be harmed by certain errors that people who are most devoted to the cause of the revolution are about to commit, or are committing. Comrade Gallacher's letter undoubtedly reveals the rudiments of *all* the mistakes that are being made by the German "Left" Communists and were made by the Russian "Left" Bolsheviks in 1908 and 1918.

The writer of the letter is full of a noble and working-class hatred for the bourgeois "class politicians" (a hatred understood and shared, however, not only by proletarians but by all working people, by all *Kleinen Leuten** to use the German expression). In a representative of the oppressed and exploited masses, this hatred is truly the "beginning of all wisdom", the basis of any socialist and communist movement and of its success. The writer, however, has apparently lost sight of the fact that politics is a science and an art that does not fall from the skies or come gratis, and that, if it wants to overcome the bourgeoisie, the proletariat must train its *own* proletarian "class politicians", of a kind in no way inferior to bourgeois politicians.

The writer of the letter fully realises that only workers' Soviets, not parliament, can be the instrument enabling the proletariat to achieve its aims; those who have failed to understand this are, of course, out-and-out reactionaries, even if they are most highly educated people, most experienced politicians, most sincere socialists, most erudite Marxists, and most honest citizens and fathers of families. But the writer of the letter does not even ask—it does not occur to him to ask—whether it is possible to bring about the Soviets' victory over parliament without getting pro-Soviet politicians *into* parliament, without disintegrating parliamentarianism from *within*, without working within parliament for the success of the Soviets in their forthcoming task of dispersing parliament. Yet the writer of the letter expresses the absolutely correct idea that the Communist Party in Great Britain must act on *scientific* principles. Science demands, first, that the experience of other countries be taken into account,

* "Small folk, little people" (Germ.).—*Ed.*

especially if these other countries, which are also capitalist, are undergoing, or have recently undergone, a very similar experience; second, it demands that account be taken of *all* the forces, groups, parties, classes and masses operating in a given country, and also that policy should not be determined only by the desires and views, by the degree of class-consciousness and the militancy of one group or party alone.

It is true that the Hendersons, the Clyneses, the MacDonalds and the Snowdens are hopelessly reactionary. It is equally true that they want to assume power (though they would prefer a coalition with the bourgeoisie), that they want to "rule" along the old bourgeois lines, and that when they are in power they will certainly behave like the Scheidemanns and Noskes. All that is true. But it does not at all follow that to support them means treachery to the revolution; what does follow is that, in the interests of the revolution, working-class revolutionaries should give these gentlemen a certain amount of parliamentary support. To explain this idea, I shall take two contemporary British political documents: (1) the speech delivered by Prime Minister Lloyd George on March 18, 1920 (as reported in *The Manchester Guardian* of March 19, 1920), and (2) the arguments of a "Left" Communist, Comrade Sylvia Pankhurst, in the article mentioned above.

In his speech Lloyd George entered into a polemic with Asquith (who had been especially invited to this meeting but declined to attend) and with those Liberals who want, not a coalition with the Conservatives, but closer relations with the Labour Party. (In the above-quoted letter, Comrade Gallacher also points to the fact that Liberals are joining the Independent Labour Party.) Lloyd George argued that a coalition—and a *close* coalition at that—between the Liberals and the Conservatives was essential, otherwise there might be a victory for the Labour Party, which Lloyd George prefers to call "Socialist" and which is working for the "common ownership" of the means of production. "It is ... known as communism in France," the leader of the British bourgeoisie said, putting it popularly for his audience, Liberal M.P.s who probably never knew it before. In Germany it was called socialism, and in Russia it is called

Bolshevism, he went on to say. To Liberals this is unacceptable on principle, Lloyd George explained, because they stand in principle for private property. "Civilisation is in jeopardy," the speaker declared, and consequently Liberals and Conservatives must unite....

"... If you go to the agricultural areas," said Lloyd George, "I agree you have the old party divisions as strong as ever. They are removed from the danger. It does not walk their lanes. But when they see it they will be as strong as some of these industrial constituencies are now. Four-fifths of this country is industrial and commercial; hardly one-fifth is agricultural. It is one of the things I have constantly in my mind when I think of the dangers of the future here. In France the population is agricultural, and you have a solid body of opinion which does not move very rapidly, and which is not very easily excited by revolutionary movements. That is not the case here. This country is more top-heavy than any country in the world, and if it begins to rock, the crash here, for that reason, will be greater than in any land."

From this the reader will see that Mr. Lloyd George is not only a very intelligent man, but one who has also learned a great deal from the Marxists. We too have something to learn from Lloyd George.

Of definite interest is the following episode, which occurred in the course of the discussion after Lloyd George's speech:

"*Mr. Wallace, M.P.:* I should like to ask what the Prime Minister considers the effect might be in the industrial constituencies upon the industrial workers, so many of whom are Liberals at the present time and from whom we get so much support. Would not a possible result be to cause an immediate overwhelming accession of strength to the Labour Party from men who at present are our cordial supporters?

"*The Prime Minister:* I take a totally different view. The fact that Liberals are fighting among themselves undoubtedly drives a very considerable number of Liberals in despair to the Labour Party, where you get a considerable body of Liberals, very able men, whose business it is to discredit the Government. The result is undoubtedly to bring a good accession of public sentiment to the Labour Party. It does not go to the Liberals who are outside, it goes to the Labour Party, the by-elections show that."

It may be said, in passing, that this argument shows in particular how muddled even the most intelligent members of the bourgeoisie have become and how they cannot help committing irreparable blunders. That, in fact, is what will bring about the downfall of the bourgeoisie. Our people, however, may commit blunders (provided, of course, that they are not too serious and are rectified in time) and yet, in the long run, will prove the victors.

The second political document is the following argument advanced by Comrade Sylvia Pankhurst, a "Left" Communist:

"... Comrade Inkpin [the General Secretary of the British Socialist Party] refers to the Labour Party as 'the main body of the working-class movement'. Another comrade of the British Socialist Party, at the Third International, just held, put the British Socialist Party position more strongly. He said: 'We regard the Labour Party as the organised working class.'

"We do not take this view of the Labour Party. The Labour Party is very large numerically though its membership is to a great extent quiescent and apathetic, consisting of men and women who have joined the trade unions because their workmates are trade unionists, and to share the friendly benefits.

"But we recognise that the great size of the Labour Party is also due to the fact that it is the creation of a school of thought beyond which the majority of the British working class has not yet emerged, though great changes are at work in the mind of the people which will presently alter this state of affairs....

"The British Labour Party, like the social-patriotic organisations of other countries, will, in the natural development of society, inevitably come into power. It is for the Communists to build up the forces that will overthrow the social patriots, and in this country we must not delay or falter in that work.

"We must not dissipate our energy in adding to the strength of the Labour Party; its rise to power is inevitable. We must concentrate on making a communist movement that will vanquish it. The Labour Party will soon be forming a government; the revolutionary opposition must make ready to attack it...."

Thus the liberal bourgeoisie are abandoning the historical system of "two parties" (of exploiters), which has been hallowed by centuries of experience and has been extremely advantageous to the exploiters, and consider it necessary for these two parties to join forces against the Labour Party. A number of Liberals are deserting to the Labour Party like rats from a sinking ship. The Left Communists believe that the transfer of power to the Labour Party is inevitable and admit that it now has the backing of most workers. From this they draw the strange conclusion which Comrade Sylvia Pankhurst formulates as follows:

"The Communist Party must not compromise.... The Communist Party must keep its doctrine pure, and its independence of reformism inviolate; its mission is to lead the way, without stopping or turning, by the direct road to the communist revolution."

On the contrary, the fact that most British workers still follow the lead of the British Kerenskys or Scheidemanns and have not yet had experience of a government composed of these people—an experience which was necessary in Russia and Germany so as to secure the mass transition of the workers to communism—undoubtedly indicates that the British Communists *should* participate in parliamentary action, that they should, from *within* parliament, help the masses of the workers see the results of a Henderson and Snowden government in practice, and that they should help the Hendersons and Snowdens defeat the united forces of Lloyd George and Churchill. To act otherwise would mean hampering the cause of the revolution, since revolution is impossible without a change in the views of the majority of the working class, a change brought about by the political experience of the masses, never by propaganda alone. "To lead the way without compromises, without turning"—this slogan is obviously wrong if it comes from a patently impotent minority of the workers who know (or at all events should know) that given a Henderson and Snowden victory over Lloyd George and Churchill, the majority will soon become disappointed in their leaders and will begin to support communism (or at all events will adopt an attitude of neutrality, and, in the main, of sympathetic neutrality, towards the Communists). It is as though 10,000 soldiers were to hurl themselves into battle against an enemy force of 50,000, when it would be proper to "halt", "take evasive action", or even effect a "compromise" so as to gain time until the arrival of the 100,000 reinforcements that are on their way but cannot go into action immediately. That is intellectualist childishness, not the serious tactics of a revolutionary class.

The fundamental law of revolution, which has been confirmed by all revolutions and especially by all three Russian revolutions in the twentieth century, is as follows: for a revolution to take place it is not enough for the exploited and oppressed masses to realise the impossibility of living in the old way, and demand changes; for a revolution to take place it is essential that the exploiters should not be able to live and rule in the old way. It is only when the "*lower classes*" *do not want* to live in the old way and the "upper classes" *cannot carry on in the old way* that the revolution can triumph. This truth can be expressed in other words: revolution is impossible without a nation-wide crisis (affecting both the exploited and the exploiters). It follows that, for a revolution to take place, it is essential, first, that a majority of the workers (or at least a majority of the class-conscious, thinking, and politically active workers) should fully realise that revolution is necessary, and that they should be prepared to die for it; second, that the ruling classes should be going through a governmental crisis, which draws even the most backward masses into politics (symptomatic of any genuine revolution is a rapid, tenfold and even hundredfold increase in the size of the working and oppressed masses—hitherto apathetic—who are capable of waging the political struggle), weakens the government, and makes it possible for the revolutionaries to rapidly overthrow it.

Incidentally, as can also be seen from Lloyd George's speech, both conditions for a successful proletarian revolution are clearly maturing in Great Britain. The errors of the Left Communists are particularly dangerous at present, because certain revolutionaries are not displaying a sufficiently thoughtful, sufficiently attentive, sufficiently intelligent and sufficiently shrewd attitude toward each of these conditions. If we are the party of the revolutionary *class*, and not merely a revolutionary group, and if we want the *masses* to follow us (and unless we achieve that, we stand the risk of remaining mere windbags), we must, first, help Henderson or Snowden to beat Lloyd George and Churchill (or, rather, compel the former to beat the latter, because the former *are afraid of their victory!*); second, we must help the majority of the working class to be convinced by their own experience that we are right, i.e., that the Hendersons and Snowdens are absolutely good for nothing, that they are petty-bourgeois and treacherous by nature, and that their bankruptcy is inevitable; third, we must bring nearer the moment when, *on the basis* of the disappointment of most of the workers in the Hendersons, it will be possible, with serious chances of success, to overthrow the government of the Hendersons at once; because if the most astute and solid Lloyd George, that big, not petty, bourgeois, is displaying consternation and is more and more weakening himself (and the bourgeoisie as a whole) by his "friction" with Churchill today and with Asquith tomorrow, how much greater will be the consternation of a Henderson government!

I will put it more concretely. In my opinion, the British Communists should unite their four parties and groups (all very weak, and some of them very, very weak) into a single Communist Party on the basis of the principles of the Third International and of *obligatory* participation in parliament. The Communist Party should propose the following "compromise" election agreement to the Hendersons and Snowdens: let us jointly fight against the alliance between Lloyd George and the Conservatives; let us share parliamentary seats in proportion to the number of workers' votes polled for the Labour Party and for the Communist Party (not in elections, but in a special ballot), and let us retain *complete freedom* of agitation, propaganda and political activity. Of course, without this latter condition, we cannot agree to a bloc, for that would be treachery; the British Communists must demand and get complete freedom to expose the Hendersons and the Snowdens in the same way as (*for fifteen years*—1903-17) the Russian Bolsheviks demanded and got it in respect of the Russian Hendersons and Snowdens, i.e., the Mensheviks.

If the Hendersons and the Snowdens accept a bloc on these terms, we shall be the gainers, because the number of parliamentary seats is of no importance to us; we are not out for seats. We shall yield on this point (whilst the Hendersons and especially their new friends—or new masters—the Liberals who have joined the Independent Labour Party are most eager to get seats). We shall be the gainers, because we shall carry *our* agitation among the *masses* at a time when Lloyd George *himself* has "incensed" them, and we shall not only be helping the Labour Party to establish its government sooner, but shall also be helping the masses sooner to understand the communist propaganda that we shall carry on against the Hendersons, without any reticence or omission.

If the Hendersons and the Snowdens reject a bloc with us on these terms, we shall gain still more, for we shall at once have shown the *masses* (note that, even in the purely Menshevik and completely opportunist Independent Labour Party, the *rank and file* are in favour of Soviets) that the Hendersons prefer *their* close relations with the capitalists to the unity of all the workers. We shall immediately gain in the eyes of the *masses*, who, particularly after the brilliant, highly correct and highly useful (to communism) explanations given by Lloyd George, will be sympathetic to the idea of uniting all the workers against the Lloyd George-Conservative alliance. We shall gain immediately, because we shall have demonstrated to the masses that the Hendersons and the Snowdens are afraid to beat Lloyd George, afraid to assume power alone, and are striving to secure the *secret* support of Lloyd George, who is *openly* extending a hand to the Conservatives, against the Labour Party. It should be noted that in Russia, after the revolution of February 27, 1917 (old style), the Bolsheviks' propaganda against the Mensheviks and Socialist-Revolutionaries (i.e., the Russian Hendersons and Snowdens) derived benefit precisely from a circumstance of this kind. We said to the Mensheviks and the Socialist-Revolutionaries: assume full power without the bourgeoisie, because you have a majority in the Soviets (at the First All-Russia Congress of Soviets, in June 1917, the Bolsheviks had only 13 per cent of the votes). But the Russian Hendersons and Snowdens were afraid to assume power without the bourgeoisie, and when the bourgeoisie held up the elections to the Constituent Assembly, knowing full well that the elections would give a majority to the Socialist-Revolutionaries and the Mensheviks* (who formed a close political bloc and in

* The results of the November 1917 elections to the Constituent Assembly in Russia, based on returns embracing over 36,000,000 voters, were as follows: the Bolsheviks obtained 25 per cent of the votes; the various parties of the landowners and the bourgeoisie obtained 13 per cent, and the petty-bourgeois-democratic parties, i.e., the Socialist-Revolutionaries, Mensheviks and a number of similar small groups obtained 62 per cent.

fact represented *only* petty-bourgeois democracy), the Socialist-Revolutionaries and the Mensheviks were unable energetically and consistently to oppose these delays.

If the Hendersons and the Snowdens reject a bloc with the Communists, the latter will immediately gain by winning the sympathy of the masses and discrediting the Hendersons and Snowdens; if, as a result, we do lose a few parliamentary seats, it is a matter of no significance to us. We would put up our candidates in a very few but absolutely safe constituencies, namely, constituencies where our candidatures would not give any seats to the Liberals at the expense of the Labour candidates. We would take part in the election campaign, distribute leaflets agitating for communism, and, in *all* constituencies where we have no candidates, we would urge the electors *to vote for the Labour candidate and against the bourgeois candidate*. Comrades Sylvia Pankhurst and Gallacher are mistaken in thinking that this is a betrayal of communism, or a renunciation of the struggle against the social-traitors. On the contrary, the cause of communist revolution would undoubtedly gain thereby.

At present, British Communists very often find it hard even to approach the masses, and even to get a hearing from them. If I come out as a Communist and call upon them to vote for Henderson and against Lloyd George, they will certainly give me a hearing. And I shall be able to explain in a popular manner, not only why the Soviets are better than a parliament and why the dictatorship of the proletariat is better than the dictatorship of Churchill (disguised with the signboard of bourgeois "democracy"), but also that, with my vote, I want to support Henderson in the same way as the rope supports a hanged man—that the impending establishment of a government of the Hendersons will prove that I am right, will bring the masses over to my side, and will hasten the political death of the Hendersons and the Snowdens just as was the case with their kindred spirits in Russia and Germany.

If the objection is raised that these tactics are too "subtle" or too complex for the masses to understand, that these tactics will split and scatter our forces, will prevent us from concentrating them on Soviet revolution, etc., I will reply to the "Left" objectors: don't ascribe your doctrinairism to the masses! The masses in Russia are no doubt no better educated than the masses in Britain; if anything, they are less so. Yet the masses understood the Bolsheviks, and the fact that, in September 1917, *on the eve* of the Soviet revolution, the Bolsheviks put up their candidates for a bourgeois parliament (the Constituent Assembly) and *on the day after* the Soviet revolution, in November 1917, took part in the elections to this Constituent Assembly, which they got rid of on January 5, 1918—this did not hamper the Bolsheviks, but, on the contrary, helped them.

I cannot deal here with the second point of disagreement among the British Communists—the question of affiliation or non-affiliation to the Labour Party. I have too little material at my disposal on this question, which is highly complex because of the unique character of the British Labour Party, whose very structure is so unlike that of the political parties usual in the European continent. It is beyond doubt, however, first, that in this question, too, those who try to deduce the tactics of the revolutionary proletariat from principles such as: "The Communist Party must keep its doctrine pure, and its independence of reformism inviolate; its mission is to lead the way, without stopping or turning, by the direct road to the communist revolution"—will inevitably fall into error. Such principles are merely a repetition of the mistake made by the French Blanquist Communards, who, in 1874, "repudiated" all compromises and all intermediate stages. Second, it is beyond doubt that, in this question too, as always, the task consists in learning to apply the general and basic principles of communism to the *specific relations* between classes and parties, to the *specific features* in the objective development towards communism, which are different in each country and which we must be able to discover, study, and predict.

This, however, should be discussed, not in connection with British communism alone, but in connection with the general conclusions concerning the development of communism in all capitalist countries. We shall now proceed to deal with this subject.

X
SEVERAL CONCLUSIONS

The Russian bourgeois revolution of 1905 revealed a highly original turn in world history: in one of the most backward capitalist countries, the strike movement attained a scope and power unprecedented anywhere in the world. In the *first month* of 1905 *alone*, the number of strikers was ten times the *annual* average for the previous decade (1895-1904); from January to October 1905, strikes grew all the time and reached enormous proportions. Under the influence of a number of unique historical conditions, backward Russia was the first to show the world, not only the growth, by leaps and bounds, of the independent activity of the oppressed masses in time of revolution (this had occurred in all great revolutions), but also that the significance of the proletariat is infinitely greater than its proportion in the total population; it showed a combination of the economic strike and the political strike, with the latter developing into an armed uprising, and the birth of the Soviets, a new form of mass struggle and mass organisation of the classes oppressed by capitalism.

The revolutions of February and October 1917 led to the all-round development of the Soviets on a nation-wide scale and to their victory in the proletarian socialist revolution. In less than two years, the international character of the Soviets, the spread of this form of struggle and organisation to the world working-class movement and the historical mission of the Soviets as the grave-digger, heir and successor of bourgeois parliamentarianism and of bourgeois democracy in general, all became clear.

But that is not all. The history of the working-class movement now shows that, in all countries, it is about to go through (and is already going through) a struggle waged by communism—emergent, gaining strength and advancing towards victory—against, primarily, Menshevism, i.e., opportunism and social-chauvinism (the home brand in each particular country), and then as a complement, so to say, Left-wing communism. The former struggle has developed in all countries, apparently without any exception, as a duel between the Second International (already virtually dead) and the Third International. The latter struggle is to be seen in Germany, Great Britain, Italy, America (at any rate, a certain *section* of the Industrial Workers of the World and of the anarcho-syndicalist trends uphold the errors of Left-wing communism alongside of an almost universal and almost unreserved acceptance of the Soviet system), and in France (the attitude of a section of the former syndicalists towards the political party and parliamentarianism, also alongside of the acceptance of the Soviet system); in other words, the struggle is undoubtedly being waged, not only on an international, but even on a world-wide scale.

But while the working-class movement is everywhere going through what is actually the same kind of preparatory school for victory over the bourgeoisie, it is achieving that development in its *own way* in each country. The big and advanced capitalist countries are travelling this road *far more rapidly* than did Bolshevism, to which history granted fifteen years to prepare itself for victory, as an organised political trend. In the brief space of a year, the Third International has already scored a decisive victory; it has defeated the yellow, social-chauvinist Second International, which only a few months ago was incomparably stronger than the Third International, seemed stable and powerful, and enjoyed every possible support—direct and indirect, material (Cabinet posts, passports, the press) and ideological—from the world bourgeoisie.

It is now essential that Communists of every country should quite consciously take into account both the fundamental objectives of the struggle against opportunism and "Left" doctrinairism, and the *concrete features* which this struggle assumes and must inevitably assume in each country, in conformity with the specific character of its economics, politics, culture, and national composition (Ireland, etc.), its colonies, religious divisions, and so on and so forth. Dissatisfaction with the Second International is felt everywhere and is spreading and growing, both because of its opportunism and because of its inability or incapacity to create a really centralised and really leading centre capable of directing the international tactics of the revolutionary proletariat in its struggle for a world Soviet republic. It should be clearly realised that such a leading centre can never be built up on stereotyped, mechanically equated, and identical tactical rules of struggle. As long as national and state distinctions exist among peoples and countries—and these will continue to exist for a very long time to come, even after the dictatorship of the proletariat has been established on a world-wide scale—the unity of the international tactics of the communist working-class movement in all countries demands, not the elimination of variety or the suppression of national distinctions (which is a pipe dream at present), but an application of the *fundamental* principles of communism (Soviet power and the dictatorship of the proletariat), which will *correctly modify* these principles in certain *particulars*, correctly adapt and apply them to national and national-state distinctions. To seek out, investigate, predict, and grasp that which is nationally specific and nationally distinctive, in the *concrete manner* in which each country should tackle a *single* international task: victory over opportunism and Left doctrinairism within the working-class movement; the overthrow of the bourgeoisie; the establishment of a Soviet republic and a proletarian dictatorship—such is the basic task in the historical period that all the advanced countries (and not they alone) are going through. The chief thing—though, of course, far from everything—the chief thing, has already been achieved: the vanguard of the working class has been won over, has ranged itself on the side of Soviet government and against parliamentarianism, on the side of the dictatorship of the proletariat and against bourgeois democracy. All efforts and all attention should now be concentrated on the *next* step, which may seem—and from a certain viewpoint actually is—less fundamental, but, on the other hand, is actually closer to a practical accomplishment of the task. That step is: the search after forms of the *transition* or the *approach* to the proletarian revolution.

The proletarian vanguard has been won over ideologically. That is the main thing. Without this, not even the first step towards victory can be made. But that is still quite a long way from victory. Victory cannot be won with a vanguard alone. To throw only the vanguard into the decisive battle, before the entire class, the broad masses, have taken up a position either of direct support for the vanguard, or at least of sympathetic neutrality towards it and of precluded support for the enemy, would be, not merely foolish but criminal. Propaganda and agitation alone are not enough for an entire class, the broad masses of the working people, those oppressed by capital, to take up such a stand. For that, the masses must have their own political experience. Such is the fundamental law of all great revolutions, which has been confirmed with compelling force and vividness, not only in Russia but in Germany as well. To turn resolutely towards communism, it was necessary, not only for the ignorant and often illiterate masses of Russia, but also for the literate and well-educated masses of Germany, to realise from their own bitter experience the absolute impotence and spinelessness, the absolute helplessness and servility to the bourgeoisie, and the utter vileness of the government of the paladins of the Second International; they had to realise that a dictatorship of the extreme reactionaries (Kornilov[37] in Russia; Kapp[38] and Co. in Germany) is inevitably the only alternative to a dictatorship of the proletariat.

The immediate objective of the class-conscious vanguard of the international working-class movement, i.e., the Communist parties, groups and trends, is to be able to *lead* the broad masses (who are still, for the most part, apathetic, inert, dormant and convention-ridden) to their new position, or, rather, to be able to lead, *not only* their own party but also these masses in their advance and transition to the new position. While the first historical objective (that of winning over the class-conscious vanguard of the proletariat to the side of Soviet power and the dictatorship of the working class) could not have been reached without a complete ideological and political victory over opportunism and social-chauvinism, the second and immediate objective, which consists in being able to lead the *masses* to a new position ensuring the victory of the vanguard in the revolution, cannot be reached without the liquidation of Left doctrinairism, and without a full elimination of its errors.

As long as it was (and inasmuch as it still is) a question

of winning the proletariat's vanguard over to the side of communism, priority went and still goes to propaganda work; even propaganda circles, with all their parochial limitations, are useful under these conditions, and produce good results. But when it is a question of practical action by the masses, of the disposition, if one may so put it, of vast armies, of the alignment of *all* the class forces in a given society *for the final and decisive battle*, then propagandist methods alone, the mere repetition of the truths of "pure" communism, are of no avail. In these circumstances, one must not count in thousands, like the propagandist belonging to a small group that has not yet given leadership to the masses; in these circumstances one must count in millions and tens of millions. In these circumstances, we must ask ourselves, not only whether we have convinced the vanguard of the revolutionary class, but also whether the historically effective forces of *all* classes—positively of all the classes in a given society, without exception—are arrayed in such a way that the decisive battle is at hand—in such a way that: (1) all the class forces hostile to us have become sufficiently entangled, are sufficiently at loggerheads with each other, have sufficiently weakened themselves in a struggle which is beyond their strength; (2) all the vacillating and unstable, intermediate elements—the petty bourgeoisie and the petty-bourgeois democrats, as distinct from the bourgeoisie—have sufficiently exposed themselves in the eyes of the people, have sufficiently disgraced themselves through their practical bankruptcy, and (3) among the proletariat, a mass sentiment favouring the most determined, bold and dedicated revolutionary action against the bourgeoisie has emerged and begun to grow vigorously. Then revolution is indeed ripe; then, indeed, if we have correctly gauged all the conditions indicated and summarised above, and if we have chosen the right moment, our victory is assured.

The differences between the Churchills and the Lloyd Georges—with insignificant national distinctions, these political types exist in *all* countries—on the one hand, and between the Hendersons and the Lloyd Georges on the other, are quite minor and unimportant from the standpoint of pure (i.e., abstract) communism, i.e., communism that has not yet matured to the stage of practical political action by the masses. However, from the standpoint of this practical action by the masses, these differences are most important. To take due account of these differences, and to determine the moment when the inevitable conflicts between these "friends", which weaken and enfeeble *all the "friends" taken together*, will have come to a head—that is the concern, the task, of a Communist who wants to be, not merely a class-conscious and convinced propagandist of ideas, but a practical leader of the *masses* in the revolution. It is necessary to link the strictest devotion to the ideas of communism with the ability to effect all the necessary practical compromises, tacks, conciliatory manoeuvres, zigzags, retreats and so on, in order to speed up the achievement and then loss of political power by the Hendersons (the heroes of the Second International, if we are not to name individual representatives of petty-bourgeois democracy who call themselves socialists); to accelerate their inevitable bankruptcy in practice, which will enlighten the masses in the spirit of our ideas, in the direction of communism; to accelerate the inevitable friction, quarrels, conflicts and complete disintegration among the Hendersons, the Lloyd Georges and the Churchills (the Mensheviks, the Socialist-Revolutionaries, the Constitutional-Democrats, the monarchists; the Scheidemanns, the bourgeoisie and the Kappists, etc.); to select the proper moment when the discord among these "pillars of sacrosanct private property" is at its height, so that, through a decisive offensive, the proletariat will defeat them all and capture political power.

History as a whole, and the history of revolutions in particular, is always richer in content, more varied, more multiform, more lively and ingenious than is imagined by even the best parties, the most class-conscious vanguards of the most advanced classes. This can readily be understood, because even the finest of vanguards express the class-consciousness, will, passion and imagination of tens of thousands, whereas at moments of great upsurge and the exertion of all human capacities, revolutions are made by the class-consciousness, will, passion and imagination of tens of millions, spurred on by a most acute struggle of classes. Two very important practical conclusions follow from this: first, that in order to accomplish its task the revolutionary class must be able to master *all* forms or aspects of social activity without exception (completing after the capture of political power—sometimes at great risk and with very great danger—what it did not complete before the capture of power); second, that the revolutionary class must be prepared for the most rapid and brusque replacement of one form by another.

One will readily agree that any army which does not train to use all the weapons, all the means and methods of warfare that the enemy possesses, or may possess, is behaving in an unwise or even criminal manner. This applies to politics even more than it does to the art of war. In politics it is even harder to know in advance which methods of struggle will be applicable and to our advantage in certain future conditions. Unless we learn to apply all the methods of struggle, we may suffer grave and sometimes even decisive defeat, if changes beyond our control in the position of the other classes bring to the forefront a form of activity in which we are especially weak. If, however, we learn to use all the methods of struggle, victory will be certain, because we represent the interests of the really foremost and really revolutionary class, even if circumstances do not permit us to make use of weapons that are most dangerous to the enemy, weapons that deal the swiftest mortal blows. Inexperienced revolutionaries often think that legal methods of struggle are opportunist because, in this field, the bourgeoisie has most frequently deceived and duped the workers (particularly in "peaceful" and non-revolutionary times), while illegal methods of struggle are revolutionary. That, however, is wrong. The truth is that those parties and leaders are opportunists and traitors to the working class that are unable or unwilling (do not say, "I can't"; say, "I shan't") to use illegal methods of struggle in conditions such as those which prevailed, for example, during the imperialist war of 1914-18, when the bourgeoisie of the freest democratic countries most brazenly and brutally deceived the workers, and smothered the truth about the predatory character of the war. But revolutionaries who are incapable of combining illegal forms of struggle with *every* form of legal struggle are poor revolutionaries indeed. It is not difficult to be a revolutionary when revolution has already broken out and is in spate, when all people are joining the revolution just because they are carried away, because it is the vogue, and sometimes even from careerist motives. After its victory, the proletariat has to make most strenuous efforts, even the most painful, so as to "liberate" itself from such pseudo-revolutionaries. It is far more difficult—and far more precious—to be a revolutionary when the conditions for direct, open, really mass and really revolutionary struggle *do not yet exist*, to be able to champion the interests of the revolution (by propaganda, agitation and organisation) in non-revolutionary bodies, and quite often in downright reactionary bodies, in a non-revolutionary situation, among the masses who are incapable of immediately appreciating the need for revolutionary methods of action. To be able to seek, find and correctly determine the specific path or the particular turn of events that will *lead* the masses to the real, decisive and final revolutionary struggle—such is the main objective of communism in Western Europe and in America today.

Britain is an example. We cannot tell—no one can tell in advance—how soon a real proletarian revolution will flare up there, and *what immediate cause* will most serve to rouse, kindle, and impel into the struggle the very wide masses, who are still dormant. Hence, it is our duty to carry on all our preparatory work in such a way as to be "well shod on all four feet" (as the late Plekhanov, when he was a Marxist and revolutionary, was fond of saying). It is possible that the breach will be forced, the ice broken, by a parliamentary crisis, or by a crisis arising from colonial and imperialist contradictions, which are hopelessly entangled and are becoming increasingly painful and acute, or perhaps by some third cause, etc. We are not discussing the kind of struggle that will *determine* the fate of the proletarian revolution in Great Britain (no Communist has any doubt on that score; for all of us this is a foregone conclusion): what we are discussing is the *immediate cause* that will bring into motion the now dormant proletarian masses, and lead them right up to revolution.

Let us not forget that in the French bourgeois republic, for example, in a situation which, from both the international and the national viewpoints, was a hundred times less revolutionary than it is today, such an "unexpected" and "petty" cause as one of the many thousands of fraudulent machinations of the reactionary military caste (the Dreyfus case[39]) was enough to bring the people to the brink of civil war!

In Great Britain the Communists should constantly, unremittingly and unswervingly utilise parliamentary elections and all the vicissitudes of the Irish, colonial and world-imperialist policy of the British Government, and all other fields, spheres and aspects of public life, and work in all of them in a new way, in a communist way, in the spirit of the Third, not the Second, International. I have neither the time nor the space here to describe the "Russian" "Bolshevik" methods of participation in parliamentary elections and in the parliamentary struggle; I can, however, assure foreign Communists that they were quite unlike the usual West-European parliamentary campaigns. From this the conclusion is often drawn: "Well, that was in Russia; in our country parliamentarianism is different." This is a false conclusion. Communists, adherents of the Third International in all countries, exist for the purpose of *changing*—all along the line, in all spheres of life—the old socialist, trade unionist, syndicalist, and parliamentary type of work into a *new* type of work, the communist. In Russia, too, there was always an abundance of opportunism, purely bourgeois sharp practices and capitalist rigging in the elections. In Western Europe and in America, the Communists must learn to create a new, uncustomary, non-opportunist, and non-careerist parliamentarianism; the Communist parties must issue their slogans; true proletarians, with the help of the unorganised and downtrodden poor, should distribute leaflets, canvass workers' houses and cottages of the rural proletarians and peasants in the remote villages (fortunately there are many times fewer remote villages in Europe than in Russia, and in Britain the number is very small); they should go into the public houses, penetrate into unions, societies and chance gatherings of the common people, and speak to the people, not in learned (or very parliamentary) language; they should not at all strive to "get seats" in parliament, but should everywhere try to get people to think, and draw the masses into the struggle, to take the bourgeoisie at its word and utilise the machinery it has set up, the elections it has appointed, and the appeals it has made to the people; they should try to explain to the people what Bolshevism is, in a way that was never possible (under bourgeois rule) outside of election times (exclusive, of course, of times of big strikes, when in Russia a *similar* apparatus for widespread popular agitation worked even more intensively). It is very difficult to do this in Western Europe and extremely difficult in America, but it can and must be done, for the objectives of communism cannot be achieved without effort. We must work to accomplish *practical* tasks, ever more varied and ever more closely connected with all branches of social life, *winning* branch after branch, and sphere after sphere *from the bourgeoisie*.

In Great Britain, further, the work of propaganda, agitation and organisation among the armed forces and among the oppressed and underprivileged nationalities in their "*own*" state (Ireland, the colonies) must also be tackled in a new fashion (one that is not socialist, but communist; not reformist, but revolutionary). That is because, in the era of imperialism in general and especially today after a war that was a sore trial to the peoples and has quickly opened their eyes to the truth (i.e., the fact that tens of millions were killed and maimed for the sole purpose of deciding whether the British or the German robbers should plunder the largest number of countries), all these spheres of social life are heavily charged with inflammable material and are creating numerous causes of conflicts, crises and an intensification of the class struggle. We do not and cannot know which spark—of the innumerable sparks that are flying about in all countries as a result of the world economic and political crisis—will kindle the conflagration, in the sense of raising up the masses; we must, therefore, with our new and communist principles, set to work to stir up all and sundry, even the oldest, mustiest and seemingly hopeless spheres, for otherwise we shall not be able to cope with our tasks, shall not be comprehensively prepared, shall not be in possession of all the weapons and shall not prepare ourselves either to gain victory over the bourgeoisie (which arranged all aspects of social life—and has now disarranged them—in its bourgeois fashion), or to bring about the impending communist reorganisation of every sphere of life, following that victory.

Since the proletarian revolution in Russia and its victories on an international scale, expected neither by the bourgeoisie nor the philistines, the entire world has become different, and the bourgeoisie everywhere has become different too. It is terrified of "Bolshevism", exasperated by it almost to the point of frenzy, and for that very reason it is, on the one hand, precipitating the progress of events and, on the other, concentrating on the forcible suppression of Bolshevism, thereby weakening its own position in a number of other fields. In their tactics the Communists in all the advanced countries must take both these circumstances into account.

When the Russian Cadets and Kerensky began furiously to hound the Bolsheviks—especially since April 1917, and more particularly in June and July 1917—they overdid things. Millions of copies of bourgeois papers, clamouring in every key against the Bolsheviks, helped the masses to make an appraisal of Bolshevism; apart from the newspapers, all public life was full of discussions about Bolshevism, as a result of the bourgeoisie's "zeal". Today the millionaires of all countries are behaving on an international scale in a way that deserves our heartiest thanks. They are hounding Bolshevism with the same zeal as Kerensky and Co. did; they, too, are overdoing things and *helping* us just as Kerensky did. When the French bourgeoisie makes Bolshevism the central issue in the elections, and accuses the comparatively moderate or vacillating socialists of being Bolsheviks; when the American bourgeoisie, which has completely lost its head, seizes thousands and thousands of people on suspicion of Bolshevism, creates an atmosphere of panic, and broadcasts stories of Bolshevik plots; when, despite all its wisdom and experience, the British bourgeoisie—the most "solid" in the world—makes incredible blunders, founds richly endowed "anti-Bolshevik societies", creates a special literature on Bolshevism, and recruits an extra number of scientists, agitators and clergymen to combat it, we must salute and thank the capitalists. They are working for us. They are helping us to get the masses interested in the essence and significance of Bolshevism, and they cannot do otherwise, for they have *already* failed to ignore Bolshevism and stifle it.

But at the same time, the bourgeoisie sees practically only one aspect of Bolshevism—insurrection, violence, and terror; it therefore strives to prepare itself for resistance and opposition primarily in *this* field. It is possible that, in certain instances, in certain countries, and for certain brief periods, it will succeed in this. We must reckon with such an eventuality, and we have absolutely nothing to fear if it does succeed. Communism is emerging in positively every sphere of public life; its beginnings are to be seen literally on all sides. The "contagion" (to use the favourite metaphor of the bourgeoisie and the bourgeois police, the one mostly to their liking) has very thoroughly penetrated the organism and has completely permeated it. If special efforts are made to block one of the channels, the "contagion" will find another one, sometimes very unexpectedly. Life will assert itself. Let the bourgeoisie rave, work itself into a frenzy, go to extremes, commit follies, take vengeance on the Bolsheviks in advance, and endeavour to kill off (as in India, Hungary, Germany, etc.) more hundreds, thousands, and hundreds of thousands of yesterday's and tomorrow's Bolsheviks. In acting thus, the bourgeoisie is acting as all historically doomed classes have done. Communists should know that, in any case, the future belongs to them; therefore, we can (and must) combine the most intense passion in the great revolutionary struggle, with the coolest and most sober appraisal of the frenzied ravings of the bourgeoisie. The Russian revolution was cruelly defeated in 1905; the Russian Bolsheviks were defeated in July 1917; over 15,000 German Communists were killed as a result of the wily provocation and cunning manoeuvres of Scheidemann and Noske, who were working hand in glove with the bourgeoisie and the monarchist generals; White terror is raging in Finland and Hungary. But in all cases and in all countries, communism is becoming steeled and is growing; its roots are so deep that persecution does not weaken or debilitate it, but only strengthens it. Only one thing is lacking to enable us to march forward more confidently and firmly to victory, namely, the universal and thorough awareness of all Communists in all countries of the necessity to display the utmost *flexibility* in their tactics. The communist movement, which is developing magnificently, now lacks, especially in the advanced countries, this awareness and the ability to apply it in practice.

That which happened to such leaders of the Second International, such highly erudite Marxists devoted to socialism as Kautsky, Otto Bauer and others, could (and should) provide a useful lesson. They fully appreciated the need for flexible tactics; they themselves learned Marxist dialectic and taught it to others (and much of what they have done in this field will always remain a valuable contribution to socialist literature); however, *in the application* of this dialectic they committed such an error, or proved to be so *un*dialectical in practice, so incapable of taking into account the rapid change of forms and the rapid acquisition of new content by the old forms, that their fate is not much more enviable than that of Hyndman, Guesde and Plekhanov. The principal reason for their bankruptcy was that they were hypnotised by a definite form of growth of the working-class movement and socialism, forgot all about the one-sidedness of that form, were afraid to see the break-up which objective conditions made inevitable, and continued to repeat simple and, at first glance, incontestable axioms that had been learned by rote, like: "three is more than two". But politics is more like algebra than arithmetic, and still more like higher than elementary mathematics. In reality, all the old forms of the socialist movement have acquired a new content, and, consequently, a new symbol, the "minus" sign, has appeared in front of all the figures; our wiseacres, however, have stubbornly continued (and still continue) to persuade themselves and others that "minus three" is more than "minus two".

We must see to it that Communists do not make a similar mistake, only in the opposite sense, or rather, we must see to it that a *similar mistake*, only made in the opposite sense by the "Left" Communists, is corrected as soon as possible and eliminated as rapidly and painlessly as possible. It is not only Right doctrinairism that is erroneous; Left doctrinairism is erroneous too. Of course, the mistake of Left doctrinairism in communism is at present a thousand times less dangerous and less significant than that of Right doctrinairism (i.e., social-chauvinism and Kautskyism); but, after all, that is only due to the fact that Left communism is a very young trend, is only just coming into being. It is only for this reason that, under certain conditions, the disease can be easily eradicated, and we must set to work with the utmost energy to eradicate it.

The old forms burst asunder, for it turned out that their new content—anti-proletarian and reactionary—had attained an inordinate development. From the standpoint of the development of international communism, our work today has such a durable and powerful content (for Soviet power and the dictatorship of the proletariat) that it can *and must* manifest itself in any form, both new and old; it can and must regenerate, conquer and subjugate all forms, not only the new, but also the old—not for the purpose of reconciling itself with the old, but for the purpose of making all and every form—new and old—a weapon for the complete and irrevocable victory of communism.

The Communists must exert every effort to direct the working-class movement and social development in general along the straightest and shortest road to the victory of Soviet power and the dictatorship of the proletariat on a world-wide scale. That is an incontestable truth. But it is enough to take one little step farther—a step that might seem to be in the same direction—and truth turns into error. We have only to say, as the German and British Left Communists do, that we recognise only one road, only the direct road, and that we will not permit tacking, conciliatory manoeuvres, or compromising—and it will be a mistake which may cause, and in part has already caused and is causing, very grave prejudice to communism. Right doctrinairism persisted in recognising only the old forms, and became utterly bankrupt, for it did not notice the new content. Left doctrinairism persists in the unconditional repudiation of certain old forms, failing to see that the new content is forcing its way through all and sundry forms, that it is our duty as Communists to master all forms, to learn how, with the maximum rapidity, to supplement one form with another, to substitute one for another, and to adapt our tactics to any such change that does not come from our class or from our efforts.

World revolution has been so powerfully stimulated and accelerated by the horrors, vileness and abominations of the world imperialist war and by the hopelessness of the situation created by it, this revolution is developing in scope and depth with such splendid rapidity, with such a wonderful variety of changing forms, with such an instructive practical refutation of all doctrinairism, that there is every reason to hope for a rapid and complete recovery of the international communist movement from the infantile disorder of "Left-wing" communism.

April 27, 1920

APPENDIX

Before publishing houses in our country—which has been plundered by the imperialists of the whole world in revenge for the proletarian revolution, and which is still being plundered and blockaded by them regardless of all promises they made to their workers—were able to bring out my pamphlet, additional material arrived from abroad. Without claiming to present in my pamphlet anything more than the cursory notes of a publicist, I shall dwell briefly upon a few points.

I
THE SPLIT AMONG THE GERMAN COMMUNISTS

The split among the Communists in Germany is an accomplished fact. The "Lefts", or the "opposition on principle", have formed a separate Communist Workers' Party, as distinct from the Communist Party. A split also seems imminent in Italy—I say "seems", as I have only two additional issues (Nos. 7 and 8) of the Left newspaper, *Il Soviet*, in which the possibility of and necessity for a split is openly discussed, and mention is also made of a congress of the "Abstentionist" group (or the boycottists, i.e., opponents of participation in parliament), which group is still part of the Italian Socialist Party.

There is reason to fear that the split with the "Lefts", the anti-parliamentarians (in part anti-politicals too, who are opposed to any political party and to work in the trade unions), will become an international phenomenon, like the split with the "Centrists" (i.e., Kautskyites, Longuetists, Independents, etc.). Let that be so. At all events, a split is better than confusion, which hampers the ideological, theoretical and revolutionary growth and maturing of the party, and its harmonious, really organised practical work which actually paves the way for the dictatorship of the proletariat.

Let the "Lefts" put themselves to a practical test on a national and international scale. Let them try to prepare for (and then implement) the dictatorship of the proletariat, without a rigorously centralised party with iron discipline, without the ability to become masters of every sphere, every branch, and every variety of political and cultural work. Practical experience will soon teach them.

Only, every effort should be made to prevent the split with the "Lefts" from impeding—or to see that it impedes as little as possible—the necessary amalgamation into a single party, inevitable in the near future, of all participants in the working-class movement who sincerely and conscientiously stand for Soviet government and the dictatorship of the proletariat. It was the exceptional good fortune of the Bolsheviks in Russia to have had fifteen years for a systematic and consummated struggle both against the Mensheviks (i.e., the opportunists and "Centrists") and against the "Lefts", long before the masses began direct action for the dictatorship of the proletariat. In Europe and America the same work has now to be done by forced marches, so to say. Certain individuals, especially among unsuccessful aspirants to leadership, may (if they lack proletarian discipline and are not honest towards themselves) persist in their mistakes for a long time; however, when the time is ripe, the masses of the workers will themselves unite easily and rapidly and unite all sincere Communists to form a single party capable of establishing the Soviet system and the dictatorship of the proletariat.*

---

* With regard to the question of future amalgamation of the "Left" Communists, the anti-parliamentarians, with the Communists in general, I would make the following additional remarks. In the measure in which I have been able to familiarise myself with the newspapers of the "Left" Communists and the Communists in general in Germany, I find that the former have the advantage of being better able than the latter to carry on agitation among the masses. I have repeatedly observed something similar to this in the history of the Bolshevik Party, though on a smaller scale, in individual local organisations, and not on a national scale. For instance, in 1907-08 the "Left" Bolsheviks, on certain occasions and in certain places, carried on more successful agitation among the masses than we did. This may partly have been due to the fact that at a revolutionary moment, or at a time when revolutionary recollections are still fresh, it is easier to approach the masses with tactics of sheer negation. This, however, is not an argument to prove the correctness of such tactics. At all events, there is not the least doubt that a Communist *party* that wishes to be the real vanguard, the advanced detachment, of the revolutionary *class*, of the proletariat—and which, in addition wishes to learn to lead the *masses*, not only the proletarian, but also the *non*-proletarian masses of working and exploited people—must know how to conduct propaganda, how to organise, and how to carry on agitation in a manner most simple and comprehensible, most clear and vivid, both to the urban, factory masses and to the rural masses.

II

THE COMMUNISTS AND THE INDEPENDENTS IN GERMANY

In this pamphlet I have expressed the opinion that a compromise between the Communists and the Left wing of the Independents is necessary and useful to communism, but will not be easy to bring about. Newspapers which I have subsequently received have confirmed this opinion on both points. No. 32 of *The Red Flag*, organ of the Central Committee, the Communist Party of Germany (*Die Rote Fahne*, Zentralorgan der Kommunistischen Partei Deutschlands, Spartakusbund,* of March 26, 1920) published a "statement" by this Central Committee regarding the Kapp-Lüttwitz military *putsch* and on the "socialist government". This statement is quite correct both in its basic premise and its practical conclusions. The basic premise is that at present there is no "objective basis" for the dictatorship of the proletariat because the "majority of the urban workers" support the Independents. The conclusion is: a promise to be a "loyal opposition" (i.e., renunciation of preparations for a "forcible overthrow") to a "socialist government if it excludes bourgeois-capitalist parties".

In the main, this tactic is undoubtedly correct. Yet, even if minor inaccuracies of formulation should not be dwelt on, it is impossible to pass over in silence the fact that a government consisting of social-traitors should not (in an official statement by the Communist Party) be called "socialist"; that one should not speak of the exclusion of "bourgeois-capitalist parties", when the parties both of the Scheidemanns and of the Kautskys and Crispiens are petty-bourgeois-democratic parties; that things should never be written that are contained in §4 of the statement, which reads:

"... A state of affairs in which political freedom can be enjoyed without restriction, and bourgeois democracy cannot operate as the

* The Spartacus League.—*Ed.*

dictatorship of capital is, from the viewpoint of the development of the proletarian dictatorship, of the utmost importance in further winning the proletarian masses over to the side of communism...."

Such a state of affairs is impossible. Petty-bourgeois leaders, the German Hendersons (Scheidemanns) and Snowdens (Crispiens), do not and cannot go beyond the bounds of bourgeois democracy, which, in its turn, cannot but be a dictatorship of capital. To achieve the practical results that the Central Committee of the Communist Party had been quite rightly working for, there was no need to write such things, which are wrong in principle and politically harmful. It would have been sufficient to say (if one wished to observe parliamentary amenities): "As long as the majority of the urban workers follow the Independents, we Communists must do nothing to prevent those workers from getting rid of their last philistine-democratic (i.e., 'bourgeois-capitalist') illusions by going through the experience of having a government of their 'own'." That is sufficient ground for a compromise, which is really necessary and should consist in renouncing, for a certain period, all attempts at the forcible overthrow of a government which enjoys the confidence of a majority of the urban workers. But in everyday mass agitation, in which one is not bound by official parliamentary amenities, one might, of course, add: "Let scoundrels like the Scheidemanns, and philistines like the Kautskys and Crispiens reveal by their deeds how they have been fooled themselves and how they are fooling the workers; their 'clean' government will itself do the 'cleanest' job of all in 'cleansing' the Augean stables of socialism, Social-Democracy and other forms of social treachery."

The real nature of the present leaders of the Independent Social-Democratic Party of Germany (leaders of whom it has been wrongly said that they have already lost all influence, whereas in reality they are even more dangerous to the proletariat than the Hungarian Social-Democrats who styled themselves Communists and promised to "support" the dictatorship of the proletariat) was once again revealed during the German equivalent of the Kornilov revolt, i.e., the Kapp-Lüttwitz *putsch.** A small but striking illustration is provided by two brief articles—one by Karl Kautsky entitled "Decisive Hours" ("Entscheidende Stunden") in *Freiheit* (*Freedom*), organ of the Independents, of March 30, 1920, and the other by Arthur Crispien entitled "On the Political Situation" (in the same newspaper, issue of April 14, 1920). These gentlemen are absolutely incapable of thinking and reasoning like revolutionaries. They are snivelling philistine democrats, who become a thousand times more dangerous to the proletariat when they claim to be supporters of Soviet government and of the dictatorship of the proletariat because, in fact, whenever a difficult and dangerous situation arises they are sure to commit treachery ... while "sincerely" believing that they are helping the proletariat! Did not the Hungarian Social-Democrats, after rechristening themselves Communists, also want to "help" the proletariat when, because of their cowardice and spinelessness, they considered the position of Soviet power in Hungary hopeless and went snivelling to the agents of the Entente capitalists and the Entente hangmen?

III

TURATI AND CO. IN ITALY

The issues of the Italian newspaper *Il Soviet* referred to above fully confirm what I have said in the pamphlet about the Italian Socialist Party's error in tolerating such members and even such a group of parliamentarians in their ranks. It is still further confirmed by an outside observer like the Rome correspondent of *The Manchester Guardian*, organ of the British liberal bourgeoisie, whose interview with Turati is published in its issue of March 12, 1920. The correspondent writes:

---

* Incidentally, this has been dealt with in an exceptionally clear, concise, precise and Marxist way in the excellent organ of the Austrian Communist Party, *The Red Banner*, of March 28 and 30, 1920. (*Die Rote Fahne*, Wien, 1920, Nos. 266 and 267; L.L.: "*Ein neuer Abschnitt der deutschen Revolution*" ["A New Stage of the German Revolution"—*Ed.*]).

"... Signor Turati's opinion is that the revolutionary peril is not such as to cause undue anxiety in Italy. The Maximalists are fanning the fire of Soviet theories only to keep the masses awake and excited. These theories are, however, merely legendary notions, unripe programmes, incapable of being put to practical use. They are likely only to maintain the working classes in a state of expectation. The very men who use them as a lure to dazzle proletarian eyes find themselves compelled to fight a daily battle for the extortion of some often trifling economic advantages so as to delay the moment when the working classes will lose their illusions and faith in their cherished myths. Hence a long string of strikes of all sizes and with all pretexts up to the very latest ones in the mail and railway services—strikes which make the already hard conditions of the country still worse. The country is irritated owing to the difficulties connected with its Adriatic problem, is weighed down by its foreign debt and by its inflated paper circulation, and yet it is still far from realising the necessity of adopting that discipline of work which alone can restore order and prosperity...."

It is clear as daylight that this British correspondent has blurted out the truth, which is probably being concealed and glossed over both by Turati himself, and his bourgeois defenders, accomplices and inspirers in Italy. That truth is that the ideas and political activities of Turati, Trèves, Modigliani, Dugoni and Co. are really and precisely of the kind that the British correspondent has described. It is downright social treachery. Just look at this advocacy of order and discipline among the workers, who are wage-slaves toiling to enrich the capitalists! And how familiar to us Russians are all these Menshevik speeches! What a valuable admission it is that the masses are *in favour of* Soviet government! How stupid and vulgarly bourgeois is the failure to understand the revolutionary role of strikes which are spreading spontaneously! Indeed, the correspondent of the British bourgeois-liberal newspaper has rendered Turati and Co. a disservice and has excellently confirmed the correctness of the demand by Comrade Bordiga and his friends on *Il Soviet*, who are insisting that the Italian Socialist Party, if it really wants to be *for* the Third International, should drum Turati and Co. out of its ranks and become a Communist Party both in name and in deed.

IV

FALSE CONCLUSIONS FROM CORRECT PREMISES

However, Comrade Bordiga and his "Left" friends draw from their correct criticism of Turati and Co. the wrong conclusion that any participation in parliament is harmful in principle. The Italian "Lefts" cannot advance even a shadow of serious argument in support of this view. They simply do not know (or try to forget) the international examples of really revolutionary and communist utilisation of bourgeois parliaments, which has been of unquestionable value in preparing for the proletarian revolution. They simply cannot conceive of any "new" ways of that utilisation, and keep on repeatedly and endlessly vociferating about the "old" non-Bolshevik way.

Herein lies their fundamental error. In *all* fields of activity, and not in the parliamentary sphere alone, communism *must introduce* (and without long and persistent effort it will be *unable* to introduce) something new in principle that will represent a radical break with the traditions of the Second International (while retaining and developing what was good in the latter).

Let us take, say, journalistic work. Newspapers, pamphlets and leaflets perform the indispensable work of propaganda, agitation and organisation. No mass movement in any country at all civilised can get along without a journalistic apparatus. No outcries against "leaders" or solemn vows to keep the masses uncontaminated by the influence of leaders will relieve us of the necessity of using, for this work, people from a bourgeois-intellectual environment or will rid us of the bourgeois-democratic, "private property" atmosphere and environment in which this work is carried out under capitalism. Even two and a half years after the overthrow of the bourgeoisie, after the conquest of political power by the proletariat, we still have this atmosphere around us, this environment of mass (peasant, artisan) bourgeois-democratic private property relations.

Parliamentarianism is one form of activity; journalism is another. The content of both can and should be communist if those engaged in these two spheres are genuine Communists, really members of a proletarian mass party.

Yet, in neither sphere—and *in no other sphere of activity* under capitalism and during the period of transition from capitalism to socialism—is it possible to avoid those difficulties which the proletariat must overcome, those special problems which the proletariat must solve so as to use, for its own purposes, the services of people from the ranks of the bourgeoisie, eradicate bourgeois-intellectualist prejudices and influences, and weaken the resistance of (and, ultimately, completely transform) the petty-bourgeois environment.

Did we not, before the war of 1914-18, witness in all countries innumerable cases of extreme "Left" anarchists, syndicalists and others fulminating against parliamentarianism, deriding bourgeois-vulgarised parliamentary socialists, castigating their careerism, and so on and so forth, and yet themselves pursuing the *same kind* of bourgeois career *through* journalism and *through* work in the syndicates (trade unions)? Is not the example of Jouhaux and Merrheim, to limit oneself to France, typical in this respect?

The childishness of those who "repudiate" participation in parliament consists in their thinking it possible to "*solve*" the difficult problem of combating bourgeois-democratic influences *within* the working-class movement in such a "simple", "easy", allegedly revolutionary manner, whereas they are actually merely running away from their own shadows, only closing their eyes to difficulties and trying to shrug them off with mere words. The most shameless careerism, the bourgeois utilisation of parliamentary seats, glaringly reformist perversion of parliamentary activity, and vulgar petty-bourgeois conservatism are all unquestionably common and prevalent features engendered everywhere by capitalism, not only outside but also within the working-class movement. But the selfsame capitalism and the bourgeois environment it creates (which disappears very slowly even after the overthrow of the bourgeoisie, since the peasantry constantly regenerates the bourgeoisie) give rise to what is essentially the same bourgeois careerism, national chauvinism, petty-bourgeois vulgarity, etc.—merely varying insignificantly in form—in positively every sphere of activity and life.

You think, my dear boycottists and anti-parliamentarians

that you are "terribly revolutionary", but in reality *you are frightened* by the comparatively minor difficulties of the struggle against bourgeois influences within the working-class movement, whereas your victory—i.e., the overthrow of the bourgeoisie and the conquest of political power by the proletariat—will create *these very same* difficulties on a still larger, an infinitely larger scale. Like children, you are frightened by a minor difficulty which confronts you today, but you do not understand that tomorrow, and the day after, you will still have to learn, and learn thoroughly, to overcome the selfsame difficulties, only on an immeasurably greater scale.

Under Soviet rule, your proletarian party and ours will be invaded by a still larger number of bourgeois intellectuals. They will worm their way into the Soviets, the courts, and the administration, since communism cannot be built otherwise than with the aid of the human material created by capitalism, and the bourgeois intellectuals cannot be expelled and destroyed, but must be won over, remoulded, assimilated and re-educated, just as we must—in a protracted struggle waged on the basis of the dictatorship of the proletariat—re-educate the proletarians themselves, who do not abandon their petty-bourgeois prejudices at one stroke, by a miracle, at the behest of the Virgin Mary, at the behest of a slogan, resolution or decree, but only in the course of a long and difficult mass struggle against mass petty-bourgeois influences. Under Soviet rule, these same problems, which the anti-parliamentarians now so proudly, so haughtily, so lightly and so childishly brush aside with a wave of the hand—*these selfsame* problems are arising anew *within* the Soviets, within the Soviet administration, among the Soviet "pleaders" (in Russia we have abolished, and have rightly abolished, the bourgeois legal bar, but it is reviving again under the cover of the "Soviet pleaders"[40]). Among Soviet engineers, Soviet school-teachers and the privileged, i.e., the most highly skilled and best situated, *workers* at Soviet factories, we observe a constant revival of absolutely *all* the negative traits peculiar to bourgeois parliamentarianism, and we are conquering this evil—gradually—only by a tireless, prolonged and persistent struggle based on proletarian organisation and discipline.

Of course, under the rule of the bourgeoisie it is very "difficult" to eradicate bourgeois habits from our own, i.e., the workers', party; it is "difficult" to expel from the party the familiar parliamentary leaders who have been hopelessly corrupted by bourgeois prejudices; it is "difficult" to subject to proletarian discipline the absolutely essential (even if very limited) number of people coming from the ranks of the bourgeoisie; it is "difficult" to form, in a bourgeois parliament, a communist group fully worthy of the working class; it is "difficult" to ensure that the communist parliamentarians do not engage in bourgeois parliamentary inanities, but concern themselves with the very urgent work of propaganda, agitation and organisation among the masses. All this is "difficult", to be sure; it was difficult in Russia, and it is vastly more difficult in Western Europe and in America, where the bourgeoisie is far stronger, where bourgeois-democratic traditions are stronger, and so on.

Yet all these "difficulties" are mere child's play compared with the *same sort* of problems which, in any event, the proletariat will have most certainly to solve in order to achieve victory, both during the proletarian revolution and after the seizure of power by the proletariat. Compared with *these* truly gigantic problems of re-educating, under the proletarian dictatorship, millions of peasants and small proprietors, hundreds of thousands of office employees, officials and bourgeois intellectuals, of subordinating them all to the proletarian state and to proletarian leadership, of eradicating their bourgeois habits and traditions—compared with these gigantic problems it is childishly easy to create, under the rule of the bourgeoisie, and in a bourgeois parliament, a really communist group of a real proletarian party.

If our "Left" and anti-parliamentarian comrades do not learn to overcome even such a small difficulty now, we may safely assert that either they will prove incapable of achieving the dictatorship of the proletariat, and will be unable to subordinate and remould the bourgeois intellectuals and bourgeois institutions on a wide scale, or they will have to *hastily complete their education*, and, by that haste, will do a great deal of harm to the cause of the proletariat, will commit more errors than usual, will manifest more than average weakness and inefficiency, and so on and so forth.

Until the bourgeoisie has been overthrown and, after that, until small-scale economy and small commodity production have entirely disappeared, the bourgeois atmosphere, proprietary habits and petty-bourgeois traditions will hamper proletarian work both outside and within the working-class movement, not only in a single field of activity—the parliamentary—but, inevitably, in every field of social activity, in all cultural and political spheres without exception. The attempt to brush aside, to fence oneself off from *one* of the "unpleasant" problems or difficulties in some one sphere of activity is a profound mistake, which will later most certainly have to be paid for. We must learn how to master every sphere of work and activity without exception, to overcome all difficulties and eradicate all bourgeois habits, customs and traditions everywhere. Any other way of presenting the question is just trifling, mere childishness.

May 12, 1920

V

In the Russian edition of this book I somewhat incorrectly described the conduct of the Communist Party of Holland as a whole, in the sphere of international revolutionary policy. I therefore avail myself of the present opportunity to publish a letter from our Dutch comrades on this question and to correct the expression "Dutch Tribunists", which I used in the Russian text, and for which I now substitute the words "certain members of the Communist Party of Holland".[41]

N. Lenin

LETTER FROM WIJNKOOP

Moscow, June 30, 1920

Dear Comrade Lenin,

Thanks to your kindness, we members of the Dutch delegation to the Second Congress of the Communist International were able to read your *"Left-Wing" Communism—an Infantile Disorder* prior to its publication in the European languages. In several places in the book you emphasise your disapproval of the part played by some members of the Communist Party of Holland in international politics.

We feel, nevertheless, that we must protest against your laying the responsibility for their actions on the Communist Party. This is highly inaccurate. Moreover, it is unjust, because these members of the Communist Party of Holland take little or no part in the Party's current activities and are endeavouring, directly or indirectly, to give effect, in the Communist Party of Holland, to opposition slogans against which the Party and all its organs have waged, and continue to wage to this day, a most energetic struggle.

Fraternally yours,
D. J. Wijnkoop
(on behalf of the Dutch delegation)

SPEECH DELIVERED AT AN ALL-RUSSIA CONGRESS OF GLASS AND PORCELAIN WORKERS APRIL 29, 1920

Yesterday brought us two pieces of news: the first is very bad—a report about a manifesto by Pilsudski, head of the Polish Government. I have not yet seen the text of this manifesto; I was told of it on the telephone. One thing is certain, however, that it is tantamount to Poland's declaration of war on the Ukraine. The French imperialists' influence has evidently gained the upper hand in Poland's government circles. The Polish Government has decided to drop its recent policy of tacking and manoeuvring around the peace negotiations with us, and to start hostilities on a wider front. The Poles have already captured Zhitomir and are marching on Kiev. This demands of us the most determined and urgent defence of the interests of the proletariat. We do not doubt that we shall be able to defend those interests; we do not doubt that this new attempt by the Entente imperialists to strangle Soviet Russia will fall through just as the Denikin and the Kolchak ventures have. Poland is obviously getting all her military support from France, Britain, and the entire Entente. It is highly characteristic, in this connection, that in the last stage of the negotiations with us about the Crimea the British Government has considerably changed its originally favourable attitude. In reply to Great Britain's call to us to show clemency to Denikin's soldiers, who are being driven into the sea, we have said that we were prepared to spare the lives of the Crimean whiteguards if, for its part, the Entente shows clemency to the defeated Hungarian Communists and allows them to enter Soviet Russia.

We do not need to shed the blood of these Crimean whiteguards; we are not vindictive. We have, however, received no reply to our Note from the British Government, which, in connection with Poland's action, seems in no hurry to reply. But we are sure that no supporters of intervention are to be found among the British workers, even the most opportunistically minded.

We have information to the effect that even in Poland the Polish Socialist Party, which has persecuted Polish Communists, has stated in its newspaper that Poland should not break off peace negotiations with Soviet Russia by presenting an ultimatum demanding that these talks should be conducted in Borisov. This newspaper considers such conduct by the Polish Government a crime. The Poles have proposed that the peace talks should take place in Borisov without any cessation of hostilities. Conducting negotiations in this particular place would prevent us from continuing hostilities during the talks, while giving Poland complete freedom of action in this respect. Of course, we could not conduct peace negotiations on such terms, and we proposed that they should be transferred to Paris, Revel, Warsaw, Moscow or some other city mutually agreed upon with Poland. The reply to this proposal was an extensive Polish offensive along the entire front. We have no doubt that the Polish Government started this war of aggression in defiance of the wishes of its workers. That is why we face this new military gamble quite calmly; we know that we shall emerge the victors. But you know, comrades, that any war is accompanied by tremendous difficulties, to overcome which we have more than onoe appealed to the worker masses for support. The war with Poland has been forced upon us. We have no designs whatever on Poland's independence, just as we have no designs on the independence of Lithuania or Byelorussia. Yet, despite all our willingness to come to terms, war has been forced upon us; that being the case, we must rise up as one man to defend both ourselves and the Ukraine from the onslaught of the Polish imperialists. (*Loud applause.*) For that purpose we must again make a certain change of plans. However much we might desire to go over to peaceful construction as soon as possible and on the greatest possible scale, the fact that war has been forced upon us makes it imperative that we subordinate everything to the demands of that war so as to achieve the most successful and rapid results. We must explain to the workers and peasants why an Entente-instigated Poland has launched a war against us. We must explain that this has been done in order to widen the barrier and deepen the gulf separating the proletariat of Germany from us.

On the other hand, we received news from Baku yesterday which shows that the position of Soviet Russia is improving. We know that our industry is at a standstill owing to lack of fuel. News has come in that the Baku proletariat has taken over power and overthrown the Azerbaijan Government. This means that we now have an economic base that may put life into our whole industry. In Baku there is a million poods* of oil which could not be sold, with the result that even Nobel, the oil magnate, tried to start talks with us for the delivery of this oil to Soviet Russia. Thus our railways and industry will receive very substantial aid from the Baku oilfields.

Comrade Tsyurupa, the People's Commissar for Food, informed me today that in Kuban Region and in the Caucasus there are vast stocks of grain which we can count on having sent here. That means that we shall have fuel for industry and bread for the people. By exerting every effort to restore the transport system, we shall be able to secure bread and oil, which will serve as a sound economic basis for relations between the workers and the peasants. We say that the peasants must give their surplus grain to the workers because under present-day conditions, the sale of these surpluses would be a crime. Consequently, as soon as we get our industry going, we shall make every effort to satisfy the peasants' need of manufactured goods from the cities.

After outlining the Republic's general position today in these few words and to the extent permitted by the time, I shall take the liberty of concluding by expressing the conviction that at the present moment, at this new stage of our relations with Poland, when both Kuban grain and Baku oil have been made available to us, the four

* 1 pood is approximately 36 lbs. avoirdupois.—*Ed.*

million workers organised in the trade unions, through whom we have conducted our Soviet policy with the backing of the broad strata of the peasants, will, without confining themselves to the narrow limits of their trade union life, go on giving every support to the further success and development of the proletariat's common cause. We know that the workers' class-consciousness and unity and the complete solidarity of the trade unions have been the only force that have made possible the brilliant victories of the Red Army, an army which has been the finest medium of spreading political enlightenment among the peasants, teaching them to oust self-seekers from their ranks so as to keep power in the hands of the workers. Now, too, we need that class-consciousness, that unity and complete solidarity of the trade unions in the war against Poland and in the work of restoring industry. What we need today is the further maintenance and tightening of the discipline necessary in all branches of production. The class-conscious workers know that if you, the workers, had not displayed this discipline hitherto, we might have suffered the fate of Hungary. Let the comrades remember that and, in their localities, ensure the complete subordination of all to the one fundamental task: we must abolish, we must eliminate as soon as possible the accursed motto—every man for himself and the devil take the hindmost. Proletarian labour discipline must be raised to the highest pitch of intensity—and then we shall be invincible. We will show that the Soviet Republic cannot be overthrown and that we shall succeed in winning the aid of all the other republics of the world. (*Continuous applause from all members of the Congress; cries of* "Long live our leader Comrade Lenin!")

Pravda No. 92,
April 30, 1920

Published according to
the *Pravda* text

FROM THE FIRST SUBBOTNIK ON THE MOSCOW-KAZAN RAILWAY TO THE ALL-RUSSIA MAY DAY SUBBOTNIK[42]

The distance indicated in the above title has been covered in a single year. This is an enormous distance. Although all our subbotniks are still weak, and each subbotnik reveals a host of defects in arrangement, organisation and discipline, the main thing has been done. A heavy and ponderous mass has been shifted, and that is the essence of the matter.

We are not deceiving ourselves in the least about the little that has yet been done and about the infinite amount of work that has yet to be done; however, only malicious enemies of the working people, only malicious supporters of the bourgeoisie, can treat the May 1 subbotnik with disdain; only the most contemptible people, who have irrevocably sold themselves to the capitalists, can condemn the utilisation of the great First of May festival for a mass-scale attempt to introduce communist labour.

This is the very first time since the overthrow of the tsars, the landowners and the capitalists that the ground is being cleared for the actual building of socialism, for the development of new social links, a new discipline of work in common and a new national (and later an international) system of economy of world-historic importance. This is a matter of transforming the very habits of the people, habits which, for a long time to come, have been defiled and debased by the accursed private ownership of the means of production, and also by the entire atmosphere of bickering, distrust, enmity, disunity and mutual intrigue that is inevitably generated—and constantly regenerated—

by petty individual economy, the economy of private owners in conditions of "free" exchange among them. For hundreds of years, freedom of trade and of exchange has been to millions of people the supreme gospel of economic wisdom, the most deep-rooted habit of hundreds and hundreds of millions of people. This freedom is just as utterly false, serving to mask capitalist deception, coercion and exploitation, as are the other "freedoms" proclaimed and implemented by the bourgeoisie, such as the "freedom to work" (actually the freedom to starve), and so on.

In the main we have broken irrevocably with this "freedom" of the property-owner to be a property-owner, with this "freedom" of capital to exploit labour, and we shall finish the job. We are combating its remnants ruthlessly, with all our might.

Down with the old social links, the old economic relationships, the old "freedom" of labour (*subordinated to capital*), the old laws, the old habits!

Let us build a new society!

We were not daunted by defeats during the great revolutionary war against tsarism, against the bourgeoisie, against the omnipotent imperialist world powers.

We shall not be daunted by the gigantic difficulties and by the errors that are inevitable at the outset of a most difficult task; the transformation of all labour habits and customs requires decades. We solemnly and firmly promise one another that we shall make every sacrifice, that we shall hold out and win in this most arduous struggle—the struggle against the force of habit—that we shall work indefatigably for years and decades. We shall work to do away with the accursed maxim: "Every man for himself and the devil take the hindmost", the habit of looking upon work merely as a duty, and of considering rightful only that work which is paid for at certain rates. We shall work to inculcate in people's minds, turn into a habit, and bring into the day-by-day life of the masses, the rule: "All for each and each for all"; the rule: "From each according to his ability, to each according to his needs"; we shall work for the gradual but steady introduction of communist discipline and communist labour.

We have shifted a huge mountain, a huge mass of conservatism, ignorance, stubborn adherence to the habits of "freedom of trade" and of the "free" buying and selling of human labour-power like any other commodity. We have begun to undermine and destroy the most deep-rooted prejudices, the firmest, age-long and ingrained habits. In a single year our subbotniks have made an immense stride forward. They are still infinitely weak, but that will not daunt us. We have seen our "infinitely weak" Soviet state, before our very eyes, gaining strength and becoming a mighty world force, as a result of our own efforts. We shall work for years and decades practising subbotniks, developing them, spreading them, improving them and converting them into a habit. We shall achieve the victory of communist labour.

Pervomaisky Subbotnik,
May 2, 1920
Signed: *N. Lenin*

Published according to the newspaper text

SPEECH AT A MEETING DEDICATED TO THE LAYING OF THE FOUNDATION STONE OF A MONUMENT TO LIBERATED LABOUR MAY 1, 1920

NEWSPAPER REPORT

(*Comrade Lenin mounts the platform to unanimous applause from the audience.*) Comrades, this was once the site of the monument to a tsar. Today we are laying the foundation stone of a monument to the glory of liberated labour. The capitalists used to speak of the freedom of labour, while the workers and the peasants were obliged to sell them their labour and, in consequence, were free to die of starvation. We call that kind of labour wage-slavery. We know that it is no easy matter to organise free labour in the proper way and to work in the conditions of the difficult times we are living through. Today's subbotnik is the first step along that road, but if we carry on in the same way we shall create a kind of labour that is genuinely free. (*Prolonged and unanimous applause.*)

Pravda No. 94,
May 4, 1920

Published according to
the newspaper text

SPEECH TO MEN OF THE RED ARMY LEAVING FOR THE POLISH FRONT MAY 5, 1920[43]

NEWSPAPER REPORT

Comrades: You know that, instigated by the Entente, the Polish landowners and capitalists have forced a new war on us. Remember, comrades, that we have no quarrel with the Polish peasants and workers; we have recognised Poland's independence and the Polish People's Republic, and shall continue to do so. We have proposed peace to Poland on the basis of the integrity of her frontiers, although these frontiers extend far beyond the purely Polish population. We have agreed to make all concessions, which is something each of you should remember at the front. Let your attitude to the Poles there prove that you are soldiers of a workers' and peasants' republic, that you are coming to them, not as aggressors but as liberators. Now that, despite our efforts, the Polish magnates have concluded an alliance with Petlyura, launched an offensive, are approaching Kiev, and are spreading rumours in the foreign press that they have already captured Kiev—which is the sheerest fabrication since only yesterday I was talking on the direct line with F. Kon, who is in Kiev—we say: Comrades, we have been able to repel a more terrible enemy; we have been able to defeat our own landowners and capitalists, and we shall defeat the Polish landowners and capitalists too! All of us here today should pledge ourselves, give a solemn promise, that we shall stand as one man so as not to allow a victory of the Polish magnates and capitalists. Long live the peasants and workers of a free independent Polish Republic! Down with the Polish magnates, landowners and capitalists! Long live our Red Workers' and Peasants' Army! (*The mighty strains of the "Internationale" and cries of* "Hurrah" *drown Comrade Lenin's final words.*)

Pravda No. 96,
May 6, 1920

Published according to
the newspaper text

SPEECH DELIVERED AT A JOINT SESSION OF THE ALL-RUSSIA CENTRAL EXECUTIVE COMMITTEE, THE MOSCOW SOVIET OF WORKERS', PEASANTS' AND RED ARMY DEPUTIES, TRADE UNIONS, AND FACTORY COMMITTEES

MAY 5, 1920[44]

(*Applause.*) Comrades, I should like to draw your attention to a feature that, from the international point of view or more correctly from the point of view of Russia's international position, distinguishes the present war from previous wars. Of course, none of you doubt, or could doubt, that this war is a link in a long chain of events revealing the international bourgeoisie's frantic resistance to the victorious proletariat, a frantic attempt by the international bourgeoisie to crush Soviet Russia, to overthrow the first Soviet state at all costs and by all means. There cannot be the least doubt that there is a connection between these events, between the international bourgeoisie's previous attempts and the present war. At the same time, however, we see the tremendous difference between this war and previous wars, from the point of view of our international position. We see the tremendous impetus our struggle has given to the international working-class movement. We see how the international proletariat reacts to Soviet Russia's victories, how the world proletarian struggle is mounting and gaining strength, and what gigantic work has been carried out in the little more than the two years of the Soviet Republic's existence.

You remember how the most responsible and most powerful ministers of the mightiest and unrivalled capitalist powers announced quite recently that they had prepared an alliance of fourteen powers against Russia; you know how, under pressure from the powerful capitalists of France and Britain, this alliance brought Yudenich, Kolchak and Denikin together, and how it drew up a really grandiose and comprehensive war plan. If we destroyed that plan, it was because the imperialists' unity was illusory, and the forces of the international bourgeoisie cannot stand up to a single trial when it comes to sacrificing oneself. It appeared that, after four years of the imperialist slaughter, the working people do not recognise the justice of a war against us, and in them we have a great ally. The Entente's plan was really destructive, but it came to grief because, despite their most powerful alliance, the capitalist states could not carry it through, proved powerless to give it effect. None of the powers, any one of which could have the advantage over us, could show unity, because the organised proletariat does not support it; no army—neither the French nor the British—could get its soldiers to fight on Russian soil, against the Soviet Republic.

If, in our mind's eye, we follow the desperate situations our republic was faced with when, in fact, it was standing up to the whole world, against powers far more powerful than it, and if we recollect how we emerged fully victorious from these formidable trials, then these recollections will give us a clear idea of what we are confronted with now. Here we see a plan that is not new and at the same time does not at all resemble the really comprehensive and single plan we were faced with six months ago. What we have is the relics of the former plan and, in the light of the international alignment of forces, this is the greatest assurance of the futility of the present attempt. The former plan was an attempt on the part of all the imperialist powers to crush the workers' and peasants' republic, in alliance with all the small border states of the former Russian Empire, which had been shamelessly and outrageously oppressed by the tsarist and capitalist government of Great Russia. At present, several powers, in alliance with one of the border states, are attempting to accomplish that which proved impossible to all the imperialist powers in alliance with all the border states, and was undertaken by them twelve and six months ago in alliance with Kolchak, Denikin and others. We now see the relics of the imperialists' plan. The great tenacity being shown by the bourgeoisie is a feature of the imperialist plans. They know that they are fighting to retain power at home, and that it is not the Russian or the Polish question that is being decided, but the question of their own survival. It is therefore to be expected that they will try to salvage the former and unsuccessful plan from the wreck.

We can all clearly see the clash of the imperialist states' interests. Despite all pronouncements by their ministers about the peaceful settlement of questions in dispute, the imperialist powers cannot in reality take a single serious step in political matters without disagreeing. The French need a powerful Poland and a powerful Russia of the tsarist brand, and they are prepared to make every sacrifice to this end. Because of her geographical position, Britain wants something else—the break-up of Russia and a weak Poland, so as to ensure a balance between France and Germany which would give the imperialist victors control of colonies acquired by robbing Germany as a consequence of the world war. Here the clash of interests is really striking; no matter how the representatives of the imperialist powers at San Remo[45] try to assure us that there is full unanimity among the Allies, we know that this is not the case.

We know that Poland's offensive is a relic of the old plan that once united the entire international bourgeoisie. If that ambitious plan failed at that time, even though from the purely military standpoint it was assured of success, it is hopeless today, even in that aspect. Furthermore, we know that the imperialist powers, who have entered into an alliance with the Polish bourgeoisie, and the Polish Government are in a bigger mess than ever. Each political move made by the Polish bourgeoisie over the past months, weeks and days has shown them up to their own working people. They have been quarrelling with their allies, and cannot make a single consistent move in their policy. At one moment they announce their unyielding attitude to Soviet Russia and the impossibility of conducting any kind of talks with her, while at the next moment they raise the blockade, and solemnly announce this on behalf of an allegedly existing alliance, an allegedly existing League of Nations, and then they again commence a policy of vacillation. In consequence of all this, the imperialists have enabled us to prove that our policy is peaceful, and that our international policy has nothing in common either with tsarist policies or those of the Russian capitalists or the Russian bourgeoisie, even a democratic bourgeoisie. We have proved to the entire world that our foreign policy has nothing in common with the policy constantly ascribed to us by all the bourgeois press. Consequently, the Poles themselves have exposed every piece of deception in their policy. The experience of three Russian revolutions has shown us how they were prepared, and how each served as the basis for the further development of home and foreign policy. This experience has proved that in the preparation of revolution those ruling classes are our most faithful assistants which, laying claim to all kinds of coalitions, constituent assemblies and so on, and asserting that they represent the will of the people, in fact reveal—through their own policy at every serious, difficult or crucial moment in the life of the country—the self-interest of squabbling bourgeois groups that cannot come to terms, rival capitalist groups that unmask themselves a hundred times more effectively than communist propaganda can do. In no country or state can the working class—even if it is most revolutionary—ever be revolutionised by any propaganda and agitation unless that agitation is backed up in practice by the behaviour of the ruling classes of that country.

What is now taking place in all capitalist countries (and this will develop even more with time, particularly in a country like Poland) makes us confident that, if we emerged victorious from a war undoubtedly far more arduous, and if we have correctly assessed the discord and the impossibility of reconciliation among the bourgeoisie of various groups and parties at times when they stand in particular need of such unity, the present improvement in our international position is enormous. This fills us with confidence, not only in view of the internal alignment of forces, but also of our international position. If we consider the entire system of present-day imperialist states, and all their strivings—and we know that their urge to use any moment for an attack on Russia is irresistible—and appraise them quite objectively in the light of the incontrovertible facts of the history of recent years and particularly of the past six months, we shall see that the international enemy is weakening, that all attempts at an alliance between the imperialists are becoming more and more futile, and that, from this aspect, our victory is assured.

However, comrades, while working on economic problems and concentrating all our attention on peaceful economic construction, we must rapidly re-form our ranks as we face the approach of a new war. Our entire army, which has recently been a labour army,[46] must now turn its attention to other matters. We must discontinue everything else and concentrate on this new war. We are perfectly aware that, after all that we have been through, we do not have to fear the enemy now facing us, but he may impose new and heavy sacrifices on the workers and peasants, may greatly impede our economic construction, and bring about the devastation and ruin of tens, hundreds and thousands of peasant households. He may also, by his temporary success, revive the extinct hopes of the imperialists we have defeated, who will of course not fail to join forces with this enemy. We must, therefore, declare that the rule we have followed throughout all previous wars must be resolutely reinforced. Since, despite all our most conciliatory intentions and the fact that we made great concessions and renounced all national claims, the Polish landowners and the Polish bourgeoisie have forced a war on us; since we are certain, and we must be certain, that the bourgeoisie of all countries, even those that at present are not helping the Poles, will help them when the war flares up, because it is not only a Russian or a Polish issue, but one of the survival of the entire bourgeoisie—then we must remember and at all costs implement the rule which we have followed in our policy and which has always been a guarantee of our success. That rule is: once things have led to war, everything must be subordinated to the war effort; the entire internal life of the country must be subordinated to wartime needs; the slightest hesitation on this score is inexcusable. No matter how hard it is for the great majority of comrades to tear themselves away from their work, which has only recently been switched onto a new course, more gratifying and essential to the tasks of peaceful construction, it must be remembered that the least oversight or inattention may often mean the deaths of tens of thousands of our best comrades, our younger generation of workers and peasants, our Communists who, as always, are in the front ranks of the fighters. Therefore, once more—everything for the war effort. No meeting, no conference should be held without having as its first item the question: have we done everything possible to help the war effort; have our forces been sufficiently mobilised; have we sent sufficient help to the front? Only those people who cannot help at the front should remain here. Every sacrifice, every assistance for the front, without the least hesitation! And, by concentrating all efforts and making every sacrifice, we shall undoubtedly triumph again. (*Applause.*)

Published in 1920 in the book *Verbatim Reports of the Plenary Meetings of the Moscow Soviet of Workers', Peasants' and Red Army Deputies*

Published according to the text in the book

TELEGRAM TO THE SOVIET SOCIALIST GOVERNMENT OF AZERBAIJAN

Baku

The Council of People's Commissars welcomes the liberation of the toiling masses of the independent Azerbaijan Republic and expresses its firm confidence that, under the leadership of its Soviet Government, the independent Republic of Azerbaijan will, together with the R.S.F.S.R., uphold its freedom and independence against imperialism, the sworn enemy of the oppressed nations of the East.

Long live the independent Soviet Republic of Azerbaijan!

Long live the workers and peasants of Azerbaijan!

Long live the alliance of the workers and peasants of Azerbaijan and Russia!

V. Ulyanov (Lenin)
Chairman of the Council of People's Commissars

May 5, 1920

Kommunist (Baku) No. 7,
May 9, 1920

Published according to
the newspaper text

SPEECH AT AN ENLARGED CONFERENCE OF WORKERS AND RED ARMY MEN IN ROGOZHSKO-SIMONOVSKY DISTRICT OF MOSCOW MAY 13, 1920

NEWSPAPER REPORT

The Soviet Republic is again going through a difficult period. After dealing with Kolchak and Denikin, the Russian proletariat was preparing to devote all its spiritual and material forces to the restoration of the country's economic life. We thought that the bourgeois government of Poland would not hazard a new venture. The Polish Communists, it is true, had said that, just because the Polish Government had nothing more to lose, it would not hesitate to drive its workers and peasants into any kind of adventure. We, however, think that the Polish proletariat, together with the proletariat of Lithuania and Byelorussia, will see to it that the Polish bourgeoisie and nobility are driven out of the country. The Russian workers' and peasants' government has made enormous concessions to Poland, wishing thereby to prove to the Polish people that it has ended with tsarism's policy towards small states.

Behind the Polish bourgeoisie stand the capitalists of France, who are manoeuvring to sell military supplies to Poland at good prices, thus recovering the losses incurred with Kolchak and Denikin.

It is significant that no Entente power dares to come out openly against Soviet Russia, for fear of showing the workers its true colours. At present it is of the utmost importance for us to make the politically illiterate and backward citizens realise that we have done everything to avoid fresh bloodshed, that the Polish worker and peasant are no enemies of ours, but that we shall fight and fight ruthlessly if the Polish bourgeoisie is out for war, hand in glove with Petlyura. In the final analysis, victory in any war depends on the spirit animating the masses that spill their own blood on the field of battle. The conviction that the war is in a just cause and the realisation that their lives must be laid down for the welfare of their brothers strengthen the morale of the fighting men and enable them to endure incredible hardships. Tsarist generals say that our Red Army men are capable of enduring hardships that the tsar's army could never have stood up to. The reason is that every mobilised worker or peasant knows what he is fighting for and is ready to shed his own blood for the triumph of justice and socialism.

The realisation by the masses of the causes and aims of the war is of tremendous importance and ensures victory.

Our country has been exhausted by war, and we are prepared to make great concessions to end the bloodshed and apply ourselves to peaceful labour. That was why, when Bullitt came to Russia and proposed a harsh peace, the Soviet Government signed it[47] so as to enable the Soviets to gain strength.

At present we are again obliged to issue the call, "Everything for the war effort!" All trade union and Party organisations must bend every effort to help the heroic Red Army.

We shall very soon convince the whole world of the justice of our cause.

A British trade union delegation arrived in Petrograd yesterday. Few of its members are in sympathy with us, but we are sure that when they return home they will be our best propagandists.[48] Even former tsarist generals consider Poland's claims unjust and are helping us. The Russian workers and peasants join us in saying, "Everything for the war effort, everything for victory". Let us devote all our forces to secure victory. (*A storm of applause.*)

Kommunistichesky Trud No. 44,
May 14, 1920

Published according to
the newspaper text

TO THE INDIAN REVOLUTIONARY ASSOCIATION[49]

I am glad to hear that the principles of self-determination and the liberation of oppressed nations from exploitation by foreign and native capitalists, proclaimed by the Workers' and Peasants' Republic, have met with such a ready response among progressive Indians, who are waging a heroic fight for freedom. The working masses of Russia are following with unflagging attention the awakening of the Indian workers and peasants. The organisation and discipline of the working people and their perseverance and solidarity with the working people of the world are an earnest of ultimate success. We welcome the close alliance of Moslem and non-Moslem elements. We sincerely want to see this alliance extended to all the toilers of the East. Only when the Indian, Chinese, Korean, Japanese, Persian, and Turkish workers and peasants join hands and march together in the common cause of liberation—only then will decisive victory over the exploiters be ensured. Long live a free Asia!

Pravda No. 108,
May 20, 1920

Published according to
the newspaper text

LETTER TO THE BRITISH WORKERS[50]

Comrades:

First of all permit me to thank you for sending your delegation here to acquaint themselves with Soviet Russia. When your delegation suggested to me that I should send a letter through them to the British workers and perhaps also proposals to the British Government, I replied that I gratefully accepted the first suggestion but that I must address myself to the government, not through a workers' delegation but directly, on behalf of our government, through Comrade Chicherin. We have on very many occasions addressed ourselves this way to the British Government, making the most formal and solemn proposals to start peace talks. All our representatives—Comrade Litvinov, Comrade Krasin and the rest—are unceasingly continuing to make these proposals. The British Government stubbornly refuses to accept them. It is not surprising, therefore, that I desired to speak to the delegates of the British workers exclusively as delegates of the workers, not as a representative of the government of Soviet Russia, but simply as a Communist.

I was not surprised to find that several members of your delegation hold a standpoint, not of the working class but of the bourgeoisie, of the exploiting class: in all capitalist countries the imperialist war fully revealed an old ulcer, namely, the desertion of the majority of the workers' parliamentary and trade union leaders to the side of the bourgeoisie. On the false pretext of "defence of country" they were actually defending the predatory interests of either of the two groups of robbers of the entire world—the Anglo-American-French group, or the German group;

they entered into an alliance with the bourgeoisie, against the revolutionary struggle of the proletariat; they covered up this treachery with sentimental petty-bourgeois reformist and pacifist phrases about peaceful evolution, constitutional methods, democracy, etc. This is what happened in all countries; it is not surprising that in Britain this state of affairs has also been reflected in the composition of your delegation.

Members of your delegation, Shaw and Guest—obviously surprised and hurt by my statement that Britain, notwithstanding our peace proposals and notwithstanding the declarations of her government, is continuing her intervention, waging war against us and helping Wrangel in the Crimea and whiteguard Poland—asked me whether I had proof of this, and whether I could show how many trainloads of military supplies Britain had provided Poland with, etc. I replied that, to obtain the secret treaties of the British Government, it was necessary to overthrow it in a revolutionary manner and to seize all its foreign policy documents in the same way as we did in 1917. Any educated man, anybody sincerely interested in politics, was aware even prior to our revolution that the tsar had secret treaties with the predatory governments of Britain, France, America, Italy and Japan concerning the division of the spoils, concerning Constantinople, Galicia, Armenia, Syria, Mesopotamia, etc. Only liars and hypocrites (excluding, of course, absolutely ignorant, backward and illiterate people) could deny this, or pretend not to know of this. However, without a revolution, we could never have obtained the secret documents of the predatory governments of the capitalist class. Those leaders or representatives of the British proletariat—whether they are members of Parliament, trade union leaders, journalists, or others—who pretend ignorance of the secret treaties between Britain, France, America, Italy, Japan and Poland concerning the plunder of other countries, concerning the division of the spoils, and who do not wage a revolutionary struggle in order to expose these treaties, are merely once again showing that they are faithful servants of the capitalists. We have known this for a long time; we are exposing this in our own country and in all other countries of the world. The visit to Russia of a delegation of the British workers will hasten the exposure of such leaders in Britain too.

I had a conversation with your delegation on Wednesday, May 26. On the following day telegrams arrived stating that Bonar Law had admitted in the British Parliament that military aid had been given to Poland in October, "for defence against Russia" (of course only for defence, and only in October! There are still "influential labour leaders" in Britain who are helping the capitalists to dupe the workers!), but the *New Statesman*, the most moderate of moderate petty-bourgeois newspapers or journals, wrote of tanks being supplied to Poland, which were more powerful than those used against the Germans during the war. After this, can one refrain from ridiculing such "leaders" of the British workers that ask with an air of injured innocence whether there is any "proof" that Britain is fighting against Russia and is helping Poland and the whiteguards in the Crimea?

Members of the delegation asked me which I considered more important: the formation in Britain of a consistently revolutionary Communist Party, or obtaining the immediate aid of the masses of the workers in Britain for the cause of peace with Russia. I replied that this is a matter of one's convictions. Sincere supporters of the emancipation of the workers from the yoke of capital cannot possibly be opposed to the formation of a Communist Party, which alone is capable of training the workers in a non-bourgeois and non-petty-bourgeois manner, and is alone capable of genuinely exposing, ridiculing and disgracing "leaders" who can doubt whether Britain is helping Poland, etc. There is no need to fear the Communists will be too numerous in Britain, because there is not even a small Communist Party there. But if anyone continues to remain in intellectual slavery to the bourgeoisie, and continues to share petty-bourgeois prejudices about "democracy" (*bourgeois* democracy), pacifism, etc., then of course such people would only do more harm to the proletariat if they took it into their heads to call themselves Communists, and affiliate to the Third International. All that these people are capable of doing is to pass sentimental "resolutions" against intervention couched exclusively in philistine phrases. In a certain sense these resolutions are also useful, namely, in the sense that the old "leaders" (adherents of bourgeois democracy, of peaceful methods, etc., etc.) will make themselves ridiculous in the eyes of the masses, and the more they pass empty, non-committal resolutions unaccompanied by revolutionary action, the sooner will they expose themselves. Let each man stick to his job: let the Communists work directly through their Party, awakening the revolutionary consciousness of the workers. Let those who supported the "defence of country" during the imperialist war for the partitioning of the world, "defence" of the secret treaty between the British capitalists and the tsar to plunder Turkey, let those who "do not see" that Britain is helping Poland and the whiteguards in Russia—let such people hasten to increase the number of their "peace resolutions" to the point of becoming ridiculous; the more they do that, the sooner will they meet with the fate of Kerensky, the Mensheviks and the Socialist-Revolutionaries in Russia.

Several members of your delegation questioned me with surprise about the Red terror, about the absence of freedom of the press in Russia, of freedom of assembly, about our persecution of Mensheviks and pro-Menshevik workers, etc. My reply was that the real cause of the terror is the British imperialists and their "allies", who practised and are still practising a White terror in Finland and in Hungary, in India and in Ireland, who have been supporting Yudenich, Kolchak, Denikin, Pilsudski and Wrangel. Our Red terror is a defence of the working class against the exploiters, the crushing of resistance from the exploiters with whom the Socialist-Revolutionaries, the Mensheviks and an insignificant number of pro-Menshevik workers have sided. Freedom of the press and assembly under bourgeois democracy is freedom for the wealthy to conspire against the working people, freedom for the capitalists to bribe and buy up the press. I have explained this in newspaper articles so often that I have derived no pleasure in repeating myself.

Two days after my talk with your delegation, the newspapers reported that, besides the arrests of Monatte and Loriot in France, Sylvia Pankhurst had been arrested in Britain. This is the best possible reply the British Government could give to a question that the non-Communist

British labour "leaders", who are captives to bourgeois prejudices, are afraid even to ask, namely, which class the terror is directed against—the oppressed and exploited, or the oppressors and exploiters? Is it a question of the "freedom" of the capitalists to rob, deceive and dupe the working people, or of the "freedom" of the toilers from the yoke of the capitalists, the speculators and the property-owners? Comrade Sylvia Pankhurst represents the interests of hundreds upon hundreds of millions of people that are oppressed by the British and other capitalists. That is why she is subjected to a White terror, has been deprived of liberty, etc. The labour "leaders" who pursue a non-Communist policy are 99 per cent representatives of the bourgeoisie, of its deceit, its prejudices.

In conclusion, I want to thank you once again, comrades, for having sent your delegation here. Despite the hostility of many of the delegates towards the Soviet system and the dictatorship of the proletariat, and although many of them are in the grip of bourgeois prejudices, their acquaintance with Soviet Russia will inevitably accelerate the collapse of capitalism throughout the world.

N. Lenin

30.5.1920

Pravda No. 130,
June 17, 1920

Published according to
the manuscript

PRELIMINARY DRAFT THESES ON THE NATIONAL AND THE COLONIAL QUESTIONS[51]

FOR THE SECOND CONGRESS OF THE COMMUNIST INTERNATIONAL

In submitting for discussion by the Second Congress of the Communist International the following draft theses on the national and the colonial questions I would request all comrades, especially those who possess concrete information on any of these very complex problems, to let me have their opinions, amendments, addenda and concrete remarks *in the most concise form* (*no more than two or three pages*), particularly on the following points:

Austrian experience;
Polish-Jewish and Ukrainian experience;
Alsace-Lorraine and Belgium;
Ireland;
Danish-German, Italo-French and Italo-Slav relations;
Balkan experience;
Eastern peoples;
The struggle against Pan-Islamism;
Relations in the Caucasus;
The Bashkir and Tatar Republics;
Kirghizia;
Turkestan, its experience;
Negroes in America;
Colonies;
China-Korea-Japan.

N. Lenin

June 5, 1920

1) An abstract or formal posing of the problem of equality in general and national equality in particular is in the very nature of bourgeois democracy. Under the guise of the equality of the individual in general, bourgeois democracy proclaims the formal or legal equality of the property-owner and the proletarian, the exploiter and the exploited, thereby grossly deceiving the oppressed classes. On the plea that all men are absolutely equal, the bourgeoisie is transforming the idea of equality, which is itself a reflection of relations in commodity production, into a weapon in its struggle against the abolition of classes. The real meaning of the demand for equality consists in its being a demand for the abolition of classes.

2) In conformity with its fundamental task of combating bourgeois democracy and exposing its falseness and hypocrisy, the Communist Party, as the avowed champion of the proletarian struggle to overthrow the bourgeois yoke, must base its policy, in the national question too, not on abstract and formal principles but, first, on a precise appraisal of the specific historical situation and, primarily, of economic conditions; second, on a clear distinction between the interests of the oppressed classes, of working and exploited people, and the general concept of national interests as a whole, which implies the interests of the ruling class; third, on an equally clear distinction between the oppressed, dependent and subject nations and the oppressing, exploiting and sovereign nations, in order to counter the bourgeois-democratic lies that play down this colonial and financial enslavement of the vast majority of the world's population by an insignificant minority of the richest and advanced capitalist countries, a feature characteristic of the era of finance capital and imperialism.

3) The imperialist war of 1914-18 has very clearly revealed to all nations and to the oppressed classes of the whole world the falseness of bourgeois-democratic phrases, by practically demonstrating that the Treaty of Versailles of the celebrated "Western democracies" is an even more brutal and foul act of violence against weak nations than was the Treaty of Brest-Litovsk of the German Junkers and the Kaiser. The League of Nations and the entire post-war policy of the Entente reveal this truth with even greater

clarity and distinctness. They are everywhere intensifying the revolutionary struggle both of the proletariat in the advanced countries and of the toiling masses in the colonial and dependent countries. They are hastening the collapse of the petty-bourgeois nationalist illusions that nations can live together in peace and equality under capitalism.

4) From these fundamental premises it follows that the Communist International's entire policy on the national and the colonial questions should rest primarily on a closer union of the proletarians and the working masses of all nations and countries for a joint revolutionary struggle to overthrow the landowners and the bourgeoisie. This union alone will guarantee victory over capitalism, without which the abolition of national oppression and inequality is impossible.

5) The world political situation has now placed the dictatorship of the proletariat on the order of the day. World political developments are of necessity concentrated on a single focus—the struggle of the world bourgeoisie against the Soviet Russian Republic, around which are inevitably grouped, on the one hand, the Soviet movements of the advanced workers in all countries, and, on the other, all the national liberation movements in the colonies and among the oppressed nationalities, who are learning from bitter experience that their only salvation lies in the Soviet system's victory over world imperialism.

6) Consequently, one cannot at present confine oneself to a bare recognition or proclamation of the need for closer union between the working people of the various nations; a policy must be pursued that will achieve the closest alliance, with Soviet Russia, of all the national and colonial liberation movements. The form of this alliance should be determined by the degree of development of the communist movement in the proletariat of each country, or of the bourgeois-democratic liberation movement of the workers and peasants in backward countries or among backward nationalities.

7) Federation is a transitional form to the complete unity of the working people of different nations. The feasibility of federation has already been demonstrated in practice both by the relations between the R.S.F.S.R. and other

Soviet Republics (the Hungarian, Finnish[52] and Latvian[53] in the past, and the Azerbaijan and Ukrainian at present), and by the relations within the R.S.F.S.R. in respect of nationalities which formerly enjoyed neither statehood nor autonomy (e.g., the Bashkir and Tatar autonomous republics in the R.S.F.S.R., founded in 1919 and 1920 respectively).

8) In this respect, it is the task of the Communist International to further develop and also to study and test by experience these new federations, which are arising on the basis of the Soviet system and the Soviet movement. In recognising that federation is a transitional form to complete unity, it is necessary to strive for ever closer federal unity, bearing in mind, first, that the Soviet republics, surrounded as they are by the imperialist powers of the whole world—which from the military standpoint are immeasurably stronger—cannot possibly continue to exist without the closest alliance; second, that a close economic alliance between the Soviet republics is necessary, otherwise the productive forces which have been ruined by imperialism cannot be restored and the well-being of the working people cannot be ensured; third, that there is a tendency towards the creation of a single world economy, regulated by the proletariat of all nations as an integral whole and according to a common plan. This tendency has already revealed itself quite clearly under capitalism and is bound to be further developed and consummated under socialism.

9) The Communist International's national policy in the sphere of relations within the state cannot be restricted to the bare, formal, purely declaratory and actually noncommittal recognition of the equality of nations to which the bourgeois democrats confine themselves—both those who frankly admit being such, and those who assume the name of socialists (such as the socialists of the Second International).

In all their propaganda and agitation—both within parliament and outside it—the Communist parties must consistently expose that constant violation of the equality of nations and of the guaranteed rights of national minorities which is to be seen in all capitalist countries, despite their "democratic" constitutions. It is also necessary, first, constantly to explain that only the Soviet system is capable of ensuring genuine equality of nations, by uniting first the proletarians and then the whole mass of the working population in the struggle against the bourgeoisie; and, second, that all Communist parties should render direct aid to the revolutionary movements among the dependent and underprivileged nations (for example, Ireland, the American Negroes, etc.) and in the colonies.

Without the latter condition, which is particularly important, the struggle against the oppression of dependent nations and colonies, as well as recognition of their right to secede, are but a false signboard, as is evidenced by the parties of the Second International.

10) Recognition of internationalism in word, and its replacement in deed by petty-bourgeois nationalism and pacifism, in all propaganda, agitation and practical work, is very common, not only among the parties of the Second International, but also among those which have withdrawn from it, and often even among parties which now call themselves communist. The urgency of the struggle against this evil, against the most deep-rooted petty-bourgeois national prejudices, looms ever larger with the mounting exigency of the task of converting the dictatorship of the proletariat from a national dictatorship (i.e., existing in a single country and incapable of determining world politics) into an international one (i.e., a dictatorship of the proletariat involving at least several advanced countries, and capable of exercising a decisive influence upon world politics as a whole). Petty-bourgeois nationalism proclaims as internationalism the mere recognition of the equality of nations, and nothing more. Quite apart from the fact that this recognition is purely verbal, petty-bourgeois nationalism preserves national self-interest intact, whereas proletarian internationalism demands, first, that the interests of the proletarian struggle in any one country should be subordinated to the interests of that struggle on a world-wide scale, and, second, that a nation which is achieving victory over the bourgeoisie should be able and willing to make the greatest national sacrifices for the overthrow of international capital.

Thus, in countries that are already fully capitalist and have workers' parties that really act as the vanguard of the proletariat, the struggle against opportunist and petty-bourgeois pacifist distortions of the concept and policy of internationalism is a primary and cardinal task.

11) With regard to the more backward states and nations, in which feudal or patriarchal and patriarchal-peasant relations predominate, it is particularly important to bear in mind:

first, that all Communist parties must assist the bourgeois-democratic liberation movement in these countries, and that the duty of rendering the most active assistance rests primarily with the workers of the country the backward nation is colonially or financially dependent on;

second, the need for a struggle against the clergy and other influential reactionary and medieval elements in backward countries;

third, the need to combat Pan-Islamism and similar trends, which strive to combine the liberation movement against European and American imperialism with an attempt to strengthen the positions of the khans, landowners, mullahs, etc.;*

fourth, the need, in backward countries, to give special support to the peasant movement against the landowners, against landed proprietorship, and against all manifestations or survivals of feudalism, and to strive to lend the peasant movement the most revolutionary character by establishing the closest possible alliance between the West-European communist proletariat and the revolutionary peasant movement in the East, in the colonies, and in the backward countries generally. It is particularly necessary to exert every effort to apply the basic principles of the Soviet system in countries where pre-capitalist relations predominate—by setting up "working people's Soviets", etc.;

fifth, the need for a determined struggle against attempts to give a communist colouring to bourgeois-democratic liberation trends in the backward countries; the Communist International should support bourgeois-democratic national

---

* In the proofs Lenin inserted a brace opposite points 2 and 3 and wrote "2 and 3 to be united".—*Ed.*

movements in colonial and backward countries only on condition that, in these countries, the elements of future proletarian parties, which will be communist not only in name, are brought together and trained to understand their special tasks, i.e., those of the struggle against the bourgeois-democratic movements within their own nations. The Communist International must enter into a temporary alliance with bourgeois democracy in the colonial and backward countries, but should not merge with it, and should under all circumstances uphold the independence of the proletarian movement even if it is in its most embryonic form;

sixth, the need constantly to explain and expose among the broadest working masses of all countries, and particularly of the backward countries, the deception systematically practised by the imperialist powers, which, under the guise of politically independent states, set up states that are wholly dependent upon them economically, financially and militarily. Under present-day international conditions there is no salvation for dependent and weak nations except in a union of Soviet republics.

12) The age-old oppression of colonial and weak nationalities by the imperialist powers has not only filled the working masses of the oppressed countries with animosity towards the oppressor nations, but has also aroused distrust in these nations in general, even in their proletariat. The despicable betrayal of socialism by the majority of the official leaders of this proletariat in 1914-19, when "defence of country" was used as a social-chauvinist cloak to conceal the defence of the "right" of their "own" bourgeoisie to oppress colonies and fleece financially dependent countries, was certain to enhance this perfectly legitimate distrust. On the other hand, the more backward the country, the stronger is the hold of small-scale agricultural production, patriarchalism and isolation, which inevitably lend particular strength and tenacity to the deepest of petty-bourgeois prejudices, i.e., to national egoism and national narrow-mindedness. These prejudices are bound to die out very slowly, for they can disappear only after imperialism and capitalism have disappeared in the advanced countries, and after the entire foundation of the backward countries' economic life has radically changed.

It is therefore the duty of the class-conscious communist proletariat of all countries to regard with particular caution and attention the survivals of national sentiments in the countries and among nationalities which have been oppressed the longest; it is equally necessary to make certain concessions with a view to more rapidly overcoming this distrust and these prejudices. Complete victory over capitalism cannot be won unless the proletariat and, following it, the mass of working people in all countries and nations throughout the world voluntarily strive for alliance and unity.

Published in June 1920

Published according to the manuscript and checked against the text of the proof-sheet, as emended by V. I. Lenin

PRELIMINARY DRAFT THESES ON THE AGRARIAN QUESTION

FOR THE SECOND CONGRESS OF THE COMMUNIST INTERNATIONAL

In his article,[54] Comrade Marchlewski gave an excellent explanation of the reasons why the Second International, which has now become the yellow International, failed, not only to define the revolutionary proletariat's tactics on the agrarian question, but even to pose that question properly. Comrade Marchlewski then went on to set forth the theoretical fundamentals of the Third International's communist agrarian programme.

These fundamentals can (and, I think, should) serve as the basis of the general resolution on the agrarian question for the Communist International Congress, which will meet on July 15, 1920.

The following is a preliminary draft of that resolution:

1) Only the urban and industrial proletariat, led by the Communist Party, can liberate the working masses of the countryside from the yoke of capital and landed proprietorship, from ruin and the imperialist wars which will inevitably break out again and again if the capitalist system remains. There is no salvation for the working masses of the countryside except in alliance with the communist proletariat, and unless they give the latter devoted support in its revolutionary struggle to throw off the yoke of the landowners (the big landed proprietors) and the bourgeoisie.

On the other hand, the industrial workers cannot accomplish their epoch-making mission of emancipating mankind from the yoke of capital and from wars if they confine themselves to their narrow craft, or trade interests, and smugly restrict themselves to attaining an improvement in their own conditions, which may sometimes be tolerable in the petty-bourgeois sense. This is exactly what happens to the "labour aristocracy" of many advanced countries, who constitute the core of the so-called socialist parties of the Second International; they are actually the bitter enemies and betrayers of socialism, petty-bourgeois chauvinists and agents of the bourgeoisie within the working-class movement. The proletariat is a really revolutionary class and acts in a really socialist manner only when it comes out and acts as the vanguard of all the working and exploited people, as their leader in the struggle for the overthrow of the exploiters; this, however, cannot be achieved unless the class struggle is carried into the countryside, unless the rural working masses are united about the Communist Party of the urban proletariat, and unless they are trained by the proletariat.

2) The working and exploited people of the countryside, whom the urban proletariat must lead into the struggle or, at all events, win over, are represented in all capitalist countries by the following classes:

first, the agricultural proletariat, wage-labourers (by the year, season, or day), who obtain their livelihood by working for hire at capitalist agricultural enterprises. The organisation of this class (political, military, trade union, co-operative, cultural, educational, etc.) independently and separately from other groups of the rural population, the conduct of intensive propaganda and agitation among this class, and the winning of its support for the Soviets and the dictatorship of the proletariat constitute the *fundamental* tasks of the Communist parties in all countries;

second, the semi-proletarians or peasants who till tiny plots of land, i.e., those who obtain their livelihood partly as wage-labourers at agricultural and industrial capitalist enterprises and partly by working their own or rented plots of land, which provide their families only with part of their means of subsistence. This group of the rural working population is very numerous in all capitalist countries; its existence and special position are played down by the representatives of the bourgeoisie and by the yellow "socialists" belonging to the Second International, partly by deliberately deceiving the workers and partly by blindly submitting to the routine of petty-bourgeois views and lumping together this group with the mass of the "peasantry". This bourgeois method of duping the workers is to be seen mostly in Germany and in France, but also in America and other countries. If the work of the Communist Party is properly organised, this group will become its assured supporter, for the lot of these semi-proletarians is a very hard one and they stand to gain enormously and immediately from Soviet government and the dictatorship of the proletariat;

third, the small peasantry, i.e., the small-scale tillers who, either as owners or as tenants, hold small plots of land which enable them to satisfy the needs of their families and their farms, and do not hire outside labour. This stratum, as such, undoubtedly stands to gain by the victory of the proletariat, which will fully and immediately bring it: (a) deliverance from the necessity of paying the big landowners rent or a share of the crop (for example, the *métayers* in France, also in Italy and other countries); (b) deliverance from mortgages; (c) deliverance from the numerous forms of oppression by and dependence on the big landowners (forest lands and their use, etc.); (d) immediate aid for their farms from the proletarian state (the use of the agricultural implements and part of the buildings on the big capitalist farms confiscated by the proletariat and the immediate conversion, by the proletarian state, of the rural co-operative societies and agricultural associations from organisations which under capitalism served above all the rich and middle peasants, into organisations that will primarily assist the poor, i.e., proletarians, semi-proletarians, small peasants, etc.), and many other things.

At the same time the Communist Party must clearly realise that during the transitional period from capitalism to communism, i.e., during the dictatorship of the proletariat, this stratum, or at all events part of it, will inevitably vacillate towards unrestricted freedom of trade and the free enjoyment of the rights of private property. That is because this stratum, which, if only in a small way, is a seller of articles of consumption, has been corrupted by profiteering and by proprietary habits. However, if a firm proletarian policy is pursued, and if the victorious proletariat deals very resolutely with the big landowners and the big peasants, this stratum's vacillation cannot be considerable and cannot alter the fact that, on the whole, it will side with the proletarian revolution.

3) Taken together, the three groups enumerated above constitute the majority of the rural population in all capitalist countries. That is why the success of the proletarian revolution is fully assured, not only in the cities but in the countryside as well. The reverse view is widespread; however, it persists only, first, because of the deception systematically practised by bourgeois science and statistics, which do everything to gloss over both the gulf that separates the above-mentioned classes in the countryside from the exploiters, the landowners and capitalists, and that which separates the semi-proletarians and small peasants from the big peasants; second, it persists because of the inability and unwillingness of the heroes of the yellow Second International and of the "labour aristocracy" in the advanced countries, which has been corrupted by imperialist privileges, to conduct genuinely proletarian revolutionary work of propaganda, agitation and organisation among the rural poor; the attention of the opportunists has always been and still is wholly concentrated on inventing theoretical and practical compromises with the bourgeoisie, including the big and middle peasants (who are dealt with below), and not on the revolutionary overthrow of the bourgeois government and the bourgeoisie by the proletariat; it persists, third, because of the obstinate refusal to understand—so obstinate as to be equivalent to a prejudice (connected with all the other bourgeois-democratic and parliamentary prejudices)—a truth which has been fully proved by Marxist theory and fully corroborated by the experience of the proletarian revolution in Russia, namely, that although the three enumerated categories of the rural population—who are incredibly downtrodden, disunited, crushed, and doomed to semi-barbarous conditions of existence in all countries, even the most advanced—are economically, socially, and culturally interested in the victory of socialism, they are capable of giving resolute

support to the revolutionary proletariat only *after* the latter has won political power, only *after* it has resolutely dealt with the big landowners and capitalists, and only *after* these downtrodden people see *in practice* that they have an organised leader and champion, strong and firm enough to assist and lead them and to show them the right path.

4) In the economic sense, one should understand by "middle peasants" those small farmers who, (1) either as owners or tenants, hold plots of land that are also small but, under capitalism, are sufficient not only to provide, as a general rule, a meagre subsistence for the family and the bare minimum needed to maintain the farm, but also produce a certain surplus which may, in good years at least, be converted into capital; (2) quite frequently (for example, one farm out of two or three) resort to the employment of hired labour. A concrete example of the middle peasants in an advanced capitalist country is provided by the group of farms of five to ten hectares in Germany, in which, according to the census of 1907, the number of farms employing hired labourers is about one-third of the total number of farms in this group.* In France, where the cultivation of special crops is more developed—for example, grape-growing, which requires a very large amount of labour—this group probably employs outside hired labour to a somewhat greater extent.

The revolutionary proletariat cannot set itself the task—at least not in the immediate future or in the initial period of the dictatorship of the proletariat—of winning over this stratum, but must confine itself to the task of neutralising it, i.e., rendering it neutral in the struggle between the proletariat and the bourgeoisie. This stratum inevitably

---

* Here are the exact figures: the number of farms of five to ten hectares—652,798 (out of a total of 5,736,082); these employed 487,704 hired labourers of various kinds, while members of the farmers' families (*Familienangehörige*) working on the farms numbered 2,003,633. In Austria, according to the census of 1902, this group comprised 383,331 farms, of which 126,136 employed hired labour; the hired labourers working on these farms numbered 146,044 and the working members of the farmers' families 1,265,969. The total number of farms in Austria was 2,856,349.

vacillates between these two forces; in the beginning of the new epoch and in the developed capitalist countries, it will, in the main, incline towards the bourgeoisie. That is because the world outlook and the sentiments of the property-owners are prevalent among this stratum, which has a direct interest in profiteering, in "freedom" of trade and in property, and stands in direct antagonism to the wage-workers. By abolishing rent and mortgages, the victorious proletariat will immediately improve the position of this stratum. In most capitalist countries, however, the proletarian state should not at once completely abolish private property; at all events, it guarantees both the small and the middle peasantry, not only the preservation of their plots of land but also their enlargement to cover the total area they usually rented (the abolition of rent).

A combination of such measures with a ruthless struggle against the bourgeoisie fully guarantees the success of the policy of neutralisation. The proletarian state must effect the transition to collective farming with extreme caution and only very gradually, by the force of example, without any coercion of the middle peasant.

5) The big peasants (*Grossbauern*) are capitalist *entrepreneurs* in agriculture, who as a rule employ several hired labourers and are connected with the "peasantry" only in their low cultural level, habits of life, and the manual labour they themselves perform on their farms. These constitute the biggest of the bourgeois strata who are open and determined enemies of the revolutionary proletariat. In all their work in the countryside, the Communist parties must concentrate their attention mainly on the struggle against this stratum, on liberating the toiling and exploited majority of the rural population from the ideological and political influence of these exploiters, etc.

Following the victory of the proletariat in the cities, all sorts of manifestations of resistance and sabotage, as well as direct armed action of a counter-revolutionary character on the part of this stratum, are absolutely inevitable. The revolutionary proletariat must therefore immediately begin the ideological and organisational preparation of the forces necessary to completely disarm this stratum and, simultaneously with the overthrow of the capitalists in industry, to deal this stratum a most determined, ruthless and smashing blow at the very first signs of resistance; for this purpose, the rural proletariat must be armed and village Soviets organised, in which the exploiters must have no place, and in which proletarians and semi-proletarians must be ensured predominance.

However, the expropriation even of the big peasants can in no way be made an immediate task of the victorious proletariat, because the material and especially the technical conditions, as well as the social conditions, for the socialisation of such farms are still lacking. In individual and probably exceptional cases, those parts of their land which they rent out in small plots or which are particularly needed by the surrounding small-peasant population will be confiscated; the small peasants should also be guaranteed, on certain terms, the free use of part of the agricultural machinery belonging to the big peasants, etc. As a general rule, however, the proletarian state must allow the big peasants to retain their land, confiscating it only if they resist the power of the working and exploited people. The experience of the Russian proletarian revolution, in which the struggle against the big peasantry was complicated and protracted by a number of special conditions, showed nevertheless that, when taught a severe lesson for the slightest attempt at resistance, this stratum is capable of loyally fulfilling the tasks set by the proletarian state, and even begins to be imbued although very slowly with respect for the government which protects all who work and is ruthless towards the idle rich.

The special conditions which, in Russia, complicated and retarded the struggle of the proletariat against the big peasants after it had defeated the bourgeoisie were, in the main, the following: after October 25 (November 7), 1917, the Russian revolution passed through the stage of the "general democratic"—that is, basically the bourgeois-democratic—struggle of the peasantry as a whole against the landowners; the cultural and numerical weakness of the urban proletariat; and, lastly, the enormous distances and extremely poor means of communication. Inasmuch as these retarding conditions do not exist in the advanced countries, the revolutionary proletariat of Europe and America should prepare far more energetically, and achieve far more rapidly, resolutely, and successfully, complete victory over the resistance of the big peasantry, completely depriving it of the slightest possibility of offering resistance. This is imperative because, until such a complete and absolute victory is achieved, the masses of the rural proletarians, semi-proletarians, and small peasants cannot be brought to accept the proletarian state as a fully stable one.

6) The revolutionary proletariat must immediately and unreservedly confiscate all landed estates, those of the big landowners, who, in capitalist countries—directly or through their tenant farmers—systematically exploit wage-labour and the neighbouring small (and, not infrequently, part of the middle) peasantry, do not themselves engage in manual labour, and are in the main descended from the feudal lords (the nobles in Russia, Germany, and Hungary, the restored seigneurs in France, the lords in Britain, and the former slave-owners in America), or are rich financial magnates, or else a mixture of both these categories of exploiters and parasites.

Under no circumstances is it permissible for Communist parties to advocate or practise compensating the big landowners for the confiscated lands, for under present-day conditions in Europe and America this would be tantamount to a betrayal of socialism and the imposition of new tribute upon the masses of working and exploited people, to whom the war has meant the greatest hardships, while it has increased the number of millionaires and enriched them.

As to the mode of cultivation of the land that the victorious proletariat confiscates from the big landowners, the distribution of that land among the peasantry for their use has been predominant in Russia, owing to her economic backwardness; it is only in relatively rare and exceptional cases that state farms have been organised on the former estates which the proletarian state runs at its own expense, converting the former wage-labourers into workers for the state and members of the Soviets, which administer the state. The Communist International is of the opinion that in the case of the advanced capitalist countries it would be correct to keep *most* of the big agricultural enterprises intact and to conduct them on the lines of the "state farms" in Russia.

It would, however, be grossly erroneous to exaggerate or to stereotype this rule and never to permit the free grant of *part* of the land that belonged to the expropriated expropriators to the neighbouring small and sometimes middle peasants.

First, the objection usually raised to this, namely, that large-scale farming is technically superior, often amounts to an indisputable theoretical truth being replaced by the worst kind of opportunism and betrayal of the revolution. To achieve the success of this revolution, the proletariat should not shrink from a temporary decline in production, any more than the bourgeois opponents of slavery in North America shrank from a temporary decline in cotton production as a consequence of the Civil War of 1863-65. What is most important to the bourgeois is production for the sake of production; what is most important to the working and exploited population is the overthrow of the exploiters and the creation of conditions that will permit the working people to work for themselves, and not for the capitalists. It is the primary and fundamental task of the proletariat to ensure the proletarian victory and its stability. There can, however, be no stable proletarian government unless the middle peasantry is neutralised and the support is secured of a very considerable section of the small peasantry, if not all of them.

Second, not merely an increase but even the preservation of large-scale production in agriculture presupposes the existence of a fully developed and revolutionarily conscious rural proletariat with considerable experience of trade union and political organisation behind it. Where this condition does not yet exist, or where this work cannot expediently be entrusted to class-conscious and competent industrial workers, hasty attempts to set up large state-conducted farms can only discredit the proletarian government. Under such conditions, the utmost caution must be exercised and the most thorough preparations made when state farms are set up.

Third, in all capitalist countries, even the most advanced, there still exist survivals of medieval, semi-feudal exploitation of the neighbouring small peasants by the big landowners as in the case of the *Instleute** in Germany, the *métayers* in France, and the sharecroppers in the United States (not only Negroes, who, in the Southern States, are mostly exploited in this way, but sometimes whites too). In such cases it is incumbent on the proletarian state to grant the small peasants free use of the lands they formerly rented, since no other economic or technical basis exists, and it cannot be created at one stroke.

The implements and stock of the big farms must be confiscated without fail and converted into state property, with the absolute condition that, *after* the requirements of the big state farms have been met, the neighbouring small peasants may have the use of these implements gratis, in compliance with conditions drawn up by the proletarian state.

In the period immediately following the proletarian revolution, it is absolutely necessary, not only to confiscate the estates of the big landowners at once, but also to deport or to intern them all as leaders of counter-revolution and ruthless oppressors of the entire rural population. However, with the consolidation of the proletarian power in the countryside as well as in the cities, systematic efforts should be made to employ (under the special control of highly reliable communist workers) those forces within this class that possess valuable experience, know-how, and organising skill, to build large-scale socialist agriculture.

7) The victory of socialism over capitalism and the consolidation of socialism may be regarded as ensured only when the proletarian state power, having completely suppressed all resistance by the exploiters and assured itself complete subordination and stability, has reorganised the whole of industry on the lines of large-scale collective production and on a modern technical basis (founded on the electrification of the entire economy). This alone will enable the cities to render such radical assistance, technical and social, to the backward and scattered rural population as will create the material basis necessary to boost the

* Tenant farmers.—*Ed.*

productivity of agricultural and of farm labour in general, thereby encouraging the small farmers by the force of example and in their own interests to adopt large-scale, collective and mechanised agriculture. Although nominally recognised by all socialists, this indisputable theoretical truth is in fact distorted by the opportunism prevalent in the yellow Second International and among the leaders of the German and the British "Independents", the French Longuetists, etc. This distortion consists in attention being directed towards the relatively remote, beautiful, and rosy future; attention is deflected from the immediate tasks of the difficult practical transition and approach to that future. In practice, it consists in preaching a compromise with the bourgeoisie and a "class truce", i.e., complete betrayal of the proletariat, which is now waging a struggle amidst the unprecedented ruin and impoverishment created everywhere by the war, and amidst the unprecedented enrichment and arrogance of a handful of millionaires resulting from that war.

It is in the countryside that a genuine possibility of a successful struggle for socialism demands, first, that all Communist parties should inculcate in the industrial proletariat a realisation of the need to make sacrifices, and be prepared to make sacrifices so as to overthrow the bourgeoisie and consolidate proletarian power—since the dictatorship of the proletariat implies both the ability of the proletariat to organise and lead all the working and exploited people, and the vanguard's ability to make the utmost sacrifices and to display the utmost heroism to that end; second, success demands that, as a result of the workers' victory, the labouring and most exploited masses in the countryside achieve an immediate and considerable improvement in their conditions at the expense of the exploiters—for without that the industrial proletariat cannot get the support of the rural areas and, in particular, will be unable to ensure the supply of food for the cities.

8) The enormous difficulty of organising and training for the revolutionary struggle the masses of rural working people, whom capitalism has reduced to a state of great wretchedness, disunity and frequently semi-medieval dependence, makes it necessary for the Communist parties

to devote special attention to the strike struggle in the rural districts, give greater support to mass strikes by the agricultural proletarians and semi-proletarians, and help develop the strike movement in every way. The experience of the Russian revolutions of 1905 and of 1917, now confirmed and extended by the experience of Germany and other advanced countries, shows that the growing mass strike struggle (into which, under certain conditions, the small peasants can and should also be drawn) is alone capable of rousing the countryside from its lethargy, awakening the class-consciousness of the exploited masses in the countryside, making them realise the need for class organisation, and revealing to them in a vivid and practical manner the importance of their alliance with the urban workers.

This Congress of the Communist International brands as traitors and renegades those socialists—to be found, unfortunately, not only in the yellow Second International, but also in the three very important European parties which have withdrawn from that International—who are not only capable of remaining indifferent to the strike struggle in the countryside, but even (like Karl Kautsky) of opposing it on the grounds that it threatens to reduce the output of articles of consumption. Neither programmes nor the most solemn declarations are of any value whatever unless it is proved in practice, in deed, that the Communists and workers' leaders are able to place above everything else in the world the development and the victory of the proletarian revolution, and to make the greatest sacrifices for it, for otherwise there is no way out, no salvation from starvation, ruin, and new imperialist wars.

In particular, it should be pointed out that the leaders of the old socialist movement and representatives of the "labour aristocracy"—who now often make verbal concessions to communism and even nominally side with it in order to preserve their prestige among the worker masses, which are rapidly becoming revolutionary—should be tested for their loyalty to the cause of the proletariat and their suitability for responsible positions in those spheres of work where the development of revolutionary consciousness and the revolutionary struggle is most marked, the resistance of the landowners and the bourgeoisie (the big peasants, the kulaks) most fierce, and the difference between the socialist compromiser and the communist revolutionary most striking.

9) The Communist parties must exert every effort to begin, as speedily as possible, to set up Soviets of Deputies in the countryside, and in the first place Soviets of hired labourers and semi-proletarians. Only if they are linked up with the mass strike struggle and with the most oppressed class can the Soviets perform their functions, and become consolidated enough to influence (and later to incorporate) the small peasants. If, however, the strike struggle has not yet developed, and the agricultural proletariat is as yet incapable of strong organisation owing both to the severe oppression by the landowners and the big peasants and to lack of support from the industrial workers and their unions, then the formation of Soviets of Deputies in the rural areas will require lengthy preparation by means of the organisation of communist cells, even if only small ones, intensified agitation—in which the demands of communism are enunciated in the simplest manner and illustrated by the most glaring examples of exploitation and oppression—and the arrangement of systematic visits of industrial workers to the rural districts, and so on.

Written at the beginning
of June 1920

Published in July 1920

Published according to
the manuscript

KOMMUNISMUS

JOURNAL OF THE COMMUNIST INTERNATIONAL FOR THE COUNTRIES OF SOUTH-EASTERN EUROPE (IN GERMAN), VIENNA, NO. 1-2 (FEBRUARY 1, 1920) TO NO. 18 (MAY 8, 1920)

This excellent journal, which is published in Vienna under the above title, contains a great deal of highly interesting material on the growth of the communist movement in Austria, Poland and other countries, together with a chronicle of the international movement, and articles on Hungary and Germany, on general tasks and tactics, etc. A shortcoming that strikes the eye even at a cursory examination cannot, however, be disregarded—the indubitable symptoms of the "infantile disorder of Left-wing Communism" that has affected the journal, a subject on which I have written a short pamphlet that has just appeared in Petrograd.

The excellent journal *Kommunismus* reveals three symptoms of this malady, which I would like at once to deal with briefly. No. 6 (March 1, 1920) contains an article by Comrade G.L.[55] entitled "On the Question of Parliamentarianism", which the editors designate as controversial, and from which Comrade B. K.,[56] the author of an article entitled "On the Question of the Parliamentary Boycott" (No. 18, May 8, 1920), directly dissociates himself (fortunately), i.e., declares that he is in disagreement with it.

G. L.'s article is very Left-wing, and very poor. Its Marxism is purely verbal; its distinction between "defensive" and "offensive" tactics is artificial; it gives no concrete analysis of precise and definite historical situations; it takes no account of what is most essential (the need to take over and to learn to take over, all fields of work and all institutions in which the bourgeoisie exerts its influence over the masses, etc.).

No. 14 (April 17, 1920), carries an article by Comrade B. K., entitled "The Events in Germany", in which he criticises a statement made by the Central Committee of the Communist Party of Germany on March 21, 1920, which statement I too criticised in the pamphlet mentioned above. However, our criticisms differ radically in character. Comrade B. K. criticises on the basis of quotations from Marx, which refer to a situation unlike the present one; he wholly rejects the tactics of the German Communist Party's Central Committee and absolutely evades what is most important, that which constitutes the very gist, the living soul, of Marxism—a concrete analysis of a concrete situation. Since most of the urban workers have abandoned the Scheidemannites for the Kautskyites, and since, within the Kautskian party (a party "independent" of correct revolutionary tactics) they are continuing to abandon its Right wing in favour of the Left, i.e., in fact, of communism—since that is the case, is it permissible to take no account of the transitional and compromise measures to be adopted with regard to *such workers*? Is it permissible to disregard and to gloss over the experience of the Bolsheviks, who, in April and May 1917, pursued what was in fact a policy of compromise, when they declared that the Provisional Government (Lvov, Milyukov, Kerensky and the rest) could not be overthrown at once, since in the Soviets, they still had the backing of the workers and it was first of all necessary to bring about a *change in views* in the majority, or a considerable part, of those workers?

I consider that impermissible.

Lastly, Comrade B. K.'s article in *Kommunismus* No. 18, which I have mentioned, very vividly, strikingly and effectively reveals his error in sympathising with the tactics of boycotting parliaments in present-day Europe. When the author dissociates himself from the "syndicalist boycott" and the "passive" boycott, but at the same time invents a special kind of "active" (Ah, how "Left"! ...) boycott, the full extent of the errors in his argument is brought out very strikingly.

"An active boycott," the author writes, "means that the Communist Party does not confine itself to disseminating the slogan advocating non-participation in elections, but, in the interests of the boycott, engages in revolutionary agitation just as extensively as if it were participating in the elections and as if its agitation and action were designed to secure the greatest possible number of proletarian votes." (P. 552).

This is a gem. This demolishes the anti-parliamentarians better than any criticism could. An "active" boycott is devised "as though" we were participating in elections!! The mass of unenlightened and semi-enlightened workers and peasants take a serious part in elections, for they still entertain bourgeois-democratic prejudices, are still under the sway of those prejudices. And instead of helping the unenlightened (although at times "highly-cultured") petty bourgeois to get rid of their prejudices by their own experience, we are to hold aloof from taking part in parliaments and to amuse ourselves by *inventing* tactics free of all commonplace and bourgeois contamination!!

Bravo, bravo, Comrade B. K.! By your defence of anti-parliamentarianism you will help us to destroy this folly much sooner than I can through my criticism.

N. Lenin

12.6.1920

Published in 1920

Published according to the manuscript

SPEECH DELIVERED AT THE SECOND ALL-RUSSIA CONFERENCE OF ORGANISERS RESPONSIBLE FOR RURAL WORK JUNE 12, 1920 [57]

Comrades, I am very glad to be able to greet you who have come to this conference to discuss work in the rural areas. Permit me first to dwell briefly on the international position of the Soviet Republic and our tasks in connection with it, and then to say a few words about the tasks in the rural districts, which, in my opinion, should now assume prime importance to Party workers.

As regards the Republic's international standing, you are of course well aware of the main facts about the Polish offensive. An incredible number of lies are being spread on this subject abroad, due to the so-called freedom of the press, which consists in all the most important organs of the press abroad being bought up by the capitalists, and being filled 99 per cent with articles by mercenary hacks. That is what they call freedom of the press, due to which there is no limit to the lies that are being spread. With regard to the Polish offensive in particular, they are trying to make out that the Bolsheviks presented impossible demands to Poland and launched an offensive, whereas you all know very well that we fully consented even to the immense frontiers held by the Poles before the offensive began. We set more store by the lives of our Red Army men than by a war for Byelorussia and Lithuania, which the Poles had seized. We declared in the most solemn terms—not only in the name of the Council of People's Commissars, but also in a special manifesto of the All-Russia Central Executive Committee,[58] the supreme body in the Soviet

Republic—we declared to the Polish Government, to the bourgeois and landowner government, besides appealing to the Polish workers and peasants, that we proposed negotiations for peace on the basis of the front that existed at the time, i.e., the front that left Lithuania and Byelorussia—non-Polish territory—in the hands of the Poles. We were and still are convinced that the Polish landowners and capitalists will be unable to retain foreign territory, and that we shall gain more even from the most unfavourable peace, since we shall save the lives of our Red Army men, and every month of peace makes us ten times as strong, whereas to every other government, including the bourgeois government of Poland, every month of peace means greater and greater disintegration. Although our peace proposals were very far-reaching, and although certain very hasty and, as far as talking goes, highly revolutionary revolutionaries, even called our proposals Tolstoyan—when, as a matter of fact, the Bolsheviks' actions have, I think, shown sufficiently that there is not a jot of Tolstoyanism in us—we considered it our duty, in the face of such a thing as war, to show that we were prepared to make the maximum possible concessions, and especially to show that we would not wage war for boundaries for which so much blood had been spilt, since to us that was a matter of little significance.

We were prepared to make concessions no other government can make; we offered Poland territory which it would be useful to compare with that described in a document published yesterday, I think, and coming from the supreme organ of the Allies, the British, French and other imperialists, in which Poland's eastern frontiers are indicated.[59]

These capitalists in Britain and France imagine that it is they who lay down boundaries. But, thank goodness, there are others besides them who do that—the workers and peasants have learnt to establish their boundaries themselves.

These capitalists have fixed the Polish boundaries much farther to the west than those we proposed. This document, coming from the Allies in Paris, is clear proof that they have arrived at a deal with Wrangel. They assure us that they want peace with Soviet Russia, that they support neither Poland nor Wrangel. We, however, say that it is an unscrupulous lie with which they are trying to shield themselves; for they say that they are not supplying any more arms, when as a matter of fact they are supplying them just as they did several months ago. Today's reports state that rich trophies have been captured—a carload of new British machine guns; Comrade Trotsky reports that brand-new French cartridges were captured the other day. What other confirmation do we need that Poland is acting with the aid of British and French equipment, with the aid of British and French cartridges, that she is acting with the aid of British and French money? If they now declare that Poland will herself establish her eastern borders, then that is in consequence of a direct deal with Wrangel. That is obvious to anybody. The entire situation makes it perfectly clear that the Polish landowners and bourgeoisie are fighting exclusively with the aid of the British and the French. The latter, however, are lying brazenly, just as they did when they assured us that they had not sent Bullitt, until he finally returned to America and came out and published the documents he had gathered here.

These gentlemen, these capitalist tradesmen, cannot act contrary to their nature. That is obvious. They can only reason like tradesmen. When our diplomats do not act like tradesmen, and when we say that the lives of our Red Army men are more precious to us than any vast boundary changes they, of course, with their purely tradesmen's reasoning, cannot understand it. When, a year ago, we proposed to Bullitt a treaty which was extremely favourable to them and extremely unfavourable to us, a treaty that would have left huge territories in the hands of Denikin and Kolchak, we did so in the certainty that, if peace were concluded, the whiteguard government would never be able to retain power.

With their tradesmen's reasoning, they could only interpret this as a confession of our weakness. "If the Bolsheviks agree to such a peace," they argued, "it must mean that they are at their last gasp." And the bourgeois press exulted, the diplomats rubbed their hands with glee, and millions of pounds sterling were advanced to Kolchak and Denikin. True, they did not give them hard cash, but supplied them with arms at usurious prices, fully convinced that the Bolsheviks could not cope with them at all. The upshot was that Kolchak and Denikin were routed and their hundreds of millions of pounds went up in smoke. We are now getting trainload after trainload of excellent British equipment; you can often meet entire divisions of Russian Red Army men clad in excellent British uniforms; the other day a comrade who arrived from the Caucasus told me that an entire division of Red Army men are wearing Italian bersagliere uniforms. I am very sorry that I am unable to show you photographs of these Russian Red Army men clad in bersagliere uniforms. All I can say is that, after all, the British equipment has been of some use and that Russian Red Army men are grateful to the British tradesmen who have fitted them out because they reasoned like tradesmen, and who have been thrashed, are being thrashed, and will be thrashed time and time again. (*Applause.*)

We find the same thing with the Polish offensive. This is another instance of God (if he exists, of course) first depriving of reason those whom he would punish. The Entente is undoubtedly headed by very shrewd men, excellent politicians, yet these people commit folly after folly. They raise up against us one country after another, enabling us to smash them one by one. Why, if only they succeeded in uniting—and they do have the League of Nations and there is no corner of the earth to which their military power does not extend. Nobody, it would seem, could unite all the enemy forces better and launch them against the Soviets. Yet they cannot unite them. They go into battle part by part. They merely threaten, boast and bluff. Six months ago they declared that they had mustered fourteen states against the Soviets, and that in a matter of months they would be in Moscow and Petrograd. But today I received a pamphlet from Finland, containing the reminiscences of a certain whiteguard officer about the offensive against Petrograd; prior to that I received a statement of protest from several Russians of the Cadet brand, members of the North-Western Government, which tells of how certain British generals invited them to a conference and suggested to them through an interpreter, and sometimes in excellent Russian, that they should form a government right away, on the spot—a Russian government, of course, a democratic government, it goes without saying, in the spirit of the Constituent Assembly—and how they were told to sign on the dotted line. And, though they were bitter enemies of the Bolsheviks, these Russian officers, these Cadets, were outraged by the brazen insolence of the British officers, who dictated to them, and ordered them, in a tone of a drill sergeant (and only like a Russian one can), to sign what they were told to—and they go on to relate how the whole affair fell through. I regret that we are unable to give extensive distribution to these documents, to these confessions of whiteguard officers who took part in the advance on Petrograd.

Why is that so? It is because their League of Nations is a league only in name; in fact it is a pack of wolves that are all the time at each other's throats and do not trust one another in the least.

As a matter of fact, they are even now boasting that Latvia, Rumania and Finland will join Poland in the attack; it is clear from the diplomatic negotiations that when Poland began her offensive the powers that were conducting peace negotiations with us changed their tone, and came out with statements whose insolence was sometimes amazing. They reason like tradesmen—and you cannot expect anything else from a tradesman. It seemed to them that this was the time to square accounts with Soviet Russia, so they turned high and mighty. Let them do so. We have seen the same thing in the case of other states, far bigger ones, but we have paid no heed to that because, as experience has shown, all the threats from Finland, Rumania, Latvia and the other bourgeois states that are wholly dependent on the Entente, have come to nought. Poland signed a treaty only with Petlyura, a general without an army, which has evoked even greater bitterness among the Ukrainian population and has induced more and more semi-bourgeois elements to side with Soviet Russia. So, once again, instead of a general offensive, you have isolated action by Poland alone. And now we see that although our forces had to spend a lot of time on the move because they were farther away from the frontiers than the Poles were and we needed more time to bring up our troops, the latter have begun to advance. Some days ago our cavalry captured

Zhitomir. Our forces have cut the last road linking Kiev with the Polish front both in the south and the north, which means that the Poles have lost Kiev irrevocably. At the same time we learn that Skólski has resigned, that the Polish Government are in a state of uncertainty and agitation and are already declaring that they will offer us new peace terms. Just as you please, you landowner and capitalist gentlemen! We will give the Polish peace terms due consideration. What we see is that their government are waging war against the wishes of their own bourgeoisie; that the Polish National Democrats,[60] who correspond to our Cadets and Octobrists—the most bitter counter-revolutionary landowners and bourgeois—are opposed to the war, for they realise that they cannot win such a war, and that it is being run by Polish adventurers, by the Socialist-Revolutionaries, the Polish Socialist Party,[61] people marked most by features characterising the Socialist-Revolutionaries, namely, revolutionary talk, boastfulness, patriotism, chauvinism, buffoonery and sheer claptrap. We are familiar with such people. When, after they have bitten off more than they can chew in this war, they begin to reshuffle their Cabinet and to say that they propose peace talks to us, we say: "Just as you please, gentlemen, have a try. We, however, are counting only on the Polish workers and peasants. We shall also talk peace, only not with you, the Polish landowners and bourgeois, but with the Polish workers and peasants, and we shall see what will come of such negotiations."

Comrades, despite the successes we are gaining on the Polish front, the position at present demands every effort of us. The most dangerous thing in a war that breaks out in conditions like those in the present war with Poland is to underrate the enemy and to reassure ourselves with the thought that we are the stronger. That is a most dangerous thing, which may lead to defeat in the war; it is the worst feature in the Russian character, which expresses itself in enervation and flabbiness. It is important, not only to begin but to carry on and hold out; that is what we Russians are not good at. Only by long training, through a proletarian disciplined struggle against all wavering and vacillation, only through such endurance can the Russian working masses be brought to rid themselves of this bad habit.

We have given Kolchak, Denikin and Yudenich a sound thrashing, but we have not yet finished the job. Wrangel is still in the Crimea. We said to ourselves: "Well, now we are the stronger"—and that has led to instance after instance of slackness and slovenliness. Meanwhile, Wrangel is receiving aid from Great Britain. This is done through traders, but it cannot be proved. Only the other day he landed troops and captured Melitopol. True, according to the latest reports we have re-captured it; but in this case, too, we had let it slip from our hands most shamefully just because we were strong. Just because Yudenich, Kolchak and Denikin have been smashed, the Russian begins to reveal his nature and take things easy, with the result that we let things slide. His slovenliness leads to tens of thousands of his comrades losing their lives. Here is a fundamental Russian trait: when not a single job has been carried through to the end he is apt to let things slide unless he is prodded. This trait must be ruthlessly combated, for it leads to tens of thousands of the finest Red Army men and peasants losing their lives, and the continued sufferings of famine. And so, though we are stronger than the Poles, our slogan in the war that has been imposed on us must be—an end to all slackness! Since war has proved inevitable, everything must be devoted to the war effort; the least slackness or lack of drive must be punished by wartime laws. War means war, and let nobody in the rear or in any peaceful occupation dare shirk this duty!

The slogan must be—everything for the war effort! Otherwise we shall be unable to cope with the Polish nobles and bourgeoisie. To finish with this war, we must teach a conclusive lesson to the last of the neighbouring powers that still dares to play at this game. We must give them so severe a lesson that they will warn their children, their grandchildren and their great-grandchildren to refrain from such things. (*Applause.*) And so, comrades, at every meeting, assembly and business conference, in all groups at all party institutions and on all executive bodies, it is the prime duty of those who are working in the countryside, of propagandists and agitators, and all the comrades engaged in any field of peaceful labour to give top priority and full effect to the slogan: "Everything for the war effort!"

Until complete victory is won in this war, we must guarantee ourselves against the errors and follies we have been committing for years. I do not know how many mistakes a Russian has to make before he learns his lesson. We have already had an instance of our thinking that the war was over before we had crushed the enemy, and we left Wrangel in the Crimea. I repeat, the slogan, "Everything for the war effort!" must be the chief item on the agenda at every conference, at every meeting, on every executive body.

We must ask ourselves: have we bent every effort, have we made every sacrifice to bring the war to an end? This is a question of saving the lives of tens of thousands of our finest comrades, who are perishing at the front, in the foremost ranks. It is a matter of saving ourselves from the famine which is imminent just because we are not fighting the war to a finish, when we can and must do that and quickly, too. For this, discipline and subordination must be enforced at all costs and with the utmost severity. The least condonement, the least slackness displayed here, in the rear, in any peaceful pursuit, will mean the loss of thousands of lives, and starvation in the rear.

That is why faults like these must be treated with ruthless severity. That is the first and principal lesson to be drawn from the civil war in Soviet Russia. It is the first and principal lesson which every Party worker must bear in mind under all circumstances, especially if his job is one of agitation and propaganda; he must know that he will be a worthless Communist and a traitor to the Soviet state if he does not, in respect to every shortcoming, however slight, implement this slogan with inflexible firmness and with ruthless determination. If this condition is observed, an early victory will be assured, and we shall be fully guaranteed against famine.

We receive reports about the situation in the outlying regions, from comrades arriving from remote parts of the country. I have seen comrades from Siberia, and also Comrades Lunacharsky and Rykov, who have returned from the Ukraine and the North Caucasus. They speak with boundless amazement of the wealth of these regions. In the Ukraine pigs are being fed on wheat; in the Northern Caucasus the peasant women, when selling milk, rinse their cans with milk. Trainloads of wool, leather and other wealth are on their way from Siberia; tens of thousands of poods of salt are lying in Siberia. In our parts, on the other hand, the peasants have been worn down, and refuse to give grain in exchange for paper money, which, as they see it, cannot restore their farms. Here, in Moscow, we may find starving workers carrying on at their machines. The continuation of the war is the chief obstacle to our keeping the workers better fed and restoring their shattered health. Just because we have slipped up on the Crimea, tens of thousands will go short of food for another six months. This is all due to poor organisation and discipline on our part. People here are dying, while in the Ukraine, in the North Caucasus and in Siberia we have wealth untold, with which we could feed the hungry workers and restore industry. To restore our economic life, we need discipline. The proletarian dictatorship should display itself primarily in the advanced, the most class-conscious and most disciplined of the urban and industrial workers—the greatest sufferers from hunger who have made great sacrifices during these two years—educating, training and disciplining all the other proletarians, who are often not class-conscious, and all working people and the peasantry. All sentimentality, all claptrap about democracy must be scrapped. Let us leave the claptrap to the Socialist-Revolutionaries and the Mensheviks; they have spoken enough about democracy to Kolchak, Denikin and Yudenich. Let them clear out and go over to Wrangel. He will complete their schooling. But that schooling must be given to those who have not yet learnt the lesson.

We maintain that the workers who have assumed the burdens and have ensured the tranquility and strength of the Soviets through their untold sacrifices, should regard themselves as a vanguard that will raise up the rest of the working masses by education and discipline. We know that the working man, as we have inherited him from capitalism, is in a state of utter benightedness and ignorance, and does not realise that work can be done, not only under the lash of capital, but also under the guidance of the organised worker. He is, however, capable of believing all that if we demonstrate it in practice. The working man cannot learn that from books but he can learn it if we demonstrate it to him in practice: he will have either to work under the guidance of the class-conscious industrial worker, or submit to the yoke of Kolchak, Wrangel and the rest. And so, we must, at any cost, have the strictest discipline, and conscious performance of what the vanguard of the proletariat prescribes, of what it has learnt from its hard experience. If all steps are taken for the achievement of our aim, that will fully guarantee our emergence from the economic chaos and disruption caused by the imperialist war. Grain collections yielded 30,000,000 poods in the season following August 1, 1917, and 110,000,000 poods in the season following August 1918. That shows that we have begun to emerge from our difficulties. Since August 1, 1919, over 150,000,000 poods have been brought in to date. That shows that we are making it. But we have not yet properly seen to the Ukraine, the North Caucasus and Siberia. If that is done we shall really be able to provide the worker with a good two pounds of bread a day.

I should also like to dwell, comrades, on a question of importance to you, rural Party workers, with whom I am in some measure acquainted from Party documents. I want to tell you that instruction, Party activities, agitation and propaganda will be your principal work. One of the main shortcomings in this work is that we do not know how to run state affairs, and that with our comrades, even with those who are in charge of work here, the habits of the old underground conditions are still too strong, i.e., habits of the time when we used to gather in small circles here or abroad, and did not have the slightest idea or inkling of how the work of the state has to be carried on. That, however, is something we have got to know, for we must remember that we have to govern millions. Any person in authority who goes to the rural districts, as delegate or representative of the Central Committee, must remember that we have a tremendous machinery of state which is still functioning poorly because we do not know how to run it properly.

In the rural districts there are hundreds of thousands of teachers who are browbeaten and intimidated by the kulaks, or who have been frightened out of their wits by the old tsarist officials, and cannot understand, are not in a position to understand, the principles of Soviet government. We have a huge military apparatus. Without the military commissars we would not have had a Red Army.

We also have the apparatus of the *Vsevobuch*,[62] which, together with its military functions, should be carrying on cultural work, should be educating the peasants. This state machinery functions very poorly; it contains no really devoted and convinced people, no real Communists. And you, who are going to the rural districts as Communists, must work not in isolation from this apparatus, but, on the contrary, in close conjunction with it. Every Party agitator who goes to a rural district must at the same time be an inspector of schools: not an inspector in the old sense of the word, not in the sense of meddling in educational affairs—that must not be permitted—but in the sense of co-ordinating his work with that of the People's Commissariat of Education, with the work of the *Vsevobuch*, with the work of the military commissars; he must regard himself as representative of the state, as representative of a party that is governing Russia. When he comes to a rural district he must not only act as propagandist and teacher; he must at the same time see to it that the school-teachers, who have never heard a living word, and those scores and hundreds of military commissars, all play a part in the Party agitator's work. Every school-teacher should have agitational pamphlets, and should not only have them, but read them to the peasants. He should know that he will lose his job unless he does that. The same applies to the military commissars; they should have these pamphlets and read them out to the peasants.

The Soviet government employs hundreds of thousands of office workers, who are either bourgeois or semi-bourgeois, or else have been so downtrodden that they have absolutely no confidence in our Soviet government, or feel so far removed from that government that they think it is somewhere far-off, over there in Moscow, while next to them are the kulaks, who have grain, but hold on to it and will not let them have any, so that they are starving. Here the Party worker has a double job. He must remember that he is not only a propagandist, that he must not only come to the assistance of the most downtrodden strata of the population —that is his principal job, not to do which means that he is no Party worker and has no right to call himself a Communist—but that, in addition, he must act as a representative of the Soviet government, he must establish contacts with the teachers, and co-ordinate his work with that of the People's Commissariat of Education. He must not be an inspector in the sense of exercising control and supervision; he must act as a representative of the governing Party, which is now administering all Russia through part of the proletariat; in this capacity he must remember that his job is one of instruction, and that he must enlist and educate all the teachers and military commissars to do the same work as his. They are not familiar with this work; you must teach it to them. They are at present defenceless against the well-fed peasant. You must help them to shake off this dependence. You must firmly remember that you are not only propagandists and agitators, but also representatives of the state; you must not destroy the existing apparatus, or interfere with it and muddle its organisation, but must organise your work so that, as efficient instructors, propagandists and agitators, even after a brief period of work in the rural districts, you will leave your mark, not only in the papers of the peasant Communists you have educated, but also in the minds of the people whose work you inspect and guide, and to whom you give assignments, demanding that every teacher and military commissar should work in the Soviet spirit under all circumstances, that he should know that this is his duty, that he must remember that if he does not perform that duty, he will lose his job; they should all sense and see in every agitator a fully empowered representative of the Soviet government.

If this is done, and if you employ your forces properly, you will multiply them, with the result that every body of agitators will leave a mark behind them in the shape of an apparatus of organisation, which already exists, but as yet functions imperfectly and unsatisfactorily.

In this sphere too, as in all others, I wish you success. (*Prolonged applause.*)

Published in 1920 in the pamphlet *Speech by V. I. Lenin at the Second All-Russia Conference of Organisers Responsible for Rural Work*

Published according to the pamphlet text

TELEPHONE MESSAGE TO THE PRESIDIUM OF THE ALL-RUSSIA FOOD CONFERENCE JULY 1, 1920

Comrades, I would have liked very much to attend your meeting and say something on the main food problems on your agenda. But, unfortunately, I am unable to indulge my wish and am obliged to content myself with addressing you briefly in this telephone message. I must inform you, comrades, that the successful outcome of your work, which is extremely onerous and responsible, recently induced the Council of People's Commissars to adopt a resolution expressing satisfaction with the results achieved by the food bodies in the matter of produce procurements. It is beyond question that the food bodies have grown in organisational strength during the past two years and more. This is largely due to your efforts.

But we cannot, of course, rest content with the results achieved. The hunger front, the next in importance after the war front, is imposing a number of new tasks upon you, and unless they are accomplished it will be impossible either to go on consolidating the workers' and peasants' government or to solve the immediate and urgent problems of economic development.

I also hope that you will help our economic development by establishing proper relations with the co-operative societies on the basis of the decisions of the Party Congress,[63] so as to properly accomplish the difficult but grateful task of transforming the petty-bourgeois co-operatives into socialist co-operatives.

The successes you have already achieved in food affairs oblige you more than ever to cope with the new tasks at all costs, and thus approach a real solution of the food problem. For to whom much has been given, of him much shall be demanded; and your work has shown that you have already been given quite a lot. Permit me then, to wish you success in solving the problems on the agenda of your conference, and also in your daily work, which I am sure, when the conference is over, you will tackle on the spot with redoubled energy.

Written on June 30, 1920
Published in *Pravda* No. 143,
July 2, 1920

Published according to the newspaper text

AID FOR THE WOUNDED OF THE RED ARMY!

Thanks to the heroism of the factory workers and of all working people, and despite the extraordinary difficulties and the terribly slow rate of progress, we are succeeding in reviving and restoring the economic life, which was shattered by the tsar and the capitalists. Matters are on the upgrade if ever so slowly. However, all our difficulties and hardships are as nothing compared with what has fallen to the lot of the wounded Red Army men, who are spilling their own blood in defence of the workers' and peasants' government, against the Polish nobles and capitalists, who are being egged on by the capitalists of Great Britain, France and America.

Let each man in the rear be mindful of his duty and help the wounded Red Army men to the best of his ability.

N. Lenin

July 2, 1920

A facsimile of the manuscript published in the magazine *Raneny Krasnoarmeyets* No. 1, July 5, 1920

Published according to the magazine text

THESES ON THE FUNDAMENTAL TASKS OF THE SECOND CONGRESS OF THE COMMUNIST INTERNATIONAL

1. The present stage in the development of the international communist movement is marked by the fact that the finest representatives of the revolutionary proletariat in all capitalist countries have fully grasped the fundamental principles of the Communist International, viz., dictatorship of the proletariat and Soviet power, and have ranged themselves with unbounded enthusiasm on the side of the Communist International. An even bigger and more important step forward is the definite sympathy with these fundamental principles that has everywhere taken shape among the broadest masses, not only of the urban proletariat, but of the advanced section of the rural workers as well.

On the other hand, two errors, or failings, are to be observed in the very rapidly growing international communist movement. One, which is very grave and constitutes an immense and immediate danger to the success of the cause of proletarian emancipation, is that a section of the old leaders and of the old parties of the Second International—some yielding half-unconsciously to the wishes and pressure of the masses, and some deliberately deceiving the masses in order to retain their function of agents and assistants of the bourgeoisie within the working-class movement—declare their qualified or even unqualified adherence to the Third International, while actually remaining in all their practical party and political work, on the level of the Second International. Such a state of affairs is absolutely intolerable, because it leads to downright corruption of the masses, detracts from the Third International's prestige, and threatens a repetition of the same acts of treachery as were perpetrated by the Hungarian Social-Democrats, who so hastily assumed the title of Communists. The other error, which is far less significant and is more in the nature of growing pains of the movement, consists in a tendency towards "Leftism" which results in a wrong appraisal of the role and the tasks of the party with regard to the class and the masses, and a wrong attitude towards the revolutionary Communists' obligation to work in bourgeois parliaments and reactionary trade unions.

Communists are in duty bound, not to gloss over shortcomings in their movement, but to criticise them openly so as to remedy them the more speedily and radically. For this purpose it is necessary: first, to define as concretely as possible, particularly on the basis of the practical experience already acquired, the content of the concepts "dictatorship of the proletariat" and "Soviet power"; second, to specify the precise content of the immediate and systematic preparatory work to be carried on in all countries so as to give effect to these slogans; and third, to specify the methods and means of rectifying the faults in our movement.

I

THE ESSENCE OF THE DICTATORSHIP OF THE PROLETARIAT AND OF SOVIET POWER

2. The victory of socialism (as the first stage of communism) over capitalism requires that the proletariat, as the only really revolutionary class, shall accomplish the following three tasks. First—overthrow the exploiters, and first and foremost the bourgeoisie, as their principal economic and political representative; utterly rout them; crush their resistance; absolutely preclude any attempt on their part to restore the yoke of capital and wage-slavery. Second—win over and bring under the leadership of the Communist Party, the revolutionary vanguard of the proletariat, not only the entire proletariat, or its vast majority, but all who labour and are exploited by capital; educate, organise, train and discipline them in the actual course of

a supremely bold and ruthlessly firm struggle against the exploiters; wrest this vast majority of the population in all the capitalist countries from dependence on the bourgeoisie; imbue it, through its own practical experience, with confidence in the leading role of the proletariat and of its revolutionary vanguard. Third—neutralise, or render harmless, the inevitable vacillation between the bourgeoisie and the proletariat, between bourgeois democracy and Soviet power, to be seen in the class of petty proprietors in agriculture, industry and commerce—a class which is still fairly numerous in nearly all advanced countries, although comprising only a minority of the population—as well as in the stratum of intellectuals, salary earners, etc., which corresponds to this class.

The first and second tasks are independent ones, each requiring its own special methods of action with regard to the exploiters and to the exploited respectively. The third task follows from the first two, and merely requires a skilful, timely and flexible combination of methods of the first and second type, depending on the specific circumstances in each separate instance of vacillation.

3. In the concrete situation created throughout the world, and above all in the most advanced, powerful, enlightened and free capitalist countries, by militarism, imperialism, the oppression of colonies and weak countries, the world-wide imperialist butchery and the "Peace" of Versailles—in that situation the very idea of the capitalists peacefully submitting to the will of the majority of the exploited, the very idea of a peaceful, reformist transition to socialism, is not merely sheer philistine stupidity but also downright deception of the workers, embellishment of capitalist wage-slavery, and concealment of the truth. That truth consists in the bourgeoisie, even the most enlightened and democratic, no longer hesitating at any fraud or crime, even the massacre of millions of workers and peasants, so as to preserve private ownership of the means of production. Only the forcible overthrow of the bourgeoisie, the confiscation of its property, the destruction of the entire bourgeois state apparatus from top to bottom—parliamentary, judicial, military, bureaucratic, administrative, municipal, etc.—right down to the wholesale deportation or internment

of the most dangerous and stubborn exploiters and the institution of strict surveillance over them so as to foil their inevitable attempts to resist and to restore capitalist slavery—only such measures can ensure real submission of the whole class of exploiters.

On the other hand, the idea, common among the old parties and the old leaders of the Second International, that the majority of the exploited toilers can achieve complete clarity of socialist consciousness and firm socialist convictions and character under capitalist slavery, under the yoke of the bourgeoisie (which assumes an infinite variety of forms that become more subtle and at the same time more brutal and ruthless the higher the cultural level in a given capitalist country) is also idealisation of capitalism and of bourgeois democracy, as well as deception of the workers. In fact, it is only after the vanguard of the proletariat, supported by the whole or the majority of this, the only revolutionary class, overthrows the exploiters, suppresses them, emancipates the exploited from their state of slavery and immediately improves their conditions of life at the expense of the expropriated capitalists—it is only after this, and only in the actual process of an acute class struggle, that the masses of the toilers and exploited can be educated, trained and organised around the proletariat under whose influence and guidance, they can get rid of the selfishness, disunity, vices and weaknesses engendered by private property; only then will they be converted into a free union of free workers.

4. Victory over capitalism calls for proper relations between the leading (Communist) party, the revolutionary class (the proletariat) and the masses, i.e., the entire body of the toilers and the exploited. Only the Communist Party, if it is really the vanguard of the revolutionary class, if it really comprises all the finest representatives of that class, if it consists of fully conscious and staunch Communists who have been educated and steeled by the experience of a persistent revolutionary struggle, and if it has succeeded in linking itself inseparably with the whole life of its class and, through it, with the whole mass of the exploited, and in completely winning the confidence of this class and this mass—only such a party is capable of leading the

proletariat in a final, most ruthless and decisive struggle against all the forces of capitalism. On the other hand, it is only under the leadership of such a party that the proletariat is capable of displaying the full might of its revolutionary onslaught, and of overcoming the inevitable apathy and occasional resistance of that small minority, the labour aristocracy, who have been corrupted by capitalism, the old trade union and co-operative leaders, etc.—only then will it be capable of displaying its full might, which, because of the very economic structure of capitalist society, is infinitely greater than its proportion of the population. Finally, it is only after they have been really emancipated from the yoke of the bourgeoisie and of the bourgeois machinery of state, only after they have found an opportunity of organising in their Soviets in a really free way (free from the exploiters), that the masses, i.e., the toilers and exploited as a body, can display, for the first time in history, all the initiative and energy of tens of millions of people who have been crushed by capitalism. Only when the Soviets have become the sole state apparatus is it really possible to ensure the participation, in the work of administration, of the entire mass of the exploited, who, even under the most enlightened and freest bourgeois democracy, have always actually been excluded 99 per cent from participation in the work of administration. It is only in the Soviets that the exploited masses really begin to learn—not in books, but from their own practical experience—the work of socialist construction, of creating a new social discipline and a free union of free workers.

II

WHAT IMMEDIATE AND UNIVERSAL PREPARATION FOR THE DICTATORSHIP OF THE PROLETARIAT SHOULD CONSIST IN

5. The present stage in the development of the international communist movement is marked by the fact that in the vast majority of capitalist countries, the proletariat's preparations to effect its dictatorship have not been completed, and, in many cases, have not even been systematically

begun. From this it does not, however, follow that the proletarian revolution is impossible in the immediate future; it is perfectly possible, since the entire economic and political situation is most inflammable and abounds in causes of a sudden flare-up; the other condition for revolution, apart from the proletariat's preparedness, viz., a general state of crisis in all the ruling and in all bourgeois parties, also exists. However, it does follow that the Communist Parties' current task consists not in accelerating the revolution, but in intensifying the preparation of the proletariat. On the other hand, the facts cited above from the history of many socialist parties make it incumbent on us to see that "recognition" of the dictatorship of the proletariat shall not remain a mere matter of words.

Hence, from the point of view of the international proletarian movement, it is the Communist parties' principal task at the present moment to unite the scattered Communist forces, to form a single Communist Party in every country (or to reinforce or renovate the already existing Party) in order to increase tenfold the work of preparing the proletariat for the conquest of political power—political power, moreover, in the form of the dictatorship of the proletariat. The ordinary socialist work conducted by groups and parties which recognise the dictatorship of the proletariat has by no means undergone that fundamental reorganisation, that fundamental renovation, which is essential before this work can be considered communist work and adequate to the tasks to be accomplished on the eve of proletarian dictatorship.

6. The proletariat's conquest of political power does not put a stop to its class struggle against the bourgeoisie; on the contrary, it renders that struggle most widespread, intense and ruthless. Owing to the extreme intensification of the struggle all groups, parties and leaders in the working-class movement who have fully or partly adopted the stand of reformism, of the "Centre", etc., inevitably side with the bourgeoisie or join the waverers, or else (what is the most dangerous of all) land in the ranks of the unreliable friends of the victorious proletariat. Hence, preparation for the dictatorship of the proletariat calls, not only for an intensification of the struggle against reformist and

"Centrist" tendencies, but also for a change in the character of that struggle. The struggle cannot be restricted to explaining the erroneousness of these tendencies; it must unswervingly and ruthlessly expose any leader of the working-class movement who reveals such tendencies, for otherwise the proletariat cannot know who it will march with into the decisive struggle against the bourgeoisie. This struggle is such that at any moment it may—and actually does, as experience has shown—substitute criticism with weapons for the weapon of criticism.[64] Any inconsistency or weakness in exposing those who show themselves to be reformists or "Centrists" means directly increasing the danger of the power of the proletariat being overthrown by the bourgeoisie, which tomorrow will utilise for the counter-revolution that which short-sighted people today see merely as "theoretical difference".

7. In particular, we must not restrict ourselves to the usual repudiation, in principle, of all collaboration between the proletariat and the bourgeoisie, of all "collaborationism". Under the dictatorship of the proletariat, which will never be able, at one stroke, to abolish private property completely, mere defence of "liberty" and "equality", while private ownership of the means of production is preserved, turns into "collaboration" with the bourgeoisie, and undermines the rule of the working class. The dictatorship of the proletariat means that the state uses its whole machinery of power to uphold and perpetuate "no-liberty" for the exploiters to continue their oppression and exploitation, "inequality" between the owner of property (i.e., one who has appropriated for himself certain means of production created by social labour) and the non-owner. That which, prior to the victory of the proletariat, seems merely a theoretical difference on the question of "democracy" inevitably becomes, on the day following victory, a question that is settled by force of arms. Consequently, even preliminary work in preparing the masses to effect the dictatorship of the proletariat is impossible without a radical change in the entire character of the struggle against the "Centrists" and the "champions of democracy".

8. The dictatorship of the proletariat is the most deter-

mined and revolutionary form of the proletariat's class struggle against the bourgeoisie. This struggle can be successful only when the most revolutionary vanguard of the proletariat has the backing of the overwhelming majority of the proletariat. Hence, preparation for the dictatorship of the proletariat entails not only explanation of the bourgeois character of all reformism, of all defence of democracy, while private ownership of the means of production is preserved; it entails, not only exposure of such trends, which are in fact a defence of the bourgeoisie within the labour movement; it also calls for old leaders being replaced by Communists in proletarian organisations of absolutely every type—not only political, but also trade union, co-operative, educational, etc. The more complete, lengthy and firmly established the rule of bourgeois democracy has been in a given country, the more the bourgeoisie will have succeeded in securing the appointment to such leading posts of people whose minds have been moulded by it and imbued with its views and prejudices, and who have very often been directly or indirectly bought by it. These representatives of the labour aristocracy, bourgeoisified workers, should be ousted from all their posts a hundred times more sweepingly than hitherto, and replaced by workers—even by wholly inexperienced men, provided they are connected with the exploited masses and enjoy their confidence in the struggle against the exploiters. The dictatorship of the proletariat will require the appointment of such inexperienced workers to the most responsible posts in the state; otherwise the workers' government will be impotent and will not have the support of the masses.

9. The dictatorship of the proletariat means that all toiling and exploited people, who have been disunited, deceived, intimidated, oppressed, downtrodden and crushed by the capitalist class, come under the full leadership of the only class trained for that leadership by the whole history of capitalism. That is why the following is one of the methods whereby preparations for the dictatorship of the proletariat should be started everywhere and immediately:

In all organisations, unions and associations without exception, and first and foremost in proletarian organisations, but also in those of the non-proletarian toiling and exploited masses (political, trade union, military, co-operative, educational, sports, etc., etc.), groups or cells of Communists should be formed—preferably open groups, but underground groups as well, the latter being essential whenever there is reason to expect their suppression, or the arrest or banishment of their members on the part of the bourgeoisie; these cells, which are to be in close touch with one another and with the Party centre, should, by pooling their experience, carrying on work of agitation, propaganda and organisation, adapting themselves to absolutely every sphere of public life and to every variety and category of the toiling masses, systematically educate themselves, the Party, the class, and the masses by means of such diversified work.

In this connection, it is of the utmost importance that necessary distinctions between the methods of work should be evolved in practice: on the one hand, in relation to the "leaders", or "responsible representatives", who are very often hopelessly beset with petty-bourgeois and imperialist prejudices—such "leaders" must be ruthlessly exposed and expelled from the working-class movement—and, on the other hand, in relation to the masses, who, particularly after the imperialist holocaust, are for the most part inclined to listen to and accept the doctrine that the guidance from the proletariat is essential, as the only way of escape from capitalist slavery. We must learn to approach the masses with particular patience and caution so as to be able to understand the distinctive features in the mentality of each stratum, calling, etc., of these masses.

10. In particular, there is a group or cell of Communists that deserves exceptional attention and care from the Party, i.e., the parliamentary group of Party members, who are deputies to bourgeois representative institutions (primarily the national, but also local, municipal, etc., representative institutions). On the one hand, it is this tribune which is held in particular regard by large sections of the toiling masses, who are backward or imbued with petty-bourgeois prejudices; it is therefore imperative for Communists to utilise this tribune to conduct propaganda, agitation and organisational work and to explain to the masses why the

dispersal of the bourgeois parliament by the national congress of Soviets was legitimate in Russia (and, at the proper time, will be legitimate in any country). On the other hand, the entire history of bourgeois democracy, particularly in the advanced countries, has converted the parliamentary rostrum into one of the principal, if not the principal, venues of unparalleled fraudulency, financial and political deception of the people, careerism, hypocrisy and oppression of the working people. The intense hatred of parliaments felt by the best representatives of the revolutionary proletariat is therefore quite justified. The Communist parties and all parties affiliated to the Third International—especially those which have not arisen by splitting away from the old parties and by waging a long and persistent struggle against them, but through the old parties accepting (often nominally) the new stand—should therefore adopt a most strict attitude towards their parliamentary groups; the latter must be brought under the full control and direction of the Central Committees of the Parties; they must consist, in the main, of revolutionary workers; speeches by members of parliament should be carefully analysed in the Party press and at Party meetings, from a strictly communist standpoint; deputies should be sent to carry on agitational work among the masses; those who manifest Second International leanings should be expelled from the parliamentary groups, etc.

11. One of the chief causes hampering the revolutionary working-class movement in the developed capitalist countries is the fact that because of their colonial possessions and the super-profits gained by finance capital, etc., the capitalists of these countries have been able to create a relatively larger and more stable labour aristocracy, a section which comprises a small minority of the working class. This minority enjoys better terms of employment and is most imbued with a narrow-minded craft spirit and with petty-bourgeois and imperialist prejudices. It forms the real social pillar of the Second International, of the reformists and the "Centrists"; at present it might even be called the social mainstay of the bourgeoisie. No preparation of the proletariat for the overthrow of the bourgeoisie is possible, even in the preliminary sense,

unless an immediate, systematic, extensive and open struggle is waged against this stratum, which, as experience has already fully shown, will no doubt provide the bourgeois White guards with many a recruit after the victory of the proletariat. All parties affiliated to the Third International must at all costs give effect to the slogans: "Deeper into the thick of the masses", "Closer links with the masses"—meaning by the masses all those who toil and are exploited by capital, particularly those who are least organised and educated, who are most oppressed and least amenable to organisation.

The proletariat becomes revolutionary only insofar as it does not restrict itself to the narrow framework of craft interests, only when in all matters and spheres of public life, it acts as the leader of all the toiling and exploited masses; it cannot achieve its dictatorship unless it is prepared and able to make the greatest sacrifices for the sake of victory over the bourgeoisie. In this respect, the experience of Russia is significant both in principle and in practice. The proletariat could not have achieved its dictatorship there, or won the universally acknowledged respect and confidence of all the toiling masses, had it not made the most sacrifices, or starved more than any other section of those masses at the most crucial moments of the onslaught, war and blockade effected by the world bourgeoisie.

In particular, the Communist Party and all advanced proletarians must give all-round and unstinted support especially to the spontaneous and mass strike movement, which, under the yoke of capital, is alone capable of really rousing, educating and organising the masses, of imbuing them with complete confidence in the leadership of the revolutionary proletariat. Without such preparation, no dictatorship of the proletariat is possible; those who are capable of publicly opposing strikes, such as Kautsky in Germany and Turati in Italy, cannot possibly be tolerated in the ranks of parties affiliated to the Third International. This applies even more, of course, to those trade union and parliamentary leaders who so often betray the workers by using the experience of strikes to teach them reformism, and not revolution (for instance, in Britain and in France in recent years).

12. In all countries, even in those that are freest, most "legal", and most "peaceful" in the sense that the class struggle is least acute there, it is now absolutely indispensable for every Communist Party to systematically combine legal and illegal work, legal and illegal organisations. Notwithstanding their false and hypocritical declarations, the governments of even the most enlightened and freest of countries, where the bourgeois-democratic system is most "stable", are already systematically and secretly drawing up blacklists of Communists and constantly violating their own constitutions so as to give secret or semi-secret encouragement to the whiteguards and to the murder of Communists in all countries, making secret preparations for the arrest of Communists, planting *agents provocateurs* among the Communists, etc., etc. Only a most reactionary philistine, no matter what cloak of fine "democratic" and pacifist phrases he may don, will deny this fact or the conclusion that of necessity follows from it, viz., that all legal Communist parties must immediately form illegal organisations for the systematic conduct of illegal work and for complete preparations for the moment the bourgeoisie resorts to persecution. Illegal work is most necessary in the army, the navy and the police because, since the imperialist holocaust, governments the world over have begun to stand in dread of people's armies which are open to the workers and peasants, and are secretly resorting to all kinds of methods to set up military units specially recruited from the bourgeoisie and equipped with the most up-to-date weapons.

On the other hand, it is likewise necessary that, in all cases without exception, the parties should not restrict themselves to illegal work, but should conduct legal work as well, overcoming all obstacles, starting legal publications, and forming legal organisations under the most varied names, which should be frequently changed if necessary. This is being practised by the illegal Communist parties in Finland, Hungary, partly in Germany, Poland, Latvia, etc. It should be practised by the Industrial Workers of the World in the U.S.A. and by all Communist parties at present legal, should public prosecutors see fit to take proceedings against them on the grounds of resolutions adopted by Congresses of the Communist International, etc.

A combination of illegal and legal work is an absolute principle dictated, not only by all features of the present period, that of the eve of the proletarian dictatorship, but also by the necessity of proving to the bourgeoisie that there is not, nor can there be, any sphere of activity that cannot be won by the Communists; above all, it is dictated by the fact that broad strata of the proletariat and even broader strata of the non-proletarian toiling and exploited masses still exist everywhere, who continue to believe in bourgeois-democratic legality and whom we must undeceive without fail.

13. In particular, the conditions of the working-class press in most advanced capitalist countries strikingly reveal the utter fraudulency of liberty and equality under bourgeois democracy, as well as the necessity of systematically combining legal work with illegal work. Both in vanquished Germany and in victorious America, the entire power of the bourgeoisie's machinery of state and all the machinations of the financial magnates are employed to deprive the workers of their press, these including legal proceedings, the arrest (or murder by hired assassins) of editors, denial of mailing privileges, the cutting off of paper supplies, and so on and so forth. Besides, the news services essential to daily newspapers are run by bourgeois telegraph agencies, while advertisements, without which a large newspaper cannot pay its way, depend on the "good will" of the capitalists. To sum up: through skulduggery and the pressure of capital and the bourgeois state, the bourgeoisie is depriving the revolutionary proletariat of its press.

To combat this, the Communist parties must create a new type of periodical press for mass distribution among the workers: first, legal publications, which, without calling themselves communist and without publicising their links with the Party, must learn to make use of any legal opportunity, however slight, just as the Bolsheviks did under the tsar, after 1905; secondly, illegal leaflets, even the briefest and published at irregular intervals, but reprinted at numerous printshops by workers (secretly, or, if the movement has become strong enough, by the revolutionary seizure of printshops), and providing the proletariat with outspoken revolutionary information and revolutionary slogans.

Preparation for the dictatorship of the proletariat is impossible without a revolutionary struggle, into which the masses are drawn, for the freedom of the communist press.

III

RECTIFICATION OF THE POLITICAL LINE—PARTLY ALSO OF THE COMPOSITION—OF PARTIES AFFILIATED OR DESIRING TO AFFILIATE TO THE COMMUNIST INTERNATIONAL

14. The measure in which the proletariat in countries most important from the viewpoint of world economics and politics is prepared to establish its dictatorship can be seen with the greatest objectivity and precision in the fact that the most influential parties of the Second International, viz., the French Socialist Party, the Independent Social-Democratic Party of Germany, the Independent Labour Party of Great Britain and the Socialist Party of America,[65] have withdrawn from this yellow International, and have decided—the first three conditionally, the latter even unconditionally—to affiliate to the Third International. This proves that not only the vanguard of the revolutionary proletariat but its majority too have begun to come over to our side, convinced by the entire course of events. The main thing now is the ability to consummate this process and to consolidate firmly in point of organisation what has been achieved, so as to advance all along the line, without the slightest wavering.

15. All the activities of the parties mentioned (to which should be added the Socialist Party of Switzerland,[66] if the telegraph reports of its decision to join the Third International are true) show—as any periodical of these parties will strikingly confirm—that they are not yet communist, and quite often run directly counter to the fundamental principles of the Third International, viz., the recognition

of the dictatorship of the proletariat and Soviet government in place of bourgeois democracy.

Accordingly, the Second Congress of the Communist International must resolve that it cannot immediately accept the affiliation of these parties; that it endorses the reply given by the Executive Committee of the Third International to the German "Independents"[67]; that it confirms its readiness to conduct negotiations with any party that withdraws from the Second International and desires to enter into closer relations with the Third International; that it will admit the delegates of such parties in a deliberative capacity to all its congresses and conferences; that it sets the following conditions for the complete adhesion of these (and similar), parties with the Communist International:

1) All decisions of all Congresses of the Communist International and of its Executive Committee to be published in all the periodicals of the parties concerned;

2) These decisions to be discussed at special meetings of all sections or local organisations of the parties;

3) After such discussion, special congresses of the parties to be convened to sum up the results, and for the purpose of—

4) Purging the parties of elements that continue to act in the spirit of the Second International;

5) All periodical publications of the parties to be placed under exclusively Communist editorship.

The Second Congress of the Third International should instruct its Executive Committee formally to accept these and similar parties into the Third International after ascertaining that all these conditions have actually been met and that the activities of the parties have assumed a communist character.

16. As to the question of the conduct of Communists now holding a minority of the responsible posts in these and similar parties, the Second Congress of the Communist International should resolve that, in view of the obvious growth of sincere sympathy for communism among workingmen belonging to these parties, it would be undesirable for Communists to resign from the latter, as long as they can carry on work within them for the recognition of the

dictatorship of the proletariat and Soviet government, and as long as it is possible to criticise the opportunists and Centrists who still remain in these parties.

At the same time, the Second Congress of the Third International should declare in favour of Communist groups and organisations, or groups and organisations sympathising with communism, joining the Labour Party in Great Britain, despite its membership in the Second International. As long as this party ensures its affiliated organisations their present freedom of criticism and freedom to carry on work of propaganda, agitation and organisation in favour of the dictatorship of the proletariat and Soviet government, and as long as this party preserves the character of a federation of all trade union organisations of the working class, it is imperative for Communists to do everything and to make certain compromises in order to be able to exercise their influence on the broadest masses of the workers, to expose their opportunist leaders from a higher tribune, that is in fuller view of the masses, and to hasten the transfer of political power from the direct representatives of the bourgeoisie to the "labour lieutenants of the capitalist class", so that the masses may be more quickly weaned away from their last illusions on this score.

17. Concerning the Socialist Party of Italy, the Second Congress of the Third International considers that the criticism of that party and the practical proposals submitted to the National Council of the Socialist Party of Italy in the name of the party's Turin section,[68] as set forth in *L'Ordine Nuovo* of May 8, 1920, are in the main correct and are fully in keeping with the fundamental principles of the Third International.

Accordingly, the Second Congress of the Third International requests the Socialist Party of Italy to convene a special congress to discuss these proposals and also all the decisions of the two Congresses of the Communist International for the purpose of rectifying the party's line and of purging it, particularly its parliamentary group, of non-Communist elements.

18. The Second Congress of the Third International considers erroneous the views on the Party's relation to the class and to the masses, and the view that it is not

obligatory for Communist parties to participate in bourgeois parliaments and in reactionary trade unions. These views have been refuted in detail in special decisions of the present Congress, and advocated most fully by the Communist Workers' Party of Germany, and partly by the Communist Party of Switzerland[69], by *Kommunismus*, organ of the East-European Secretariat of the Communist International in Vienna, by the now dissolved secretariat in Amsterdam, by several Dutch comrades, by several Communist organisations in Great Britain, as, for example, the Workers' Socialist Federation, etc., and also by the Industrial Workers of the World in the U.S.A. and the Shop Stewards' Committees in Great Britain, etc.

Nevertheless, the Second Congress of the Third International considers it possible and desirable that those of the above-mentioned organisations which have not yet officially affiliated to the Communist International should do so immediately; for in the present instance, particularly as regards the Industrial Workers of the World in the U.S.A. and Australia, as well as the Shop Stewards' Committees in Great Britain, we are dealing with a profoundly proletarian and mass movement, which in all essentials actually stands by the basic principles of the Communist International. The erroneous views held by these organisations regarding participation in bourgeois parliaments can be explained, not so much by the influence of elements coming from the bourgeoisie, who bring their essentially petty-bourgeois views into the movement—views such as anarchists often hold—as by the political inexperience of proletarians who are quite revolutionary and connected with the masses.

For this reason, the Second Congress of the Third International requests all Communist organisations and groups in the Anglo-Saxon countries, even if the Industrial Workers of the World and the Shop Stewards' Committees do not immediately affiliate to the Third International, to pursue a very friendly policy towards these organisations, to establish closer contacts with them and the masses that sympathise with them, and to explain to them in a friendly spirit—on the basis of the experience of all revolutions, and particularly of the three Russian revolutions of the twentieth century—the erroneousness of their views as set forth above, and not to desist from further efforts to amalgamate with these organisations to form a single Communist party.

19. In this connection, the Congress draws the attention of all comrades, particularly in the Latin and Anglo-Saxon countries, to the fact that, since the war, a profound ideological division has been taking place among anarchists all over the world regarding the attitude to be adopted towards the dictatorship of the proletariat and Soviet government. Moreover, a proper understanding of these principles is particularly to be seen among proletarian elements that have often been impelled towards anarchism by a perfectly legitimate hatred of the opportunism and reformism of the parties of the Second International. That understanding is growing the more widespread among them, the more familiar they become with the experience of Russia, Finland, Hungary, Latvia, Poland and Germany.

The Congress therefore considers it the duty of all Communists to do everything to help all proletarian mass elements to abandon anarchism and come over to the side of the Third International. The Congress points out that the measure in which genuinely Communist parties succeed in winning mass proletarian elements rather than intellectual, and petty-bourgeois elements away from anarchism, is a criterion of the success of those Parties.

July 4, 1920

Published in July 1920

REPLY TO A LETTER FROM THE JOINT PROVISIONAL COMMITTEE FOR THE COMMUNIST PARTY OF BRITAIN[70]

I have received a letter from the Joint Provisional Committee for the Communist Party of Britain, dated June 20, and, in accordance with their request, I hasten to reply that I am in complete sympathy with their plans for the immediate organisation of a single Communist Party of Britain. I consider erroneous the tactics pursued by Comrade Sylvia Pankhurst and the Workers' Socialist Federation, who refuse to collaborate in the amalgamation of the British Socialist Party, the Socialist Labour Party and others to form a single Communist party. Personally I am in favour of participation in Parliament and of affiliation to the Labour Party, given wholly free and independent communist activities. I shall defend these tactics at the Second Congress of the Third International on July 15, 1920 in Moscow. I consider it most desirable that a single Communist party be speedily organised on the basis of the decisions of the Third International, and that such a party should establish the closest contact with the Industrial Workers of the World and the Shop Stewards' Committees, in order to bring about a complete merger with them in the near future.

N. Lenin

8.7.1920

Published in English in *The Call* No. 224, July 22, 1920

First published in Russian in the Fourth Edition of the *Collected Works*

Published according to the manuscript

TELEPHONE MESSAGE TO J. V. STALIN

By telephone to *Stalin, Kharkov*

A Note has been received from Curzon. He proposes an armistice with Poland on the following terms: the Polish army to withdraw beyond the line fixed by last year's peace conference,[71] viz., Grodno, Yalovka, Nemirov, Brest-Litovsk, Dorogusk, Ustilug, Krylov. This line cuts across Galicia between Przemysl and Rava-Russkaya, right up to the Carpathians. We keep everything east of this line. Our army is to withdraw 50 kilometres east of *this* line. A conference of representatives of Soviet Russia, Poland, Latvia, Lithuania and Finland is to be held in London under the auspices of the peace conference. Representatives of Eastern Galicia will be allowed to attend. We can send anybody we like as our representative. It has been proposed to us that we conclude an armistice with Wrangel, provided he withdraws to the Crimea. Wrangel is going to London to discuss the fate of his army, but not as member of the conference. We have been given a week for our reply. Besides, the Curzon Note says that the Polish Government has given its consent to a peace with Russia, on the basis of these terms.

Such is the Curzon Note. I ask Stalin:

1) to expedite execution of the order to furiously intensify the offensive;

2) to inform me of his (Stalin's) opinion.

For my part, I think that all this is a piece of knavery aimed at the annexation of the Crimea, which is advanced so insolently in the Note. The idea is to snatch victory out of our hands with the aid of false promises.

Lenin

Stalin's *reply* to be recorded and sent on to me by *telephone*.

Lenin

Written July 12 or 13, 1920
First published in the Fourth (Russian) Edition of the *Collected Works*

Published according to the manuscript copy revised and emended by V. I. Lenin

TELEGRAM TO J. V. STALIN

Kharkov

Revolutionary Council of the South-Western Front
To Stalin, urgent

17.7.1920

The Central Committee plenum has adopted almost in full the proposals I have made.[72] You will receive the full text. Keep me informed without fail, twice weekly in cipher and in detail, regarding the development of operations and the course of events.

Lenin

First published in the Fourth (Russian) Edition of the *Collected Works*

Published according to the manuscript

THE TERMS OF ADMISSION INTO THE COMMUNIST INTERNATIONAL

The First, Inaugural Congress of the Communist International[73] did not draw up precise conditions for the admission of parties into the Third International. When the First Congress was convened, only communist *trends* and *groups* existed in most countries.

It is in a different situation that the Second World Congress of the Communist International is meeting. In most countries, Communist *parties* and *organisations*, not merely trends, now exist.

Parties and groups only recently affiliated to the Second International are more and more frequently applying for membership in the Third International, though they have not become really Communist. The Second International has definitely been smashed. Aware that the Second International is beyond hope, the intermediate parties and groups of the "Centre" are trying to lean on the Communist International, which is steadily gaining in strength. At the same time, however, they hope to retain a degree of "autonomy" that will enable them to pursue their previous opportunist or "Centrist" policies. The Communist International is, to a certain extent, becoming the vogue.

The desire of certain leading "Centre" groups to join the Third International provides oblique confirmation that it has won the sympathy of the vast majority of class-conscious workers throughout the world, and is becoming a more powerful force with each day.

In certain circumstances, the Communist International may be faced with the danger of dilution by the influx of wavering and irresolute groups that have not as yet broken with their Second International ideology.

Besides, some of the big parties (Italy, Sweden), in which the majority have adopted the communist standpoint, still contain a strong reformist and social-pacifist wing that is only waiting for an opportune moment to raise its head again, begin active sabotage of the proletarian revolution, and thereby help the bourgeoisie and the Second International.

No Communist should forget the lessons of the Hungarian Soviet Republic. The Hungarian proletariat paid dearly for the Hungarian Communists having united with the reformists.

In view of all this, the Second World Congress deems it necessary to lay down absolutely precise terms for the admission of new parties, and also to set forth the obligations incurred by the parties already affiliated.

The Second Congress of the Communist International resolves that the following are the terms of Comintern membership:

* * *

1. Day-by-day propaganda and agitation must be genuinely communist in character. All press organs belonging to the parties must be edited by reliable Communists who have given proof of their devotion to the cause of the proletarian revolution. The dictatorship of the proletariat should not be discussed merely as a stock phrase to be learned by rote; it should be popularised in such a way that the practical facts systematically dealt with in our press day by day will drive home to every rank-and-file working man and working woman, every soldier and peasant, that it is indispensable to them. Third International supporters should use all media to which they have access—the press, public meetings, trade unions, and co-operative societies—to expose systematically and relentlessly, not only the bourgeoisie but also its accomplices—the reformists of every shade.

2. Any organisation that wishes to join the Communist International must consistently and systematically *dismiss* reformists and "Centrists" from positions of any responsibility in the working-class movement (party organisations,

editorial boards, trade unions, parliamentary groups, co-operative societies, municipal councils, etc.), replacing them by reliable Communists. The fact that in some cases rank-and-file workers may at first have to replace "experienced" leaders should be no deterrent.

3. In countries where a state of siege or emergency legislation makes it impossible for Communists to conduct their activities legally, it is absolutely essential that legal and illegal work should be combined. In almost all the countries of Europe and America, the class struggle is entering the phase of civil war. In these conditions, Communists can place no trust in bourgeois legality. They must *everywhere* build up a parallel illegal organisation, which, at the decisive moment, will be in a position to help the Party fulfil its duty to the revolution.

4. Persistent and systematic propaganda and agitation must be conducted in the armed forces, and Communist cells formed in every military unit. In the main Communists will have to do this work illegally; failure to engage in it would be tantamount to a betrayal of their revolutionary duty and incompatible with membership in the Third International.

5. Regular and systematic agitation is indispensable in the countryside. The working class cannot consolidate its victory without support from at least a section of the farm labourers and poor peasants, and without neutralising, through its policy, part of the rest of the rural population. In the present period communist activity in the countryside is of primary importance. It should be conducted, in the main, through revolutionary *worker*-Communists who have contacts with the rural areas. To forgo this work or entrust it to unreliable semi-reformist elements is tantamount to renouncing the proletarian revolution.

6. It is the duty of any party wishing to belong to the Third International to expose, not only avowed social-patriotism, but also the falsehood and hypocrisy of social-pacifism. It must systematically demonstrate to the workers that, without the revolutionary overthrow of capitalism, no international arbitration courts, no talk about a reduction of armaments, no "democratic" reorganisation of the League of Nations will save mankind from new imperialist wars.

7. It is the duty of parties wishing to belong to the Communist International to recognise the need for a complete and absolute break with reformism and "Centrist" policy, and to conduct propaganda among the party membership for that break. Without this, a consistent communist policy is impossible.

The Communist International demands imperatively and uncompromisingly that this break be effected at the earliest possible date. It cannot tolerate a situation in which avowed reformists, such as Turati, Modigliani and others, are entitled to consider themselves members of the Third International. Such a state of affairs would lead to the Third International strongly resembling the defunct Second International.

8. Parties in countries whose bourgeoisie possess colonies and oppress other nations must pursue a most well-defined and clear-cut policy in respect of colonies and oppressed nations. Any party wishing to join the Third International must ruthlessly expose the colonial machinations of the imperialists of its "own" country, must support—in deed, not merely in word—every colonial liberation movement, demand the expulsion of its compatriot imperialists from the colonies, inculcate in the hearts of the workers of its own country an attitude of true brotherhood with the working population of the colonies and the oppressed nations, and conduct systematic agitation among the armed forces against all oppression of the colonial peoples.

9. It is the duty of any party wishing to join the Communist International to conduct systematic and unflagging communist work in the trade unions, co-operative societies and other mass workers' organisations. Communist cells should be formed in the trade unions, and, by their sustained and unflagging work, win the unions over to the communist cause. In every phase of their day-by-day activity these cells must unmask the treachery of the social-patriots and the vacillation of the "Centrists". The cells must be completely subordinate to the party as a whole.

10. It is the duty of any party belonging to the Communist International to wage a determined struggle against the Amsterdam "International" of yellow trade unions.[74] Its indefatigable propaganda should show the organised

workers the need to break with the yellow Amsterdam International. It must give every support to the emerging international federation of Red trade unions[75] which are associated with the Communist International.

11. It is the duty of parties wishing to join the Third International to re-examine the composition of their parliamentary groups, eliminate unreliable elements and effectively subordinate these groups to the Party Central Committees. They must demand that every Communist proletarian should subordinate all his activities to the interests of truly revolutionary propaganda and agitation.

12. The periodical and non-periodical press, and all publishing enterprises, must likewise be fully subordinate to the Party Central Committee, whether the party as a whole is legal or illegal at the time. Publishing enterprises should not be allowed to abuse their autonomy and pursue any policies that are not in full accord with that of the Party.

13. Parties belonging to the Communist International must be organised on the principle of democratic *centralism*. In this period of acute civil war, the Communist parties can perform their duty only if they are organised in a most centralised manner, are marked by an iron discipline bordering on military discipline, and have strong and authoritative party centres invested with wide powers and enjoying the unanimous confidence of the membership.

14. Communist parties in countries where Communists can conduct their work legally must carry out periodic membership purges (re-registrations) with the aim of systematically ridding the party of petty-bourgeois elements that inevitably percolate into it.

15. It is the duty of any party wishing to join the Communist International selflessly to help any Soviet republic in its struggle against counter-revolutionary forces. Communist parties must conduct incessant propaganda urging the workers to refuse to transport war materials destined for the enemies of the Soviet republics; they must conduct legal or illegal propaganda in the armed forces dispatched to strangle the workers' republics, etc.

16. It is the duty of parties which have still kept their old Social-Democratic programmes to revise them as speedily as possible and draw up new communist programmes

in conformity with the specific conditions in their respective countries, and in the spirit of Communist International decisions. As a rule, the programmes of all parties belonging to the Communist International must be approved by a regular Congress of the Communist International or by its Executive Committee. In the event of the Executive Committee withholding approval, the party is entitled to appeal to the Congress of the Communist International.

17. All decisions of the Communist International's congresses and of its Executive Committee are binding on all affiliated parties. Operating in conditions of acute civil war, the Communist International must be far more centralised than the Second International was. It stands to reason, however, that in every aspect of their work the Communist International and its Executive Committee must take into account the diversity of conditions in which the respective parties have to fight and work, and adopt decisions binding on all parties only on matters in which such decisions are possible.

18. In view of the foregoing, parties wishing to join the Communist International must change their name. Any party seeking affiliation must call itself the *Communist* Party of the country in question (Section of the Third, Communist International). The question of a party's name is not merely a formality, but a matter of major political importance. The Communist International has declared a resolute war on the bourgeois world and all yellow Social-Democratic parties. The difference between the Communist parties and the old and official "Social-Democratic", or "socialist", parties, which have betrayed the banner of the working class, must be made absolutely clear to every rank-and-file worker.

19. After the conclusion of the proceedings of the Second World Congress of the Communist International, any party wishing to join the Communist International must at the earliest date convene an extraordinary congress for official acceptance of the above obligations on behalf of the entire party.

Published in July 1920

ARTICLE TWENTY OF THE TERMS OF ADMISSION INTO THE COMMUNIST INTERNATIONAL[76]

Parties which now wish to join the Third International but have not yet radically changed their previous tactics must do everything necessary, before joining the International, for at least two-thirds of their respective Central Committees and all the principal central Party bodies to be made up of comrades who came out publicly, prior to the Second Congress of the Communist International, with unambiguous statements in favour of joining the Third International. Exceptions may be allowed with the consent of the Executive Committee of the Third International. The latter has the right to make exceptions also for representatives of the "Centre", named in § 7.

First published in 1921 in the book *The Second Congress of the Communist International. Verbatim Report*. Published by the Communist International, Petrograd

Published according to the text of the book

THE SECOND CONGRESS OF THE COMMUNIST INTERNATIONAL[77]

JULY 19-AUGUST 7, 1920

First published in full in 1921 in the book *The Second Congress of the Communist International. Verbatim Report*. Published by the Communist International, Petrograd

The Report on the International Situation is published according to the text of the book, checked against the verbatim report as emended by Lenin; speeches are published according to the text of the book, checked against the verbatim report in German

1

REPORT ON THE INTERNATIONAL SITUATION AND THE FUNDAMENTAL TASKS OF THE COMMUNIST INTERNATIONAL JULY 19

(*An ovation breaks out. All present rise to their feet and applaud. The speaker tries to begin, but the applause and cries in all languages continue. The ovation does not abate.*) Comrades, the theses on the questions of the fundamental tasks of the Communist International have been published in all languages and contain nothing that is materially new (particularly to the Russian comrades). That is because, in a considerable measure, they extend several of the main features of our revolutionary experience and the lessons of our revolutionary movement to a number of Western countries, to Western Europe. My report will therefore deal at greater length, if in brief outline, with the first part of my subject, namely, the international situation.

Imperialism's economic relations constitute the core of the entire international situation as it now exists. Throughout the twentieth century, this new, highest and final stage of capitalism has fully taken shape. Of course, you all know that the enormous dimensions that capital has reached are the most characteristic and essential feature of imperialism. The place of free competition has been taken by huge monopolies. An insignificant number of capitalists have, in some cases, been able to concentrate in their hands entire branches of industry; these have passed into the hands of combines, cartels, syndicates and trusts, not infrequently of an international nature. Thus, entire branches of industry, not only in single countries, but all over the world, have been taken over by monopolists in the field of finance, property rights, and partly of production. This has formed the basis for the unprecedented domination exercised by an insignificant number of very big banks, financial tycoons, financial magnates who have, in fact, transformed even the freest republics into financial monarchies. Before the war this was publicly recognised by such far from revolutionary writers as, for example, Lysis in France.

This domination by a handful of capitalists achieved full development when the whole world had been partitioned, not only in the sense that the various sources of raw materials and means of production had been seized by the biggest capitalists, but also in the sense that the preliminary partition of the colonies had been completed. Some forty years ago, the population of the colonies stood at somewhat over 250,000,000, who were subordinated to six capitalist powers. Before the war of 1914, the population of the colonies was estimated at about 600,000,000, and if we add countries like Persia, Turkey, and China, which were already semi-colonies, we shall get, in round figures, a population of a thousand million people oppressed through colonial dependence by the richest, most civilised and freest countries. And you know that, apart from direct political and juridical dependence, colonial dependence presumes a number of relations of financial and economic dependence, a number of wars, which were not regarded as wars because very often they amounted to sheer massacres, when European and American imperialist troops, armed with the most up-to-date weapons of destruction, slaughtered the unarmed and defenceless inhabitants of colonial countries.

The first imperialist war of 1914-18 was the inevitable outcome of this partition of the whole world, of this domination by the capitalist monopolies, of this great power wielded by an insignificant number of very big banks—two, three, four or five in each country. This war was waged for the repartitioning of the whole world. It was waged in order to decide which of the small groups of the biggest states—the British or the German—was to obtain the opportunity and the right to rob, strangle and exploit the whole world. You know that the war settled this question in favour of the British group. And, as a result of this war, all capitalist contradictions have become immeasurably more acute. At a single stroke the war relegated about 250,000,000 of the world's inhabitants to what is equivalent to colonial status, viz., Russia, whose population can be taken at about 130,000,000, and Austria-Hungary, Germany and Bulgaria, with a total population of not less than 120,000,000. That means 250,000,000 people living in countries, of which some, like Germany, are among the most advanced, most enlightened, most cultured, and on a level with modern technical progress. By means of the Treaty of Versailles, the war imposed such terms upon these countries that advanced peoples have been reduced to a state of colonial dependence, poverty, starvation, ruin, and loss of rights: this treaty binds them for many generations, placing them in conditions that no civilised nation has ever lived in. The following is the post-war picture of the world: at least *1,250 million* people are at once brought under the colonial yoke, exploited by a brutal capitalism, which once boasted of its love for peace, and had some right to do so some fifty years ago, when the world was not yet partitioned, the monopolies did not as yet rule, and capitalism could still develop in a relatively peaceful way, without tremendous military conflicts.

Today, after this "peaceful" period, we see a monstrous intensification of oppression, the reversion to a colonial and military oppression that is far worse than before. The Treaty of Versailles has placed Germany and the other defeated countries in a position that makes their economic existence physically impossible, deprives them of all rights, and humiliates them.

How many nations are the beneficiaries? To answer this question we must recall that the population of the United States—the only full beneficiary from the war, a country which, from a heavy debtor, has become a general creditor—is no more than 100,000,000. The population of Japan—which gained a great deal by keeping out of the European-American conflict and by seizing the enormous Asian continent—is 50,000,000. The population of Britain, which next to the above-mentioned countries gained most, is about 50,000,000. If we add the neutral countries with their very small populations, countries which were enriched by the war, we shall get, in round figures, some 250,000,000 people.

Thus you get the broad outlines of the picture of the world as it appeared after the imperialist war. In the oppressed colonies—countries which are being dismembered, such as Persia, Turkey and China, and in countries that were defeated and have been relegated to the position of colonies—there are 1,250 million inhabitants. Not more than 250,000,000 inhabit countries that have retained their old positions, but have become economically dependent upon America, and all of which, during the war, were militarily dependent, once the war involved the whole world and did not permit a single state to remain really neutral. And, finally, we have not more than 250,000,000 inhabitants in countries whose top stratum, the capitalists alone, benefited from the partition of the world. We thus get a total of about 1,750 million comprising the entire population of the world. I would like to remind you of this picture of the world, for all the basic contradictions of capitalism, of imperialism, which are leading up to revolution, all the basic contradictions in the working-class movement that have led up to the furious struggle against the Second International, facts our chairman has referred to, are all connected with this partitioning of the world's population.

Of course, these figures give the economic picture of the world only approximately, in broad outline. And, comrades, it is natural that, with the population of the world divided in this way, exploitation by finance capital, the capitalist monopolies, has increased many times over.

Not only have the colonial and the defeated countries been reduced to a state of dependence; within each victor state the contradictions have grown more acute; all the capitalist contradictions have become aggravated. I shall illustrate this briefly with a few examples.

Let us take the national debts. We know that the debts of the principal European states increased no less than *sevenfold* in the period between 1914 and 1920. I shall quote another economic source, one of particular significance—Keynes, the British diplomat and author of *The Economic Consequences of the Peace*, who, on instructions from his government, took part in the Versailles peace negotiations, observed them on the spot from the purely bourgeois point of view, studied the subject in detail, step by step, and took part in the conferences as an economist. He has arrived at conclusions which are more weighty, more striking and more instructive than any a Communist revolutionary could draw, because they are the conclusions of a well-known bourgeois and implacable enemy of Bolshevism, which he, like the British philistine he is, imagines as something monstrous, ferocious, and bestial. Keynes has reached the conclusion that after the Peace of Versailles, Europe and the whole world are heading for bankruptcy. He has resigned, and thrown his book in the government's face with the words: "What you are doing is madness". I shall quote his figures, which can be summed up as follows.

What are the debtor-creditor relations that have developed between the principal powers? I shall convert pounds sterling into gold rubles, at a rate of ten gold rubles to one pound. Here is what we get: the United States has assets amounting to 19,000 million, its liabilities are nil. Before the war it was in Britain's debt. In his report on April 14, 1920, to the last congress of the Communist Party of Germany, Comrade Levi very correctly pointed out that there are now only two powers in the world that can act independently, viz., Britain and America. America alone is absolutely independent financially. Before the war she was a debtor; she is now a creditor only. All the other powers in the world are debtors. Britain has been reduced to a position in which her assets total 17,000 million, and her liabilities 8,000 million. She is already half-way to becoming a debtor nation. Moreover, her assets include about 6,000 million owed to her by Russia. Included in the debt are military supplies received by Russia during the war. When Krasin, as representative of the Russian Soviet Government, recently had occasion to discuss with Lloyd George the subject of debt agreements, he made it plain to the scientists and politicians, to the British Government's leaders, that they were labouring under a strange delusion if they were counting on getting these debts repaid. The British diplomat Keynes has already laid this delusion bare.

Of course, it is not only or even not at all a question of the Russian revolutionary government having no wish to pay the debts. No government would pay, because these debts are usurious interest on a sum that has been paid twenty times over, and the selfsame bourgeois Keynes, who does not in the least sympathise with the Russian revolutionary movement, says: "It is clear that these debts cannot be taken into account."

In regard to France, Keynes quotes the following figures: her assets amount to 3,500 million, and her liabilities to 10,500 million! And this is a country which the French themselves called the world's money-lender, because her "savings" were enormous; the proceeds of colonial and financial pillage—a gigantic capital—enabled her to grant thousands upon thousands of millions in loans, particularly to Russia. These loans brought in an enormous revenue. Notwithstanding this and notwithstanding victory, France has been reduced to debtor status.

A bourgeois American source, quoted by Comrade Braun, a Communist, in his book *Who Must Pay the War Debts*? (Leipzig, 1920), estimates the ratio of debts to national wealth as follows: in the victor countries, Britain and France, the ratio of debts to aggregate national wealth is over 50 per cent; in Italy the percentage is between 60 and 70, and in Russia 90. As you know, however, these debts do not disturb us, because we followed Keynes's excellent advice just a little before his book appeared—we annulled all our debts. (*Stormy applause.*)

In this, however, Keynes reveals the usual crankiness of the philistine: while advising that all debts should be annulled, he goes on to say that, of course, France only stands to gain by it, that, of course, Britain will not lose very much, as nothing can be got out of Russia in any case; America will lose a fair amount, but Keynes counts on American "generosity"! On this point our views differ from those of Keynes and other petty-bourgeois pacifists. We think that to get the debts annulled they will have to wait for something else to happen, and will have to try working in a direction other than counting on the "generosity" of the capitalists.

These few figures go to show that the imperialist war has created an impossible situation for the victor powers as well. This is further shown by the enormous disparity between wages and price rises. On March 8 of this year, the Supreme Economic Council, an institution charged with protecting the bourgeois system throughout the world from the mounting revolution, adopted a resolution which ended with an appeal for order, industry and thrift, provided, of course, the workers remain the slaves of capital. This Supreme Economic Council, organ of the Entente and of the capitalists of the whole world, presented the following summary.

In the United States of America food prices have risen, on the average, by 120 per cent, whereas wages have increased only by 100 per cent. In Britain, food prices have gone up by 170 per cent, and wages 130 per cent; in France, food prices—300 per cent, and wages 200 per cent; in Japan—food prices 130 per cent, and wages 60 per cent (I have analysed Comrade Braun's figures in his pamphlet and those of the Supreme Economic Council as published in *The Times* of March 10, 1920).

In such circumstances, the workers' mounting resentment, the growth of a revolutionary temper and ideas, and the increase in spontaneous mass strikes are obviously inevitable, since the position of the workers is becoming intolerable. The workers' own experience is convincing them that the capitalists have become prodigiously enriched by the war and are placing the burden of war costs and debts upon the workers' shoulders. We recently learnt by cable that America wants to deport another 500 Communists to Russia so as to get rid of "dangerous agitators".

Even if America deports to our country, not 500 but 500,000 Russian, American, Japanese and French "agitators" that will make no difference, because there will still be the disparity between prices and wages, which they can do nothing about. The reason why they can do nothing about it is because private property is most strictly safeguarded, is "sacred" there. That should not be forgotten, because it is only in Russia that the exploiters' private property has been abolished. The capitalists can do nothing about the gap between prices and wages, and the workers cannot live on their previous wages. The old methods are useless against this calamity. Nothing can be achieved by isolated strikes, the parliamentary struggle, or the vote, because "private property is sacred", and the capitalists have accumulated such debts that the whole world is in bondage to a handful of men. Meanwhile the workers' living conditions are becoming more and more unbearable. There is no other way out but to abolish the exploiters' "private property".

In his pamphlet *Britain and the World Revolution*, valuable extracts from which were published by our *Bulletin of the People's Commissariat of Foreign Affairs* of February 1920, Comrade Lapinsky points out that in Britain coal export prices have doubled as against those anticipated by official industrial circles.

In Lancashire things have gone so far that shares are at a premium of 400 per cent. Bank profits are at least 40-50 per cent. It should, moreover, be noted that, in determining bank profits, all bank officials are able to conceal the lion's share of profits by calling them, not profits but bonuses, commissions, etc. So here, too, indisputable economic facts prove that the wealth of a tiny handful of people has grown prodigiously and that their luxury beggars description, while the poverty of the working class is steadily growing. We must particularly note the further circumstance brought out very clearly by Comrade Levi in the report I have just referred to, namely, the change in the value of money. Money has everywhere depreciated as a result of the debts, the issue of paper currency, etc. The same bourgeois source I have already mentioned, namely, the statement of the Supreme Economic Council of March 8, 1920, has calculated that in Britain the depreciation in the value of currency as against the dollar is approximately one-third, in France and Italy two-thirds, and in Germany as much as 96 per cent.

This fact shows that the "mechanism" of the world capitalist economy is falling apart. The trade relations on which the acquisition of raw materials and the sale of commodities hinge under capitalism cannot go on; they cannot continue to be based on the subordination of a number of countries to a single country—the reason being the change in the value of money. No wealthy country can exist or trade unless it sells its goods and obtains raw materials.

Thus we have a situation in which America, a wealthy country that all countries are subordinate to, cannot buy or sell. And the selfsame Keynes who went through the entire gamut of the Versailles negotiations has been compelled to acknowledge this impossibility despite his unyielding determination to defend capitalism, and all his hatred of Bolshevism. Incidentally, I do not think any communist manifesto, or one that is revolutionary in general, could compare in forcefulness with those pages in Keynes's book which depict Wilson and "Wilsonism" in action. Wilson was the idol of philistines and pacifists like Keynes and a number of heroes of the Second International (and even of the "Two-and-a-Half" International[78]), who exalted the "Fourteen Points" and even wrote "learned" books about the "roots" of Wilson's policy; they hoped that Wilson would save "social peace", reconcile exploiters and exploited, and bring about social reforms. Keynes showed vividly how Wilson was made a fool of, and all these illusions were shattered at the first impact with the practical, mercantile and huckster policy of capital as personified by Clemenceau and Lloyd George. The masses of the workers now see more clearly than ever, from their own experience—and the learned pedants could see it just by reading Keynes's book—that the "roots" of Wilson's policy lay in sanctimonious piffle, petty-bourgeois phrase-mongering, and an utter inability to understand the class struggle.

In consequence of all this, two conditions, two fundamental situations, have inevitably and naturally emerged. On the one hand, the impoverishment of the masses has grown incredibly, primarily among 1,250 million people, i.e., 70 per cent of the world's population. These are the colonial and dependent countries whose inhabitants possess no legal rights, countries "mandated" to the brigands of finance. Besides, the enslavement of the defeated countries has been sanctioned by the Treaty of Versailles and by existing secret treaties regarding Russia, whose validity, it is true, is sometimes about as real as that of the scraps of paper stating that we owe so many thousands of millions.

For the first time in world history, we see robbery, slavery, dependence, poverty and starvation imposed upon 1,250 million people by a legal act.

On the other hand, the workers in each of the creditor countries have found themselves in conditions that are intolerable. The war has led to an unprecedented aggravation of all capitalist contradictions, this being the origin of the intense revolutionary ferment that is ever growing. During the war people were put under military discipline, hurled into the ranks of death, or threatened with immediate wartime punishment. Because of the war conditions people could not see the economic realities. Writers, poets, the clergy, the whole press were engaged in nothing but glorifying the war. Now that the war has ended, the exposures have begun: German imperialism with its Peace of Brest-Litovsk has been laid bare; the Treaty of Versailles, which was to have been a victory for imperialism but proved its defeat, has been exposed. Incidentally, the example of Keynes shows that in Europe and America tens and hundreds of thousands of petty-bourgeois, intellectuals, and simply more or less literate and educated people, have had to follow the road taken by Keynes, who resigned and threw in the face of the government a book exposing it. Keynes has shown what is taking place and will take place in the minds of thousands and hundreds of thousands of people when they realise that all the speeches about a "war for liberty", etc., were sheer deception, and that as a result only a handful of people were enriched, while the others were ruined and reduced to slavery. Is it not a fact that the bourgeois Keynes declares that, to survive and save the British economy, the British must secure the resumption of free commercial intercourse between Germany and Russia? How can this be achieved? By cancelling all debts, as Keynes proposes. This is an idea that has been arrived at not only by Keynes, the learned economist; millions of people are or will be getting the same idea. And millions of people hear bourgeois economists declare that there is no way out except annulling the debts; therefore "damn the Bolsheviks" (who have annulled the debts), and let us appeal to America's "generosity"! I think that, on behalf of the Congress of the Communist International, we should send a message of thanks to these economists, who have been agitating for Bolshevism.

If, on the one hand, the economic position of the masses has become intolerable, and, on the other hand, the disintegration described by Keynes has set in and is growing among the negligible minority of all-powerful victor countries, then we are in the presence of the maturing of the two conditions for the world revolution.

We now have before us a somewhat more complete picture of the whole world. We know what dependence upon a handful of rich men means to 1,250 million people who have been placed in intolerable conditions of existence. On the other hand, when the peoples were presented with the League of Nations Covenant, declaring that the League had put an end to war and would henceforth not permit anyone to break the peace, and when this Covenant, the last hope of working people all over the world, came into force, it proved to be a victory of the first order for us. Before it came into force, people used to say that it was impossible not to impose special conditions on a country like Germany, but when the Covenant was drawn up, everything would come out all right. Yet, when the Covenant was published, the bitterest opponents of Bolshevism were obliged to repudiate it! When the Covenant came into operation, it appeared that a small group of the richest countries, the "Big Four"—in the persons of Clemenceau, Lloyd George, Orlando and Wilson—had been put on the job of creating the new relations! When the machinery of the Covenant was put into operation, this led to a complete breakdown.

We saw this in the case of the wars against Russia. Weak, ruined and crushed, Russia, a most backward country, fought against all the nations, against a league of the rich and powerful states that dominate the world, and emerged victorious. We could not put up a force that was anything like the equal of theirs, and yet we proved the victors. Why was that? Because there was not a jot of unity among them, because each power worked against the other. France wanted Russia to pay her debts and become a formidable force against Germany; Britain wanted to partition Russia, and attempted to seize the Baku oilfields and conclude a treaty with the border states of Russia. Among the official

British documents there is a Paper which scrupulously enumerates all the states (fourteen in all) which some six months ago, in December 1919, pledged themselves to take Moscow and Petrograd. Britain based her policy on these states, to whom she granted loans running into millions. All these calculations have now misfired, and all the loans are unrecoverable.

Such is the situation created by the League of Nations. Every day of this Covenant's existence provides the best propaganda for Bolshevism, since the most powerful adherents of the capitalist "order" are revealing that, on every question, they put spokes in one another's wheels. Furious wrangling over the partitioning of Turkey, Persia, Mesopotamia and China is going on between Japan, Britain, America and France. The bourgeois press in these countries is full of the bitterest attacks and the angriest statements against their "colleagues" for trying to snatch the booty from under their noses. We see complete discord at the top, among this handful, this very small number of extremely rich countries. There are 1,250 million people who find it impossible to live in the conditions of servitude which "advanced" and civilised capitalism wishes to impose on them: after all, these represent 70 per cent of the world's population. This handful of the richest states—Britain, America and Japan (though Japan was able to plunder the Eastern, the Asian countries, she cannot constitute an independent financial and military force without support from another country)—these two or three countries are unable to organise economic relations, and are directing their policies toward disrupting policies of their colleagues and partners in the League of Nations. Hence the world crisis; it is these economic roots of the crisis that provide the chief reason of the brilliant successes the Communist International is achieving.

Comrades, we have now come to the question of the revolutionary crisis as the basis of our revolutionary action. And here we must first of all note two widespread errors. On the one hand, bourgeois economists depict this crisis simply as "unrest", to use the elegant expression of the British. On the other hand, revolutionaries sometimes try to prove that the crisis is absolutely insoluble.

This is a mistake. There is no such thing as an absolutely hopeless situation. The bourgeoisie are behaving like barefaced plunderers who have lost their heads; they are committing folly after folly, thus aggravating the situation and hastening their doom. All that is true. But nobody can "prove" that it is absolutely impossible for them to pacify a minority of the exploited with some petty concessions, and suppress some movement or uprising of some section of the oppressed and exploited. To try to "prove" in advance that there is "absolutely" no way out of the situation would be sheer pedantry, or playing with concepts and catchwords. Practice alone can serve as real "proof" in this and similar questions. All over the world, the bourgeois system is experiencing a tremendous revolutionary crisis. The revolutionary parties must now "prove" in practice that they have sufficient understanding and organisation, contact with the exploited masses, and determination and skill to utilise this crisis for a successful, a victorious revolution.

It is mainly to prepare this "proof" that we have gathered at this Congress of the Communist International.

To illustrate to what extent opportunism still prevails among parties that wish to affiliate to the Third International, and how far the work of some parties is removed from preparing the revolutionary class to utilise the revolutionary crisis, I shall quote the leader of the British Independent Labour Party, Ramsay MacDonald. In his book, *Parliament and Revolution*, which deals with the basic problems that are now engaging our attention, MacDonald describes the state of affairs in what is something like a bourgeois pacifist spirit. He admits that there is a revolutionary crisis and that revolutionary sentiments are growing, that the sympathies of the workers are with the Soviets and the dictatorship of the proletariat (note that this refers to Britain) and that the dictatorship of the proletariat is better than the present dictatorship of the British bourgeoisie.

But MacDonald remains a thorough-paced bourgeois pacifist and compromiser, a petty bourgeois who dreams of a government that stands above classes. Like all bourgeois liars, sophists and pedants, MacDonald recognises the class struggle merely as a "descriptive fact". He ignores the experience of Kerensky, the Mensheviks and the Socialist-Revolutionaries of Russia, the similar experience of Hungary, Germany, etc., in regard to creating a "democratic" government allegedly standing above classes. MacDonald lulls his party and those workers who have the misfortune to regard this bourgeois as a socialist, this philistine as a leader, with the words: "We know that all this [i.e., the revolutionary crisis, the revolutionary ferment] will pass... settle down." The war, he says, inevitably provoked the crisis, but after the war it will all "settle down", even if not at once!

That is what has been written by a man who is leader of a party that wants to affiliate to the Third International. This is a revelation—the more valuable for its rare outspokenness—of what is no less frequently to be seen in the top ranks of the French Socialist Party and the German Independent Social-Democratic Party, namely, not merely an inability, but also an unwillingness to take advantage, in a revolutionary sense, of the revolutionary crisis, or, in other words, both an inability and an unwillingness to really prepare the party and the class in revolutionary fashion for the dictatorship of the proletariat.

That is the main evil in very many parties which are now leaving the Second International. This is precisely why, in the theses I have submitted to the present Congress, I have dwelt most of all on the tasks connected with *preparations* for the dictatorship of the proletariat, and have given as concrete and exact a definition of them as possible.

Here is another example. A new book against Bolshevism was recently published. An unusually large number of books of this kind are now coming out in Europe and America; the more anti-Bolshevik books are brought out, the more strongly and rapidly mass sympathy for Bolshevism grows. I am referring to Otto Bauer's *Bolshevism or Social-Democracy?* This book clearly demonstrates to the Germans the essence of Menshevism, whose shameful role in the Russian revolution is understood well enough by the workers of all countries. Otto Bauer has produced a thoroughgoing Menshevik pamphlet, although he has concealed his own sympathy with Menshevism. In Europe and America, however, more precise information should now be disseminated about what Menshevism actually is, for it is a generic term for all allegedly socialist, Social-Democratic and other trends that are hostile to Bolshevism. It would be dull writing if we Russians were to explain to Europeans what Menshevism is. Otto Bauer has shown that in his book, and we thank in advance the bourgeois and opportunist publishers who will publish it and translate it into various languages. Bauer's book will be a useful if peculiar supplement to the textbooks on communism. Take any paragraph, any argument in Otto Bauer's book and indicate the Menshevism in it, where the roots lie of views that lead up to the actions of the traitors to socialism, of the friends of Kerensky, Scheidemann, etc.—this is a question that could be very usefully and successfully set in "examinations" designed to test whether communism has been properly assimilated. If you cannot answer this question, you are not yet a Communist, and should not join the Communist Party. (*Applause.*)

Otto Bauer has excellently expressed in a single sentence the essence of the views of world opportunism; for this, if we could do as we please in Vienna, we would put up a monument to him in his lifetime. The use of force in the class struggle in modern democracies, Otto Bauer says, would be "violence exercised against the social factors of force".

You may think that this sounds queer and unintelligible. It is an example of what Marxism has been reduced to, of the kind of banality and defence of the exploiters to which the most revolutionary theory *can* be reduced. A German variety of philistinism is required, and you get the "theory" that the "social factors of force" are: number; the degree of organisation; the place held in the process of production and distribution; activity and education. If a rural agricultural labourer or an urban working man practises revolutionary violence against a landowner or a capitalist, that is no dictatorship of the proletariat, no violence against the exploiters and the oppressors of the people. Oh, no! This is "violence against the social factors of force".

Perhaps my example sounds something like a jest. However, such is the nature of present-day opportunism that its struggle against Bolshevism becomes a jest. The task of involving the working class, all its thinking elements, in the struggle between international Menshevism (the MacDonalds, Otto Bauers and Co.) and Bolshevism is highly useful and very urgent .to Europe and America.

Here we must ask: how is the persistence of such trends in Europe to be explained? Why is this opportunism stronger in Western Europe than in our country? It is because the culture of the advanced countries has been, and still is, the result of their being able to live at the expense of a thousand million oppressed people. It is because the capitalists of these countries obtain a great deal more in this way than they could obtain as profits by plundering the workers in their own countries.

Before the war, it was calculated that the three richest countries—Britain, France and Germany—got between eight and ten thousand million francs a year from the export of capital alone, apart from other sources.

It goes without saying that, out of this tidy sum, at least five hundred millions can be spent as a sop to the labour leaders and the labour aristocracy, i.e., on all sorts of bribes. The whole thing boils down to nothing but bribery. It is done in a thousand different ways: by increasing cultural facilities in the largest centres, by creating educational institutions, and by providing co-operative, trade union and parliamentary leaders with thousands of cushy jobs. This is done wherever present-day civilised capitalist relations exist. It is these thousands of millions in superprofits that form the economic basis of opportunism in the working-class movement. In America, Britain and France we see a far greater persistence of the opportunist leaders, of the upper crust of the working class, the labour aristocracy; they offer stronger resistance to the Communist movement. That is why we must be prepared to find it harder for the European and American workers' parties to get rid of this disease than was the case in our country. We know that enormous successes have been achieved in the treatment of this disease since the Third International was formed, but we have not yet finished the job; the purging of the workers' parties, the revolutionary parties of the proletariat all over the world, of bourgeois influences, of the opportunists in their ranks, is very far from complete.

I shall not dwell on the concrete manner in which we must do that; that is dealt with in my published theses. My task consists in indicating the deep economic roots of this phenomenon. The disease is a protracted one; the cure takes longer than the optimists hoped it would. Opportunism is our principal enemy. Opportunism in the upper ranks of the working-class movement is bourgeois socialism, not proletarian socialism. It has been shown in practice that working-class activists who follow the opportunist trend are better defenders of the bourgeoisie than the bourgeois themselves. Without their leadership of the workers, the bourgeoisie could not remain in power. This has been proved, not only by the history of the Kerensky regime in Russia; it has also been proved by the democratic republic in Germany under its Social-Democratic government, as well as by Albert Thomas's attitude towards his bourgeois government. It has been proved by similar experience in Britain and the United States. This is where our principal enemy is, an enemy we must overcome. We must leave this Congress firmly resolved to carry on this struggle to the very end, in all parties. That is our main task.

Compared with this task, the rectification of the errors of the "Left" trend in communism will be an easy one. In a number of countries anti-parliamentarianism is to be seen, which has not been so much introduced by people of petty-bourgeois origin as fostered by certain advanced contingents of the proletariat out of hatred for the old parliamentarianism, out of a legitimate, proper and necessary hatred for the conduct of members of parliament in Britain, France, Italy, in all lands. Directives must be issued by the Communist International and the comrades must be made more familiar with the experience of Russia, with the significance of a genuinely proletarian political party. Our work will consist in accomplishing this task. The fight against these errors in the proletarian movement, against these shortcomings, will be a thousand times easier than fighting against those bourgeois who, in the guise of reformists, belong to the old parties of the Second International and conduct the whole of their work in a bourgeois, not proletarian, spirit.

Comrades, in conclusion I shall deal with one other aspect of the subject. Our comrade, the chairman, has said that our Congress merits the title of a World Congress. I think he is right, particularly because we have here quite a number of representatives of the revolutionary movement in the colonial and backward countries. This is only a small beginning, but the important thing is that a beginning has been made. At this Congress we see taking place a union between revolutionary proletarians of the capitalist, advanced countries, and the revolutionary masses of those countries where there is no or hardly any proletariat, i.e., the oppressed masses of colonial, Eastern countries. It is on ourselves that the consolidation of unity depends, and I am sure we shall achieve it. World imperialism shall fall when the revolutionary onslaught of the exploited and oppressed workers in each country, overcoming resistance from petty-bourgeois elements and the influence of the small upper crust of labour aristocrats, merges with the revolutionary onslaught of hundreds of millions of people who have hitherto stood beyond the pale of history, and have been regarded merely as the object of history.

The imperialist war has helped the revolution: from the colonies, the backward countries, and the isolation they lived in, the bourgeoisie levied soldiers for this imperialist war. The British bourgeoisie impressed on the soldiers from India that it was the duty of the Indian peasants to defend Great Britain against Germany; the French bourgeoisie impressed on soldiers from the French colonies that it was their duty to defend France. They taught them the use of arms, a very useful thing, for which we might express our deep gratitude to the bourgeoisie—express our gratitude on behalf of all the Russian workers and peasants, and particularly on behalf of all the Russian Red Army. The imperialist war has drawn the dependent peoples into world history. And one of the most important tasks now confronting us is to consider how the foundation-stone of the organisation of the Soviet movement can be laid in the *non*-capitalist countries. Soviets are possible there; they will not be workers' Soviets, but peasants' Soviets, or Soviets of working people.

Much work will have to be done; errors will be inevitable; many difficulties will be encountered along this road. It is the fundamental task of the Second Congress to elaborate or indicate the practical principles that will enable the work, till now carried on in an unorganised fashion among hundreds of millions of people, to be carried on in an organised, coherent and systematic fashion.

Now, a year or a little more after the First Congress of the Communist International, we have emerged victors over the Second International; it is not only among the workers of the civilised countries that the ideas of the Soviets have spread; it is not only to them that they have become known and intelligible. The workers of all lands are ridiculing the wiseacres, not a few of whom call themselves socialists and argue in a learned or almost learned manner about the Soviet "system", as the German systematists are fond of calling it, or the Soviet "idea" as the British Guild Socialists[79] call it. Not infrequently, these arguments about the Soviet "system" or "idea" becloud the workers' eyes and their minds. However, the workers are brushing this pedantic rubbish aside and are taking up the weapon provided by the Soviets. A recognition of the role and significance of the Soviets has now also spread to the lands of the East.

The groundwork has been laid for the Soviet movement all over the East, all over Asia, among all the colonial peoples.

The proposition that the exploited must rise up against the exploiters and establish their Soviets is not a very complex one. After our experience, after two and a half years of the existence of the Soviet Republic in Russia, and after the First Congress of the Third International, this idea is becoming accessible to hundreds of millions of people oppressed by the exploiters all over the world. We in Russia are often obliged to compromise, to bide our time, since we are weaker than the international imperialists, yet we know that we are defending the interests of this mass of a thousand and a quarter million people. For the time being, we are hampered by barriers, prejudices and ignorance which are receding into the past with every passing hour; but we are more and more becoming representatives and genuine defenders of this 70 per cent of the world's population, this mass of working and exploited people. It is with pride that we can say: at the First Congress we were in fact merely propagandists; we were only spreading the fundamental ideas among the world's proletariat; we only issued the call for struggle; we were merely asking where the people were who were capable of taking this path. Today the advanced proletariat is everywhere with us. A proletarian army exists everywhere, although sometimes it is poorly organised and needs reorganising. If our comrades in all lands help us now to organise a united army, no shortcomings will prevent us from accomplishing our task. That task is the world proletarian revolution, the creation of a world Soviet republic. (*Prolonged applause.*)

2

SPEECH ON THE ROLE OF THE COMMUNIST PARTY JULY 23

Comrades, I would like to make a few remarks concerning the speeches of Comrades Tanner and McLaine. Tanner says that he stands for the dictatorship of the proletariat, but he does not see the dictatorship of the proletariat quite in the way we do. He says that by the dictatorship of the proletariat we actually mean the dictatorship of the organised and class-conscious minority of the proletariat.

True enough, in the era of capitalism, when the masses of the workers are subjected to constant exploitation and cannot develop their human capacities, the most characteristic feature of working-class political parties is that they can involve only a minority of their class. A political party can comprise only a minority of a class, in the same way as the really class-conscious workers in any capitalist society constitute only a minority of all workers. We are therefore obliged to recognise that it is only this class-conscious minority that can direct and lead the broad masses of the workers. And if Comrade Tanner says that he is opposed to parties, but at the same time is in favour of a minority that represents the best organised and most revolutionary workers showing the way to the entire proletariat, then I say that there is really no difference between us. What is this organised minority? If this minority is really class-conscious, if it is able to lead the masses, if it is able to reply to every question that appears on the order of the day, then it is a party in reality. But if comrades like

Tanner, to whom we pay special heed as representatives of a mass movement—which cannot, without a certain exaggeration, be said of the representatives of the British Socialist Party—if these comrades are in favour of there being a minority that will fight resolutely for the dictatorship of the proletariat and will educate the masses of the workers along these lines, then this minority is in reality nothing but a party. Comrade Tanner says that this minority should organise and lead the entire mass of workers. If Comrade Tanner and the other comrades of the Shop Stewards' group and the Industrial Workers of the World accept this—and we see from the daily talks we have had with them that they do accept it—if they approve the idea that the class-conscious Communist minority of the working class leads the proletariat, then they must also agree that this is exactly the meaning of all our resolutions. In that case the only difference between us lies in their avoidance of the word "party" because there exists among the British comrades a certain mistrust of political parties. They can conceive of political parties only in the image of the parties of Gompers and Henderson,[80] parties of parliamentary smart dealers and traitors to the working class. But if, by parliamentarianism, they mean what exists in Britain and America today, then we too are opposed to such parliamentarianism and to such political parties. What we want is new and different parties. We want parties that will be in constant and real contact with the masses and will be able to lead those masses.

I now come to the third question I want to touch upon in connection with Comrade McLaine's speech. He is in favour of the British Communist Party affiliating to the Labour Party. I have already expressed my opinion on this score in my theses on affiliation to the Third International.[81] In my pamphlet I left the question open.[82] However, after discussing the matter with a number of comrades, I have come to the conclusion that the decision to remain within the Labour Party is the only correct tactic. But here is Comrade Tanner, who declares, "Don't be too dogmatic." I consider his remark quite out of place here. Comrade Ramsay says: "Please let us British Communists decide this question for ourselves." What would the International be like if every little group were to come along and say: "Some of us are in favour of this thing and some are against; leave it to us to decide the matter for ourselves"? What then would be the use of having an International, a congress, and all this discussion? Comrade McLaine spoke only of the role of a political party. But the same applies to the trade unions and to parliamentarianism. It is quite true that a larger section of the finest revolutionaries are against affiliation to the Labour Party because they are opposed to parliamentarianism as a means of struggle. Perhaps it would be best to refer this question to a commission, where it should be discussed and studied, and then decided at this very Congress of the Communist International. We cannot agree that it concerns only the British Communists. We must say, in general, which are the correct tactics.

I will now deal with some of Comrade McLaine's arguments concerning the question of the British Labour Party. We must say frankly that the Party of Communists can join the Labour Party only on condition that it preserves full freedom of criticism and is able to conduct its own policy. This is of supreme importance. When, in this connection Comrade Serrati speaks of class collaboration, I affirm that this will not be class collaboration. When the Italian comrades tolerate, in their party, opportunists like Turati and Co., i.e., bourgeois elements, that is indeed class collaboration. In this instance, however, with regard to the British Labour Party, it is simply a matter of collaboration between the advanced minority of the British workers and their vast majority. Members of the Labour Party are all members of trade unions. It has a very unusual structure, to be found in no other country. It is an organisation that embraces four million workers out of the six or seven million organised in trade unions. They are not asked to state what their political opinions are. Let Comrade Serrati prove to me that anyone there will prevent us from exercising our right of criticism. Only by proving that, will you prove Comrade McLaine wrong. The British Socialist Party can quite freely call Henderson a traitor and yet remain in the Labour Party. Here we have collaboration between the vanguard of the working class and the rearguard, the backward workers. This collaboration is so important to the entire movement that we categorically insist on the British Communists serving as a link between the Party, that is, the minority of the working class, and the rest of the workers. If the minority is unable to lead the masses and establish close links with them, then it is not a party, and is worthless in general, even if it calls itself a party or the National Shop Stewards' Committee—as far as I know, the Shop Stewards' Committees in Britain have a National Committee, a central body, and that is a step towards a party. Consequently, until it is refuted that the British Labour Party consists of proletarians, this is co-operation between the vanguard of the working class and the backward workers; if this co-operation is not carried on systematically, the Communist Party will be worthless and there can be no question of the dictatorship of the proletariat at all. If our Italian comrades cannot produce more convincing arguments, we shall have to definitely settle the question later here, on the basis of what we know—and we shall come to the conclusion that affiliation is the correct tactic.

Comrades Tanner and Ramsay tell us that the majority of British Communists will not accept affiliation. But must we always agree with the majority? Not at all. If they have not yet understood which are the correct tactics, then perhaps it would be better to wait. Even the parallel existence for a time of two parties would be better than refusing to reply to the question as to which tactics are correct. Of course, acting on the experience of all Congress delegates and on the arguments that have been brought forward here, you will not insist on passing a resolution here and now, calling for the immediate formation of a single Communist Party in each country. That is impossible. But we can frankly express our opinion, and give directives. We must study in a special commission the question raised by the British delegation and then we shall say: affiliation to the Labour Party is the correct tactic. If the majority is against it, we must organise a separate minority. That will be of educational value. If the masses of the British workers still believe in the old tactics, we shall verify our conclusions at the next congress. We cannot, however, say that this question concerns Britain alone—that would mean copying the worst habits of the Second International. We must express our opinion frankly. If the British Communists do not reach agreement, and if a mass party is not formed, a split is inevitable one way or another.*

---

* Issue No. 5 of the *Bulletin of the Second Congress of the Communist International* gave the concluding sentences of this speech as follows:

"We must express our opinion frankly, whatever it may be. If the British Communists do not reach agreement on the question of the organisation of the mass movement, and if a split takes place on this issue, then better a split than rejection of the organisation of the mass movement. It is better to rise to definite and sufficiently clear tactics and ideology than to go on remaining in the previous chaos."—*Ed.*

3
REPORT
OF THE COMMISSION ON THE NATIONAL AND THE COLONIAL QUESTIONS
JULY 26[83]

Comrades, I shall confine myself to a brief introduction, after which Comrade Maring, who has been secretary to our commission, will give you a detailed account of the changes we have made in the theses. He will be followed by Comrade Roy, who has formulated the supplementary theses. Our commission have unanimously adopted both the preliminary theses, as amended, and the supplementary theses. We have thus reached complete unanimity on all major issues. I shall now make a few brief remarks.

First, what is the cardinal idea underlying our theses? It is the distinction between oppressed and oppressor nations. Unlike the Second International and bourgeois democracy, we emphasise this distinction. In this age of imperialism, it is particularly important for the proletariat and the Communist International to establish the concrete economic facts and to proceed from concrete realities, not from abstract postulates, in all colonial and national problems.

The characteristic feature of imperialism consists in the whole world, as we now see, being divided into a large number of oppressed nations and an insignificant number of oppressor nations, the latter possessing colossal wealth and powerful armed forces. The vast majority of the world's population, over a thousand million, perhaps even 1,250 million people, if we take the total population of the world as 1,750 million, in other words, about 70 per cent of the world's population, belong to the oppressed nations, which are either in a state of direct colonial dependence or are semi-colonies, as, for example, Persia, Turkey and China, or else, conquered by some big imperialist power, have become greatly dependent on that power by virtue of peace treaties. This idea of distinction, of dividing the nations into oppressor and oppressed, runs through the theses, not only the first theses published earlier over my signature, but also those submitted by Comrade Roy. The latter were framed chiefly from the standpoint of the situation in India and other big Asian countries oppressed by Britain. Herein lies their great importance to us.

The second basic idea in our theses is that, in the present world situation following the imperialist war, reciprocal relations between peoples and the world political system as a whole are determined by the struggle waged by a small group of imperialist nations against the Soviet movement and the Soviet states headed by Soviet Russia. Unless we bear that in mind, we shall not be able to pose a single national or colonial problem correctly, even if it concerns a most outlying part of the world. The Communist parties, in civilised and backward countries alike, can pose and solve political problems correctly only if they make this postulate their starting-point.

Third, I should like especially to emphasise the question of the bourgeois-democratic movement in backward countries. This is a question that has given rise to certain differences. We have discussed whether it would be right or wrong, in principle and in theory, to state that the Communist International and the Communist parties must support the bourgeois-democratic movement in backward countries. As a result of our discussion, we have arrived at the unanimous decision to speak of the national-revolutionary movement rather than of the "bourgeois-democratic" movement. It is beyond doubt that any national movement can only be a bourgeois-democratic movement, since the overwhelming mass of the population in the backward countries consists of peasants who represent bourgeois-capitalist relationships. It would be utopian to believe that proletarian parties in these backward countries, if indeed they can emerge in them, can pursue communist tactics and a communist policy, without establishing definite relations with the peasant movement and without giving it effective support. However, the objections have been raised that, if we speak of the bourgeois-democratic movement, we shall be obliterating all distinctions between the reformist and the revolutionary movements. Yet that distinction has been very clearly revealed of late in the backward and colonial countries, since the imperialist bourgeoisie is doing everything in its power to implant a reformist movement among the oppressed nations too. There has been a certain *rapprochement* between the bourgeoisie of the exploiting countries and that of the colonies, so that very often—perhaps even in most cases—the bourgeoisie of the oppressed countries, while it does support the national movement, is in full accord with the imperialist bourgeoisie, i.e., joins forces with it against all revolutionary movements and revolutionary classes. This was irrefutably proved in the commission, and we decided that the only correct attitude was to take this distinction into account and, in nearly all cases, substitute the term "national-revolutionary" for the term "bourgeois-democratic". The significance of this change is that we, as Communists, should and will support bourgeois-liberation movements in the colonies only when they are genuinely revolutionary, and when their exponents do not hinder our work of educating and organising in a revolutionary spirit the peasantry and the masses of the exploited. If these conditions do not exist, the Communists in these countries must combat the reformist bourgeoisie, to whom the heroes of the Second International also belong. Reformist parties already exist in the colonial countries, and in some cases their spokesmen call themselves Social-Democrats and socialists. The distinction I have referred to has been made in all the theses with the result, I think, that our view is now formulated much more precisely.

Next, I would like to make a remark on the subject of peasants' Soviets. The Russian Communists' practical activities in the former tsarist colonies, in such backward countries as Turkestan, etc., have confronted us with the question of how to apply the communist tactics and policy in pre-capitalist conditions. The preponderance of pre-capitalist relationships is still the main determining feature in these countries, so that there can be no question of a purely proletarian movement in them. There is practically no industrial proletariat in these countries. Nevertheless, we have assumed, we must assume, the role of leader even there. Experience has shown us that tremendous difficulties have to be surmounted in these countries. However, the practical results of our work have also shown that despite these difficulties we are in a position to inspire in the masses an urge for independent political thinking and independent political action, even where a proletariat is practically non-existent. This work has been more difficult for us than it will be for comrades in the West-European countries, because in Russia the proletariat is engrossed in the work of state administration. It will readily be understood that peasants living in conditions of semi-feudal dependence can easily assimilate and give effect to the idea of Soviet organisation. It is also clear that the oppressed masses, those who are exploited, not only by merchant capital but also by the feudalists, and by a state based on feudalism, can apply this weapon, this type of organisation, in their conditions too. The idea of Soviet organisation is a simple one, and is applicable, not only to proletarian, but also to peasant feudal and semi-feudal relations. Our experience in this respect is not as yet very considerable. However, the debate in the commission, in which several representatives from colonial countries participated, demonstrated convincingly that the Communist International's theses should point out that peasants' Soviets, Soviets of the exploited, are a weapon which can be employed, not only in capitalist countries but also in countries with pre-capitalist relations, and that it is the absolute duty of Communist parties and of elements prepared to form Communist parties, everywhere to conduct propaganda in favour of peasants' Soviets or of working people's Soviets, this to include backward and colonial countries. Wherever conditions permit, they should at once make attempts to set up Soviets of the working people.

This opens up a very interesting and very important field for our practical work. So far our joint experience in this respect has not been extensive, but more and more data will gradually accumulate. It is unquestionable that the proletariat of the advanced countries can and should give help to the working masses of the backward countries, and that the backward countries can emerge from their present stage of development when the victorious proletariat of the Soviet Republics extends a helping hand to these masses and is in a position to give them support.

There was quite a lively debate on this question in the commission, not only in connection with the theses I signed, but still more in connection with Comrade Roy's theses, which he will defend here, and certain amendments to which were unanimously adopted.

The question was posed as follows: are we to consider as correct the assertion that the capitalist stage of economic development is inevitable for backward nations now on the road to emancipation and among whom a certain advance towards progress is to be seen since the war? We replied in the negative. If the victorious revolutionary proletariat conducts systematic propaganda among them, and the Soviet governments come to their aid with all the means at their disposal—in that event it will be mistaken to assume that the backward peoples must inevitably go through the capitalist stage of development. Not only should we create independent contingents of fighters and party organisations in the colonies and the backward countries, not only at once launch propaganda for the organisation of peasants' Soviets and strive to adapt them to the pre-capitalist conditions, but the Communist International should advance the proposition, with the appropriate theoretical grounding, that with the aid of the proletariat of the advanced countries, backward countries can go over to the Soviet system and, through certain stages of development, to communism, without having to pass through the capitalist stage.

The necessary means for this cannot be indicated in advance. These will be prompted by practical experience. It has, however, been definitely established that the idea of the Soviets is understood by the mass of the working people in even the most remote nations, that the Soviets should be adapted to the conditions of a pre-capitalist social system, and that the Communist parties should immediately begin work in this direction in all parts of the world.

I would also like to emphasise the importance of revolutionary work by the Communist parties, not only in their own, but also in the colonial countries, and particularly among the troops employed by the exploiting nations to keep the colonial peoples in subjection.

Comrade Quelch of the British Socialist Party spoke of this in our commission. He said that the rank-and-file British worker would consider it treasonable to help the enslaved nations in their uprisings against British rule. True, the jingoist and chauvinist-minded labour aristocrats of Britain and America present a very great danger to socialism, and are a bulwark of the Second International. Here we are confronted with the greatest treachery on the part of leaders and workers belonging to this bourgeois International. The colonial question has been discussed in the Second International as well. The Basle Manifesto[84] is quite clear on this point, too. The parties of the Second International have pledged themselves to revolutionary action, but they have given no sign of genuine revolutionary work or of assistance to the exploited and dependent nations in their revolt against the oppressor nations. This, I think, applies also to most of the parties that have withdrawn from the Second International and wish to join the Third International. We must proclaim this publicly for all to hear, and it is irrefutable. We shall see if any attempt is made to deny it.

All these considerations have formed the basis of our resolutions, which undoubtedly are too lengthy but will nevertheless, I am sure, prove of use and will promote the development and organisation of genuine revolutionary work in connection with the national and the colonial questions. And that is our principal task.

4
SPEECH ON THE TERMS OF ADMISSION INTO THE COMMUNIST INTERNATIONAL JULY 30[85]

Comrades, Serrati has said that we have not yet invented a sincerometer—meaning by this French neologism an instrument for measuring sincerity. No such instrument has been invented yet. We have no need of one. But we do already have an instrument for defining trends. Comrade Serrati's error, which I shall deal with later, consists in his having failed to use this instrument, which has been known for a long time.

I would like to say only a few words about Comrade Crispien. I am very sorry that he is not present. (*Dittmann*: "He is ill.") I am very sorry to hear it. His speech is a most important document, and expresses explicitly the political line of the Right wing of the Independent Social-Democratic Party. I shall speak, not of personal circumstances or individual cases but only of the ideas clearly expressed in Crispien's speech. I think I shall be able to prove that the entire speech was thoroughly in the Kautskian spirit, and that Comrade Crispien shares the Kautskian views on the dictatorship of the proletariat. Replying to a rejoinder, Crispien said: "Dictatorship is nothing new, it was already mentioned in the Erfurt Programme."[86] The Erfurt Programme says nothing about the dictatorship of the proletariat, and history has proved that this was not due to chance. When in 1902-03, we were drawing up our Party's first programme, we always had before us the example of the Erfurt Programme; Plekhanov, that very Plekhanov who rightly said at the time, "Either Bernstein will bury Social-Democracy, or Social-Democracy will bury Bernstein", laid special emphasis on the fact that the Erfurt Programme's failure to mention the dictatorship of the proletariat was erroneous from the standpoint of theory and, in practice was a cowardly concession to the opportunists. The dictatorship of the proletariat has been in our programme since 1903.[87]

When Comrade Crispien now says that the dictatorship of the proletariat is nothing new, and goes on to say: "We have always stood for the conquest of political power", he is evading the gist of the matter. Conquest of political power is recognised, but not dictatorship. All the socialist literature—not only German, but French and British as well—shows that the leaders of the opportunist parties, for instance, MacDonald in Britain, stand for the conquest of political power. They are, in all conscience, sincere socialists, but they are against the dictatorship of the proletariat! Since we have a good revolutionary party worthy of the name of Communist, it should conduct propaganda for the dictatorship of the proletariat, as distinct from the old conception of the Second International. This has been glossed over and obscured by Comrade Crispien, which is the fundamental error common to all of Kautsky's adherents.

"We are leaders elected by the masses," Comrade Crispien continues. This is a formal and erroneous point of view, since a struggle of trends was clearly to be seen at the latest Party congress of the German Independents. There is no need to seek for a sincerometer and to wax humorous on the subject, as Comrade Serrati does, in order to establish the simple fact that a struggle of trends must and does exist: one trend is that of the revolutionary workers who have just joined us and are opposed to the labour aristocracy; the other is that of the labour aristocracy, which in all civilised countries is headed by the old leaders. Does Crispien belong to the trend of the old leaders and the labour aristocracy, or to that of the new revolutionary masses of workers, who are opposed to the labour aristocracy? That is a question Comrade Crispien has failed to clarify.

In what kind of tone does Comrade Crispien speak of the split? He has said that the split was a bitter necessity, and deplored the matter at length. That is quite in the Kautskian spirit. Who did they break away from? Was it not from Scheidemann? Of course, it was. Crispien has said: "We have split away." In the first place, this was done too late. Since we are on the subject, that has to be said. Second, the Independents should not deplore this, but should say: "The international working class is still under the sway of the labour aristocracy and the opportunists." Such is the position both in France and in Great Britain. Comrade Crispien does not regard the split like a Communist, but quite in the spirit of Kautsky, who is supposed to have no influence. Then Crispien went on to speak of high wages. The position in Germany, he said, is that the workers are quite well off compared with the workers in Russia or in general, in the East of Europe. A revolution, as he sees it, can be made only if it does not worsen the workers' conditions "too much". Is it permissible, in a Communist Party, to speak in a tone like this, I ask? This is the language of counter-revolution. The standard of living in Russia is undoubtedly lower than in Germany, and when we established the dictatorship, this led to the workers beginning to go more hungry and to their conditions becoming even worse. The workers' victory cannot be achieved without sacrifices, without a temporary deterioration of their conditions. We must tell the workers the very opposite of what Crispien has said. If, in desiring to prepare the workers for the dictatorship, one tells them that their conditions will not be worsened "too much", one is losing sight of the main thing, namely, that it was by helping their "own" bourgeoisie to conquer and strangle the whole world by imperialist methods, with the aim of thereby ensuring better pay for themselves, that the labour aristocracy developed. If the German workers now want to work for the revolution they must make sacrifices, and not be afraid to do so.

In the general and world-historical sense, it is true that in a backward country like China, the coolie cannot bring about a proletarian revolution; however, to tell the workers in the handful of rich countries where life is easier, thanks to imperialist pillage, that they must be afraid of "too great" impoverishment, is counter-revolutionary. It is the reverse that they should be told. The labour aristocracy that is afraid of sacrifices, afraid of "too great" impoverishment during the revolutionary struggle, cannot belong to the Party. Otherwise the dictatorship is impossible, especially in West-European countries.

What does Crispien say about terror and coercion? He has said that these are two different things. Perhaps such a distinction is possible in a manual of sociology, but it cannot be made in political practice, especially in the conditions of Germany. We are forced to resort to coercion and terror against people who behave like the German officers did when they murdered Liebknecht and Rosa Luxemburg, or against people like Stinnes and Krupp, who buy up the press. Of course, there is no need to proclaim in advance that we shall positively resort to terror but if the German officers and the Kappists remain the same as they now are and if Krupp and Stinnes remain the same as they now are, the employment of terror will be inevitable. Not only Kautsky, but Ledebour and Crispien as well, speak of coercion and terror in a wholly counter-revolutionary spirit. A party that makes shift with such ideas cannot participate in the dictatorship. That is self-evident.

Then there is the agrarian question. Here Crispien has got very worked up and tried to impute a petty-bourgeois spirit to us: to do anything for the small peasant at the expense of the big landowner is alleged to be petty-bourgeois action. He says the landed proprietors should be dispossessed and their land handed over to co-operative associations. This is a pedantic viewpoint. Even in highly developed countries, including Germany, there are a sufficient number of latifundia, landed estates that are cultivated by semi-feudal, not large-scale capitalist, methods. Part of such land may be cut off and turned over to the small peasants, without injury to farming. Large-scale farming can be preserved, and yet the small peasants can be provided with something of considerable importance to them. No thought is given to this, unfortunately, but in practice that has to be done, for otherwise you will fall into error. This has been borne out, for example, in a book by Varga (former People's Commissar for the National Economy in the Hungarian Soviet Republic), who writes that the establishment of the proletarian dictatorship hardly changed anything in the Hungarian countryside, that the day-labourers saw no changes, and the small peasants got nothing. There are large latifundia in Hungary, and a semi-feudal economy is conducted in large areas. Sections of large estates can and must always be found, part of which can be turned over to the small peasants, perhaps not as their property, but on lease, so that even the smallest peasant may get some part of the confiscated estates. Otherwise, the small peasant will see no difference between the old order and the dictatorship of the Soviets. If the proletarian state authority does not act in this way, it will be unable to retain power.

Although Crispien did say: "You cannot deny that we have our revolutionary convictions", I shall reply that I do deny them. I do not say that you would not like to act in revolutionary manner, but I do say that you are unable to reason in a revolutionary fashion. I am willing to wager that if we chose any commission of educated people, and gave them a dozen Kautsky's books and then Crispien's speech, the commission would say: "The whole speech is thoroughly Kautskian, is imbued through and through with Kautsky's views." The entire method of Crispien's argumentation is fundamentally Kautskian, yet Crispien comes along and says, "Kautsky no longer has any influence whatever in our party." No influence, perhaps, on the revolutionary workers who have joined recently. However, it must be accepted as absolutely proved that Kautsky has had and still has an enormous influence on Crispien, on his entire line of thought, all his ideas. This is manifest in his speech. That is why, without inventing any sincerometers, any instruments for measuring sincerity, we can say that Crispien's orientation is not that of the Communist International. In saying this, we are defining the orientation of the entire Communist International.

Comrades Wijnkoop and Münzenberg have expressed dissatisfaction with the fact that we have invited the Independent Socialist Party and are holding talks with its representatives. I think they are wrong. When Kautsky attacks us and brings out books against us, we polemise with him as our class enemy. But when the Independent Social-Democratic Party, which has expanded as a result of an influx of revolutionary workers, comes here for negotiations, we must talk to its representatives, since they are a section of the revolutionary workers. We cannot reach an immediate agreement with the German Independents, or with the French and the British, regarding the International. In every speech he delivers, Comrade Wijnkoop reveals that he shares almost all the errors of Comrade Pannekoek. Wijnkoop has stated that he does not share Pannekoek's views, but his speeches prove the reverse. Herein lies the main error of this "Left" group, but this, in general, is an error of a proletarian movement that is developing. The speeches of Comrades Crispien and Dittmann are imbued with a bourgeois spirit which will not help us prepare for the dictatorship of the proletariat. When Comrades Wijnkoop and Münzenberg go still further on the subject of the Independent Social-Democratic Party, we are not in agreement with them.

Of course, we have no instrument for measuring sincerity, as Serrati has put it, for testing a man's conscience; we quite agree that the matter is not one of forming an opinion of people, but of appraising a situation. I am sorry to say that although Serrati did speak he said nothing new. His was the sort of speech we used to hear in the Second International as well.

Serrati was wrong in saying: "In France the situation is not revolutionary; in Germany it is revolutionary; in Italy it is revolutionary."

Even if the situation is non-revolutionary, the Second International is in error and carries a heavy responsibility if it is really unwilling to organise revolutionary propaganda and agitation, since, as has been proved by the entire history of the Bolshevik Party, revolutionary propaganda can and should be conducted even in a situation that is not revolutionary. The difference between the socialists and the Communists consists in the former refusing to act in the way we act in any situation, i.e., conduct revolutionary work.

Serrati merely repeats what Crispien has said. We do not mean to say that Turati should be expelled on such and such a date. That question has already been touched upon by the Executive Committee, and Serrati has said to us: "Not expulsions, but a Party purge." We must simply tell the Italian comrades that it is the line of *L'Ordine Nuovo* members that corresponds to the line of the Communist International, and not that of the present majority of the Socialist Party's leaders and their parliamentary group. They claim that they want to defend the proletariat against the reactionaries. Chernov, the Mensheviks and many others in Russia are also "defending" the proletariat against the reactionaries, but that is not sufficient reason for accepting them into our midst.

That is why we must say to the Italian comrades and all parties that have a Right wing: this reformist tendency has nothing in common with communism.

We ask our Italian comrades to call a congress and have our theses and resolutions submitted to it. I am sure that the Italian workers will want to remain in the Communist International.

5
SPEECH ON PARLIAMENTARIANISM
AUGUST 2

Comrade Bordiga seems to have wanted to defend the Italian Marxists' point of view here, yet he has failed to reply to any of the arguments advanced by other Marxists in favour of parliamentary action.

Comrade Bordiga has admitted that historical experience is not created artificially. He has just told us that the struggle must be carried into another sphere. Is he not aware that every revolutionary crisis has been attended by a parliamentary crisis? True, he has said that the struggle must be carried into another sphere, into the Soviets. Bordiga, however, has himself admitted that Soviets cannot be created artificially. The example of Russia shows that Soviets can be organised either during a revolution or on the eve of a revolution. Even in the Kerensky period, the Soviets (which were Menshevik Soviets) were organised in such a way that they could not possibly constitute a proletarian government. Parliament is a product of historical development, and we cannot eliminate it until we are strong enough to disperse the bourgeois parliament. It is only as a member of the bourgeois parliament that one can, in the given historical conditions, wage a struggle against bourgeois society and parliamentarianism. The same weapon as the bourgeoisie employs in the struggle must also be used by the proletariat, of course, with entirely different aims. You cannot assert that that is not the case, and if you want to challenge it, you will have thereby to erase the experience of all revolutionary developments in the world.

You have said that the trade unions are also opportunist, that they, too, constitute a danger. On the other hand, however, you have said that an exception must be made in the case of trade unions, because they are workers' organisations. But that is true only up to a certain point. There are very backward elements in the trade unions too: a section of the proletarianised petty bourgeoisie, the backward workers, and the small peasants. All these elements really think that their interests are represented in parliament. This idea must be combated by work within parliament and by citing the facts, so as to show the masses the truth. Theory will have no effect on the backward masses; they need practical experience.

This was to be seen in the case of Russia too. We were obliged to convene the Constituent Assembly even after the victory of the proletariat, so as to prove to the backward proletarians that they had nothing to gain from that Assembly. To bring home the difference between the two, we had to concretely contrapose the Soviets and the Constituent Assembly and to show the Soviets as the only solution.

Comrade Souchy, a revolutionary syndicalist, advocated the same theory, but he had no logic on his side. He said that he was not a Marxist, so everything can be readily understood. But you, Comrade Bordiga, assert that you are a Marxist, so we must expect more logic from you. You must know how parliament can be smashed. If you can do it by an armed uprising in all countries, well and good. You are aware that we in Russia proved our determination to destroy the bourgeois parliament, not only in theory, but in practice as well. You, however, have lost sight of the fact that this is impossible without fairly long preparations, and that in most countries it is as yet impossible to destroy parliament at one stroke. We are obliged to carry on a struggle within parliament for the destruction of parliament. For the conditions determining the political line of all classes in modern society you substitute your revolutionary determination; that is why you forget that to destroy the bourgeois parliament in Russia we were first obliged to convene the Constituent Assembly, even after our victory. You say: "It is a fact that the Russian revolution is a case that is not in accord with conditions in Western Europe", but you have not produced a single weighty argument to prove that to us. We went through a period of bourgeois democracy. We went through it rapidly at a time when we had to agitate for elections to the Constituent Assembly. Later, when the working class was able to seize power, the peasants still believed in the necessity of a bourgeois parliament.

Taking account of these backward elements, we had to proclaim the elections and show the masses, by example and by facts, that the Constituent Assembly, which was elected at a time of dire and universal need, did not express the aspirations and demands of the exploited classes. In this way the conflict between Soviet and bourgeois government became quite clear, not only to us, the vanguard of the working class, but also to the vast majority of the peasantry, to the petty office employees, the petty bourgeoisie, etc. In all capitalist countries there are backward elements in the working class who are convinced that parliament is the true representative of the people and do not see the unscrupulous methods employed there. You say that parliament is an instrument with the aid of which the bourgeoisie deceive the masses. But this argument should be turned against you, and it does turn against your theses. How will you reveal the true character of parliament to the really backward masses, who are deceived by the bourgeoisie? How will you expose the various parliamentary manoeuvres, or the positions of the various parties, if you are not in parliament, if you remain outside parliament? If you are Marxists, you must admit that, in capitalist society, there is a close link between the relations of classes and the relations of parties. How, I repeat, will you show all this if you are not members of parliament, and if you renounce parliamentary action? The history of the Russian revolution has clearly shown that the masses of the working class, the peasantry, and petty office employees could not have been convinced by any arguments, unless their own experience had convinced them.

It has been claimed here that it is a waste of time to participate in the parliamentary struggle. Can one conceive of any other institution in which all classes are as interested as they are in parliament? This cannot be created artificially. If all classes are drawn into the parliamentary struggle, it is because the class interests and conflicts are reflected in parliament. If it were possible everywhere and immediately to bring about, let us say, a decisive general strike so as to overthrow capitalism at a single stroke, the revolution would have already taken place in a number of countries. But we must reckon with the facts, and parliament is a scene of the class struggle. Comrade Bordiga and those who share his views must tell the masses the truth. Germany provides the best example that a Communist group in parliament is possible. That is why you should have frankly said to the masses: "We are too weak to create a party with a strong organisation." That would be the truth that ought to be told. But if you confessed your weakness to the masses, they would become your opponents, not your supporters; they would become supporters of parliamentarianism.

If you say: "Fellow workers, we are so weak that we cannot form a party disciplined enough to compel its members of parliament to submit to it", the workers would abandon you, for they would ask themselves: "How can we set up a dictatorship of the proletariat with such weaklings?"

You are very naïve if you think that the intelligentsia, the middle class, and the petty bourgeoisie will turn Communist the day the proletariat is victorious.

If you do not harbour this illusion, you should begin right away to prepare the proletariat to pursue its own line. You will find no exceptions to this rule in any branch of state affairs. On the day following the revolution, you will everywhere find advocates of opportunism who call themselves Communists, i.e., petty bourgeois who refuse to recognise the discipline of the Communist Party or of the proletarian state. Unless you prepare the workers for the creation of a really disciplined party, which will compel its members to submit to its discipline, you will never prepare for the dictatorship of the proletariat. I think that this accounts for your unwillingness to admit that the repudiation of parliamentary action by a great many of the new Communist parties stems from their weakness. I am convinced that the vast majority of the really revolutionary workers will follow us and speak up against your anti-parliamentary theses.

6

SPEECH ON AFFILIATION TO THE BRITISH LABOUR PARTY[88]
AUGUST 6

Comrades, Comrade Gallacher began his speech by expressing regret at our having been compelled to listen here for the hundredth and the thousandth time to sentences that Comrade McLaine and other British comrades have reiterated a thousand times in speeches, newspapers and magazines. I think there is no need for regret. The old International used the method of referring such questions for decision to the individual parties in the countries concerned. That was a grave error. We may not be fully familiar with the conditions in one country or another, but in this case we are dealing with the principles underlying a Communist Party's tactics. That is very important and, in the name of the Third International, we must herewith clearly state the communist point of view.

First of all, I should like to mention a slight inaccuracy on the part of Comrade McLaine, which cannot be agreed to. He called the Labour Party the political organisation of the trade union movement, and later repeated the statement when he said that the Labour Party is "the political expression of the workers organised in trade unions". I have met the same view several times in the paper of the British Socialist Party. It is erroneous, and is partly the cause of the opposition, fully justified in some measure, coming from the British revolutionary workers. Indeed, the concepts "political department of the trade unions" or "political expression" of the trade union movement, are erroneous. Of course, most of the Labour Party's members are workingmen. However, whether or not a party is really a political party of the workers does not depend solely upon a membership of workers but also upon the men that lead it, and the content of its actions and its political tactics. Only this latter determines whether we really have before us a political party of the proletariat. Regarded from this, the only correct, point of view, the Labour Party is a thoroughly bourgeois party, because, although made up of workers, it is led by reactionaries, and the worst kind of reactionaries at that, who act quite in the spirit of the bourgeoisie. It is an organisation of the bourgeoisie, which exists to systematically dupe the workers with the aid of the British Noskes and Scheidemanns.

We have also heard another point of view, defended by Comrade Sylvia Pankhurst and Comrade Gallacher, who have voiced their opinion in the matter. What was the substance of the speeches delivered by Gallacher and many of his friends? They have told us that they are insufficiently linked with the masses. But take the instance of the British Socialist Party, they went on. It is still less linked with the masses and it is a very weak party. Comrade Gallacher has told us here how he and his comrades have organised, and done so really splendidly, the revolutionary movement in Glasgow, in Scotland, how in their wartime tactics they manoeuvred skilfully, how they gave able support to the petty-bourgeois pacifists Ramsay MacDonald and Snowden when they came to Glasgow, and used this support to organise a mass movement against the war.

It is our aim to integrate this new and excellent revolutionary movement—represented here by Comrade Gallacher and his friends—into a Communist Party with genuinely communist, i.e., Marxist tactics. That is our task today. On the one hand, the British Socialist Party is too weak and incapable of properly carrying on agitation among the masses; on the other hand, we have the younger revolutionary elements so well represented here by Comrade Gallacher, who, although in touch with the masses, are not a political party, and in this sense are even weaker than the British Socialist Party and are totally unable to organise their political work. Under these circumstances, we must express our frank opinion on the correct tactics. When, in speaking of the British Socialist Party, Comrade Gallacher said that it is "hopelessly reformist", he was undoubtedly exaggerating. But the general tenor and content of all the resolutions we have adopted here show with absolute clarity that we demand a change, in this spirit, in the tactics of the British Socialist Party; the only correct tactics of Gallacher's friends will consist in their joining the Communist Party without delay, so as to modify its tactics in the spirit of the resolutions adopted here. If you have so many supporters that you are able to organise mass meetings in Glasgow, it will not be difficult for you to bring more than ten thousand new members into the Party. The latest Conference of the British Socialist Party, held in London three or four days ago, decided to assume the name of the Communist Party and introduced into its programme a clause providing for participation in parliamentary elections and affiliation to the Labour Party. Ten thousand organised members were represented at the Conference. It will therefore not be at all difficult for the Scottish comrades to bring into this "Communist Party of Great Britain" more than ten thousand revolutionary workers who are better versed in the art of working among the masses, and thus to modify the old tactics of the British Socialist Party in the sense of better agitation and more revolutionary action. In the commission, Comrade Sylvia Pankhurst pointed out several times that Britain needed "Lefts". I, of course, replied that this was absolutely true, but that one must not overdo this "Leftism". Furthermore she said that they were better pioneers, but for the moment were rather noisy. I do not take this in a bad sense, but rather in a good one, namely, that they are better able to carry on revolutionary agitation. We do and should value this. We expressed this in all our resolutions, for we always emphasise that we can consider a party to be a workers' party only when it is really linked up with the masses and fights against the old and quite corrupt leaders, against both the Right-wing chauvinists and those who, like the Right Independents in Germany, take up an intermediate position. We have asserted and reiterated this a dozen times and more in all our resolutions, which means that we demand a transformation of the old party, in the sense of bringing it closer to the masses.

Sylvia Pankhurst also asked: "Is it possible for a Communist Party to join another political party which still belongs to the Second International?" She replied that it was not. It should, however, be borne in mind that the British Labour Party is in a very special position: it is a highly original type of party, or rather, it is not at all a party in the ordinary sense of the word. It is made up of members of all trade unions, and has a membership of about four million, and allows sufficient freedom to all affiliated political parties. It thus includes a vast number of British workers who follow the lead of the worst bourgeois elements, the social-traitors, who are even worse than Scheidemann, Noske and similar people. At the same time, however, the Labour Party has let the British Socialist Party into its ranks, permitting it to have its own press organs, in which members of the selfsame Labour Party can freely and openly declare that the party leaders are social-traitors. Comrade McLaine has cited quotations from such statements by the British Socialist Party. I, too, can certify that I have seen in *The Call*, organ of the British Socialist Party, statements that the Labour Party leaders are social-patriots and social-traitors. This shows that a party affiliated to the Labour Party is able, not only to severely criticise but openly and specifically to mention the old leaders by name, and call them social-traitors. This is a very original situation: a party which unites enormous masses of workers, so that it might seem a political party, is nevertheless obliged to grant its members complete latitude. Comrade McLaine has told us here that, at the Labour Party Conference, the British Scheidemanns were obliged to openly raise the question of affiliation to the Third International, and that all party branches and sections were obliged to discuss the matter. In such circumstances, it would be a mistake not to join this party.

In a private talk, Comrade Pankhurst said to me: "If we are real revolutionaries and join the Labour Party, these gentlemen will expel us." But that would not be bad at all. Our resolution says that we favour affiliation insofar as the Labour Party permits sufficient freedom of criticism. On that point we are absolutely consistent. Comrade McLaine has emphasised that the conditions now prevailing in Britain are such that, should it so desire, a political party may remain a revolutionary workers' party even if it is connected with a special kind of labour organisation of four million members, which is half trade union and half political and is headed by bourgeois leaders. In such circumstances it would be highly erroneous for the best revolutionary elements not to do everything possible to remain in such a party. Let the Thomases and other social-traitors, whom you have called by that name, expel you. That will have an excellent effect upon the mass of the British workers.

The comrades have emphasised that the labour aristocracy is stronger in Britain than in any other country. That is true. After all, the labour aristocracy has existed in Britain, not for decades but for centuries. The British bourgeoisie, which has had far more experience—democratic experience—than that of any other country, has been able to buy workers over and to create among them a sizable stratum, greater than in any other country, but one that is not so great compared with the masses of the workers. This stratum is thoroughly imbued with bourgeois prejudices and pursues a definitely bourgeois reformist policy. In Ireland, for instance, there are two hundred thousand British soldiers who are applying ferocious terror methods to suppress the Irish. The British Socialists are not conducting any revolutionary propaganda among these soldiers, though our resolutions clearly state that we can accept into the Communist International only those British parties that conduct genuinely revolutionary propaganda among the British workers and soldiers. I emphasise that we have heard no objections to this either here or in the commissions.

Comrades Gallacher and Sylvia Pankhurst cannot deny that. They cannot refute the fact that, in the ranks of the Labour Party, the British Socialist Party enjoys sufficient freedom to write that certain leaders of the Labour Party are traitors; that these old leaders represent the interests of the bourgeoisie; that they are agents of the bourgeoisie in the working-class movement. They cannot deny all this because it is the absolute truth. When Communists enjoy such freedom, it is their duty to join the Labour Party if they take due account of the experience of revolutionaries in all countries, not only of the Russian revolution (for here we are not at a Russian congress but at one that is international). Comrade

Gallacher has said ironically that in the present instance we are under the influence of the British Socialist Party. That is not true; it is the experience of all revolutions in all countries that has convinced us. We think that we must say that to the masses. The British Communist Party must retain the freedom necessary to expose and criticise the betrayers of the working class, who are much more powerful in Britain than in any other country. That is readily understandable. Comrade Gallacher is wrong in asserting that by advocating affiliation to the Labour Party we shall repel the best elements among the British workers. We must test this by experience. We are convinced that all the resolutions and decisions that will be adopted by our Congress will be published in all British revolutionary socialist newspapers and that all the branches and sections will be able to discuss them. The entire content of our resolutions shows with crystal clarity that we are representatives of working-class revolutionary tactics in all countries and that our aim is to fight against the old reformism and opportunism. The events reveal that our tactics are indeed defeating the old reformism. In that case the finest revolutionary elements in the working class, who are dissatisfied with the slow progress being made—and progress in Britain will perhaps be slower than in other countries—will all come over to us. Progress is slow because the British bourgeoisie are in a position to create better conditions for the labour aristocracy and thereby to retard the revolutionary movement in Britain. That is why the British comrades should strive, not only to revolutionise the masses—they are doing that splendidly (as Comrade Gallacher has shown), but must at the same time strive to create a real working-class political party. Comrade Gallacher and Comrade Sylvia Pankhurst, who have both spoken here, do not as yet belong to a revolutionary Communist Party. That excellent proletarian organisation, the Shop Stewards' movement, has not yet joined a political party. If you organise politically you will find that our tactics are based on a correct understanding of political developments in the past decades, and that a real revolutionary party can be created only when it absorbs the best elements of the revolutionary class and uses every opportunity to fight the reactionary leaders, wherever they show themselves.

If the British Communist Party starts by acting in a revolutionary manner in the Labour Party, and if the Hendersons are obliged to expel this Party, that will be a great victory for the communist and revolutionary working-class movement in Britain.

TELEGRAM TO J. V. STALIN

To Stalin

We have just decided, in the Political Bureau, that the Army Groups shall be separated, so that you will deal exclusively with Wrangel. Following the uprisings, especially in the Kuban and then in Siberia, the Wrangel danger is becoming enormous, and the opinion is mounting in the Central Committee that peace with bourgeois Poland should be concluded immediately. Please study the Wrangel situation very carefully and let us know your conclusions. I have arranged with the Commander-in-Chief that you are to get more ammunition, reinforcements and aircraft. Together with his friends, Dzerzhinsky has set up a Polish revolutionary committee and has issued a manifesto.

Lenin

Written on August 2, 1920

First published in 1945
in *Lenin Miscellany XXXV*

Published according to
the manuscript

TELEGRAM TO J. V. STALIN

To Stalin

A plenary session of the Central Committee has been called for 1800 hours tomorrow. Try to send us, before that hour, your conclusions on the nature of the difficulties encountered by Budyonny and those on the Wrangel front, as well as the military prospects on both fronts. Political decisions of the utmost importance may depend on your conclusions.

Lenin

Written on August 4, 1920
First published in 1942

Published according to the manuscript

TELEGRAM TO J. V. STALIN

To Stalin

We have just received a dispatch from the head of the Soviet delegation in London. Great Britain has flinched from a general strike, and Lloyd George has declared that he advises Poland to accept our armistice terms, including disarmament, the handing over of weapons to the workers, land distribution, etc. Our victory is a great one, and will be complete if we smash Wrangel. Here we are taking all measures. You, for your part, should make every effort to take the whole of the Crimea without fail, during the present offensive. Everything now depends on that. The Poles are temporising, and have not arrived in time. This is of tremendous advantage to us.

Lenin

Written on August 11, 1920
First published in 1942

Published according to the manuscript

LETTER TO THE AUSTRIAN COMMUNISTS[89]

The Austrian Communist Party has decided to boycott the elections to the bourgeois-democratic parliament. The Second Congress of the Communist International which ended recently recognised as the correct tactics Communist *participation* in elections to and the activities in bourgeois parliaments.

Judging by reports of the Austrian Communist Party's delegates, I have no doubt that it will set a decision by the Communist International above that of one of the parties. Neither can it be doubted that the Austrian Social-Democrats, those traitors to socialism who have gone over to the bourgeoisie, will gloat over the Communist International decision, which is at variance with the Austrian Communist Party's boycott decision. However, politically-conscious workers will, of course, pay no heed to the malicious glee of people like the Austrian Social-Democrats, those confederates of the Scheidemanns and Noskes, Thomases and Gomperses. The Renners' servility to the bourgeoisie has revealed itself sufficiently, and in all countries the workers' indignation at the heroes of the yellow Second International is ever mounting and spreading.

The Austrian Social-Democrats are behaving in the bourgeois parliament, as in all spheres of their "work", including their own press, in the manner of petty-bourgeois democrats who are capable only of spineless vacillation, while in fact they are totally dependent on the capitalist class. We Communists enter bourgeois parliaments in order to unmask from their rostrums the deception practised by these thoroughly corrupt capitalist institutions, which dupe the workers and all working people.

One of the Austrian Communists' arguments against participation in the bourgeois parliaments deserves somewhat more careful consideration. Here it is:

> "Parliament is of importance to Communists only as a platform for agitation. We in Austria have the Council of Workers' Deputies as a platform for agitation. We therefore refuse to take part in elections to the bourgeois parliament. In Germany there is no Council of Workers' Deputies which can be taken in earnest. That is why the German Communists pursue different tactics."

I consider this argument erroneous. As long as we are unable to disband the bourgeois parliament, we must work against it both from without and within. As long as a more or less appreciable number of working people (not only proletarians, but also semi-proletarians and small peasants) still have confidence in the bourgeois-democratic instruments employed by the bourgeoisie for duping the workers, we must expose that deception *from the very platform* which the backward sections of the workers, particularly of the non-proletarian working people, consider most important, and authoritative.

As long as we Communists are unable to take over state power and hold elections, with working people alone voting for *their* Soviets against the bourgeoisie; as long as the bourgeoisie exercise state power and call upon the different classes of the population to take part in the elections, we are in duty bound to take part in the elections with the purpose of conducting agitation among all working people, not only among proletarians. As long as the bourgeois parliament remains a means of duping the workers, and phrases about "democracy" are used to cover up financial swindling and every kind of bribery (the particularly "subtle" brand of bribery the bourgeoisie practise with regard to writers, M.P.s, lawyers, and others is nowhere to be seen on so wide a scale as in the bourgeois parliament), we Communists are in duty bound to be in this very institution (which is supposed to *express the people's will* but actually covers up the *deception of the people by the wealthy*) to untiringly expose this deception, and expose each and every case of the Renners and Co.'s desertion to the capitalists, against the workers. It is in parliament that the relations between bourgeois parties and groups manifest themselves most frequently and reflect the relations between all the classes of bourgeois society. That is why it is in the bourgeois parliament, from within it, that we Communists must tell the people the *truth* about the relation between classes and parties, and the attitude of the landowners to the farm labourers, of the rich peasants to the poor peasants, of big capital to employees and petty proprietors, etc.

The proletariat *must* know all this, so as to learn to see through all the vile and refined machinations of the capitalists, and to learn to influence the petty-bourgeois masses, the non-proletarian masses of the working people. Without this "schooling" the proletariat cannot cope successfully with the tasks of the *dictatorship of the proletariat*, for even then the bourgeoisie, operating from its new position (that of a deposed class), will carry on, in different forms and in different fields, its policy of duping the peasants, of bribing and intimidating employees, of covering up its self-seeking and unsavoury aspirations with phrases about "democracy".

No, the Austrian Communists will not be frightened by the malicious glee of the Renners and similar lackeys of the bourgeoisie. The Austrian Communists will not be afraid to declare their open and forthright recognition of international proletarian discipline. We are proud that we settle the great problems of the workers' struggle for their emancipation by submitting to the international discipline of the revolutionary proletariat, with due account of the experience of the workers in different countries, reckoning with their knowledge and their will, and thus giving effect in deed (and not in word, as the Renners, Fritz Adlers and Otto Bauers do) to the unity of the workers' class struggle for communism throughout the world.

N. Lenin

August 15, 1920

Published in German
in *Die Rote Fahne* (Vienna)
No. 396, August 31, 1920

First published in Russian
in 1925

Published according to
the manuscript

THE SECOND CONGRESS OF THE COMMUNIST INTERNATIONAL

The Second Congress of the Communist International ended on August 7. A little over a year has elapsed since its foundation, during which brief period immense and decisive successes have been achieved.

Held a year ago, the First Congress only unfurled the banner of communism, around which the forces of the revolutionary proletariat were to rally. War was declared on the yellow Second International, which unites the social-traitors, who have sided with the bourgeoisie against the proletariat and are in alliance with the capitalists against the workers' revolution.

The huge measure of success achieved in a year can be seen, among other things, in the fact that the growing sympathy with communism among the masses of workers has compelled the withdrawal from the Second International of some of its leading European and American parties, namely, the French Socialist Party, the German and the British "Independent" parties, and the American Socialist Party.

In every country of the world the finest representatives of the revolutionary workers have already ranged themselves on the side of communism, Soviet rule and the dictatorship of the proletariat. In all the advanced countries of Europe and America, there already exist Communist parties or numerous Communist groups. At the Congress which ended on August 7, it was not only the heralds of the proletarian revolution who joined forces, but delegates from strong and powerful organisations linked with the proletarian masses. A world army of the revolutionary proletariat—that is what now stands for communism, and, at the Congress just ended, received organisational form and a clear, precise and detailed programme of action.

The Congress refused to admit immediately into the Communist International such parties that still retain in their ranks influential representatives of "Menshevism", social-treachery and opportunism, similar to the above-mentioned parties which have withdrawn from the yellow Second International.

In a number of precisely worded resolutions, the Congress blocked every avenue of access for opportunism, and demanded a total break with it. The incontestable facts reported to the Congress showed that the working-class masses are with us, and that the opportunists shall now be utterly routed.

The Congress rectified the errors committed in certain countries by Communists who were bent on turning to the "Left" and denied the need to work in bourgeois parliaments, reactionary trade unions, and wherever there are millions of workers who are still being duped by the capitalists and by their lackeys from among the workers, i.e., by members of the yellow Second International.

The Congress created a degree of unity and discipline among the world's Communist parties such as has never before existed and will make it possible for the vanguard of the workers' revolution to march forward with giant strides to its great goal, the overthrow of the yoke of capital.

Thanks to the international conference of working women which was organised simultaneously, the Congress will strengthen ties with the communist women's movement.

Communist parties and groups in the East, in the colonial and backward countries, which are so brutally robbed, oppressed and enslaved by the "civilised" league of predatory nations, were likewise represented at the Congress. The revolutionary movement in the advanced countries would in fact be nothing but a sheer fraud if, in their struggle against capital, the workers of Europe and America were not closely and completely united with the hundreds upon hundreds of millions of "colonial" slaves, who are oppressed by that capital.

Great are the military victories of the workers' and peasants' Soviet Republic over the landowners and the capitalists, over the Yudeniches, the Kolchaks, and the Denikins, the Polish Whites and their accomplices—France, Britain, America and Japan.

But greater still is our victory over the minds and hearts of the masses of the workers, of all those who toil and are oppressed by capital—the victory of the communist ideas and communist organisations all over the world.

The revolution of the proletariat, the overthrow of the yoke of capitalism, is on the march and shall come about in every country in the world.

Kommunistka No. 3-4, August-September 1920

Published according to the journal text

Signed: *N. Lenin*

REPLY TO MR. SEGRUE, *DAILY NEWS* CORRESPONDENT

With reference to your telegraphic inquiry of September 3, 1920,[90] I would like to inform you that the attacks on Bolshevism on the part of the German Independents' Right wing, by people like Dittmann, for instance, do not surprise me. In my speech at the Comintern Congress in Moscow, I showed that Crispien's ideas are quite Kautskian. Kautskians like Crispien and Dittmann are, of course, dissatisfied with Bolshevism. It would be deplorable if such people were satisfied with us. It is quite natural that, in the decisive struggle between the proletariat and the bourgeoisie, petty-bourgeois democrats like Dittmann, who is very similar to our Mensheviks, are often to be found on the side of the bourgeoisie. Dittmann is indignant at the shootings, but it is natural that, in such cases, Mensheviks are shot at by revolutionary workers, which cannot be altogether to Dittmann's liking. The Third, Communist International would not be worth much if it admitted into its ranks Dittmanns of the German, French or any other variety.

If, however, you consider that the reports by the French, the German and the British workers' delegations have done more harm to Bolshevism than the entire anti-Bolshevik propaganda has done, I willingly accept the conclusion that logically follows.

Let the two of us reach an understanding—you on behalf of the anti-Bolshevik bourgeoisie of all countries, and I on behalf of the Russian Soviet Republic. Accordingly, let delegations consisting of workers and small peasants (i.e., of working people, those whose labour creates profit on capital) be sent to Russia from all countries, each delegation to stay here for about two months. If these delegations' reports are useful to the cause of anti-Bolshevik propaganda, the entire cost of their visit shall be borne by the international bourgeoisie. However, as the bourgeoisie is very weak and poor in all countries in the world, while we in Russia are rich and strong, I agree to secure the consent of the Soviet Government to defray three-quarters of the expenses, a mere quarter to be borne by the millionaires of all lands.

I hope that you, who in your telegram call yourself an honest journalist, will not refuse always and everywhere to publicise this understanding between the Soviet Republic and the international bourgeoisie—of course, in the interests of anti-Bolshevik propaganda.

Lenin

September 8, 1920

Pravda No. 202 and
Izvestia No. 202,
September 12, 1920

Published according to
the manuscript

SPEECH
DELIVERED AT THE NINTH ALL-RUSSIA CONFERENCE OF THE RUSSIAN COMMUNIST PARTY (BOLSHEVIKS)[91]
SEPTEMBER 22, 1920

NEWSPAPER REPORT

The war against Poland, or, to be more precise, the July-August campaign, has radically changed the international political situation.

The Poles' attack against us was preceded by an episode typical of the international relations existing at the time. When, in January, we offered Poland peace terms that were most favourable to her and most unfavourable to us, the diplomatists of all lands interpreted the fact in their own way: since the Bolsheviks were making such tremendous concessions, that should be taken to mean that they were very weak. This was merely more confirmation of bourgeois diplomacy's inability to understand the methods employed by our new diplomacy, that of direct and frank declarations. That was why our proposals evoked merely an outburst of savage chauvinism in Poland, France and other countries, and prompted Poland to attack us. At first the Poles captured Kiev, but our forces' counter-attack then brought them right up to Warsaw. Then came a turn in the events, and we fell back for over a hundred versts.

The undoubtedly difficult situation that resulted has not been a total loss to us. We have completely upset the diplomatists' expectations to make use of our weakness and have proved that Poland cannot defeat us, whereas we have never been and are not far from victory over Poland. At present we still hold a hundred versts of captured territory.

Finally, our advance on Warsaw has had such a powerful effect on Western Europe and on the entire world situation that it has profoundly changed the alignment of the struggling internal and external political forces.

Our army's close approach to Warsaw has incontestably shown that the centre of world imperialism's entire system, which rests on the Treaty of Versailles, lies somewhere very close to the Polish capital. Poland, the last anti-Bolshevik stronghold fully controlled by the Entente, is such an important element in that system that when the Red Army threatened that stronghold the entire structure was shaken. The Soviet Republic has become a major factor in world politics.

The new situation which has arisen has, in the first place, revealed the tremendously significant fact that the bourgeoisie of the Entente-oppressed countries is in the main for us, and these countries contain seventy per cent of the world's population. We have already seen that the small states, which have had such a bad time under Entente tutelage (Estonia, Georgia, etc.), and have been hanging their Bolsheviks, have made peace with us, against the will of the Entente. This has been manifesting itself with special force throughout the world. All Germany began to seethe when our forces approached Warsaw. In that country a situation arose very much like that which could be seen in Russia in 1905, when the Black Hundreds aroused and involved in political life large and most backward sections of the peasantry, which were opposed to the Bolsheviks one day, and on the next were demanding all the land from the landed proprietors. In Germany too we have seen a similar unnatural bloc between the Black Hundreds and the Bolsheviks. There has appeared a strange type of Black-Hundred revolutionary, like the backward rustic youth from East Prussia who, as I read in a German non-Bolshevik newspaper the other day, says that the Kaiser will have to return because there is no order, but one has to follow the Bolsheviks.

Our presence at the walls of Warsaw has had, as another consequence, a powerful effect on the revolutionary movement in Europe, particularly in Britain. Though we have not been able to affect the industrial proletariat of Poland beyond the Vistula and in Warsaw (this being one of the main reasons for our defeat), we have succeeded in influencing the British proletariat and in raising the movement there to an unprecedented level, to an absolutely new stage in the revolution. When the British Government presented an ultimatum to us, it transpired that it would first have to consult the British workers. The latter, nine-tenths of whose leaders are out-and-out Mensheviks, replied to the ultimatum by forming a Council of Action.[92]

Alarmed by these developments, the British press raised a hullabaloo about what it called this "duality of government". It had every reason to say so. Britain found herself at the same stage of political relationships as Russia after February 1917, when the Soviets were obliged to scrutinise every step taken by the bourgeois government. This Council of Action unites all workers, irrespective of party, just like our All-Russia Central Executive Committee of the period when Gotz, Dan and others were running things, a kind of association which runs parallel with the government, and in which the Mensheviks are forced to act in a semi-Bolshevik way. Just as our Mensheviks finally got confounded and helped win over the masses to our side, the Mensheviks in the Council of Action have been forced by the inexorable course of events to clear the way to the Bolshevist revolution for the worker masses of Britain. According to testimony by competent persons, the British Mensheviks already consider themselves a government, and are prepared to replace the bourgeois government in the near future. This will be the next step in the general process of the British proletarian revolution.

These tremendous changes in the British working-class movement are exerting a powerful influence on the world working-class movement, and first and foremost on the working-class movement in France.

Such are the results of our recent Polish campaign in its effect on world politics and the relations emerging in Western Europe.

We are now faced with the question of war or peace with Poland. We want to avoid a winter campaign that will be hard on us, and are again offering Poland a peace that is to her advantage and our disadvantage. However, the bourgeois diplomatists, following their old habit, may possibly interpret our frank statement as a sign of weakness. They have probably decided on a winter campaign. At this stage we have to ascertain the conditions in which we shall probably have to enter a new period of the war.

In Western Europe our defeat has brought about certain changes and rallied against us heterogeneous elements that are hostile to us. However, we have on more than one occasion seen even more powerful groups and currents hostile to us, which nevertheless could not achieve anything.

We have against us a bloc consisting of Poland, France and Wrangel. France pins her hopes on the latter. However, this bloc suffers from the same old malady—the antagonism among its elements, and the fear felt by the Polish petty bourgeoisie with regard to Black-Hundred Russia and to Wrangel, its typical representative. Petty-bourgeois and patriotic Poland, the Polish Socialist Party, the Ludowa Party, i.e., the well-to-do peasants—all of these want peace. Here is what spokesmen of these parties said to us in Minsk, "We know that it was not the Entente that saved Warsaw and Poland; it was unable to save us. It was the upsurge of patriotism that saved us." Such lessons are not to be forgotten. The Poles realise very clearly that this war will ruin them financially. War has to be paid for, and France upholds the "sanctity of private property". The representatives of the petty-bourgeois parties are aware that Poland was on the eve of a crisis even before the war, and that a war will mean further ruination; that is why they prefer peace. We want to make use of this by offering peace to Poland.

Another factor of the utmost importance has appeared—the change in the social composition of the Polish army. We defeated Kolchak and Denikin only after the social composition of their armies had changed, when their basic cadres were watered down in the mass of mobilised peasants. The same kind of process is under way in the Polish army, the government has been obliged to call up workers and peasants of the older age groups, who have gone through the even harsher imperialist war. This army is now made up, not of youngsters, who can easily be "brain-washed", but of older men, who will not let themselves be talked over.

Poland has passed the point which at first assured her total victory, and then total defeat.

If we have to wage a winter campaign, we shall win despite exhaustion and fatigue. There can be no doubt on that score. Our economic situation also vouches for that outcome. It has improved considerably. Compared with last year, we have acquired a firm economic basis. In 1917-18 we gathered in 30 million poods of grain, in 1918-19—110 million poods, and in 1919-20—260 million; next year we expect to collect 400 million poods. These are far higher figures than those of the time when we struggled desperately to make both ends meet. No longer shall we look with such horror upon the multi-coloured banknotes that run into the thousands of millions, and today clearly show us that they are the wreckage, the tatters, of the old bourgeois vestments.

We now have over a hundred million poods of oil. The Donets Basin now provides us with between twenty and thirty million poods of coal a month. The firewood situation has greatly improved. As recently as last year we had only firewood—no oil or coal.

All this gives us the right to say that, if we close our ranks and bend every effort, we shall win the victory.

Pravda No. 216,
September 29, 1920

Published according to
the *Pravda* text

LETTER TO THE GERMAN AND THE FRENCH WORKERS

REGARDING THE DISCUSSION ON THE SECOND CONGRESS OF THE COMMUNIST INTERNATIONAL[98]

Comrades, the bourgeois press of Germany and France is devoting much attention to the discussion within the German Independent Social-Democratic Party and the Socialist Party of France on affiliation to the Communist International. It is vigorously supporting the views of the Right-wing opportunist sections in the two parties.

That can be readily understood, for these Right-wing elements are in essence petty-bourgeois democrats, who, like Dittmann and Crispien, cannot think in terms of revolution, and are incapable of helping the working class prepare for and carry out the revolution. A break with these Right-wing and opportunist elements is necessary; it is the only way to rally all the genuinely revolutionary and genuinely proletarian masses.

All the clamour about Moscow's "dictates", etc., is simply a red herring. As a matter of fact, only five of the twenty members of the Communist International's Executive Committee belong to the Russian Communist Party. All this talk about "dictates", etc., is either self-deception or deception of the workers. It serves to cover up the bankruptcy of certain opportunist leaders, just as similar talk in the *K.A.P.D.* (Communist *Workers'* Party of Germany) has served to cover up the bankruptcy of several of its leaders, who have abandoned the path of proletarian revolutionism. The outcry that the "Moscow dictators", making use of the terms of admission to the Communist International, are persecuting certain individuals is likewise self-deception or deception of others. Article 20 of the terms of admission says clearly in black and white that "*exceptions*" (*Ausnahmen*) *to the strict rules* in regard of Right-wing leaders and members of central bodies *can be made with the consent of the Executive Committee of the Third International.*

Since exceptions are expressly declared to be permissible, there can be no talk of an absolute bar against specific individuals. Consequently, there is full recognition of the need to take into account, not the past but the present, the change in the views and conduct of individuals, of individual leaders. Since exceptions are declared to be permissible with the consent of the Executive Committee of the Third International—in which Russians constitute only one-fourth of the membership—it follows that the clamour about "dictates", etc., is stuff and nonsense, sheer falsehood.

All this clamour is simply a red herring. In fact, a struggle is going on between the revolutionary *proletarian* elements and the opportunist *petty-bourgeois* elements. Today as in the past, the latter include the Hilferdings, the Dittmanns, the Crispiens, numerous members of the parliamentary groups in Germany and France, etc. A struggle between these two *political trends* is in progress in every country without exception. This struggle has a long history. It grew extremely acute everywhere during the imperialist war, and has become aggravated since then. Opportunism is represented by elements of the "labour aristocracy", the old bureaucracy in the trade unions, co-operative societies, etc., by the intellectualist petty-bourgeois strata, etc. Without the elimination of this *trend*—which, by its vacillation and its "Menshevism" (the Dittmanns and Crispiens fully resemble our Mensheviks) in fact exerts the bourgeoisie's influence on the proletariat *from within* the working-class movement, *from within* the socialist parties—without the elimination of this trend, a break with it, and the expulsion of all its prominent representatives, it will be impossible to rally the revolutionary proletariat.

By their constant veering towards reformism and Menshevism, and their inability to think and act in terms of revolution, the Dittmanns, the Crispiens, etc., without realising the fact, are actually carrying bourgeois influence into the proletariat from within the proletarian party—they *subordinate* the proletariat to *bourgeois reformism*. Only a break with such and similar people can lead to *international unity* of the revolutionary proletariat, *against* the bourgeoisie, and for the overthrow of the bourgeoisie.

The events in Italy should open eyes most stubbornly closed to the harmfulness of "unity" and "peace" with the Crispiens and the Dittmanns. The Italian Crispiens and Dittmanns (Turati, Prampolini and D'Aragona) began at once to *hinder* the revolution in Italy as soon as things *reached the stage of a real revolution*. Throughout Europe and the world things are moving in that direction more or less rapidly, and more or less arduously and painfully.

It is high time to discard, once and for all, these most harmful illusions about the possibility of "unity" or "peace" with the Dittmanns and the Crispiens, with the Right wing of the German Independent Social-Democratic Party, the British Independent Labour Party, the French Socialist Party, etc. It is high time for all revolutionary workers to purge their parties of these trends, and form genuinely united Communist parties of the proletariat.

N. Lenin

September 24, 1920

Pravda No. 213,
September 25, 1920

Published according to
the manuscript

THE TASKS OF THE YOUTH LEAGUES*

SPEECH DELIVERED AT THE THIRD ALL-RUSSIA CONGRESS OF THE RUSSIAN YOUNG COMMUNIST LEAGUE OCTOBER 2, 1920[94]

(*The Congress greets Lenin with a tremendous ovation.*) Comrades, today I would like to talk on the fundamental tasks of the Young Communist League and, in this connection, on what the youth organisations in a socialist republic should be like in general.

It is all the more necessary to dwell on this question because in a certain sense it may be said that it is the youth that will be faced with the actual task of creating a communist society. For it is clear that the generation of working people brought up in capitalist society can, at best, accomplish the task of destroying the foundations of the old, the capitalist way of life, which was built on exploitation. At best it will be able to accomplish the tasks of creating a social system that will help the proletariat and the working classes retain power and lay a firm foundation, which can be built on only by a generation that is starting to work under the new conditions, in a situation in which relations based on the exploitation of man by man no longer exist.

And so, in dealing from this angle with the tasks confronting the youth, I must say that the tasks of the youth in general, and of the Young Communist Leagues and all other organisations in particular, might be summed up in a single word: learn.

Of course, this is only a "single word". It does not reply to the principal and most essential questions: what to learn,

---

* Revised translation by Julius Katzer.

and how to learn? And the whole point here is that, with the transformation of the old, capitalist society, the upbringing, training and education of the new generations that will create the communist society cannot be conducted on the old lines. The teaching, training and education of the youth must proceed from the material that has been left to us by the old society. We can build communism only on the basis of the totality of knowledge, organisations and institutions, only by using the stock of human forces and means that have been left to us by the old society. Only by radically remoulding the teaching, organisation and training of the youth shall we be able to ensure that the efforts of the younger generation will result in the creation of a society that will be unlike the old society, i.e., in the creation of a communist society. That is why we must deal in detail with the question of what we should teach the youth and how the youth should learn if it really wants to justify the name of communist youth, and how it should be trained so as to be able to complete and consummate what we have started.

I must say that the first and most natural reply would seem to be that the Youth League, and the youth in general, who want to advance to communism, should learn communism.

But this reply—"learn communism"—is too general. What do we need in order to learn communism? What must be singled out from the sum of general knowledge so as to acquire a knowledge of communism? Here a number of dangers arise, which very often manifest themselves whenever the task of learning communism is presented incorrectly, or when it is interpreted in too one-sided a manner.

Naturally, the first thought that enters one's mind is that learning communism means assimilating the sum of knowledge that is contained in communist manuals, pamphlets and books. But such a definition of the study of communism would be too crude and inadequate. If the study of communism consisted solely in assimilating what is contained in communist books and pamphlets, we might all too easily obtain communist text-jugglers or braggarts, and this would very often do us harm, because such people, after learning by rote what is set forth in communist books and pamphlets, would prove incapable of combining the various branches of knowledge, and would be unable to act in the way communism really demands.

One of the greatest evils and misfortunes left to us by the old, capitalist society is the complete rift between books and practical life; we have had books explaining everything in the best possible manner, yet in most cases these books contained the most pernicious and hypocritical lies, a false description of capitalist society.

That is why it would be most mistaken merely to assimilate book knowledge about communism. No longer do our speeches and articles merely reiterate what used to be said about communism, because our speeches and articles are connected with our daily work in all fields. Without work and without struggle, book knowledge of communism obtained from communist pamphlets and works is absolutely worthless, for it would continue the old separation of theory and practice, the old rift which was the most pernicious feature of the old, bourgeois society.

It would be still more dangerous to set about assimilating only communist slogans. Had we not realised this danger in time, and had we not directed all our efforts to averting this danger, the half million or million young men and women who would have called themselves Communists after studying communism in this way would only greatly prejudice the cause of communism.

The question arises: how is all this to be blended for the study of communism? What must we take from the old schools, from the old kind of science? It was the declared aim of the old type of school to produce men with an all-round education, to teach the sciences in general. We know that this was utterly false, since the whole of society was based and maintained on the division of people into classes, into exploiters and oppressed. Since they were thoroughly imbued with the class spirit, the old schools naturally gave knowledge only to the children of the bourgeoisie. Every word was falsified in the interests of the bourgeoisie. In these schools the younger generation of workers and peasants were not so much educated as drilled in the interests of that bourgeoisie. They were trained in such a way as to be useful servants of the bourgeoisie, able to create profits for it without disturbing its peace and leisure. That is why, while rejecting the old type of schools, we have made it our task to take from it only what we require for genuine communist education.

This brings me to the reproaches and accusations which we constantly hear levelled at the old schools, and which often lead to wholly wrong conclusions. It is said that the old school was a school of purely book knowledge, of ceaseless drilling and grinding. That is true, but we must distinguish between what was bad in the old schools and what is useful to us, and we must be able to select from it what is necessary for communism.

The old schools provided purely book knowledge; they compelled their pupils to assimilate a mass of useless, superfluous and barren knowledge, which cluttered up the brain and turned the younger generation into bureaucrats regimented according to a single pattern. But it would mean falling into a grave error for you to try to draw the conclusion that one can become a Communist without assimilating the wealth of knowledge amassed by mankind. It would be mistaken to think it sufficient to learn communist slogans and the conclusions of communist science, without acquiring that sum of knowledge of which communism itself is a result. Marxism is an example which shows how communism arose out of the sum of human knowledge.

You have read and heard that communist theory—the science of communism created in the main by Marx, this doctrine of Marxism—has ceased to be the work of a single socialist of the nineteenth century, even though he was a genius, and that it has become the doctrine of millions and tens of millions of proletarians all over the world, who are applying it in their struggle against capitalism. If you were to ask why the teachings of Marx have been able to win the hearts and minds of millions and tens of millions of the most revolutionary class, you would receive only one answer: it was because Marx based his work on the firm foundation of the human knowledge acquired under capitalism. After making a study of the laws governing the development of human society, Marx realised the inevitability of capitalism developing towards communism. What is most important is that he proved this on the sole basis of a most precise, detailed and profound study of this capitalist society, by fully assimilating all that earlier science had produced. He critically reshaped everything that had been created by human society, without ignoring a single detail. He reconsidered, subjected to criticism, and verified on the working-class movement everything that human thinking had created, and therefrom formulated conclusions which people hemmed in by bourgeois limitations or bound by bourgeois prejudices could not draw.

We must bear this in mind when, for example, we talk about proletarian culture.[95] We shall be unable to solve this problem unless we clearly realise that only a precise knowledge and transformation of the culture created by the entire development of mankind will enable us to create a proletarian culture. The latter is not clutched out of thin air; it is not an invention of those who call themselves experts in proletarian culture. That is all nonsense. Proletarian culture must be the logical development of the store of knowledge mankind has accumulated under the yoke of capitalist, landowner and bureaucratic society. All these roads have been leading, and will continue to lead up to proletarian culture, in the same way as political economy, as reshaped by Marx, has shown us what human society must arrive at, shown us the passage to the class struggle, to the beginning of the proletarian revolution.

When we so often hear representatives of the youth, as well as certain advocates of a new system of education, attacking the old schools, claiming that they used the system of cramming, we say to them that we must take what was good in the old schools. We must not borrow the system of encumbering young people's minds with an immense amount of knowledge, nine-tenths of which was useless and one-tenth distorted. This, however, does not mean that we can restrict ourselves to communist conclusions and learn only communist slogans. You will not create communism that way. You can become a Communist only when you enrich your mind with a knowledge of all the treasures created by mankind.

We have no need of cramming, but we do need to develop and perfect the mind of every student with a knowledge of fundamental facts. Communism will become an empty word, a mere signboard, and a Communist a mere boaster, if all the knowledge he has acquired is not digested in his mind. You should not merely assimilate this knowledge, but assimilate it critically, so as not to cram your mind with useless lumber, but enrich it with all those facts that are indispensable to the well-educated man of today. If a Communist took it into his head to boast about his communism because of the cut-and-dried conclusions he had acquired, without putting in a great deal of serious and hard work and without understanding facts he should examine critically, he would be a deplorable Communist indeed. Such superficiality would be decidedly fatal. If I know that I know little, I shall strive to learn more; but if a man says that he is a Communist and that he need not know anything thoroughly, he will never become anything like a Communist.

The old schools produced servants needed by the capitalists; the old schools turned men of science into men who had to write and say whatever pleased the capitalists. We must therefore abolish them. But does the fact that we must abolish them, destroy them, mean that we should not take from them everything mankind has accumulated that is essential to man? Does it mean that we do not have to distinguish between what was necessary to capitalism and what is necessary to communism?

We are replacing the old drill-sergeant methods practised in bourgeois society, against the will of the majority, with the class-conscious discipline of the workers and peasants, who combine hatred of the old society with a determination, ability and readiness to unite and organise their forces for this struggle so as to forge the wills of millions and hundreds of millions of people—disunited, and scattered over the territory of a huge country—into a single will, without which defeat is inevitable. Without this solidarity, without this conscious discipline of the workers and peasants, our cause is hopeless. Without this, we shall be unable to vanquish the capitalists and landowners of the whole world. We shall not even consolidate the foundation, let alone build a new, communist society on that foundation. Likewise, while condemning the old schools, while harbouring an absolutely justified and necessary hatred for the old schools, and appreciating the readiness to destroy them, we must realise that we must replace the old system of instruction, the old cramming and the old drill, with an ability to acquire the sum total of human knowledge, and to acquire it in such a way that communism shall not be something to be learned by rote, but something that you yourselves have thought over, something that will embody conclusions inevitable from the standpoint of present-day education.

That is the way the main tasks should be presented when we speak of the aim: learn communism.

I shall take a practical example to make this clear to you, and to demonstrate the approach to the problem of how you must learn. You all know that, following the military problems, those of defending the republic, we are now confronted with economic tasks. Communist society, as we know, cannot be built unless we restore industry and agriculture, and that, not in the old way. They must be re-established on a modern basis, in accordance with the last word in science. You know that electricity is that basis, and that only after electrification of the entire country, of all branches of industry and agriculture, only when you have achieved that aim, will you be able to build for yourselves the communist society which the older generation will not be able to build. Confronting you is the task of economically reviving the whole country, of reorganising and restoring both agriculture and industry on modern technical lines, based on modern science and technology, on electricity. You realise perfectly well that illiterate people cannot tackle electrification, and that elementary literacy is not enough either. It is insufficient to understand what electricity is; what is needed is the knowledge of how to apply it technically in industry and agriculture, and in the individual branches of industry and agriculture. This has to be learnt for oneself, and it must be taught to the entire rising generation of working people. That is the task confronting every class-conscious Communist, every young person who regards himself a Communist and who clearly understands that, by joining the Young Communist League, he has pledged himself to help the Party build communism and to help the whole younger generation create a communist society. He must realise that he can create it only

10-988

on the basis of modern education, and if he does not acquire this education communism will remain merely a pious wish.

It was the task of the older generation to overthrow the bourgeoisie. The main task then was to criticise the bourgeoisie, arouse hatred of the bourgeoisie among the masses, and foster class-consciousness and the ability to unite their forces. The new generation is confronted with a far more complex task. Your duty does not lie only in assembling your forces so as to uphold the workers' and peasants' government against an invasion instigated by the capitalists. Of course, you must do that; that is something you clearly realise, and is distinctly seen by the Communist. However, that is not enough. You have to build up a communist society. In many respects half of the work has been done. The old order has been destroyed, just as it deserved, it has been turned into a heap of ruins, just as it deserved. The ground has been cleared, and on this ground the younger communist generation must build a communist society. You are faced with the task of construction, and you can accomplish that task only by assimilating all modern knowledge, only if you are able to transform communism from cut-and-dried and memorised formulas, counsels, recipes, prescriptions and programmes into that living reality which gives unity to your immediate work, and only if you are able to make communism a guide in all your practical work.

That is the task you should pursue in educating, training and rousing the entire younger generation. You must be foremost among the millions of builders of a communist society in whose ranks every young man and young woman should be. You will not build a communist society unless you enlist the mass of young workers and peasants in the work of building communism.

This naturally brings me to the question of how we should teach communism and what the specific features of our methods should be.

I first of all shall deal here with the question of communist ethics.

You must train yourselves to be Communists. It is the task of the Youth League to organise its practical activities in such a way that, by learning, organising, uniting and fighting, its members shall train both themselves and all those who look to it for leadership; it should train Communists. The entire purpose of training, educating and teaching the youth of today should be to imbue them with communist ethics.

But is there such a thing as communist ethics? Is there such a thing as communist morality? Of course, there is. It is often suggested that we have no ethics of our own; very often the bourgeoisie accuse us Communists of rejecting all morality. This is a method of confusing the issue, of throwing dust in the eyes of the workers and peasants.

In what sense do we reject ethics, reject morality?

In the sense given to it by the bourgeoisie, who based ethics on God's commandments. On this point we, of course, say that we do not believe in God, and that we know perfectly well that the clergy, the landowners and the bourgeoisie invoked the name of God so as to further their own interests as exploiters. Or, instead of basing ethics on the commandments of morality, on the commandments of God, they based it on idealist or semi-idealist phrases, which always amounted to something very similar to God's commandments.

We reject any morality based on extra-human and extra-class concepts. We say that this is deception, dupery, stultification of the workers and peasants in the interests of the landowners and capitalists.

We say that our morality is entirely subordinated to the interests of the proletariat's class struggle. Our morality stems from the interests of the class struggle of the proletariat.

The old society was based on the oppression of all the workers and peasants by the landowners and capitalists. We had to destroy all that, and overthrow them but to do that we had to create unity. That is something that God cannot create.

This unity could be provided only by the factories, only by a proletariat trained and roused from its long slumber. Only when that class was formed did a mass movement arise which has led to what we have now—the victory of the proletarian revolution in one of the weakest of countries, which for three years has been repelling the onslaught of the bourgeoisie of the whole world. We can see how the proletarian revolution is developing all over the world. On the basis of experience, we now say that only the proletariat could have created the solid force which the disunited and scattered peasantry are following and which has withstood all onslaughts by the exploiters. Only this class can help the working masses unite, rally their ranks and conclusively defend, conclusively consolidate and conclusively build up a communist society.

That is why we say that to us there is no such thing as a morality that stands outside human society; that is a fraud. To us morality is subordinated to the interests of the proletariat's class struggle.

What does that class struggle consist in? It consists in overthrowing the tsar, overthrowing the capitalists, and abolishing the capitalist class.

What are classes in general? Classes are that which permits one section of society to appropriate the labour of another section. If one section of society appropriates all the land, we have a landowner class and a peasant class. If one section of society owns the factories, shares and capital, while another section works in these factories, we have a capitalist class and a proletarian class.

It was not difficult to drive out the tsar—that required only a few days. It was not very difficult to drive out the landowners—that was done in a few months. Nor was it very difficult to drive out the capitalists. But it is incomparably more difficult to abolish classes; we still have the division into workers and peasants. If the peasant is installed on his plot of land and appropriates his surplus grain, that is, grain that he does not need for himself or for his cattle, while the rest of the people have to go without bread, then the peasant becomes an exploiter. The more grain he clings to, the more profitable he finds it; as for the rest, let them starve: "The more they starve, the dearer I can sell this grain." All should work according to a single common plan, on common land, in common factories and in accordance with a common system. Is that easy to attain? You see that it is not as easy as driving out the tsar, the landowners and the capitalists. What is required is that the proletariat re-educate a section of the peasantry; it must win over the working peasants in order to crush the resistance of those peasants who are rich and are profiting from the poverty and want of the rest. Hence the task of the proletarian struggle is not quite completed after we have overthrown the tsar and driven out the landowners and capitalists; to accomplish that is the task of the system we call the dictatorship of the proletariat.

The class struggle is continuing; it has merely changed its forms. It is the class struggle of the proletariat to prevent the return of the old exploiters, to unite in a single union the scattered masses of unenlightened peasants. The class struggle is continuing and it is our task to subordinate all interests to that struggle. Our communist morality is also subordinated to that task. We say: morality is what serves to destroy the old exploiting society and to unite all the working people around the proletariat, which is building up a new, a communist society.

Communist morality is that which serves this struggle and unites the working people against all exploitation, against all petty private property; for petty property puts into the hands of one person that which has been created by the labour of the whole of society. In our country the land is common property.

But suppose I take a piece of this common property and grow on it twice as much grain as I need, and profiteer on the surplus? Suppose I argue that the more starving people there are, the more they will pay? Would I then be behaving like a Communist? No, I would be behaving like an exploiter, like a proprietor. That must be combated. If that is allowed to go on, things will revert to the rule of the capitalists, to the rule of the bourgeoisie, as has more than once happened in previous revolutions. To prevent the restoration of the rule of the capitalists and the bourgeoisie, we must not allow profiteering; we must not allow individuals to enrich themselves at the expense of the rest; the working people must unite with the proletariat and form a communist society. This is the principal feature of the fundamental task of the League and the organisation of the communist youth.

The old society was based on the principle: rob or be robbed; work for others or make others work for you; be a slave-owner or a slave. Naturally, people brought up in such a society assimilate with their mother's milk, one might say, the psychology, the habit, the concept which says: you are either a slave-owner or a slave, or else, a small owner, a petty employee, a petty official, or an intellectual—in short, a man who is concerned only with himself, and does not care a rap for anybody else.

If I work this plot of land, I do not care a rap for anybody else; if others starve, all the better, I shall get the more for my grain. If I have a job as a doctor, engineer, teacher, or clerk, I do not care a rap for anybody else. If I toady to and please the powers that be, I may be able to keep my job, and even get on in life and become a bourgeois. A Communist cannot harbour such a psychology and such sentiments. When the workers and peasants proved that they were able, by their own efforts, to defend themselves and create a new society—that was the beginning of the new and communist education, education in the struggle against the exploiters, education in alliance with the proletariat against the self-seekers and petty proprietors, against the psychology and habits which say: I seek my own profit and don't care a rap for anything else.

That is the reply to the question of how the young and rising generation should learn communism.

It can learn communism only by linking up every step in its studies, training and education with the continuous struggle the proletarians and the working people are waging against the old society of exploiters. When people tell us about morality, we say: to a Communist all morality lies in this united discipline and conscious mass struggle against the exploiters. We do not believe in an eternal morality, and we expose the falseness of all the fables about morality. Morality serves the purpose of helping human society rise to a higher level and rid itself of the exploitation of labour.

To achieve this we need that generation of young people who began to reach political maturity in the midst of a disciplined and desperate struggle against the bourgeoisie. In this struggle that generation is training genuine Communists; it must subordinate to this struggle, and link up with it, each step in its studies, education and training. The education of the communist youth must consist, not in giving them suave talks and moral precepts. This is not what education consists in. When people have seen the way in which their fathers and mothers lived under the yoke of the landowners and capitalists; when they have themselves experienced the sufferings of those who began the struggle against the exploiters; when they have seen the sacrifices made to keep what has been won, and seen what deadly enemies the landowners and capitalists are—they are taught by these conditions to become Communists. Communist morality is based on the struggle for the consolidation and completion of communism. That is also the basis of communist training, education, and teaching. That is the reply to the question of how communism should be learnt.

We could not believe in teaching, training and education if they were restricted only to the schoolroom and divorced from the ferment of life. As long as the workers and peasants are oppressed by the landowners and capitalists, and as long as the schools are controlled by the landowners and capitalists, the young generation will remain blind and ignorant. Our schools must provide the youth with the fundamentals of knowledge, the ability to evolve communist views independently; they must make educated people of the youth. While they are attending school, they must learn to become participants in the struggle for emancipation from the exploiters. The Young Communist League will justify its name as the League of the young communist generation only when every step in its teaching, training and education is linked up with participation in the common struggle of all working people against the exploiters. You are well aware that, as long as Russia remains the only workers' republic and the old, bourgeois system exists in the rest of the world, we shall be weaker than they are, and be constantly threatened with a new attack; and that only if we learn to be solidly united shall we win in the further struggle and—having gained strength—become really invincible. Thus, to be a Communist means that you must organise and unite the entire young generation and set an example of training and discipline in this struggle. Then you will be able to start building the edifice of communist society and bring it to completion.

To make this clearer to you, I shall quote an example. We call ourselves Communists. What is a Communist? Communist is a Latin word. *Communis* is the Latin for "common". Communist society is a society in which all things—the land, the factories—are owned in common and the people work in common. That is communism.

Is it possible to work in common if each one works separately on his own plot of land? Work in common cannot be brought about all at once. That is impossible. It does not drop from the skies. It comes through toil and suffering; it is created in the course of struggle. The old books are of no use here; no one will believe them. One's own experience of life is needed. When Kolchak and Denikin were advancing from Siberia and the South, the peasants were on their side. They did not like Bolshevism because the Bolsheviks took their grain at a fixed price. But when the peasants in Siberia and the Ukraine experienced the rule of Kolchak and Denikin, they realised that they had only one alternative: either to go to the capitalists, who would at once hand them over into slavery under the landowners; or to follow the workers, who, it is true, did not promise a land flowing with milk and honey, and demanded iron discipline and firmness in an arduous struggle, but would lead them out of enslavement by the capitalists and landowners. When even the ignorant peasants saw and realised this from their own experience, they became conscious adherents of communism, who had gone through a severe school. It is such experience that must form the basis of all the activities of the Young Communist League.

I have replied to the questions of what we must learn, what we must take from the old schools and from the old science. I shall now try to answer the question of how this must be learnt. The answer is: only by inseparably linking each step in the activities of the schools, each step in training, education and teaching, with the struggle of all the working people against the exploiters.

I shall quote a few examples from the experience of the work of some of the youth organisations so as to illustrate how this training in communism should proceed. Everybody is talking about abolishing illiteracy. You know that a communist society cannot be built in an illiterate country. It is not enough for the Soviet government to issue an order, or for the Party to issue a particular slogan, or to assign a certain number of the best workers to this task. The young generation itself must take up this work. Communism means that the youth, the young men and women who belong to the Youth League, should say: this is our job; we shall unite and go into the rural districts to abolish illiteracy, so that there shall be no illiterates among our young people. We are trying to get the rising generation to devote their activities to this work. You know that we cannot rapidly transform an ignorant and illiterate Russia into a literate country. But if the Youth League sets to work on the job, and if all young people work for the benefit of all, the League, with a membership of 400,000 young men and women, will be entitled to call itself aYoung Communist League. It is also a task of the League, not only to acquire knowledge itself, but to help those young people who are unable to extricate themselves by their own efforts from the toils of illiteracy. Being a member of the Youth League means devoting one's labour and efforts to the common cause. That is what a communist education means. Only in the course of such work do young men and women become real Communists. Only if they achieve practical results in this work will they become Communists.

Take, for example, work in the suburban vegetable gardens. Is that not a real job of work? It is one of the tasks of the Young Communist League. People are starving; there is hunger in the factories. To save ourselves from starvation, vegetable gardens must be developed. But farming is being carried on in the old way. Therefore, more class-conscious elements should engage in this work, and then you will find that the number of vegetable gardens will increase, their acreage will grow, and the results will improve. The Young Communist League must take an active part in this work. Every League and League branch should regard this as its duty.

The Young Communist League must be a shock force, helping in every job and displaying initiative and enterprise. The League should be an organisation enabling any worker to see that it consists of people whose teachings he perhaps does not understand, and whose teachings he may not immediately believe, but from whose practical work and activity he can see that they are really people who are showing him the right road.

If the Young Communist League fails to organise its work in this way in all fields, it will mean that it is reverting to the old bourgeois path. We must combine our education with the struggle of the working people against the exploiters, so as to help the former accomplish the tasks set by the teachings of communism.

The members of the League should use every spare hour to improve the vegetable gardens, or to organise the education of young people at some factory, and so on. We want to transform Russia from a poverty-stricken and wretched country into one that is wealthy. The Young Communist League must combine its education, learning and training with the labour of the workers and peasants, so as not to confine itself to schools or to reading communist books and pamphlets. Only by working side by side with the workers and peasants can one become a genuine Communist. It has to be generally realised that all members of the Youth League are literate people and at the same time are keen at their jobs. When everyone sees that we have ousted the old drill-ground methods from the old schools and have replaced them with conscious discipline, that all young men and women take part in subbotniks, and utilise every suburban farm to help the population—people will cease to regard labour in the old way.

It is the task of the Young Communist League to organise assistance everywhere, in village or city block, in such matters as—and I shall take a small example—public hygiene or the distribution of food. How was this done in the old, capitalist society? Everybody worked only for himself and nobody cared a straw for the aged and the sick, or whether housework was the concern only of the women, who, in consequence, were in a condition of oppression and servitude. Whose business is it to combat this? It is the business of the Youth Leagues, which must say: we shall change all this; we shall organise detachments of young people who will help to assure public hygiene or distribute food, who will conduct systematic house-to-house inspections, and work in an organised way for the benefit of the whole of society, distributing their forces properly and demonstrating that labour must be organised.

The generation of people who are now at the age of fifty

cannot expect to see a communist society. This generation will be gone before then. But the generation of those who are now fifteen will see a communist society, and will itself build this society. This generation should know that the entire purpose of their lives is to build a communist society. In the old society, each family worked separately and labour was not organised by anybody except the landowners and capitalists, who oppressed the masses of the people. We must organise all labour, no matter how toilsome or messy it may be, in such a way that every worker and peasant will be able to say: I am part of the great army of free labour, and shall be able to build up my life without the landowners and capitalists, able to help establish a communist system. The Young Communist League should teach all young people to engage in conscious and disciplined labour from an early age. In this way we can be confident that the problems now confronting us will be solved. We must assume that no less than ten years will be required for the electrification of the country, so that our impoverished land may profit from the latest achievements of technology. And so, the generation of those who are now fifteen years old, and will be living in a communist society in ten or twenty years' time, should tackle all its educational tasks in such a way that every day, in every village and city, the young people shall engage in the practical solution of some problem of labour in common, even though the smallest or the simplest. The success of communist construction will be assured when this is done in every village, as communist emulation develops, and the youth prove that they can unite their labour. Only by regarding our every step from the standpoint of the success of that construction, and only by asking ourselves whether we have done all we can to be united and politically-conscious working people will the Young Communist League succeed in uniting its half a million members into a single army of labour and win universal respect. (*Stormy applause.*)

Pravda Nos. 221, 222 and 223, October 5, 6 and 7, 1920

Published according to the *Pravda* text, verified against the text of the pamphlet: N. Lenin (V. I. Ulyanov), *The Tasks of the Youth Leagues*, 1920

SPEECH DELIVERED AT A CONGRESS OF LEATHER INDUSTRY WORKERS OCTOBER 2, 1920[96]

Comrades, in compliance with the wish expressed by the organisers of your congress, the political position of our Republic will be the subject of my report. In this respect, the chief thing I have to deal with is undoubtedly our war with Poland, the general course of events in connection with that war, and what has consequently become revealed concerning the domestic and international position of our Republic.

You are all, of course, aware of the present gravity of our position at the front. In this connection it will be natural if we examine the circumstances that have made the situation so acute, and given it such a turn for the worse. You will of course remember that last April, when the Polish offensive had not yet begun, the line of the front lay farther eastward, in many places very much farther eastward, than at present. As it then was, the line left Minsk in Polish hands; the Poles held the whole of Byelorussia. Not only the Council of People's Commissars, but the Presidium of the All-Russia Central Executive Committee itself—the highest body in the R.S.F.S.R.—solemnly declared in a manifesto to the Polish people that they proposed peace, and rejected the idea of deciding by force of arms the fate of Byelorussia, which had never been Polish, and whose peasant population had long suffered from the Polish landowners and did not regard themselves as Poles. Nevertheless, we declared in the most official and solemn terms that we proposed peace on the basis of the then existing line, since we set so high a value on the workers who would have to lay down their lives in case of war that we considered no concessions too important by comparison. We presumed that the question of Byelorussia would be settled, not by force of arms, but exclusively through the development of the struggle within Poland. We knew that we could contribute to the liberation of Poland's toilers, not so much by the force of arms as through the force of our propaganda.

That was last April, and you know that at first Poland replied to our solemn offer of peace with a manoeuvre, a proposal that peace should be signed in Borisov, a highly important strategic point, which was in their hands. Negotiations in Polish-held Borisov would have meant that the Poles could advance in the south-west while we would have been prevented from advancing in the north-west. Any other city but Borisov, was our reply. The Poles refused. I remind you of this so that, whenever you have to speak on this subject, you may the more emphatically stress the point that at first we proposed peace on the basis of a line lying farther eastward than the present one, that is, we agreed to a peace which was most disadvantageous to ourselves.

The Poles have forced the war on us; we know that it was not even the Polish landowners or the Polish capitalists that have played the chief role here, since Poland's position was as desperate then as it is now. She has embarked on this venture in sheer desperation. But, of course, international capital, and in the first place French capital, was the chief force driving the Poles into a war with us. It has so far been established that hundreds of French officers have been serving with the Polish army, and that all the weapons, all the financial and military support Poland has received, have come from France.

Such are the conditions in which this war began. It marked a new attempt by the Allies to destroy the Soviet Republic, an attempt, following the collapse of the Yudenich plan, to crush the Soviet Republic, this time with the help of Poland. You are acquainted with the main events in this war with Poland, which began against our wish. You know that at first the Poles were successful, and captured Kiev in the south-west. Then there was a fairly long interval in which the Red Army was able to concentrate its forces and to start an offensive, whereupon the Poles began to lose one point after another. They lost Polotsk, and so on. But it was not until July that the Red Army began a decisive offensive, which proved so successful that we effected an advance almost unparalleled in military history. The Red Army advanced 500, 600, and in many cases even 800 versts without a stop, and almost reached Warsaw. Warsaw was considered practically lost to Poland. That, at least, was the opinion of the world press. Then the tide turned. By the time our troops had got within reach of Warsaw they were too exhausted to press home the victory, whereas the Polish troops supported by a wave of patriotism in Warsaw, and with a feeling that they were now on their own soil, found encouragement and a fresh opportunity to advance. The war, as it turned out, had enabled us almost to rout Poland completely, but at the decisive moment our strength failed us.

I could speak of this at greater length, but, in keeping with the topic of my report, I must dwell on the political situation that had developed at the time. We have seen that when, before the April offensive, we proposed peace to the Polish Republic on terms that were most advantageous to the Poles and disadvantageous to us, the bourgeois press all over the world raised a hullabaloo, and our outspoken declaration was taken as a sign of weakness. If the Bolsheviks were proposing peace on the basis of the line then held by the Polish troops, and if the Bolsheviks were even surrendering Minsk, then they must surely be weak. On the outbreak of the war, even the British monarch sent a message of congratulations to the head of the Polish landowner government.

On July 12, as you very likely remember, we suddenly received a telegram from the Secretary of the League of Nations to the effect that the Polish Government were willing to start negotiations for peace on the basis of ethnographic boundaries, and provided the whole of Galicia were given to Poland. An unparalleled uproar was raised in the world press. This time they were all for peace. When we proposed peace in April, or even earlier, in the spring of 1920, all these newspapers were silent, or else urged Poland to fight. But when we had defeated Poland and it was Poland that was asking for peace—to which we replied by clearly and frankly stating our opinion that the League of Nations did not represent any force and that we could not rely on any promise it made—they all raised a hullabaloo and demanded that we should call a halt. Now that the fortunes of war have changed, and we announced yesterday that we were offering Poland peace on terms more favourable than the League of Nations had proposed, on condition peace was signed before October 5, the whole bourgeois press has again fallen silent. They are silent about peace when the Bolsheviks are attacked, but raise an outcry when it is the Bolsheviks who are attacking. And after all this, they want us to believe that the bourgeois press wants peace. At our Party's conference, which ended a few days ago, we were able to hear a report by a Polish worker, representative of one of the largest trade unions in Poland,[97] who managed to get through from Warsaw. He told us of the persecution of the workers in Poland, how the Warsaw workers looked to the Red Army as their liberator, and how they were waiting for the coming of the Russian Red Army, which they regard, not as their enemy but, on the contrary, as their friend in their struggle against the landowners and the bourgeois oppressors of Poland. It is quite clear that Poland is the Entente's cat's-paw in a new attempt to destroy the Soviet Republic; however, when this attempt threatened to lead to a diametrically opposite result and we were on the point of helping the Polish workers overthrow their government, the entire European bourgeois press turned on us. Comrade Kamenev, who visited London, has told us here in the Bolshoi Theatre how he daily heard ultimatums and threats from the British Government, which was already prepared to mobilise its whole navy against Petrograd and concentrate it at Kronstadt, allegedly to defend Poland against us. Now that the fortunes of war have changed and we are withdrawing from our terms everything Poland has declared unacceptable, the bourgeois press has fallen silent. It is quite clear that French and British imperialism is inciting Poland to make a fresh attempt to overthrow the Soviets.

I think that this is a last attempt (and this is undoubtedly important) at an offensive against Soviet Russia. It appears that Poland is too closely bound up with the whole system of international imperialism. You know that, after defeating Germany, the Allied imperialists—France, Great Britain, America and Japan—signed the Peace of Versailles, which, to say the least, was far more brutal than the infamous Peace of Brest-Litovsk, over which such an outcry was raised. But while the French, the Americans and the British proclaimed from the house-tops that this was a war of liberation, that its purpose was to save Europe and the world from the barbarian Huns, as they called the Germans, to save the world from German militarism and the German Kaiser, we now find that the Peace of Versailles outdoes in atrocity anything the Kaiser was capable of when he was victor. The interference of British and French officers in economic life has proved to all the defeated countries, to Germany and to all the countries that made up the Austro-Hungarian Empire, that it is impossible to live under such conditions. One of the pillars of this monstrous peace is Poland's cutting across Germany, since Polish territory stretches to the sea. Relations between Germany and Poland are at present strained to the utmost. In oppressing the German population, the Poles have the support of the Entente troops and officers. The Versailles Peace has turned Poland into a buffer state which is to guard against German contact with Soviet communism and is regarded by the Entente as a weapon against the Bolsheviks. Through Poland and with the help of Poland, the French are hoping to recover the tens of thousands of millions loaned to the tsarist government. That is why, when the war with Poland broke out, which we tried to avert even at the price of heavy concessions, it proved to be a more direct war against the Entente than previous wars had been. The latter, in which Kolchak, Denikin and Yudenich attacked us, were also conducted with the aid of officers and hundreds of millions provided by the Allies, with the aid of their guns and tanks. The previous wars were also wars against the Entente, but they were fought on Russian territory against Russian whiteguard officers and the peasants they had mobilised and they could not become wars that could shake the Peace of Versailles. That is where they differed from the war against Poland. The war against Yudenich, Kolchak and Denikin was also a war against the Entente, but at the same time it was a war of working-class Russia against the whole of bourgeois Russia. When it ended in victory and when we smashed Yudenich, Kolchak and Denikin, this was not a direct attack on the Peace of Versailles. The reverse is true of Poland; that is what distinguishes the war against Poland, and constitutes Poland's international significance.

When we were victoriously pressing our offensive on Poland, the whole of Europe began to vociferate that they wanted peace, that the whole world was tired of war, and that it was time to make peace. But now that the Poles are advancing, there is no outcry that people are tired of war. Why is that? It is because, by defeating Yudenich, Kolchak and Denikin, we could not destroy the Peace of Versailles; we were merely falling upon Yudenich, Kolchak and Denikin and driving them into the sea. However, in attacking Poland we are thereby attacking the Entente itself; by destroying the Polish army we are destroying the Peace of Versailles, on which the whole present system of international relations rests.

Had Poland turned Soviet, had the Warsaw workers received from Soviet Russia help they awaited and welcomed, the Peace of Versailles would have been smashed, and the entire international system set up as a result of the victory over Germany would have collapsed. France would then not have had a buffer protecting Germany against Soviet Russia. She would not have had a battering-ram against the Soviet Republic. She would have had no hope of recovering her tens of thousands of millions, and would be heading for disaster even more rapidly than she now is. France is up to her ears in debt. Once the wealthiest of money-lenders, she now owes America three times as much as other countries do. She is heading for bankruptcy. Her position is hopeless. That is why the approach of the Red troops to Warsaw meant an international crisis; that is why the entire bourgeois press was so agitated by it. Such was the position that, had the Red Army advanced victoriously another few days, not only would Warsaw have been captured (that would not have mattered so much), but the Peace of Versailles would have been destroyed.

Therein lies the international significance of this Polish war. You know that we harboured no plans of conquest. I said at the beginning of my speech that in April 1920 we stood east of Minsk and proposed peace on those terms, if only we could save the workers and peasants of Russia from a new war. But since war has been forced upon us, we must fight it to a victorious finish. The Peace of Versailles is oppressing hundreds of millions of people. It is robbing Germany of coal, robbing her of her milch herds, and is reducing her to an unparalleled and unprecedented state of servitude. Even the most backward sections of Germany's peasant population have declared that they are for the Bolsheviks, that they are allies of the Bolsheviks; that is quite natural, for, in its struggle for existence, the Soviet Republic is the only force in the world which is combating imperialism—and imperialism now means an alliance of France, Britain and America. We are approaching the hub of the present international system. When the Red troops approached the frontier of Poland, the Red Army's victorious advance created an unprecedented political crisis. The main feature of this crisis was that, when the British Government threatened us with war, and told us that if we advanced any farther they would fight us and send their warships against us, the British workers declared that they would not permit this war. Let me tell you that Bolshevism is spreading among the British workers. However, the Communists there are just as weak today as we were in March, April and May 1917, when we had one-tenth of the votes at conferences and congresses. At the First All-Russia Congress of Soviets in June 1917, we had no more than 13 per cent of the votes. A similar situation exists in Great Britain: there the Bolsheviks are in an insignificant minority. But the point is that the British Mensheviks have always been opposed to Bolshevism and direct revolution, and have favoured an alliance with the bourgeoisie. Today, however, the old leaders of the British workers have begun to waver and have changed their minds: they were opposed to the dictatorship of the working class, but now they have come over to our side. They have set up a Council of Action over there in Britain. This is a radical change in British politics. Alongside of Parliament, which in Great Britain is now elected by almost universal suffrage (since 1918), there has arisen a self-appointed Council of Action which relies on support from the workers' trade unions with a membership of over six million. When the government wanted to begin a war against Soviet Russia, the workers declared that they would not allow it, and said they would not let the French fight either, because the French depend upon British coal, and should this industry come to a standstill it would be a severe blow to France.

I repeat that this was a tremendous turning-point in British politics. Its significance to Great Britain is as great as the revolution of February 1917 was to us. The revolution of February 1917 overthrew tsarism and set up a bourgeois republic in Russia. There is no republic in Great Britain, but her thoroughly bourgeois monarchy has existed for many centuries. The workers can vote in the parliamentary elections, but all foreign policy is conducted outside Parliament, for it is the province of the Cabinet. We have long known that the British Government are waging an undercover war on Russia and are helping Yudenich, Kolchak and Denikin. We have often met with statements in the British press to the effect that Great Britain has no right to send a single soldier to Russia. Who, then, voted for this measure? What act of Parliament authorised war on Russia in aid of Yudenich and Kolchak? There have been no such acts, and by actions like this Great Britain has violated her own constitution. What then is this Council of Action? Independently of Parliament, this Council of Action has presented an ultimatum to the government on behalf of the workers. This is a step towards dictatorship, and there is no other way out of the situation. This is taking place in Great Britain, which is an imperialist country with 400 or 500 million people enslaved in her colonies. She is a most important country, which rules the greater part of the population of the earth. The advance on Poland has led to such a turn of affairs that the British Mensheviks have entered into an alliance with the Russian Bolsheviks. That is what this offensive has done.

The entire British bourgeois press declared that the Council of Action meant the Soviets. They were right. It did not call itself by that name, but actually that is what it was. It is the same kind of dual power as we had under Kerensky from March 1917 onwards, a time when the Provisional Government was considered the only government, but actually could do nothing of significance without the Soviet of Workers' and Peasants' Deputies, a time when we said to the Soviets: "Take over all power." A similar situation has now arisen in Britain, and the Mensheviks on this "Council of Action" have been obliged to adopt an anti-constitutional course. This will give you some idea of what our war with Poland has meant. Though the international bourgeoisie are still immeasurably stronger than we are, and the British Government has put the whole blame on Kamenev, expelled him from Great Britain, and will not let him return, this is but an empty and ridiculous threat, for the best defenders of the American and British capitalists, the moderate British labour leaders—those Right Mensheviks and Right Socialist-Revolutionaries—have joined the Council of Action, and Great Britain is now facing a new crisis. She is now threatened with a coal miners' general strike. The strikers are demanding, not only higher pay but a cut in coal prices. One wave of strikes is following another in Great Britain. The strikers are demanding higher wages. However, if the workers win a 10 per cent wage rise today, prices go up 20 per cent tomorrow. Prices are rising, and the workers see that their struggle gets them nowhere and that, despite wage increases, they are losing, because of the higher prices. So the workers are demanding, not only higher pay for the coal miners but lower coal prices as well. This has led to the British bourgeois press panicking in even greater horror than when the Red Army entered Poland.

You know how the European crisis has affected Italy. Italy is one of the victor powers, and when the Red Army's successes led to a movement in Germany and a change in British policy, the struggle in Italy became so acute that the workers began to seize the factories, take over the factory owners' dwellings, and rouse the rural population.

The present situation in Italy is far removed from any form of class peace.

That was the course taken by the Polish war. That is why, while realising that the Polish war was closely linked up with the international imperialism's entire position, we agreed to make the greatest concessions to save the workers and peasants from the hardships of war. Then we clashed with the Peace of Versailles, and found that the bourgeoisie was just as incensed against us as ever; however, we also found that the workers were maturing daily and hourly, and that the workers' revolution was steadily approaching, although all too slowly as compared with the speed of developments in Russia. It was possible to accomplish the revolution so rapidly in Russia because it took place in wartime. During the war tens of millions of Russian workers and peasants were armed, and against such a force the bourgeoisie and the officers were powerless. During the October days they threatened to lead an army against Petrograd. We used to receive tens of thousands of telegrams from all the fronts saying: "We are marching against you to wipe you out." "Well have a try," we said to ourselves. When delegates arrived from each of the armies, a thirty minutes' talk was enough to show that the soldiers were with us, and the officers had to hold their tongues. The attempts at resistance, the plots of Yudenich, Kolchak and Denikin came later, after the army had been demobilised. That is why the revolution could succeed so rapidly in Russia. The people were armed. The workers and peasants proved to be on our side to a man. In Europe, however, the war is over. The armies have been demobilised; the soldiers have returned to their homes; the workers and peasants are disarmed. Developments there are slow now, but they are on the move. The international bourgeoisie has only to raise a hand against us to have it seized by its own workers. That is the international significance of the war with Poland. That is the source of the international crisis. That, too, is the source of our new difficulties now. It was when, as you know, we lacked just a little strength to reach Warsaw, hand over power to the Warsaw workers, convene Soviets of Workers' and Peasants' Deputies in Warsaw, and say to them "We have come to your aid", when, after heroic efforts without parallel or precedent in the past, our army's strength was spent, that the moment of our military defeat came.

We have now fallen back very far to the east. In the north we have even lost the town of Lida; in the south we are almost on the line we held in April 1919—the Pilsudski line. In the north we are retreating very rapidly, and in the meantime Wrangel is making ever new attempts to advance. He recently threatened Ekaterinoslav, approached Sinelnikovo and got control of it. He has now captured Slavgorod. In the east, he has captured Mariupol, is approaching Taganrog and threatening the Donets Basin. We are again in difficult straits, and again we see the international imperialists attempting to strangle the Soviet Republic with both hands: the Polish offensive and the Wrangel offensive. In fact, Poland and Wrangel are the two hands of the French imperialists, who are supplying the troops both of Poland and of Wrangel with munitions. But these three forces are not getting along very well together. France tells the Poles that they should not grab too many resources, too much territory, because a tsarist Russia will never let them keep it. Then she tells Wrangel that he must not act so as to restore the power of the old landowners, for the example of Denikin, Kolchak and Yudenich shows that when the old landowners direct the whiteguard armies, or when their officers command the armies, the more territory they seize, the sooner that leads to their ruin, because in the end the peasants rise up in revolt against them.

As long as Wrangel has a crack officer army he can rely on it; Wrangel's strength lies in his possessing splendid weapons of the most up-to-date type and a crack officer army. When he effected a landing in the Kuban region, his army was so selected that every company and regiment could be developed into an entire division, because it consisted entirely of officers. But as soon as he attempts to repeat what Kolchak, Denikin and Yudenich did in the past, i.e., seize more territory, so as to mobilise a larger peasant population and create a mass army, his success will at once give way to defeat; just as the peasant army was opposed to Kolchak, Denikin and Yudenich, so it will never march with Wrangel's officer army. The Warsaw worker who addressed the Party Conference formulated it as follows: the Polish army, which formerly consisted of youngsters (raw lads just called up for service), has been destroyed. Men up to the age of 35 have now been mobilised; these are adults who have been through the imperialist war, and this army, as far as the Polish landowners and capitalists are concerned, is by no means as reliable as an army of youngsters.

That is how matters stand with regard to the international situation. In the war against the Entente, owing to the defeat we have suffered at Warsaw and the offensive now continuing on the Western and Wrangel fronts, our position is again highly critical. I must therefore conclude my brief report by appealing to our comrades in the leather industry and pointing out to them that we must once again bend every effort, for the defeat of Wrangel is now our principal task. This will call for tremendous effort and initiative on the part of the workers, the trade unions, the proletarian masses, and first and foremost of those workers who are closely associated with the branches of industry that are connected with defence. Our chief difficulty in the present war is not manpower—we have enough of that—but supplies. The chief difficulty on all the fronts is the shortage of supplies, the shortage of warm clothing and footwear. Greatcoats and boots—that is the main thing our soldiers lack, and it is on that account that quite successful advances have so often failed. That is the difficulty which prevents us from rapidly utilising for a victorious advance the new units, which we possess in sufficient numbers, but which, without sufficient supplies, cannot be formed and cannot be of any real combat value.

Both the leather workers' union and this assembly, which represents the entire proletariat in this industry, must give their most serious attention to this. Comrades, it depends on you to make the forthcoming offensive against Wrangel, for which we are mustering all our forces, as rapid and successful as it can possibly be. It depends on you, because the measures being taken by the Soviet Government and the Communist Party are not enough. To give real help to the Red Army men, to secure a decisive turn for the better, and to improve supplies, the assistance of Soviet institutions, the decrees of the Council of People's Commissars and the Council of Defence,[98] and Party decisions are not enough: what is required is help from the trade unions. The trade unions must realise that, despite our repeated offers of peace, the very existence of the workers' and peasants' power is once more at stake. You know how this power gained in strength after the collapse of Denikin, Kolchak and Yudenich. You know how the grain collections improved thanks to the recovery of Siberia and the Kuban region; you know that the capture of Baku has now enabled us to secure over a hundred million poods of oil, and how our industry has at last begun to acquire the foundation on which it is possible to create stocks of grain and bring the workers back to the factories, accumulate raw material and provide fuel, so that the factories may be started and economic life restored at last. But for all these possibilities to materialise, we must at all costs put an end to the war, and speed up the offensive against Wrangel. The Crimea must be recovered before winter comes in the south and that will depend on the energy and initiative of the workers themselves, and above all, perhaps, on the energy and initiative of every Russian leather worker and of the Leather Workers' Union.

I appeal to you to follow the example of our Petrograd workers, who recently, after a report by a representative of the Communist International on the situation at the fronts, once more began to make tremendous efforts to help the cause, again beginning with munitions for the Red Army men, and building up the strength of the Red Army. You know that each step taken in the rear to help the Red Army has an immediate effect on the morale of the Red Army men. You know that the autumn cold affects the Red Army men, depresses them, creates new difficulties, increases the number of sick men and results in great hardships. All aid given by the rear to the Red Army men immediately helps strengthen the Red Army, fortify its morale, bring down the number of sick and increase its offensive power. At every meeting and in every workshop, every worker must now make the slogan "Everything for the Red Army!" the chief topic of his talks, reports and meetings.

What we must ask ourselves is: have we done everything in our power to help the Red Army? On this help depends how soon we settle final accounts with Wrangel and fully ensure for ourselves peace and the possibility of constructive work in the economic field. (*Applause.*)

Pravda Nos. 225 and 226,
October 9 and 10, 1920

Published according to
the *Pravda* text

TO THE POOR PEASANTS OF THE UKRAINE

Comrades, the tsarist general Wrangel is building up his offensive against the Ukraine and Russia. With backing from the French capitalists, he is pushing forward, threatening the Donets Basin and Ekaterinoslav. The danger is grave. Once again the landowners are trying to re-establish their power, get their estates back, and re-enslave the peasants.

Comrades, the Ukrainian countryside has endured unparalleled sufferings under the yoke of the landowners. The latter have more than once been able to overthrow the Soviets, the workers' and peasants' power; more than once they have been helped by the kulaks, the rich peasants, who either went over openly to their side or hampered the poor and working peasants' efforts to introduce the new order, the new way of life, the new organisation in the villages. Each such attempt to restore the rule of the landowners has ended in a new victory for the workers and peasants. Today, all over the Ukraine, the poor villagers have begun to set up their committees so as to smash the resistance of the handful of the rich, and finally to establish the rule of the working people. Wrangel, general of the landowners, is increasing his pressure with the intention of routing these organisations of the working people.

Comrades, rise up to a man to hurl Wrangel back. Let all committees of poor peasants bend every effort to help the Red Army crush Wrangel. Not a single working peasant should stand aside in the struggle for the cause of the workers and peasants, or remain inactive or indifferent. Comrades, remember that this is a matter of saving the lives of your families, of defending the peasants' land and their rule.

Rally for aid to the Red Army!

Death to the oppressor landowners!

Lenin

2.10.1920

Kommunist (Kiev) No. 199, October 13, 1920

Published according to the manuscript

ON PROLETARIAN CULTURE[99]

We see from *Izvestia* of October 8 that, in his address to the Proletcult Congress, Comrade Lunacharsky said things that were *diametrically opposite* to what he and I had agreed upon yesterday.[100]

It is necessary that a draft resolution (of the Proletcult Congress) should be drawn up with the utmost urgency, and that it should be endorsed by the Central Committee, in time to have it put to the vote *at this very* session of the Proletcult. On behalf of the Central Committee it should be submitted not later than today, for endorsement both by the Collegium of the People's Commissariat of Education and by the Proletcult Congress, because the Congress is closing today.

DRAFT RESOLUTION

1) All educational work in the Soviet Republic of workers and peasants, in the field of political education in general and in the field of art in particular, should be imbued with the spirit of the class struggle being waged by the proletariat for the successful achievement of the aims of its dictatorship, i.e., the overthrow of the bourgeoisie, the abolition of classes, and the elimination of all forms of exploitation of man by man.

2) Hence, the proletariat, both through its vanguard—the Communist Party—and through the many types of proletarian organisations in general, should display the utmost activity and play the leading part in all the work of public education.

3) All the experience of modern history and, particularly, the more than half-century-old revolutionary struggle of the proletariat of all countries since the appearance of the *Communist Manifesto* has unquestionably demonstrated

that the Marxist world outlook is the only true expression of the interests, the viewpoint, and the culture of the revolutionary proletariat.

4) Marxism has won its historic significance as the ideology of the revolutionary proletariat because, far from rejecting the most valuable achievements of the bourgeois epoch, it has, on the contrary, assimilated and refashioned everything of value in the more than two thousand years of the development of human thought and culture. Only further work on this basis and in this direction, inspired by the practical experience of the proletarian dictatorship as the final stage in the struggle against every form of exploitation, can be recognised as the development of a genuine proletarian culture.

5) Adhering unswervingly to this stand of principle, the All-Russia Proletcult Congress rejects in the most resolute manner, as theoretically unsound and practically harmful, all attempts to invent one's own particular brand of culture, to remain isolated in self-contained organisations, to draw a line dividing the field of work of the People's Commissariat of Education and the Proletcult, or to set up a Proletcult "autonomy" within establishments under the People's Commissariat of Education and so forth. On the contrary, the Congress enjoins all Proletcult organisations to fully consider themselves in duty bound to act as auxiliary bodies of the network of establishments under the People's Commissariat of Education, and to accomplish their tasks under the general guidance of the Soviet authorities (specifically, of the People's Commissariat of Education) and of the Russian Communist Party, as part of the tasks of the proletarian dictatorship.

* *
*

Comrade Lunacharsky says that his words have been distorted. In that case this resolution is needed *all the more* urgently.

Written on October 8, 1920
First published in 1926

Published according to the manuscript

SPEECH DELIVERED AT A CONFERENCE OF CHAIRMEN OF UYEZD, VOLOST AND VILLAGE EXECUTIVE COMMITTEES OF MOSCOW GUBERNIA OCTOBER 15, 1920[101]

Comrades, in my report on the domestic and the external position of the Republic, which you wished to hear, I shall naturally have to devote most of my remarks to the war with Poland and its causes. It was this war which in the main determined the Republic's domestic and external position during the past six months. Now that the preliminaries for a peace with Poland have just been signed, it is possible and necessary to take a general look at this war and its significance and try to give thought to the lessons we have all learnt from the war which has just ended, though nobody knows whether it has ended for good. I would therefore like first to remind you that it was on April 26 of this year that the Poles began their offensive. The Soviet Republic solemnly and formally proposed a peace to the Poles, the Polish landowners and the Polish bourgeoisie, on terms more favourable than those we have offered them now, despite the tremendous reverses our troops suffered at Warsaw, and the even greater reverses during the retreat from Warsaw. At the end of the April of this year, the Poles held a line between 50 and 150 versts to the east of the one they now regard as the line of a preliminary peace; though at that time the line was manifestly an unfair one, we solemnly proposed peace to them on behalf of the All-Russia Central Executive Committee, since, as you all of course know and remember, the Soviet government was mainly concerned at the time with ensuring the transition to peaceful construction. We had no reason for wishing to resort to arms in settling questions in dispute between ourselves and the Polish state. We were fully aware that the Polish state was, and still is, a state of the landowners and capitalists, and that it is fully dependent on the capitalists of the Entente countries, in particular on France. Though at the time Poland controlled, not only the whole of Lithuania but also Byelorussia, to say nothing of Eastern Galicia, we considered it our duty to do everything possible to avert a war, so as to give the working class and the peasantry of Russia at least a brief respite from imperialist and civil wars, and at last enable them to get down in earnest to peaceful work. The events that ensued have happened all too frequently: our straightforward and public offer of peace on the line the Poles actually held was taken as a sign of weakness. Bourgeois diplomats of all countries are unaccustomed to such frank statements and our readiness to accept a peace along a line so disadvantageous to us was taken and interpreted as proof of our extreme weakness. The French capitalists succeeded in inciting the Polish capitalists to go to war. You will remember how, after a brief interval following upon the Polish offensive, we replied by dealing a counter-blow and almost reached Warsaw, after which our troops suffered a heavy defeat, and were thrown back.

For over a month and right down to the present, our troops were retreating and suffered reverses, for they were utterly worn out, exhausted by their unparalleled advance from Polotsk to Warsaw. But, I repeat, despite this difficult situation, peace was signed on terms less advantageous to Poland than the earlier ones. The earlier frontier lay 50 versts to the east, whereas it is now 50 versts to the west. Thus, though we signed a peace at a time favourable only to the enemy, when our troops were on the retreat and Wrangel was building up his offensive, we signed a peace treaty on more favourable terms. This once again proves to you that when the Soviet Government proposes peace, its words and statements have to be treated seriously; otherwise what will happen is that we shall offer peace on terms less favourable to us, and get this peace on better terms. This is a lesson the Polish landowners and capitalists will not, of course, forget; they realise that they have gone too far; the peace terms now give them less territory than was offered previously. This is not the first lesson either. You all probably remember that, in the spring of 1919, a representative of the U.S. Government came to Moscow and proposed a preliminary peace with us and with all the whiteguard commanders at the time: Kolchak, Denikin and others, a peace which would have been extremely unfavourable to us. When he returned and reported on our peace terms, they were not considered advantageous, and the war went on. You are aware of the outcome of the war. This is not the first time that the Soviet state has proved that it is considerably stronger than it appears, and that our diplomatic Notes do not contain the boasts and threats that are usual with all bourgeois governments; consequently, rejecting an offer of peace from Soviet Russia means getting that peace some time later on terms that are far worse. Such things are not forgotten in international politics; after proving to the Polish landowners that they have now obtained a peace worse than the one which we originally offered, we shall teach the Polish people, the Polish peasants and workers, to weigh and compare the statements of their government and ours.

Many of you may have read in the newspapers the American Government's Note, in which it declares: "we do not wish to have any dealings with the Soviet Government because it does not honour its obligations."[102] This does not surprise us, because it has been said for many years, the only outcome being that all their attempts to invade Soviet Russia have ended in disaster. The Polish newspapers, nearly all of which are in the pay of the landowners and the capitalists—there this is called freedom of the press—assert that the Soviet government cannot be trusted, since it is a government of tyrants and frauds. All Polish newspapers say the same thing, but the Polish workers and peasants compare these words with the facts, and the facts show that we demonstrated our attachment to peace the very first time we made our peace offer; by concluding peace in October we proved this again. You will not find proof of this kind in the history of any bourgeois government, a fact that cannot but leave its impress on the minds of the Polish workers and peasants. The Soviet Government signed a peace when it was not to its advantage to do so. It is only in this way that we shall teach the governments that are controlled by the landowners and capitalists to stop lying; only in this way shall we destroy the faith the workers and peasants have in them. We must give more thought to this than to anything else. Soviet power in Russia is surrounded by countless enemies, and yet these enemies are impotent. Think of the course and outcome of the Polish war. We now know that the French capitalists stood behind Poland, that they supplied Poland with money and munitions, and sent them French officers. We quite recently received information that African troops, namely French colonial troops, had appeared on the Polish front. This means that the war was waged by France with aid from Britain and America. At the same time, France recognised the lawful government of Russia in the person of Wrangel—so Wrangel too was backed by France, who provided him with the means to equip and maintain an army. Britain and America are also aiding Wrangel's army. Consequently, three allies stood against us: France, supported by the world's wealthy countries, Poland, and Wrangel—yet we have emerged from this war by concluding a favourable peace. In other words, we have won. Anyone who examines the map will see that we have won, that we have emerged from this war with more territory than we had before it started. But is the enemy weaker than we are? Is he weaker in the military sense? Has he got fewer men and munitions? No, he has more of everything. This enemy is stronger than we are, and yet he has been beaten. This is what we must give thought to in order to understand Soviet Russia's position with respect to all other countries.

When we Bolsheviks started the revolution, we said that it could and should be started, but at the same time we did not forget that it could be successfully ended and brought to an absolutely victorious conclusion, without confining ourselves to Russia alone, but, in alliance with a number of countries, after defeating international capital. Russian capital is linked up with international capital. When our enemies say to us: even if you were to win in Russia, your cause will nevertheless perish because the other capitalist states will crush you, we now have an answer—the highly important experience of the war with Poland, which shows how things have actually turned out. Indeed, why did it happen that, within six months and even less, if we take April as the beginning of the offensive, France, Poland and Wrangel, who were stronger than we are, were full of hatred of Bolshevism, and were determined to overthrow Soviet power, have been defeated, and the war has ended in our favour? How could it have happened that Soviet Russia, exhausted by the imperialist and civil wars, surrounded by enemies, and cut off from every source of supplies and equipment—this Soviet Russia has proved the victor? We must reflect on this because, if we go deeper into this question, we begin to understand the mechanism, not only of the Russian but of the world revolution as well. We see confirmation of the fact that the Russian revolution is but a single link in the chain of the world revolution, and that our cause is strong and invincible because the cause of revolution is developing throughout the world; economic conditions are evolving in a way that is making our enemies weaker and us stronger with every day. The Polish war has again proved that this is neither exaggeration, boasting nor over-enthusiasm. Three allies were fighting against us. One might have thought that uniting these three allies should present no difficulty but it appeared that, taught by the great experience of Yudenich, Kolchak and Denikin campaigns, they were unable to unite against us and squabbled at every step. In this connection, the history of the Polish war, which has only just ended, is particularly instructive. Our march on Warsaw—the Red Army's march, in which weary, exhausted and poorly-clad soldiers covered over 600 versts, inflicting one defeat after another on the Polish troops, who were excellently trained, with hundreds of the best French officer instructors—showed us the kind of relations that existed among our enemies. On July 12, when the Red Army troops were approaching the Polish frontier, we received a telegram from Britain's Foreign Secretary, Curzon, on behalf of the League of Nations, that notorious League of Nations, an alliance which professes to unite Britain, France, America, Italy and Japan, countries with a tremendous military potential and possessing all the navies of the world, and against whom military resistance might seem perfectly impossible and absurd. On behalf of this League of Nations, Curzon proposed that we stop the war and enter into negotiations with the Poles in London. According to this telegram, the boundary should pass near Grodno, Byelostok, Brest-Litovsk and along the River San in Eastern Galicia. To this proposal we replied that we recognised no League of Nations, since we had seen its insignificance and the disregard that even its members had for its decisions. The French Government considered our reply insolent, and one would have thought that this League of Nations would come out against us. But what happened? The League of Nations fell apart at our very first declaration, and Britain and France fell on each other.

For several years Britain's Secretary for War Churchill has been employing every means, both lawful and more often unlawful from the viewpoint of British law, to help the whiteguards against Russia, so as to supply them with military equipment. He hates Soviet Russia bitterly, yet immediately after our declaration Britain fell out with France, because France needs the forces of a whiteguard Russia to protect her against Germany, while Britain needs no such protection. Britain, a naval power, fears no such action because she has a most powerful navy. Thus, the League of Nations, which has sent such unprecedented threats to Russia, was itself helpless from the very outset. At every step the interests of the League's member states are patently in conflict. France desires the defeat of Britain, and vice versa. When Comrade Kamenev was negotiating with the British Government in London and asked the British Prime Minister, "Let us suppose that you will really do what you say, what about France?", the British Prime Minister had to reply that France would go her own way. He said that Britain could not take the same road as France. It became plain that the League of Nations was non-existent, that the alliance of the capitalist powers is sheer fraud, and that in actual fact it is an alliance of robbers, each trying to snatch something from the others. When at the conclusion of peace in Riga, we discovered what divided Poland, Britain, France and Wrangel, and why they could not act in unison, we learnt that their interests differed: Britain wanted to have the small succession states—Finland, Estonia, Latvia and Lithuania—in her sphere of influence and was not interested in the restoration of tsarist or whiteguard or even bourgeois Russia; she even stood to lose from it. That was why Britain was acting counter to France and could not unite with Poland and Wrangel. France's concern was to fight to the last Polish soldier for her interests and the debts owed to her. She hoped we would pay her the 20-thousand-million debt incurred by the former tsar and recognised by the Kerensky government. Any sensible person will realise that the French capitalists will never see the colour of their money; the French capitalists realise that the French workers and peasants cannot be made to fight, while Polish soldiers are plentiful and can be driven into battle—so let them die that the French capitalists may get their millions back. However, the Polish workers too can see that the French, British and other officers behave in Poland just as if they were in a conquered country. That was why, during the Riga negotiations, we saw that the party of the Polish workers and peasants which is undoubtedly patriotic and undoubtedly hostile to Bolshevism, just like our Right-wing Mensheviks and the Socialist-Revolutionary Party, stood for peace and was opposed to the government of the Polish landowners and capitalists, who up to the last moment tried to wreck the peace treaty, and even now want to do so and will go on doing so for a long time to come. I shall have to speak on this point when I come to the question of whether the preliminary peace we have just concluded will last.

The third ally, Wrangel, who fought for the return of the whole of Russia to the landowners and the capitalists, regards Poland as part of Russia. All the Russian tsars, landowners and capitalists were accustomed to regarding Poland as their prey; they never forgot that Poland had long ago been crushed by the Russian serf army led to war by the tsar. That meant that, had Wrangel been victorious, he would have used his victory in order to restore full power, both in Russia and in Poland, to the landowners. What happened, however, was that, when the three allies stood ready to attack us, they began by falling out among themselves. France's aims are alien to both the Polish peasant and the Polish worker, while Wrangel's aims are alien even to any Polish landowner. And now, when we hear Wrangel's radio or the French Government radio from Paris, we learn that France and Wrangel are gnashing their teeth because they realise the implication of this peace which we have concluded with Poland, though they assert that this is no peace, and that Poland cannot sign it. We shall see what we shall see, but meanwhile a peace has been signed. Actually, neither Wrangel nor France understands how it could have come about. They cannot stomach the miracle of a devastated Soviet Russia defeating civilised countries far stronger than she is. They do not understand that these victories stem from the fundamental doctrine of the Communists, which says that property divides whereas labour unites. Private property is robbery, and a state based on private property is a state of robbers, who are fighting for a share of the spoils. Though they have not yet finished this war, they are already fighting among themselves. A year ago fourteen states were threatening us, yet the alliance of these fourteen states at once fell apart. Why did it fall apart? Simply because the agreement between these states only existed on paper, and not one of them went to war. When a war started and France, Poland and Wrangel joined forces, their alliance too fell apart, because they were trying to trip one another up. As the Russian proverb says, they were trying to share out the skin of a bear they had not yet killed. They were, in fact, squabbling over a bear they would never kill.

The experience of world politics has shown that the alliance against Soviet Russia is irretrievably doomed to failure, because it is an imperialist alliance, an alliance of plunderers who are not united, and are bound by no genuine or permanent interests. They lack that which unites the working class; they have no common interests, which was again revealed during the Polish war. When our Red Army crushed the resistance of the Poles, captured Byelostok and Brest-Litovsk and approached the Polish frontier, this signified the collapse of the entire established system of international politics, for it is based on the Treaty of Versailles, which is a treaty of robbers and plunderers. When the Peace of Brest-Litovsk was imposed on us, a burden we bore so long, there was a world-wide outcry that it was a robber s peace. After Germany's defeat, the

League of Nations which had declared, during the war against Germany, that it was being fought for liberation and democracy, imposed a peace on the vanquished country, but it was a usurer's peace, an oppressor's peace, a butcher's peace, because Germany and Austria were looted and carved up. They deprived them of all means of subsistence, and left the children hungry and starving; this was a predatory peace, without any parallel. What then is the Treaty of Versailles? It is an unparalleled and predatory peace, which has made slaves of tens of millions of people, including the most civilised. This is no peace, but terms dictated to a defenceless victim by armed robbers. Through the Treaty of Versailles, Germany's enemies have deprived her of all her colonies. Turkey, Persia and China have been enslaved. A situation has arisen wherein seven-tenths of the world's population are in a condition of servitude. These slaves are to be found throughout the world and are at the mercy of a handful of countries—Britain, France and Japan. That is why this international system in its entirety, the order based on the Treaty of Versailles, stands on the brink of a volcano, for the enslaved seven-tenths of the world's population are waiting impatiently for someone to give them a lead in a struggle which will shake all these countries. France hopes that her loans will be repaid to her, but is herself in debt to America whom she cannot repay because she has not the wherewithal, and private property is sacred over there. What is the essence of this sacrosanct private property? It is that the tsars and capitalists borrow money, while the workers and the peasants have to repay the debt for them. They are on the verge of bankruptcy. They cannot meet their debts. At that very moment, the Red Army broke through the Polish frontier and approached the German borders. At the time it was common talk in Germany, even among the reactionaries and the monarchists, that the Bolsheviks would save them, it being evident that the Versailles peace was falling apart, that there existed a Red Army which had declared war on all capitalists. What has come to pass? It has come to pass that the Peace of Versailles now hinges on Poland. True, we lacked the strength to bring the war to an end. It should, however, be remembered that our workers and peasants were ill-clad and practically barefooted, yet they marched on and overcame all difficulties, fighting in conditions never before experienced by any other army in the world. We lacked the strength to take Warsaw and finish off the Polish landowners, whiteguards and capitalists, but our army showed the whole world that the Treaty of Versailles is not the force it is made out to be, that hundreds of millions of people are condemned to repay loans for many years to come and have their grandchildren and great-grandchildren do the same in order that the French, British and other imperialists may be enriched. The Red Army proved that the Treaty of Versailles is not so very stable. After the Treaty of Versailles our army showed that in the summer of 1920, the Soviet land, devastated as it was, was on the eve of complete victory thanks to that Red Army. The world saw that a force exists to which the Treaty of Versailles holds no terror, and that no Versailles treaties will subdue the power of the workers and peasants once they have learnt to deal with the landowners and capitalists.

Thus, the campaign against the Peace of Versailles, the campaign against all the capitalists and landowners of every country and against their oppression of other countries, has not been in vain. Millions upon millions of workers and peasants in all lands have been watching this and giving it thought, and they now look upon the Soviet Republic as their deliverer. They say: the Red Army has shown that it can give blow for blow, though it was not strong enough for victory in the first year or, you might even say, in the first month of its peaceful construction. That first month of peaceful construction, however, will be followed by many years, and with each passing year its strength will multiply tenfold. It was thought that the Peace of Versailles was one of the all-powerful imperialists, but after the summer of 1920 it became clear that they were weaker than the workers and peasants of even a weak country who know how to unite their forces and repulse the capitalists. In the summer of 1920 Soviet Russia showed herself as a force that not only defended herself against attack, against the onslaught of the Polish whiteguards, but showed herself in fact as a world force capable of smashing the Treaty of Versailles and freeing hundreds of millions of people in most countries of the world. That is the significance of the Red Army's campaign of this summer. That is why events took place in Britain during this war, which marked a turning-point in the whole of British policy. When we refused to halt our troops Britain replied by threatening to send her fleet against Petrograd. The order was given to attack Petrograd. That is what the British Prime Minister announced to Comrade Kamenev, and all countries were notified. But on the day following the dispatch of this telegram, mass meetings were held throughout Britain, and Councils of Action sprang up. The workers united. All the British Mensheviks, who are even viler than the Russian brand, and fawn upon the capitalists far more assiduously—even they had to join in, because the workers were demanding it, because the British workers said they would not tolerate a war against Russia. All over Britain Councils of Action were formed, the British imperialists' war plans were frustrated, and it once more turned out that, in her war against the imperialists of all lands, Soviet Russia has allies in each of them. When we Bolsheviks said: "We are not alone in our revolt against the landowners and capitalists of Russia, because in every country we have allies—the worker and peasant; moreover, those allies are to be found in most countries", we were ridiculed and were asked: "Where are these working people?" Yes, it is true that in Western Europe, where the capitalists are far stronger and live by fleecing hundreds of millions in the colonies, it is far more difficult to rise up in revolt. There the working-class revolution is developing incomparably more slowly. Nevertheless, it is developing. When, in July 1920, Britain threatened Russia with war, the British workers prevented that war from taking place. The British Mensheviks followed the lead of the British Bolsheviks. They had to do so and come out against the Constitution, against the law declaring they would not tolerate the war. If the latter was declared on the morrow, they would call a strike and give no coal to Britain and to France as well. The British workers declared that they wanted to determine foreign policy; they are directing it in the same way as the Bolsheviks in Russia, and not like the capitalists in other countries.

That is an example of what the Polish war has brought to light. That is why we have emerged victorious within six months. That is why devastated, weak and backward Soviet Russia is defeating an alliance of states infinitely more powerful than she is. That is because they lack strength at home, and the workers, the working people in general, are against them. This is apparent at every crisis. This is apparent because they are robbers who attack each other and cannot unite against us; because, in the final analysis, private property divides people and brutalises them, whereas labour unites them. Labour has not only united the workers and peasants of Russia, it has united them with the workers and peasants of all lands. Consequently, in all these countries the people can now see that Soviet Russia is a force that is smashing the Peace of Versailles. Soviet Russia will become stronger, and the Treaty of Versailles will collapse just as it all but collapsed at the first blow by the Red Army in July 1920. That is why the Polish war has ended in a manner no imperialist state had bargained for. This is a lesson of the utmost importance to us, for it shows by the example and behaviour of all countries taking part in international politics that our cause is strong; that no matter what attempts are made to invade Russia and no matter what military moves are made against us—and in all probability many more will be made—all these attempts will go up in smoke as we know from our actual experience, which has steeled us. After every such attempt by our enemies, we shall emerge stronger than ever.

I shall now turn from international politics, where the clash with the Peace of Versailles demonstrated our strength, to problems that are more immediate and practical, to the situation which has arisen in connection with the Treaty of Versailles. I shall not dwell on the significance of the Second Congress of the Communist International, which took place in Moscow in July, a congress of the Communists of the whole world, and also of the Congress of the Peoples of the East, which took place afterwards in Baku.[103] These were international congresses which united the Communists and showed that in all civilised countries and in all the backward countries of the East, the banner of Bolshevism, the programme of Bolshevism, the line of Bolshevik action are an emblem of salvation, an emblem of struggle to the workers of all civilised countries and the peasants of all the backward colonial countries. They showed that, during the past three years, Soviet Russia not only beat off those who fell upon her in order to throttle her, but won the sympathy of the working people of the whole world; that we not only defeated our enemies, but acquired and are still acquiring new allies daily and by the hour. That which was achieved by the congress of Communists in Moscow and by the Baku congress of Communist representatives of the peoples of the East cannot be immediately assessed or directly calculated, but it has been an achievement of greater significance than some military victories are, because it proves to us that the Bolsheviks' experience, their activities and programme, and their call for a revolutionary struggle against the capitalists and imperialists have won world-wide recognition; that which was achieved in Moscow in July and in Baku in September will for many months to come provide food for thought and assimilation by the workers and peasants of the world. This is a force which, in any conflict or crisis, will come out for Soviet Russia, as we have seen on more than one occasion. Such is the fundamental lesson of the Polish war, from the angle of the alignment of world forces.

In dealing with events at home, I must say that Wrangel is the chief force in the field against us. France, Poland and Wrangel joined forces against us. While our forces were wholly engaged in the war on the Western front, Wrangel mustered his forces, aided by the French and British navies. When Wrangel was approaching the Kuban, he was counting on support from the rich Cossack kulaks. Who helped Wrangel at the time? Who supplied him with fuel and a fleet to enable him to hold on to the Donets Basin? It was the British and the American navies. We know, however, that this landing operation failed, because the Kuban Cossack, though he was rich in grain, saw perfectly through those promises of a constituent assembly, rule by the people and the other fine things that the Mensheviks, the Socialist-Revolutionaries, etc., try to fool simpletons with. Perhaps the Kuban peasants believed them while they were holding forth so eloquently, but in the long run they put their faith in action not words, and saw that though the Bolsheviks were severe people to deal with, they were to be preferred. As a result, Wrangel fled from the Kuban, and many hundreds and thousands of his troops were shot. Despite this, Wrangel assembled more and more of his forces in the Crimea, his troops consisting in the main of officers. He hoped that, at the first favourable moment, it would be possible to build up these forces, provided they had the backing of the peasants.

Wrangel's troops are better equipped with guns, tanks, and aircraft than all the other armies that fought in Russia. Wrangel was assembling his forces when we were fighting the Poles; that is why I say that the peace with Poland is unstable. According to the preliminary peace signed on the 12th, the armistice will come into force only on the 18th, and the Poles still have two days in which they can repudiate it.[104] The entire French press and the capitalists there are striving to get Poland to start a new war against Soviet Russia; Wrangel is hastening to use all his connections in order to wreck this peace, because he can see that when the war with Poland is ended the Bolsheviks will turn against him. The only practical conclusion for us, therefore, is to direct all our forces against Wrangel. In April this year we proposed peace on terms which were unfavourable to us, only in order to spare tens of thousands of workers and peasants the carnage of a new war. To us frontiers do not matter so much; we do not mind losing some territory in the frontier regions. To us it is more important to preserve the lives of tens of thousands of workers and peasants and to retain the possibility of peaceful construction, than to keep a small piece of territory. That is why we submitted this peace proposal and now repeat that Wrangel is the main threat, that his troops, which have meanwhile grown enormously in strength, are fighting desperately, at points have crossed the Dnieper and have assumed the offensive. The Wrangel front and the Polish front are one and the same thing, and the question of the war against Wrangel is a question of the war against Poland; to convert the preliminary peace with Poland into a permanent peace we must crush Wrangel in the shortest possible space of time. If that is not done, we cannot be certain that the Polish landowners and capitalists, under pressure from the French landowners and capitalists and with their help, will not once again try to embroil us in war. That is why I am taking advantage of this broadly representative meeting to draw your attention to this fundamental question and to ask you to make use of your position and authority in order to influence the masses of workers and peasants and ensure that the greatest possible efforts are made towards the full accomplishment of our immediate task—at all costs to crush Wrangel in the shortest space of time, because the possibility of our engaging in the work of peaceful construction depends only on this.

We know that in our devastated country the peasant economy has been destroyed, and that the peasant needs goods, and not the paper money which is being showered on him in such profusion. However, to supply him with goods such as paraffin oil, salt, clothing, etc., industry must be restored. We are approaching a position in which that can be done. We know that we now have more grain than last year; we now have fuel for industry: over 100 million poods of oil from Baku; the Donets Basin, which provides an enormous quantity of fuel, has been rehabilitated, though some industrial enterprises had to be evacuated during Wrangel's advance to the south of the Donets Basin. Donets industry can be considered completely restored. Supplies of firewood are growing. Last year they totalled seven million cubic metres; we now have considerably more. Our industry is reviving. In Ivanovo-Voznesensk Gubernia, where for a number of years the mills were at a standstill, putting all the workers in low spirits, the mills are now being supplied with fuel and are beginning to operate. Thanks to the victories in Turkestan, they have received Turkestan cotton, and are starting to work. We are now confronted with a vast field of productive work, and we must do everything possible to rehabilitate industry, and supply the peasant with clothing, footwear and food and thus commence a fair exchange of the peasants' grain for urban products. We must begin to give aid to agriculture. Yesterday, in the Council of People's Commissars, we decided to encourage with extra rations the workers of the factory that will manufacture the first plough that proves best suited to our Russian conditions, so that we may restore our agriculture and raise it to a higher level, despite the shortage of cattle.

The workers and peasants are working together, without the landowners and the capitalists, and are achieving successes. However, the main thing in tackling this problem in earnest is the need to remember firmly that tens of thousands of workers and peasants are giving up their lives on the Wrangel front, that the enemy is better armed than we are, and that it is there, on the Wrangel front, that the last desperate battle is being fought out; it is there that the matter is being decided whether Soviet Russia will be able to strengthen herself for peaceful labour, so that no imperialist world-wide alliance, and not only the Polish whiteguards, will be able to threaten her. It is up to you, comrades. You must bend every effort, and remember that Soviet Russia has been able to solve all the problems in her struggle, not because decrees have been issued from the centre, but because these decrees have met with the enthusiastic and ardent sympathy of the workers and peasants throughout the country. Only when the workers and peasants saw that they were fighting against Kolchak, Denikin and Wrangel for their own land, their own factories and workshops, for their own interests and against the landowners and capitalists—only then did every one of them give the Red Army every possible support and assistance. When the Red Army men saw that the people in the rear were doing all they could for them, they were filled with the spirit which led them to victory. Everything depends on our defeating Wrangel, and I call on you to do everything possible in your organisations and factories, and in your villages, voluntarily and in accordance with the interests of the workers and peasants of the whole of Russia to come to the aid of the Wrangel front, and then we shall be victorious, both on the Wrangel and on the international fronts. (*Stormy applause.*)

Published in 1920 in the book: *Verbatim Reports of the Plenary Sessions of the Moscow Soviet of Workers', Peasants' and Red Army Deputies*

Published according to the text in the book

CONCLUDING REMARKS AT A CONFERENCE OF CHAIRMEN OF UYEZD, VOLOST AND VILLAGE EXECUTIVE COMMITTEES OF MOSCOW GUBERNIA
OCTOBER 15, 1920

Comrades, I shall have to confine myself to some brief concluding remarks, because from the very beginning of the meeting it has been clear that there is quite a strong desire, in fact a very strong desire, to upbraid the central government. That would, of course, have been useful, and I have considered it my duty to listen to everything said in criticism of the government and its policy. I think that the discussion should not have been wound up. (*Hear, hear!*) However, while listening to your remarks, I have been surprised to see how few precise and specific proposals you have put forward. Of the two questions—the foreign affairs and the home affairs of our Republic—I think that home affairs interest you more. That is how it should be. But, comrades, you forget that home affairs depend on foreign affairs, and I therefore have thought it my duty to tell you how and why the Polish war brought us up against the international imperialists and then led to peace; how and why this peace is precarious, and what has to be done to consolidate it. I hope that, in this matter, after you have discussed all the other questions and set forth all the problems in a calm fashion, you will not behave like certain personages in the fable mentioned by one of the speakers,[105] about the lynx which waits for the goat and the ram to fall out, so as to devour them both. You will not give that satisfaction to the lynx—of that I am sure. However furiously the goat and the ram may clash, we shall give no satisfaction to the lynx. (*Applause and cheers.*) Comrades, if extreme dissatisfaction and impatience have been expressed here so often, we all know that freedom of speech is the primary rule of procedure at meetings. At this meeting you have broken this rule—it is because the majority of the peasants are experiencing all too severely the effects of the very grave situation that has arisen in the localities. Most of the peasants are feeling all too severely the effects of famine, cold and excessive taxation. ("*Hear, Hear!*" *and applause.*) It was, in the main, for this that most of the speakers upbraided the central government, directly and indirectly. One got a feeling that the comrades did not even want to give a full hearing to speakers in whose speeches they heard no replies to this acute problem. One of the speakers, I do not remember which, said that in his opinion I had evaded this issue. I consider this assertion groundless.

The position of the Soviet Republic is most grave, which made us hurry to conclude peace before the winter campaign set in. That haste stemmed from a desire to avoid a winter campaign, a realisation that it is better to have a worse frontier, that is to say, to get less Byelorussian territory and be in a position to wrest fewer Byelorussian peasants from the yoke of the bourgeoisie, than to impose fresh hardships and another winter campaign on the peasants of Russia. Such were our reasons. You know that the poor harvest of this year has aggravated the peasants' need. However, the measure in which this ties us in our home policy is not generally realised. I think that you will all be fully informed on the subject of taxation. You will also hear what the speaker on the food policy will have to say. And all I want is to draw your attention to the close connection between the internal situation and the external. Let us take, for example, the sittings of our Council of Defence and the Council of People's Commissars. At these meetings we even have to deal with the question of the running of each train, the grain-requisitioning quotas imposed upon the Great Russia gubernias—quotas that are often extremely rigorous. Two or three weeks ago the Council of People's Commissars considered the question of the excessively rigorous quotas, established by the central authorities; it decided that they should be reduced. At whose expense is this to be done? There can be only one reply to this question: only at the expense of outlying regions that are richer in grain, namely, Siberia and the Kuban, and by making it possible to obtain grain from the Ukraine. We are getting grain from Siberia and from the Kuban, but we cannot get grain from the Ukraine because warfare is raging there, and the Red Army has to fight the bands that infest that area. We have to settle the problem of almost every train. We have seen what this meeting has turned into, the dissatisfaction expressed here, and the voices raised in loud protest. We know the reason for all this. We know that all those who have revealed such emotion here are sick at heart because there is no fodder, livestock is perishing, and taxation is so heavy. The comrade who said that these cries of protest were something new to us was wrong. Both from telegrams and reports from the provinces we know of the heavy loss of cattle as a result of the grave fodder situation, and we all realise the difficulties. But we also know the solution. There is only one solution—Siberia, the Kuban and the Ukraine.

From Siberia we had to bring up troops to the Wrangel front, and in the Council of Defence there were two or three very painful meetings when comrades came with the demand that we should cancel the special food trains. After the most bitter wrangling and bargaining, we ended by deciding to somewhat curtail the number of food trains. However, we would like to hear more weighty and serious criticism. We know all about the outcries and lamentations that the farms are being ruined. That is why even the truce that comes into force on the 18th, even though the Poles are entitled to cancel it at forty-eight hours' notice, will give us some respite and relief; in any case there will be more trainloads of grain from Siberia and the Kuban in the next few weeks. Of course, the need is so acute and the crop shortage so severe that the relief this will provide will not be very great. We should not, of course, deceive ourselves and say that it will remove all our difficulties and enable us to discontinue the grain requisitioning quotas.

That is something I cannot and will not say. State your views precisely, let us have your definite suggestions for relieving the heavy taxation, and the representatives of the workers' and peasants' government will examine them with the closest attention, because we must find a way of easing this exceedingly painful situation. There is no less grain in the Ukraine than in the Kuban; there is perhaps even more, but so far we have been able to get hardly anything from the Ukraine under the grain quotas, which have been fixed at 600,000,000 poods, and which could meet all the needs of our industries and help restore them. We have struck the Ukraine off our accounts: not a single pood can be expected from the Ukraine, because of the bandits there, and because the war with Wrangel compels us to say that we cannot be sure of getting a single pood from the Ukraine. Such is the situation, which, notwithstanding your legitimate impatience and quite justified indignation, makes us divert all our attention to the Polish and the Wrangel fronts. That is why when comrades say that they are not against giving help, but they want that help to be given freely, we say: "Go and help the front!"

I shall conclude my brief remarks by reminding you of what I said at the end of my report, namely, that every time the Soviets have had to get out of a difficult situation—when Denikin was in Orel, or when Yudenich was within five versts of Petrograd—when the situation seemed not only difficult, but desperate, a hundred times as difficult as it is now, the Soviet government got out of that situation by calling together meetings of workers and peasants like the present one and telling them the unvarnished truth. That is why I say that whether or not Wrangel will soon be crushed depends, not on a decision of the central government but on the way in which the representatives from the localities, after giving vent to their dissatisfaction, after finishing the struggle which the above-mentioned comrade has called a clash between the goats and the rams—an indispensable thing—and after voicing their complaints, accusations and recriminations—the way in which local representatives reply to the question whether they themselves want freedom, quite apart from any decision by the central government. Here we cannot give orders; it will depend on your own decisions, when you come to discuss the state of affairs, the grain-requisitioning quotas, taxation, Wrangel, etc.—it will depend on you. Let each man have his say; give vent to all your reproaches; censure us ten times more severely—that is your right and your duty. You have come here to express your opinion plainly and bluntly. But when you have done all that, just reflect calmly what you want to contribute and do so as to finish with Wrangel as quickly as possible. I think that we shall reach such thorough agreement on this question that—I repeat in conclusion—never will the lynx benefit from our arguments, recriminations and accusations. (*Applause.*)

Published in 1920 in the book: *Verbatim Reports of the Plenary Sessions of the Moscow Soviet of Workers', Peasants' and Red Army Deputies*

Published according to the text in the book

TELEGRAM TO THE SOVIET GOVERNMENT OF THE UKRAINE AND THE GENERAL HEADQUARTERS OF THE SOUTHERN FRONT

In reply to your telegram concerning the poor peasants I am informing you of my *personal* opinion. If their temper is really revolutionary, the following should be regarded as a programme: 1) collective cultivation; 2) hiring stations; 3) confiscation of the kulaks' land over and above the labour norm; 4) grain surpluses to be collected in full, part of the grain to be turned over to the poor peasants; 5) the kulaks' agricultural implements to be handed over to the hiring stations; 6) these measures to be applied only given successful collective cultivation of the soil, and effective control. The question of communes should be posed last, since nothing is more dangerous than the formation of pseudo-communes, with the participation of individual militants who thus become detached from the main body of the peasantry. The greatest prudence should be exercised in introducing innovations, and the possibility of achieving what is being undertaken should be triple-checked.

Lenin

Chairman of the Council of People's Commissars

Written on October 16, 1920
First published in 1942

Published according to the carbon copy

A CONTRIBUTION TO THE HISTORY OF THE QUESTION OF THE DICTATORSHIP [106]

A NOTE

The question of the dictatorship of the proletariat is the fundamental question of the modern working-class movement in all capitalist countries without exception. To elucidate this question fully, a knowledge of its history is required. On an international scale, the history of the doctrine of revolutionary dictatorship in general, and of the dictatorship of the proletariat in particular, coincides with the history of revolutionary socialism, and especially with the history of Marxism. Moreover—and this, of course, is the most important thing of all—the history of all revolutions by the oppressed and exploited classes, against the exploiters, provides the basic material and source of our knowledge on the question of dictatorship. Whoever has failed to understand that dictatorship is essential to the victory of any revolutionary class has no understanding of the history of revolutions, or else does not want to know anything in this field.

With reference to Russia, special importance attaches, as far as theory is concerned, to the Programme of the Russian Social-Democratic Labour Party as drafted in 1902-03 by the editorial board of *Zarya* and *Iskra*, or, more exactly, drafted by G. Plekhanov, and edited, amended and endorsed by that editorial board. In this Programme, the question of the dictatorship of the proletariat is stated in clear and definite terms, and, moreover, is linked up with the struggle against Bernstein, against opportunism. Most important of all, however, is of course the experience of revolution, i.e., in the case of Russia, the experience of the year 1905.

The last three months of that year—October, November and December—were a period of a remarkably vigorous and broad mass revolutionary struggle, a period that saw a combination of the two most powerful methods of that struggle: the mass political strike and an armed uprising. (Let us note parenthetically that as far back as *May* 1905 the Bolshevik congress, the "Third Congress of the Russian Social-Democratic Labour Party", declared that "the task of organising the proletariat for direct struggle against the autocracy by means of the armed uprising" was "one of the major and most urgent tasks of the Party", and instructed all Party organisations to "explain the role of mass political strikes, which may be of great importance at the beginning and during the progress of the uprising".[107])

For the first time in world history, the revolutionary struggle attained such a high stage of development and such an impetus that an armed uprising was combined with that specifically proletarian weapon—the mass strike. This experience is clearly of world significance to *all* proletarian revolutions. It was studied by the Bolsheviks with the greatest attention and diligence in both its political and its economic aspects. I shall mention an analysis of the month-by-month statistics of economic and political strikes in 1905, of the relations between them, and the level of development achieved by the strike struggle for the first time in world history. This analysis was published by me in 1910 and 1911 in the *Prosveshcheniye* journal, a summary of it being given in Bolshevik periodicals brought out abroad at the time.[108]

The mass strikes and the armed uprisings raised, as a matter of course, the question of the revolutionary power and dictatorship, for these forms of struggle inevitably led—initially on a local scale—to the ejection of the old ruling authorities, to the seizure of power by the proletariat and the other revolutionary classes, to the expulsion of the landowners, sometimes to the seizure of factories, and so on and so forth. The revolutionary mass struggle of the time gave rise to organisations previously unknown in world history, such as the *Soviets of Workers' Deputies*, followed by the Soviets of Soldiers' Deputies, Peasants' Committees, and the like. Thus the fundamental questions (Soviet power and the dictatorship of the proletariat) that are now engaging the minds of class-conscious workers all over the world were posed in a practical form at the end of 1905. While such outstanding representatives of the revolutionary proletariat and of unfalsified Marxism as Rosa Luxemburg, immediately realised the significance of this practical experience and made a critical analysis of it at meetings and in the press, the vast majority of the official representatives of the official Social-Democratic and socialist parties—including both the reformists and people of the type of the future "Kautskyites", "Longuetists", the followers of Hillquit in America, etc.—proved absolutely incapable of grasping the significance of this experience and of performing their duty as *revolutionaries*, i.e., of setting to work to study and propagate the lessons of this experience.

In Russia, immediately after the defeat of the armed uprising of December 1905, both the Bolsheviks and the Mensheviks set to work to sum up this experience. This work was especially expedited by what was called the Unity Congress of the Russian Social-Democratic Labour Party, held in Stockholm in April 1906, where both Mensheviks and Bolsheviks were represented, and formally united. The most energetic preparations for this Congress were made by both these groups. Early in 1906, prior to the Congress, both groups published drafts of their resolutions on all the most important questions. These draft resolutions—reprinted in my pamphlet, *Report on the Unity Congress of the R.S.D.L.P.* (*A Letter to the St. Petersburg Workers*), Moscow, 1906 (110 pages, nearly half of which are taken up with the draft resolutions of both groups and with the resolutions finally adopted by the Congress)—provide the most important material for a study of the question as it stood at the time.

By that time, the disputes as to the significance of the Soviets were already linked up with the question of dictatorship. The Bolsheviks had raised the question of the dictatorship even *prior to* the revolution of October 1905 (see my pamphlet *Two Tactics of Social-Democracy in the Democratic Revolution*, Geneva, July 1905; reprinted in a volume of collected articles entitled *Twelve Years*). The Mensheviks took a negative stand with regard to the "dictatorship" slogan; the Bolsheviks emphasised that the Soviets of Workers' Deputies were "*actually an embryo of a new revolutionary power*", as was literally said in the draft of the Bolshevik resolution (p. 92 of my *Report*). The Mensheviks acknowledged the importance of the Soviets; they were in favour of "helping to organise" them, etc., but they did not regard them as embryos of revolutionary power, did not in general say anything about a "new revolutionary power" of this or some similar type, and flatly rejected the slogan of dictatorship. It will easily be seen that this attitude to the question already contained the seeds of *all* the present disagreements with the Mensheviks. It will also be easily seen that, in their attitude to this question, the Mensheviks (both Russian and non-Russian, such as the Kautskyites, Longuetists and the like) have been behaving like reformists or opportunists, who recognise the proletarian revolution in word, but *in deed reject what is most essential and fundamental in the concept of "revolution"*.

Even before the revolution of 1905, I analysed, in the afore-mentioned pamphlet, *Two Tactics*, the arguments of the Mensheviks, who accused me of having "imperceptibly substituted 'dictatorship' for 'revolution'" (*Twelve Years*, p. 459). I showed in detail that, by this very accusation, the Mensheviks revealed their opportunism, their true political nature, as toadies to the liberal bourgeoisie and conductors of its influence in the ranks of the proletariat. When the revolution becomes an unquestioned force, I said, even its opponents begin to "recognise the revolution"; and I pointed (in the summer of 1905) to the example of the Russian liberals, who remained constitutional monarchists. At present, in 1920, one might add that in Germany and Italy the liberal bourgeois—or at least the most educated and adroit of them—are ready to "recognise the revolution". But by "recognising" the revolution, and at the same time refusing to recognise the *dictatorship* of a definite class (or of definite classes), the Russian liberals and the Mensheviks of that time, and the present-day German and Italian liberals, Turatists and Kautskyites, have revealed their *reformism*, their absolute unfitness to be revolutionaries.

Indeed, when the revolution has already become an unquestioned force, when even the liberals "recognise" it, and when the ruling classes not only see but also feel the invincible might of the oppressed masses, then the *entire question*—both to the theoreticians and the leaders of practical policy—reduces itself *to an exact class definition of the revolution*. However, without the concept of "dictatorship", this precise class definition *cannot* be given. One cannot be a revolutionary *in fact* unless one prepares for dictatorship. This truth was not understood in 1905 by the Mensheviks, and it is not understood in 1920 by the Italian, German, French and other socialists, who are afraid of the severe "conditions" of the Communist International; this truth is feared by people who are capable of recognising the dictatorship *in word*, but are incapable of *preparing for it in deed*. It will therefore not be irrelevant to quote at length the explanation of Marx's views, which I published in July 1905 in opposition to the Russian Mensheviks, but is equally applicable to the West-European Mensheviks of 1920. (Instead of giving titles of newspapers, etc., I shall merely indicate whether Mensheviks or Bolsheviks are referred to.)

"In his notes to Marx's articles in *Die Neue Rheinische Zeitung* of 1848, Mehring tells us that one of the reproaches levelled at this newspaper by bourgeois publications was that it had allegedly demanded 'the immediate introduction of a dictatorship as the sole means of achieving democracy' (Marx, *Nachlass*, Vol. III, p. 53). From the vulgar bourgeois standpoint the terms of dictatorship and democracy are mutually exclusive. Failing to understand the theory of class struggle and accustomed to seeing in the political arena the petty squabbling of the various bourgeois circles and coteries, the bourgeois understands by dictatorship the annulment of all liberties and guarantees of democracy, arbitrariness of every kind, and every sort of abuse of power, in a dictator's personal interests. In fact, it is precisely this vulgar bourgeois view that is to be observed among our Mensheviks, who attribute the partiality of the Bolsheviks for the slogan of 'dictatorship' to Lenin's 'passionate desire to try his luck' (*Iskra* No. 103, p. 3, column 2). In order to explain to the Mensheviks the meaning of the term class dictatorship as distinct from a personal dictatorship, and the tasks of a democratic dictatorship as distinct from a socialist dictatorship, it would not be amiss to dwell on the views of *Die Neue Rheinische Zeitung*.[109]

"'After a revolution,' *Die Neue Rheinische Zeitung* wrote on September 14, 1848, 'every provisional organisation of the state requires a dictatorship, and an energetic dictatorship at that. From the very beginning we have reproached Camphausen [the head of the Ministry after March 18, 1848] for not acting dictatorially, for not having immediately smashed up and eliminated the remnants of the old institutions. And while Herr Camphausen was lulling himself with constitutional illusions, the defeated party [i.e., the party of reaction) strengthened its positions in the bureaucracy and in the army, and here and there even began to venture upon open struggle.'[110]

"These words, Mehring justly remarks, sum up in a few propositions all that was propounded in detail in *Die Neue Rheinische Zeitung* in long articles on the Camphausen Ministry. What do these words of Marx tell us? That a provisional revolutionary government *must* act dictatorially (a proposition which the Mensheviks were totally unable to grasp since they were fighting shy of the slogan of dictatorship), and that the task of such a dictatorship is to destroy the remnants of the old institutions (which is precisely what was clearly stated in the resolution of the Third Congress of the Russian Social-Democratic Labour Party [Bolsheviks] on the struggle against counter-revolution, and was omitted in the Mensheviks' resolution as shown above). Third, and last, it follows from these words that Marx castigated the bourgeois democrats for entertaining 'constitutional illusions' in a period of revolution and open civil war. The meaning of these words becomes particularly obvious from the article in *Die Neue Rheinische Zeitung* of June 6, 1848.

"'A Constituent National Assembly', Marx wrote, 'must first of all be an active, revolutionary active assembly. The Frankfurt Assembly,[111] however, is busying itself with school exercises in parliamentarianism while allowing the government to act. Let us assume that this learned assembly succeeds, after mature consideration, in evolving the best possible agenda and the best constitution, but what is the use of the best possible agenda and of the best possible constitution, if the German governments have in the meantime placed the bayonet on the agenda?'[112]

"That is the meaning of the slogan: dictatorship....

"Major questions in the life of nations are settled only by force. The reactionary classes themselves are usually the first to resort to violence, to civil war; they are the first to 'place the bayonet on the agenda', as the Russian autocracy has systematically and unswervingly been doing everywhere ever since January 9.[113] And since such a situation has arisen, since the bayonet has really become the main point on the political agenda, since insurrection has proved imperative and urgent—the constitutional illusions and school exercises in parliamentarianism become merely a screen for the bourgeois betrayal of the revolution, a screen to conceal the fact that the bourgeoisie is 'recoiling' from the revolution. It is precisely the slogan of dictatorship that the genuinely revolutionary class must advance, in that case."[114]

That was how the Bolsheviks reasoned on the dictatorship before the revolution of October 1905.

After the experience of this revolution, I made a detailed study of the question of dictatorship in the pamphlet, *The Victory of the Cadets and the Tasks of the Workers' Party*, St. Petersburg, 1906 (the pamphlet is dated March 28, 1906). I shall quote the most important arguments from this pamphlet, only substituting for a number of proper names a simple indication as to whether the reference is to the Cadets or to the Mensheviks. Generally speaking, this pamphlet was directed against the Cadets, and partly also against the non-party liberals, the semi-Cadets, and the semi-Mensheviks. But, actually speaking, everything said therein about dictatorship applies in fact to the Mensheviks, who were constantly sliding to the Cadets' position on this question.

"At the moment when the firing in Moscow was subsiding, and when the military and police dictatorship was indulging in its savage orgies, when repressions and mass torture were raging all over Russia, voices were raised in the Cadet press against the use of force by the Lefts, and against the strike committees organised by the revolutionary parties. The Cadet professors on the Dubasovs' pay roll, who are peddling their science, went to the length of translating the word 'dictatorship' by the words 'reinforced security'. These 'men of science' even distorted their high-school Latin in order to discredit the revolutionary struggle. Please note once and for all, you Cadet gentlemen, that dictatorship means unlimited power, based on force, and not on law. In civil war, any victorious power can only be a dictatorship. The point is, however, that there is the dictatorship of a minority over the majority, the dictatorship of a handful of police officials over the people; and there is the dictatorship of the overwhelming majority of the people over a handful of tyrants, robbers and usurpers of the people's power. By their vulgar distortion of the scientific concept 'dictatorship', by their outcries against the violence of the Left at a time when the Right are resorting to the most lawless and outrageous violence the Cadet gentlemen have given striking evidence of the position the 'compromisers' take in the intense revolutionary struggle. When the struggle flares up, the 'compromiser' cravenly runs for cover. When the revolutionary people are victorious (October 17), the 'compromiser' creeps out of his hiding-place, boastfully preens himself, shouting and raving until he is hoarse: 'That was a "glorious" political strike!' But when victory goes to the counter-revolution, the 'compromiser' begins to heap hypocritical admonitions and edifying counsel on the vanquished. The successful strike was 'glorious'. The defeated strikes were criminal, mad, senseless, and anarchistic. The defeated insurrection was folly, a riot of surging elements, barbarity and stupidity. In short, his political conscience and political wisdom prompt the 'compromiser' to cringe before the side that for the moment is the strongest, to get in the way of the combatants, hindering first one side and then the other, to tone down the struggle and to blunt the revolutionary consciousness of the people who are waging a desperate struggle for freedom."[115]

To proceed. It would be highly opportune at this point to quote the explanations on the question of dictatorship, directed against Mr. R. Blank. In 1906, this R. Blank, in a newspaper actually Menshevik though formally non-partisan,[116] set forth the Mensheviks' views and extolled their efforts "to direct the Russian Social-Democratic movement along the path that is being followed by the whole of the international Social-Democratic movement, led by the great Social-Democratic Party of Germany".

In other words, like the Cadets, R. Blank contraposed the Bolsheviks, as unreasonable, non-Marxist, rebel, etc., revolutionaries, to the "reasonable" Mensheviks, and presented the German Social-Democratic Party as a Menshevik party as well. This is the usual method of the international trend of social-liberals, pacifists, etc., who in all countries extol the reformists and opportunists, the Kautskyites and the Longuetists, as "reasonable" socialists in contrast with the "madness" of the Bolsheviks.

This is how I answered Mr. R. Blank in the above-mentioned pamphlet of 1906:

"Mr. Blank compares two periods of the Russian revolution. The first period covers approximately October-December 1905. This is the period of the revolutionary whirlwind. The second is the present period, which, of course, we have a right to call the period of Cadet victories in the Duma elections, or, perhaps, if we take the risk of running ahead somewhat, the period of a Cadet Duma.

"Regarding this period, Mr. Blank says that the turn of intellect and reason has come again, and it is possible to resume deliberate, methodical and systematic activities. On the other hand, Mr. Blank describes the first period as a period in which theory diverged from practice. All Social-Democratic principles and ideas vanished; the tactics that had always been advocated by the founders of Russian Social-Democracy were forgotten, and even the very pillars of the Social-Democratic world outlook were uprooted.

"Mr. Blank's main assertion is merely a statement of fact: the whole theory of Marxism diverged from 'practice' in the period of the revolutionary whirlwind.

"Is that true? What is the first and main 'pillar' of Marxist theory? It is that the only thoroughly revolutionary class in modern society, and therefore, the advanced class in every revolution, is the proletariat. The question is then: has the revolutionary whirlwind uprooted this 'pillar' of the Social-Democratic world outlook? On the contrary, the whirlwind has vindicated it in the most brilliant fashion.

It was the proletariat that was the main and, at first, almost the only *fighter* in this period. For the first time in history, perhaps, a bourgeois revolution was marked by the employment of a purely proletarian weapon, i.e., the mass political strike, on a scale unprecedented even in the most developed capitalist countries. The proletariat marched into battle that was definitely revolutionary, at a time when the Struves and the Blanks were calling for participation in the Bulygin Duma and when the Cadet professors were exhorting the students to keep to their studies. With its proletarian weapon, the proletariat won for Russia the whole of that so-called 'constitution', which since then has only been mutilated, chopped about and curtailed. The proletariat in October 1905 employed those tactics of struggle that *six months before* had been laid down in the resolution of the *Bolshevik* Third Congress of the Russian Social-Democratic Labour Party, which had strongly emphasised the necessity of combining the mass political strike with insurrection; and it is this combination that characterises the whole period of the 'revolutionary whirlwind', the whole of the last quarter of 1905. Thus our ideologist of petty bourgeoisie has distorted reality in the most brazen and glaring manner. He has not cited a single fact to prove that Marxist theory diverged from practical experience in the period of the 'revolutionary whirlwind'; he has tried to obscure the main feature of this whirlwind, which most brilliantly confirmed the correctness of 'all Social-Democratic principles and ideas', of 'all the pillars of the Social-Democratic world outlook'.

"But what was the real reason that induced Mr. Blank to come to the monstrously wrong conclusion that all Marxist principles and ideas vanished in the period of the 'whirlwind'? It is very interesting to examine this circumstance; it still further exposes the real nature of philistinism in politics.

"What is it that mainly distinguished the period of the 'revolutionary whirlwind' from the present 'Cadet' period, as regards the various forms of political activity and the various methods by which the people make history? First and mainly it is that during the period of the 'whirlwind' certain special methods of making history were employed which are foreign to other periods of political life. The following were the most important of these methods: 1) the '*seizure' by the people of political liberty*—its exercise without any rights and laws, and without any limitations (freedom of assembly, even if only in the universities, freedom of the press, freedom of association, the holding of congresses, etc.); 2) the creation of new organs of *revolutionary authority*—Soviets of Workers', Soldiers', Railwaymen's and Peasants' Deputies, new rural and urban authorities, and so on, and so forth. These bodies were set up exclusively by the *revolutionary* sections of the people, they were formed irrespective of all laws and regulations, entirely in a revolutionary way, as a product of the native genius of the people, as a manifestation of the independent activity of the people which had rid itself, or was ridding itself, of its old police fetters. Lastly, they were indeed organs of *authority*, for all their rudimentary, spontaneous, amorphous and diffuse character, in composition and in activity. They acted as a government, when, for example, they seized printing plants (in St. Petersburg), and arrested police officials who were preventing the revolutionary people from exercising their rights (such cases also occurred in St. Petersburg, where the new organ of authority concerned was weakest, and where the old government was strongest). They acted as a government when they appealed to the whole people to withhold money from the old government. They confiscated the old government's funds (the railway strike committees in the South) and used them for the needs of the new, the people's government. Yes, these were undoubtedly the embryos of a new, people's, or, if you will, revolutionary government. In their social and political character, they were the rudiments of the dictatorship of the revolutionary elements of the people. This surprises you, Mr. Blank and Mr. Kiesewetter! You do not see here the 'reinforced security', which for the bourgeois is tantamount to dictatorship? We have already told you that you have not the faintest notion of the scientific concept 'dictatorship'. We will explain it to you in a moment; but first we will deal with the *third* 'method' of activity in the period of the 'revolutionary whirlwind': *the use by the people of force against those who used force against the people.*

"The organs of authority that we have described represented a dictatorship in embryo, for they recognised *no* other authority, *no* law and *no* standards, no matter by whom established. Authority—unlimited, outside the law, and based on force in the most direct sense of the word—is dictatorship. But the force on which this new authority was based, and sought to base itself, was not the force of bayonets usurped by a handful of militarists, not the power of the 'police force', not the power of money, nor the power of any previously established institutions. It was nothing of the kind. The new organs of authority possessed neither arms, nor money, nor old institutions. Their power—can you imagine it, Mr. Blank and Mr. Kiesewetter?—had nothing in common with the old instruments of power, nothing in common with 'reinforced security', if we do not have in mind the reinforced security established to protect the people from the tyranny of the police and of the other organs of the old regime.

"What was the power based on, then? It was based on the mass of the people. That is the *main* feature that distinguished this new authority from all preceding organs of the old regime. The latter were the instruments of the rule of the minority over the people, over the masses of workers and peasants. The former was an instrument of the rule of the people, of the workers and peasants, over the minority, over a handful of police bullies, over a handful of privileged nobles and government officials. That is the difference between dictatorship *over* the people and dictatorship *of* the revolutionary people: mark this well, Mr. Blank and Mr. Kiesewetter! As the dictatorship of a minority, the old regime was able to maintain itself solely with the aid of police devices, solely by preventing the masses of the people from taking part in the government, and from supervising the government. The old authority persistently distrusted the masses, feared the light, maintained itself by deception. As the dictatorship of the overwhelming majority, the new authority maintained itself and could maintain itself solely because it enjoyed the confidence of the vast masses, solely because it, in the freest, widest, and most resolute manner, enlisted all the masses in the task of government. It concealed nothing, it had no secrets, no regulations, no formalities. It said, in effect: are you a working man? Do you want to fight to rid Russia of the gang of police bullies? You are our comrade. Elect your deputy. Elect him at once, immediately, whichever way you think best. We will willingly and gladly accept him as a full member of our Soviet of Workers' Deputies, Peasant Committee, Soviet of Soldiers' Deputies, and so forth. It was an authority open to all, it carried out all its functions before the eyes of the masses, was accessible to the masses, sprang directly from the masses; and was a direct and immediate instrument of the popular masses, of their will. Such was the new authority, or, to be exact, its embryo, for the victory of the old authority trampled down the shoots of this young plant very soon.

"Perhaps, Mr. Blank or Mr. Kiesewetter, you will ask: why 'dictatorship', why 'force'? Is it necessary for a vast mass to use force against a handful? Can tens and hundreds of millions be dictators over a thousand or ten thousand?

"That question is usually put by people who for the first time hear the term 'dictatorship' used in what to them is a new connotation. People are accustomed to see only a police authority and only a police dictatorship. The idea that there can be government without any police, or that dictatorship need not be a police dictatorship, seems strange to them. You say that millions need not resort to force against thousands? You are mistaken; and your mistake arises from the fact that you do not regard a phenomenon in its process of development. You forget that the new authority does not drop from the skies, but grows up, arises parallel with, and in opposition to the old authority, in struggle against it. Unless force is used against tyrants armed with the weapons and instruments of power, the people cannot be liberated from tyrants.

"Here is a very simple analogy, Mr. Blank and Mr. Kiesewetter, which will help you to grasp this idea, which seems so remote and 'fantastic' to the Cadet mind. Let us suppose that Avramov is injuring and torturing Spiridonova. On Spiridonova's side, let us say, are tens and hundreds of unarmed people. On Avramov's side there is a handful of Cossacks. What would the people do if Spiridonova were being tortured, not in a dungeon but in public? They would resort to force against Avramov and his body-guard. Perhaps they would sacrifice a few of their comrades, shot down by Avramov; but in the long run they would forcibly disarm Avramov and his Cossacks, and in all probability would kill on the spot some of these brutes in human form; they would clap the rest into some gaol to prevent them from committing any more outrages and to bring them to judgement before the people.

"So you see, Mr. Blank and Mr. Kiesewetter, when Avramov and his Cossacks torture Spiridonova, that is military and police dictatorship over the people. When a revolutionary people (that is to say, a people capable of fighting the tyrants, and not only of exhorting, admonishing, regretting, condemning, whining and whimpering; not a philistine narrow-minded, but a revolutionary people) resorts to force against Avramov and the Avramovs, that is a dictatorship of the revolutionary people. It is a *dictatorship*, because it is the authority of the people over Avramov, an authority unrestricted by any laws (the philistines, perhaps, would be opposed to rescuing Spiridonova from Avramov by force, thinking it to be against the 'law'. They would no doubt ask: Is there a 'law' that permits the killing of Avramov? Have not some philistine ideologists built up the 'resist not evil' theory?). The scientific term 'dictatorship' means nothing more nor less than authority untrammeled by any laws, absolutely unrestricted by any rules whatever, and based directly on force. The term 'dictatorship' *has no other meaning but this*—mark this well, Cadet gentlemen. Again, in the analogy we have drawn, we see the dictatorship *of the people*, because the people, the mass of the population, unorganised, 'casually' assembled at the given spot, itself appears on the scene, exercises justice and metes out punishment, exercises power and creates a new, revolutionary law. Lastly, it is the dictatorship of the *revolutionary* people. Why only of the revolutionary, and not of the whole people? Because among the whole people, constantly suffering, and most cruelly, from the brutalities of the Avramovs, there are some who are physically cowed and terrified; there are some who are morally degraded by the 'resist not evil' theory, for example, or simply degraded not by theory, but by prejudice, habit, routine; and there are indifferent people, whom we call philistines, petty-bourgeois people who are more inclined to hold aloof from intense struggle, to pass by or even to hide themselves (for fear of getting mixed up in the fight and getting hurt). That is why the dictatorship is exercised, not by the whole people, but by the revolutionary people who, however, do not shun the whole people, who explain to all the people the motives of their actions in all their details, and who willingly enlist the *whole* people not only in 'administering' the state, but in governing it too, and indeed in organising the state.

"Thus our simple analogy contains *all the elements* of the scientific concept 'dictatorship of the revolutionary people', and also of the concept 'military and police dictatorship'. We can now pass from this simple analogy, which even a learned Cadet professor can grasp, to the more complex developments of social life.

"Revolution, in the strict and direct sense of the word, is a period in the life of a people when the anger accumulated during centuries of Avramov brutalities breaks forth into *actions*, not merely into words; and into the actions of *millions of the people*, not merely of individuals. The people awaken and rise up to rid themselves of the Avramovs. The people rescue the countless numbers of Spiridonovas in Russian life from the Avramovs, use force against the Avramovs, and establish their authority over the Avramovs. Of course, this does not take place so easily, and not 'all at once', as it did in our analogy, simplified for Professor Kiesewetter. This struggle of the people against the Avramovs, a struggle in the strict and direct sense of the word, this act of the people in throwing the Avramovs off their backs, stretches over months and years of 'revolutionary whirlwind'. This act of the people in throwing the Avramovs off their backs is the real content of what is called the great Russian revolution. This act, regarded from the standpoint of the methods of making history, takes place in the forms we have just described in discussing the revolutionary whirlwind, namely: the people seize political freedom, that is, the freedom which the Avramovs had prevented them from exercising; the people create a new, revolutionary authority, authority over the Avramovs, over the tyrants of the old police regime; the people use force against the Avramovs in order to remove, disarm and make harmless these wild dogs, all the Avramovs, Durnovos, Dubasovs, Mins, etc., etc.

"Is it good that the people should apply such unlawful, irregular, unmethodical and unsystematic methods of struggle as seizing their liberty and creating a new, formally unrecognised and revolutionary authority, that it should use force against the oppressors of the people? Yes, it is very good. It is the supreme manifestation of the people's struggle for liberty. It marks that great period when the dreams of liberty cherished by the best men and women of Russia *come true*, when liberty becomes the cause of the masses of the people, and not merely of individual heroes. It is as good as the rescue by the crowd (in our analogy) of Spiridonova from Avramov, and the forcible disarming of Avramov and making him harmless.

"But this brings us to the very pivot of the Cadets' hidden thoughts and apprehensions. A Cadet is the ideologist of the philistines precisely because he looks at politics, at the liberation of the whole people, at revolution, through the spectacles of that same philistine who, in our analogy of the torture of Spiridonova by Avramov, would try to restrain the crowd, advise it not to break the law, not to hasten to rescue the victim from the hands of the torturer, since he is acting in the name of the law. In our analogy, of course, that philistine would be morally a monster; but in social life as a whole, we repeat, the philistine monster is not an individual, but a social phenomenon, conditioned, perhaps, by the deep-rooted prejudices of the bourgeois-philistine theory of law.

"Why does Mr. Blank hold it as self-evident that all Marxist principles were forgotten during the period of 'whirlwind'? Because he distorts Marxism into Brentanoism,[117] and thinks that such 'principles' as the seizure of liberty, the establishment of revolutionary authority and the use of force by the people are not Marxist. This idea runs through the whole of Mr. Blank's article; and not only Mr. Blank's, but the articles of all the Cadets, and of all the writers in the liberal and radical camp who, today, are praising Plekhanov for his love of the Cadets; all of them, right up to the Bernsteinians of *Bez Zaglaviya*,[118] the Prokopoviches, Kuskovas and *tutti quanti*.

"Let us see how this opinion arose and why it was bound to arise.

"It arose directly out of the Bernsteinian or, to put it more broadly, the opportunist concepts of the West-European Social-Democrats. The fallacies of these concepts, which the 'orthodox' Marxists in Western Europe have been systematically exposing all along the line, are now being smuggled into Russia 'on the sly', in a different dressing and on a different occasion. The Bernsteinians accepted and accept Marxism *minus* its directly revolutionary aspect. They do not regard the parliamentary struggle as one of the weapons particularly suitable for definite historical periods, but as the main and almost the sole form of struggle making 'force , 'seizure', 'dictatorship' unnecessary. It is this vulgar philistine distortion of Marxism that the Blanks and other liberal eulogisers of Plekhanov are now smuggling into Russia. They have become so accustomed to this distortion that they do not even think it necessary to prove that Marxist principles and ideas were forgotten in the period of the revolutionary whirlwind.

"Why was such an opinion bound to arise? Because it accords very well with the class standing and interests of the petty bourgeoisie. The ideologists of 'purified' bourgeois society agree with *all* the methods used by the Social-Democrats in their struggle *except those to which the revolutionary people resort in the period of a 'whirlwind'*, and which revolutionary Social-Democrats approve of and help in using. The interests of the bourgeoisie demand that the proletariat should take part in the struggle against the autocracy, but only in a way that does not lead to the supremacy of the proletariat and the peasantry, and does not completely eliminate the old, feudal-autocratic and police organs of state power. The bourgeoisie wants to preserve these organs, only establishing its direct control over them. It needs them *against the proletariat*, whose struggle would be too greatly facilitated if they were completely abolished. That is why the interests of the bourgeoisie as a class require both a monarchy and an Upper Chamber, and the prevention of the dictatorship of the revolutionary people.

Fight the autocracy, the bourgeoisie says to the proletariat, but do not touch the old organs of state power, for I need them. Fight in a 'parliamentary' way, that is, within the limits that we will prescribe by agreement with the monarchy. Fight with the aid of organisations, only not organisations like general strike committees, Soviets of Workers', Soldiers' Deputies, etc., but organisations that are recognised, restricted and made safe for capital by a law that we shall pass by agreement with the monarchy.

"It is clear, therefore, why the bourgeoisie speaks with disdain, contempt, anger and hatred about the period of the 'whirlwind', and with rapture, ecstasy and boundless philistine infatuation for . . . reaction, about the period of constitutionalism as protected by Dubasov. It is once again that constant, invariable quality of the Cadets: seeking to lean on the people and at the same time dreading their revolutionary initiative.

"It is also clear why the bourgeoisie is in such mortal fear of a repetition of the 'whirlwind', why it ignores and obscures the elements of the new revolutionary crisis, why it fosters constitutional illusions and spreads them among the people.

"Now we have fully explained why Mr. Blank and his like declare that in the period of the 'whirlwind' all Marxist principles and ideas were forgotten. Like all philistines, Mr. Blank accepts Marxism *minus* its revolutionary aspect; he accepts Social-Democratic methods of struggle *minus* the most revolutionary and directly revolutionary methods.

"Mr. Blank's attitude towards the period of 'whirlwind' is extremely characteristic as an illustration of bourgeois failure to understand proletarian movements, bourgeois horror of acute and resolute struggle, bourgeois hatred for every manifestation of a radical and directly revolutionary method of solving social historical problems, a method that breaks up old institutions. Mr. Blank has betrayed himself and all his bourgeois narrow-mindedness. Somewhere he heard and read that during the period of whirlwind the Social-Democrats made 'mistakes'—and he had hastened to conclude, and to declare with self-assurance, in tones that brook no contradiction and require no proof, that all the 'principles' of Marxism (of which he has not the least notion!) were forgotten. As for these 'mistakes', we will remark: Has there been a period in the development of the working-class movement, in the development of Social-Democracy, when no mistakes were made, when there was no deviation to the right or the left? Is not the history of the parliamentary period of the struggle waged by the German Social-Democratic Party—the period which all narrow-minded bourgeois all over the world regard as the utmost limit—filled with such mistakes? If Mr. Blank were not an utter ignoramus on problems of socialism, he would easily call to mind Mülberger, Dühring, the *Dampfersubvention*[119] question, the 'Youth',[120] and Bernsteiniad and many, many more. But Mr. Blank is not interested in studying the actual course of development of the Social-Democratic movement; all he wants is to minimise the scope of the proletarian struggle in order to exalt the bourgeois paltriness of his Cadet Party.

"Indeed, if we examine the question in the light of the deviations that the Social-Democratic movement has made from its ordinary, 'normal' course, we shall see that even in this respect there was *more* and not less solidarity and ideological integrity among the Social-Democrats in the period of 'revolutionary whirlwind' than there was before it. The tactics adopted in the period of 'whirlwind' did not further estrange the two wings of the Social-Democratic Party, but brought them closer together. Former disagreements gave way to unity of opinion on the question of armed uprising. Social-Democrats of both factions were active in the Soviets of Workers' Deputies, these peculiar instruments of embryonic revolutionary authority; they drew the soldiers and peasants into these Soviets, they issued revolutionary manifestos jointly with the petty-bourgeois revolutionary parties. Old controversies of the pre-revolutionary period gave way to unanimity on practical questions. The upsurge of the revolutionary tide pushed aside disagreements, compelling Social-Democrats to adopt militant tactics; it swept the question of the Duma into the background and put the question of insurrection on the order of the day; and it brought closer together the Social-Democrats and revolutionary bourgeois democrats in carrying out immediate tasks. In *Severny Golos*,[121] the Mensheviks, jointly with the Bolsheviks, called for a general strike and insurrection; and they called upon the workers to continue this struggle until they had captured power. The revolutionary situation itself suggested practical slogans. There were arguments only over matters of detail in the appraisal of events: for example, *Nachalo*[122] regarded the Soviets of Workers' Deputies as organs of revolutionary local self-government, while *Novaya Zhizn*[123] regarded them as embryonic organs of revolutionary state power that united the proletariat with the revolutionary democrats. *Nachalo* inclined towards the dictatorship of the proletariat. *Novaya Zhizn* advocated the democratic dictatorship of the proletariat and the peasantry. But have not disagreements of this kind been observed at every stage of development of every socialist party in Europe?

"Mr. Blank's misrepresentation of the facts and his gross distortion of recent history are nothing more nor less than a sample of the smug bourgeois banality, for which periods of revolutionary whirlwind seem folly ('all principles are forgotten', 'even intellect and reason almost vanish'), while periods of suppression of revolution and philistine 'progress' (protected by the Dubasovs) seem to be periods of reasonable, deliberate and methodical activity. This comparative appraisal of two periods (the period of 'whirlwind' and the Cadet period) runs through the whole of Mr. Blank's article. When human history rushes forward with the speed of a locomotive, he calls it a 'whirlwind', a 'torrent', the 'vanishing' of all 'principles and ideas'. When history plods along at dray-horse pace, it becomes the very symbol of reason and method. When the masses of the people themselves, with all their virgin primitiveness and simple, rough determination begin to make history, begin to put 'principles and theories' immediately and directly into practice, the bourgeois is terrified and howls that 'intellect is retreating into the background' (is not the contrary the case, heroes of philistinism? Is it not the intellect of the masses, and not of individuals, that invades the sphere of history at such moments? Does not mass intellect at such a time become a verile, effective, and not an armchair force?). When the direct movement of the masses has been crushed by shootings, repressive measures, floggings, unemployment and starvation, when all the parasites of professorial science financed by Dubasov come crawling out of their crevices and begin to administer affairs *on behalf of* the people, *in the name of the masses*, selling and betraying their interests to a privileged few—then the knights of philistinism think that an era of calm and peaceful progress has set in and that 'the turn of intellect and reason has come'. The bourgeois always and everywhere remains true to himself: whether you take *Polyarnaya Zvezda* or *Nasha Zhizn*,[124] whether you read Struve or Blank, you will always find this same narrow-minded, professorially pedantic and bureaucratically lifeless appraisal of periods of revolution and periods of reform. The former are periods of madness, *tolle Jahre*, the disappearance of intellect and reason. The latter are periods of 'deliberate and systematic' activities.

"Do not misinterpret what I am saying. I am not arguing that the Blanks prefer some periods to others. It is not a matter of preference; our subjective preferences do not determine the changes in historical periods. The thing is that *in analysing the characteristics* of this or that period (quite apart from our preferences or sympathies), the Blanks shamelessly *distort the truth*. The thing is that it is just the revolutionary periods which are distinguished by wider, richer, more deliberate, more methodical, more systematic, more courageous and more vivid making of history than periods of philistine, Cadet, reformist progress. But the Blanks turn the truth inside out! They palm off paltriness as magnificent making of history. They regard the inactivity of the oppressed or downtrodden masses as the triumph of 'system' in the work of bureaucrats and bourgeois. They shout about the disappearance of intellect and reason when, instead of the picking of draft laws to pieces by petty bureaucrats and liberal *penny-â-liner** journalists, there begins a period of direct political activity of the 'common people', who simply set to work without more ado to smash all the instruments for oppressing the people, seize power and take what was regarded as belonging to all kinds of robbers of the people—in short, when the intellect and

* In the original these words are in English.—*Ed.*

reason of millions of downtrodden people awaken not only to read books, but for action, vital human action, to make history."[125]

Such was the controversy that was waged in Russia in the years 1905 and 1906 on the question of the dictatorship.

Actually, the Dittmanns, Kautskys, Crispiens, and Hilferdings in Germany, Longuet and Co. in France, Turati and his friends in Italy, the MacDonalds and Snowdens in Britain, etc., argue about the dictatorship exactly as Mr. R. Blank and the Cadets did in Russia in 1905. They do not understand what dictatorship means, do not know how to prepare for it, and are incapable of understanding it and implementing it.

20.10.1920

Published in 1920

Published according to the manuscript

TELEGRAM TO J. V. STALIN

To Stalin, Member of the Revolutionary Military Council of the Republic, *Baku* (wherever he may be)

29.10

I consider it beyond doubt that Georgia will hand Batum over to the Entente, probably secretly, and that the Entente will march on Baku. Study the matter and take urgent steps to fortify the land and sea approaches to Baku, and to bring up heavy artillery, etc. Communicate your decisions.

Lenin

Written on October 29, 1920
First published in 1942

Published according to the manuscript

SPEECH DELIVERED AT AN ALL-RUSSIA CONFERENCE OF POLITICAL EDUCATION WORKERS OF GUBERNIA AND UYEZD EDUCATION DEPARTMENTS NOVEMBER 3, 1920[126]

Comrades, allow me to speak on several ideas, some of which were dealt with by the Central Committee of the Communist Party and by the Council of People's Commissars in connection with the formation of the Chief Committee for Political Education, while others came to me in connection with the draft submitted to the Council of People's Commissars. This draft was adopted yesterday as a basis; its details have still to be discussed.

I shall permit myself only to say, for my part, that at first I was highly averse to any change in the name of your institution. In my opinion, the function of the People's Commissariat of Education is to help people learn and teach others. My Soviet experience has taught me to regard titles as childish jokes; after all, any title is a joke in its way. Another name has now been endorsed: the Chief Committee for Political Education.

As this matter has already been decided, you must take this as nothing more than a personal remark. If the matter is not limited merely to a change of label, it is only to be welcomed.

If we succeed in drawing new people into cultural and educational work, it will not be just a change of title, and then we can reconcile ourselves to the "Soviet" weakness of sticking a label on every new undertaking and every new institution. If we succeed, we shall have achieved something more than ever before.

The link between education and our policy should be the chief inducement in making people join us in our cultural and educational work. A title may express something if there is a need for it, for along the whole line of our educational work we have to abandon the old standpoint that education should be non-political; we cannot conduct educational work in isolation from politics.

That idea has always predominated in bourgeois society. The very term "apolitical" or "non-political" education is a piece of bourgeois hypocrisy, nothing but humbuggery practised on the masses, 99 per cent of whom are humiliated and degraded by the rule of the church, private property and the like. That, in fact, is the way the bourgeoisie, still in the saddle in all bourgeois countries, is deceiving the masses.

The greater the importance of a political apparatus in such countries, the less its independence of capital and its policy.

In all bourgeois states the connection between the political apparatus and education is very strong, although bourgeois society cannot frankly acknowledge it. Nevertheless, this society indoctrinates the masses through the church and the institution of private property.

It is one of our basic tasks to contrapose our own truth to bourgeois "truth", and win its recognition.

The transition from bourgeois society to the policy of the proletariat is a very difficult one, all the more so for the bourgeoisie incessantly slandering us through its entire apparatus of propaganda and agitation. It bends every effort to play down an even more important mission of the dictatorship of the proletariat, its educational mission, which is particularly important in Russia, where the proletariat constitutes a minority of the population. Yet in Russia this mission must be given priority, for we must prepare the masses to build up socialism. The dictatorship of the proletariat would have been out of the question if, in the struggle against the bourgeoisie, the proletariat had not developed a keen class-consciousness, strict discipline and profound devotion, in other words, all the qualities required to assure the proletariat's complete victory over its old enemy.

We do not hold the utopian view that the working masses are ready for a socialist society. From precise facts provided by the entire history of working-class socialism we know that this is not the case, and that preparedness for socialism is created only by large-scale industry, by the strike struggle and by political organisation. To win the victory and accomplish the socialist revolution, the proletariat must be capable of concerted action, of overthrowing the exploiters. We now see that it has acquired all the necessary qualities, and that it translated them into action when it won power.

Education workers, and the Communist Party as the vanguard in the struggle, should consider it their fundamental task to help enlighten and instruct the working masses, in order to cast off the old ways and habituated routine we have inherited from the old system, the private property habits the masses are thoroughly imbued with. This fundamental task of the entire socialist revolution should never be neglected during consideration of the particular problems that have demanded so much attention from the Party's Central Committee and the Council of People's Commissars. What kind of structure should the Chief Committee for Political Education have? How should it be linked up with other institutions? How should it be linked up, not only with the centre but with local bodies? These questions will be answered by comrades who are more competent in the matter, have already gained considerable experience, and have made a special study of the matter. I would like merely to stress the main principles involved. We must put the matter frankly and openly affirm, despite all the old untruths, that education cannot but be linked up with politics.

We are living in an historic period of struggle against the world bourgeoisie, which is far stronger than we are. At this stage of the struggle, we have to safeguard the development of the revolution and combat the bourgeoisie in the military sense and still more by means of our ideology through education, so that the habits, usages and convictions acquired by the working class in the course of many decades of struggle for political liberty—the sum total of these habits, usages and ideas—should serve as an instrument for the education of all working people. It is for the proletariat to decide how the latter are to be educated. We must inculcate in the working people the realisation that it is impossible and inexcusable to stand aside in the proletariat's struggle, which is now spreading more and more to all capitalist countries in the world, and to stand aside in international politics. An alliance of all the world's powerful capitalist countries against Soviet Russia—such is the real basis of international politics today. And it must, after all, be realised that on this will depend the fate of hundreds of millions of working people in the capitalist countries. We know that, at the present moment, there is not a corner of the earth which is not under the control of a small group of capitalist countries. Thus the situation is shaping in such a way that one is faced with the alternative of standing aloof from the present struggle and thereby proving one's utter lack of political consciousness, just like those benighted people who have held aloof from the revolution and the war and do not see the bourgeoisie's gross deception of the masses, the deliberate way in which the bourgeoisie is keeping the masses in ignorance; or else of joining the struggle for the dictatorship of the proletariat.

It is with absolute frankness that we speak of this struggle of the proletariat; each man must choose between joining our side or the other side. Any attempt to avoid taking sides in this issue must end in fiasco.

Observation of the many remnants of the Kerensky gang, the Socialist-Revolutionaries and the Social-Democrats, as represented by the Yudeniches, Kolchaks, Petlyuras, Makhnos and others, has shown us such a variety of forms and shades of counter-revolution in various parts of Russia that we have every reason to consider ourselves far more steeled in the struggle than anybody else is. A glance at Western Europe shows the same thing happening there as in our country—a repetition of our own history. Almost everywhere elements similar to the Kerensky gang are to be met alongside the bourgeoisie. They predominate in a number of countries, especially Germany. One can see the same thing everywhere—the impossibility of taking an intermediate position, and a clear realisation that there must be either a whiteguard dictatorship (for which the bourgeoisie of all the countries of Western Europe are preparing by arming against us), or the dictatorship of the proletariat. We have experienced this so acutely and profoundly that there is no need for me to talk at length about the Russian Communists. Hence there can be only a single conclusion, one that should be the corner-stone of all arguments and theories about the Chief Committee for Political Education: the primacy of the Communist Party's policy must be frankly recognised in the work of that body. We know of no other form of guidance; and no other has been evolved in any country. Parties may represent the interests of their class in one degree or another; they may undergo changes or modifications, but we do not yet know of any better form. The entire course of the struggle waged by Soviet Russia, which for three years has withstood the onslaught of world imperialism, is bound up with the fact that the Party has consciously set out to help the proletariat perform its function of educator, organiser and leader, without which the collapse of capitalism is impossible. The working masses, the masses of peasants and workers, must oust the old intellectualist habits and re-educate themselves for the work of building communism. Otherwise the work of construction cannot be undertaken. Our entire experience shows that this is a very serious matter, and we must therefore give prominence to Party primacy and never lose sight of it when discussing our activities and our organisational development. How this is to be done will still have to be discussed at length; it will have to be discussed in the Party's Central Committee and in the Council of People's Commissars. The decree which was endorsed yesterday laid down the fundamentals in respect of the Chief Committee for Political Education, but it has not yet gone through all the stages in the Council of People's Commissars. The decree will be published within the next few days, and you will see that its final form makes no direct mention of relations with the Party.

We must, however, know and remember that, in law and in practice, the Constitution of the Soviet Republic is based on the tenet that the Party rectifies, prescribes and builds according to a single principle—to enable the communist elements linked with the proletariat to imbue the proletariat with their own spirit, win its adherence, and open its eyes to the bourgeois deceit which we have been trying so long to eliminate. The People's Commissariat of Education has gone through a long struggle; for a long time the teachers' organisation resisted the socialist revolution. Bourgeois prejudices have struck very deep root among the teachers. There has been a long struggle in the form of direct sabotage and of tenacious bourgeois prejudices, and we have to fight for the communist positions slowly, step by step and win them. The Chief Committee for Political Education, which is concerned with extra-mural education, the work of educating and enlightening the masses, is faced with the clear task of combining Party leadership with the effort to gain the adherence of, to imbue with its spirit and to animate with its initiative, this half-million strong army of teachers, this vast institution which is now in the service of the workers. Education workers—the teachers—were trained in the spirit of bourgeois prejudices and habits, in a spirit hostile to the proletariat, with which they have had no ties whatever. We must now train a new army of teachers and instructors who must be in close touch with the Party and its ideas, be imbued with its spirit, and attract the masses of workers, instilling the spirit of communism into them and arousing their interest in what is being done by the Communists.

Since the old customs, habits and ideas must be discarded, the Chief Committee for Political Education and its personnel are faced with a most important task, which they must keep uppermost in their minds. Here we indeed have a dilemma: how can we establish a link between the teachers, most of whom are of the old school, with Party members, with the Communists? That is an extremely difficult problem, one that will require a considerable amount of thought.

Let us consider the means of establishing organisational links between people who are so different. In principle, we cannot for a moment doubt the need of the Communist Party's primacy. Consequently, the purpose of political culture, of political instruction, is to train genuine Communists capable of stamping out falsehood and prejudices and helping the working masses to vanquish the old system and build up a state without capitalists, without exploiters, and without landowners. How can that be done? Only by acquiring the sum total of knowledge that the teachers have inherited from the bourgeoisie. Without this the technical achievements of communism will be impossible, and all hopes for those achievements would be pipe dreams. So the question arises: how are we to organise these people, who are not used to bringing politics into their work, especially the politics that is to our advantage, i.e., politics essential to communism? That, as I have said, is a very difficult problem. We have discussed the matter in the Central Committee, and in discussing it have tried to take into account the lessons of experience. We think that a congress like the one I am addressing today, a conference like yours, will be of great value in this respect. Every Party Committee now has to look from a new angle upon every propagandist, who used to be regarded merely as a man belonging to a definite circle, a definite organisation. Each of them belongs to a ruling party which directs the whole state, and the Soviet Russia's world struggle against the bourgeois system. He is a representative of a fighting class and of a party which runs, and must run, an enormous machine of state. Many a Communist who has been through the splendid school of underground work and has been tested and steeled in the struggle is unwilling or unable to understand the full significance of this change, of this transition, which turns the agitator and propagandist into a leader of agitators, a leader in a huge political organisation. The kind of title he is given, even if it is an embarrassing one—such as superintendent of general schools—does not matter much; what is important is that he should be capable of directing the mass of teachers.

It should be said that the hundreds of thousands of teachers constitute a body that must get the work moving, stimulate thought, and combat the prejudices that to this day still persist among the masses. The heritage of capitalist culture, the fact that the mass of the teachers are imbued with its defects, which prevent them from being Communists, should not deter us from admitting these teachers into the ranks of the political education workers, for these teachers possess the knowledge without which we cannot achieve our aim.

We must put hundreds of thousands of useful people to work in the service of communist education. That is a task that was accomplished at the front, in our Red Army, into which tens of thousands of representatives of the old army were incorporated. In the lengthy process of re-education, they became welded with the Red Army, as they ultimately proved by their victories. This is an example that we must follow in our cultural and educational work. True, this work is not so spectacular, but it is even more important. We need every agitator and propagandist; he will be doing his job if he works in a strictly Party spirit but at the same time does not limit himself to Party work, and remembers that it is his duty to direct hundreds of thousands of teachers, whet their interest, overcome their old bourgeois prejudices, enlist them in the work we are doing, and make them realise the immensity of our work. It is only by tackling that job that we can lead this mass of people, whom capitalism suppressed and drew away from us, along the right path.

Such are the aims that every agitator and propagandist working in the sphere of extra-mural education must pursue and constantly keep in sight. A host of practical difficulties will be encountered in the process, and you must help the cause of communism by becoming representatives and leaders, not only of Party study-circles, but of the entire state administration, which is now in the hands of the working class.

We must overcome resistance from the capitalists in all its forms, not only in the military and the political spheres, but also ideological resistance, which is the most deep-seated and the strongest. It is the duty of our educational workers to accomplish the re-education of the masses. The interest, the thirst for education and knowledge of communism which are to be seen among them are a guarantee of our victory in this field too, although, perhaps, not as rapid as at the front and only after great difficulties and at times even reverses. However, we shall ultimately win.

Last, I should like to dwell on one more point. Perhaps the title of Chief Committee for Political Education is not properly understood. Inasmuch as it makes mention of the political concept, politics is the main thing here.

But how is politics to be understood? If politics is understood in the old sense, one may fall into a grave and profound error. Politics means a struggle between classes; means the relations of the proletariat in its struggle for its emancipation, against the world bourgeoisie. However, in our struggle two aspects of the matter stand out: on the one hand, there is the task of destroying the heritage of the bourgeois system, of foiling the repeated attempts of the whole bourgeoisie to crush the Soviet state. This task has absorbed most of our attention hitherto and has prevented us from proceeding to the other task, that of construction. According to the bourgeois world-outlook, politics was divorced, as it were, from economics. The bourgeoisie said: peasants, you must work for your livelihood; workers, you must work to secure your means of subsistence on the market; as for economic policy, that is the business of your masters. That, however, is not so; politics should be the business of the people, the business of the proletariat. Here we must emphasise the fact that nine-tenths of our time and our work is devoted to the struggle against the bourgeoisie. The victories over Wrangel, of which we read yesterday, and of which you will read today and probably tomorrow, show that one stage of the struggle is coming to an end and that we have secured peace with a number of Western countries; every victory on the war front leaves our hands freer for the internal struggle, for the politics of state organisation. Every step that brings us closer to victory over the whiteguards gradually shifts the focus of the struggle to economic policy. Propaganda of the old type describes and illustrates what communism is. This kind of propaganda is now useless, for we have to show in practice how socialism is to be built. All our propaganda must be based on the political experience of economic development. That is our principal task; whoever interprets it in the old sense will show himself to be a retrograde, one who is incapable of conducting propaganda work among the masses of the peasants and workers. Our main policy must now be to develop the state economically, so as to gather in more poods of grain and mine more poods of coal, to decide how best to utilise these poods of grain and coal and preclude starvation—that is our policy. All our agitation and propaganda must be focussed on this aim. There must be less fine talk, for you cannot satisfy the working people with fine words. As soon as the war enables us to shift the focus from the struggle against the bourgeoisie, from the struggle against Wrangel and the whiteguards, we shall turn to economic policy. And then agitation and propaganda will play a role of tremendous and ever growing importance.

Every agitator must be a state leader, a leader of all the peasants and workers in the work of economic development. He must tell them what one should know, what pamphlets and books one should read to become a Communist.

That is the way to improve our economic life and make it more secure, more social; that is the way to increase production, improve the food situation and distribution of the goods produced, increase coal output, and restore industry without capitalism and without the capitalist spirit.

What does communism consist in? All propaganda for communism must be conducted in a way that will amount to practical guidance of the state's development. Communism must be made comprehensible to the masses of the workers so that they will regard it as their own cause. That task is being poorly accomplished, and thousands of mistakes are being made. We make no secret of the fact. However, the workers and the peasants must themselves build up and improve our apparatus, with our assistance, feeble and inadequate as it is. To us, that is no longer a programme, a theory, or a task to be accomplished; it has become a matter of actual and practical development. Although we suffered some cruel reverses in our war, we have at least learnt from these reverses and won complete victory. Now, too, we must learn a lesson from every defeat and must remember that the workers and peasants have to be instructed by taking the work already performed as an example. We must point out what is bad, so as to avoid it in future.

By taking constructive work as an example, by repeating it time and again, we shall succeed in turning inefficient communist managers into genuine builders, and, in the first place, into builders of our economic life. We shall achieve our targets and overcome all the obstacles which we have inherited from the old system and cannot be eliminated at a single stroke. We must re-educate the masses; they can be re-educated only by agitation and propaganda. The masses must be brought, in the first place, into the work of building the entire economic life. That must be the principal and basic object in the work of each agitator and propagandist, and when he realises this, the success of his work will be assured. (*Loud applause.*)

Bulletin of the All-Russia Conference of Political Education Workers (November 1-8, 1920), Moscow

Published according to the text of the *Bulletin*

DRAFT RESOLUTION ON "THE TASKS OF THE TRADE UNIONS, AND THE METHODS OF THEIR ACCOMPLISHMENT"[127]

In accordance with the decisions of the Ninth Congress of the Communist Party of Russia, the Conference once again draws the attention of the trade unions to the necessity of these decisions being scrupulously fulfilled, and points out in particular that the imperative need of a single economic plan establishing the order of priority of objectives in the general scheme of economic construction is indisputable. At the same time, as was recognised by the Party Conference of September 1920, a gradual but steady transition must be effected from urgency procedures to a more even distribution of forces, particularly in the secondment of the individual unions' best organisers to the All-Russia Central Council of Trade Unions with a view to consolidating that body as a whole, improving the functioning of its apparatus, achieving greater system in the work of all trade unions, and thereby strengthening the entire trade union movement.

This measure should be applied in particular to the Central Committee of the General Transport Workers' Union (*Tsektran*)[128]; an end must be put to its disproportionate growth as compared with the other unions, and the best elements thus released should extend to the entire trade union movement those methods of the broader application of democracy, the promotion of initiative, participation in the management of industry, the development of emulation, and so forth, which have yielded the best practical results.

In conformity with the decisions of the Ninth Congress of the Communist Party of Russia, and recognising as absolutely indispensable the development, extension and consolidation of trade union participation in production management, the Conference instructs the All-Russia Central Council of Trade Unions to sum up immediately the practical experience gained in this respect by the leading unions and enterprises, and to draw up detailed instructions, which will help all trade unions make use of that practical experience and will enjoin them to utilise the latter in a more energetic and systematic fashion.

This refers especially to the utilisation of specialists.

Written in early November 1920

First published in the Fourth (Russian) edition of the *Collected Works*

Published according to the manuscript

ON THE STRUGGLE WITHIN THE ITALIAN SOCIALIST PARTY [129]

Published in 1920

Published according to the manuscript

Pravda No. 213 of September 25, 1920, published a short letter of mine entitled: "Letter to the German and the French Workers Regarding the Discussion on the Second Congress of the Communist International."[130] In its issue of October 5, *Avanti!*, the central organ of the Italian Socialist Party, carried a reprint of this letter with comments of its own, which are worth examining since they strikingly reveal the fallacy of the stand taken by Comrade Serrati, editor of *Avanti!*

"Lenin's explanation," we read, "to some extent mitigates the draconic conditions dictated by comrades who are not quite in a position to correctly appraise men and circumstances at such a distance and in such a different situation...."

"... Lenin spared one of his victims: Modigliani...."

"... Lenin now says—whether on his own behalf or on behalf of the Executive Committee of the Communist International, we do not know—that 'exceptions' [to the general rule] are permissible [with the consent of the Executive Committee]."

The ironical remark about the "victim", which Modigliani, one of the reformists, is supposed to be, is pointless. Despite Serrati's opinion, my failure to mention the name of Modigliani (and of Longuet) was unintentional. I took one name or another as an example, in order to characterise a *trend*, leaving aside, as I still do, the question of *individuals*; I did not undertake to decide this question, considering it of secondary importance, and spoke of the possibility of exceptions. Notwithstanding his statement, Serrati is fully aware (for he makes precise reference to my article in *Pravda*) that I speak, and can do so, *only* on my own behalf, and in no way on behalf of the Executive Committee.

By his remarks, Serrati distracts *Avanti!* readers from the principal, basic and vital question of whether reformists can now be tolerated in the ranks of the Italian party of the revolutionary proletariat. Serrati covers up the falseness of his stand by trying to divert attention from the essential to the secondary and insignificant.

That must be combated. The essentials must be elucidated.

Both in the comment we are dealing with and in other articles, Serrati says that the Moscow Congress (the Second Congress of the Communist International) was not adequately informed about Italian affairs. One might think that the gist of the matter did not lie in the struggle between two fundamental trends, or in the answer to the fundamental question of whether "unity" with the reformists is permissible, but in differences over points that "Moscow" is not precisely informed about!

The glaring fallacy of this view—and of this attempt to distract attention from the main point—is best of all exposed in the *official report* of the discussion *in the Central Committee* of the Italian Socialist Party. This discussion took place in Milan on September 28, 29 and 30 and October 1, only a few days prior to the publication of the issue of *Avanti!* referred to above.

The discussion closed with a vote on two resolutions, one of which may be called a communist, and the other a "Centrist" or evasive resolution, which in a masked form advocated an alliance ("unity"!) with the reformists. The first resolution was carried, seven voting for it (Terracini, Gennari, Regent, Tuntar, Casucci, Marziali, and Bellone); the second resolution was rejected (five in favour: Baratono, Zannerini, Bacci, Giacomini and Serrati).

The first resolution is of a remarkable clarity and precision. It opens with a reference to the "present conditions" of the revolutionary struggle in Italy calling for "greater homogeneity" in the party. It goes on to say that the right to remain in the party was extended to all, on condition of submission to party discipline; however, this condition has not been observed. It would be erroneous, it goes on to say, to expect submission to discipline from those whose convictions are opposed to the principles and tactics of the Third International; consequently, since the twenty-one points of the Moscow conditions have been accepted, a "radical purge" of the party is necessary so as to *eliminate* all reformist and opportunist elements.

Here no reference is made to names or particular instances. A clear political line is laid down. The grounds for the decision are precisely stated, viz., concrete facts from the history of the party in Italy, and concrete features in the revolutionary situation there.

The second resolution is a model of evasiveness and poor diplomacy: we accept the twenty-one points, but consider that "these conditions leave a loop-hole for dubious interpretations", and that "the political criterion of each section of the Third, Communist International should be adapted to the historical conditions and the actual specific features of its country, and submitted for approval to this International". The resolution emphasises "the need to preserve the unity of the Italian Socialist Party on the basis of the twenty-one points"; individual breaches of discipline are to be sternly punished by the Central Committee of the Party.

The communist resolution says that the revolutionary situation calls for greater homogeneity in the party. That is undeniable. The resolution of those who advocate "unity" with the reformists attempts to *evade* this undeniable truth, without daring to dispute it.

The Communist resolution says that it is a feature of the situation in Italy that the condition demanding submission to party decisions by the reformists *has not been observed*. That is the gist of the matter. That being so, it is not merely a mistake *but a crime* to allow the reformists to remain in the party at a time when the general revolutionary situation is *becoming acute*, and the country may even be on the eve of decisive revolutionary battles.

Is this true or not? Have the reformists carried out party decisions? Have they in fact submitted to the party? Have they pursued its policy? The resolution of the defenders of the reformists cannot give an affirmative answer; it cannot challenge the Communists' negative answer, and avoids a reply. It twists and turns, makes general references to the different specific features in the various countries, and does so *in order* to evade and to present in a false light the most important "specific feature" of Italy herself at the moment. What constitutes this specific feature of Italy is the fact that the reformists have already proved incapable in practice of carrying out party decisions and pursuing party policy. By evading this fundamental issue, the resolution of the advocates of unity with the reformists utterly defeats itself.

By this fact alone, Serrati, Baratono, Zannerini, Bacci, and Giacomini have *already* shown quite clearly and irrefutably that they are *fundamentally* wrong, that their political line is *fundamentally false*.

The discussion in the Italian party's Central Committee has ever more forcefully revealed the total falsity of Serrati's line. The Communists were right in saying that as long as the reformists remained what they were they could not but sabotage the revolution, as they had already sabotaged it during the recent revolutionary movement of the Italian workers who were taking over the factories.

That is the pith and marrow of the matter! How is it possible to prepare for revolution and advance towards decisive battles, when there are people in the party who sabotage the revolution? That is not merely a mistake but a crime.

If, as he frankly declared in his letter to *l'Humanité*[131] of October 14, Serrati counted on the expulsion of Turati alone,* this mistake of his has also *already* been revealed by the *facts*. The Italian reformists not only held a factional congress of their own (in Reggio Emilia on October 11, 1920); at this congress they not only reiterated the essence of their reformist views; not only did they give a triumphant reception to Filippo Turati at the congress, but they also declared, through Trèves: "We shall either remain in the

---

* Here is the principal passage in this letter: "We all stand for the Moscow conditions. *The question is how they are to be applied.* I assert that the party must be *purged* of harmful elements, and I proposed that Turati be expelled; but we must not lose the masses belonging to the syndicates [trade unions] and co-operative societies. Others want a *radical split*. That is where we differ." (*l'Humanité*, October 14, Serrati's italics.)

party, or to a man leave it." Let us note in this connection that the bourgeois press and the reformists themselves did their utmost to play up the importance of their factional congress. But in *Avanti!* of October 13 (the Milan edition) we find it frankly stated that the reformists were able to get representatives from only two hundred branches of a party with *thousands* of branches.

But let us dwell in greater detail on Serrati's main argument on the essence of the question. Serrati fears a split that may weaken the party and especially the trade unions, the co-operative societies and the municipalities. These institutions, which are essential to the construction of socialism, must not be destroyed—that is Serrati's main idea. He asks (*Avanti!*, October 2, 1920, the Milan edition): "Where shall we find enough 'Communists', even if only the most ardent new-fledged Communists, to fill the public posts from which we shall drive their holders, as Terracini proposes?" The same idea is expressed by Serrati in an article on the Second Congress of the Third International, in the journal *Comunismo* (No. 24, p. 1627), which he edits: "Picture to yourselves the Milan commune [i.e., the Milan municipality] administered, not by competent people but by novices who only yesterday declared themselves ardent Communists."

Serrati fears the destruction of the trade unions, the co-operative societies and municipalities, and the inefficiency and mistakes of the novices.

What the Communists fear is the reformists' sabotage of the revolution.

This difference reveals Serrati's error of principle. He keeps reiterating a simple idea: the need for flexible tactics. This idea is incontestable. The trouble is that Serrati *leans to the right* when, in the present-day conditions in Italy one should *lean to the left*. To successfully accomplish the revolution and safeguard it, the Italian party must take a *definite step to the left* (without in any way keeping its hands tied or forgetting that subsequent events may well call for definite steps to the right).

Victory in the proletarian revolution *cannot* be achieved, and that revolution *cannot* be safeguarded, while there are reformists and Mensheviks in one's ranks. That is obvious in principle, and has been strikingly confirmed by the experience both of Russia and of Hungary. This is a decisive consideration. It is simply ridiculous to compare with this danger the danger of "losing" the trade unions, co-operative societies, municipalities, etc., or of their failures, mistakes, or collapse. It is not only ridiculous, but criminal. Anyone who would subject the entire revolution to risk for fear of injuring the municipal affairs of Milan and so forth, has completely lost his head, has no idea of the fundamental task of the revolution, and is totally incapable of preparing its victory.

We in Russia made thousands of mistakes and suffered thousands of reverses, losses, etc., owing to the inefficiency of novices and incompetent people in the co-operative societies, municipalities, trade unions, etc. We have no doubt that other and more civilised nations will make *fewer* mistakes of this kind. Notwithstanding these mistakes, we have achieved what is most important, viz., the conquest of power by the proletariat. Moreover, we have maintained that power for three years.

The mistakes mentioned by Comrade Serrati are minor ones and are infinitely easier to rectify than the "mistake" of allowing the sabotage of the revolution by the Mensheviks and the wrecking of the revolution itself. That is self-evident. It has been strikingly demonstrated in the case of Hungary. It has also been confirmed by our experience; during the three years of proletarian government in Russia difficult situations have arisen *many times*, when the Soviet regime would *most certainly* have been overthrown if Mensheviks, reformists, petty-bourgeois democrats had remained in our Party, or even if they had remained in any considerable numbers in the central Soviet bodies, such as the Central Executive Committee.

Serrati has failed to understand the specific features of the transitional situation that exists in Italy, where, as is generally admitted, decisive battles are in store between the proletariat and the bourgeoisie for possession of state power. At such a moment, it is not only absolutely essential to remove the Mensheviks, reformists, Turatists from the party, but it may even be useful to remove some very good Communists too, to remove them from all responsible posts, if they are inclined to waver, and reveal a tendency to drift towards "unity" with the reformists.

Let me give a practical illustration. On the eve of the October Revolution in Russia, and immediately after it, a number of very good Communists in Russia committed an error, one which our people are now loth to recall. Why are they loth to recall it? Because, unless there is particular reason for it, it is wrong to recall mistakes which have been completely set right. But it will be useful to recall this mistake for the benefit of the Italian workers. At the time mentioned, prominent Bolsheviks and Communists, such as Zinoviev, Kamenev, Rykov, Nogin and Milyutin, wavered and expressed the fear that the Bolsheviks were isolating themselves excessively, were taking too much risk in heading for an uprising, and were too unyielding in their attitude towards a certain section of the Mensheviks and Socialist-Revolutionaries. The conflict became so acute that these comrades demonstratively resigned from all responsible posts in Party and government, to the great glee of the enemies of the Soviet revolution. It developed so far that the Central Committee of our Party conducted a very heated controversy in the press with the comrades who had resigned. But a few weeks later—at most a few months—all these comrades realised their mistake and returned to their posts, some of the most responsible in the Party and the Soviets.

Why this happened can readily be understood. On the eve of revolution or at the height of the struggle for its victory, the slightest wavering in the ranks of the Party may *wreck everything*, frustrate the revolution, and wrest power from the hands of the proletariat, for that power has not yet been consolidated, and the onslaught against it is still very strong. If wavering leaders resign at *such* a time, that does not weaken the party, the working-class movement and the revolution, but strengthens them.

Italy is going through a *similar* period. It is generally seen and admitted that a nation-wide revolutionary crisis is maturing The proletariat has proved in deed that it is capable of rising spontaneously, and of rousing the masses for a mighty revolutionary movement. The poor peasants, or semi-proletarians (it is a pity that Comrade Serrati has acquired the bad habit of putting a question mark after this word whenever he uses it; it is a correct Marxist term and expresses a correct idea, which has been confirmed by facts both in Russia and in Italy, viz., that the poor peasants are half property-owners and half proletarians)—the poor peasants in Italy have shown in deed that they are capable of rising for a revolutionary struggle, in the wake of the proletariat. What is most essential now, in fact absolutely essential for the victory of the revolution in Italy, is that the Italian revolutionary proletariat should have a real vanguard in the shape of a truly Communist Party, one that is *incapable* of wavering and flinching at the decisive moment, a party that will concentrate within itself the utmost fervour, devotion to the revolution, energy and boundless courage and determination. Victory has to be achieved in a very hard and painful struggle that will entail great sacrifice; when captured, power will have to be upheld in the face of incredibly fierce attacks, intrigues, slander, calumny, intimidation and violence on the part of the bourgeoisie of the *whole world*, in the face of the most dangerous waverings on the part of every petty-bourgeois democrat, every Turati supporter, every "Centrist", every Social-Democrat, socialist and anarchist. At such a time and in such surroundings, the Party must be a hundred times firmer, bolder, more determined, devoted and ruthless than in ordinary or in less difficult times. At such a time and in such surroundings, the Party will become a hundred times *stronger*, not weaker, if Mensheviks, like those who foregathered in Reggio Emilia on October 11, 1920, withdraw from it altogether, and even if some excellent Communists—such as Baratono, Zannerini, Bacci, Giacomini and Serrati, members of the present Central Committee of the party, probably are—withdraw from its leadership.

Even if the people of the latter category resigned now, most of them would undoubtedly very soon see their mistake and return after the victory of the proletariat, after its victory had been consolidated. In all probability, even a section of the Italian Mensheviks, of the Turati supporters, would return, too, and be received into the party when the period of greatest difficulties had passed, just as a section of the Mensheviks and Socialist-Revolutionaries, who were on the other side of the barricades in 1917-18, have come over to us now (after we have been through three difficult years since the revolution).

The Italian revolutionary proletariat is about to face a period of battles that will be not merely extremely difficult, as I have said, but truly the most difficult of all. The greatest trials lie ahead. I would consider it frivolous and criminal to shrug off these difficulties. It surprises me how Comrade Serrati could have published in his journal *Comunismo* (No. 24, September 15-30, 1920), without any comment, such a superficial article as that by G. C. entitled "Will We Be Blockaded?" Despite what the author of this article says, I personally think that in the event of the proletariat's victory in Italy, the blockade of that country by Great Britain, France and America is possible and probable. In my opinion, Comrade Graziadei was much closer to the truth in his speech at the meeting of the Italian party's Central Committee (*Avanti!*, October 1, 1920, the Milan edition), when he admitted that the problem of a possible blockade was "very grave" ("*problema gravissima*"). He said that Russia had held out despite the blockade, partly because of the sparseness of her population and her enormous territory, but the revolution in Italy "could not resist (*resistere*) for long if it were not co-ordinated with a revolution in some other country in Central Europe", and that "such co-ordination is difficult but not impossible", because the whole of continental Europe is passing through a revolutionary period.

Though put very cautiously, this is true. I would merely add that Italy is *assured* of a *certain amount* of co-ordination—although that may as yet be inadequate and incomplete—and that *complete* co-ordination will have to be *fought* for. When the reformists speak of the possibility of a blockade they do so in order to sabotage the revolution, instil apprehension of the revolution, and imbue the masses with *their own* panic, fear, indecision and vacillation. Revolutionaries and Communists must not deny the dangers and difficulties of the struggle in order to put *greater* firmness into the masses, *purge* the party of those that are weak, wavering and unstable, and inspire the entire movement with greater enthusiasm, a higher spirit of internationalism, and a greater preparedness to make sacrifices for the sake of a great aim, namely, hastening the revolution in Great Britain, France and America *should* these countries dare to blockade the proletarian and Soviet Italian republic.

The question of replacing experienced reformist or "Centrist" leaders by novices is not a particular question, of concern to a single country in special circumstances. It is a general question which arises in every proletarian revolution, and as such it is formulated and quite specifically answered in the resolution of the Second Congress of the Communist International on "The Fundamental Tasks of the Communist International". In point 8 we read: "Preparation for the dictatorship of the proletariat, not only entails explaining the bourgeois character of all reformism; ... it also entails replacing the old leaders by Communists in proletarian organisations of absolutely every type—not only political, but also trade union, co-operative, educational, etc. ...These representatives of the labour aristocracy, or the bourgeoisified workers, should be eliminated from all their posts a hundred times more boldly than hitherto, and replaced by workers, even if wholly inexperienced, as long as they are connected with the exploited masses and enjoy the latter's confidence in the struggle against the exploiters. The dictatorship of the proletariat will require the appointment of such inexperienced workers to the most responsible posts in the state; otherwise the workers' government will be impotent, and will not have the support of the masses."[132]

Serrati is therefore wrong in saying that "all" in the Italian party agree to accept the decisions of the Communist Congress. In fact the reverse is to be seen.

In the above-mentioned letter to *l'Humanité* Serrati says among other things:

"... As for the recent events, one should know that the leaders of the General Confederation of Labour (the Italian variant of the T.U.C.) proposed that the leadership of the movement should be turned over to those who wanted to expand it to a revolution. Our comrades of the General Confederation of Labour declared that they were willing to remain disciplined soldiers if the extremists assumed leadership of the insurrection. But the latter did not assume leadership of the movement...."

It would be highly naïve on Serrati's part to take at its face value this statement from the reformists in the General Confederation of Labour. In fact, threatening to resign at crucial moments is a variety of sabotage of the revolution. This is in no way a question of loyalty, but simply of the victory of the revolution being *impossible* if at every difficult turn the leaders are faced with hesitation, vacillation and resignations on the part of their "own" colleagues, those at the top, the "leaders". It may be useful to Comrade Serrati to know that at the end of September 1917, when the coalition of Russian Mensheviks and Socialist-Revolutionaries with the bourgeoisie had obviously fallen through politically, none other than our Socialist-Revolutionaries, Chernov's party, wrote in their newspaper: "The Bolsheviks will be obliged to form a cabinet.... Let them not make futile attempts to hide behind a hastily concocted theory that it is impossible for them to take power. The democracy will not accept these theories. At the same time, the advocates of coalition must guarantee them full support" (the Socialist-Revolutionary newspaper, the newspaper of their party, Chernov's newspaper—*Dyelo Naroda*, September 21, 1917, quoted in my pamphlet *Can the Bolsheviks Retain State Power?*, Petrograd, 1917, p. 4).[133]

It would be just as fatal a mistake for the revolutionary workers to believe in the loyalty of such statements as it was to believe the Hungarian Turatists, who promised Bela Kun their help and joined the Communist Party, but, nevertheless, proved to be saboteurs of the revolution and wrecked it by their vacillation.

* * *

To sum up:

1) The party of the revolutionary proletariat in Italy should display the utmost self-restraint, circumspection and coolness for a correct appraisal of the conditions in general, and the appropriate moment in particular, in the impending decisive battles for political power between the Italian working class and the bourgeoisie.

2) At the same time, all propaganda and agitation conducted by that party should be imbued with the firmest determination to wage that struggle to a victorious conclusion, come what may, in a united and centralised manner, and with supreme heroism, ruthlessly eliminating the vacillation, indecision and wavering with which the Turati supporters are so thoroughly imbued.

3) The propaganda conducted by the Milan edition of *Avanti!*, which is edited by Serrati, does not prepare the proletariat for the struggle, but brings disintegration into its ranks. At a moment like the present, the party's Central Committee should give the workers leadership, prepare them for the revolution, and challenge wrong views. This can (and should) be done, while allowing all trends to express themselves. Serrati is giving leadership, but doing so in the wrong direction.

4) The expulsion from the party of all who attended the Reggio Emilia Congress on October 11, 1920, will not weaken the party but strengthen it; such "leaders" are capable only of wrecking the revolution in the "Hungarian style", *even if they do remain loyal.* The whiteguards and the bourgeoisie will be able to utilise the hesitation, vacillation, doubts, uncertainty, etc., of even quite "loyal" socialists, Social-Democrats, etc.

5) If people such as Baratono, Zannerini, Bacci, Giacomini and Serrati display vacillation and resign, they should not be asked to remain; their resignations should be immediately accepted. They will return after the period of decisive battles and will then be of greater use to the proletariat.

6) Comrades, workers of Italy, do not forget the lessons of the history of all revolutions, the lessons of Russia and Hungary in 1917-20. Great battles, great difficulties and great sacrifices await the proletariat in Italy. Victory over the bourgeoisie, the assumption of power by the proletariat and the consolidation of the Soviet Republic in Italy all depend on the outcome of these battles, and on the solidarity, discipline and devotion of the masses of the workers. The bourgeoisie of Italy and of all countries of the world will do their utmost and resort to any crime and atrocity to prevent the proletariat from taking power, and to over-

throw its power. The hesitation, vacillation and irresolution of the reformists and of all who attended the Reggio Emilia Congress on October 11, 1920, are inevitable, because, even though many of them are quite honest, such people have always and in all countries, wrecked the cause of revolution by their vacillation. It was such as these who wrecked the revolution (the first revolution; it will be followed by another ...) in Hungary, and would have wrecked the revolution in Russia had they not been removed from all responsible posts and surrounded by a wall of proletarian distrust, vigilance and surveillance.

The toiling and exploited masses of Italy will follow the revolutionary proletariat. It will prove victorious in the end, for its cause is that of the workers of the whole world, and there is no way to avoid the continuation of the present imperialist wars, the advent of the new imperialist wars that are being prepared, and the horrors of capitalist slavery and oppression, otherwise than in a Soviet Workers' Republic.

4.11.1920

FALSE TALK ON FREEDOM
(INSTEAD OF AN EPILOGUE)

Comrade Nobs, editor of *Volksrecht*, the Swiss Left-Socialist newspaper in Zurich, recently published a letter by Zinoviev on the need to break with the opportunists, together with his own lengthy reply to this letter. Nobs's reply amounts to an emphatic rejection of the twenty-one conditions and of affiliation to the Communist International, this, of course, being done in the name of "freedom"—the freedom to criticise, freedom from excessive demands or the dictatorship of Moscow (I have not kept Nobs's article and am therefore obliged to quote from memory; I can vouch for the idea, but not for the exact wording).

Incidentally, Comrade Nobs has enrolled Comrade Serrati as an ally, who is also known to be displeased with "Moscow", i.e., particularly with the Russian members of the Communist International's Executive Committee and who also complains that Moscow violates the "freedom" of the constituent sections, the individual parties and individual members of the Communist International. It will not be superfluous, therefore, to say a few words about freedom.

After three years of the dictatorship of the proletariat, we may safely say that the most common and popular objection to it all over the world is its alleged violation of freedom and equality. The entire bourgeois press in all countries, including the press of the petty-bourgeois democrats, i.e., of the Social-Democrats and socialists, among them Kautsky, Hilferding, Martov, Chernov, Longuet, etc., etc., rail against the Bolsheviks for the latter's violation of freedom and equality. From the standpoint of theory, this can be readily understood. The reader will recall Marx's celebrated and sarcastic words in *Capital*:

"This sphere [of the circulation or exchange of commodities], within whose boundaries the sale and purchase of labour power goes on, is in fact a very Eden of the innate rights of man. There alone rule Freedom, Equality, Property and Bentham." (*Capital*, Vol. I, Part II, end of Chapter 4, Russian language edition, 1920, p. 152.)[134]

This sarcastic remark has a profound historical and philosophical meaning. It should be compared with the popular explanation of the same question given by Engels in *Anti-Dühring*, particularly with what Engels said about the idea of equality being a prejudice or an absurdity, if it does not mean the abolition of classes.[135]

The abolition of feudalism and of its vestiges, and the establishment of the foundations of the bourgeois order (one may quite correctly say: the bourgeois-democratic order) occupied an entire epoch of world history. It was inevitable for freedom, equality, property and Bentham to become the slogans of this epoch of world history. The abolition of capitalism and its vestiges, and the establishment of the fundamentals of the communist order comprise the content of the new era of world history that has set in. It is inevitable that the slogans of our era are and must be: the abolition of classes; the dictatorship of the proletariat for the purpose of achieving that aim; the ruthless exposure of petty-bourgeois democratic prejudices concerning freedom and equality and ruthless war on these prejudices. Whoever does not understand this has no understanding of the dictatorship of the proletariat, Soviet government, and the fundamental principles of the Communist International.

Until classes are abolished, all talk about freedom and equality in general is self-deception, or else deception of the workers and of all who toil and are exploited by capital; in any case, it is a defence of the interests of the bourgeo sie. Until classes are abolished, all arguments about freedom and equality should be accompanied by the questions: freedom for which class, and for what purpose; equality between which classes, and in what respect? Any direct or indirect, witting or unwitting evasion of these questions inevitably turns into a defence of the interests of the bourgeoisie, the interests of capital, the interests of the exploiters. If these questions are glossed over, and nothing is said about the private ownership of the means of production, then the slogan of freedom and equality is merely the lies and humbug of bourgeois society, whose formal recognition of freedom and equality conceals actual economic servitude and inequality for the workers, for all who toil and are exploited by capital, i.e., for the overwhelming majority of the population in all capitalist countries.

Thanks to the fact that, in present-day Russia, the dictatorship of the proletariat has posed in a practical manner the fundamental and *final* problems of capitalism, one can see with particular clarity *whose interests are served* (*cui prodest?*—"who benefits?") by talk about freedom and equality in general. When the Socialist-Revolutionaries and the Mensheviks, the Chernovs and the Martovs, favour us with arguments about freedom and equality *within the limits of labour democracy* (for, you see, they are never guilty of reasoning about freedom and equality in general! They never forget Marx!) we ask them: what about the distinction between the class of wage-workers and the class of small property-owners in the period of the dictatorship of the proletariat?

Freedom and equality *within the limits of labour democracy* mean freedom for the small peasant owner (even if he farms on nationalised land) to sell his surplus grain at profiteering prices, i.e., *to exploit the workers*. Anyone who talks about freedom and equality within the limits of labour democracy when the capitalists have been overthrown but private property and freedom to trade still survive is a champion of the exploiters. In exercising its dictatorship, the proletariat must treat these champions as it does the exploiters, even though they say they are Social-Democrats or socialists, or admit that the Second International is putrid, and so on and so forth.

As long as private ownership of the means of production (e.g., of agricultural implements and livestock, even if private ownership of land has been abolished) and freedom to trade remain, so does the economic basis of capitalism. The dictatorship of the proletariat is the only means of successfully fighting for the demolition of that basis, the only way to abolish classes (without which abolition there can be no question of genuine freedom for the individual—*and not for the property-owner*—of real equality, in the social and political sense, between man and man—*and not the humbug of equality between those who possess property and those who do not*, between the well-fed and the hungry, between the exploiters and the exploited). The dictatorship of the proletariat leads to the abolition of classes; it leads to that end, on the one hand, by the overthrow of the exploiters and the suppression of their resistance, and on the other hand by neutralising and rendering harmless the small property-owner's vacillation between the bourgeoisie and the proletariat.

The falsity of Comrade Nobs's and Comrade Serrati's statements does not, of course, consist in their being falsely or insincerely meant. Nothing of the kind. They are quite sincere, and there is nothing subjectively false in what they have said. However, their statements are false objectively, in content, for they are a defence of the prejudices of petty-bourgeois democracy; they amount to a defence of the bourgeoisie.

The Communist International cannot under any circumstances recognise freedom and equality for all who wish to subscribe to certain statements, irrespective of their political conduct. To Communists this would be no less suicidal both as regards theory and practical politics than the recognition of freedom and equality "within the limits of labour democracy", etc. To anyone able to read and *willing* to understand what he reads, it must be quite clear that *none* of the decisions, theses, resolutions and conditions of the Communist International recognise the *absolute* "freedom and equality" of those who desire to affiliate to the Communist International.

What is our stipulation for recognising "freedom and equality", the freedom and equality of members of the Communist International?

It is that no opportunists and "Centrists", such as the well-known representatives of the Right wing of the Swiss and Italian socialist parties, shall be able to become members. No matter how these opportunists and "Centrists" may claim that they recognise the dictatorship of the proletariat, they actually remain advocates and defenders of the prejudices, weaknesses and vacillations of the petty-bourgeois democrats.

You must first break with these prejudices, weaknesses and vacillations, with those who preach, defend and give practical expression to these views and qualities. Then, and only on this condition, can you be "free" to join the Communist International; only then can the genuine Communist, a Communist in deed and not merely in word, be the "equal" of any other Communist, of any other member of the Communist International.

Comrade Nobs, you are "free" to defend the views you hold. But we, too, are "free" to declare that these views are petty-bourgeois prejudices, which are injurious to the proletarian cause and of use to capitalism; we, too, are "free" to refuse to join in an alliance or league with people who defend those views or a policy that corresponds to them. We have *already* condemned that policy and those views on behalf of the Second Congress of the Communist International as a whole. We have already said that we absolutely demand a rupture with the opportunists as a first and preliminary step.

Do not talk of freedom and equality in general, Comrade Nobs and Comrade Serrati! Talk of freedom *not to carry out* the decisions of the Communist International on the absolute duty of breaking with the opportunists and the "Centrists" (who cannot but undermine, cannot but sabotage the dictatorship of the proletariat). Talk of the equality of the opportunists and "Centrists" with the Communists. Such freedom and such equality cannot be recognised by us for the Communist International; as for any other kind of freedom and equality—you may enjoy them to your heart's content!

On the eve of the proletarian revolution, the liberation, the freedom, of the parties of the revolutionary proletariat from opportunists and "Centrists", from their influence, their prejudices, their weaknesses and vacillations, is the main and essential condition of success.

11.12.1920

SPEECH AT A JOINT PLENUM OF THE MOSCOW SOVIET OF WORKERS', PEASANTS' AND RED ARMY DEPUTIES, THE MOSCOW COMMITTEE OF THE R.C.P.(B.) AND THE MOSCOW CITY TRADE UNION COUNCIL, DEDICATED TO THE THIRD ANNIVERSARY OF THE OCTOBER REVOLUTION

NOVEMBER 6, 1920

(*Prolonged applause.*) Comrades, we have gathered here today to commemorate our proletariat's days of struggle and our revolutionary achievements. Today we can celebrate our victory. Despite the unparalleled difficulties of life and the unparalleled efforts of our enemies, we have won. We have been winning for three years. This is a gigantic victory, one that previously none of us would have believed possible. Three years ago, when we were at Smolny, the Petrograd workers' uprising showed us that it was more unanimous than we could have expected, but had we been told that night that, three years later, we would have what now exists, that we would have this victory of ours, nobody, not even the most incurable optimist, would have believed it. We knew at that time that our victory would be a lasting one only when our cause had triumphed the world over, and so when we began working for our cause we counted exclusively on the world revolution. The imperialist war changed all the forms of life we had lived in till then, and we had no way of knowing what forms would be assumed by the struggle, which had dragged on much longer than could have been expected. Now, after three years, it turns out that we are immeasurably stronger than we were before, but the world bourgeoisie are still very strong, too; yet, despite the fact that they are far stronger than we are, we can say that we have won. We have directed all our energies to disintegrating this bourgeoisie, and in this respect our work has not been without success. The reason for this is that we staked our chances on world revolution, and were undoubtedly right in doing so. We knew that the whole world was heading for destruction; we knew that, after the imperialist war, things could not go on in the old way because the imperialist war had thoroughly destroyed all the old economic and legal relations, all the conditions of existence on which the old order had till then been based. And if, at a time when the imperialist war had done a thousand times more than our propaganda did to pave the way for a *débâcle*, the proletariat in even a single country took action ending in victory, this would be sufficient to undermine the forces of the world bourgeoisie.

If we now cast a glance at the international situation—and we have always stressed that we regard things from the international standpoint—and examine the history of the wars that have been waged against Soviet Russia, we shall see that we are at peace with almost all the little bourgeois states bordering on us, states in which Bolsheviks are persecuted and executed. These states are servants and slaves to the Entente, and they want to ruin and destroy Soviet Russia, yet we have concluded peace with them—against the Entente's wishes. Three such mighty powers as Britain, France and America could not unite against us, and were defeated in a war they had begun against us with their joint forces. Why has that been? It has been because their economies and life in their countries have been undermined, because they are moribund, because they cannot go on living in the old way, and because the class at whose will they exist—the bourgeois class—has gone rotten. That class drove over 10 million people into the imperialist war and to destruction. For what purpose? For the purpose of partitioning the world among a handful of capitalists. In doing so, however, it has come to the end of its strength, and has undermined the foundations of its own existence; however strong it may seem militarily, it is internally impotent. This is no longer a proclamation in the Bolshevik spirit, but a fact that has been proved with fire and sword. However rich and strong that class may be, it is doomed, whereas we are a class that is advancing towards victory. Even though we are weaker than our enemies, we have been winning for three years, and we have the right to say, without the least boasting, that we have won.

In saying that, we should not forget another aspect of the matter. We should not forget that we have won no more than half of the victory. We have won because we have been able to hold out against states that are stronger than we are, and moreover have joined forces with our émigré exploiters—the landowners and capitalists. We have always known and shall never forget that ours is an international cause, and until the revolution takes place in all lands, including the richest and most highly civilised ones, our victory will be only a half-victory, perhaps still less. At present we are gaining the upper hand in the fighting against Wrangel; we are expecting news that will bear out our expectations.[136] We are confident that if we do not succeed in capturing the Crimea within the next few days, we shall do so several days later, but we have no guarantee that this is the last effort against us on the part of the world bourgeoisie. On the contrary, facts in our possession show that this effort will be repeated in the spring. We know that their chances of success will be negligible, and we know too that our military forces will be more powerful than those of any other country. For all that, however, the danger is not yet over; it still exists and will continue to do so until the revolution is victorious in one or in several advanced countries.

We know that things are moving in that direction; we know that the Second Congress of the Third International, which was held in Moscow during the summer, did an immense job, one that has no precedent. Some of you may have been present when Comrade Zinoviev delivered his report, in which he dealt in detail with the congress of German Independents at Halle.[137] Many of you may have heard his graphic description of developments in a country in which the chances of a revolution are the greatest. Similar things are taking place in all countries. Communism has developed, grown strong, and created parties in all the leading countries. During this period, the cause of the international revolution has suffered a number of reverses in some small countries, where assistance in crushing the movement has come from such huge predators as Germany, which helped to crush the Finnish revolution, or those giants of capitalism, Britain, France and Austria, which crushed the revolution in Hungary. By doing so, however, they have multiplied a thousandfold the elements of revolution in their own countries. Today the main reason why they have been weakened by the struggle is that their rear lines are not assured, because in all countries the workers and peasants do not want to fight against us, and heroic sailors have come to the fore, not only in our country, in Kronstadt, but also in their countries. Throughout France the names of the sailors who served in our Black Sea are associated with recollections of the Russian revolution; the French workers know that those who are now serving terms of penal servitude in France mutinied in the Black Sea because they refused to become butchers of the Russian workers and peasants.[138] That is why the Entente has grown weak; that is why we say with confidence that our position is secure in the international field.

However, our victory is far from complete, comrades; we have won less than half of it. Yes, we have won a gigantic victory thanks to the self-sacrifice and enthusiasm of the Russian workers and peasants; we have been able to show that Russia is capable of producing not only the individual heroes who entered the struggle against tsarism and died at a time when the workers and peasants did not support them. We were right when we said that Russia would produce such heroes from among the masses, that she would be able to do so by the hundreds and thousands. We said that it would come about, and that then capitalism would be a lost cause. The main reason of our victory, its chief source, is the heroism, the self-sacrifice, and the unparalleled tenacity displayed by our Red Army men who have laid down their lives at the front, and by the workers and peasants who have suffered so much, especially the industrial workers, most of whom have suffered more during these three years than the workers did during the early years of capitalist slavery. They have endured cold, hunger and suffering—all this in order to retain power. Thanks to this tenacity and this heroism, they have created a rear that has proved the only strong rear existing at the moment among the belligerent forces. That is why we are strong and firm, whereas the Entente is steadily disintegrating before our very eyes.

However, with this enthusiasm and heroism alone, the cause of the revolution cannot be completed, carried on to full victory. These qualities were sufficient to hurl back the enemy when he flung himself on us and tried to strangle us; they were sufficient for victory in a bloody conflict, but not for the ultimate goal. They are not enough because we are now faced with the second half of our task, the major and more difficult part. Our triumph of today, our confidence that we shall win, must be imbued with a quality that will enable us to gain a victory just as decisive in the second half of the task. Mere enthusiasm, the mere readiness of the workers and peasants to face death in accomplishing the second half of our task are not enough, because the second task is a most difficult one of constructive and creative work. From capitalism we inherited not only a ruined culture, not only wrecked factories, not only a despairing intelligentsia; we inherited a disunited and backward mass of individual proprietors; we inherited inexperience, an absence of the team spirit and of an understanding that the past must be buried.

Such are the problems we have to solve today. We must remember that today's temper has to be put to work for a long time to come, so that fragmentation of our economic life may be done away with. We cannot return to the old ways. By overthrowing the rule of the exploiters we have already accomplished the greater part of the job. We must now unite all working men and women and get them to work together. We have come here like conquerors entering new territory; yet, despite difficult conditions we are working in, we have been victorious at the front. We see that our work is progressing today better than it did a year ago. We know that we cannot provide sufficient food for all, and we are not certain that hunger and cold will not knock at the doors of homes and cottages, but we do know that we have won. We know that our productive power is enormous even now, after the severe imperialist and civil wars; we know that we shall not let the workers and peasants starve and freeze; however, to be able to do that, we must count all our resources and share them out properly. We do not yet know how to do that because capitalism taught every petty proprietor to look after his own interests, to think of how to get rich, and become one of the money-bags as quickly as possible; it did not teach anybody how to wage a common struggle for some definite idea. We must now be guided by another principle. The other and more difficult part of our task now faces us. The enthusiasm that now fills us may last another year, perhaps even five years. However we should remember that the struggle we shall have to wage is made up of ordinary workaday tasks. Around us are small-scale economic tasks. Furthermore, you know that the little units that keep our economic life going are the same that served in the past—petty officials, petty bureaucrats accustomed to the old and selfish way of doing things. The struggle against such things must become the task of the hour. On the occasion of these festivities, the occasion of this triumphant mood of ours, the occasion of the third anniversary of the establishment of Soviet rule we must become imbued with the labour enthusiasm, the will to work, and the persistence on which the speedy salvation of the workers and peasants, the salvation of the national economy now depends. We shall then see that our victory in the accomplishment of this task will be more effective and lasting than in all bloody battles of the past. (*Prolonged applause.*)

Published in 1920 in *Verbatim Reports of the Plenums of the Moscow Soviet of Workers', Peasants' and Red Army Deputies*

Published according to the text in the book

TELEGRAM TO J. V. STALIN

To Stalin

How is the struggle against the bands progressing? Is it true that they have over 20,000 rifles and sabres? Are the reinforcements designated for the Caucasus front sufficient? Do you consider a peaceful settlement of relations with Georgia and Armenia possible, and on what basis? Then, is the work on the fortification of the approaches to Baku being conducted in real earnest? I also ask for information on Turkey and Persia, briefly by telegram, and in detail by letter.

Lenin

Written on November 13, 1920

First published in *Pravda* No. 21, January 21, 1937

Published according to the manuscript

THESES ON PRODUCTION PROPAGANDA[139]

ROUGH DRAFT

1. In connection with the R.S.F.S.R.'s military victories and its international position in general, production propaganda must now be given special prominence, and be accentuated and organised.

2. The leading newspapers, *Izvestia* and *Pravda* in the first place, should: a) reduce the space devoted to politics, and increase space for production propaganda; b) influence all the work of the Party and of Soviet institutions, in the sense of mobilising greater forces for production propaganda; c) endeavour to work systematically to place production propaganda on a nation-wide footing, and evolve extensive measures for its encouragement and improvement, with a special view to verifying the successes actually achieved in practice.

3. In just the same way, work should be systematised, extended and developed in selecting able administrators, organisers and inventors from the masses of workingmen and peasants.

4. Throughout the R.S.F.S.R. production propaganda should be placed under the direction of a single body, with the aim of economising forces and improving guidance of this work. In this, the greatest autonomy, both local and within each trade, is indispensable. Any marked success should be systematically and judiciously rewarded (bonuses in kind, etc.). Verification of successes to be organised impartially and competently.

5. The editorial board of a mass newspaper with a circulation of between 500,000 and 1,000,000 should be made the sole body guiding production propaganda.

Bednota[140] is the right newspaper for the purpose.

It would be harmful to have a division into an industrial newspaper and an agricultural newspaper, since it is the aim of socialism to bring industry and agriculture closer together and unite them. In practice, the guiding role of the industrial proletariat both in the cities and in the rural areas, particularly in the urbanisation of agriculture and the electrification of the entire country, calls precisely for a single newspaper devoted to problems of production (and for a single body in charge of production propaganda) both for the workers and the peasants.

6. This guiding collegiate body should consist of five members representing: 1) the All-Russia Central Council of Trade Unions; 2) the Supreme Council of the National Economy; 3) the People's Commissariat of Agriculture; 4) the Chief Committee for Political Education; 5) the Central Committee of the R.C.P. (or an editor-in-chief). This collegiate body and the newspaper should be attached to the All-Russia Central Council of Trade Unions (perhaps there should also be a representative of the Central Board for Vocational Training?).

7. This newspaper, devoted to matters of production, should be a popular one, in the sense of being understood by millions of readers, without falling into vulgarisation. The paper should not descend to the level of the uncultivated reader, but should work steadily—and by very gradual degrees—to promote his development. Little space—not exceeding a quarter of the total—should be devoted to politics. Top priority should be given to a single economic plan, to the labour front, production propaganda, the training of workers and peasants in the work of administration, to seeing that Soviet laws and measures established by Soviet institutions are given due effect, and to an extensive and properly organised exchange of opinions with the rank-and-file reader.

8. Materials published in the newspaper or addressed to it, as well as all other kinds of material, should be systematically and periodically brought out in pamphlet or leaflet form and compulsorily supplied to libraries, as well as to factories and enterprises in the given field of production (the pamphlets and leaflets should systematise all the

material relating to each particular branch of production). Together with manuals and reviews of foreign technology, this material should serve to spread vocational training and *polytechnical* education.

A more rational distribution of the newspaper, as well as of pamphlets and leaflets dealing with questions of production, among *all* libraries in the R.S.F.S.R. should, in particular, be the object of special attention.

9. It is indispensable that engineers, agronomists, school-teachers, and also Soviet functionaries possessing definite professional qualifications, should be drawn into systematic participation in production propaganda (this in connection with the liquidation of illiteracy).

The organisation of lectures, talks, reports, etc.

Compulsory labour service on the part of all those who are able to acquaint the population with problems of electrification, with the Taylor system, etc.

10. The more extensive and systematic use of films for production propaganda. Joint work with the cinema section.

Soviet gramophone records. Displays of diagrams and cartograms at clubs, village reading-rooms, in streets, etc. Bills and placards to be displayed near factories, workshops, technical schools, etc.

11. The organisation, jointly with the People's Commissariat of Labour and other institutions, of an inspectorate of production. The latter's work to be co-ordinated with that of production propaganda, as well as with the work of instructors, exhibition trains and ships, and the like.

12. Extensive publicity for exemplary enterprises. Organisation of factory workers with foreign industrial experience—this to be done in special workshops, sections or groups, etc. Such workers to be utilised for the training of backward workingmen, for the dissemination of vocational-technical and polytechnical instruction, etc.

N. Lenin

18.11.1920

Published in 1928

Published according to the manuscript

EXTRACT FROM DIRECT-LINE TALK BETWEEN V. I. LENIN AND J. V. STALIN

I can give no reply without convening the Political Bureau. I advise that you immediately submit a concrete proposal and at once table it for the Political Bureau, or act independently on the basis of the powers conferred on Stalin, or else expedite your coming to Moscow to settle the entire Caucasus question as a whole. In any case, the bringing up of reinforcements should be intensified and speeded up. Communicate your exact opinion.

Lenin

November 20, 1920 or earlier

First published in 1945
in *Lenin Miscellany XXXV*

Published according to
the text
of the telegraph tape

OUR FOREIGN AND DOMESTIC POSITION AND THE TASKS OF THE PARTY

SPEECH DELIVERED TO THE MOSCOW GUBERNIA CONFERENCE OF THE R.C.P.(B.), NOVEMBER 21, 1920[141]

(*Applause.*) Comrades, in speaking of the international position of the Soviet Republic we naturally have to deal mainly with the Polish war and Wrangel's defeat. I think that at a meeting of Party workers who have, of course, followed the Party press and have frequently heard major reports on this question, there is no need and indeed it would be superfluous, for me to speak in detail on this period or on each phase of the war against Poland, on the character of our offensives, or on the significance of our defeat at Warsaw. I presume that most of the comrades are so familiar with this aspect of the matter that I would only be repeating myself, which would be unsatisfactory to these comrades. I shall therefore speak, not on the various episodes and turns of our Polish campaign but on the results we now have before us.

After the Red Army's brilliant victories in the summer, the serious defeat at Warsaw, and the conclusion of a preliminary peace with Poland, which at this very moment, in Riga, is being or at least should be turned a conclusive peace, the chances of that preliminary peace really becoming conclusive have greatly increased as a result of Wrangel's *débâcle*. Now that the latter has become an established fact the imperialist press in the Entente countries is beginning to show its cards and disclose what it has most of all kept in the dark.

I do not know whether you noticed a brief news item published in the papers today or some days ago to the effect that the newspaper *Temps*, mouthpiece of the French imperialist bourgeoisie, now speaks of the peace with Poland having been signed against France's advice. There can be no doubt that the French bourgeoisie's spokesmen are admitting a truth they would have preferred to cover up and indeed have covered up for a very long time. Despite the unfavourable terms of the Polish peace (which are more advantageous than those we ourselves offered to the Polish landowners this April in order to avoid any war), and they are indeed unfavourable as compared to what might have been achieved but for the extremely serious situation at Warsaw, we succeeded in getting terms that frustrate the greater part of the imperialists' over-all plan. The French bourgeoisie have now acknowledged that they insisted on Poland continuing the war, and were opposed to the conclusion of a peace, because they feared the rout of Wrangel's army and wished to support a new intervention and campaign against the Soviet Republic. Though Polish imperialism's conditions have impelled it to go to war against Russia—despite this—the French imperialists' plans have collapsed, and as a result we now have gained something more than a mere breathing-space.

Of the small states formerly belonging to the Russian Empire, Poland has been among those that have been most of all at odds with the Great-Russian nation during the last three years, and made the greatest claims to a large slice of territory inhabited by non-Poles. We concluded peace with Finland, Estonia and Latvia[142] also against the wishes of the imperialist Entente, but this was easier because the bourgeoisie of Finland, Estonia and Latvia entertained no imperialist aims that would call for a war against the Soviet Republic, whereas the Polish bourgeois republic had an eye, not only to Lithuania and Byelorussia but the Ukraine as well. Furthermore, it was impelled along the same direction by the age-old struggle of Poland, who used to be a great power and is now pitting herself against another great power—Russia. Even at present, Poland cannot hold back from this age-long struggle. That is why Poland has been far more bellicose and stubborn in her war plans against our Republic, and why our present success in concluding peace against the wishes of the Entente is so much more resounding. Among the states which have preserved the bourgeois system and border on Russia, there is no other country but Poland on which the Entente can rely in a long-term plan of military intervention; that is why in their common hate of the Soviets, all the bourgeois states are directly interested in having Eastern Galicia under the control of the Polish landed proprietors.

Moreover, Poland lays claim to the Ukraine and Lithuania. This gives the campaign a particularly acute and stubborn character. Keeping Poland supplied with war materials has, naturally, been the main concern of France and certain other powers, and it is quite impossible to estimate just how much money has gone into this. Therefore, the importance of the Red Army's final victory despite our defeat at Warsaw, is particularly great, for it has placed Poland in a position in which she is unable to prosecute the war. She has had to agree to peace terms that have given her less than those we proposed in April 1920, before the Polish offensive, when we, unwilling to discontinue our work of economic construction, proposed boundaries that were highly disadvantageous to us. At that time, the press of the petty-bourgeois patriots, to whose number both our Socialist-Revolutionaries and Mensheviks belong, accused the Bolsheviks of submissiveness, and an almost Tolstoyan attitude displayed by the Soviet government. The latter term was used to qualify our acceptance of peace along the proposed Pilsudski line, which left Minsk in Polish hands, the boundary lying some 50 versts and at places some 100 versts east of the present line. Of course, I do not have to tell a meeting of Party workers why we accepted, and had to accept, worse boundaries if indeed our work of economic construction was to go on. The outcome was that, by waging war, Poland, which had retained her bourgeois system, brought about an acute dislocation of her entire economy, a tremendous growth of discontent, and a bourgeois reign of terror, not only against the industrial workers but against the farm labourers as well. Poland's entire position as a bourgeois state became so precarious that there could be no question of continuing the war.

The successes scored in this respect by the Soviets have been tremendous. When, three years ago, we raised the question of the tasks and the conditions of the proletarian revolution's victory in Russia, we always stated emphatically that victory could not be permanent unless it was followed up by a proletarian revolution in the West, and that a correct appraisal of our revolution was possible only from the international point of view. For victory to be lasting, we must achieve the victory of the proletarian revolution in all, or at any rate in several, of the main capitalist countries. After three years of desperate and stubborn struggle, we can see in what respect our predictions have or have not materialised. They have not materialised in the sense that there has been no rapid or simple solution of the problem. None of us, of course, expected that such an unequal struggle as the one waged by Russia against the whole of the capitalist world could last for three years. It has emerged that neither side—the Russian Soviet Republic or the capitalist world—has gained victory or suffered defeat; at the same time it has turned out that, while our forecasts did not materialise simply, rapidly and directly, they were fulfilled insofar as we achieved the main thing—the possibility has been maintained of the existence of proletarian rule and the Soviet Republic even in the event of the world socialist revolution being delayed. In this respect it must be said that the Republic's international position today provides the best and most precise confirmation of all our plans and all our policy.

Needless to say, there can be no question of comparing the military strength of the R.S.F.S.R. with that of all the capitalist powers. In this respect we are incomparably weaker than they are, yet, after three years of war, we have forced almost all of these states to abandon the idea of further intervention. This means that what we saw as possible three years ago, while the imperialist war was not yet over, i.e., a highly protracted situation, without any final decision one way or the other, has come about. That has been, not because we have proved militarily stronger and the Entente weaker, but because throughout this period the disintegration in the Entente countries has intensified, whereas our inner strength has grown. This has been confirmed and proved by the war. The Entente was unable to fight us with its own forces. The workers and peasants of the capitalist countries could not be forced to fight us. The bourgeois states were able to emerge from the imperialist war with their bourgeois regimes intact. They were able to stave off and delay the crisis hanging over them, but basically they so undermined their own position that, despite all their gigantic military forces, they had to acknowledge, after three years, that they were unable to crush the Soviet Republic with its almost non-existent military forces. It has thus turned out that our policy and our predictions have proved fundamentally correct in all respects and that the oppressed people in any capitalist country have indeed shown themselves our allies, for it was they who stopped the war. Without having gained an international victory, which we consider the only sure victory, we are in a position of having won conditions enabling us to exist side by side with capitalist powers, who are now compelled to enter into trade relations with us. In the course of this struggle we have won the right to an independent existence.

Thus a glance at our international position as a whole will show that we have achieved tremendous successes and have won, not only a breathing-space but something much more significant. By a breathing-space we understand a brief period during which the imperialist powers have had many opportunities to renew in greater force the war against us. Today, too, we do not underestimate the danger and do not deny the possibility of future military intervention by the capitalist countries. It is essential for us to maintain our military preparedness. However, if we cast a glance at the conditions in which we defeated all attempts made by the Russian counter-revolutionaries and achieved a formal peace with all the Western states, it will be clear that we have something more than a breathing-space: we have entered a new period, in which we have won the right to our fundamental international existence in the network of capitalist states. Domestic conditions have not allowed a single powerful capitalist state to hurl its army against Russia; this has been due to the revolution having matured within such countries, preventing them from overcoming us as quickly as they might have done. There were British, French and Japanese armies on Russian territory for three years. There can be no doubt that the most insignificant concentration of forces by these three powers would have been quite enough to win a victory over us in a few months, if not in a few weeks. We were able to contain that attack only on account of the demoralisation among the French troops and the unrest that set in among the British and Japanese. We have made use of this divergence of imperialist interests all the time. We defeated the interventionists only because their interests divided them, thereby enhancing our strength and unity. This gave us a breathing-space and rendered impossible the complete victory of German imperialism at the time of the Peace of Brest-Litovsk.

These dissensions have become more aggravated of late, especially because of the project of an agreement on concessions with a group of American capitalist sharks, with the toughest of them, headed by a multimillionaire who expects to form a group of multimillionaires.[143] We know that almost all reports from the Far East bear witness to the extreme resentment felt in Japan over the conclusion of this agreement, although so far there has been no agreement, but only the draft of one. Japanese public opinion, however, is already seething, and today I read a communication which said that Japan is accusing Soviet Russia of wanting to set Japan against America.

We have correctly appraised the intensity of the imperialist rivalry and have told ourselves that we must make systematic use of the dissension between them so as to hamper their struggle against us. Political dissension is already apparent in the relations between Britain and France. Today we can speak, not merely of a breathing-space, but of a real chance of a new and lengthy period of development. Until now we have actually had no basis in the international sense. We now have this basis, the reason being the attitude of the smaller powers that are completely dependent on the Great Powers both in the military and in the economic sense. It now appears that, despite the pressure brought to bear by France, Poland has signed a peace with us. The Polish capitalists have a hate of Soviet power; they crush the most ordinary strikes with unparalleled ferocity. They want war with Soviet Russia more than anything else, yet they prefer to make peace with us rather than carry out the conditions set by the Entente. We see that the imperialist powers dominate the whole world although they comprise an insignificant part of the world's population. The fact that a country has appeared that for three years has resisted world imperialism has considerably changed the international situation; the minor powers—and they form the majority of the world's population—are therefore all inclined to make peace with us.

The entry of the socialist country into trade relations with capitalist countries is a most important factor ensuring our existence in such a complex and absolutely exceptional situation.

I have had occasion to observe a certain Spargo, an American social-chauvinist close to our Right Socialist-Revolutionaries and Mensheviks, one of the leaders of the Second International and member of the American Socialist Party, a kind of American Alexinsky, and author of a number of anti-Bolshevik books, who has reproached us—and has quoted the fact as evidence of the complete collapse of communism—for speaking of transactions with capitalist powers. He has written that he cannot imagine better proof of the complete collapse of communism and the breakdown of its programme. I think that anybody who has given thought to the matter will say the reverse. No better proof of the Russian Soviet Republic's material and moral victory over the capitalists of the whole world can be found than the fact that the powers that took up arms against us because of our terror and our entire system have been compelled, against their will, to enter into trade relations with us in the knowledge that by so doing they are strengthening us. This might have been advanced as proof of the collapse of communism only if we had promised, with the forces of Russia alone, to transform the whole world, or had dreamed of doing so. However, we have never harboured such crazy ideas and have always said that our revolution will be victorious when it is supported by the workers of all lands. In fact, they went half-way in their support, for they weakened the hand raised against us, yet in doing so they were helping us.

I shall not dwell any further on this question but shall only remark that at the moment conditions in the Caucasus are becoming most complex and extremely difficult to analyse, with the likelihood that war may be forced on us any day. But with the peace with Poland almost assured and Wrangel wiped out, this war cannot be so alarming and, if forced on us, only promises to strengthen and fortify our position even more. Newspaper reports of events in Armenia and Turkey give us some idea of this.[144] An extremely confused situation has arisen, but I am absolutely confident that we shall emerge from it, preserving peace on the present basis, which in some respects is extremely favourable, on a basis that is satisfactory to us and permits our economic existence. We are doing all we can to ensure this. It is, however, quite likely that circumstances may arise which will directly force war on us or indirectly lead to it. We can view this prospect quite calmly—this will be a war in a distant region, with the balance of forces fully in our favour, probably ensuring greater advantages than the Polish war. The Polish war was a war on two fronts, with a threat from Wrangel, and it could not be called peripheral, because the Pilsudski line did not run so far from Moscow. With this, I shall conclude my review of the international situation.

I now turn to the state of affairs at home. The failure of a number of attempts at military intervention has led to a considerable improvement in our economic position. The main cause of our former desperate position was that we in Central Russia, industrial Russia, proletarian Russia—Petrograd, Moscow, and Ivanovo-Voznesensk—were cut off from all the main grain-producing areas such as Siberia, the South and the South-East; we were cut off from the Donets Basin, one of the main sources of fuel, and from the sources of oil, and it seemed absolutely impossible for the Republic to hold out. You know what appalling distress, what extreme privation, what grain shortages and famine we experienced because we were cut off from the richest grain-producing areas and the most important economic regions. The return of these territories is to a considerable extent responsible for the improvement now to be seen. Thanks to the possibility of drawing on Siberia and the Caucasus, and to the social changes developing in our favour in the Ukraine, there is promise that with the state food procurements in the forthcoming food campaign we shall not only emerge without an actual shortage as we did this year, but shall have sufficient food for all industrial workers. This is the first campaign when we can hope that, as a result of the doubtless improvement in the transport system, the government will dispose of such food stocks—between 250 and 300 million poods of grain—that we shall not merely be talking about socialist construction and doing precious little, as at present, but shall actually operate with real armies of labour; we shall be able to transfer hundreds of thousands of industrial workers, or workers now engaged in provisioning for industry, to really urgent and essential work, and to improve that work in the same way as the improved fuel situation made it possible to restore the textile industry. The Ivanovo-Voznesensk Gubernia mills have begun to work. At first, not more than a quarter of a million spindles were operating but at present there are already half a million, perhaps 600,000, and by the end of the year we count on a million spindles in operation. We think the number will go up to four million next year. Whereas quite recently we made both ends meet with the greatest difficulty by using up old stocks, conditions have now set in in which we are starting to rehabilitate Russia's ruined industry, and shall be able, while collecting grain from the countryside, to supply the peasants in return with salt and paraffin oil, and, though in small quantities, with textiles. Without this it is useless to talk of socialist construction.

While in the international sense we have gained a footing by concluding a series of military campaigns and by wresting peace treaties from a number of states, it has only now become economically possible for us to supply the industrial workers with bread and to provide the bread of industry, namely fuel, on a scale enabling us to set about the construction of socialism. That is our main task, the root of the problem, a transition we have several times tried to make. I remember that at a meeting of the All-Russia Central Executive Committee in April 1918, I said that our military tasks appeared to be ending and that we had not only convinced Russia, not only won her from the exploiters, for the working people but had now to tackle other tasks in order to govern Russia in the interests of her economic construction.[145] Our breathing-space at the time proved quite brief. The war that was forced on us, starting with the Czechoslovak revolt in the summer of 1918, was most ferocious. However, we made several attempts, both in the spring of 1918 and, on a broader scale, in the spring of this year when the question of labour armies was posed in practice. We must now once again give top priority to this transitional stage and exert every effort to achieve it. Regarded from the international point of view, from the standpoint of victory over capitalism in general, this is a paramount task of the entire socialist revolution. To defeat capitalism in general, it is necessary, in the first place, to defeat the exploiters and to uphold the power of the exploited, namely, to accomplish the task of overthrowing the exploiters by revolutionary forces; in the second place, to accomplish the constructive task, that of establishing new economic relations, of setting an example of how this should be done. These two aspects of the task of accomplishing a socialist revolution are indissolubly connected, and distinguish our revolution from all previous ones, which never went beyond the destructive aspect.

If we do not accomplish this second task, nothing will follow from our successes, from our victories in overthrowing the exploiters, and from our military rebuff to international imperialism, and a return to the old system will be inevitable. In the theoretical sense, that is beyond question. In this instance, the transitional stage is abrupt and most difficult, and calls for new methods, a different deployment and use of forces, a different emphasis, a new psychological approach, and so on. In the place of methods of the revolutionary overthrow of the exploiters and of repelling the tyrants, we must apply the methods of constructive organisation; we must prove to the whole world that we are a force capable, not only of resisting any attempt to crush us by force of arms but of setting an example to others. All the writings of the greatest socialists have always provided guidance on these two aspects of the task of the socialist revolution which, as two aspects of the same task, refer both to the outside world, to those states that have remained in capitalist hands, and to the non-proletarians of one's own country. We have convinced the peasants that the proletariat provides them with better conditions of existence than the bourgeoisie did; we have convinced them of this in practice. When the peasants, though they were dissatisfied with Bolshevik government, compared it in practice with the rule of the Constituent Assembly, Kolchak and the others they drew the conclusion that the Bolsheviks guaranteed them a better existence and defended them militarily from violence by world imperialism. Yet, under conditions of bourgeois rule, half of the peasantry lived in a bourgeois fashion, and this could not have been otherwise. The proletariat must now solve the second problem: it must prove to the peasant that the proletariat can provide him with the example and practice of economic relations of a higher level than those under which every peasant family farms on its own. The peasant still believes only in this old system; he still considers this the normal state of affairs. That is beyond doubt. It would be absurd to think that the peasant will change his attitude to vital economic problems, as a result of our propaganda. His is a wait-and-see attitude. From being neutrally hostile, he has become neutrally sympathetic. He prefers us to any other form of government because he sees that the workers', the proletarian state, the proletarian dictatorship, does not mean brute force or usurpation, as it has been described, but is a better defender of the peasants than Kolchak, Denikin, and the rest are.

But all that is not enough; we have not achieved the main object: to show that the proletariat will restore large-scale industry and the national economy so that the peasants can be transferred to a higher economic system. After proving that, by revolutionary organisation, we can repel any violence directed against the exploited, we must prove the same thing in another field by setting an example that will convince the vast mass of the peasants and petty-bourgeois elements, and other countries as well, not in word but in deed, that a communist system and way of life, can be created by a proletariat which has won a war. This is a task of world-wide significance. To achieve the second half of the victory in the international sense, we must accomplish the second half of the task, that which bears upon economic construction. We discussed this at the last Party conference, so I think there is hardly any need or possibility to go into detail on the various points; this is a task that embraces every aspect of economic construction. I have briefly described the conditions ensuring bread for the industrial workers and fuel for industry. These conditions are fundamental in providing the possibility of further construction. I should add that, as you have seen from the agenda published in the newspapers, the question of economic construction will be the main item to be discussed at the forthcoming Congress of Soviets. The entire agenda has been drawn up so that the entire attention and concern of all delegates and of the whole mass of Government and Party workers throughout the Republic will be concentrated on the economic aspect, on the restoration of transport and industry, on what is cautiously termed "aid to the peasant economy" but which implies far more—a system of carefully thought-out measures to raise to the appropriate level the peasant economy, which will continue to exist for some time to come.

The Congress of Soviets will, therefore, discuss a report on the electrification of Russia, so that an all-over economic plan for the rehabilitation of the national economy, of which we have spoken, can be drawn up in the technological aspect. There can be no question of rehabilitating the national economy or of communism unless Russia is put on a different and a higher technical basis than that which has existed up to now. Communism is Soviet power plus the electrification of the whole country, since industry cannot be developed without electrification. This is a long-term task which will take at least ten years to accomplish, provided a great number of technical experts are drawn into the work. A number of printed documents in which this project[146] has been worked out in detail by technical experts will be presented to the Congress. We cannot achieve the main objects of this plan—create 30 large regions of electric power stations which would enable us to modernise our industry—in less than ten years. Without this reconstruction of all industry on lines of large-scale machine production, socialist construction will obviously remain only a set of decrees, a political link between the working class and the peasantry, and a means of saving the peasants from the rule by Kolchak and Denikin; it will remain an example to all powers of the world, but it will not have its own basis. Communism implies Soviet power as a political organ, enabling the mass of the oppressed to run all state affairs—without that, communism is unthinkable. We see proof of this throughout the world, because the idea of Soviet power and its programme are undoubtedly becoming victorious throughout the world. We see this in every phase of the struggle against the Second International, which is living on support from the police, the church and the old bourgeois functionaries in the working-class movement.

This guarantees political success. Economic success, however, can be assured only when the Russian proletarian state effectively controls a huge industrial machine built on up-to-date technology; that means electrification. For this, we must know the basic conditions of the application of electricity, and accordingly understand both industry and agriculture. This is an enormous task, to accomplish which will require a far longer period than was needed to defend our right to existence against invasion. However, we are not afraid of such a period and we think we have won a victory by attracting to this work tens and hundreds of engineers and scientists imbued with bourgeois ideas, whom we have given the mission of reorganising the entire economy, industry and agriculture, in whom we have aroused interest and from whom we have received a great deal of information being summarised in a number of pamphlets. Each region earmarked for electrification is dealt with in a separate pamphlet. The plan for the electrification of the Northern region is ready, and those interested may receive it. Pamphlets dealing with each region, with the over-all plan for reorganisation, will be published by the time the Congress of Soviets meets. It is now our task to carry on systematic work throughout the country, in all Party cells, in every Soviet institution, according to this all-over plan covering many years, so that we may in the near future have a clear idea of how and in what measure we are progressing, without deceiving ourselves or concealing the difficulties confronting us. The entire Republic is faced with the task of accomplishing this single economic plan at any cost. All the Communist Party's activities, propaganda and agitation must be focussed on this task. From the angle of theory, it has been dealt with on more than one occasion; nobody argues against it, but scarcely a hundredth part of what has to be done has been accomplished.

It is natural that we have grown used to a period of political warfare; we have all been steeled in the political and military struggle and, therefore, what has been accomplished by the present Soviet government is only an approach to a task which demands that the train should be switched over to other rails; this is a train which has to carry tens of millions of people. The switching of this heavy load on to other rails, along a track on which there are no rails at all in places, calls for concentrated attention, knowledge and very great persistence. The cultural level of the peasants and the workers has not been high enough for this task and, at the same time, we have become almost totally accustomed to tackling political and military tasks; this has led to a revival of bureaucratic methods. This is generally admitted. It is the task of the Soviet government to completely destroy the old machinery of state as it was destroyed in October, and to transfer power to the Soviets. However, our Programme recognises that there has been a revival of bureaucratic methods and that at present no economic foundation yet exists for a genuinely socialist society. A cultural background, literacy, and in general a higher standard of culture are lacking in the mass of workers and peasants. That is because the best forces of the proletariat have been engaged with military tasks. The proletariat has made tremendous sacrifices to assure the success of military tasks into which tens of millions of peasants had to be drawn, and elements imbued with bourgeois views had to be put to work, because no others were available. That is why we had to state in the Programme—in a document like the Party Programme—that there has been a revival of bureaucratic methods, against which a systematic struggle has to be waged. It is natural that the bureaucratic methods that have reappeared in Soviet institutions were bound to have a pernicious effect even on

Party organisations, since the upper ranks of the Party are at the same time the upper ranks of the state apparatus; they are one and the same thing. Since we recognise that the evil consists in the old bureaucratic methods which have been able to appear in the Party apparatus, it is obvious and natural that all the symptoms of this evil have revealed themselves in the Party organisations. Since that is so, the question has been placed on the agenda of the Congress of Soviets and has received a great deal of attention from this Conference. That is how it should be, because a disease that has affected the Party and has been acknowledged in the resolutions of the general Party Conference[147] exists, not in Moscow alone, but has spread throughout the entire republic. It is a result of the need to carry on political and military work, when we had to involve the peasant masses and were unable to increase our demands for a broader plan to raise the level of the peasant economy, and that of the mass of peasants.

Allow me in conclusion to say a few words about the situation within the Party, about the struggle and the appearance of an opposition, of which all those present are fully aware and which took up a great deal of energy and attention at the Moscow City and Gubernia Conference, perhaps considerably more than we would have all liked. It is quite natural that the great transition now in progress, at a time when all the forces drawn by the Republic from the proletariat and the Party during three years of struggle have been exhausted, has placed us in a difficult position in the face of a task to accurately assess which is beyond our powers. We have to acknowledge that we do not know the real extent of the evil, and that we cannot determine the relationships and the exact groupings. The Party Conference's main task is to raise the question, not cover up the existing evil, but to draw the Party's attention to it, and call on all Party members to work on remedying the evil. From the point of view of the Central Committee and also, I think, of the immense majority of Party comrades, it is perfectly natural and beyond doubt (as far as I am aware of the views, which nobody has repudiated), that in connection with the crisis in the Party the opposition which exists, not only in Moscow but throughout

Russia, reveals many tendencies that are absolutely healthy, necessary and inevitable at a time of the Party's natural growth and the transition from a situation in which all attention was concentrated on political and military tasks to a period of construction and organisation, when we have to take care of dozens of bureaucratic institutions, this at a time when the cultural level of the majority of the proletariat and the peasants is unequal to the task. After all, the Workers' and Peasants' Inspection exists more as a pious wish; it has been impossible to set it in motion because the best workers have been sent to the front, and the cultural level of the peasant masses is such that they have been unable to produce a sufficient number of officials.

Of course the opposition, whose slogan urges a more speedy transition, the enlistment of the greatest number of fresh and young forces and the promotion of local workers to more responsible posts, has extremely sound aspirations, trend and programme. No doubts on this score exist either in the Central Committee or among comrades who hold positions of any responsibility, as far as can be seen from their statements. It is, however, equally beyond doubt that, besides the sound elements which are united on the platform of fulfilment of Conference decisions, others also exist. At all meetings, including preliminary meetings attended by a larger number of delegates than this Conference, opinions on this question were unanimous. Our general Programme must be carried out—that is beyond doubt, and difficult work awaits us. Of course, the important thing is not to confine ourselves to overthrowing the opponent and repelling him. Here we have petty-bourgeois elements surrounding us and numbering tens of millions. We are fewer in number; there are very few of us compared with this petty-bourgeois mass. We must educate this mass and prepare it, but it has so happened that all the organised forces engaged in such preparatory work have had to be directed elsewhere and employed in an undertaking that is essential, arduous and very risky, involving great sacrifices, i.e., warfare. War calls for every ounce of effort, and there is no getting away from this fact.

The question we must ask ourselves in connection with this state of affairs is: is the Party quite healthy again?

Have we a complete victory over bureaucratic methods so as to place economic construction on a more correct foundation, and get the Workers' and Peasants' Inspection operating, not only in the sense of issuing decrees but by actually drawing the masses of workers into the work? This is a difficult matter, and our main task—if we are to speak of Party tasks—must be the speediest possible elimination of the so-called line of the opposition. If this is a question of diverging views, differing interpretations of current events, different programmes or even of future activities, the Central Committee must devote the greatest attention to the matter at all meetings of the Political Bureau and at plenary meetings, where various shades of opinion are voiced. Harmonious work by the entire Party will ensure the accomplishment of this task. We regard this as a matter of the utmost importance. We now face an economic effort that is more taxing than the military task we have accomplished thanks to the enthusiasm of the peasants, who undoubtedly preferred the workers' state to that of Kolchak. Things are quite different today when the peasant masses have to be switched over to construction work that is quite unfamiliar to them, which they do not understand and cannot have any faith in. This task calls for more systematic work, greater perseverance, and greater organising skill, and so far as the latter quality is concerned, the Russian is not in the picture. This is our weakest point, so we must try rapidly to eliminate everything that hampers this work. The opposition, which is a reflection of this period of transition, no doubt contains a sound element, but when it turns into an opposition for the sake of opposition, we should certainly put an end to it. We have wasted a great deal of time on altercations, quarrels and recrimination and we must put an end to all that, and try to come to some agreement to work more effectively. We must make certain concessions, better greater than smaller, to those who are dissatisfied, who call themselves the opposition, but we must succeed in making our work harmonious, for otherwise we cannot exist when we are surrounded by enemies at home and abroad.

There can be no doubt that the old petty-bourgeois elements—small property-owners—outnumber us. They are stronger than the socialist sector of an economy geared to meet the requirements of the workers. Anyone who has had contacts with the rural areas and has seen the speculation in the cities, realises perfectly well that this social sector, which is based on small-scale economy units is stronger than we are: hence the necessity of absolutely harmonious effort. We must achieve it at all costs. When I had occasion to observe the controversies and the struggle in the Moscow organisations, and saw the numerous debates at meetings, and the altercations, and quarrels there, I came to the conclusion that it was high time to put an end to all this and to achieve general unity on the Conference platform. It should be said that we have paid a heavy price for this. It was sad, for example, to see hours wasted at Party meetings on altercation as to whether someone had arrived at the meeting punctually or not, or whether a particular individual had made his stand clear in one way or another. Do people attend meetings for this sort of thing? For that we have a special commission, which decides whether or not an individual on the list of delegates has made his stand clear in one way or another. Here, however, it is a question of the content of the meeting. For instance, take an experienced Party comrade like Bubnov. I heard his speech on the platform proposed by the Conference. This platform boils down to greater freedom of criticism. The Conference, however, was held in September, and it is now November. Freedom of criticism is a splendid thing—but once we are agreed on this, it would be no bad thing to concern ourselves with the content of criticism. For a long time the Mensheviks, Socialist-Revolutionaries and others tried to scare us with freedom of criticism, but we were not afraid of that. If freedom of criticism means freedom to defend capitalism then we shall suppress it. We have passed that stage. Freedom of criticism has been proclaimed, but thought should be given to the content of criticism.

And here we have to admit something that is highly regrettable: criticism is devoid of content. You visit a district and ask yourself what criticism actually contains. The Party organisations cannot overcome illiteracy by using the old bureaucratic methods. What methods of defeating red tape are there other than bringing workers and peasants into the work? Meanwhile, criticism at district meetings is concerned with trifles, and I have not heard a single word about the Workers' and Peasants' Inspection. I have not heard of a single district encouraging workers and peasants to take part in this work. Genuine construction work means applying criticism which must be constructive. For instance, the management of every small block of flats, every large plant, every factory in Moscow must have its own experience. If we wish to combat bureaucratic methods, we must draw people from below into this work. We must acquaint ourselves with the experience of certain factories, learn what steps they have taken to remove their bureaucrats, and study the experience of a house management or of a consumers' society. A most rapid functioning of the entire economic machine is needed, but meanwhile you do not hear a word about this, although there is plenty of altercation and recrimination. Of course, such a gigantic upheaval could not have taken place without a certain amount of dirt and some scum coming to the surface. It is time we posed the question, not only of freedom of criticism but also of its content. It is time we said that, in view of our experience, we must make a number of concessions but that in future we shall not tolerate the slightest tendency to recrimination. We must break with the past, set about genuine economic construction, and completely overhaul all Party work so as to enable it to guide Soviet economic construction, ensure practical successes, and conduct propaganda more by example than by precept. Today neither the worker nor the peasant will be convinced by words; that can be done only by example. They have to be persuaded that they can improve the economy without the capitalists, and that conflicts can be abolished without the policeman's truncheon or capitalist starvation; for that they need Party leadership. This is the attitude we must adopt; if we do so, we shall achieve successes in future economic construction which will lead to our complete victory on a world-wide scale.

Published in 1920 in the pamphlet *Current Questions of the Party's Present Work*. Published by the Moscow Committee, R.C.P.(B.)

Published according to the text of the pamphlet

SPEECH DELIVERED AT THE MOSCOW GUBERNIA CONFERENCE OF THE R.C.P.(B.) ON ELECTIONS TO THE MOSCOW COMMITTEE NOVEMBER 21, 1920

Comrades, I have often—perhaps too often—had to take part in elections: in Party elections following on a struggle waged by various groups, trends and even factions, and in conditions of a most furious struggle marked by mutual control to such a degree that no voting at any Party cell was considered valid unless conducted in the presence of scrutineers from both groups, who counted the votes cast. Never, however, has the principle of proportional representation been practised in the election of guiding bodies—the Petrograd Committee, the Moscow Committee or the Central Committee. When two groups, two trends or factions, are contesting elections, proportional representation is essential in calling a Party conference as a directing body, or a Party congress. When, however, it is a question of setting up an executive body charged with the conduct of practical work, proportional representation has never been applied, and can hardly be considered justified. I think that, in this connection, the preceding speaker departed from the proportional principle when he declared, together with Ignatov, that it stood to the credit of the list presented by him that it proposed eleven candidates, as he said. I am not in a position to verify eleven out of the thirty-eight, but I think that the concession should be greater than that desired by the effective majority at this assembly, or by the group that consider themselves adherents of the Moscow Committee. I have already elaborated on the motives behind this view, but what should stand first now is the selection of persons. I do not know most of the comrades on these lists, but you, who have the decisive votes at this Conference, evidently know them all. I think that, in choosing the comrades you know personally, you will no doubt be guided exclusively by a desire to set up a group that will be able to work harmoniously, a group that will give expression to any Party trend with something healthy in it, whether or not it has assumed definite shape, or has perhaps remained indeterminate in some respects; however, it has to be a group that, on the whole, directs practical politics, does not proportionally represent all the shades of opinion at this assembly, but carries on militant work—the struggle against the internal and external enemies, in the spirit of Conference decisions, and in a way that leaves no room for discord or lack of harmony. That is why the decisive consideration must be that you, members of this Conference, should have a personal knowledge of each candidate, and give preference to that group which may be expected to work harmoniously, and not the principle of proportionality in the election of an executive body, a principle that has never been applied, and to apply which would hardly be right at present.

Published for the first time in the Fourth (Russian) edition of the *Collected Works*

Published according to the verbatim report

SPEECH DELIVERED AT A CONFERENCE OF FACTORY TRADE UNION COMMITTEES OF MOSCOW ENTERPRISES OF THE PRINTING AND PUBLISHING INDUSTRY NOVEMBER 25, 1920 [148]

BRIEF NEWSPAPER REPORT

(*Comrade Lenin, who was met with a storm of applause from all present, spoke on the first item on the agenda—the international and domestic situation of the Republic and the immediate tasks of the working class.*) Comrade Lenin indicated the causes that have prevented world imperialism from carrying out its plan to crush the proletarian republic, causes stemming in the main from the decay of the capitalist system and the development of the revolutionary movement among the workers of all lands. The language used by our Red Army is the one that is most convincing and comprehensible to the plunderers and robbers, and they have now been forced to talk to us about trade. However, the Red Army's victory will not be complete or lasting unless we cope with the next task, which is more formidable and gigantic, that of rehabilitating industry and improving the national economy.

Lenin touched on the question of electrification, without which the renascence of the country is impossible. After dealing with the question of the invitation of foreign capital and the granting of concessions, the speaker went on to the part played by the printing and publishing industry in the national economy as a whole, and concluded by expressing the confidence that the workers and peasants of Russia will show a splendid example of victory on the peace front, just as they have done so often on the war fronts. (*Prolonged applause.*)

Pravda No. 269,
November 30, 1920

Published according to
the *Pravda* text

SPEECH DELIVERED AT A MEETING OF CELLS' SECRETARIES OF THE MOSCOW ORGANISATION OF THE R.C.P.(B.) NOVEMBER 26, 1920 [149]

NEWSPAPER REPORT

In the first written question submitted, a comrade asks whether it is true that all institutions of administration are to be transferred to Petrograd. That is inaccurate. The rumour has arisen from the fact that the Moscow Soviet has had the idea of transferring non-essential institutions from Moscow to Petrograd because of the housing shortage in the capital. It appears that Petrograd can accept up to 10,000 Soviet office workers, who number 200,000 in Moscow. To study all aspects of the matter, a committee has been set up, which is now working. Its findings will be submitted to the Council of People's Commissars.[150] So you see that this rumour is inaccurate in some respects.

The second question and the third ask about concessions. You will allow me to dwell on the subject.

In one of his books, Spargo, the American Socialist, a man who is something like our Alexinsky, and has a vindictive hate of the Bolsheviks, speaks of concessions as proof of the collapse of communism. Our Mensheviks say the same thing. The challenge has been made, and we are ready to take it up. Let us consider the question in terms of the facts. Who has got the worse of it, we or the European bourgeoisie? For three years they have been calumniating us, calling us usurpers and bandits; they have had recourse to all and every means to overthrow us, but have now had to confess to failure, which is in itself a victory for us. The Mensheviks assert that we are pledged to defeating the world bourgeoisie on our own. We have, however, always said that we are only a single link in the chain of the world revolution, and have never set ourselves the aim of achieving victory by our own means. The world revolution has not yet come about, but then we have not yet been overcome. While militarism is decaying, we are growing stronger; not we, but they have had the worse of it.

They now want to subdue us by means of a treaty. Until the revolution comes about, bourgeois capital will be useful to us. How can we speed up the development of our economy whilst we are an economically weaker country? We can do that with the aid of bourgeois capital. We now have before us two drafts of concessions. One of them is for a ten-year concession in Kamchatka. We were recently visited by an American multimillionaire, who told us very frankly of the reasons behind the treaty, viz., that America wants to have a base in Asia in case of a war against Japan. This multimillionaire said that if we sold Kamchatka to America, he could promise us such enthusiasm among the people of the United States that the American Government would immediately recognise the Soviets of Russia. If we gave them only the lease, there would be less enthusiasm. He is now on his way to America, where he will make it known that Soviet Russia is a far cry from what people believed her to be.

We have till now been more than a match for the world bourgeoisie, because they are incapable of uniting. The Treaties of Brest-Litovsk and Versailles[151] have both divided them. An intense hostility is now developing between America and Japan. We are making use of this and are offering a lease of Kamchatka instead of giving it away gratis; after all, Japan has taken a huge expanse of our territory in the Far East,[152] this by force of arms. It is far more to our advantage to run no risk, grant a lease of Kamchatka, and receive part of its products, the more so for our being unable, in any case, to run or exploit it. The treaty has not been signed, but it is already being spoken of in Japan with the utmost anger. Through this treaty we have aggravated the differences between our enemies.

The second kind of concession is represented by our granting the lease of several million dessiatines* of timberland in Archangel Gubernia which, despite all our efforts, we cannot fully exploit. We are arranging a kind of checkerboard pattern, with sections of timberland we shall be exploiting alternating with the leased sections, so that our workers will be able to learn the use of felling equipment from their neighbours. All this is very much to our advantage.

And now for the final aspect of the question.

Concessions do not mean peace; they too are a kind of warfare, only in another form, one that is to our advantage. Previously war was waged with the aid of tanks, cannon and the like, which hindered our work; the war will now be conducted on the economic front. They may perhaps try to restore the freedom to trade, but they cannot get along without us. Besides, they have to submit to all our laws, and our workers can learn from them; in case of war—and we must always be prepared for war against the bourgeoisie—the property will remain in our hands by virtue of the laws of war. I repeat: concessions are a continuation of war on the economic front, but here we do not destroy our productive forces, but develop them. They will no doubt try to evade our laws and deceive us, but we have the appropriate bodies to deal with that, such as the All-Russia Cheka, the Moscow Cheka, the Gubernia Cheka, and so on, and we are sure that we shall win.

Eighteen months ago we wanted to sign a peace that would have given Denikin and Kolchak a vast territory. They turned this down and in consequence lost everything.[153] We have mapped out the right road to the world revolution, but this road is not a straight one, but goes in zigzags. We have weakened the bourgeoisie, so that it cannot overcome us by force of arms. They used to ban our conduct of communist propaganda; but there can be no question of that at present, and it would be ridiculous to demand such things. They are decaying from within, and that gives us strength. We do not imagine that we shall defeat the world bourgeoi-

---

* *Dessiatine*—a Russian unit of land measure equal to 2.7 acres.—*Ed.*

sie by force of arms alone, and the Mensheviks are wrong in ascribing that intention to us.

I did not hear Comrade Kamenev's report on the Conference, but I shall say that the latter teaches us a lesson: no matter how the struggle proceeded and whatever memories remain, we must put a complete end to everything. It should be remembered that the consolidation of our forces is the main and most important task. Tasks of economic construction await us. That transition will be difficult after six years of war, and we have to tackle the problem with united forces, on the platform of the All-Russia Conference's resolutions, which must be carried out. The struggle against red-tape methods, and economic and administrative work call for unity. What is expected of us is propaganda by example; the non-Party masses have to be set an example. It will be no easy matter to carry out the resolutions, but we must concentrate all our forces on that task and set about working in all earnest. I call upon you to do that.

Pravda No. 269,
November 30, 1920

Published according to the *Pravda* text checked against the verbatim report

SPEECH DELIVERED AT A GENERAL MEETING OF COMMUNISTS OF ZAMOSKVORECHYE DISTRICT, MOSCOW NOVEMBER 29, 1920

BRIEF NEWSPAPER REPORT

Comrade Lenin dwelt in detail on the problem of the struggle against bureaucratic methods which, in its differences with the majority at the gubernia conference, our so-called "opposition" is advancing almost as a matter of principle. Though he thought that the fact that the "opposition" had raised this question was in itself a healthy sign, Lenin at the same time attacked the opposition for its frivolous attitude to the question. Indicating the causes of the recrudescence of bureaucratic methods in our Soviet state and the roots now nourishing them, Lenin very emphatically warned the comrades against the idea that this evil could be combated by resolutions on paper and by abstract criticism devoid of any substance. The Mensheviks and the Socialist-Revolutionaries, who were out to make capital out of this question, both reproached us with being unable to combat red tape in our Soviet apparatus. There had been a time when these gentlemen had said that we would be unable to preserve our Soviet state; now they said: "They have preserved it, it is true, but bureaucratic methods remain in the Soviet institutions, even though Lenin said in such-and-such a book that red tape would be abolished under the rule of the Soviets."

But that was not how the matter stood.

First of all, general living standards had to be raised, so that the worker would not have to go about in search of flour, with a sack on his back, and hundreds of thousands and millions of working people should pass through the school of the Workers' and Peasants' Inspection and learn to administer the state (which was something nobody had taught us), so that they might replace hundreds of thousands of bourgeois bureaucrats.

Incidentally, a reference to the Workers' and Peasants' Inspection. That body had been set up nearly a year before, but it had so far made itself felt very little as a school training people in the administration of the state. It would not be amiss for comrades who really wanted to expedite the fight against bureaucratic methods to work in this sphere and learn some useful lessons.

Lenin remarked that the question of combating red tape was particularly acute in Moscow, because there the comrades came up against, not only Moscow bureaucrats but bureaucrats on a national scale, since central institutions were concentrated there. There were 200,000 Soviet functionaries in Moscow, of whom only 10,000 could be transferred with their institutions to Petrograd in the near future.

It was only to be expected that red tape in the Soviet apparatus would penetrate into the Party apparatus, for these apparatuses are interwoven most intimately. The fight against the evil could and should be placed on the order of the day—not, however, in the sense of criticism for criticism's sake, but of practical suggestions as to the methods of waging that struggle, and better still, of a real struggle in the institutions in which the criticising comrades were working, and of publicity for the results and lessons of the struggle.

CONCLUDING REMARKS

In his concluding remarks Comrade Lenin pointed out to his "opponents", in sharp terms, that it was not befitting for Communists to indulge in such unsubstantiated criticism, such sweeping accusations against the Central Committee, without citing a single fact, such bandying about of names even of experts, and lumping them all together as "bourgeois elements", without even trying to find out what kind of people they were. Lenin mentioned by name a number of workers who had been able to make a success of joint work with experts, establish correct relations with the latter, and obtain from them what was needed. Such workers did not complain of the experts; the grumbling came from those who had not coped with the work. An example was Shlyapnikov (one of the opponents, who had presented himself as a member of the Workers' Opposition[154]), a man who was sparing no effort, as Lenin put it, "to hatch differences", a man who objected to what Lenin had said in his report about our deep debt to the peasantry, and went on to say that the "opposition disagrees with Comrade Lenin". The selfsame Shlyapnikov would turn a blind eye to his own poor work, and was out to present his mission to Archangel as exile imposed by the Central Committee. Another instance was Comrade Bubnov, who spoke so much about the struggle against red tape, without saying a single word about the way he was combating the evil at least in the Central Administration of the Textile Industry which he headed, and where there was no less red tape, perhaps even more, than in other institutions. That was why Vladimir Ilyich warned the Zamoskvorechye comrades in the following terms: "When you hear such criticism, criticism without any content, criticism for the sake of criticism, be on your guard; make inquiry to find out whether the criticising comrade's vanity has not been injured in some way; perhaps he has been offended or is irritated, which drives him towards groundless opposition, opposition for its own sake."

In conclusion, Comrade Lenin replied to written questions handed to him, and then dealt in detail with the question of concessions.

Pravda No. 273,
December 4, 1920

Published according to
the *Pravda* text

TELEGRAM TO THE CHAIRMAN OF THE REVOLUTIONARY MILITARY COMMITTEE OF ARMENIA [155]

To Comrade Kasyan, Chairman of the Revolutionary Military Committee of Armenia, Yerevan

Through you I send greetings to the Soviet Armenia of the working people, liberated from the yoke of imperialism. I have no doubt that you will exert every effort to establish fraternal solidarity between the working people of Armenia, Turkey and Azerbaijan.

Lenin

Chairman of the Council of People's Commissars

Moscow, December 2, 1920

Pravda No. 273,
December 4, 1920

Published according to the *Pravda* text

SPEECH DELIVERED AT A MEETING OF ACTIVISTS OF THE MOSCOW ORGANISATION OF THE R.C.P.(B.) DECEMBER 6, 1920

Comrades, I have noticed with great pleasure, although, I must confess, with surprise, that the question of concessions is arousing enormous interest. Cries are to be heard on all sides, mostly from the rank and file. "How can that be?" they ask. "We have driven out our own exploiters, and yet we are inviting others from abroad."

It will readily be understood why these outcries give me pleasure. The fact that a cry of alarm has gone up from the rank and file about the possibility of the old capitalists returning, and that this cry has gone up in connection with an act of such tenth-rate significance as the decree on concessions, shows that there is a very keen consciousness of the danger of capitalism and the great danger of the struggle against it. That is excellent, of course, and it is all the more excellent because, as I have already said, alarm is being voiced by the rank and file.

From the political point of view, the fundamental thing in the question of concessions—and here there are both political and economic considerations—is a rule we have not only assimilated in theory, but have also applied in practice, a rule which will remain fundamental with us for a long time until socialism finally triumphs all over the world: we must take advantage of the antagonisms and the contradictions that exist between the two imperialisms, the two groups of capitalist states, and play them off against each other. Until we have conquered the whole world, and as long as we are economically and militarily weaker than the capitalist world, we must stick to the rule that we must be able to take advantage of the antagonisms and contradictions existing among the imperialists. Had we not adhered to this rule, every one of us would have long ago been strung up by the neck, to the glee of the capitalists. We gained our chief experience in this respect when we concluded the Treaty of Brest-Litovsk. It should not be inferred that all treaties must be like that of Brest-Litovsk, or the Treaty of Versailles. That is not true. There may be a third kind of treaty, one that is advantageous to us.

Brest-Litovsk was significant in being the first time that we were able, on an immense scale and amidst vast difficulties, to take advantage of the contradictions among the imperialists in such a way as to make socialism the ultimate gainer. During the Brest-Litovsk period there were two immensely powerful groups of imperialist predators—the Austro-German and the Anglo-Franco-American. They were locked in a furious struggle which was to decide the fate of the world for the immediate future. That we were able to hold on—though from the military standpoint our forces were non-existent, we possessed nothing and were steadily sinking into the depths of economic chaos—the fact that we were able to hold on was a miracle that resulted from our having taken due advantage of the conflict between German and American imperialism. We made a tremendous concession to German imperialism; by doing so we at once safeguarded ourselves against persecution by both imperialisms. Germany was unable to concentrate on stifling Soviet Russia either economically or politically; she was too busy for that. We let her have the Ukraine, from which she could get all the grain and coal she wanted—provided, of course, she was able to get them, and had the strength for the purpose. Anglo-Franco-American imperialism was unable to attack us because we first made an offer of peace. A big book by Robins has just appeared in America, in which the author describes the U.S. talks with Lenin and Trotsky, who gave their consent to the conclusion of peace. Although the Americans were helping the Czechoslovaks and making them take part in the military intervention, they were unable to interfere because they were busy with their own war.

The outcome might have seemed something like a bloc between the first Socialist Republic and German imperialism, against another imperialism. However, we did not conclude a bloc of any kind; we nowhere exceeded the borderline that would undermine or defame the socialist state; we simply took advantage of the conflict between the two imperialisms in such a way that both were ultimately the losers. Germany obtained nothing from the Brest Peace except several million poods of grain, but she brought the disintegrating force of Bolshevism into the country. We, however, gained time, in the course of which the formation of the Red Army began. Even the tremendous distress suffered by the Ukraine proved reparable, although at a heavy price. What our antagonists had counted on, namely, the rapid collapse of Soviet rule in Russia, did not come to pass. We made use of the interval history had accorded us as a breathing-space in order to consolidate ourselves to a degree that would make it impossible to vanquish us by military force. We gained time, a little time, but in return had to sacrifice a great deal of territory. In those days, I recall, people used to philosophise and say that to gain time we must surrender territory. It was in accordance with the philosophers' theory of time and space that we acted in practice and in policy: we sacrificed a great deal of territory, but won sufficient time to enable us to muster strength. Then, when all the imperialists wanted to launch a full-scale war against us, that proved impossible: they had neither the means nor the forces for such a war. At that time we sacrificed no fundamental interests; we conceded minor interests and preserved what was fundamental.

This, incidentally, raises the question of opportunism. Opportunism means sacrificing fundamental interests so as to gain temporary and partial advantages. That is the gist of the matter, if we consider the theoretical definition of opportunism. Many people have gone astray on this point. In the case of the Brest-Litovsk Peace, we sacrificed Russia's interests, as understood in the patriotic sense, which were, in fact, secondary from the socialist point of view. We made immense sacrifices, yet they were only minor ones. The Germans hated Britain implacably. They hated the Bolsheviks too, but we held out a bait, and they fell for it.

They had all the time asserted that they would not go as far as Napoleon did. Indeed, they did not reach Moscow, but they penetrated into the Ukraine where they came to grief. They thought they had learnt a lot from Napoleon, but things worked out otherwise. We, on the other hand, gained a great deal.

The example of the Peace of Brest-Litovsk has taught us a lot. At present, we stand between two foes. If we are unable to defeat both of them, we must be able to dispose our forces in such a way as to make them fall out among themselves; whenever thieves fall out, honest men come into their own. However, as soon as we are strong enough to overcome capitalism as a whole, we shall immediately seize it by the scruff of the neck. Our strength is growing, and very rapidly. The Peace of Brest-Litovsk was a lesson we shall never forget, one which, in respect of the conclusions to be drawn from it, was worth more than any propaganda or preaching. We have now won in the sense that we stand on our own feet. We are surrounded by imperialist states which detest the Bolsheviks and are spending vast sums of money, using ideological means, the power of the press, and so on, and yet have been unable to defeat us in three years of war, although we are infinitely weak from the military and economic standpoint. We do not possess one-hundredth of the forces of the combined imperialist states, yet they are unable to stifle us. They cannot crush us because their soldiers will not obey; their war-weary workers and peasants do not want a war against the Soviet Republic. Such is the position now, and that is what we must proceed from. We do not know what the position will be like several years from now, since with every year the Western powers are recovering from the war.

Since the Second Congress of the Third International we have secured a firm foothold in the imperialist countries, not only in the sphere of ideology but also in that of organisation. In all countries there are groups which are carrying on independent work and will continue to do so. That has been accomplished. But the rate, the tempo of development of the revolution in the capitalist countries is far slower than in our country. It was evident that the revolutionary movement would inevitably slow down when the nations secured peace. Therefore, without surmising as to the future, we cannot now rely on this tempo becoming rapid. We have to decide what we are to do at the present time. Every people lives in a state, and every state belongs to a system of states, which are in a certain system of political equilibrium in relation to one another.

Let us bear in mind that all over the world the capitalists have bought up the vast majority of the richest sources of raw materials, or, if they have not actually bought them, they have seized them politically; since there is a balance based on capitalism, that must be reckoned with and turned to account. We cannot go to war with the present-day Entente. Our agitation has been and is being conducted splendidly—of that we are certain. We must take political advantage of the differences among our opponents, but only of major differences that are due to profound economic causes. If we try to exploit minor and fortuitous differences, we shall be behaving like petty politicians and cheap diplomats. There is nothing of value to be gained by that. There are swarms of diplomats who play this game; they do so for several months, make careers, and then come to grief.

Are there any radical antagonisms in the present-day capitalist world that must be utilised? Yes, there are three principal ones, which I should like to enumerate. The first, the one that affects us closest, is the relations between Japan and America. War is brewing between them. They cannot live together in peace on the shores of the Pacific, although those shores are three thousand versts apart. This rivalry arises incontestably from the relation between their capitalisms. A vast literature exists on the future Japanese-American war. It is beyond doubt that war is brewing, that it is inevitable. The pacifists are trying to ignore the matter and obscure it with general phrases, but no student of the history of economic relations and diplomacy can have the slightest doubt that war is ripe from the economic viewpoint and is being prepared politically. One cannot open a single book on this subject without seeing that a war is brewing. The world has been partitioned. Japan has seized vast colonies. Japan has a population of fifty million, and she is comparatively weak economically. America has a population of a hundred and ten million, and although she is many times richer than Japan she has no colonies. Japan has seized China, which has a population of four hundred million and the richest coal reserves in the world. How can this plum be kept? It is absurd to think that a stronger capitalism will not deprive a weaker capitalism of the latter's spoils. Can the Americans remain indifferent under such circumstances? Can strong capitalists remain side by side with weak capitalists and not be expected to grab everything they can from the latter? What would they be good for if they did not? But that being the case, can we, as Communists, remain indifferent and merely say: "We shall carry on propaganda for communism in these countries." That is correct, but it is not everything. The practical task of communist policy is to take advantage of this hostility and to play one side off against the other. Here a new situation arises. Take the two imperialist countries, Japan and America. They want to fight and will fight for world supremacy, for the right to loot. Japan will fight so as to continue to plunder Korea, which she is doing with unprecedented brutality, combining all the latest technical inventions with purely Asiatic tortures. We recently received a Korean newspaper which gives an account of what the Japanese are doing. Here we find all the methods of tsarism and all the latest technical perfections combined with a purely Asiatic system of torture and unparalleled brutality. But the Americans would like to grab this Korean titbit. Of course, defence of country in such a war would be a heinous crime, a betrayal of socialism. Of course, to support one of these countries against the other would be a crime against communism; we Communists have to play one off against the other. Are we not committing a crime against communism? No, because we are doing that as a socialist state which is carrying on communist propaganda and is obliged to take advantage of every hour granted it by circumstances in order to gain strength as rapidly as possible. We have begun to gain strength, but very slowly. America and the other capitalist countries are growing in economic and military might at tremendous speed. We shall develop far more slowly, however we muster our forces.

We must take advantage of the situation that has arisen. That is the whole purpose of the Kamchatka concessions.

We have had a visit from Vanderlip, a distant relative of the well-known multimillionaire, if he is to be believed; but since our intelligence service in the Cheka, although splendidly organised, unfortunately does not yet extend to the United States of America, we have not yet established the exact kinship of these Vanderlips. Some even say there is no kinship at all. I do not presume to judge: my knowledge is confined to having read a book by Vanderlip, not the one that was in our country and is said to be such a very important person that he has been received with all the honours by kings and ministers—from which one must infer that his pocket is very well lined indeed. He spoke to them in the way people discuss matters at meetings such as ours, for instance, and told them in the calmest tones how Europe should be restored. If ministers spoke to him with so much respect, it must mean that Vanderlip is in touch with the multimillionaires. His book reveals the outlook of a man of business who knows nothing else but business and who, after observing Europe, says: "It looks as if nothing will come of it and everything will go to the devil." The book is full of hatred of Bolshevism, but it does take up the matter of establishing business contacts. It is a most interesting book from the point of view of agitation too, better than many a communist book, because its final conclusion is: "I'm afraid this patient is incurable—though we have lots of money and the means for his treatment."

Well, Vanderlip brought a letter to the Council of People's Commissars. It was a very interesting letter, for, with the utter frankness, cynicism and crudity of an American tightfist, the writer of the letter said: "We are very strong now, in 1920, and in 1923 our navy will be still stronger. However, Japan stands in the way of our growing might and we shall have to fight her, and you cannot fight without oil. Sell us Kamchatka, and I can vouch that the enthusiasm of the American people will be so great that we shall recognise you. The presidential elections in March will result in a victory for our party. If, however, you let us have only the lease of Kamchatka, I assure you there will be no such enthusiasm." That is almost literally what he said in his letter. Here we have an unblushing imperialism, which does not even consider it necessary to veil itself in any way because it thinks it is magnificent just as it is. When this letter was received, we said that we must grasp at the opportunity with both hands. That he is right, economically speaking, is shown by the fact that in America the Republican Party is on the eve of victory. For the first time in the history of America, people in the South have voted against the Democrats. It is therefore clear that here we have the economically correct reasoning of an imperialist. Kamchatka belonged to the former Russian Empire. That is true. Who it belongs to at the present moment is not clear. It seems to be the property of a state called the Far Eastern Republic, but the boundaries of that state have not been precisely fixed.[156] True, certain documents are being drawn up on the subject, but, first, they have not yet been drawn up, and, second, they have not yet been ratified. The Far East is dominated by Japan, who can do anything she pleases there. If we lease to America Kamchatka, which legally belongs to us but has actually been seized by Japan, we shall clearly be the gainers. That is the basis of my political reasoning, and on that basis we at once decided to conclude an immediate agreement with America. Of course, we have to bargain, as no businessman will respect us if we do not. Comrade Rykov accordingly began to bargain, and we drafted an agreement. But when it came to the actual signing, we said: "Everybody knows who we are, but who are you?" It transpired that Vanderlip could provide no guarantee, whereupon we said that we were ready to accommodate. Why, we said, this is merely a draft, and you said yourself that it would come into force when your party gained the upper hand; it has not gained the upper hand as yet, so we shall wait. Things worked out as follows: we drew up a draft of the treaty, as yet unsigned, giving Kamchatka—a big slice of the territory of the Far East and North-East Siberia to America for a period of sixty years, with the right to build a naval harbour in a port that is ice-free the year round, and has oil and coal.

A draft agreement is not binding in any way. We can always say that it contains unclear passages, and back out at any moment. In that case we shall only have lost time in negotiating with Vanderlip, and a few sheets of paper; yet we have already gained something. One has only to take the reports from Europe to see that. There is hardly a report from Japan which does not speak of the great concern caused by the expected concessions. "We shall not tolerate it," Japan declares, "it infringes our interests." Go ahead then, and defeat America; we have no objections. We have already set Japan and America at loggerheads, to put it crudely, and have thereby gained a point. We have also gained as far as the Americans are concerned.

Who is Vanderlip? We have not established who he is—but it is a fact that in the capitalist world telegrams are not dispatched all over the world about rank-and-file citizens. And when he left us, telegrams went to all corners of the earth. Well, he went about saying that he had obtained a good concession and, wherever he went, began to praise Lenin. That was rather funny, but let me tell you that there is a bit of politics in this funny situation. When Vanderlip had concluded all his negotiations here, he wanted to meet me. I consulted representatives of the appropriate departments and asked whether I should receive him. They said, "Let him leave with a sense of satisfaction." Vanderlip came to see me. We talked about all these things, and when he began to tell me that he had been in Siberia, that he knew Siberia and came of a worker's family, just like most American multimillionaires, and so on, that they valued only practical things, and that they believed a thing only when they saw it, I replied, "Well, you are a practical people, and when you see the Soviet system you will introduce it in your own country." He stared at me in amazement at this turn in the conversation, and said to me in Russian (the whole conversation had been in English), "Mozhet byt."* I asked in surprise where he had got his knowledge of Russian. "Why, I covered most of Siberia on horseback when I was twenty-five". I will tell you of a remark by Vanderlip which belongs to the sphere of the humorous. At parting he said: "I shall have to tell them in America that Mr. Lenin has no horns." I did not grasp his meaning at once, as I don't understand English very well. "What did you say? Will you please repeat that?" He is a spry old fellow; pointing to his temple, he said, "No horns here."

---

* Perhaps.—*Ed.*

There was an interpreter present who said, "That is exactly what he says." In America they are convinced that I have horns here, that is, the bourgeois say that I have been marked by the devil. "And now I shall have to tell them that you have no horns," said Vanderlip. We parted very amicably. I expressed the hope that friendly relations between the two states would be a basis not only for the granting of a concession, but also for the normal development of reciprocal economic assistance. It all went off in that kind of vein. Then telegrams came telling what Vanderlip had said on arriving home from abroad. Vanderlip had compared Lenin with Washington and Lincoln. Vanderlip had asked for my autographed portrait. I had declined, because when you present a portrait you write, "To Comrade So-and-so", and I could not write, "To Comrade Vanderlip". Neither was it possible to write: "To the Vanderlip we are signing a concession with" because that concession agreement would be concluded by the Administration when it took office. I did not know what to write. It would have been illogical to give my photograph to an out-and-out imperialist. Yet these were the kind of telegrams that arrived; this affair has clearly played a certain part in imperialist politics. When the news of the Vanderlip concessions came out, Harding—the man who has been elected President, but who will take office only next March issued an official denial, declaring that he knew nothing about it, had no dealings with the Bolsheviks and had heard nothing about any concessions. That was during the elections, and, for all we know, to confess, during elections, that you have dealings with the Bolsheviks may cost you votes. That was why he issued an official denial. He had this report sent to all the newspapers that are hostile to the Bolsheviks and are on the pay roll of the imperialist parties. The political advantages we can gain in respect of America and Japan are perfectly clear to us. This report is significant because it concretely shows the kind of concessions we want to sign, and on what terms. Of course this cannot be told to the press. It can be told only to a Party meeting. We must not be silent in the press about this agreement. It is to our advantage, and we must not say a single word that may hamper the conclusion of such an agreement because it promises us tremendous advantages and a weakening of both U.S. and Japanese imperialism with regard to us.

All this deal means deflecting the imperialist forces away from us—while the imperialists are sighing and waiting for an opportune moment to strangle the Bolsheviks, we are deferring that moment. When Japan was becoming involved in the Korean venture, the Japanese said to the Americans: "Of course, we can beat the Bolsheviks, but what will you give us for it? China? We shall take her anyway, whereas here we have to go ten thousand versts to beat the Bolsheviks, with you Americans in our rear. No, that is not politics." Even then the Japanese could have beaten us in a few weeks, had there been a double-track railway and America's aid in transport facilities. What saved us was the fact that while Japan was busy gobbling up China she could not advance westward, through all of Siberia, with America in her rear; moreover, she did not want to pull America's chestnuts out of the fire.

A war between the imperialist powers would have saved us even more. If we are obliged to put up with such scoundrels as the capitalist robbers, each of whom is ready to knife us, it is our prime duty to make them turn their knives against each other. Whenever thieves fall out, honest men come into their own. The second gain is purely political. Even if this concession agreement does not materialise, it will be to our advantage. As for the economic gain, it will provide us with part of the products. If the Americans received part of the products, it would be to our advantage. There is so much oil and ore in Kamchatka that we are obviously not in a position to work them.

I have shown you one of the imperialist antagonisms we must take advantage of—that which exists between Japan and America. There is another—the antagonism between America and the rest of the capitalist world. Practically the entire capitalist world of "victors" emerged from the war tremendously enriched. America is strong; she is everybody's creditor and everything depends on her; she is being more and more detested; she is robbing all and sundry and doing so in a unique fashion. She has no colonies. Britain emerged from the war with vast colonies. So did France. Britain offered America a mandate—that is the language they use nowadays—for one of the colonies she had seized, but America did not accept it. U.S. businessmen evidently reason in some other way. They have seen that, in the devastation it produces and the temper it arouses among the workers, war has very definite consequences, and they have come to the conclusion that there is nothing to be gained by accepting a mandate. Naturally, however, they will not permit this colony to be used by any other state. All bourgeois literature testifies to a rising hatred of America, while in America there is a growing demand for an agreement with Russia. America signed an agreement with Kolchak giving him recognition and support but here they have already come to grief, the only reward for their pains being losses and disgrace. Thus we have before us the greatest state in the world, which by 1923 will have a navy stronger than the British, and this state is meeting with growing enmity from the other capitalist countries. We must take this trend of things into account. America cannot come to terms with the rest of Europe—that is a fact proved by history. Nowhere has the Versailles Treaty been analysed so well as in the book by Keynes, a British representative at Versailles. In his book Keynes ridicules Wilson and the part he played in the Treaty of Versailles. Here, Wilson proved to be an utter simpleton, whom Clemenceau and Lloyd George twisted round their little fingers. Thus everything goes to show that America cannot come to terms with the other countries because of the profound economic antagonism between them, since America is richer than the rest.

We shall therefore examine all questions of concessions from this angle: if the least opportunity arises of aggravating the differences between America and the other capitalist countries, it should be grasped with both hands. America stands in inevitable contradiction with the colonies, and if she attempts to become more involved there she will be helping us ten times as much. The colonies are seething with unrest, and when you touch them, whether or not you like it, whether or not you are rich—and the richer you are the better—you will be helping us, and the Vanderlips will be sent packing. That is why to us this antagonism is the main consideration.

15-988

The third antagonism is that between the Entente and Germany. Germany has been vanquished, crushed by the Treaty of Versailles, but she possesses vast economic potentialities. Germany is the world's second country in economic development, if America is taken as the first. The experts even say that as far as the electrical industry is concerned she is superior to America, and you know that the electrical industry is tremendously important. As regards the extent of the application of electricity, America is superior, but Germany has surpassed her in technical perfection. It is on such a country that the Treaty of Versailles has been imposed, a treaty she cannot possibly live under. Germany is one of the most powerful and advanced of the capitalist countries. She cannot put up with the Treaty of Versailles. Although she is herself imperialist, Germany is obliged to seek for an ally against world imperialism, because she has been crushed. That is the situation we must turn to our advantage. Everything that increases the antagonism between America and the rest of the Entente or between the entire Entente and Germany should be used by us from the viewpoint of the concessions. That is why we must try and attract their interest; that is why the pamphlet Milyutin promised to bring, and has brought and will distribute, contains the decrees of the Council of People's Commissars written in a way that will attract prospective concessionaires. The booklet contains maps with explanations. We shall get it translated into all languages and encourage its distribution with the aim of setting Germany against Britain, because concessions will be a lifeline to Germany. We shall likewise set America against Japan, the entire Entente against America, and all Germany against the Entente.

These, then, are the three antagonisms that are upsetting the imperialists' apple-cart. That is the crux of the matter; that is why, from the political standpoint, we should be heart and soul—or rather with all our wits—in favour of concessions.

I now go over to the economics. When we were speaking of Germany we came up to the question of economics. Germany cannot exist from the economic standpoint following the Peace of Versailles; neither can all the defeated countries, such as Austria-Hungary in her former boundaries, for although parts of that country now belong to the victor states, she cannot exist under the Treaty of Versailles. These countries form, in Central Europe, a vast group with enormous economic and technical might. From the economic standpoint they are all essential to the restoration of the world economy. If you carefully read and re-read the Decree on Concessions of November 23, you will find that we stress the significance of the world economy, and we do so intentionally. That is undoubtedly correct. For the world economy to be restored, Russian raw materials must be utilised. You cannot get along without them—that is economcally true. It is admitted even by a bourgeois of the first water, a student of economics, who regards things from a purely bourgeois standpoint. That man is Keynes, author of *The Economic Consequences of the Peace*. Vanderlip, who has travelled all over Europe as a financial magnate, also admits that the world economy cannot be restored because it appears that there is very little raw material available in the world, it having been dissipated in the war. He says that Russia must be relied on. And Russia now comes forward and declares to the world: we undertake to restore the international economy—here is our plan. That is sound economics. During this period Soviet government has grown stronger; not only has it grown stronger, but it has advanced a plan for the restoration of the entire world economy. The rehabilitation of the international economy by means of a plan of electrification is scientifically sound. With our plan we shall most certainly attract the sympathy, not only of all the workers but of sensible capitalists as well, regardless of the fact that in their eyes we are "those terrible Bolshevik terrorists", and so forth. Our economic plan is therefore correct; when they read this plan, all the petty-bourgeois democrats will swing over towards us, for while the imperialists have already fallen out among themselves, here is a plan to which engineers and economists can offer no objection. We are entering the field of economics and are offering the world a positive programme of construction; we are opening up prospects based on economic considerations, prospects which Russia regards not as a selfish plan to destroy the economies of other lands, as was the rule in the past, but as a way to restore those economies in the interests of the whole world.

We are shifting the question to the anti-capitalist plane. We say that we undertake to build the whole world on a rational economic foundation; there can be no doubt that this idea is a correct one. There can be no doubt that if we set to work properly, with modern machinery and the help of science, the whole world economy can be restored at once.

We are conducting a kind of industrial propaganda when we say to the master class: "You capitalists are useless; while you are going to rack and ruin, we are building in our own way; so don't you think, gentlemen, it is time to come to terms with us?" To which all the capitalists of the world will have to reply, though grudgingly: "Yes, perhaps it is. Let us sign a trade agreement."

The British have already made a draft and sent it to us.[157] It is under discussion. New times are setting in. Their war schemes have miscarried and they now have to fight in the economic field. We fully understand that. We never imagined that with the fighting over and the advent of peace, the capitalist wolf would lie down with the socialist lamb. No, we did not. Yet the fact that you have to fight us in the economic field is a tremendous step forward. We have presented you with a world programme by regarding concessions from the standpoint of the world economy. That is indisputable from the viewpoint of economics. No engineer or agronomist who has anything to do with the national economy will deny that. Many capitalists say there cannot be a stable system of capitalist states without Russia. Yet we have advanced such a programme in the capacity of builders of a world economy based on a different plan. That is of tremendous propaganda value. Even if they do not sign a single concession—which I regard as quite possible—even if the sole outcome of all this talk of concessions will be a certain number of Party meetings and decrees, without a single concession being granted, we shall still have gained something. Besides advancing a plan of economic reconstruction, we are winning over all states that have been ruined by the war. At the congress of the Third, Communist International I said that the whole world is divided into oppressed and oppressor nations.

The oppressed nations constitute not less than seventy per cent of the population of the earth. To these the Peace of Versailles has added another hundred or hundred and fifty million people.

We now stand, not only as representatives of the proletarians of all countries but as representatives of the oppressed peoples as well. A journal of the Communist International recently appeared under the title of *Narody Vostoka.*[158] It carries the following slogan issued by the Communist International for the peoples of the East: "Workers of all countries and all oppressed peoples, unite!" "When did the Executive Committee give orders for slogans to be modified?" one of the comrades asked. Indeed, I do not remember that it ever did. Of course, the modification is wrong from the standpoint of the *Communist Manifesto*, but then the *Communist Manifesto* was written under entirely different conditions. From the point of view of present-day politics, however, the change is correct. Relations have become tense. All Germany is seething; so is all of Asia. You have read how the revolutionary movement is developing in India. In China there is a fierce hatred of the Japanese, and also of the Americans. In Germany there is such seething hatred of the Entente as can only be understood by those who have seen the hatred of the German workers for their own capitalists. As a result, they have made Russia the immediate representative of the entire mass of the oppressed population of the earth; the events are teaching the peoples to regard Russia as a centre of attraction. A Menshevik newspaper in Georgia recently wrote: "There are two forces in the world: the Entente and Soviet Russia." What are the Mensheviks? They are people who trim their sails to the wind. When we were weak internationally, they cried, "Down with the Bolsheviks!" When we began to grow stronger, they cried, "We are neutral!" Now that we have beaten off the enemies, they say, "Yes, there are two forces."

In the concessions decree we come forward, on behalf of all humanity, with an economically irreproachable programme for the restoration of the world's economic forces by utilising all raw materials, wherever they are to be found. What we consider important is that there should be no starvation anywhere. You capitalists cannot eliminate it; we can. We are speaking for seventy per cent of the population of the earth. This is sure to exert an influence. Whatever comes of the project, no exception can be taken to it from the angle of economics. The economic aspect of concessions is important, regardless of whether they are signed or not.

As you see, I have been obliged to make a rather long introduction and to demonstrate the advantages of concessions. Of course, concessions are important to us also as a means of obtaining commodities. That is unquestionably true, but the chief thing is the political aspect. By the time the Congress of Soviets meets you will receive a book of six hundred pages—the plan for the electrification of Russia. This plan has been devised by the leading agronomists and engineers. We cannot expedite its realisation without the help of foreign capital and means of production. But if we want assistance, we must pay for it. So far, we have been fighting the capitalists, and they said that they would either strangle us or compel us to pay up twenty thousand millions. However they are in no position to strangle us, and we shall not pay the debts. For the time being we are enjoying a certain respite. As long as we are in need of economic assistance we are willing to pay you—that is the way we put the matter, and any other way would be economically unsound. Russia is in a state of industrial ruin; she is ten times or more worse off than before the war. Had we been told three years ago that we would be fighting the entire capitalist world for three years, we would not have believed it. But now we shall be told that to restore the economy, with only one-tenth of the pre-war national wealth is a still more difficult task. And indeed it is more difficult than fighting. We could fight with the help of the enthusiasm of the working-class masses and the peasants, who were defending themselves against the landowners. At present it is not a question of defence against the landowners, but of restoring economic life along lines the peasants are not accustomed to. Here victory will not depend on enthusiasm, dash, or self-sacrifice, but on day-by-day, monotonous, petty and workaday effort. That is undoubtedly a more difficult matter. Where are we to procure the means of production we need? To attract the Americans, we must pay: they are men of business. And what are we to pay with? With gold? But we cannot throw gold about. We have little gold left. We have too little even to cover the programme of electrification. The engineer who drew up the programme has estimated that we need at least a thousand and one hundred million rubles of gold to carry it out. We do not have such a stock of gold. Neither can we pay in raw materials, because we have not yet fed all our own people. When, in the Council of People's Commissars, the question arises of giving 100,000 poods of grain to the Italians, the People's Commissar for Food gets up and objects. We are bargaining for every trainload of grain. Without grain we cannot develop foreign trade. What then shall we give? Rubbish? They have enough rubbish of their own. They say, let us trade in grain; but we cannot give them grain. We therefore propose to solve the problem by means of concessions.

I pass to the next point. Concessions create new dangers. I shall mention what I said at the beginning of my speech, namely, that an outcry is going up from the rank and file, from the working-class masses: "Don't yield to the capitalists; they are clever and crafty." It is good to hear that, because it is a sign of the development of that vast mass which will fight the capitalists tooth and nail. There are some sound ideas in the articles of Comrade Stepanov, which he planned on pedagogical lines (first set forth all the arguments against concessions, and then say that they must be accepted; but certain readers, before they get to the good part, may stop reading, convinced that concessions are unnecessary); but when he says that we must not give concessions to Britain because that will mean some Lockhart coming here, I cannot agree. We coped with him at a time when the Cheka was still in its infancy, not as effective as it is now. If we cannot catch spies after three years of war, then all that can be said is that such people should not undertake to run the state. We are solving far more difficult problems. For instance, there are at present 300,000 bourgeois in the Crimea. These are a source of future profiteering, espionage and every kind of aid to the capitalists. However, we are not afraid of them. We say that we shall take and distribute them, make them submit, and assimilate them.

To say after this that foreigners who will be attached to the various concessions will be a danger to us, or that we shall not be able to keep an eye on them, is ridiculous. Why, then, should we have started the whole business? Why, then, should we have undertaken to run the state? The task here is purely one of organisation, and it is not worth dwelling on at length.

It would, of course, be a great mistake to think that concessions imply peace. Nothing of the kind. Concessions are nothing but a new form of warfare. Europe waged war on us, and now the war is shifting to a new sphere. Previously, the war was conducted in a field in which the imperialists were infinitely stronger than we were—the military field. If you count the number of cannon and machine-guns they have and the number we have, the number of soldiers their governments can mobilise and the number our government can mobilise, then we certainly ought to have been crushed in a fortnight. Nevertheless, we held our own in this field, and we undertake to continue the fight and are going over to an economic war. We definitely stipulate that next to a concession area, a concession square of territory, there will be our square, and then again their square; we shall learn from them how to organise model enterprises by placing what is ours next to theirs. If we are incapable of doing that, there is no use talking about anything. Operating up-to-date equipment nowadays is no easy matter, and we have to learn to do so, learn it in practice. That is something that no school, university or course will teach you. That is why we are granting concessions on the chequer-board system. Come and learn on the job.

We shall get a tremendous economic gain from concessions. Of course, when their dwelling areas are created they will bring capitalist customs along with them and will try to demoralise the peasantry. We must be on the alert and exercise our communist counter-influence at every step. That too is a kind of war, a duel between two methods, two political and economic systems—the communist and the capitalist. We shall prove that we are the stronger. We are told: "Very good, you have held your own on the external front; well, start construction, go ahead and build, and we shall see who wins...." Of course, the task is a difficult one, but we have said, and still say, that socialism has the force of example. Coercion is effective against those who want to restore their rule. But at this stage the significance of force ends, and after that only influence and example are effective. We must show the significance of communism in practice, by example. We have no machinery; the war has impoverished us and deprived Russia of her economic resources. Yet we do not fear this duel, because it will be advantageous to us in all respects.

That, too, will be a war in which we will not yield an inch. This war will be to our advantage in every respect; the transition from the old war to this new one will also be of advantage, to say nothing of the fact that there is a certain indirect guarantee of peace. At the meeting which was so poorly reported in *Pravda*, I said that we had passed from war to peace, but that we had not forgotten that war will return. While capitalism and socialism exist side by side, they cannot live in peace: one or the other will ultimately triumph—the last obsequies will be observed either for the Soviet Republic or for world capitalism. This is some respite from war. The capitalists will seek pretexts for going to war. If they accept our proposal and agree to concessions, that will be harder for them. On the one hand, we shall have the best conditions in the event of war; on the other hand, those who want to go to war will not agree to take concessions. The existence of concessions is an economic and political argument against war. States that might go to war with us will not be able to do so if they take concessions. This will bind them. We set such a high value by this that we shall not be afraid to pay, the more so that we shall be paying from the means of production that we cannot develop. For Kamchatka we shall pay in terms of 100,000 poods of oil, taking only 2 per cent for ourselves. If we do not pay up we shall not get even two poods. This is an exorbitant price, but while capitalism exists we cannot expect a fair price from it. Yet the advantages are beyond doubt. From the angle of the danger of a collision between capitalism and Bolshevism, it can be said that concessions are a continuation of the war, but in a different sphere.

Each step of the enemy will have to be watched. Every means of administration, supervision, influence and action will be required. And that is also warfare. We have fought a much bigger war; in this war we shall mobilise even larger numbers of people than in the preceding. In this war all working people will be mobilised to a man. They will be told and given to understand: "If capitalism does this or that, you workers and peasants who have overthrown the capitalists must do no less. You must learn!"

I am convinced that the Soviets will overtake and outstrip the capitalists and that our gain will not be a purely economic one. We shall get the miserable two per cent—very little indeed, yet it is something. But then we shall be getting knowledge and training; no school or university is worth anything without practical knowledge. You will see from the map appended to the pamphlet Comrade Milyutin will show you that we are granting concessions principally in the outlying regions. In European Russia there are 70,000,000 dessiatines of northern forest land. About 17,000,000 dessiatines are being set aside for concessions. Our timber enterprises are mapped out chequerwise: these forests are in West Siberia and in the Far North. We have nothing to lose. The principal enterprises are located in West Siberia, whose wealth is immense. We cannot develop a hundredth part of it in ten years. However, with the help of foreign capitalists, by letting them have, say, a single mine, we shall be able to work our own mines. In granting concessions, we do the choosing of the locations.

How are the concessions to be organised as regards supervision? They will try to demoralise our peasantry, our masses. A small master by his very nature, the peasant is inclined to freedom of trade, something we consider criminal. That is a matter for the state to combat. Our task here is to contrapose the socialist system of economy to the capitalist system. That, too, will be a war in which we shall have to fight a decisive battle. We are suffering from a tremendous crop failure, lack of fodder and loss of livestock, yet at the same time vast areas of land are uncultivated. In a few days a decree will be issued providing that every effort be exerted to achieve the largest possible sowing of crops and the greatest possible improvement of agriculture.[159]

Next, we have a million dessiatines of virgin soil which we cannot bring under the plough because we have not enough draught animals and implements, whereas with tractors this land can be ploughed to any depth. It is therefore to our advantage to let out this land on lease. Even if we surrender half of the produce, or even three-quarters, we shall be the gainers. That is the policy we are guided by, and I can say that our actions must be guided, not only by economic considerations and the trend of the world economy, but also by profound political considerations. Any other approach to the matter would be short-sighted. If it is a question of whether concessions are economically advantageous or disadvantageous, the reply is that the economic advantages are beyond dispute. Without concessions, we shall not be able to carry out our programme and the electrification of the country; without them, it will be impossible to restore our economic life in ten years; once we have restored it we shall be invincible to capital. Concessions do not mean peace with capitalism, but war in a new sphere. The war of guns and tanks yields place to economic warfare. True, it also holds out new difficulties and new dangers, but I am certain that we shall overcome them. I am convinced that if the question of concessions is posed in this way, we shall easily be able to convince the vast majority of the Party comrades of the necessity of concessions. The instinctive apprehension I have spoken of is a good and healthy sentiment, which we shall convert into a driving force that will secure us a more rapid victory in the impending economic war.

First published in 1923

Published according to the verbatim report

MESSAGE OF GREETINGS TO THE ALL-RUSSIA CONFERENCE OF GUBERNIA DEPARTMENTS FOR WORK AMONG WOMEN[160]

TELEPHONE MESSAGE

Comrades, I very much regret that I have not been able to attend your conference. Please convey to the delegates, both men and women, my sincere greetings and wishes for every success.

The participation of women in Party and Soviet activities has acquired a gigantic significance today, when the war has ended, and the peaceful work of organisation has—for a long time to come, as I hope—advanced into the foreground. In this work the women must play a leading part, and will of course do so.

V. Ulyanov (Lenin)
Chairman of the Council of People's Commissars

December 6, 1920

Pravda No. 286,
December 19, 1920

Published according to the manuscript

THE EIGHTH ALL-RUSSIA CONGRESS OF SOVIETS[161]

DECEMBER 22-29, 1920

Report on concessions; speech to the R.C.P.(B.) group on December 24 and draft resolutions of the Congress were first published in 1930; report on the work of the Council of People's Commissars, and reply to the debate were published in 1921 in the book *The Eighth All-Russia Congress of Soviets. Verbatim Report*

Report on concessions and speech to the R.C.P.(B.) group are published according to the verbatim report; report on the work of the Council of People's Commissars, and reply to the debate—according to the text in the book

1

REPORT ON CONCESSIONS DELIVERED TO THE R.C.P.(B.) GROUP AT THE EIGHTH CONGRESS OF SOVIETS DECEMBER 21

Comrades, I think you have made a fully correct decision by preferring the discussion on concessions to be held first in the Party group. To the best of our knowledge, the question of concessions has everywhere aroused considerable concern and even anxiety, not only in Party circles and among the working-class masses but also among the masses of the peasantry. All comrades have pointed out that, since the decree of November 23 of this year, the questions most frequently raised and the written questions submitted at most meetings held on a variety of subjects have dealt with concessions, and the general tone of the questions, as well as of talk on the subject, has been one of apprehension: we have driven out our own capitalists, and now we want to admit others. I believe that this apprehension, this widespread interest in concessions—displayed, not only by Party comrades but by many others—is a good sign, which shows that in three years of incredibly hard struggle the workers' and peasants' state power has become so strong and our experience of the capitalists has become so fixed in the mind that the broad masses consider the workers' and peasants' state power stable enough to manage without concessions; they also consider their lesson learnt well enough to avoid any deals with the capitalists unless there is a dire necessity to do so. This sort of supervision from below, this kind of apprehension emanating from the masses, and this kind of anxiety among non-Party circles show the highly vigilant attention that is being paid to relations between us and the capitalists. I believe that on this score we should absolutely welcome this apprehension as revealing the temper of the masses.

Yet I think that we shall come to the conclusion that, in the question of concessions, we cannot be guided by this revolutionary instinct alone. When we have analysed all aspects of the question we shall see that the policy we have adopted—the policy of offering concessions—is the correct one. I can tell you briefly that the main subject of my report—or rather the repetition of a talk I had very recently in Moscow with several hundred leading executives,[162] because I have not prepared a report and cannot present it to you—the main subject of this talk is to offer proof of two premises: first, that any war is merely the continuation of peacetime politics by other means, and second, that the concessions which we are giving, which we are forced to give, are a continuation of war in another form, using other means. To prove these two premises, or rather to prove only the second because the first does not require any special proof, I shall begin with the political aspect of the question. I shall dwell on those relations existing between the present-day imperialist powers, which are important for an understanding of present-day foreign policy in its entirety, and of our reasons for adopting this policy.

The American Vanderlip sent a letter to the Council of People's Commissars in which he said that the Republicans, members of the Republican Party of America, the party of the banking interests, which is linked with memories of the war against the Southern States for liberation, were not in power at the time. He wrote this before the November elections, which he hoped the Republicans would win (they have won them) and have their own president in March. The Republicans' policy, he went on, would not repeat the follies that had involved America in European affairs, they would look after their own interests. American interests would lead them to a clash with Japan, and they would fight Japan. It might interest you to know, he went on, that in 1923 the U.S. navy would be stronger than Britain's. To fight, they needed control of oil, without which they could not wage a modern war. They not only needed oil, but also had to take steps to ensure that the enemy did not get any. Japan was in a bad way in that respect. Somewhere near Kamchatka there is an inlet (whose name he had forgotten) with oil deposits, and they did not want the Japanese to get that oil. If we sold them that land, Vanderlip could vouch that the Americans would grow so enthusiastic that the U.S. would immediately recognise our government. If we offered a concession, and did not sell them the land, he could not say that they would refuse to examine the project, but he could not promise the enthusiasm that would guarantee recognition of the Soviet Government.

Vanderlip's letter is quite outspoken; with unparalleled cynicism he outlines the point of view of an imperialist who clearly sees that a war with Japan is imminent, and poses the question openly and directly—enter into a deal with us and you will get certain advantages from it. The issue is the following: the Far East, Kamchatka and a piece of Siberia are *de facto* in the possession of Japan insofar as her troops are in control there, and circumstances made necessary the creation of a buffer state, the Far Eastern Republic. We are well aware of the unbelievable sufferings that the Siberian peasants are enduring at the hands of the Japanese imperialists and the atrocities the Japanese have committed in Siberia. The comrades from Siberia know this; their recent publications have given details of it.[163] Nevertheless, we cannot go to war with Japan and must make every effort, not only to put off a war with Japan but, if possible, to avert it because, for reasons known to you, it is beyond our strength. At the same time Japan is causing us tremendous losses by depriving us of our links with world trade through the Pacific Ocean. Under such conditions, when we are confronted with a growing conflict, an imminent clash between America and Japan—for a most stubborn struggle has been going on for many decades between Japan and America over the Pacific Ocean and the mastery of its shores, and the entire diplomatic, economic and trade history of the Pacific Ocean and its shores is full of quite definite indications that the struggle is developing and making war between America and Japan inevitable—we return to a situation we were in for three years: we are a Socialist Republic surrounded by imperialist countries that are far stronger than us in the military sense, are using every means of agitation and propaganda to increase hatred for the Soviet Republic, and will never miss an opportunity for military intervention, as they put it, i.e., to strangle Soviet power.

If, remembering this, we cast a glance over the history of the past three years from the point of view of the international situation of the Soviet Republic, it becomes clear that we have been able to hold out and have been able to defeat the Entente powers—an alliance of unparalleled might that was supported by our whiteguards—only because there has been no unity among these powers. We have so far been victorious only because of the most profound discord among the imperialist powers, and only because that discord has not been a fortuitous and internal dissension between parties, but a most deep-seated and ineradicable conflict of economic interests among the imperialist countries which, based on private property in land and capital, cannot but pursue a predatory policy which has stultified their efforts to unite their forces against the Soviets. I take Japan, who controlled almost the whole of Siberia and could, of course, have helped Kolchak at any time. The main reason she did not do so was that her interests differ radically from those of America, and she did not want to pull chestnuts out of the fire for U.S. capital. Knowing this weakness, we could of course pursue no other policy than that of taking advantage of this enmity between America and Japan so as to strengthen ourselves and delay any possibility of an agreement between Japan and America against us; we have had an instance of the possibility of such an agreement: American newspapers carried the text of an agreement between all countries who had promised to support Kolchak.[164]

That agreement fell through, of course, but it is not impossible that an attempt will be made to restore it at the first opportunity. The deeper and more formidable the communist movement grows, the greater will be the number of new attempts to strangle our Republic. Hence our policy of utilising the discord among the imperialist powers so as to hamper an agreement or to make one temporarily impossible. This has been the fundamental line of our policy for three years; it necessitated the conclusion of the Peace of Brest-Litovsk, as well as the signing, with Bullitt, of a peace treaty and an armistice agreement most disadvantageous to us. This political line of conduct enjoins us to grasp at a proposal on the granting of concessions. Today we are giving America Kamchatka, which in any case is not actually ours because it is held by Japanese troops. At the moment we are in no condition to fight Japan. We are giving America, for economic exploitation, a territory where we have absolutely no naval or military forces, and where we cannot send them. By doing so we are setting American imperialism against Japanese imperialism and against the bourgeoisie closest to us, the Japanese bourgeoisie, which still maintains its hold on the Far Eastern Republic.

Thus, our main interests were political at the concessions negotiations. Recent events, moreover, have shown with the greatest clarity that we have been the gainers from the mere fact of negotiations on concessions. We have not yet granted any concessions, and shall not be able to do so until the American president takes office, which will not be before March; besides, we reserve the possibility of renouncing the agreement when the details are being worked out.

It follows, therefore, that in this matter the economic interest is secondary, its real value lying in its political interest. The contents of the press we have received goes to show that we have been the gainers. Vanderlip himself insisted that the concessions plan should be kept secret for the time being, until the Republican Party had won the elections. We agreed not to publish either his letter or the entire preliminary draft. However, it appeared that such a secret could not be kept for long. No sooner had Vanderlip returned to America than exposures of various kinds began. Before the elections Harding was candidate for the presidency; he has now been elected. The selfsame Harding published in the press a denial of the report that he was in touch with the Soviets through Vanderlip. That denial was categorical, almost in the following words: I don't know Vanderlip and recognise no relations with the Soviets. The reason behind this denial is quite obvious. On the eve of the elections in bourgeois America, it might have meant losing several hundred thousand votes for Harding to become known as a supporter of an agreement with the Soviets, and so he hastened to announce in the press that he did not know any Vanderlip. As soon as the elections were over, however, information of a quite different kind began to come in from America. In a number of newspaper articles Vanderlip came out in full support of an agreement with the Soviets and even wrote in one article that he compared Lenin to Washington. It turns out, therefore, that in the bourgeois countries we have propagandists for an agreement with us, and have won these propagandists from among representatives of exploiters of the worst type, such as Vanderlip, and not in the person of the Soviet ambassador or among certain journalists.

When I told a meeting of leading executives what I am now telling you, a comrade just back from America where he had worked in Vanderlip's factories, said he had been horrified; nowhere had he seen such exploitation as at Vanderlip's factories. And now in the person of this capitalist shark we have won a propagandist for trade relations with Soviet Russia, and even if we do not get anything except the proposed agreement on concessions we shall still be able to say that we have gained something. We have received a number of reports, secret ones, of course, to the effect that the capitalist countries have not given up the idea of launching a new war against Soviet Russia in the spring. We have learnt that preliminary steps are being taken by some capitalist states, while whiteguard elements are, it may be said, making preparations in all countries. Our chief interest therefore, lies in achieving the re-establishment of trade relations, and for that purpose we need to have at least a section of the capitalists on our side.

In Britain the struggle has been going on for a long time. We have gained by the mere fact that among those who represent the worst capitalist exploitation we have people who back the policy of restoring trade relations with Russia. The agreement with Britain—a trade agreement—has not yet been signed. Krasin is now actively negotiating it in London. The British Government has submitted its draft to us and we have presented our counterdraft, but all the same we see that the British Government is dragging out the negotiations and that there is a reactionary military group hard at work there which is hindering the conclusion of trade agreements and has so far been successful. It is our prime interest and prime duty to support anything that can strengthen the parties and groups working for the conclusion of this agreement with us. In Vanderlip we have gained such a supporter, not by mere chance or because Vanderlip is particularly enterprising or knows Siberia very well. The causes here lie much deeper and are linked with the development of the interests of British imperialism, which possesses a huge number of colonies. This rift between American and British imperialism is deep, and it is our imperative duty to base ourselves on it.

I have mentioned that Vanderlip is particularly knowledgeable in respect of Siberia. When our talks were coming to a close, Comrade Chicherin pointed out that Vanderlip should be received because it would have an excellent effect on his further actions in Western Europe. Of course, the prospect of talking to such a capitalist shark was not of the pleasantest, but then I had had to talk very politely, by way of duty, even to the late Mirbach, so I was certainly not afraid of a talk with Vanderlip. It is interesting that when Vanderlip and I exchanged all sorts of pleasantries and he started joking and telling me that the Americans are an extremely practical people and do not believe what they are told until they see it with their own eyes, I said to him, half in banter: "Now you can see how good things are in Soviet Russia and you can introduce the same in America." He answered me, not in English but in Russian: "Mozhet byt."* "Why, you even know Russian?" He answered: "A long time ago I travelled five thousand versts through Siberia and the country interested me greatly." This humorous exchange of pleasantries with Vanderlip ended by his saying as he was leaving, "Yes, it is true Mr. Lenin has no horns and I must tell that to my friends in America." It would have seemed simply ridiculous had it not been for the further reports in the European press to the effect that the Soviets are a monster no relations can be established with. We were given an opportunity to throw

* Perhaps.—*Ed.*

into that swamp a stone in the person of Vanderlip, who favours the re-establishment of trade relations with us.

There has not been a single report from Japan that has not spoken of the extraordinary alarm in Japanese commercial circles. The Japanese public say that they will never go against their own interests, and are opposed to concessions in Soviet Russia. In short, we have a terrific aggravation of the enmity between Japan and America and thus an undoubted slackening of both Japanese and American pressure on us.

At the meeting of executives in Moscow where I had to mention the fact, the following question was asked. "It appears," one of the comrades wrote, "that we are driving Japan and America to war, but it is the workers and peasants who will do the fighting. Although these are imperialist powers, is it worthy of us socialists to drive two powers into a war against each other, which will lead to the shedding of workers' blood?" I replied that if we were really driving workers and peasants to war that would be a crime. All our politics and propaganda, however, are directed towards putting an end to war and in no way towards driving nations to war. Experience has shown sufficiently that the socialist revolution is the only way out of eternal warfare. Our policy, therefore, is not that of involving others in a war. We have not done anything justifying, directly or indirectly, a war between Japan and America. All our propaganda and all our newspaper articles try to drive home the truth that a war between America and Japan would be just as much an imperialist war as the one between the British and the German groups in 1914, and that socialists should think, not of defending their respective countries but of overthrowing the power of the capitalists; they should think of the workers' revolution. Is it the correct policy for us to use the discord between the imperialist bandits to make it more difficult for them to unite against us, who are doing everything in our power to accelerate that revolution, but are in the position of a weak socialist republic that is being attacked by imperialist bandits? Of course, it is the correct policy. We have pursued that policy for four years. The Treaty of Brest-Litovsk was the chief expression of this policy. While the German imperialists were offering resistance, we were able to hold out even when the Red Army had not yet been formed, by using the contradictions existing between the imperialists.

Such was the situation in which our concessions policy in respect to Kamchatka emerged. This type of concession is quite exceptional. I shall speak later of the way the other concessions are taking shape. For the moment I shall confine myself to the political aspect of the question. I want to point out that the relations between Japan and America show why it is to our advantage to offer concessions or to use them as an inducement. Concessions presume some kind of re-establishment of peaceful agreements, the restoration of trade relations; they presume the possibility for us to begin direct and extensive purchases of the machinery we need. We must turn all our efforts to achieving this. That has not yet been done.

The comrade who has asked about the resumption of trade relations with Britain wants to know why the signing of the agreement with that country has been held up. My answer is that it is being delayed because the British Government is hesitant. Most of the trade and industrial bourgeoisie in Britain are in favour of relations being resumed and clearly realise that any action for war means taking enormous risks and speeding up the revolution. You will remember that during our drive on Warsaw the British Government presented us with an ultimatum, threatening to order its navy to sail against Petrograd. You will remember that Councils of Action sprang up all over Britain at the time and the Menshevik leaders of the British working class declared that they were against war and would not permit one. On the other hand, the reactionary section of the British bourgeoisie and the military clique at court are in favour of the war continuing. The delay in signing the trade agreement must undoubtedly be ascribed to their influence. I shall not go into all the details of these trade relations with Britain, or of this agreement on trade relations with Britain, because it would take me too far afield. This delicate problem had recently to be very thoroughly discussed by the Central Committee of the Party. We have returned to it again and again, and our policy in this matter has been marked by the greatest degree of accommodation. Our aim now is to obtain a trade agreement with Britain so as to start more regular trade and be able to buy as soon as possible the machinery necessary for our extensive plan to rehabilitate the national economy. The sooner we do this the greater will be the basis ensuring our economic independence of the capitalist countries. At present, after having burnt their fingers in the armed invasion of Russia, they cannot think of an immediate resumption of the war. We must seize the opportunity and bend every effort to achieve trade relations even at the cost of maximum concessions, for we cannot for a moment believe in lasting trade relations with the imperialist powers; the respite will be temporary. The experience of the history of revolutions and great conflicts teaches us that wars, a series of wars, are inevitable. The existence of a Soviet Republic alongside of capitalist countries—a Soviet Republic surrounded by capitalist countries—is so intolerable to the capitalists that they will seize any opportunity to resume the war. The peoples are weary of the imperialist war and threaten to make their indignation felt if war continues, but the possibility of the capitalists being able to resume it in a few years is not precluded. That is why we must exert every effort to utilise the opportunity, since it exists, and conclude trade agreements. I can say the following here (this is not for the record). I think that we shall ultimately emerge on top as a result of our firm stand that the Communist International is not a governmental institution. That is the more probable for the British bourgeoisie having to realise the ridiculousness of rising up against the Third International. The Third International was formed in March 1919. Its Second Congress was held in July 1920, following which the terms proposed in Moscow were made publicly known in all countries. An open struggle is going on for adhesion to the Communist International. The organisational foundations for the formation of Communist parties exist everywhere. In these circumstances, any attempt to present us seriously with an ultimatum that we get rid of the Communist International is inexcusable. However, the emphasis laid on the matter shows where the shoe pinches and what displeases them in our policy. Even without that, we have known what it is in our policy that is not to their liking. The East is another question that can be spoken of at a Party meeting, and is alarming Britain. The latter wants us to give assurances that we will do nothing against Britain's interests in the East. We are willing and ready to give such an undertaking. As an example I might mention that the Congress of Peoples of the East, a Communist congress, took place, not in the R.S.F.S.R. but in Baku, in the independent republic of Azerbaijan. The British Government will have no reason to accuse us of doing anything against British interests. In their ignorance of our Constitution, they sometimes confuse the Azerbaijan Republic with the Russian Soviet Republic. Our laws are definite and precise on that score, and it will be easy to refute the false interpretations of the British ministers. However, there are still differences on this subject, and Krasin is engaged with the ministers in talks on these two sore points.

In July, when Poland was threatened with utter defeat, and the Red Army was about to crush her, the complete text of an agreement was presented by Britain, which in effect said that we had to declare as a matter of principle that we would not carry on official propaganda or do anything contrary to British interests in the East. That was to be laid down at a subsequent political conference, but at the moment they were concluding a definite trade agreement. They asked whether we would like to sign it. We replied that we would. Today we say again that we will sign such an agreement. The political conference will specify Britain's interests in the East. We also have certain interests in the East, and we shall set them forth in detail when the need arises. Britain cannot say outright that she is abandoning her July proposal and so she is dragging things out and concealing from her own people the truth about the negotiations. The outcome of the negotiations is uncertain and we cannot guarantee that an agreement will be signed. The very powerful court and military circles in Britain are opposed to the agreement. We are, however, proposing maximum concessions, and we believe it to be in our interests to sign a trade pact and purchase with all possible dispatch some of the essentials for the restoration of the railways (i.e., locomotives), for the rehabilitation of industry, and for electrification. This is more important to us than anything else. If we achieve that, we shall become so strong in a few years that even, if the worst comes to the worst and there is armed intervention in a few years' time, it will fail because we shall be stronger than we are now. The line we in the Central Committee are following is one of maximum concessions to Britain. If these gentlemen think they will catch us breaking promises, we declare that our government will not carry on any official propaganda and that we have no intention of infringing on any of Britain's interests in the East. If they hope to derive some advantage from this, let them try; we shall not be the losers.

I now come to the question of the relations between Britain and France. These are confused. On the one hand, Britain and France belong to the League of Nations and are obliged to act jointly; on the other hand, whenever any tension arises they fail to do so. When Comrade Kamenev was in London conducting negotiations together with Krasin, this became quite obvious. France was in favour of supporting Poland and Wrangel, but the British Government declared it would not support France. Concessions are more acceptable to Britain than to France, which still aspires to get her debts paid back, while in Britain capitalists with any business sense no longer think about it. From that angle, too, it is to our advantage to use the dissension between Britain and France, and we must therefore insist on the political proposal of concessions to Britain. We now have a draft agreement on timber concessions in the Far North. Since there is no political unity between Britain and France, our position imposes on us the duty of even incurring a certain risk, if only we succeed in hampering a military alliance between Britain and France against us. A new war that Britain and France will support against us will be an immense burden on us (even if it ends, as the war with Wrangel has done, in our complete victory); it will hinder our economic development and worsen the condition of the workers and peasants. We must therefore be ready to do whatever involves the least loss. Obviously, the losses from concessions are negligible compared with those that would arise from a delay in our economic development and the loss of thousands of workers and peasants that would ensue were we unable to withstand the alliance of the imperialists. Negotiations on concessions with Britain are one of the means of standing up to their alliance. That is the political aspect of the issue.

Last, the final aspect of the matter is the attitude of Britain and the entire Entente to Germany. If we exclude America, Germany is the most advanced country. In the development of electricity her technical level is even higher than America's. The conditions obtaining in Germany in consequence of the Treaty of Versailles make her existence impossible. Because of that situation it is natural for Germany to be prompted towards an alliance with Russia. When the Russian troops were approaching Warsaw, all Germany was seething. An alliance between Russia and Germany, a country that has been strangled, a country that is able to set gigantic productive forces in motion—this situation has led to a political mix up in Germany: the German Black Hundreds sympathise with the Russian Bolsheviks in the same way as the Spartacus League does. This can well be understood because it derives from economic causes, and is the basis of the entire economic situation and of our foreign policy.

While we stand alone and the capitalist world is strong, our foreign policy consists, on the one hand, in our having to utilise disagreements (to vanquish all the imperialist powers would, of course, be a most pleasant thing, but for a fairly long time we shall not be in a position to do so). On the one hand, our existence depends on the presence of radical differences between the imperialist powers, and, on the other, on the Entente's victory and the Peace of Versailles having thrown the vast majority of the German nation into a situation it is impossible for them to live in. The Peace of Versailles has created a situation in which Germany cannot even dream of a breathing-space, or of not being plundered, of not having the means of subsistence taken away from her, of her people not being doomed to starvation and extinction; Germany cannot even dream of any of these things, so that, naturally, her only means of salvation lies in an alliance with Soviet Russia, a country towards which her eyes are therefore turning. They are furiously opposing Soviet Russia; they detest the Bolsheviks, and shoot down their own Communists in the manner of real whiteguards. The

German bourgeois government has an implacable hatred of the Bolsheviks, but such is its international position that, against its own desires, the government is driven towards peace with Soviet Russia. That, comrades, is the second corner-stone of our international policy, our foreign policy; it is to show peoples that are conscious of the bourgeois yoke that there is no salvation for them without the Soviet Republic. Since the Soviet Republic withstood the onslaught of the imperialists for three years, this goes to show that one country, and that country alone, has been successful in hurling back this imperialist yoke. That country has been called a country of "robbers", "plunderers", "bandits", Bolsheviks, etc.—let that be so, but still it is impossible to improve the economic situation without that country.

In a situation such as this, the question of concessions acquires still another aspect. The pamphlet I have in my hands is the Decree on Concessions of November 23. It will be distributed to all members of the Congress. We intend to publish this pamphlet abroad, in several languages.[165] It is our immediate object to do everything possible to arouse interest in concessions among the population of the greatest number of countries, to interest those countries that are the most oppressed. The divergence of interests between Japan and America is very great. They are unable to agree between themselves over China, a number of islands, etc. The divergence of interests between Germany and the Entente is of another kind. Germany's existence has been made impossible by the conditions in which the Entente has placed her. People are dying there because the Entente has been requisitioning their motors and their cattle. Such a situation urges Germany towards a *rapprochement* with Soviet Russia. I do not know the details of the treaty between Germany and the Entente, but in any case the treaty is known to ban direct trade relations between Germany and Soviet Russia. When we arranged for the purchase of German locomotives, that was done through the agency of Sweden. Germany will hardly be able to restore direct trade relations with us before April 1921. However, progress in restoring our trade relations with Germany is more rapid than with the Entente. The conditions of existence in

Germany are compelling the German people as a whole, including the Black Hundreds and the capitalists, to seek relations with Soviet Russia. Germany is already linked with us by certain trade relations. These links can become closer inasmuch as we are offering Germany agricultural concessions. It is therefore clear that we must advance concessions as an economic method, even irrespective of the measure in which we are able to put the project into effect. The interest in concessions is so obvious that even if we do not succeed in granting a single concession, or none of our agreements are put into effect (and even that is quite possible)—even in that case we shall still have gained something, and we still have to pursue our policy because by so doing we make it more difficult for the imperialist countries to attack us.

Irrespective of this, we must tell all the oppressed peoples that a handful of countries are overtly or covertly, consciously or unconsciously, strangling other peoples—this derives from the Treaty of Versailles—and these peoples are turning to us for help, and are becoming more and more aware of the economic necessity of an alliance with Soviet Russia against international imperialism. Agricultural concessions, therefore, are of a wider scope than the old bourgeois concessions; they are different from the old capitalist concessions. They remain capitalist in character inasmuch as we tell the German capitalists to bring so many tractors into our country, in exchange for which we shall give them so much excellent virgin land and grain. We are attracting capital with the prospect of tremendous profits. In this respect the concessions are a purely capitalist undertaking, but they acquire an immeasurably greater significance because Germany as a nation, Austria and other countries cannot exist because they need aid in food and because the entire people, irrespective of whether the capitalists make a profit of a hundred or two hundred per cent, can, despite anti-Bolshevik prejudices, see that the Bolsheviks are establishing completely different international relations, which make it possible for all oppressed peoples to rid themselves of the imperialist yoke. That is why our successes of the last three years will lead to still greater successes in foreign policy during the coming year. Our policy is grouping around the Soviet Republic those capitalist countries which are being strangled by imperialism. That is why our concessions proposal has more than a capitalist significance; that is why it is a hand held out, not only to the German capitalists with the offer, "Bring us hundreds of tractors and make as much as three hundred per cent on each ruble if you like"; it is a hand held out to oppressed peoples, an alliance of the oppressed masses, which is a factor in the future proletarian revolution. The doubts and fears that still exist in the advanced countries, which assert that Russia could risk a socialist revolution because she is a vast country with her own means of subsistence while they, the industrial countries of Europe, cannot do so because they have no allies—these doubts and fears are groundless. We say: "You now have an ally, Soviet Russia." Since we are granting concessions, this will be an alliance that will consolidate the alliance against world imperialism. This is a postulate that must not be lost sight of, it justifies our concessions policy and proves the need to grant concessions.

And now for several purely economic considerations. I shall now go on to these considerations and read out the stipulations of the law, although I hope that the comrades present here have read the law of November 23. I shall, however, remind you briefly that it says that concessionaires shall be paid with part of the products, that when special technical improvements have been introduced, we are prepared to offer trade advantages, and that the term of concessions will be more or less prolonged, depending on the volume and character of the expenditures involved. We guarantee that property invested in an enterprise shall not be confiscated or requisitioned.

Without such a guarantee owners of private capital and private property will not, of course, enter into relations with us. The question of courts, which was at first raised in the draft agreement, was subsequently removed, since we saw that this was not to our advantage. Thus the judicial authority on our territory remains in our hands. In the event of a dispute, the issue will be settled by our judges. This will be not requisitioning but the lawful exercise of jurisprudence by our judicial bodies.

The fifth clause in the agreement deals with the code of labour laws. In the original draft of the agreement, which was discussed with Vanderlip, provision was made for the withdrawal of the application of the labour code in localities inhabited by underdeveloped tribes, we cannot say which. In such places no code of labour laws is possible. The labour code was to be replaced in such areas by a special agreement on guarantees for the workers.

In the final clause we guarantee the concessionaire against any unilateral changes. Without this guarantee, there can, of course, be no question of granting concessions. The question of what is meant by non-unilateral changes has, however, been left open. That will depend on the text of the agreement on each individual concession. Arbitration may be possible through some of the neutral powers. This is a point that may lead to differences, and leaves a certain latitude in determining the actual terms of a concession. It should, incidentally, be pointed out that in the capitalist countries the Menshevik leaders of the working class are considered reliable people. They enter bourgeois governments, and it is very difficult for bourgeois governments to challenge such mediators or arbitrators as the Mensheviks or social-traitors of the European countries. Experience has shown, however, that when any serious tension arises, the American and European Mensheviks behave just like the Russian Mensheviks do, i.e., they do not know how to behave, and are obliged to yield to the pressure of the revolutionary masses, though they themselves remain opposed to the revolution. The question remains open; we shall not decide it in advance.

From the terms that I have read out to you, you will see that economic relations between the capitalist concessionaires and the Socialist Republic are far from stable or durable. It is obvious that a capitalist who retains private property and exploitation relations cannot be anything but a foreign body in a socialist republic. Hence one of the main themes in my report: concessions are a continuation of war by other means. I shall deal with that in detail in a moment, but first I want to mention the three main forms or kinds of the concessions.

In this pamphlet we have given a list of the chief concessions; the comrades from the Supreme Council of the National Economy who provided the material for the pamphlet and edited it, have appended maps showing these objects. These maps show that the concessions fall into three main groups—first, timber concessions in the Far North, second, agricultural concessions and third, mining concessions in Siberia.

Our economic interest in timber concessions in the Far North of European Russia is obvious; there are tens and even hundreds of millions of dessiatines of forest land which we are quite unable to exploit because we lack the railways, the means of production and the possibility of providing the workers there with food, but which could be exploited by a country that owns a big merchant fleet and could fell and saw timber properly and export it in tremendous quantities.

If we want to trade with foreign countries—and we do want to, because we realise its necessity—our chief interest is in obtaining as quickly as possible, from the capitalist countries, the means of production (locomotives, machinery, and electrical equipment) without which we cannot more or less seriously rehabilitate our industry, or perhaps may even be unable to do so at all, because the machinery needed by our factories cannot be made available. It is with the motive of extra profit that we must attract the capitalist. He will get surplus profit—well, let him have that surplus profit; we shall obtain the fundamentals that will help strengthen us; we shall stand firmly on our own feet, and shall win in the economic field. We shall have to pay up if we want to get the best machinery, etc. What are we to pay with? We still dispose of gold reserves totalling several millions. You will see from the special plan for the electrification of Russia, drawn up for several decades, that this plan, together with the additional work for the rehabilitation of industry, will involve an approximate expenditure of something like 17,000 million gold rubles. Electrification alone will require the direct expenditure of more than 1,000 million rubles in gold. We cannot cover this with our gold reserves; it is extremely undesirable and dangerous for us to export foodstuffs because we have not got sufficient for our own industry, and yet this need has to be met. In this case there is no concession project economically more suitable for us than the forests of the Far North which cover an enormous area, and where the timber is rotting away and a total loss because we are economically unable to exploit these timber reserves. Timber, however, is of tremendous value on the world market. Besides, the Far North is also convenient politically because it is an outlying border area. This concession is convenient to us both politically and economically, and we must make the best possible use of it. At the Moscow Conference I have told you about,[166] Milyutin said that negotiations with Britain about concessions in the north of European Russia are progressing. There are several scores of millions of dessiatines of standing timber there. If we grant three or five million dessiatines disposed chequerwise, we shall get an opportunity to derive advantage from up-to-date enterprises, an opportunity to learn, by stipulating that our technicians take part in the work; we shall thus gain a lot and make it difficult for capitalist powers that enter into deals with us to take part in military action against us, because war cancels everything, and should one break out we shall get possession of all the buildings, installations and railways. Any possible action against us by new Kolchaks, Denikins and others will not be made the easier.

The second type is agricultural concessions. With the exception of West Siberia with its vast expanses of excellent land, inaccessible to us because of its great distance from railways, there are in European Russia and along the River Ural alone (our Commissariat of Agriculture has taken the necessary steps and has calculated the amount of land we cannot cultivate, which is no less than 3,000,000 dessiatines along the River Ural, abandoned by entire Cossack villages as a result of the victorious culmination of the Civil War) excellent lands that must be brought under the plough, but which we cannot cultivate because of the shortage of draught animals and our weakened productive forces.

The state farms of the Don Region have about 800,000 dessiatines which we cannot cultivate; to cultivate this land we shall need a tremendous number of draught animals or entire tractor columns that we cannot put on the fields, while some capitalist countries, including those that urgently need foodstuffs—Austria, Germany and Bohemia—could put tractors to work and obtain excellent wheat in good season. We do not know to what extent we shall be able to carry that out. At present we have two tractor plants functioning, in Moscow and Petrograd, but in consequence of the difficult conditions that obtain they cannot produce tractors in large numbers. We could ease the situation by purchasing a greater number of tractors. Tractors are the most important means of effecting a radical change in the old farming methods and of extending the area cultivated. By such concessions we shall show a large number of countries that we are able to develop the world economy on a gigantic scale.

If our propaganda and our proposal do not meet with success, and if our proposal is not accepted, we shall still reap an advantage that is not only political but socialist as well. What is going on in the capitalist world is not only a waste of wealth, but madness and a crime, for in some countries there is a food surplus that cannot be sold because of currency revolutions, since money has depreciated in a number of countries that have suffered defeat. Huge stocks of foodstuffs are rotting away, while tens of millions of people in countries like Germany are actually starving. This absurdity, this crime of capitalism, is becoming obvious to all capitalist countries and to the small countries that surround Russia. To the capitalist countries the Soviet Republic says: "We have hundreds of thousands of dessiatines of excellent land that can be ploughed with tractors; you have the tractors, the petrol and the trained technicians; we propose to all peoples, including the peoples of the capitalist countries, to make the rehabilitation of the economy and the salvation of all peoples from hunger their main object." If the capitalists do not understand this, it is an argument demonstrating the corruption, madness and criminal nature of the capitalist system. That will be of more than mere propaganda value: it will be a communist call for revolution, for it shows beyond doubt that capitalism is falling apart and cannot satisfy the people's needs, a fact that is more and more penetrating into the consciousness of all peoples. An insignificant minority of imperialist countries are growing rich, while a large number of other countries are actually on the verge of ruin. The world economy needs reorganisation, and the Soviet Republic comes forward with a plan of reconstruction, with the following incontestable business-like, and realisable proposal: "You are starving under capitalism, despite the fabulous wealth of machinery. We can solve the crisis by bringing together your machinery and our raw materials, but the capitalists are in the way. We have proposed to them that they should accept our offer, but they are holding back and wrecking our plan." That is the second type of concession, the agricultural or tractor type.

Mining concessions are the third type. These are indicated on the map of Siberia, with details of each area in which concessions are being considered. Siberia's mineral wealth is literally boundless, and at best, even given significant progress, we cannot exploit even a hundredth part of it for many years. The minerals are to be found in conditions that demand the best machinery. There are such products as copper ore, which the capitalists need badly for their electrical industry because it is in such short supply. It is possible to rehabilitate the world economy and improve the world's technology if they enter into regular relations with us.

It is, of course, more difficult to implement these concessions, i.e., they present greater difficulties than timber or agricultural concessions do. As far as agricultural concessions are concerned, it is only a matter of a brief working period with tractors being used. Timber concessions are also easier, especially as they concern an area we cannot avail ourselves of; but mining concessions are frequently at no great distance from the railways, frequently in densely populated areas. Here the danger is serious and we shall weigh the pros and cons very carefully to see whether or not they should be granted; we shall do so on definite terms, for there is no doubt that concessions are a new kind of war. The capitalists are coming to us to wage a new kind of war—the very existence of the capitalists is in itself a war against the socialist world surrounding them. Capitalist enterprises in a socialist state are in the economic sense a war for freedom of trade, against the policy of compulsory deliveries, a war for private property against a republic that has abolished that property. On this economic basis there develop a variety of relationships (similar to the hostility between the Sukharevka Market[167] and our institutions). We may be told that we are closing down the Sukharevka black market but opening up a number of other "Sukharevkas" by letting the capitalists in. We have not closed our eyes to this, and say: if we have been victorious till now, if we were victorious when our enemies used every means to disrupt our enterprises, when there was disruption from within combined with that from without, then we must surely be able to deal with such things, to keep an eye on them when they are in certain limited areas and there are definite conditions and relations. We have practical experience of the struggle against military espionage and against capitalist sabotage. We fought against them when they were under cover in our own institutions; surely we shall be able to handle them when the capitalists have been let in according to a definite list and under definite conditions. We know, of course, that they will try to break these conditions, and we shall combat such infractions. But, comrades, concessions on a capitalist foundation means war. Until we have overthrown capital in other countries, and while capital is much stronger than we are, its forces can be sent against us at any time and it can start another war against us. For this reason we have to make ourselves stronger, and to do that we must develop large-scale industry and get our transport going. In carrying this out, we are taking a risk; here we again have relations of warfare, of struggle, and if they try to undermine our policy, we shall fight them. It would be grossly mistaken to think that a peaceful agreement on concessions is a peaceful agreement with capitalists. It is an agreement concerning war, but an agreement that is less dangerous to us, besides being less burdensome for the workers and peasants, less burdensome than at the time when the best tanks and guns were being thrown into action against us; we must therefore use all methods, and, at the cost of economic concessions, develop our economic forces and facilitate our economic rehabilitation. The capitalists will, of course, not honour their agreements, say comrades who are afraid of concessions. It is quite impossible, of course, to be sure that the capitalists will honour agreements. It will be a war, and war is the ultimate argument, which in general remains an argument entering the relations of the socialist republic.

War threatens us at any hour. We are conducting peace negotiations with Poland, and there is every chance that peace will be concluded, or at least, to be more exact, the vast majority of chances are that peace will be concluded. There is no doubt, however, that the Savinkovs and the French capitalists are working to prevent the treaty from being signed. To the capitalists war is possible tomorrow if not today, and they would willingly start a war today if they had not learnt something from three years' experience. Concessions constitute a certain risk; they are a loss; they are the continuation of war. There is no doubt of this, but it is a war that is more to our advantage. When we have obtained a certain minimum of the means of production, locomotives and machines, then we shall be different, in the economic sense, from what we have been till now, and the imperialist countries will be still less dangerous to us.

We have been told that the concessionaires will create exclusive conditions for their workers, and supply them with better clothes, better footwear, and better food. That will be their propaganda among our workers, who are suffering privation and will have to suffer privation for a long time to come. We shall then have a socialist republic in which the workers are poverty-stricken and next to it a capitalist island, in which the workers get an excellent livelihood. This apprehension is frequently voiced at our Party meetings. Of course, there is a danger of that kind, and it shows that concessions are a continuation of war and do not constitute peace. We have, however, experienced far greater deprivations and have seen that workers from capitalist countries nevertheless come to our country, knowing that the economic conditions awaiting them in Russia are far worse; surely, then, we ought to be able to defend ourselves against such propaganda with counter-propaganda; surely we should be able to show the workers that capitalism can, of course, provide better conditions for certain groups of its workers, but that this does not improve the conditions of the rest of the workers. And lastly, why is it that at every contact with bourgeois Europe and America we, not they, have always won? Why is it that to this day it is they who fear to send delegations to us, and not we to them? To this day we have always managed to win over to our side at least a small part of the delegations, despite the fact that such delegations consisted in the main of Menshevik elements, and that they were people who came to us for short periods. Should we be afraid of being unable to explain the truth to the workers?! We should be in a bad way if we had such fears, if we were to place such considerations above the direct interest which is a matter of the greatest significance as far as concessions are concerned. The position of our peasants and workers remains a difficult one. It must be improved. We cannot have any doubt on that score. I think we shall agree that the concessions policy is a policy of continuation of the war, but we must also agree that it is our task to ensure the continued existence of an isolated socialist republic surrounded by capitalist enemies, to preserve a republic that is infinitely weaker than the capitalist enemies surrounding it, thereby eliminating any possibility of our enemies forming an alliance among themselves for the struggle against us, and to hamper their policies and not give them an opportunity to win a victory. It is our task to secure for Russia the necessary machinery and funds for the restoration of the economy; when we have obtained that, we shall stand so firmly on our own feet that no capitalist enemies can overawe us. That is the point of view which has guided us in our policy on concessions, the policy I have outlined.

2

REPORT ON THE WORK OF THE COUNCIL OF PEOPLE'S COMMISSARS DECEMBER 22

(*Shouts from the hall:* "Long live Comrade Lenin!" *Storm of applause. An ovation.*) Comrades, I have to present a report on the home and foreign policy of the government. I do not think it is the purpose of my report to give you a list of at least the most outstanding or most important laws and measures adopted by the workers' and peasants' government. Nor do I think that you would be interested in an account of the events of this period, or that it is very important that I should give one. As I see it, general conclusions should be drawn from the principal lessons we have learnt during this year, which was no less abundant in abrupt political changes than the preceding years of the revolution were. From the general lessons of this year's experience we must deduce the most urgent political and economic tasks that face us, tasks to which the Soviet government—both through the legislative acts which are being submitted for your examination and endorsement and through the sum total of its measures—at present attaches the greatest hopes and significance, and from the fulfilment of which it expects important progress in our economic development. Permit me, therefore, to confine myself to brief comments on the Republic's international situation and on the chief results of our foreign policy during the past year.

You all know, of course, how the Polish landowners and capitalists forced a war on us under the pressure and at the insistence of the capitalist countries of Western Europe, and not of Western Europe alone. You know that in April of this year we made peace proposals to the Polish Government, on terms which were incomparably more advantageous to it than the present terms, and that it was only under pressure of dire necessity, after our negotiations for an armistice with Poland had ended in a complete breakdown, that we were obliged to fight. Despite the heavy defeat our forces suffered near Warsaw, as a result of their undoubted exhaustion, this war has ended in a peace that is far more favourable to us than the one we proposed to Poland in April. A preliminary treaty with Poland has been signed, and negotiations are now under way for the conclusion of a final peace treaty. We certainly do not conceal from ourselves the danger presented by the pressure being exerted by some of the more stubborn capitalist countries and by certain Russian whiteguard circles with the aim of preventing these negotiations from ending in a peace. It should, however, be said that the Entente's policy, which aims at military intervention and the armed suppression of the Soviets, is steadily coming to nought, and that we are winning over to our policy of peace a steadily increasing number of states which are undoubtedly hostile towards the Soviets. The number of countries that have signed peace treaties is increasing, and there is every probability that a final peace treaty with Poland will be signed in the immediate future. Thus, another severe blow will be struck at the alliance of the capitalist forces which are trying to wrench the power of government from us by means of war.

Comrades, you also know, of course, that the temporary setbacks we suffered in the war with Poland and the difficulty of our position at certain moments of the war were due to our being obliged to fight Wrangel, who was officially recognised by one imperialist power,[168] and received vast material, military and other aid. To end the war as quickly as possible, we had to effect a rapid concentration of troops so as to strike a decisive blow at Wrangel. You, of course, know what dauntless heroism was displayed by the Red Army in surmounting obstacles and fortifications which even military experts and military authorities considered impregnable. The complete, decisive and remarkably swift victory the Red Army gained over Wrangel is one of the most brilliant pages in its history. That was how the war forced on us by the whiteguards and the imperialists ended.

It is with far greater assurance and determination that we can now set about a task that is dear to us, an essential task, one that has long been attracting us—that of economic development. We can do so with the assurance that the capitalist tycoons will not find it as easy to frustrate this work as in the past. Of course, we must be on our guard. In no case can we say that we are already guaranteed against war. It is not because of the absence of formal peace treaties that we are still without that guarantee. We are very well aware that the remnants of Wrangel's army have not been destroyed, that they are lying low close at hand, that they are under ward and tutelage, and are being re-formed with the aid of the capitalist powers. We know that the white-guard Russian organisations are working actively to re-create certain military units and, together with Wrangel's forces, to prepare them for a new onslaught on Russia at a favourable moment.

That is why we must maintain our military preparedness under all circumstances. Irrespective of the blows already struck at imperialism, we must keep our Red Army in a state of combat readiness at all costs, and increase its fighting efficiency. The release of a certain section of the army and its rapid demobilisation does not, of course, militate against this. We rely on the tremendous experience gained by the Red Army and its leaders during the war to enable us now to improve its quality. And we shall see to it that although the army is reduced we shall retain a cadre whose maintenance will not entail an undue burden on the Republic, while at the same time, with the reduction in the number of effectives, we shall be in a better position than before, in case of need, to mobilise and equip a still larger military force.

We are certain that all the neighbouring states, which have already lost a great deal by supporting the whiteguard conspiracies against us, have learnt the hard lesson of experience and have duly appreciated our conciliatory spirit, which was generally considered as weakness on our part. Three years of experience have no doubt shown them that, while we are persistently striving for peace, we are prepared from the military point of view. Any attempt to start a war against us will mean, to the states involved, that the terms they will get following such a war will be worse than those they could have obtained without a war or prior to it. This has been proved in respect of several countries. This is an achievement we shall not forego, one that will not be forgotten by any of the powers surrounding us or in political contact with Russia. Thanks to this, our relations with neighbouring countries are steadily improving. You know that a final peace has been signed with a number of states bordering on the Western frontiers of Russia. These were part of the former Russian Empire, and the Soviet government has unequivocally recognised their independence and sovereignty, in conformity with the fundamental principles of our policy. Peace on such a basis has every chance of being far more durable than is to the liking of the capitalists and certain West-European states.

As regards the Latvian Government, I must say that at one time there was a danger of our relations becoming strained, so much so that the idea even arose of severing diplomatic relations. But the latest report from our representative in Latvia indicates that a change of policy has already taken place, and that many misunderstandings and legitimate causes of dissatisfaction have been removed. There is good reason to hope that in the near future we shall have close economic ties with Latvia, which will naturally be even more useful to us in our trade with Western Europe than Estonia and the other states bordering on the R.S.F.S.R.

I must also say, comrades, that during this year our policy in the East has been very successful. We must welcome the formation and consolidation of the Soviet Republics of Bokhara, Azerbaijan and Armenia, which have not only recovered their complete independence, but have placed the power of government in the hands of the workers and peasants. These republics are proof and corroboration of the fact that the ideas and principles of Soviet government are understood and immediately applicable, not only in the industrially developed countries, not only in those which have a social basis like the proletariat, but also in those which have the peasantry as their basis. The idea of peasants' Soviets has triumphed. The peasants' power has been assured: they own the land and the means of production. The friendly relations between the peasant Soviet Republics and the Russian Socialist Republic have already been consolidated by the practical results of our policy.

We can also welcome the forthcoming signing of a treaty with Persia,[169] friendly relations with whom are assured by the fact that the fundamental interests of all peoples suffering from the yoke of imperialism coincide.

We must also note that friendly relations with Afghanistan, and still more so with Turkey, are being steadily established and strengthened. As for the latter power, the Entente countries have done everything they could to render impossible any more or less normal relations between her and the West-European countries. This circumstance, coupled with consolidation of the Soviets, is steadily strengthening the alliance and the friendly relations between Russia and the oppressed nations of the East, despite the bourgeoisie's resistance and intrigues and the continuing encirclement of Russia by bourgeois countries. The chief factor in politics today is the violence being used by the imperialists against peoples which have not had the good fortune to be among the victors; this world policy of imperialism is leading to closer relations, alliance and friendship among all the oppressed nations. The success we have achieved in this respect in the West as well, in relation to more Europeanised states, goes to show that the present principles of our foreign policy are correct and that the improvement in our international position rests on a firm basis. We are confident that, by continuing our peace policy and by making concessions (and we must do so if we wish to avoid war), the basic line of our policy and the fundamental interests which stem from the very nature of imperialist policy will come into their own and will make it more and more imperative for the R.S.F.S.R. to establish closer relations with a growing number of neighbouring states, despite the intrigues and machinations of the imperialists, who, of course, are always capable of provoking a quarrel between us and some other state. Such relations are our guarantee that we shall be able to devote ourselves whole-heartedly to economic development and that we shall be able, for a longer period, to work calmly, steadfastly and confidently.

I must add that negotiations for the conclusion of a trade agreement with Great Britain are now under way. Unfortunately, these negotiations have been dragging out much longer than we would wish, but we are not at all to blame for that. When, as far back as July—at the moment the Soviet troops were achieving their greatest successes—the British Government officially submitted to us the text of an agreement assuring the establishment of trade relations, we replied by giving our full consent, but since then the conflict of the various trends within the British Government and the British state has held this up. We see how the British Government is vacillating, and is threatening to sever relations with us and immediately to dispatch warships to Petrograd. We have seen all this, but at the same time we have seen that, in reply to this threat, Councils of Action have sprung up all over Great Britain. We have seen how, under pressure from the workers, the most extreme adherents of the opportunist trend and their leaders have been obliged to resort to this quite "unconstitutional" policy, one that they had themselves condemned a short while before. It appears that, despite the Menshevik prejudices which have hitherto prevailed in the British trade union movement, the pressure brought to bear by the working people and their political consciousness have become strong enough to blunt the edge of the imperialists' bellicose policy. Continuing our policy of peace. we have taken our stand on the proposals made by the British Government in July. We are prepared to sign a trade agreement at once; if it has not yet been signed, the blame rests wholly with those trends and tendencies in British ruling circles that are anxious to frustrate the trade agreement and, against the will of the majority, not only of the workers but even of the British bourgeoisie, want a free hand to attack Soviet Russia again. That is their affair.

The longer this policy is pursued by certain influential circles in Great Britain, by financial and imperialist circles there, the more it will aggravate the financial situation, the longer it will delay the semi-agreement which has now become essential between bourgeois Britain and the Soviet

Republic, and the nearer it will bring the imperialists to a situation that will oblige them to accept a full agreement, not merely a semi-agreement.

Comrades, I must say that this trade agreement with Great Britain is connected with one of the most important questions in our economic policy, that of concessions. One of the important acts passed by the Soviet government during the period under review is the law on concessions of November 23, this year. You are, of course, all familiar with the text of this law. You all know that we have now published additional material, from which delegates to the Congress of Soviets can obtain full information on this question. We have published a special pamphlet containing, not only the text of the decree but also a list of the chief concessions we are offering: agricultural, timber and mining. We have taken steps to make the published text of this decree available in the West-European countries as early as possible, and we hope that our concessions policy will also be a practical success. We do not in the least close our eyes to the dangers this policy presents to the Socialist Soviet Republic, a country that, moreover, is weak and backward. While our Soviet Republic remains the isolated borderland of the capitalist world, it would be absolutely ridiculous, fantastic and utopian to hope that we can achieve complete economic independence and that all dangers will vanish. Of course, as long as the radical contrasts remain, the dangers will also remain, and there is no escaping them. What we have to do is to get firmly on our feet in order to survive these dangers; we must be able to distinguish between big dangers and little dangers, and incur the lesser dangers rather than the greater.

We were recently informed that, at a Congress of Soviets of Arzamas Uyezd in Nizhni-Novgorod Gubernia, a peasant, not a member of the Party, said on the subject of concessions: "Comrades, we are delegating you to the All-Russia Congress and declare that we peasants are prepared to endure hunger and cold and do our duty for another three years, but don't sell Mother Russia in the form of concessions." I heartily welcome such sentiments, which are very widespread. I think it is highly indicative that during these three years the masses of non-Party working people—not only industrial workers but peasants as well—have acquired the political and economic experience which enables and compels them to value their liberation from the capitalists above all else, which compels them to exercise redoubled caution and to treat with extreme suspicion every step that involves the possibility of new dangers of the restoration of capitalism. Of course, we give the greatest consideration to all declarations of this kind, but we must say that there is no question of selling out Russia to the capitalists. It is a question of concessions; any concessions agreement is limited to a definite period and by definite terms. It is hedged around with all possible guarantees, by guarantees that have been carefully considered and will be considered and discussed with you again and again, at the present Congress and at various other conferences. These temporary agreements have nothing to do with any selling out. There is not a hint in them of selling Russia. What they do represent is a certain economic concession to the capitalists, the purpose of which is to enable us, as soon as possible, to secure the necessary machinery and locomotives without which we cannot effect the restoration of our economy. We have no right to neglect anything that may, in however small a measure, help us to improve the conditions of the workers and peasants.

We must do all we possibly can to bring about the rapid restoration of trade relations, and negotiations are at present being carried on in a semi-legal framework. We are ordering locomotives and machines in far from adequate numbers, but we have begun to order them. When we conduct these negotiations officially, the possibilities will be vastly expanded. With the aid of industry we shall achieve a great deal, and in a shorter period; but even if the achievements are very great, the period will cover years, a number of years. It must be borne in mind that although we have now gained a military victory and have secured peace, history teaches us that no big question has ever been settled, and no revolution accomplished, without a series of wars. And we shall not forget this lesson. We have already taught a number of powerful countries not to wage war on us, but we cannot guarantee that this will be for long. The imperialist predators will attack us again if there is the slightest change in the situation. We must be prepared for it. Hence, the first thing is to restore the economy and place it firmly on its feet. Without equipment, without machinery obtained from capitalist countries, we cannot do this rapidly. And we should not grudge the capitalist a little extra profit if only we can effect this restoration. The workers and peasants must share the sentiments of those non-Party peasants who have declared that they are not afraid to face sacrifice and privation. Realising the danger of capitalist intervention, they do not regard concessions from a sentimental point of view, but as a continuation of the war, as the transfer of the ruthless struggle to another plane; they see in them the possibility of fresh attempts on the part of the bourgeoisie to restore the old capitalism. That is splendid; it is a guarantee that not only the organs of Soviet power but all the workers and peasants will make it their business to keep watch and ward over our interests. We are, therefore, confident that we shall be able to place the protection of our interests on such a basis that the restoration of the power of the capitalists will be totally out of the question even in carrying out the concessions agreements; we shall do everything to reduce the danger to a minimum, and make it less than the danger of war, so that it will be difficult to resume the war and easier for us to restore and develop our economy in a shorter period, in fewer years (and it is a matter of a good many years).

Comrades, economic tasks, the economic front, are again and again assuming prominence as the chief and fundamental factor. While studying the texts of the various laws on which I have to report to you, I saw that the vast majority of the measures and decisions of the Council of People's Commissars and the Council of Defence consist at present of specific, detailed and frequently minute measures connected with this economic activity. You, of course, do not expect me to give you a list of these measures. It would be extremely tedious and quite uninteresting. I should only like to remind you that this is by no means the first time that we are attaching primary importance to the labour front. Let us recall the resolution passed by the All-Russia Central Executive Committee on April 29, 1918.[170] That was a time when Russia was economically dismembered by the Peace of Brest-Litovsk that was forced upon us, and when this extremely rapacious treaty had placed us in an extremely difficult position. It then appeared possible to count on a respite which would create conditions for the restoration of peaceful economic activities, and—although we now know that this respite was a very brief one—the All-Russia Central Executive Committee, in its resolution of April 29, at once focussed all attention on economic development. This resolution, which has not been rescinded and remains one of our laws, provides a proper perspective, enabling us to judge how we approached this task and to what we must now devote greater attention in the interests of our work and in order to complete it successfully.

An examination of this resolution clearly shows that many of the problems we now have to tackle were presented in a clear-cut, firm and sufficiently decisive way as far back as April 1918. Remembering this, we say that repetition is the mother of learning. We are not dismayed by our having to repeat the basic axioms of economic development. We shall repeat them time and again, but see what a difference there is between the declaration of abstract principles in 1918 and the practical economic work that has already been begun. Despite the tremendous difficulties and the constant interruptions in our work, we are approaching closer and closer to a concrete and practical solution of our economic problems. We shall repeat things over and over again. In constructive work you cannot avoid a vast number of repetitions, or avoid turning back every now and again, testing what you have done, making certain corrections, adopting new methods, and bending every effort to convince the backward and the untrained.

The essential feature of the present political situation is that we are now passing through a crucial period of transition, something of a zigzag transition from war to economic development. This has occurred before, but not on such a wide scale. This should constantly remind us of what the general political tasks of the Soviet government are, and what constitutes the particular feature of this transition. The dictatorship of the proletariat has been successful because it has been able to combine compulsion with persuasion. The dictatorship of the proletariat does not fear any resort to compulsion and to the most severe, decisive and ruthless forms of coercion by the state. The advanced class, the class most oppressed by capitalism, is entitled to use compulsion, because it is doing so in the interests of the working and exploited people, and because it possesses means of compulsion and persuasion such as no former classes ever possessed, although they had incomparably greater material facilities for propaganda and agitation than we have.

If we ask ourselves what the results of our experience in these three years have been (for it is difficult, on certain fundamental points, to sum up the results of a single year), if we ask ourselves how, after all, our victory over an enemy much stronger than ourselves is to be explained, it must be said that it was because the organisation of the Red Army splendidly embodied the consistency and firmness of proletarian leadership in the alliance of the workers and the working peasantry against all exploiters. What was the reason? Why did the vast masses of the peasantry willingly consent to this? Because they were convinced, though their vast majority were not Party members, that there was no way of salvation except by supporting the Soviet government. It was, of course, not books that convinced them of this, nor was it propaganda. It was all through experience. They were convinced by the experience of the Civil War, in particular by the alliance between our Mensheviks and Socialist-Revolutionaries, which is more closely akin to certain fundamental features of small-scale peasant economy. Their experience of the alliance between these parties of the small property-owners and the landowners and the capitalists, and their experience of Kolchak and Denikin, convinced the peasant masses that no middle course was possible, that the plain and straightforward Soviet policy was the right one, and that the iron leadership of the proletariat was their only means of salvation from exploitation and violence. It has been only because of our ability to convince the peasants of this that our policy of coercion, which is based on this firm and absolute conviction, has met with such tremendous success.

We must now bear in mind that, in going over to the labour front, we are faced with the same problem, under new conditions and on a much wider scale, that confronted us when we were fighting the whiteguards and witnessed a degree of enthusiasm and concentration of energy on the part of the worker and peasant masses such as has never been, and never could have been, displayed in any war in any other state. From their own observations and their knowledge of life, the non-Party peasants, like the Arzamas peasant whose words I have just quoted, did really come to the conclusion that the exploiters are ruthless enemies and that a ruthless state power is required to crush them. We succeeded in rousing unprecedented numbers of people to display an intelligent attitude towards the war, and to support it actively. Never before, under any political regime, has there been even one-tenth of the sympathy with a war and an understanding of it as that unanimously displayed by our Party and non-Party workers and non-Party peasants (and the mass of the peasants are non-Party) under Soviet power. That is the main reason for our having ultimately defeated a powerful enemy. That is corroboration of one of the most profound and at the same time most simple and comprehensible precepts of Marxism. The greater the scope and extent of historical events, the greater is the number of people participating in them, and, contrariwise, the more profound the change we wish to bring about, the more must we rouse an interest and an intelligent attitude towards it, and convince more millions and tens of millions of people that it is necessary. In the final analysis, the reason our revolution has left all other revolutions far behind is that, through the Soviet form of government, it has aroused tens of millions of people, formerly uninterested in state development, to take an active part in the work of building up the state. Let us now consider, from this aspect, the new tasks which confronted us and were expressed in tens and hundreds of decisions passed by the Soviet government during this period; they accounted for nine-tenths of the work of the Council of Labour and Defence (we shall speak of this later), and probably more than half of the work of the Council of People's Commissars, namely, the economic tasks, the elaboration of a single economic plan, the reorganisation of the very foundations of the economy of Russia, the very foundations of small-scale peasant economy. These tasks require that all members of trade unions, without exception, should be drawn into this absolutely new work, something that was alien to them under capitalism. Now ask yourselves whether we at present have the condition for the rapid and unequivocal success that we had during the war, the condition of the masses being drawn into the work. Are the members of the trade unions and the majority of the non-Party people convinced that our new methods and our great tasks of economic development are necessary? Are they as convinced of this as they were of the necessity of devoting everything to the war, of sacrificing everything for the sake of victory on the war front? If the question is presented in that way, you will be compelled to answer that they are certainly not. They are far from being as fully convinced of this as they should be.

War was a matter which people understood and were used to for hundreds and thousands of years. The acts of violence and brutality formerly committed by the landowners were so obvious that it was easy to convince the people; it was not difficult to convince even the peasants of the richer grain regions, who are least connected with industry, that we were waging war in the interests of the working people, and it was therefore possible to arouse almost universal enthusiasm. It will be more difficult to get the peasant masses and the members of the trade unions to understand these tasks now, to get them to understand that we cannot go on living in the old way, that however firmly capitalist exploitation has been implanted in the course of decades, it must be overcome. We must get everybody to understand that Russia belongs to us, and that only we, the masses of workers and peasants, can by our activities and our strict labour discipline remould the old economic conditions of existence and put a great economic plan into practice. There can be no salvation apart from this. We are lagging behind the capitalist powers and shall continue to lag behind them; we shall be defeated if we do not succeed in restoring our economy. That is why we must repeat the old truths I have just reminded you of, the old truths regarding the importance of organisational problems, of labour discipline, regarding the immense role of the trade unions—an absolutely exclusive role in this sphere, because there is no other organisation which unites the broad masses; that is why we must not only repeat these old truths, but must with every fibre of our being realise that the transition from military tasks to economic tasks has begun.

We have been completely successful in the military sphere, and we must now prepare to achieve similar successes in tasks which are more difficult and which demand enthusiasm and self-sacrifice from the vast majority of workers and peasants. The conviction that the new tasks are necessary must be instilled in hundreds of millions of people who from generation to generation have lived in a state of slavery and oppression and whose every initiative has been suppressed. We must convince the millions of workers who belong to trade unions but who are still not politically conscious and are unaccustomed to regarding themselves as masters. They must be organised, not to resist the government but to support and develop the measures of their workers' government and to carry them out to the full. This transition will be accompanied by difficulties. Regarded merely as a formulation, it is not a new task; it is a new task insofar as the economic problem is being raised on such a vast scale for the first time; we must realise and remember that the war on the economic front will be more difficult and prolonged. To achieve success on this front, a larger number of workers and peasants must be educated to be self-reliant, active and devoted. This can be done, as is borne out by the experience we have gained in economic development, because the masses fully realise that the misfortunes, cold, hunger and privation have been caused by the inadequacy of our productive forces. We must now transfer all our agitation and propaganda from political and military interests to economic development. We have proclaimed this many times, but insufficiently; it seems to me that the most outstanding measures adopted by the Soviet government during the past year are the creation of the Central Bureau for Production Propaganda of the All-Russia Central Council of Trade Unions,[171] the amalgamation of its work with that of the Chief Committee for Political Education, and the publication of additional newspapers for the respective industries, which are to devote attention, not only to production propaganda but also to its organisation on a country-wide scale.

The necessity of organising production propaganda on a nation-wide scale follows from the special features of the political situation. It is equally necessary to the working class, the trade unions, and the peasantry. It is absolutely essential to our state apparatus, which we have used far from enough for this purpose. We have a thousand times more knowledge, book knowledge, of how to run industry and how to interest the masses than is being applied in practice. We must see to it that literally every member of the trade unions becomes interested in production, and remembers that only by increasing production and raising labour productivity will Soviet Russia be in a state to win. Only in this way will Soviet Russia be able to shorten by about ten years the period of the frightful conditions she is now experiencing, the hunger and cold she is now suffering. If we do not understand this task, we may all perish, because we shall have to retreat owing to the weakness of our apparatus, since, after a short respite, the capitalists may at any moment renew the war, while we shall not be in a state to continue it. We shall not be able to bring the pressure of the millions of our masses to bear, and in this last war we shall be smashed. That is how the matter stands. Hitherto, the fate of all revolutions, of all great revolutions, has been decided by a long series of wars. Our revolution too is such a great revolution. We have passed through one period of wars, and we must prepare for another. We do not know when it will come, but we must see to it that when it does come we shall be prepared for all contingencies. That is why we must not give up measures of compulsion, and not merely because we are preserving the dictatorship of the proletariat, which the mass of peasants and non-Party workers already understand. They know all about our dictatorship, and it holds out no terrors to them. It does not frighten them. They regard it as a bulwark and a stronghold, that is, something with which they can resist the landowners and capitalists, and without which victory is impossible.

This realisation, this conviction, which has already become deep-rooted among the peasant masses as far as military and political tasks are concerned, must now be extended to economic problems. We may not, perhaps, succeed in bringing about this transition at once. It may, possibly, not be effected without certain vacillations and reversions to the old flabbiness and petty-bourgeois ideology. We must tackle this work with still greater energy and zeal, remembering that we can convince the non-Party peasants and insufficiently class-conscious trade union members, because the truth is on our side, and because it cannot be denied that in the second period of wars we shall not be able to defeat our enemies unless the country's economy is restored. Let us only see to it that the millions take a more enlightened attitude towards the war on the economic front. This is the task of the Central Bureau of Production Propaganda, the task of the All-Russia Central Council of Trade Unions, the task of all Party workers, the task of all the departments of the Soviet government, the task of all our propaganda, with the help of which we have secured successes of world-wide significance, because our propaganda throughout the world has always told the workers and peasants the truth, while all other propaganda tells them lies. We must now switch our propaganda over to something which is far more difficult and concerns the everyday work of the workers in the factory shop, no matter how difficult the conditions of this work may be, and no matter how strong the memories of the old capitalist system may be, which taught the workers and peasants to mistrust governments. We must convince both workers and peasants that, without a new combination of forces, new forms of state amalgamation, and the new forms associated with compulsion, we shall not cope with our difficulties, and we shall not escape the abyss of economic collapse on the brink of which we are standing—and we have already begun to cope with the situation.

Comrades, I shall now deal with certain facts of our economic policy and the economic problems which seem to me to be characteristic of the present political situation and of the transition now confronting us. I must first mention our agrarian bill, the bill of the Council of People's Commissars for the consolidation and development of agricultural production and for assistance to peasant farms. This bill was published on December 14 of this year, and before that date the substance and principles of it were communicated to all local officials by wireless.

Arrangements should at once be made to have this bill thoroughly discussed—in the light of local experience (on which it is actually based), and this is being done in the localities—by the Congress and also by the representatives of the local Executive Committees and the departments of the latter. I think that no comrade now doubts the necessity of specific and very energetic measures of assistance—not only in the form of encouragement but also in the form of compulsion—to improve our agricultural production.

Our country has been and still is a country of small peasants, and the transition to communism is far more difficult for us than it would be under any other conditions. To accomplish this transition, the peasants' participation in it must be ten times as much as in the war. The war could demand, and was bound to demand, part of the adult male population. However, our country, a land of peasants which is still in a state of exhaustion, has to mobilise the entire male and female population of workers and peasants without exception. It is not difficult to convince us Communists, workers in the Land Departments, that state labour conscription is necessary. In the discussion of the bill of December 14, which has been submitted for your consideration, I hope that on this point there will not be even a shadow of difference in principle. We must realise that there is another difficulty, that of convincing the non-Party peasants. The peasants are not socialists. To base our socialist plans on the assumption that they are would be building on sand; it would mean that we do not understand our tasks and that, during these three years, we have not learnt to adjust our programmes and carry out our new undertakings with due account of the poverty and often squalor that surround us. We must have a clear picture of the problems that face us. The first task is to unite the Communists working in the Land Departments, draw general conclusions from their experience, grasp what has been done in the localities, and embody it in the legislative acts which will be promulgated at the centre, by government departments, and by the All-Russia Congress of Soviets. We hope that we shall be able to do that. However, that is only the first step. The second step is to convince the non-Party peasants, yes, the non-Party peasants, because they form the majority and because what we are in a position to do can be done only by making this mass, which is in itself active and full of initiative, realise to a greater degree that the task must be tackled. Peasant farming cannot continue in the old way. While we were able to extricate ourselves from the first period of wars, we shall not extricate ourselves so easily from the second period, and must therefore pay special attention to this aspect.

Every non-Party peasant must be made to understand this undoubted truth, and we are sure that he will understand it. He has not lived through these last six painful and difficult years in vain. He is not like the pre-war muzhik. He has suffered severely, has done a lot of thinking, and has borne many political and economic hardships that have induced him to give up a good deal of their old habits. It seems to me that he already realises that he cannot live in the old way, that he must live in a different way. All our means of propaganda, all the resources of the state, all our educational facilities and all our Party resources and reserves must be devoted in full force to convincing the non-Party peasant. Only then will our agrarian bill—which I hope you will adopt unanimously, with necessary amendments and addenda, of course—be placed on a sound basis. Only when we convince the majority of the peasants and draw them into this work will this measure become just as firm as our policy is. That is because—as Comrade Kurayev has rightly said in an article based on the experience of the Tatar Republic—the working middle peasant and poor peasant are friends of the Soviet government, while the idlers are its enemies. That is the real truth, a truth in which there is nothing socialist, but which is so indisputable and obvious that any village assembly and any meeting of non-Party peasants will understand it, and it will become the conviction of the overwhelming majority of the working peasants.

Comrades, here is what I particularly want to bring home to you now that we have turned from the phase of war to economic development. In a country of small peasants, our chief and basic task is to be able to resort to state compulsion in order to raise the level of peasant farming, beginning with measures that are absolutely essential, urgent and fully intelligible and comprehensible to the peasant. We shall be able to achieve this only when we are able to convince more millions of people who are not yet ready for it. We must devote all our forces to this and see to it that the apparatus of compulsion, activated and reinforced, shall be adapted and developed for a new drive of persuasion. Another campaign in the war will then end in victory. We are now declaring war on the relics of inertness, ignorance and mistrust that prevail among the peasant masses. We shall achieve nothing by the old methods, but we shall achieve victory by the methods of propaganda, agitation and organised influence which we have learnt. We shall also see to it that, besides decrees being adopted, institutions created and documents written—it is not enough to send orders flying all over the country—all the fields are sown better than before by the spring, and a definite improvement is achieved in small peasant farming. Let it be even the most elementary improvement—the more cautious we are the better—but it must be achieved at all costs and on a mass scale. If we correctly understand the task that faces us, and if we devote our whole attention to the non-Party peasant, and concentrate on this all the skill and experience we have gained during these three years, we shall succeed. And unless we succeed, unless we achieve a practical and massive improvement in small-scale peasant farming, there is no salvation for us. Unless this basis is created, no economic development will be possible and the most ambitious plans will be valueless. The comrades must remember this and must bring it home to the peasants. They must tell the non-Party peasants of Arzamas—and there are about ten or fifteen million of them—that we cannot go on starving and freezing endlessly, for then we shall be overthrown in the next period of wars. This is a state matter; it concerns the interests of our state. Whoever reveals the least weakness, the least slackness in this matter, is an out-and-out criminal towards the workers' and peasants' government; he is helping the landowner and the capitalist. And the landowner and the capitalist have their armies nearby, holding them in readiness to launch against us the instant they see us weakening. There is no way to strengthen ourselves otherwise than by building up our main bulwark—agriculture and urban industry. These cannot be improved except by convincing the non-Party peasant of the need to do so, by mobilising all our forces to help him, and by actually helping him in practice.

We admit that we are in debt to the peasant. We have had grain from him in return for paper money, and have taken it from him on credit. We must repay that debt, and we shall do so when we have restored our industry. To restore it we need a surplus of agricultural products. That is why the agrarian bill is important, not only because we must secure practical results, but also because around it, as on a focal point, are grouped hundreds of decisions and legislative measures of the Soviet government.

I now pass on to the question of how the basis for our industrial development is being created to enable us to begin restoring Russia's economic forces. In this connection I must first draw your attention—from among the mass of reports which you have received or will receive in the next few days from all the Commissariats—to a passage in the report of our Commissariat of Food. In the next few days each Commissariat will present you with a profusion of figures and reports, which taken together are overwhelming in their abundance. We must extract from them what is most essential to success, however modest it may be, and what is fundamental for the realisation of our economic plan, for the restoration of our economy and our industry. One of these essentials is the state of our food procurements. In the booklet which has been distributed to you—the report of the Commissariat of Food for three years—you will find a table from which I shall read only the totals, and even those in round figures, because reading figures, and particularly listening to figures, is a difficult matter. These are the figures showing the total procurements for each year. From August 1, 1916 to August 1, 1917, 320,000,000 poods were procured; 50,000,000 were procured in the following year, then 100,000,000 and then 200,000,000 poods. These figures—320, 50, 100 and 200—give you the basis of the economic history of Soviet government, of the work of the Soviet government in the economic field, the preparations for that foundation which, when laid down, will enable us to really start developing. The pre-revolutionary 320,000,000 poods is the approximate minimum without which development is impossible. In the first year of the revolution, with only 50,000,000 poods, there was starvation, cold and poverty. In the second year we had 100,000,000 poods; in the third year, 200,000,000 poods. The total has doubled with each year. According to figures I received yesterday from Svidersky, we had 155,000,000 poods on December 15. We are beginning to stand on our feet for the first time, but with the utmost efforts, with unparalleled difficulties, very often having to accomplish the task without any supplies from Siberia, the Caucasus and the South. At present, with a procurement of over 150,000,000 poods, we can say without any exaggeration that despite the tremendous difficulties, this task has been accomplished. We shall have a total of about 300,000,000 poods, perhaps more. Without such a supply, however, it will be impossible to restore the country's industry; it will be hopeless to expect the revival of the transport system and it will be impossible even to approach the great task of electrifying Russia. There can be no socialist country, no state with a workers' and peasants' government unless, by the joint efforts of the workers and peasants, it can accumulate a stock of food sufficient to guarantee the subsistence of the workers engaged in industry and to make it possible to send tens and hundreds of thousands of workers wherever the Soviet government deems it necessary. Without this there can be nothing but empty talk. Food stocks are the real basis of the economic system. In this we have achieved a signal success. Having achieved this success and with such a reserve, we can set about restoring our economy. We know that these successes have been achieved at the cost of tremendous privation, hunger and lack of cattle fodder among the peasants, which may become still more acute. We know that the year of drought increased the hardships and privations of the peasants to an unparalleled extent. We therefore lay prime stress on the measures of assistance contained in the bill I have referred to. We regard stocks of food as a fund for the restoration of industry, as a fund for helping the peasants. Without such a fund the state power is nothing. Without such a fund socialist policy is but a pious wish.

We must remember that the production propaganda which we have firmly decided to launch will be supplemented with a different kind of persuasion, namely, bonuses in kind.[172] The law on bonuses in kind has been one of the most important decrees and decisions of the Council of People's Commissars and the Council of Defence. We were not able to pass this law immediately. If you examine the matter, you will find that ever since April there has been a long chain of decisions and resolutions, and that this law was passed only when, as the result of strenuous efforts on the part of our transport system, we were able to accumulate a food reserve of 500,000 poods. Five hundred thousand poods is a very modest figure. The reports which you no doubt read in *Izvestia* yesterday show that out of these 500,000 poods 170,000 poods have already been expended. As you see the reserve is nothing to boast of, and is far from adequate; nevertheless, we have entered on a road along which we shall advance. It is proof that we are not relying on persuasion alone in the transition to new methods of work. It is not enough to tell the peasants and the workers to maintain the utmost labour discipline. We must also help them; we must reward those who, after suffering tremendous hardships, continue to display heroism on the labour front. We have already created a reserve fund, but it is being utilised in a way that is far from satisfactory. We in the Council of People's Commissars have numerous indications that in practice a bonus in kind often amounts simply to an increase in wages. A good deal still remains to be done in this respect. The work of conferences and of drafting supplementary schemes at the centre must be coupled with very important work of another kind, namely, on the spot and among the masses. When the state not only persuades, but also rewards good workers by creating better living conditions for them, that is something that is not hard to understand; one does not have to be a socialist to understand it, and here we are assured in advance of the sympathy of the non-Party masses of workers and peasants. We have only to make this idea much more widely known and to organise this work in a more practical way in the localities.

Now with regard to fuel; you will find in Comrade Rykov's theses figures that show the improvement that has been achieved, not only in firewood, but also in oil supplies. Thanks to the great zeal displayed by the workers in the Azerbaijan Republic, the friendly relations we have established with them and the capable managers provided by the Supreme Council of the National Economy, the oil situation is now favourable, so that we are beginning to stand on our own feet in the matter of fuel as well. Coal deliveries from the Donets Basin are being increased from 25,000,000 poods to 50,000,000 poods per month, thanks to the work of the authorised commission which was sent there under the chairmanship of Comrade Trotsky. This commission has decided to send responsible and experienced men to the Donets Basin, and Comrade Pyatakov has now been sent there to take charge.

Thus, to achieve success, we have adopted certain measures with regard to fuel. The Donets Basin, one of the largest sources, is already under our control. In the minutes of the Council of People's Commissars and the Council of Defence, decisions may be found relating to the Donets Basin. These make reference to the dispatch of commissions invested with considerable powers and consisting of representatives of the central government and of local officials. We must stimulate work in the localities, and it appears to me that we can do so with the help of these commissions. You will see the results of the work of these commissions, which we shall continue to set up in the future. We must give a definite boost to fuel production, the principal branch of our industry.

I must say that, in the matter of fuel, the hydraulic method of extracting peat is a great achievement. Peat is a fuel we possess in very large quantities, but which we have been unable to utilise till now because of the deplorable working conditions. This new method will enable us to overcome the fuel shortage, which presents one of the greatest dangers on our economic front. We shall not be able to get out of this impasse for many years to come, if we stick to the old methods and do not restore our industry and transport. The members of our Peat Committee have helped two Russian engineers to perfect this new invention, with the result that the new method is on the verge of completion. We are thus on the eve of a great revolution, which will be an important aid to us economically. It must not be forgotten that we possess vast deposits of peat, which we cannot utilise because we cannot send people to do such back-breaking work. The capitalist system could send people to work under such harsh conditions. In the capitalist state people were driven to work there by hunger, but in the socialist state we cannot consign people to such intolerable work, and nobody will go there voluntarily. The capitalist system did everything for the upper crust. It was not concerned with the lower classes.

We must introduce more machines everywhere, and resort to machine technology as widely as possible. The extraction of peat by the hydraulic method, which has been so successfully promoted by the Supreme Council of the National Economy, makes it possible to extract fuel in vast quantities and eliminates the need for skilled workers, since even unskilled workers can perform the work under this method. We have produced these machines; I would advise the delegates to see the cinema film on peat extraction which has been shown in Moscow and which can be demonstrated for the Congress delegates. It will give you a definite idea of one of the means for coping with the fuel shortage. We have made the machines required for the new method, but we have made them badly. If we send our people abroad, with the establishment of trade with foreign countries, with even the existing semi-legal trade relations, the machines designed by our inventors could be made properly there. The number of these machines and the success gained in this field by the Chief Peat Committee and the Supreme Council of the National Economy will serve as a measure of all our economic achievements. Unless we overcome the fuel shortage, it will be impossible to win on the economic front. Vital success in restoring the transport system will also depend on this.

Incidentally, you have already seen from the theses of Comrades Yemshanov and Trotsky that in this field we have a real plan worked out for a number of years. Order No. 1042 was designed for a period of five years[173]; in five years we can restore our transport and reduce the number of broken-down locomotives. I should like to stress as probably the most difficult problem the statement made in the ninth thesis, to the effect that this period has already been reduced.

When extensive plans appear, designed for a number of years, sceptics are frequently to be found who say: how can we plan for a number of years ahead? The best we can hope for is to do what is required at the moment. Comrades, we must be able to combine the two things; we cannot work without a long-term plan that envisages important achievements. The truth of this is borne out by the undoubted improvement in the work of the transport system. I draw your attention to the passage in the ninth thesis which says that the period for the restoration of transport was fixed at five years, but it has already been reduced because we are ahead of the schedule. The period is now being fixed at three and a half years. That is the way to work in the other branches of economic activity too. The real and practical task of the Council of Labour and Defence is being steadily reduced to that. We must avail ourselves of the progress of science and practice, and must steadfastly strive to get the plan fulfilled in the localities ahead of schedule, so that the masses will see that the long period separating us from the complete restoration of industry can be reduced in practice. It depends on us. Let us improve our methods in every workshop, in every railway depot, in every sphere, and we shall shorten this period. It is already being reduced. Do not be afraid of long-term plans, for without them you cannot achieve an economic revival; let us devote all our energies in the localities to their fulfilment.

Economic plans must be carried out in accordance with a definite programme, and the increasing fulfilment of this programme must be noted and encouraged. The masses must not only realise, but also feel that the shortening of the period of hunger, cold and poverty depends entirely upon how quickly they fulfil our economic plans. The plans of the various branches of production must be soundly coordinated, and linked up so as to constitute the single economic plan we stand in such great need of.

In this connection, we are confronted with the task of unifying the People's Commissariats for the various branches of the economy under a single economic centre. We have begun to tackle this task and we are submitting for your consideration a decision of the Council of People's Commissars and the Council of Labour and Defence regarding the reorganisation of the latter body.

You will examine this project, and I trust that with the necessary amendments it will be adopted unanimously. Its contents are very modest but its significance is great, because we need a body which definitely knows what its position is and unites all economic work; it is on economic work that the chief stress is now being laid.

This has been dealt with in the literature which appeared before and in connection with the Congress, in a pamphlet by Comrade Gusev, which, incidentally, is not as well written as his earlier one. The pamphlet contains a sweeping plan for the organisation of the Council of Labour and Defence, to which it is proposed to transfer many prominent workers, among whom we find the names of Trotsky and Rykov. I would say that we need somewhat fewer flights of fancy like this. We cannot burst out of an apparatus which it has taken three years to build up. We realise its immense shortcomings, of which we shall speak in detail at this Congress. This question has been placed on the agenda; it is one of the most important questions. I am referring to the question of improving the Soviet apparatus. But we must at present act with circumspection, confine ourselves to what is essential, and change our apparatus on the basis of practical experience. Comrade Gusev has derided the project we have submitted and says that we are proposing to add the People's Commissariat of Agriculture to the Council of Labour and Defence. Quite right, we are proposing such a project. In it we assign a very modest place to the Council of Labour and Defence, making it a Commission of Labour and Defence under the Council of People's Commissars. Until now we have been working in the Council of Labour and Defence without any constitution. The powers of the Council of People's Commissars and the Council of Labour and Defence have been poorly defined; we have sometimes exceeded these powers and acted as a legislative body. But there has never been any conflict on these grounds. Such cases have been settled by immediately referring them to the Council of People's Commissars. When it became apparent that the Council of Labour and Defence must be converted into a body for the closer co-ordination of economic policy, the question arose how to give legal definition to these relations. There are two plans before us. One of them calls for the demarcation of the competence of the Council of People's Commissars and that of the Council of Labour and Defence. To do this, numerous codifiers must be engaged and reams of paper used, and even then there will be no guarantee that mistakes will not be made.

Let us set about it in a different way. The Council of Labour and Defence has been regarded as something almost equal to the Council of People's Commissars. Let us abandon that idea. Let it be a commission of the Council of People's Commissars. We shall avoid a great deal of friction and shall achieve more rapid practical realisation. If any member of the Council of People's Commissars is dissatisfied, let him bring his complaint before the Council of People's Commissars; it can be summoned in a few hours, as you know. In this way we shall avoid friction between departments and will make the Council of Labour and Defence a rapidly acting body. That is no easy problem. It is bound up with the actual creation of a single economic plan. The problem, for the solution of which we have done something and for which we have been preparing for two years, is to achieve the unification of the Commissariats for the various branches of the economy. That is why I draw your attention to this bill on the Council of Labour and Defence, and I hope that, with the necessary amendments, you will endorse it. The work of uniting these Commissariats will then proceed more smoothly, rapidly, firmly and energetically.

I now come to the last item—the question of electrification, which stands on the agenda of the Congress. You are to hear a report on this subject. I think that we are witnessing a momentous change, one which in any case marks the beginning of important successes for the Soviets. Henceforth the rostrum at All-Russia Congresses will be mounted, not only by politicians and administrators but also by engineers and agronomists. This marks the beginning of that very happy time when politics will recede into the

17-988

background, when politics will be discussed less often and at shorter length, and engineers and agronomists will do most of the talking. To really proceed with the work of economic development, this custom must be initiated at the All-Russia Congress of Soviets and in all Soviets and organisations, newspapers, organs of propaganda and agitation, and all institutions, from top to bottom.

We have, no doubt, learnt politics; here we stand as firm as a rock. But things are bad as far as economic matters are concerned. Henceforth, less politics will be the best politics. Bring more engineers and agronomists to the fore, learn from them, keep an eye on their work, and turn our congresses and conferences, not into propaganda meetings but into bodies that will verify our economic achievements, bodies in which we can really learn the business of economic development.

You will hear the report of the State Electrification Commission, which was set up in conformity with the decision of the All-Russia Central Executive Committee of February 7, 1920. On February 21, the Presidium of the Supreme Council of the National Economy signed the final ordinance determining the composition of the commission, and a number of leading experts and workers, mainly from the Supreme Council of the National Economy, over a hundred of them, and also from the People's Commissariat of Railways and the People's Commissariat of Agriculture, are devoting their entire energy to this work. We have before us the results of the work of the State Commission for the Electrification of Russia in the shape of this small volume which will be distributed to you today or tomorrow.[174] I trust you will not be scared by this little volume. I think I shall have no difficulty in convincing you of the particular importance of this book. In my opinion it is the second programme of our Party. We have a Party programme which has been excellently explained by Comrades Preobrazhensky and Bukharin in the form of a book which is less voluminous, but extremely useful. That is the political programme; it is an enumeration of our objectives, an explanation of the relations between classes and masses. It must, however, also be realised that the time has come to take this road in actual fact and to measure the practical results achieved. Our Party programme must not remain solely a programme of the Party. It must become a programme of our economic development, or otherwise it will be valueless even as a programme of the Party. It must be supplemented with a second Party programme, a plan of work aimed at restoring our entire economy and raising it to the level of up-to-date technical development. Without a plan of electrification, we cannot undertake any real constructive work. When we discuss the restoration of agriculture, industry and transport, and their harmonious co-ordination, we are obliged to discuss a broad economic plan. We must adopt a definite plan. Of course, it will be a plan adopted as a first approximation. This Party programme will not be as invariable as our real Party programme is, which can be modified by Party congresses alone. No, day by day this programme will be improved, elaborated, perfected and modified, in every workshop and in every volost. We need it as a first draft, which will be submitted to the whole of Russia as a great economic plan designed for a period of not less than ten years and indicating how Russia is to be placed on the real economic basis required for communism. What was one of the most powerful incentives that multiplied our strength and our energies to a tremendous degree when we fought and won on the war front? It was the realisation of danger. Everybody asked whether it was possible that the landowners and capitalists might return to Russia. And the reply was that it was. We therefore multiplied our efforts a hundredfold, and we were victorious.

Take the economic front, and ask whether capitalism can be restored economically in Russia. We have combated the Sukharevka black market. The other day, just prior to the opening of the All-Russia Congress of Soviets, this not very pleasant institution was closed down by the Moscow Soviet of Workers' and Red Army Deputies. (*Applause.*) The Sukharevka black market has been closed but it is not that market that is so sinister. The old Sukharevka market on Sukharevskaya Square has been closed down, an act that presented no difficulty. The sinister thing is the "Sukharevka" that resides in the heart and behaviour of every petty proprietor. This is the "Sukharevka" that must be closed down. That "Sukharevka" is the basis of capitalism. While it exists, the capitalists may return to Russia and may grow stronger than we are. That must be clearly realised. It must serve as the mainspring of our work and as a condition and yardstick of our real success. While we live in a small-peasant country, there is a firmer economic basis for capitalism in Russia than for communism. That must be borne in mind. Anyone who has carefully observed life in the countryside, as compared with life in the cities, knows that we have not torn up the roots of capitalism and have not undermined the foundation, the basis, of the internal enemy. The latter depends on small-scale production, and there is only one way of undermining it, namely, to place the economy of the country, including agriculture, on a new technical basis, that of modern large-scale production. Only electricity provides that basis.

Communism is Soviet power plus the electrification of the whole country. Otherwise the country will remain a small-peasant country, and we must clearly realise that. We are weaker than capitalism, not only on the world scale, but also within the country. That is common knowledge. We have realised it, and we shall see to it that the economic basis is transformed from a small-peasant basis into a large-scale industrial basis. Only when the country has been electrified, and industry, agriculture and transport have been placed on the technical basis of modern large-scale industry, only then shall we be fully victorious.

We have already drawn up a preliminary plan for the electrification of the country; two hundred of our best scientific and technical men have worked on it. We have a plan which gives us estimates of materials and finances covering a long period of years, not less than a decade. This plan indicates how many million barrels of cement and how many million bricks we shall require for the purpose of electrification. To accomplish the task of electrification from the financial point of view, the estimates are between 1,000 and 1,200 million gold rubles. You know that we are far from being able to meet this sum from our gold reserves. Our stock of foodstuffs is not very large either. We must therefore meet the expenditure indicated in these estimates by means of concessions, in accordance with the plan I have mentioned. You will see the calculation showing how the restoration of our industry and our transport is being planned on this basis.

I recently had occasion to attend a peasant festival held in Volokolamsk Uyezd, a remote part of Moscow Gubernia, where the peasants have electric lighting.[175] A meeting was arranged in the street, and one of the peasants came forward and began to make a speech welcoming this new event in the lives of the peasants. "We peasants were unenlightened," he said, "and now light has appeared among us, an 'unnatural light, which will light up our peasant darkness'." For my part, these words did not surprise me. Of course, to the non-Party peasant masses electric light is an "unnatural" light; but what we consider unnatural is that the peasants and workers should have lived for hundreds and thousands of years in such backwardness, poverty and oppression under the yoke of the landowners and the capitalists. You cannot emerge from this darkness very rapidly. What we must now try is to convert every electric power station we build into a stronghold of enlightenment to be used to make the masses electricity-conscious, so to speak. All should be made aware of the reason why these small electric power stations, whose numbers run into the dozens, are linked up with the restoration of industry. We have an established plan of electrification, but the fulfilment of this plan is designed to cover a number of years. We must fulfil this plan at all costs, and the period of its fulfilment must be reduced. Here we must have the same thing as was the case with one of our first economic plans, the plan for the restoration of transport—Order No. 1042—which was designed to cover a period of five years, but has now been reduced to three and a half years because we are ahead of the schedule. To carry out the electrification plan we may need a period of ten or twenty years to effect the changes that will preclude any return to capitalism. This will be an example of rapid social development without precedent anywhere in the world. The plan must be carried out at all costs, and its deadline brought nearer.

This is the first time that we have set about economic work in such a fashion that, besides separate plans which have arisen in separate sections of industry as, for instance, in the transport system and have been brought into other branches of industry, we now have an all-over plan calculated for a number of years. This is hard work, designed to bring about the victory of communism.

It should, however, be realised and remembered that we cannot carry out electrification with the illiterates we have. Our commission will endeavour to stamp out illiteracy—but that is not enough. It has done a good deal compared with the past, but it has done little compared with what has to be done. Besides literacy, we need cultured, enlightened and educated working people; the majority of the peasants must be made fully aware of the tasks awaiting us. This programme of the Party must be a basic book to be used in every school. You will find in it, in addition to the general plan of electrification, separate plans for every district of Russia. Thus every comrade who goes to the provinces will have a definite scheme of electrification for his district, a scheme for transition from darkness and ignorance to a normal life. And, comrades, you can and must compare the theses you have been presented with, elaborate and check them on the spot; you must see to it that when the question "What is communism?" is asked in any school and in any study circle, the answer should contain not only what is written in the Party programme but should also say how we can emerge from the state of ignorance.

Our best men, our economic experts, have accomplished the task we set them of drawing up a plan for the electrification of Russia and the restoration of her economy. We must now see to it that the workers and peasants should realise how great and difficult this task is, how it must be approached and tackled.

We must see to it that every factory and every electric power station becomes a centre of enlightenment; if Russia is covered with a dense network of electric power stations and powerful technical installations, our communist economic development will become a model for a future socialist Europe and Asia. (*Stormy and prolonged applause.*)

3

REPLY TO THE DEBATE ON THE REPORT ON THE WORK OF THE COUNCIL OF PEOPLE'S COMMISSARS DECEMBER 23

(*Applause.*) Comrades, I must confine myself to a few remarks on the speeches and declarations you have just heard. One of the notes I have received expresses perplexity and asks what is the use of the Congress of Soviets hearing such declarations and speeches. I think most of you will disagree with this opinion. It is no doubt always very useful to have a reminder of what some catchwords, now perhaps quite popular—as set forth by certain parties, sections of which have just made their declarations—may lead to in the present political situation. Take for example the reasoning of the representative of the Menshevik Party, or to be more exact, a certain section of that party. It is not our fault that the Menshevik Party and the Socialist-Revolutionaries, which still preserve their old titles, constitute a conglomeration of heterogeneous parts that are constantly changing camps, which turns them into voluntary or involuntary, conscious or unconscious, accomplices of international imperialism. This is evident from their declarations and speeches at this Congress.

For example, I have been reproached for advancing a new theory about an impending new period of wars. I need not go far back into history to show what my statements were based upon. We have only just finished with Wrangel; but Wrangel's troops exist somewhere, not very far from the frontiers of our Republic, and are biding their time. Therefore, whoever forgets about the danger that is constantly threatening us and will never cease as long as world imperialism exists, whoever forgets about this forgets about our working people's republic. To say to us that we are conducting secret diplomacy; to say that we must wage only a war of defence, at a time when the sword still hangs over us, when to this day, despite the hundreds of offers we have made and the incredible concessions we are prepared to make, not a single big power has concluded peace with us—to say such things means repeating the old phrases of petty-bourgeois pacifism which have long become meaningless. If, in the face of these ever actively hostile forces, we pledged ourselves—as we have been advised to do—never to resort to certain actions which from a military-strategical point of view may prove to be aggressive, we would be, not only fools but criminals. This is what these pacifist phrases and resolutions lead to. They lead to a situation wherein the Soviets, surrounded by enemies, will be tied hand and foot and thrown to the predators of world imperialism to be torn to pieces.

When, further, we hear talk about the unity of the proletariat and about our disrupting that unity, it is hard not to smile. We in this country have heard about the unity of the proletariat and now see in fact that the unity of the proletariat in the epoch of social revolution can be achieved only by the extreme revolutionary party of Marxism, and only through a relentless struggle against all other parties. (*Stormy applause.*)

Further, we are told about the arming of the whole people; we hear the ABC of the old bourgeois-democratic slogan repeated at a time when a most decisive class struggle is raging among the people.

Yesterday I had the pleasure of being present—regrettably, for only a short while—at a small private conference of non-Party peasant delegates to our Congress and I learned a great deal from their discussion of some of the most burning questions of rural life, the questions of food supplies, of their destitution and want, of which you all know.[176] The most striking impression that I obtained from this discussion was the depth of the struggle between the poor peasants—the real toilers—and the kulaks and idlers. The supreme significance of our revolution lies in our having helped the lowest sections in the rural districts, the mass of politically the least educated, the mass of the non-Party peasantry, to raise this fundamental question of the social revolution, not only from the theoretical but also from the broad and practical point of view. In all the villages and hamlets throughout our boundless Soviet Russia, people are discussing and finding out who benefits from our political and economic measures. Everywhere, even in the most remote villages, people understand the problem of the working peasantry and the kulaks. Sometimes they accuse each other too heatedly and passionately, but at any rate they look into the matter and realise that it is necessary, imperatively necessary, to help the working peasant and put him on his feet and to repulse all sorties by the insolent kulaks.

The class struggle has become a reality in the rural districts, deep down among the masses of the peasantry; we have been doing all we can to make this struggle a conscious one. And when, after all this, the leaders of a certain special "International" come before us and talk about arming the people, one feels as if one has been transformed into a pupil of a preparatory class on questions of Marxism and socialism. To forget about the class struggle which is raging all over the world means involuntarily aiding the imperialists of the whole world against the fighting proletariat. The arming of the people is the slogan of our enemies; we stand on the basis of an armed class; we have achieved victory on this basis, and on it we will always win. (*Stormy applause.*)

The representatives of the Mensheviks and the Socialist-Revolutionaries asked how we could think of such a thing as granting concessions without a special referendum, and why we did not make labour equality the corner-stone of our economic policy (in the Socialist Revolutionaries' resolution this labour equality was called "rule of labour", while in the Mensheviks' resolution it was paraphrased and called equality between toilers of town and countryside). But what else are tllese phrases about the "rule of labour" but agitation for the trade unions' independence of the class rule of the proletariat? Jointly with the Mensheviks and Socialist-Revolutionaries, the whole of the West-European bourgeois press is showing concern for, and wailing about, this "independence" of the trade unions.

What happened when Martov appeared at the Congress of the Independent Social-Democrats in Halle, where, free of any constraint from the dictatorship of the Bolsheviks, which he dislikes, he said everything he wanted to say? A few days later Martov's speech was published in its entirety, as a titbit, in the most reactionary and imperialist newspapers in Britain. These newspapers thanked Citizen Martov for having disclosed the designs of the Bolsheviks. (Incidentally, over there they use Mr., not Citizen as the form of address.) When such speeches are made in the thick of a world-wide struggle against us, what are they but a piece of Entente politics? You may, of course, say that such a presentation of your ideas of the rule of labour, etc., is petty-bourgeois nonsense, but in actual fact, I repeat, it is nothing more and nothing less than a piece of Entente politics. Tomorrow, if there is an agent of the Entente present here, your speech will be sent to all the capitalist countries and there printed in millions of copies, so that your speech, Citizen Dan, may mislead and dupe the politically unintelligent section of the European workers.

Citizen Dan argued that when I spoke about labour discipline, I was advocating only coercion. The Socialist-Revolutionary Party's representative was more explicit and said that I advocated compulsion based on persuasion. Our entire policy is a clear reply to this. We do not claim that we make no mistakes; but please point out these mistakes and show us better ways of doing things. We have heard nothing like that here. Neither the Mensheviks nor the Socialist-Revolutionaries say: "Here there is want, here there is destitution among the peasants and workers; here is the way to get rid of this poverty." No, they do not say anything of the kind. They only say that what we are doing is compulsion. Yes, that cannot be denied. But we ask you, Citizen Dan: Are you for or against? That is the essence, the crux of the matter. Answer categorically: yes or no? "Neither yes nor no," is the reply. You see, they only want to talk about the rule of labour, to say that we are encroaching on the freedom of the peasants. But who are the peasants? Does not our Soviet Constitution say that the peasants are toilers, working people? We respect such peasants and regard them as the equals and brothers of the workers. Without such a peasantry we could not take a single step in our Soviet policy. Between the working peasantry and the workers there is a fraternal understanding, embodied in our Constitution. But there is another element in the peasantry, the element that constitutes a vast "Sukharevka". I hope that any assembly, even of non-Party people, will be able to see that after careful examination. Do the profiteering peasants represent the working people? This is the crux of the economic problems in the rural districts. The peasants, as petty proprietors, and the workers are two different classes, and we shall abolish the difference between them when we abolish the basis of small-scale production, and create a new basis of gigantic, large-scale, machine production, as I have already pointed out in my report. This is economically inevitable, but the Mensheviks and Socialist-Revolutionaries who spoke here came out with incoherent talk of some kind of labour equality between all the peasants and the workers. These are mere phrases, which are fallacious in terms of economics and are refuted by scientific Marxism. Take our revolution in Siberia and in Georgia, take the experience of the international revolution, and you will see for yourselves that these resonant words about labour equality are false. They are part and parcel of the policy the bourgeoisie is pursuing against us, and nothing more.

Dan has asserted here that, in the offices of the Cheka, there is a document to the effect that the Mensheviks are not to come under the October amnesty; from this Citizen Dan draws the conclusion that the Cheka instructs and controls the Presidium of the All-Russia Central Executive Committee. Can we, who are in power, believe a thing like that? Do not the Communists here, who constitute 70 to 80 per cent of all delegates, know that the Cheka is headed by Comrade Dzerzhinsky, a member of the Central Executive Committee and of the Central Committee of the Party, and that in the Presidium of the All-Russia Central Executive Committee there are six members of the Central Committee of our Party? There are no grounds whatever for believing that, under these circumstances, the Presidium of the Cheka or its Operations Department instructs and runs the Presidium of the Central Executive Committee. That is simply ridiculous. Of course, there is nothing of interest in this, and the representative of the Menshevik Party was simply putting on a comedy. I would, however, like you to take up, in a few days' time, any bourgeois newspaper published in Western Europe or America in half a million or a million copies. There you will find printed in the boldest type that Citizen Dan has disclosed that the Cheka instructs and controls the Presidium of the All-Russia Central Executive Committee.

4

SPEECH DELIVERED AT A MEETING OF THE R.C.P.(B.) GROUP OF THE EIGHTH CONGRESS OF SOVIETS DECEMBER 24 [177]

Comrades, in the first place I will say a word or two about the wrong construction that has been put on the question of force. To bring out this wrong construction, I shall read three lines from the minutes of the Eighth Congress.[178]

The whole argument against force was connected with the question of the communes. I think that the slightest use of force in this sphere will be harmful. Attempts have been made to apply this argument—i.e., that it is foolish to resort to force in establishing communes—to the entire question of persuasion and compulsion in general. This is obviously stretching the point, and is wrong. As regards the bill we are introducing and the exchange of opinions that has commenced, I must say that I think that the effort to give the question a more Leftist bias is the least business-like. I saw nothing concrete or business-like in the proposal made by Comrade Khanov, who claimed to belong to the extreme Left. I considered that Comrade Schlichter's advice to refrain from passing the bill, and leave it to the next session of the All-Russia Central Executive Committee to do so, was most reprehensible. We in the Council of People's Commissars tried to lick the bill into shape as quickly as possible so that the Congress of Soviets, consisting in the main of representatives from the localities, might adopt a final decision. We are threatened with the danger of being too late in conducting this campaign at district level. To conduct the campaign instructions are needed. It must take at least two or three weeks to draw up such instructions. There can be nothing more injurious than the advice given by Schlichter in his speech on another item of the agenda, regarding the rights of the Gubernia Executive Committees. In substance, the bill proposes that practical measures should at once be taken to assist individual peasant farming, which is the predominating system, and that this assistance should take the form, not only of encouragement but of compulsion as well.

I must say that the bill definitely indicates the measures we have in mind. Clause 11, the most important one, states that the Gubernia Sowing Committees may, under the direction and control of the People's Commissariat of Agriculture, issue "compulsory regulations governing the principal methods of mechanical cultivation of the fields and of improving meadows, sowing, and the methods of preserving the natural fertility of the soil". Where are these compulsory regulations to come from? The bill goes on to say that the methods mainly employed by the more efficient farmers should be adopted. What methods should we make compulsory by law? Well-known methods of improving agriculture—these must be made compulsory by law and popularised. At the end we read the following: "It is forbidden to introduce regulations and demands: 1) that will cause a radical change in peasant farming, unless such regulations and demands are proposed by volost congresses, or unless the state supplies the given locality with improved implements and means of production; 2) that are difficult of fulfilment by the household of average means, and 3) that involve risks."

A comrade expressed the opinion that the shortcoming in Comrade Osinsky's report consisted in its being too practical and specific; this, he said, prevented him from presenting the problem properly. On the contrary, the most valuable feature of Comrade Osinsky's report was that he took the bull by the horns and called upon you to set to work and discuss immediate practical questions, such as the question of seeds, of taking measures to prevent seed grain from being consumed. In European Russia this will be much more difficult than in the extremely rich Altai

Region, where, it appears, it is so easy to issue orders. If it is so easy to issue orders there, and if you can achieve practical results by issuing orders, then every gubernia land department—the Altai or any other—will deserve the utmost encouragement.

Unfortunately, this is far from being the case in the poorer gubernias of European Russia. Here, the whole task of the present campaign, like the whole task of our Congress, is to keep this question as far away as possible from all arguments of a general character, which Schlichter and other comrades called upon us to indulge in. I would like to call for a more practical and business-like presentation of questions, and I welcome the turn which Osinsky has given to the matter. Let us discuss the question of seeds. They will be consumed, unless we do something about preserving them. What is the most practical method of doing that? They must be stored in the public granaries, and the peasants must be given guarantees that they will not be tied up by red tape and improperly distributed. We must convince them that our object at present is to put in the safekeeping of the state the quantity of seeds required to sow all the fields. We shall certainly convince the middle peasant of this, because it is an obvious necessity. If any objection is raised, and if some say that they cannot work for Tsyurupa, and try to depict him as some sort of beast of prey, we will say: "Stop joking; give us a straight reply to the question: How do you propose to restore industry?" The peasants must be supplied with agricultural machinery and implements. If the state is to be in a position to meet all requirements and to provide all the necessary agricultural and technical equipment it will need a steadily growing fund. But we are reaching this position very slowly. That is why I think it is wrong to confuse the issue with the tasks of the state farms and collective farms. The collective farms are not an immediate problem. I know that the collective farms are still in such a state of disorganisation, in such a deplorable position, that they deserve the name of alms-houses. I have no objection to the delegates of the Eighth All-Russia Congress impressing on the Council of People's Commissars or the All-Russia Central Executive Committee, the necessity of taking special measures to improve the work of the All-Russia Union of Land and Forest Workers. In this respect, this union is a bulwark, if only it unites in its ranks real semi-proletarian elements who are capable of helping us to become real business-like organisers. I have no objection to that whatever.

However, the object of the present bill is a different one. The present condition of the overwhelming majority of the state farms is below the average. We must base ourselves on the individual peasant; we must take him as he is, and he will remain what he is for some time to come, and so it is no use dreaming about going over to socialism and collectivisation at present. We must drop general arguments and discuss the first practical steps we must take this very spring, and no later; only such a presentation of the question will be business-like. To do that, we must at once pass this bill in the form it has been drafted by the Council of People's Commissars, introduce the necessary changes and amendments at once, and not delay matters for a moment.

As for the socialisation of agricultural implements, I think you are best able to judge what compulsory regulations may be issued in the name of the state. I would warn you against that. We already have a law which grants the right to socialise the implements of the rich peasants.[179] In the districts where this can be successfully carried out, complete freedom to municipalise these implements is allowed by this law; however, the methods to be used are not always and everywhere fully established. Therefore, to introduce that into an act whose immediate object is different would create the danger of scattering our forces instead of concentrating on the most urgent tasks and wherever pressure may be needed. Let us rather concentrate all our efforts on what is absolutely urgent, on collecting a sufficient quantity of seeds at all costs so as to ensure that the entire plan of sowing is carried out, and on introducing, on a mass scale, and wherever the toilers, the poor and middle peasants, predominate, improved methods of farming that have been tested by experience. That is the point. The fewer measures of this kind we draw up now, the better, because, by making sure of carrying out a few measures, we shall put on the proper basis the entire machinery for improving agriculture, and thoroughly convince the peasants that the road we have taken is the right one. If, however, we undertake more than we can do we shall discredit ourselves in the eyes of the peasants. If there are gubernias where more can be done by issuing orders, there is nothing to prohibit that. The bill says: take into account your own peasant experience; consider what you are able to do in the way of collecting livestock and implements. If agricultural implements in good condition are still available in the gubernia, that will be done successfully. However, to apply the law in gubernias where the situation in this respect is far worse and where the peasants are unable to carry out such orders means that the orders will remain a dead letter and will be left hanging in mid-air, as it were; instead of understanding the importance of these measures, the peasants will be disappointed, and that is what I fear most of all for the future. That is why we must first of all start with what is absolutely essential, that is, with preserving the seeds.

Let us now go over to the measures for improving small-peasant individual farming, which are quite feasible and must be discussed immediately, in detail, and here decreed and made compulsory by law, to be enforced by order and compulsion, so that what is passed after repeated discussion shall be carried out without fail. I would propose that we at once set up committees, without waiting until the committees are formed officially at the plenary session of the Congress after the report. This unofficial committee can be set up at once, or at all events some time today. The official committee can be set up later, but it would be a mistake to put this off for a day, or even half a day. We have a total of 2,500 delegates, and I think that at least one-tenth of this number have a practical knowledge of this question, after several years of work; if we have 250, that is, over 25 for each district, since our Republic is divided up into nine agricultural districts, I think this number of representatives is sufficient to enable us to proceed at once to a discussion of the practical questions, the concrete measures we should adopt.

What measures to improve agriculture should be adopted in the various districts? In one district, perhaps, steps may be taken towards compulsory sowing; in another, perhaps, the ground may be prepared for a more vigorous order, like the one proposed by the comrade who investigated conditions in the Altai Gubernia only this spring. In still another district, perhaps, measures could be taken, with the help of agronomists and non-Party peasants, for more timely ploughing and harrowing. I think we ought at once to form committees and divide the regions into districts, since the same measures cannot be employed in all districts, and devote a half a day or a day to the discussion of questions that are not directly mentioned in the decree, but constitute the most important part of the bill. This bill says: appropriate measures should be taken to convince the non-Party peasants. If we are lagging behind in this respect, then, with the mass agitation which we are developing and will develop a hundred times more vigorously and widely than we have done up to now, we can draw up measures for each district and each gubernia; we shall endeavour to make them successful, and do that no less strenuously than we did when we strove to achieve success in our food policy. In the latter case the task was not so complex: we demanded that the peasants yield up a certain quantity of foodstuffs. Here, however, we are demanding that the peasants introduce on their own farms the changes which the state regards as necessary. The chief thing is to make no mistake in defining these changes. That is the most important thing. The fact that Comrade Kurayev put these questions concretely indicates that he is on the right track; however to go over from this to arguments about the general plan of collectivisation, the role of the state farms, which sometimes play a very nasty role, and the Marxist method of approach to purchases, means dragging us away from the immediately practical affairs, back to general arguments which may be useful, but not at a Congress of Soviets which is to pass a law of supreme importance. To prepare the ground for this step, we must carefully consider what the activities and role of the village Soviets should be. We must carefully consider whether the chairman of a village Soviet is the person to be consulted, since he is mainly responsible for carrying out these measures among the peasants. Will it be useful to combine the functions of chairman of the village Soviet and of chairman of the Committee of Assistance in one person? I am throwing this out as a suggestion. I would like the comrades who are familiar with the work at district level to pay careful attention to this question. The Committees of Assistance ought to discuss what measures should be made compulsory by law. In discussing this question there is no need to be afraid of non-Party people. We shall carefully weigh all their proposals, and we shall know definitely who is for us and who is against us. Clarity must be achieved in every volost and every village. The demands proposed are quite feasible and, with a certain amount of effort, they can be carried out this spring. I would propose that this conference of the group now adjourn. When you consider that the general debate has ended, we should form committees for the various districts with specific agricultural conditions, and immediately proceed to discuss the question. That will be the proper thing to do from the practical point of view, and will ensure the success of the bill.

5

DRAFT RESOLUTION OF THE EIGHTH CONGRESS OF SOVIETS ON THE REPORT ON ELECTRIFICATION

The Eighth All-Russia Congress of Soviets,

after hearing the report of the Chairman of the State Commission for the Electrification of Russia, expresses its thanks, in the first place, to the Presidium of the Supreme Council of the National Economy and also to the People's Commissariat of Agriculture and the People's Commissariat of Railways, and particularly to the Commission for the Electrification of Russia for their work in drawing up the plan for the electrification of Russia.

The Congress instructs the All-Russia Central Executive Committee, the Council of People's Commissars, the Council of Labour and Defence, the Presidium of the Supreme Council of the National Economy and also the other People's Commissariats to complete the elaboration of this plan and to endorse it without fail at the earliest date.

The Congress further instructs the government and requests the All-Russia Central Council of Trade Unions and the All-Russia Congress of Trade Unions to take all measures to conduct the widest possible propaganda for this plan and to make the broadest sections of the population in town and countryside familiar with it. The study of this plan must be introduced into all educational establishments in the Republic without exception; every electric power station and every tolerably well organised factory and state farm must become a centre for teaching the principles of electricity and modern industry, a centre of propaganda for the plan of electrification, and of its systematic study.

All persons possessing sufficient scientific or practical knowledge must be mobilised for the purpose of conducting propaganda for the electrification plan and for imparting to others the knowledge necessary to understand it.

The Congress expresses its firm conviction that all Soviet institutions, all Soviets, and all industrial workers and working peasants will exert every effort and shrink from no sacrifice to carry out the plan for the electrification of Russia at all costs, and despite all obstacles.

Published according to
the manuscript

6

DRAFT RESOLUTION OF THE R.C.P.(B.) GROUP OF THE EIGHTH CONGRESS OF SOVIETS

It is obligatory upon all members of the R.C.P., by the time the Tenth Congress of the R.C.P. is held (February 6, 1921):

1) to make the fullest possible study of the plan of electrification;

2) to take measures to ensure the widest and most detailed study of the local plan in every district;

3) to draw up, for the Tenth Congress of the R.C.P., practical proposals:

for methods of making all working people more widely familiar with the plan of electrification,

as well as for ways and means of immediately proceeding with the practical fulfilment of this plan in all its aspects.

Published according to the manuscript

LETTER TO THE WORKERS OF RED PRESNYA DISTRICT OF MOSCOW DECEMBER 25, 1920

Fifteen years ago the proletariat of Moscow raised the banner of revolt against tsarism.[180] This was the culmination in the development of the first working-class revolution against tsarism. The workers suffered defeat and workers' blood was shed in Presnya District. The unmatched heroism of the Moscow workers provided the toiling masses of Russia with a model in the struggle. However, the masses were then as yet too unprepared and too divided, and did not give support to the heroes of Presnya District and Moscow, who had risen up in an armed struggle against the tsarist monarchy of landowners.

The defeat of the Moscow workers was followed by the defeat of the first revolution. For twelve long years the most ferocious reaction maintained by the landowners tormented all the workers and peasants, all the peoples of Russia.

The exploit of the Presnya workers was not useless. Their sacrifices were not in vain. The first breach was made in the edifice of the tsarist monarchy, a breach that slowly but steadily grew wider and undermined the old and medieval order.

The exploit of the Moscow workers deeply agitated the urban and rural working masses, a frame of mind whose impress has persisted despite all persecution.

Prior to the armed uprising of December 1905, the people of Russia had proved incapable of a mass armed struggle against the exploiters.

The December events brought about profound changes in the people. It became transformed. It had gone through its baptism of fire. It had become steeled in the insurrection, and brought forth numerous fighters who triumphed in 1917 and today—despite immense difficulties, the torments of famine, and the destruction caused by the imperialist war—are defending the cause of socialism's world-wide victory.

Long live the workers of Red Presnya District, a detachment in the vanguard of the world working-class revolution!

N. Lenin

Daily Bulletin of the Eighth All-Russia Congress of Soviets No. 5, December 25, 1920

Published according to the *Bulletin* text

NOTES

1 "*Left-Wing*" *Communism—an Infantile Disorder* was written by Lenin in April, and the appendix—on May 12, 1920. It came out on June 8-10, in Russian and almost simultaneously in July in German, English and French. Lenin gave personal attention to the book's type-setting and printing schedule so that it should be published before the opening of the Second Congress of the Communist International, each delegate receiving a copy. Between July and November 1920, the book was re-published in Leipzig, Paris and London, in the German, French and English languages respectively.

The manuscript of the book is subtitled: "An Attempt to Conduct a Popular Discussion on Marxist Strategy and Tactics." This subtitle was deleted in all editions published in Lenin's lifetime. In the fourth (Russian) edition of Lenin's *Works*, "*Left-Wing*" *Communism—an Infantile Disorder* is published according to the first edition, the proofs of which were read by Lenin himself. p. 17

2 The old *Iskra*—the first illegal Marxist newspaper in Russia. It was founded by V. I. Lenin in 1900, and played a decisive role in the formation of revolutionary Marxist party of the working class in Russia. *Iskra*'s first issue appeared in Leipzig in December 1900, the following issues being brought out in Munich, and then beginning with July 1902—in London, and after the spring of 1903—in Geneva.

On Lenin's initiative and with his participation, the editorial staff drew up a draft of the Party's Programme (published in *Iskra* No. 21), and prepared the Second Congress of the R.S.D.L.P., at which the Russian revolutionary Marxist party was actually founded.

Soon after the Second Congress, the Mensheviks, supported by Plekhanov, won control of *Iskra*. Beginning with issue No. 52, *Iskra* ceased to be an organ of the revolutionary Marxists. p. 22

3 The reference is to the Mensheviks (who formed the Right and opportunist wing of Social-Democracy in the R.S.D.L.P.), and to the Socialist-Revolutionaries. p. 26

4 The reference is to the Bolshevik deputies to the Fourth Duma, namely, A. Y. Badayev, M. K. Muranov, G. I. Petrovsky, F. N. Samoilov and N. R. Shagov. At the Duma's session of July 26 (August 8), 1914, at which the representatives of all the bour-

geois-landowner Duma groups approved tsarist Russia's entry into the imperialist war, the Bolshevik Duma group declared a firm protest; they refused to vote for war credits and launched revolutionary propaganda among the people. In November 1914 the Bolshevik deputies were arrested, in February 1915 they were brought to trial, and exiled for life to Turukhansk Territory in Eastern Siberia. The courageous speeches made by the Bolshevik deputies at their trial, exposing the autocracy, played an important part in anti-war propaganda and in revolutionising the toiling masses. p. 29

5 *Longuetism*—the Centrist trend within the French Socialist Party, headed by Jean Longuet. During the First World War of 1914-18, the Longuetists conducted a policy of conciliation with the social-chauvinists. They rejected the revolutionary struggle and came out for "defence of country" in the imperialist war. Lenin called them petty-bourgeois nationalists. After the victory of the October Socialist Revolution in Russia, the Longuetists called themselves supporters of the proletarian dictatorship, but in fact they remained opposed to it. In December 1920 the Longuetists, together with the avowed reformists, broke away from the Party and joined the so-called Two-and-a-Half International. p. 29

6 *Fabians*—members of the Fabian Society, a British reformist organisation founded in 1884. The membership consisted, in the main, of bourgeois intellectuals. The Fabians denied the necessity of the proletariat's class struggle and the socialist revolution, and contended that the transition from capitalism to socialism was possible only through petty reforms and the gradual reorganisation of society. In 1900 the Fabian Society joined the Labour Party. The Fabians are characterised by Lenin in "British Pacifism and British Dislike of Theory" (see present edition, Vol. 21, pp. 260-65) and elsewhere. p. 29

7 The *Independent Labour Party of Britain* (I.L.P.)—a reformist organisation founded in 1893 by leaders of the "new trade unions", in conditions of a revival of the strike struggle and the mounting movement for British working-class independence of the bourgeois parties. The I.L.P. included members of the "new trade unions" and those of a number of the old trade unions, as well as intellectuals and petty bourgeoisie who were under the influence of the Fabians. The I.L.P. was headed by James Keir Hardie and Ramsay MacDonald. From its very inception, the I.L.P. took a bourgeois-reformist stand, laying particular stress on parliamentary forms of struggle and parliamentary deals with the Liberals. Lenin wrote of the I.L.P. that "in reality it is an opportunist party always dependent on the bourgeoisie". p. 29

8 *Ministerialism* (or "ministerial socialism", or else Millerandism)—the opportunist tactic of socialists' participation in reactionary bourgeois governments. The term appeared when in 1899, the

French socialist Millerand joined the bourgeois government of Waldeck-Rousseau. p. 30

9 The *Independent Social-Democratic Party of Germany*—a Centrist party founded in April 1917.

A split took place at the Congress of the Independent Social-Democratic Party, held in Halle in October 1920, the majority joining the Communist Party of Germany in December 1920. The Right wing formed a separate party, retaining the old name of the Independent Social-Democratic Party. In 1922 the "Independents" re-joined the German Social-Democratic Party. p. 30

10 Lenin is referring probably to his article "What Should Not Be Copied from the German Labour Movement", published in the Bolshevik magazine *Prosveshcheniye* in April 1914 (see present edition, Vol. 20, pp. 254-58). Here Lenin exposed the treacherous behaviour of Karl Legien, the German Social-Democrat who in 1912, in addressing the Congress of the U.S.A., praised U.S. official circles and bourgeois parties. p. 34

11 *Spartacists*—members of the Spartacus League founded in January 1916, during the First World War, under the leadership of Karl Liebknecht, Rosa Luxemburg, Franz Mehring and Clara Zetkin. The Spartacists conducted revolutionary anti-war propaganda among the masses, and exposed the expansionist policy of German imperialism and the treachery of the Social-Democratic leaders. However, the Spartacists—the German Left wing—did not get rid of their semi-Menshevik errors on the most important questions of theory and tactics. A criticism of the German Left-wing's mistakes is given in Lenin's works "On Junius's Pamphlet" (see present edition, Vol. 22, pp. 297-305), "A Caricature of Marxism and Imperialist Economism" (see Vol. 23, pp. 28-76) and elsewhere.

In April 1917, the Spartacists joined the Centrist Independent Social-Democratic Party of Germany, preserving their organisational independence. After the November 1918 revolution in Germany, the Spartacists broke away from the "Independents", and in December of the same year founded the Communist Party of Germany. p. 34

12 The reference is to Frederick Engels's letter to August Bebel, written on March 18-28, 1875. p. 34

13 The *Treaty of Brest-Litovsk* was signed between Soviet Russia and the powers of the Quadruple Alliance (Germany, Austria-Hungary, Bulgaria and Turkey) on March 3, 1918, at Brest-Litovsk and ratified on March 15 by the Fourth (Extraordinary) All-Russia Congress of Soviets. The peace terms were very harsh for Soviet Russia. According to the treaty, Poland, almost all the Baltic states, and part of Byelorussia were placed under the control of Germany and Austria-Hungary. The Ukraine was

separated from Soviet Russia, becoming a state dependent on Germany. Turkey gained control of the cities of Kars, Batum and Ardagan. In August 1918, Germany imposed on Soviet Russia a supplementary treaty and a financial agreement containing new and exorbitant demands.

The signing of the Peace of Brest-Litovsk was linked with a persistent struggle against Trotsky and the anti-Party group of "Left-wing Communists". It was only through great efforts on the part of Lenin that the peace treaty with Germany was signed. The Peace of Brest-Litovsk was a splendid instance of the wisdom and flexibility of Lenin's tactics and skill in working out the only correct policy in an extremely complex situation.

The treaty was a reasonable political compromise. It gave the Soviet state a breathing-space, an opportunity to disband the old decaying army and create the new Red Army, develop socialist construction, and muster strength for the struggle against the counter-revolution at home and military intervention by other countries. The signing of the Treaty of Brest-Litovsk promoted the struggle for peace among the broad masses of all the warring nations. On November 13, 1918, following the November revolution in Germany, which overthrew the monarchist regime, the All-Russia Central Executive Committee annulled the predatory Treaty of Brest-Litovsk. p. 35

[14] The reference is to the otzovists* and ultimatumists, the struggle against whom developed in 1908, and in 1909 resulted in the expulsion of A. Bogdanov, the otzovist leader, from the Bolshevik Party. Behind a screen of revolutionary phrases, the otzovists demanded the recall of the Social-Democrat deputies from the Third Duma and the cessation of activities in legal organisations such as the trade unions, the co-operatives, etc. Ultimatumism was a variety of otzovism. The ultimatumists did not realise the necessity of conducting persistent day-by-day work with the Social-Democrat deputies, so as to make them consistent revolutionary parliamentarians. They proposed that an ultimatum should be presented to the Social-Democratic group in the Duma, demanding their absolute subordination to decisions of the Party's Central Committee; should the deputies fail to comply, they were to be recalled from the Duma. A conference of the enlarged editorial board of the Bolshevik paper *Proletary*, held in June 1909, pointed out in its decision that "Bolshevism, as a definite trend in the R.S.D.L.P., had nothing in common either with otzovism or with ultimatumism". The conference urged the Bolsheviks "to wage a most resolute struggle against these deviations from the path of revolutionary Marxism" (*KPSS v rezolutsiyakh i resheniyakh syezdov, konferentsii i plenumov TsK* [*The C.P.S.U. in the Resolutions and Decisions of Its Congresses, Conferences and Plenums of the Central Committee*], Part I, 1954, p. 221). p. 35

* The term *otzovist* derives from the Russian verb "otozvat", meaning "to recall".—*Ed.*

15 On August 6 (19), 1905, the tsar's manifesto was made public, proclaiming the law on the setting up of the Duma and the election procedures. This body was known as the Bulygin Duma, after A. G. Bulygin, the Minister of the Interior, whom the tsar entrusted with drawing up the Duma draft. According to the latter, the Duma had no legislative functions, but could merely discuss certain questions as a consultative body under the tsar. The Bolsheviks called upon the workers and peasants to actively boycott the Bulygin Duma, and concentrate all agitation on the slogans of an armed uprising, a revolutionary army, and a provisional revolutionary government. The boycott campaign against the Bulygin Duma was used by the Bolsheviks to mobilise all the revolutionary forces, organise mass political strikes, and prepare for an armed uprising. Elections to the Bulygin Duma were not held and the government was unable to convene it. The Duma was swept away by the mounting tide of the revolution and the all-Russia October political strike of 1905. p. 35

16 Lenin is referring to the *all-Russia October political strike of 1905*, during the first Russian revolution. This strike, which involved over two million people, was conducted under the slogan of the overthrow of the tsarist autocracy, an active boycott of the Bulygin Duma, the summoning of a Constituent Assembly and the establishment of a democratic republic. The all-Russia political strike showed the strength of the working-class movement, fostered the development of the revolutionary struggle in the countryside, the army and the navy. The October strike led the proletariat to the December armed uprising. Concerning the October strike, see the article by V. I. Lenin "The All-Russia Political Strike" (present edition, Vol. 9, pp. 392-95). p. 35

17 The "*opposition on principle*"—a group of German Left-wing Communists advocating anarcho-syndicalist views. When the Second Congress of the Communist Party of Germany, which was held in Heidelberg in October 1919, expelled the opposition, the latter formed the so-called Communist Workers' Party of Germany, in April 1920. To facilitate the unification of all German communist forces and win over the finest proletarian elements in the C.W.P.G., the opposition was temporarily admitted into the Communist International in November 1920 with the rights of a sympathising member.

However, the Executive Committee of the Communist International still considered the United Communist Party of Germany to be the only authoritative section of the Comintern. C.W.P.G.'s representatives were admitted into the Comintern on the condition that they merged with the United Communist Party of Germany and supported all its activities. The C.W.P.G. leaders, however, failed to observe these conditions. The Third Congress of the Communist International, which was held in June-July 1921, and wanted solidarity with workers who still followed the C.W.P.G. leaders, resolved to give the C.W.P.G. two months to call a congress and settle the question of affiliation. The C.W.P.G. leaders did not obey the Third Congress's resolution and thus placed themselves outside the Communist International. Later the C.W.P.G. degenerated into a small sectarian group without any support in the working class. p. 39

[18] *Horner, Karl*—Anton Pannekoek. p. 43

[19] *Kommunistische Arbeiterzeitung* (The Communist Workers' Newspaper)—organ of the anarcho-syndicalist group of the German Left-wing Communists (see Note 17). The newspaper was published in Hamburg from 1919 till 1927. Karl Erler, who is mentioned by V. I. Lenin, was Heinrich Laufenberg's pen-name. p. 43

[20] The reference is to the *League of Struggle for the Emancipation of the Working Class* organised by V. I. Lenin in the autumn of 1895. The League of Struggle united about twenty Marxist circles in St. Petersburg. It was headed by the Central Group including V. I. Lenin, A. A. Vaneyev, P. K. Zaporozhets, G. M. Krzhizhanovsky, N. K. Krupskaya, L. Martov, M. A. Silvin, V. V. Starkov, and others; five members headed by V. I. Lenin directed the League's activities. The organisation was divided into district groups. Progressive workers such as I. V. Babushkin, V. A. Shelgunov and others linked these groups with the factories.

The St. Petersburg League of Struggle for the Emancipation of the Working Class was, in V. I. Lenin's words, the embryo of a revolutionary party based on the working-class movement and giving leadership to the class struggle of the proletariat. p. 45

[21] The Congress was held in Moscow from March 29 to April 5, 1920. The Ninth Congress was more numerous than any previous Party congresses. It was attended by 715 delegates — 553 of them with full votes, and 162 with deliberative votes—representing a membership of 611,978. Represented were the Party organisations of Central Russia, the Ukraine, the Urals, Siberia and other regions recently liberated by the Red Army. Many of the delegates came to the Congress straight from the front.

The agenda of the Congress was as follows: 1. The report of the Central Committee. 2. The immediate tasks of economic construction. 3. The trade union movement. 4. Organisational questions. 5. The tasks of the Communist International. 6. The attitude towards the co-operatives. 7. The change-over to the militia system. 8. Elections to the Central Committee. 9. Miscellaneous.

The Congress was held under the guidance of V. I. Lenin, who was the main speaker on the political work of the Central Committee and replied to the debate on the report. He also spoke on economic construction and co-operation, made the speech at the closing of the Congress, and submitted a proposal on the list of candidates to the Party's Central Committee.

In the resolution "The Immediate Tasks of Economic Development" the Congress noted that "the basic condition of economic rehabilitation of the country is a steady implementation of the single economic plan for the coming historical epoch" (*KPSS v rezolutsiyakh i resheniyakh syezdov, konferentsii i plenumov TsK* [*The C.P.S.U. in the Resolutions and Decisions of Its Congresses, Conferences and Plenums of the Central Committee*], Part I, 1954, p. 478). The kingpin of the single economic plan was electrification, which V. I. Lenin considered a great programme for a period of 10 to 20 years. The directives of the Ninth Congress were the basis of the plan conclusively drawn up by the State Commission for the Electrification of Russia (the GOELRO plan) and approved by the All-Russia Congress of Soviets in December 1920.

The Congress paid particular attention to the organisation of industrial management. The resolution on this question called for the establishment of competent, firm and energetic one-man management. Taking its guidance from Lenin, the Congress especially stressed the necessity to extensively enlist old and experienced experts.

The anti-Party group of Democratic Centralists, consisting of Sapronov, Osinsky, V. Smirnov and others, came out against the Party line. Behind a cover of phrases about Democratic Centralism but in fact distorting that principle, they denied the need for one-man management at factories, came out against strict Party and state discipline, and alleged that the Central Committee did not give effect to the principle of collective leadership.

The group of Democratic Centralists was supported at the Congress by Rykov, Tomsky, Milyutin and Lomov. The Congress rebuffed the Democratic Centralists and rejected their proposals.

The Congress gave special attention to labour emulation and communist *Subbotniks*. To stimulate such emulation, the extensive application of the bonus system of wages was recommended. The Congress resolved that May 1, the international proletarian holiday, which in 1920 fell on Saturday, should be a mass *Subbotnik* organised throughout Russia.

An important place in the work of the Congress was held by the question of trade unions, which was considered from the viewpoint of adapting the entire work of the trade unions to the accomplishment of the economic tasks. In a resolution on this question, the Congress distinctly defined the trade unions' role, their relations with the state and the Party, forms and methods of guidance of trade unions by the Communist Party, as well as forms of their participation in communist construction. The Congress decisively rebuffed the anarcho-syndicalist elements (Shlyapnikov, Lozovsky, Tomsky and Lutovinov), who advocated the "independence" of the trade unions and contraposed them to the Communist Party and the Soviet government.

At a closed meeting held on April 4, the Congress elected a new Central Committee of 19 members and 12 candidate members. The former included V. I. Lenin, A. A. Andreyev, F. E. Dzerzhinsky, M. I. Kalinin, Y. E. Rudzutak, F. A. Sergeyev (Artyom), and J. V. Stalin. On April 5 the Congress concluded its work. p. 45

[22] Between the February 1917 Revolution and 1919 inclusively, the Party's membership changed as follows: by the Seventh All-Russia Conference of the R.S.D.L.P.(B.) (April 1917) the Party numbered 80,000 members; by the Sixth R.S.D.L.P.(B.) Congress in July-August 1917—about 240,000; by the Seventh Congress of the R.C.P.(B.) in March 1918—not less than 270,000; by the Eighth Congress of the R.C.P.(B.) in March 1919—313,766 members. p. 47

[23] The reference is to *Party Week*, which was held in accordance with the resolution of the Eighth Congress of the R.C.P.(B.) on building up the Party's membership. The Party Week was conducted in conditions of the bitter struggle waged by the Soviet state against the foreign intervention and domestic counter-revolution. Party Week was first held in the Petrograd organisation of the R.C.P.(B.), August 10-17, 1919 (the second Party Week was held in Petrograd in October-November 1919); between September 20 and 28 a Party Week was held in the Moscow Gubernia organisation. Summarising the experience of the first Party Weeks, the Plenum of the Central Committee of the R.C.P.(B.), held on September 26, 1919, resolved that Party Weeks should be held in cities, the countryside and the army. At the end of September, the Central Committee addressed a circular to all Party organisations pointing out that, as the re-registration and purge of the membership had been accomplished in almost all Party organisations, new members might be enrolled. The Central Committee stressed that during Party Weeks only industrial workers, peasants, and Red Army and Navy men should be admitted into the Party. As a result of Party Weeks, over 200,000 joined the Party in 38 gubernias of the European part of the R.S.F.S.R., more than a half of them being industrial workers. Over 25 per cent of the armed forces' strength joined the Party at the fronts. p. 47

[24] See present edition, Vol. 30, pp. 253-75. p. 52

[25] The *Communist International*—a journal, organ of the Executive Committee of the Communist International. It was published in Russian, German, French, English, Spanish and Chinese, the first issue appearing on May 1, 1919.

The journal published theoretical articles and documents of the Comintern, including a number of articles by Lenin. It elucidated the fundamental questions of Marxist-Leninist theory in connection with problems confronting the international working-class and communist movement and the experience of socialist construction in the Soviet Union. It also waged a struggle against various anti-Leninist tendencies.

Publication of the journal ceased in June 1943 in connection with the resolution adopted by the Presidium of the Comintern's Executive Committee on May 15, 1943, on the dissolution of the Communist International. p. 52

[26] See Karl Marx and Frederick Engels, *Selected Correspondence*, Moscow, 1965, p. 110. p. 53

[27] The *Industrial Workers of the World (I.W.W.)*—a workers' trade union organisation, founded in the U.S.A. in 1905, and in the main organising unskilled and low-paid workers of various trades. Among its founders were such working-class leaders as Daniel De Leon, Eugene Debs and William Haywood. I.W.W. organisations were also set up in Canada, Australia, Britain, Latin America and South Africa. In conditions of the mass strike movement in the U.S.A., which developed under the influence of the Russian revolution of 1905-07, the I.W.W. organised a number of successful mass strikes, waged a struggle against the policy of class collaboration conducted by reformist leaders of the American Federation of Labor and Right-wing socialists. During the First World War of 1914-18, the organisation led a number of mass anti-war actions by the American working class. Some I.W.W. leaders, among them William Haywood, welcomed the Great October Socialist Revolution and joined the Communist Party of the U.S.A. At the same time, anarcho-syndicalist features showed up in I.W.W. activities: it did not recognise the proletariat's political struggle, denied the Party's leading role and the necessity of the proletarian dictatorship, and refused to carry on work among the membership of the American Federation of Labor. In 1920 the organisation's anarcho-syndicalist leaders took advantage of the imprisonment of many revolutionaries and, against the will of the trade union masses, rejected appeal by the Comintern's Executive Committee that they join the Communist International. As a result of the leaders' opportunist policy, the I.W.W. degenerated into a sectarian organisation, which soon lost all influence on the working-class movement. p. 54

[28] From its foundation in 1892, the *Italian Socialist Party* saw a bitter ideological struggle between the opportunist and the revolutionary trends within it. At the Reggio Emilia Congress of 1912, the most outspoken reformists who supported the war and collaboration with the government and the bourgeoisie (Ivanoe Bonomi, Leonida Bissolati and others) were expelled from the party under pressure from the Left wing. After the outbreak of the First World War and prior to Italy's entry into it, the I.S.P. came out against the war and advanced the slogan: "Against war, for neutrality!" In December 1914, a group of renegades including Benito Mussolini, who advocated the bourgeoisie's imperialist policy and supported the war, were expelled from the party. When Italy entered the war on the Entente's side (May 1915), three distinct trends emerged in the Italian Socialist Party: 1) the Right wing, which aided the bourgeoisie in the conduct of the war; 2) the Centre, which united most of party members and came out under the slogan: "No part in the war, and no sabotage of the war" and 3) the Left wing, which took a firmer anti-war stand, but could not organise a consistent struggle

against the war. The Left wing did not realise the necessity of converting the imperialist war into a civil war, and of a decisive break with the reformists.

After the October Socialist Revolution in Russia, the Left wing of the I.S.P. grew stronger, and the 16th Party Congress held on October 5-8, 1919, in Bologna, adopted a resolution on affiliation to the Third International. I.S.P. representatives took part in the work of the Second Congress of the Comintern. After the Congress Centrist Serrati, head of the delegation, declared against a break with the reformists. At the 17th Party Congress in Leghorn in January 1921, the Centrists, who were in the majority, refused to break with the reformists and to accept all the terms of admission into the Comintern. On January 21, 1921, the Left-wing delegates walked out of the Congress and founded the Communist Party of Italy. p. 66

[29] Soviet rule was established in Hungary on March 21, 1919. The socialist revolution in Hungary was a peaceful one, the Hungarian bourgeoisie being unable to resist the people. Incapable of overcoming its internal and external difficulties, it decided to hand over power for a while to the Right-wing Social-Democrats so as to prevent the development of the revolution. However, the Hungarian Communist Party's prestige had grown so great, and the demands of rank-and-file Social-Democrats for unity with the Communists had become so insistent that the leaders of the Social-Democratic Party proposed to the arrested Communist leaders the formation of a joint government. The Social-Democratic leaders were obliged to accept the terms advanced by the Communists during the negotiations, i.e., the formation of a Soviet government, disarmament of the bourgeoisie, the creation of a Red Army and people's militia, confiscation of the landed estates, the nationalisation of industry, an alliance with Soviet Russia, etc.

An agreement was simultaneously signed on the merging of the two parties to form the Hungarian Socialist Party. While the two parties were being merged, errors were made which later became clear. The merger was carried out mechanically, without isolation of the reformist elements.

At its first meeting, the Revolutionary Governmental Council adopted a resolution on the formation of the Red Army. On March 26, the Soviet Government of Hungary issued decrees on the nationalisation of industrial enterprises, transport, and the banks; on April 2, a decree was published on the monopoly of foreign trade. Workers' wages were increased by an average of 25 per cent, and an 8-hour working day was introduced. On April 3, land-reform law was issued, by which all estates exceeding 57 hectares in area were confiscated. The confiscated land, however, was not distributed among the land-starved and landless peasants, but was turned over to agricultural producers' co-operatives and state farms organised after the reform. The poor peasants, who had hoped to get land, were disappointed. This prevented the establishment of a firm alliance between the proletariat and the peasantry, and weakened Soviet power in Hungary.

The Entente imperialists instituted an economic blockade of the Soviet Republic. Armed intervention against the Hungarian Soviet Republic was organised, the advance of interventionist troops stirring up the Hungarian counter-revolutionaries. The treachery of the Right-wing Social-Democrats, who entered into an alliance with international imperialism, was one of the causes of the Hungarian Soviet Republic's downfall.

The unfavourable international situation in the summer of 1919, when Soviet Russia was encircled by enemies and therefore could not help the Hungarian Soviet Republic, also played a definite role. On August 1, 1919, as a result of joint actions by the foreign imperialist interventionists and the domestic counter-revolutionaries, Soviet power in Hungary was overthrown. p. 66

[30] See Marx/Engels, *Werke*, Dietz Verlag, Berlin, 1962, Bd. 18, S. 533. p. 67

[31] The *League of Nations* was an international body which existed between the First and the Second World Wars. It was founded in 1919 at the Paris Peace Conference of the victor powers of the First World War. The Covenant of the League of Nations formed part of the Treaty of Versailles of 1919, and was signed by 44 nations. The Covenant was designed to produce the impression that this organisation's aim was to combat aggression, reduce armaments, and consolidate peace and security. In practice, however, its leaders shielded the aggressors, fostered the arms race and preparations for the Second World War.

Between 1920 and 1934, the League's activities were hostile towards the Soviet Union. It was one of the centres for the organising of armed intervention against the Soviet state in 1920-21.

On September 15, 1934, on French initiative, 34 member states invited the Soviet Union to join the League of Nations, which the U.S.S.R. did, with the aim of strengthening peace. However, the Soviet Union's attempts to form a peace front met with resistance from reactionary circles in the Western powers. With the outbreak of the Second World War the League's activities came to an end, the formal dissolution taking place in April 1946, according to a decision by the specially summoned Assembly. p. 69

[32] Lenin is referring to a passage from Frederick Engels's letter to F. A. Sorge of November 29, 1886, in which, criticising German Social-Democrat political exiles living in America, Engels wrote that for them the theory was "a credo, not a guide to action" (see Karl Marx and Frederick Engels, *Selected Correspondence*, Moscow, 1965, p. 395). p. 71

[33] The reference is to the international socialist conferences in Zimmerwald and Kienthal (Switzerland).

The *Zimmerwald Conference*, the first international socialist conference, was held on September 5-8, 1915. The *Kienthal Conference*, the second international socialist conference, was held in the small town of Kienthal on April 24-30, 1916.

The Zimmerwald and Kienthal conferences contributed to the ideological unity, on the basis of Marxism-Leninism, of the Left-wing elements in West-European Social-Democracy, who later played an active part in the formation of Communist parties in their countries and the establishment of the Third, Communist International. p. 72

34 "*Revolutionary Communists*"—a Narodnik group which broke away from the Left Socialist-Revolutionaries after the latter's mutiny in July 1918. In September 1918, they formed the "Party of Revolutionary Communism", which favoured co-operation with the R.C.P.(B.), and pledged support for Soviet power. Their programme, which remained on the platform of Narodnik utopianism, was muddled and eclectic. While recognising that Soviet rule created preconditions for the establishment of a socialist system, the "revolutionary communists" denied the necessity of the proletarian dictatorship during the transitional period from capitalism to socialism. Throughout the lifetime of the "Party of Revolutionary Communism", certain of its groups broke away from it, some of them joining the R.C.P.(B.) (A. Kolegayev, A. Bitsenko, M. Dobrokhotov and others), and others, the Left Socialist-Revolutionaries. Two representatives of the "Party of Revolutionary Communism" were allowed to attend the Second Congress of the Comintern, in a deliberative capacity, but with no votes. In September 1920, following the Congress decision that there must be a single Communist Party in each country, the "Party of Revolutionary Communism" decided to join the R.C.P.(B.). In October of the same year, the R.C.P.(B.) Central Committee permitted Party organisations to enrol members of the former "Party of Revolutionary Communism" in the R.C.P.(B.). p. 72

35 The *British Socialist Party* was founded in 1911, in Manchester, as a result of a merger of the Social-Democratic Party and other socialist groups. The B.S.P. conducted agitation in the spirit of Marxism; it was "not opportunist and was *really* independent of the Liberals" (see present edition, Vol. 19, p. 273). However, its small membership and its poor links with the masses gave the B.S.P. a somewhat sectarian character. During the First World War, a bitter struggle developed within the British Socialist Party between the internationalists (William Gallacher, Albert Inkpin, John Maclean, Theodore Rothstein and others), and the social-chauvinists, headed by Hyndman. Within the internationalist trend were inconsistent elements that took a Centrist stand on a number of issues. In February 1916, a group of B.S.P. leaders founded the newspaper *The Call*, which played an important role in uniting the internationalists. The B.S.P.'s annual

conference, held in Salford in April 1916, condemned the social-chauvinist stand of Hyndman and his supporters, who, after the conference, left the party.

The British Socialist Party welcomed the Great October Socialist Revolution, its members playing an important part in the "Hands Off Russia" movement. In 1919, the overwhelming majority of its organisations (98 against 4) declared for affiliation to the Communist International. The British Socialist Party, together with the Communist Unity Group formed the core of the Communist Party of Great Britain. At the First (Unity) Congress, held in 1920, the vast majority of B.S.P. local organisations entered the Communist Party. p. 77

36 The *Socialist Labour Party* was organised in 1903 by a group of the Left-wing Social-Democrats who had broken away from the Social-Democratic Federation. The *South Wales Socialist Society* was a small group consisting mostly of Welsh coal miners. The *Workers' Socialist Federation* was a small organisation which emerged from the Women's Suffrage League and consisted mostly of women.

The Leftist organisations did not join the Communist Party of Great Britain when it was formed (its Inaugural Congress was held on July 31-August 1, 1920) since the Party's programme contained a clause on the Party participation in parliamentary elections and on affiliation to the Labour Party. At the Communist Party's Congress in January 1921, the South Wales Socialist Society and the Workers' Socialist Federation, which had assumed the names of the Communist Workers' Party and the Communist Party respectively, united with the Communist Party of Great Britain under the name of the United Communist Party of Great Britain. The leaders of the Socialist Labour Party refused to join. p. 77

37 This refers to the counter-revolutionary mutiny organised in August 1917 by the bourgeoisie and the landowners, under the Supreme Commander-in-Chief, the tsarist general Kornilov. The conspirators hoped to seize Petrograd, smash the Bolshevik Party, break up the Soviets, establish a military dictatorship in the country, and prepare the restoration of the monarchy.

The mutiny began on August 25 (September 7), Kornilov sending the 3rd Cavalry Corps against Petrograd, where Kornilov counter-revolutionary organisations were ready to act.

The Kornilov mutiny was crushed by the workers and peasants led by the Bolshevik Party. Under pressure from the masses, the Provisional Government was forced to order that Kornilov and his accomplices be arrested and brought to trial. p. 93

38 The reference is to the military-monarchist coup d'état, the so-called Kapp *putsch* organised by the German reactionary militarists. It was headed by the monarchist landowner Kapp and Generals Ludendorff, Seeckt and Lüttwitz. The conspirators

prepared the coup with the connivance of the Social-Democratic government. On March 13, 1920, the mutinous generals moved troops against Berlin and, meeting with no resistance from the government, proclaimed a military dictatorship. The German workers replied with a general strike. Under pressure from the proletariat, the Kapp government was overthrown on March 17, and the Social-Democrats again took power. p. 93

[39] The *Dreyfus case*—a provocative trial organised in 1894 by the reactionary-monarchist circles of the French militarists. On trial was Dreyfus, a Jewish officer of the French General Staff, falsely accused of espionage and high treason. Dreyfus's conviction—he was condemned to life imprisonment—was used by the French reactionaries to rouse anti-Semitism and to attack the republican regime and democratic liberties. When, in 1898, socialists and progressive bourgeois democrats such as Emile Zola, Jean Jaurès, and Anatole France launched a campaign for Dreyfus's re-trial, the case became a major political issue and split the country into two camps—the republicans and democrats on the one hand, and a bloc of monarchists, clericals, anti-Semites and nationalists, on the other. Under the pressure of public opinion, Dreyfus was released in 1899, and in 1906 was acquitted by the Court of Cassation and reinstated in the Army. p. 98

[40] "*Soviet pleaders*"—collegiums of advocates established in February 1918, under the Soviets of Workers', Soldiers', Peasants' and Cossacks' Deputies. In October 1920, these collegiums were abolished. p. 115

[41] On the basis of this directive from Lenin the words "certain members of the Communist Party of Holland" have been substituted everywhere in this volume, in the text of *"Left-Wing" Communism—an Infantile Disorder* for the expression "Dutch Tribunists". p. 117

[42] The first communist subbotnik was held on April 12, 1919, by railwaymen of the Sortirovochnaya marshalling yards of the Moscow-Kazan Railway. Subbotniks were soon being held at many other enterprises in various cities. The experience of the first communist subbotniks was summed up by V. I. Lenin in *A Great Beginning (Heroism of the Workers in the Rear. "Communist Subbotniks")* (see present edition, Vol. 29, pp. 409-34).

An all-Russia subbotnik was held on May 1, 1920, with over 425,000 people in Moscow alone participating, including V. I. Lenin, who, together with Kremlin army cadets, worked on clearing away building rubble on the territory of the Kremlin.

Lenin's article "From the First Subbotnik on the Moscow-Kazan Railway to the All-Russia May Day Subbotnik" was brought out on May 2, 1920, in a specially published handbill *Pervomaisky Subbotnik*, which was drawn up, set and printed during the May Day subbotnik by the staff of the newspapers *Pravda*, *Izvestia*, *Ekonomicheskaya Zhizn*, *Bednota*, the ROSTA Telegraph Agency, and by workers at the printing-house of the All-Russia Central Executive Committee. p. 123

[43] This speech was made by V. I. Lenin on May 5, 1920, in Teatralnaya Square (now Sverdlov Square), where a parade of the Moscow garrison troops took place. Petrograd Communists leaving for the Polish front were also present at the parade. p. 127

[44] The *joint session of the All-Russia Central Executive Committee, the Moscow Soviet, and representatives of Moscow trade unions and factory committees*, held on May 5, 1920, was called in connection with the offensive launched by the whiteguard Poles against Soviet Russia. The session was also attended by 300 worker Communists from Petrograd who were going to the Polish front. A single item was discussed—the position on the Polish front. The session unanimously adopted a resolution calling upon the workers and peasants to bend every effort for the defeat of bourgeois-landowner Poland. p. 129

[45] The reference is to the *Conference of the Entente Powers* held at San Remo (Italy) in April 1920. Among questions discussed at the Conference were the draft peace treaty with Turkey, and Germany's observation of the Treaty of Versailles. p. 131

[46] The use of Red Army regular units as labour detachments for construction work was occasioned by the situation in the country during the peaceful respite early in 1920, when any day could bring a resumption of the imperialists' armed intervention. In February 1920, in connection with the formation of the labour army, Lenin pointed out, "The task of the transition from war to peaceful development arises in such peculiar conditions that we cannot disband the army, since we have to allow, say, for the possibility of an attack by that selfsame Poland or any of the powers which the Entente continues to incite against us" (see present edition, Vol. 30, pp. 331-32).

The war that broke out against bourgeois-landowner Poland and Wrangel made necessary the transfer of the labour detachments to a wartime footing. p. 133

[47] Lenin has in view the arrival in Moscow, in March 1919, of Bullitt, on instructions from U.S. President Wilson and British Prime Minister Lloyd George, with the proposal that the Soviet Government should sign a peace with the whiteguard governments existing at the time on the territory of Russia. A draft of the treaty was drawn up, but then the imperialists, who, in view of the temporary successes of Kolchak's army, hoped that the Soviet Republic would be crushed, refused to continue peace talks. p. 137

[48] The *British trade union delegation* was sent to Russia by decision of the British Trade Unions Congress held in December 1919, for a first-hand study of the economic and political situation in Soviet

Russia. The delegation consisted of: Ben Turner (head of the delegation), Ethel Snowden, Tom Shaw, Robert Williams—from the Labour Party, and Margaret Bondfield, A. Purcell, and H. Skinner, from the trade unions; Charles Roden Buxton and Haden L. Guest were secretaries to the delegation. R. C. Wallhead and Allen Clifford, representing the Independent Labour Party, came to Russia together with the delegation, but were not official members.

V. I. Lenin attached great importance to the delegation's visit to Russia. He instructed the All-Russia Central Council of Trade Unions to give the delegation a hearty welcome and acquaint them with the life of the Soviet people, so that they could tell the truth about Soviet Russia when they returned home.

The delegation arrived in Petrograd on May 12, 1920, and went to Moscow on May 17. They were warmly welcomed by the working people of Soviet Russia, as representatives of the British working masses. Meetings were held in their honour, as well as a great rally in the Bolshoi Theatre and a parade of the Moscow garrison. The delegation became acquainted in detail with the life of the Soviet Republic, visited a number of cities along the Volga, went to the front, and took part in *Subbotniks*. The delegation members expressed their determination to strengthen fraternal solidarity between British and Soviet working people, and voiced a protest against any aid, whether overt or covert, given by Britain to the Polish Government in the new offensive, and against any threat to force Russia to meet Polish demands. The delegation were received by V. I. Lenin on May 26. On their return home, the British workers' delegation published a report on the situation in Russia (see "British Labour Delegation to Russia. 1920. Report". London, 1920). p. 137

49 Lenin's message of greetings "To the Indian Revolutionary Association" was broadcasted on May 10, 1920, in reply to the resolution of the Assembly of Indian Revolutionaries held in Kabul on February 17, 1920. The Assembly's resolution, which was addressed to Lenin, read as follows: "The Indian revolutionaries express their deep gratitude and their admiration of the great struggle carried on by Soviet Russia for the liberation of all oppressed classes and peoples, and especially for the liberation of India. Great thanks to Soviet Russia for her having heard the cries of agony from the 315,000,000 people suffering under the yoke of imperialism. The mass meeting accepts with joy the hand of friendship and help extended to oppressed India" (*Pravda* No. 108, May 20, 1920). p. 138

50 "Letter to the British Workers" was published on June 17, 1920, in *Pravda*, *Izvestia*, *Kommunistichesky Trud*, and *Gudok;* on the same day it was published in Britain in *The Call*, the weekly of the British Socialist Party. On June 19, the letter was published in *The Workers' Dreadnought*, organ of the Workers' Socialist Federation of England and in the journal *The Russia Outlook*,

and on June 22, in the Labour *The Daily Herald*. Later the "Letter to the British Workers" was repeatedly published both in Russia and abroad. p. 139

51 Notes to "Preliminary Draft Theses on the National and the Colonial Questions" were received by Lenin from G. V. Chicherin, N. N. Krestinsky, J. V. Stalin, M. G. Rafes, Y. A. Preobrazhensky, N. D. Lapinsky, and I. Nedelkov (N. Shablin), representative of the Bulgarian Communists, as well as from a number of leaders in Bashkiria, Kirghizia, and Turkestan. Along with correct ideas, the notes contained certain grave errors. Thus, Chicherin gave a wrong interpretation to Lenin's theses on the necessity of support for national liberation movements and on agreements with the national bourgeoisie, without due regard for Lenin's distinction between the bourgeoisie and the peasantry. With regard to this Lenin wrote: "I lay *greater* stress on the alliance with the *peasantry* (which does *not quite* mean the bourgeoisie)" (Central Party Archives of the Institute of Marxism-Leninism of the C.C. C.P.S.U.). Referring to the relations between the future socialist Europe and the economically underdeveloped and dependent countries, Preobrazhensky wrote: "... if it proves impossible to reach economic agreement with the leading national groups, the latter will inevitably be suppressed by force and economically important regions will be compelled to join a union of European Republics." Lenin decisively objected to this remark: "... it goes too far. It cannot be proved, and it is wrong to say that *suppression* by force is "inevitable". That is radically wrong" (see *Voprosy Istorii KPSS* [*Problems of the C.P.S.U. History*] 1958, No. 2, p. 16).

A grave error was made by Stalin, who did not agree with Lenin's proposition on the difference between federal relations among the Soviet republics based on autonomy, and federal relations among independent republics. In a letter to Lenin, dated June 12, 1920, he declared that in reality "there is no difference between these two types of federal relations, or else it is so small as to be negligible". Stalin continued to advocate this later, when, in 1922, he proposed the "autonomisation" of the independent Soviet republics. These ideas were criticised in detail by Lenin in his article "The Question of Nationalities or 'Autonomisation'", and in his letter to members of the Political Bureau "On the Formation of the U.S.S.R." (see present edition, Vol. 36, and *Lenin Miscellany XXXVI*, pp. 496-98). p. 144

52 As a result of the revolution which commenced in Finland on January 27, 1918, the bourgeois government of Svinhufvud was overthrown and the working class assumed power. On January 29, the revolutionary government of Finland, the Council of People's Representatives was formed by Edvard Gylling, Yrjö Sirola, Otto Kuusinen, A. Taimi and others. The following were among the most important measures taken by the workers' government: the law on the transfer to landless peasants, without indemnification,

of the land they actually tilled; tax-exemption for the poorest sections of the population; the expropriation of enterprises whose owners had fled the country; the establishment of state control over private banks (their functions being assumed by the State Bank).

On March 1, 1918, a treaty between the Finnish Socialist Workers' Republic and the R.S.F.S.R. was signed in Petrograd. Based on the principle of complete equality and respect for the sovereignty of the two sides, this was the first treaty in world history to be signed between two socialist countries.

The proletarian revolution, however, was victorious only in the south of Finland. The Svinhufvud government concentrated all counter-revolutionary forces in the north of the country, and appealed to the German Kaiser's government for help. As a result of German armed intervention, the Finnish revolution was put down in May 1918, after a desperate civil war. White terror reigned in the country; thousands of revolutionary workers and peasants were executed or tortured to death in the prisons. p. 147

[53] As a result of mass action by the Lettish proletariat and peasantry against the German invaders and the counter-revolutionary government of Ulmanis, a provisional Soviet government was established in Latvia on December 17, 1918, which issued a Manifesto on the assumption of state power by the Soviets. Soviet Russia gave fraternal help to the Lettish people in their struggle to establish Soviet rule and strengthen the Latvian Soviet Socialist Republic.

Under the leadership of the Latvian Communist Party and the Latvian Soviet Government, a Red Army was formed, the landed estates were confiscated, the banks and big commercial and industrial enterprises were nationalised, social insurance and an eight-hour working day were introduced, and a system of public catering for working people was organised.

In March 1919, German troops and the whiteguards, armed and equipped by the U.S. and the Entente imperialists, attacked Soviet Latvia. In May they captured Riga, the capital of Soviet Latvia. After fierce fighting the entire territory of Latvia had been overrun by the interventionists by the beginning of 1920. The counter-revolutionary bourgeoisie established a regime of bloody terror, thousands of revolutionary workers and peasants being killed or thrown into prison. p. 147

[54] Lenin is referring to the article by J. Marchlewski "The Agrarian Question and World Revolution" published in the journal *The Commnnist International* No. 12, July 20, 1920. Lenin read the article before the issue appeared. p. 152

[55] *G. L.*—György Lukács (b. 1885). After 1919 he was several times elected member of the Central Committee of the Communist Party of Hungary. In the early twenties made Left-sectarian

mistakes. Author of a number of works on philosophy, aesthetics, history, and the theory of literature. p. 165

56 *B. K.*—Béla Kun (1886-1939), an outstanding figure in the Hungarian and the international working-class movement; one of the founders and leaders of the Communist Party of Hungary. p. 165

57 Called by the Central Committee of the R.C.P.(B.), the *Second All-Russia Conference of Organisers Responsible for Rural Work* was held in Moscow from June 10 to 15, 1920. It was attended by gubernia, uyezd and volost organisers for rural work, a total of over 300 delegates from 61 gubernias. The third meeting of the Conference, held on June 12, was addressed by Lenin. M. I. Kalinin greeted the delegates on behalf of the All-Russia Central Executive Committee.

A report on the activities of the Department for Rural Work under the Party's Central Committee was made by V. I. Nevsky. The Conference adopted a resolution on this report; it stressed the importance of Party work in the countryside, and expressed the firm confidence that "the Department for Rural Work will unswervingly carry out the directive of the Party's Ninth Congress, on improving agitation and propaganda work among the peasantry" (see *Rezolutsii Vtorogo Vserossiiskogo Soveshchaniya rabotnikov v derevne* [*Resolutions of the Second All-Russia Conference of Party Rural Workers*], Moscow, 1920, pp. 4-5). Reports from the various localities were also heard, and organisational and other matters discussed. The Conference adopted an appeal "To All Workers of the World", greeting the British, Hungarian, Italian and other workers who had decided to prevent the dispatch of troops and military supplies to help bourgeois-landowner Poland in her war against Soviet Russia. p. 168

58 Lenin is referring to the Declaration by the R.S.F.S.R. Council of People's Commissars addressed to the Government of Poland and the Polish people, made on January 28, 1920, and the Appeal of the All-Russia Central Executive Committee to the Polish people on February 2, 1920. p. 168

59 The reference is to the declaration of the Entente's Supreme Council "On the Temporary Eastern Borders of Poland", made on December 8, 1919, and published on June 11, 1920, in the newspaper *Izvestia* No. 125. p. 169

60 *National Democrats* ("*Narodowa Democracya*")—the main reactionary and nationalist party of the Polish landowners and bourgeoisie, founded in 1897 and closely connected with the Catholic church. The National Democrats advanced the slogans of "class harmony" and "the national interests", trying to influence the masses and draw them into the wake of their reactionary policy. They propagated extreme militant nationalism and chauvinism

as a means of struggle against the socialist and democratic movement of the Polish people, which they strove to isolate from the Russian revolutionary movement. During the First World War (1914-18) the National Democrats unreservedly supported the Entente, counting on the victory of tsarist Russia, the unification of the Polish territories then under the yoke of Austria and Germany, and autonomy for Poland within the framework of the Russian Empire. The downfall of tsarism drove the National Democrats towards a pro-French orientation. Though bitterly opposed to the October Socialist Revolution and the Soviet state, the National Democrats, following their traditional anti-German policy, did not always support the adventurist anti-Soviet foreign policy of the Pilsudski clique, which ruled the country after 1926. At present, separate National-Democrat groups are carrying on their activities among reactionary émigré elements.
p. 173

61 The *Polish Socialist Party* (*Polska Partia Socjalistyczna*, the P.S.P.)—a reformist nationalist party founded in 1892. Throughout its history, Left-wing groups arose in it under the influence of the worker rank and file in the party. Some of these groups subsequently joined the revolutionary wing of the Polish working-class movement.
p. 173

62 *Vsevobuch*—the universal military training of the population of the Soviet Republic. The question of organising the *Vsevobuch* was raised in the resolution "On War and Peace" adopted by the Seventh Congress of the R.C.P.(B.), which was held in March 1918. The resolution said that one of the most important and urgent tasks of the Party was the all-round, systematic and universal military training of the adult population, irrespective of sex. The Decree of the All-Russia Central Executive Committee of April 22, 1918, authorised the calling up of all citizens between the ages of 18 and 40, who did not exploit the labour of others. The *Vsevobuch* bodies were entrusted with the registration of all working people of military age, their unified military training, and the formation of army units. On June 5-25, 1918, the first conference on universal military training was held; it drew up a programme for the training and testing of *Vsevobuch* instructors and discussed the organisation of *Vsevobuch* departments, the calling of conferences on the military training and the registration of the population. The conference also adopted a resolution on permanent bureaus of *Vsevobuch* conferences and the statute of inspections.
p. 178

63 Lenin is referring to the resolution adopted by the Ninth Congress of the R.C.P.(B.) "On the Attitude to the Co-operatives" (see *KPSS v rezolutsiyakh i resheniyakh syezdov, konferentsii i plenumov TsK* [*The C.P.S.U. in the Resolutions and Decisions of Its Congresses, Conferences and Plenums of the Central Committee*], Part I, 1940, pp. 340-42).
p. 181

[64] Lenin is quoting from Marx's work "Zur Kritik der Hegelschen Rechtsphilosophie" (see Marx/Engels, *Werke*, Bd. 1, S. 385). p. 190

[65] The *American Socialist Party* was formed in July 1901 at a congress held in Indianapolis, as the result of a merger of groups that had broken away from the Socialist Workers' Party and the Social-Democratic Party of the U.S.A. Among the new party's organisers was Eugene Debs, a popular figure in the U.S. labour movement. The social composition of the party was not uniform, it contained native-born and immigrant workers, as well as small farmers and people of petty-bourgeois origin. The Centrist and the Right-wing opportunist leaders of the party (Victor Berger, Morris Hillquit and others) denied the necessity of the proletarian dictatorship, renounced revolutionary methods of struggle, and reduced all party activities to participation in election campaigns. During the First World War (1914-18) three trends appeared in the Socialist Party: the social-chauvinists, who supported the imperialist policy of the Administration, the Centrists, who opposed the imperialist war only in word, and the revolutionary minority, who took an internationalist stand and struggled against the war.

The Socialist Party's Left wing, headed by Charles Ruthenberg, William Foster, William Haywood and others, relying on the proletarian elements, waged a struggle against the party's opportunist leadership, for independent proletarian action and the formation of industrial trade unions based on the principles of the class struggle. In 1919 a split took place in the Socialist Party. The party's Left wing broke away, becoming the initiator and nucleus of the Communist Party of the U.S.A. At present the Socialist Party is a small sectarian organisation. p. 197

[66] The *Social-Democratic Party of Switzerland* (known as the *Swiss Socialist Party*) was formed in the seventies of the last century and affiliated to the First International. The party was re-formed in 1888. The opportunists were very influential in the party, and during the First World War took a social-chauvinist stand. In the autumn of 1916, the party's Right wing broke away to form their own organisation. The majority, headed by Robert Grimm, took a Centrist, social-pacifist stand, while the Left wing of the party adhered to an internationalist stand. The Great October Socialist Revolution in Russia influenced and strengthened the Left wing which, in December 1920, broke away and joined the Communist Party of Switzerland in 1921 (see Note 69). p. 197

[67] "Draft (or the Theses) of the R.C.P.'s Reply to a Letter from the German Independent Social-Democratic Party" (see present edition, Vol. 30, pp. 337-44). p. 198

[68] The *Turin section* accused the Italian Socialist Party with its conciliatory leadership, of failing to give a correct analysis of events, in the conditions of the revolutionary upsurge in Italy

(1919-20) that had created the possibility of the seizure of political power by the proletariat, and of having failed to advance any slogan acceptable to the revolutionary masses; and expel the reformists from its ranks. The section made a number of practical proposals: the expulsion of the opportunists from the party; the formation of communist groups in each factory, in the trade unions, co-operatives, and army barracks; the setting-up of factory T.U. committees to organise control of production in industry and agriculture. The section demanded that work to prepare the working masses for the creation of Soviets should be begun at once. p. 199

69 In October 1918, part of the Social-Democrat Left wing united to form the *Communist Party of Switzerland*. It was not a big party at the time, being represented by two delegates at the Second Congress of the Comintern.

In December 1920, the Left wing of the Swiss Social-Democratic Party broke away from it, and raised the question of forming a strong section of the Communist International in Switzerland. At a congress held in Zurich in March 1921, attended by 28 delegates from the Communist Party and 145 delegates representing the former Left wing of the Social-Democratic Party, the two groups officially united to form a single Communist Party of Switzerland. p. 200

70 "Reply to a Letter from the Joint Provisional Committee for the Communist Party of Britain" was broadcasted and published in English in *The Call* (No. 224, July 22, 1920), organ of the British Socialist Party. The reply was also read to the Congress of British Communists, which took place on July 31-August 1, 1920. p. 202

71 The reference is to the *Paris Peace Conference* called after the First World War of 1914-18. Its deliberations ended in the signing of the Treaty of Versailles. Among the questions discussed was that of Poland's boundaries. The temporary eastern frontiers of Poland were arbitrarily established by decision of the Allies' Supreme Council on December 8, 1919. p. 203

72 The reference is to Lenin's proposals regarding the reply to the Curzon Note of July 12, 1920. These proposals were accepted by the Central Committee Plenum on July 16, 1920. p. 205

73 The *First Congress of the Communist International* was held on March 2-6, 1919, in Moscow. Fifty-two delegates attended, 34 with the right to vote and 18—with voice but no vote. The following Communist and Socialist parties, organisations and groups were represented: the Communist Parties of Russia, Germany, German Austria, Hungary, Poland, Finland, the Ukraine, Latvia, Lithuania and Byelorussia, Estonia, Armenia, of the German colonies in Russia, the Swedish Left Social-Democratic Party, the Nor-

wegian Social-Democratic Party, the Swiss Social-Democratic Party (Opposition), the Revolutionary Balkan Federation, the United Group of the Eastern Tribes of Russia, the French Zimmerwaldian Left, the Czech, Bulgarian, Yugoslav, British, French, and Swiss Communist groups, the Dutch Social-Democratic Party, the American League of Socialist Propaganda, the American Socialist Labour Party, the Chinese Socialist Labour Party, the Korean Workers' League, the Turkestan, Turkish, Georgian, Azerbaijan and Persian Sections of the Central Bureau of Eastern Nations and the Zimmerwald Commission.

The first meeting of the Comintern passed a decision "to consider this meeting as an international communist conference", and adopted the following agenda: 1) the inauguration, 2) reports, 3) the platform of the international communist conference, 4) bourgeois democracy and proletarian dictatorship, 5) the Berne Conference and the attitude towards socialist trends, 6) the international situation and the policy of the Entente, 7) the Manifesto, 8) the White terror, 9) elections to the Bureau, and various organisational questions.

The conference, whose work centred on Lenin's theses and report on bourgeois democracy and proletarian dictatorship, unanimously expressed solidarity with Lenin's theses and adopted a decision to refer them to the Bureau for dissemination in the various countries. The conference also adopted a resolution tabled by Lenin, in addition to the theses.

On March 4, after the theses and the resolution on Lenin's report had been adopted, the conference decided to constitute itself as the Third International, and to take the name of the Communist International. On the same day a resolution was unanimously passed to consider the Zimmerwald Left dissolved, and the Comintern platform was approved, on the following main principles: 1) the inevitability of the capitalist social system being replaced by a communist system; 2) the necessity of the proletariat's revolutionary struggle to overthrow bourgeois governments; 3) the abolition of the bourgeois state and its replacement by a state of a new type, i.e., the state of the proletariat, of the Soviet type, which will ensure the transition to a communist society.

One of the most important documents of the Congress was the Manifesto to the world proletariat, which declared that the Communist International was the successor of Marx's and Engels's ideas as expressed in the Communist Manifesto. The Congress called upon the workers of the world to support Soviet Russia, and demanded non-interference by the Entente in the internal affairs of the Soviet Republic, the withdrawal of the interventionist troops from Russian territory, recognition of the Soviet state, the raising of the economic blockade, and the resumption of trade relations.

In its resolution on "The Attitude Towards the 'Socialist' Parties and the Berne Conference", the Congress condemned the attempts to re-establish the Second International, which was "an instrument of the bourgeoisie only", and declared that the revolutionary proletariat had nothing in common with that conference.

The establishment of the Third, Communist International played a tremendous part in restoring links between the working people of many countries, in forming and consolidating Communist parties, and in exposing opportunism in the working-class movement. p. 206

[74] The *Amsterdam "International" of yellow trade unions* (the International Federation of Trade Unions) was established by reformist trade union leaders of a number of countries, at a conference held in Amsterdam on July 26-August 2, 1919. The trade union organisations of 14 countries merged to form this federation, viz., Britain, France, Germany, the U.S.A., Belgium, Denmark, Holland, Luxemburg, Norway, Sweden, Austria, Czechoslovakia, Switzerland and Spain. The reactionary trade union leaders of Britain and France were predominant in the Amsterdam International of trade unions, whose entire activities were connected with the policies of the opportunist parties of the Second International. The Amsterdam International came out in favour of the proletariat's collaboration with the bourgeoisie, and rejected revolutionary forms of the proletariat's struggle. The leaders of the Amsterdam International pursued a policy of splitting the working-class movement, excluded Left-wing trade unions from the organisation, and rejected all proposals by the Red International of Labour Unions for joint action against capital, the threat of war, reaction and fascism, and to establish world-wide trade union unity. The leaders of the Amsterdam International supported the anti-Soviet policy of the ruling circles of the imperialist states.

During the Second World War the Amsterdam International's activities ceased. p. 209

[75] The *Red International of Labour Unions* (the *Profintern*)—an international organisation of revolutionary trade unions. It was organised in 1921, and existed till the end of 1937. It amalgamated trade union centres which had not entered the reformist Amsterdam International of trade unions, i.e., the All-Russia Central Council of Trade Unions, the Unitary General Confederation of Labour of France, the national revolutionary trade union centres of Australia, Belgium, Holland, Indonesia, Ireland, Canada, China, Colombia, Korea, Lithuania, Mongolia, Iran, Peru, Uruguay, Czechoslovakia, Chile and Estonia, as well as opposition groups and trends within the reformist trade unions in a number of capitalist countries. The Red Trade Union International waged a struggle for unity in the trade union movement, on the basis of a revolutionary struggle, in defence of the demands of the working class, against capital and fascism, against the danger of imperialist war, and for solidarity with the working class of Soviet Russia. p. 210

[76] This article was proposed by Lenin at a sitting of the commission of the Comintern Second Congress on July 25, 1920, during

the discussion of his theses on the terms of admission into the Communist International. Both the commission and the Congress approved the article. Lenin's theses entitled "The Terms of Admission into the Communist International" and published before the Congress met contained 19 articles. The Congress adopted 21 articles, the last article reading as follows: "Party members who reject in principle the obligations and theses laid down by the Communist International shall be expelled from the Party.

"This shall also apply to delegates to extraordinary Party congresses." p. 212

77 The *Second Congress of the Communist International* met from July 19 to August 7, 1920. The opening session was held in Petrograd and the subsequent sessions in Moscow. It was attended by over 200 delegates who represented workers' organisations of 37 countries. Apart from delegates representing the Communist parties and organisations of 31 countries, there were delegates from the Independent Social-Democratic Party of Germany, the Socialist parties of Italy and France, Industrial Workers of the World (Australia, Britain and Ireland), the National Confederation of Labour of Spain and other organisations.

Lenin directed all the preparatory work before the Congress. At its first session he made a report on the international situation and the fundamental tasks of the Communist International. Throughout the Congress, in his reports and speeches, Lenin fought uncompromisingly against the opportunist Centrist parties, who were attempting to penetrate into the Third International, and levelled sharp criticism at the anarcho-syndicalist trends and "Left" sectarianism of a number of communist organisations. Lenin took part in the work of various commissions and delivered reports and speeches on the international situation and the fundamental tasks of the Communist International, the national and the colonial questions, the agrarian question and the terms of admission into the Communist International. Lenin's theses on the fundamental tasks of the Second Congress of the Communist International, the national and the colonial questions, the agrarian question and the terms of admission into the Communist International were endorsed as Congress decisions.

The Second Congress laid the foundations of the programme, organisational principles, strategy and tactics of the Communist International. p. 213

78 This international organisation was being set up at the time by the Centrist socialist parties and groups which had left the Second International under pressure from the revolutionary masses. The International Union of the Socialist Parties, as the new organisation was officially called, was formed at a conference in Vienna in February 1921 and was also known as the Two-and-a-Half or Vienna International. Professing opposition to the Second International, the leaders of the Two-and-a-Half International actually pursued the same opportunist and splitting

policy on the most important questions of the proletarian movement and tried to make the new organisation a counter-balance to the growing influence of the Communists among the workers. Lenin wrote, "The gentlemen of the Two-and-a-Half International pose as revolutionaries; but in every serious situation they prove to be counter-revolutionaries because they shrink from the violent destruction of the old state machine; they have no faith in the forces of the working class" (see present edition, Vol. 33, "New Times and Old Mistakes in a New Guise").

In May 1923 the Second International and the Two-and-a-Half International united to form the so-called Labour and Socialist International. p. 223

[79] *Guild socialists*—a reformist trend in the British trade unions, which arose before the First World War. They denied the class character of the state and sowed illusions among the workers that it was possible to get rid of exploitation without the class struggle, by establishing, on the basis of the existing trade unions, special associations of producers, so-called guilds whose federation was to take over industrial management. In this way the guild socialists hoped to build socialism.

After the October Socialist Revolution the guild socialists stepped up their propaganda, contraposing the "theory" of guild socialism to the ideas of the class struggle and the dictatorship of the proletariat. In the 1920s guild socialism lost all its influence on the British workers. p. 233

[80] The reference is to the American Federation of Labor and the British Labour Party.

The *American Federation of Labor* was formed in 1881, on the guild principle. In the main it organised the labour aristocracy. The reformist A.F.L. leaders denied the principles of socialism and the class struggle, preached "class co-operation" and championed the capitalist system. They followed a splitting policy in the international working-class movement, giving active support to the aggressive policy of the U.S. imperialists. In 1955 the A.F.L. merged with the C.I.O. p. 236

[81] See pp. 198-99 in this volume. p. 236

[82] See p. 89 in this volume. p. 236

[83] The commission on the national and the colonial questions, formed by the Second Congress of the Communist International, included representatives of the Communist parties of Russia, Bulgaria, France, Holland, Germany, Hungary, the U.S.A., India, Persia, China, Korea and Britain. The work of the commission was guided by Lenin, whose theses on the national and the colonial questions were discussed at the fourth and fifth sessions of the Congress, and were adopted on July 28. p. 240

84 The *Basle Manifesto* was adopted by the Extraordinary International Socialist Congress held in Basle on November 24-25, 1912. It gave a warning against the imminent world imperialist war, whose predatory aims it unmasked, and called upon the workers of all countries to wage a determined fight for peace and "to pit against the might of capitalist imperialism the international solidarity of the proletariat". The Manifesto denounced the expansionist policy of the imperialist countries and urged socialists to fight against all oppression of small nations and manifestations of chauvinism. p. 245

85 The terms of admission into the Communist International were first discussed by a commission appointed by the Congress. The commission included representatives of the Communist parties of Russia, Germany, Bulgaria, the U.S.A., Hungary, Austria, Holland, the Irish I.W.W., the Left wing of the Socialist Party of Switzerland and the French Communist group. In its work the commission proceeded from Lenin's theses "The Terms of Admission into the Communist International". Lenin also worked on the commission. The terms of admission into the Communist International were discussed at three Congress sessions, July 29 and 30, and were adopted on August 6. p. 246

86 Lenin is referring to the German Social-Democratic Party's programme which was adopted at its congress in Erfurt in October 1891. This programme marked an advance over the Gotha Programme of 1875, since it was based on the Marxist thesis that the capitalist mode of production was doomed and would be inevitably replaced by the socialist mode of production; it stressed the need for the working class to wage a political struggle and defined the party's role as leader in that struggle, but it too made serious concessions to opportunism. Engels gave a profound criticism of the draft of the programme in his work "*Zur Kritik des sozialdemokratischen Programmentwurfes 1891*" (see Marx/Engels, *Werke*, Dietz Verlag, Berlin, 1963, Bd. 22, S. 225-40). In fact, Engels criticised the opportunism of the entire Second International. However, in working out the final version of the programme, the German Social-Democratic leaders concealed Engels's criticism from the party rank and file and disregarded his most important remarks. According to Lenin, the fact that the Erfurt Programme made no mention of the dictatorship of the proletariat was the main defect in the programme, and a cowardly concession to opportunism. p. 246

87 See *KPSS v rezolutsiyakh i resheniyakh syezdov, konferentsii i plenumov TsK* (*The C.P.S.U. in the Resolutions and Decisions of Its Congresses, Conferences and Plenums of the Central Committee*), Part I, 1954, p. 39. p. 247

88 The question of the Communist Party's affiliation to the Labour Party was dealt with during the discussion on Lenin's theses on

the fundamental tasks of the Communist International, at the closing session of the Congress on August 6. Following Lenin's speech the majority (58 votes against 24, with 2 abstentions) approved affiliation. The Labour leaders, however, refused to grant membership to the Communist Party. p. 257

89 Lenin wrote this letter in connection with the Austrian Communist Party's decision to boycott parliamentary elections. On September 1, 1920, the Party Conference decided to participate in the elections. The Party's election campaign was conducted under the slogan of the revolutionary unity of the working class. p. 267

90 The radio message of the correspondent of the London *Daily News* Mr. Segrue was published in *Pravda* No. 202, September 12, 1920, along with Lenin's reply. In his message, Segrue pointed out that some socialists who had visited Soviet Russia had published anti-Soviet articles, and asked Lenin to comment on this. p. 273

91 The *Ninth All-Russia Conference of the R.C.P.(B.)*, held in Moscow from September 22 to September 25, 1920, was attended by 241 delegates (116 with the right to vote and 125 with voice but no vote). Among the items on the agenda were: the political and organisational reports of the Central Committee; the immediate tasks of Party development; a report of the commission in charge of the Party history studies, and a report on the Second Congress of the Communist International. The Conference also heard a report from the Polish Communists' delegate. Lenin opened the Conference, delivered the Central Committee's political report, and took the floor during the debate on the immediate tasks of Party development. The political report dealt mainly with the two subjects—the question of war and peace with Poland, and the organisation of Wrangel's defeat. The Conference passed a unanimous resolution on the conditions of peace with Poland, and approved the statement by the All-Russia Central Executive Committee on the specific peace terms drawn up on Lenin's instructions and edited by Lenin. The resolution on "The Immediate Tasks of Party Development" provided for practical measures to extend inner-Party democracy, strengthen Party unity and discipline, combat red tape in government and economic bodies and improve the communist training of young Party members. The Conference deemed it necessary to set up a Control Commission, to be elected at Party congresses, and Party commissions under gubernia Party committees, to be elected at gubernia Party conferences. The Conference gave a rebuff to the "Democratic Centralism" group, who denied Party discipline and the Party's guiding role in the Soviets and the trade unions. p. 275

92 The *Council of Action* was set up at a joint conference of representatives from the Parliamentary Committee of the trade unions, the Labour Party Executive Committee and the Parliamentary

Labour Party on August 9, 1920. Its aim was to prevent Britain making war on Russia. Besides the Central Council of Action in London, local councils of action were also set up. There were 150 councils by the end of August, the figure doubling within the next month. The Communist Party was largely instrumental in getting councils organised. It called upon its members to extend Communist representation in the councils and to win key positions on the strike committees in order to "withstand any attempts by trade union and Labour leaders to frustrate the desires of the rank and file, by capitulating at the crucial moment" (*The (Communist* No. 2, London, August 12, 1920). p. 277

93 The letter was published in *Die Rote Fahne*, organ of the Communist Party of Germany, *l'Humanité*, organ of the Socialist Party of France and *The Communist*, organ of the Communist Party of Great Britain, in the period from September to November 1920. p. 280

94 The *Third All-Russia Congress of the Russian Young Communist League* took place in Moscow between October 2 and 10, and was attended by some 600 delegates. Lenin addressed the Congress at the first session in the evening of October 2. p. 283

95 Lenin is referring to *Proletcult*. a cultural and educational organisation which arose in September 1917 as an independent workers' organisation. After the October Revolution Proletcult, whose leadership fell into the hands of Bogdanov and his supporters, continued to insist on independence, thus setting itself in opposition to the proletarian state. This led to the infiltration of bourgeois intellectuals, who began to exert a decisive influence on Proletcult. Its members actually denied the cultural legacy of the past, neglected cultural and educational work among the masses, isolated themselves from life and aimed at setting up a special "proletarian culture". Bogdanov, the chief Proletcult ideologist, paid lip service to Marxism, but actually preached subjective idealism, Machism. Besides bourgeois intellectuals who held leading positions in many organisations, Proletcult also included young workers who sincerely wished to promote cultural development in the Soviet state. Proletcult organisations had their heyday in 1919. In the early 1920s they began to decline, ceasing to exist in 1932. p. 287

96 This was the *Third All-Russia Congress of Leather Industry Workers*. It was held in Moscow between October 2 and 6, 1920, and was attended by some 300 delegates. It discussed the tasks of the trade unions, a report by the Central Committee of the Leather Industry Workers' Union, the organisation of management in leather industry, wages policy, labour protection, the cultural and educational work of the union, organisational questions, etc. Lenin spoke at the first sitting of the Congress. p. 300

[97] Lenin is referring to the speech made by the Polish Communist Uljanowski at the Ninth All-Russia Conference of the R.C.P.(B.). p. 303

[98] The *Council of Workers' and Peasants' Defence* was formed by the All-Russia Central Executive Committee on November 30, 1918. Its task was to implement the decree of the All-Russia Central Executive Committee of September 2, 1918, which proclaimed the country a military camp. The Council of Defence was an extraordinary organ brought into being by the extremely difficult situation in the country. It was vested with full powers to mobilise manpower and resources for the country's defence. Lenin was appointed Chairman of the Council.

Decisions of the Council were binding on all central and local bodies and all citizens of the Soviet Republic. The Council became the main military, economic and planning body of the Republic during the foreign intervention and the Civil War. The Revolutionary Military Council and other military bodies were brought under its control.

Early in April 1920, it was reorganised as the Council of Labour and Defence. By a decision of the Eighth All-Russia Congress of Soviets, adopted in December 1920, it was vested with the rights of a commission of the Council of People's Commissars and set the task of co-ordinating the work of all departments in the sphere of economic development. It existed until 1937. p. 312

[99] Lenin drew up this draft resolution for the First All-Russia Congress of Proletcult, which met in Moscow from October 5 to October 12, 1920. When the Political Bureau of the Central Committee of the Party discussed the question of Proletcult on October 9 and 11, it proceeded from Lenin's draft resolution. It was proposed to the Communist group of the Congress that it pass a resolution putting central and local Proletcult organisations under the control of the People's Commissariat of Education. The resolution was in keeping with Lenin's ideas and was unanimously approved by the Congress. However, after the Congress, some Proletcult leaders began to voice disagreement with the resolution and misinterpreted it to the rank and file, alleging that the Central Committee of the Communist Party was hamstringing the workers in the sphere of the arts and aiming at dissolving Proletcult. The Central Committee of the Party refuted these demagogical insinuations in its letter "On Proletcult Organisations" which gave a detailed analysis of Proletcult mistakes. The letter was published in *Pravda* No. 270 on December 1, 1920. p. 316

[100] On October 8, 1920, *Izvestia* reported Lunacharsky as saying in his speech at the Proletcult Congress that Proletcult must be assured a special status and complete autonomy. Recalling this episode, Lunacharsky wrote in his reminiscences: "At the time of the Proletcult Congress in October 1920, Vladimir Ilyich instructed me to attend it and pointed out quite definitely that

Proletcult should be subordinated to the People's Commissariat of Education, should regard itself as one of its institutions, and so on. In short, he wanted us to bring Proletcult closer to the state. At the same time, he took steps to bring it closer to the Party. I spoke at the Congress in a rather non-committal and conciliatory way, and the version sent to Vladimir Ilyich was even milder. He summoned me and gave me a good talking-to." p. 316

101 The conference was held between October 15 and 17, 1920, and was attended by some 3,000 delegates. Following Lenin's report a resolution was passed expressing satisfaction with the signing of a peace with Finland and a preliminary truce with Poland. It also recognised as correct the peaceful policy of the Soviet government which "has set out to save the lives of hundreds of thousands of Russian and Polish workers and peasants and to spare the Russian and Polish working people the hardships and privations of a winter campaign". The conference went on record that "the immediate task in winning a lasting peace is the complete rout of surviving bands in the South" and urged the working people of Russia "to give all possible help to the fronts and to bend every effort to wipe out Wrangel" (*Pravda* No. 231, October 16, 1920). The conference also discussed the organisation of aid for the Western front, the food situation, labour and cart service, and education. p. 318

102 Lenin is referring to a Note from the U.S. Secretary of State B. Colby to the Italian Government, on the attitude of the U.S. Administration towards Soviet Russia. The Note was published in *Izvestia* No. 198 of September 8, 1920. p. 320

103 Lenin is referring to the *First Congress of the Peoples of the East*, which was held in Baku between September 1 and 7, 1920, and attended by 1,891 delegates representing 37 nationalities (1,273 delegates were Communists). On the national and the colonial questions the Congress expressed solidarity with the relevant resolution of the Second Congress of the Communist International. p. 329

104 Under the armistice and the preliminary conditions of peace signed in Riga on October 12, 1920, between the R.S.F.S.R. and the Ukraine, on the one hand, and Poland on the other, the latter received the western regions of the Ukraine and Byelorussia. The parties to the treaty undertook to abstain from giving support to hostile activities directed against any of the parties, and disclaimed indemnities. The Soviet Government also agreed to return to Poland the cultural treasures appropriated by the tsarist government. p. 331

105 The reference is to a speech made by the peasant Belayev, who said that the lynx (world capital) was lying low waiting for a clash between the goat and the ram (the workers and the peasants). p. 334

[106] Lenin sent the manuscript of this article to the editors of the journal *The Communist International* in Petrograd. On the next day he informed the editors that he had sent the article, and requested them "to register, check up and set the material (everything to be returned to me)" (Central Party Archives at the Institute of Marxism-Leninism of the C.C. C.P.S.U.). He himself read and made a number of corrections in the proofs, which he had received from Petrograd.

A large part of the article was taken by Lenin from his pamphlet *The Victory of the Cadets and the Tasks of the Workers' Party* which he wrote in 1906 (see present edition, Vol. 10, pp. 199-276). He used Chapter V of the pamphlet entitled "A Sample of Cadet Smugness". p. 340

[107] See present edition, Vol. 8, pp. 373-74. p. 341

[108] See present edition, Vol. 16, pp. 374-92 and 393-421. p. 341

[109] *Die Neue Rheinische Zeitung* was a daily published in Cologne under the editorship of Marx, from June 1, 1848 to May 19, 1849. The editorial board consisted of Frederick Engels, Wilhelm Wolff, Georg Weerth, Ferdinand Wolff, Ernst Dronke, Ferdinand Freiligrath and Heinrich Bürgers. This militant organ of the proletarian wing of democracy did much to educate the masses and rouse them for struggle against the counter-revolution. Most of the leading articles defining the newspaper's stand on the key problems of the German and European revolution were written by Marx and Engels.

Despite police persecution, the newspaper boldly championed the interests of revolutionary democracy and the proletariat. Publication of the newspaper was discontinued following Marx's deportation from Prussia in May 1849 and reprisals against other editors. p. 345

[110] Karl Marx, "Die Krisis und die Konterrevolution" (see Marx/Engels, *Werke*, Dietz Verlag, Berlin, 1959, Bd. 5, S. 402). p. 345

[111] This refers to the All-Germany National Assembly convened after the March 1848 revolution in Germany in Frankfort on the Main in May of the same year. The Assembly faced the task of putting an end to the political fragmentation of Germany and of drawing up a constitution for all Germany. Due to the cowardice and the vacillation of its Liberal majority, and the irresoluteness and inconsistency of the petty-bourgeois Left wing, the Assembly did not dare to assume supreme power in the country and failed to take a resolute stand on the major questions of the German revolution of 1848-49. It did nothing to alleviate the position of the workers and peasants and did not support the national liberation movement in Poland and Bohemia, but approved the policy of oppression of subject peoples pursued by Austria and Prussia. The deputies did not have the courage to mobilise the

people for the defeat of the counter-revolutionary offensive and the defence of the Imperial Constitution which they had framed in March 1849.

Shortly afterwards the Austrian and then the Prussian governments recalled their deputies, and the Liberal deputies of other German states followed suit. The remaining deputies, who belonged to the petty-bourgeois Left wing, had the Assembly moved to Stuttgart. In June 1849 the Assembly was disbanded by the troops of the Württemberg government. p. 345

112 See Marx/Engels, *Werke*, Dietz Verlag, Berlin, 1959, Bd. 5, S. 40. p. 346

113 On January 9, 1905, over 140,000 St. Petersburg workers carrying gonfalons and icons, marched to the Winter Palace to submit a petition to the tsar. The march was staged by the priest Gapon, an agent of the secret police, at a time when the strike of the Putilov workers, which began on January 3 (16), had already spread to the other factories in the city. The Bolsheviks exposed Gapon's venture, warning the workers that the tsar might unleash a massacre. The Bolsheviks were right. On orders from the tsar, the troops met the demonstrating workers, their wives and children with rifle shots, sabres and Cossack whips. More than a thousand workers were killed and five thousand wounded. January 9, or Bloody Sunday as it came to be known, sparked off the 1905 Revolution. p. 346

114 See present edition, Vol. 9, pp. 131-32. p. 346

115 See present edition, Vol. 10, pp. 216-17. p. 347

116 Lenin is referring to the daily newspaper *Nasha Zhizn* (Our Life) which was published at intervals in St. Petersburg, from November 6 (19), 1904 to July 11 (24), 1906. p. 347

117 *Brentanoism*—a political trend originated by the German bourgeois economist Lujo Brentano (1844-1931), who preached "class peace" in capitalist society and maintained that it was possible to eliminate social contradictions without the class struggle and that the labour question could be settled and the interests of the workers and the capitalists reconciled through the establishment of reformist trade unions, and factory legislation. p. 355

118 *Bez Zaglaviya* (Without a Title)—political weekly published in St. Petersburg from January 24 (February 6) to May 14 (27), 1906. It was edited by Prokopovich, who worked in close cooperation with Kuskova, Bogucharsky, Khizhnyakov and others. The *Bez Zaglaviya* supporters formed a semi-Cadet, semi-Menshevik group of Russian bourgeois intellectuals who, under the guise of non-partisanship, propagated the ideas of bourgeois liberalism

and opportunism, and supported revisionists in the Russian and international Social-Democratic movement. p. 356

119 Lenin is referring to the disagreements in the Social-Democratic group of the German Reichstag over the shipping subsidies (*Dampfersubvention*). Late in 1884 Bismarck, in pursuance of the expansionist colonial policy, demanded from the Reichstag that it approve subsidies to shipping companies for establishing regular shipping routes to East Asia, Australia and Africa. The Left wing of the Social-Democratic group led by Bebel and Liebknecht rejected the subsidies, but the Right wing, under Auer, Dietz and others, which constituted the majority, declared themselves in favour of granting subsidies, even before the official debate on the question. During the Reichstag debate in March 1885, the Social-Democratic Right wing voted for subsidies for shipping lines to East Asia and Australia, making a number of reservations, in particular that the ships for the new lines should be built at German shipyards. Only after the Reichstag declined this demand did the whole group unanimously come out against the government bill. The behaviour of the majority of the group came in for criticism from the newspaper *Sozialdemokrat* and Social-Democratic organisations. At one time the disagreements within the group were so acute that they threatened to lead to a split in the Party. Engels sharply criticised the opportunist stand taken by the group's Right wing (see Marx/Engels, *Werke*, Dietz Verlag, Berlin, Bd. 36). p. 358

120 The "*Youth*" group in the German Social-Democratic Party—a petty-bourgeois, semi-anarchist opposition which took shape in 1890. The nucleus of the opposition was made up of young writers and students, who posed as Party theoreticians and leaders. Blind to the changes brought about by the abrogation of the Anti-Socialist Law in 1878, they denied the need for the Party to make use of legal forms of struggle, opposed the participation of Social-Democrats in parliament, and accused the Party of opportunism and defending the interests of the petty bourgeoisie. Engels wrote that the theoretical views and tactics of the opposition were "'Marxism' distorted beyond recognition". Their unrealistic and adventurist tactics, he said, might "ruin even the strongest party numbering millions of members" (see Marx/Engels, *Werke*, Dietz Verlag, Berlin, 1963, Bd. 22, S. 69). Some leaders of the "Left" opposition were expelled from the Party at the Erfurt Congress in October 1891. p. 358

121 *Severny Golos* (Voice of the North)—a legal daily newspaper, organ of the R.S.D.L.P., which appeared in St. Petersburg from December 6 (19), 1905 and was edited jointly by the Bolsheviks and the Mensheviks. It was closed down after its third issue had appeared, on December 8 (21), 1905. p. 358

122 *Nachalo* (The Beginning)—a legal daily Menshevik newspaper, published in St. Petersburg from November to December 1905. p. 359

[123] *Novaya Zhizn* (New Life)—the first legal Bolshevik newspaper published daily in St. Petersburg from October 27 (November 9) to December 3 (16), 1905. From the beginning of November, after Lenin's return to St. Petersburg from abroad, it was published under his direct guidance. The paper was actually the Central Organ of the R.S.D.L.P. p. 359

[124] *Polyarnaya Zvezda* (The Pole Star)—a weekly journal, mouthpiece of the Right wing of the Constitutional-Democratic Party. It was edited by P. B. Struve and appeared in St. Petersburg in 1905-06.

Nasha Zhizn (Our Life)—a daily newspaper that was close to the Left wing of the Constitutional-Democratic Party; appeared in St. Petersburg at intervals, from 1904 to 1906. p. 360

[125] See present edition, Vol. 10, pp. 241-54. p. 361

[126] The Conference met in Moscow from November 2 to 8, 1920, with 283 delegates attending. The main question discussed was the establishment of the Chief Committee for Political Education. A. V. Lunacharsky delivered the opening address, in which he dealt with the work done in the sphere of political education. The Conference also heard a report by N. K. Krupskaya on the current plan of work of the Chief Committee for Political Education, and Y. A. Litkens's report on the organisation of local political education departments. Other items on the agenda concerned the food campaign and political education, production propaganda in the light of the rehabilitation of economic activity, and the elimination of illiteracy. Lenin spoke after Krupskaya at the third session of the Conference, on the second day of the proceedings. p. 363

[127] This document formed the basis of the resolution on the tasks of the trade union movement, which was passed by the R.C.P.(B.) group of the Fifth All-Russia Conference of Trade Unions on November 8, 1920, and published in *Pravda* on November 13. 200 delegates supported the resolution, with 12 delegates abstaining.

At the Conference, which took place in Moscow between November 2 and 6, the Party raised the question of reorganising the work of the trade unions in keeping with the tasks of peaceful socialist construction, extending democracy and abandoning purely administrative methods. Trotsky came out against the proposed reorganisation. At a sitting of the Communist group on November 3, he spoke "fine words", as Lenin said, about "shaking up" the trade unions, "tightening the screws" and immediate "governmentalisation of trade unions". Trotsky's speech, which sparked off a discussion in the Party, was duly rebuffed by the Communist delegates. Disagreement with Trotsky over trade unions concerned the methods of approaching the masses, of winning over and establishing ties with them. Had Trotsky had his way, the trade unions would have been ruined and the dictatorship of the proletariat undermined. The Central Committee of the Party, therefore, could not leave the matter at that. On November 8 Lenin read his theses at a plenary meeting of the Central Committee, in which he opposed Trotsky's views. Trotsky's theses won 7 votes, and Lenin's, 8 votes.

Lenin's theses formed the basis of his draft resolution on "The Tasks of the Trade Unions, and the Methods of Their Accomplishment", which was passed by 10 votes against 4, with 1 abstention. p. 374

128 The *Central Committee of the General Transport Workers' Union* was formed in September 1920. The amalgamation was necessitated by the need to provide a stable centralised leadership capable of coping with the speedy rehabilitation of transport, whose dislocation threatened to disrupt the country's economy. This called for temporary extraordinary measures, and made it necessary to put the trade unions on a wartime footing. The new body did much to rehabilitate the transport facilities, but then lost its ties with the trade union rank and file. The red tape and the purely administrative methods of the Trotskyite union leaders, who made arbitrary appointments and abandoned democratic methods of work—all this set the transport workers against the Party and tended to create a split among them. The Central Committee of the Party condemned these reprehensible methods, and the plenary meetings of the Central Committee held on November 8 and December 7, 1920, decided to incorporate the union in the system of the All-Russia Central Council of Trade Unions on an equal footing with the other trade unions, recommending to the union leaders that they change their methods of work: extend democracy within the union, apply the principle of election of trade union bodies on a broad scale, discontinue the practice of arbitrary appointments, etc. The First All-Russia Congress of Transport Workers, which was called by the Central Committee of the R.C.P.(B.) in March 1921, expelled the Trotskyites from the union leadership and defined various measures to improve the work of the union. p. 374

129 This work consists of two articles on a single subject. The first article, whose title covers the two articles in the present edition, was written on November 4, 1920, and first published in *Pravda* No. 250 on November 7, 1920. In the note to the article, the editors wrote: "Comrade Lenin wrote the article before he received the news of the despicable behaviour of D'Aragona and the opportunist trade unionists, Party members, who insisted on their policy in opposition to the Central Committee of their own Party and, acting in collusion with Minister Giolitti, frustrated an immense movement of the working class. These facts, of which we shall speak in greater detail in one of our next issues, confirm still more strikingly that Lenin is right." The second article, which Lenin entitled "False Talk on Freedom (Instead of an Epilogue)" was written on December 11, 1920. The following note

is to be found in the MS: "NB: if you are going to publish it at all, then publish it as an epilogue to the article on the struggle in the Italian Socialist Party. NB" (Central Party Archives at the Institute of Marxism-Leninism of the C.C. C.P.S.U.). Both articles were published in issue No. 15 of the journal *The Communist International* in December 1920 under a common title "False Talk on Freedom". p. 377

130 See pp. 280-82 in this volume. p. 379

131 *l'Humanité*—French daily founded by Jean Jaurès in 1904 as organ of the French Socialist Party. During the First World War it was the mouthpiece of the extreme Right wing of the Party and took a social-chauvinist stand. Shortly after the split in the Party at the congress in December 1920 and the formation of the Communist Party, it became the organ of the latter and has since then been published as such. p. 382

132 See p. 191 in this volume. p. 388

133 See present edition, Vol. 26, pp. 91-92. p. 389

134 See Karl Marx, *Capital*, Moscow, Vol. I, 1962, p. 176. p. 392

135 See Frederick Engels, *Anti-Dühring*, Moscow, 1959, p. 148. p. 392

136 The Red Army's drive against Wrangel began at the end of October 1920. After heavy fighting Wrangel was hurled back into the Crimea. On the night of November 7 the Red Army troops launched an offensive on the Perekop Isthmus and by November 16 cleared the Crimea of the whiteguards. Thus the period of the Civil war and foreign intervention was in the main brought to an end. p. 399

137 The extraordinary congress of the Independent Social-Democratic Party of Germany met in Halle on October 12-17, 1920. The main question on the agenda was the terms of admission into the Communist International. The fierce struggle over this question caused a split in the party, 237 delegates voting for affiliation to the Comintern, and 156 against. The Right wing called its own congress and elected an executive committee, retaining the old name of the party. The Left wing and the Communist Party (the Spartacists) formed the United Communist Party of Germany. p. 399

138 The mutiny in the Second Black Sea squadron of the French navy, which broke out in April-May 1919, was directed against the French Government's policy in sending 300,000 soldiers and sailors to Russia to crush Soviet power. The interventionists' troops in the South numbered over 130,000 men. The Odessa underground committee of the Bolshevik Party headed by Smirnov (Lastoch-

kin), and its Foreign Collegium with Jeanne Labourbe as a member of its Bureau, played an important role in fostering the revolutionary spirit of the soldiers and sailors of the interventionist troops. The Collegium included such experienced Communist agitators as Yakov Yelin, Vladimir Dyogot and others, who established contacts with soldiers and the crews of a number of ships. The mutiny began on April 20 on the battleships *France* and *Jean Bart*, which were riding off Sevastopol harbour. Other ship crews and soldiers of the 175th French Infantry Regiment supported their action. Then the mutiny spread to the ships in Odessa harbour. The mutineers demanded that the intervention should be stopped at once and the troops sent home, threatening to join the Red Army if their demands were not granted. The French command arrested the mutineers' leaders and sent them off to France, where they were treated most harshly. The mutiny was defeated because the mutineers did not have a clear revolutionary aim or capable leadership, as no Communist Party yet existed in France. However, the action of the French soldiers and sailors, who gave revolutionary support to the world's first working people's state stimulated the growth of the revolutionary movement in France.

The successes of the Red Army, revolutionary action in the French army and navy, and the workers' pressure compelled the French Government to withdraw its troops from Russia. p. 400

139 This document served as a basis for the draft theses of the Chief Committee for Political Education, which were published in *Prarda* No. 267 on November 27, 1920, under the heading "Production Propaganda (Draft Theses of the Chief Committee for Political Education)".

The question of production propaganda was first raised in connection with the discussion of the immediate tasks of economic development, at the Ninth Party Congress held from March 29 to April 5, 1920. But after Poland's attack on the Soviet Republic, the brief respite came to an end and the questions of economic development receded into the background. Only at the end of 1920, after the signing of a preliminary peace with Poland and the defeat of Wrangel, did the question of production propaganda aimed at drawing the masses into the work of economic rehabilitation come up again with renewed urgency. Production propaganda, first suggested by Lenin, remains to this day one of the main tasks of the political, cultural and educational activities of the Party and the Soviet state. p. 404

140 *Bednota* (The Poor)—a daily newspaper published by the C.C. C.P.S.U.(B.) from March 27, 1918 to January 31, 1931. On February 1, 1931 it merged with *Sotsialisticheskoye Zemledeliye* (Socialist Farming), which is published to this day. p. 405

141 The Conference was held in the Kremlin between November 20 and 22, 1920, during the discussion on trade unions, which had begun

in the Party. The acute struggle waged by opposition groups against the Party's policy created a tense atmosphere at the Conference. The anti-Party "Democratic Centralism", "Workers' Opposition" and Ignatov's groups demagogically attacked the Party's policy. Before and during the Conference they tried to gain decisive influence in the Party's Moscow organisation. In an attempt to get the maximum number of their supporters elected to the Moscow Committee the "Workers' Opposition" group held a special conference of their supporters from among the worker delegates.

Directed by Lenin, the Conference repulsed the anti-Party attacks and pointed to the need of combating the unscrupulous groups bred by an atmosphere of recriminations. After hearing the report of the Moscow Committee, the Conference passed a resolution reflecting the viewpoint of the Central Committee. The list of candidate members of the Moscow Committee, drawn up by the opposition at the private conference was blackballed, and only those delegates were elected who had been nominated by the Political Bureau of the Central Committee. p. 408

142 *Peace between the R.S.F.S.R. and Finland* was signed on October 14, 1920. The treaty terminated the state of war, confirmed Finland's independence and sovereignty as granted by the Soviet Government in 1917, and laid down the state frontiers between the two countries.

Peace between the R.S.F.S.R. and Estonia was signed in Yuryev (now Tartu) on February 2, 1920. Under the treaty Soviet Russia recognised Estonia's independence.

Latvian ruling circles were also compelled to sign peace with the R.S.F.S.R., following the defeat of the foreign interventionists and the whiteguards in 1919 and the resulting consolidation of Soviet Russia's international position. On March 25, 1920, the Latvian Foreign Ministry approached the Soviet Government suggesting that peace talks be started. On April 16, the Soviet and Latvian representatives started peace talks in Moscow and on August 11 a treaty was signed with Latvia in Riga. p. 409

143 In the autumn of 1920 Washington Vanderlip, who represented the U.S. Vanderlip Syndicate, arrived in Moscow to negotiate a concession for fishing, prospecting and extracting oil and coal in Kamchatka and elsewhere in Siberia, east of the 160th meridian.

In agreeing to the concession, the Soviet Government intended not only to establish mutually advantageous co-operation with American businessmen but also to normalise relations between Soviet Russia and the United States. Vanderlip's move, however, did not get the support of the U.S. Administration and financial tycoons, and the agreement was never signed. p. 413

144 To incite Turkey against Soviet Russia and torpedo the talks between the two countries on the establishment of friendly

relations, the Entente diplomats provoked Dashnak Armenia's attack on Turkey. The Dashnak nationalist party, then in power in Armenia (1918-20), pursued an aggressive policy with regard to Turkey and aimed at establishing a "Greater Armenia" that would include nearly half of Asia Minor. On September 24, 1920 the Dashnak government began hostilities against Turkey, but five days later the Turkish troops checked the Dashnak offensive and, in a counter-offensive lasting from September to November occupied Sarykamysh, Kars and Alexandropol. The Turkish Government decided to take advantage of the adventurist Dashnak policy and occupy the whole of Armenia.

On November 11 the People's Commissariat for Foreign Affairs of the R.S.F.S.R. offered its mediation to the warring parties. Turkey rejected Soviet mediation, and the Dashnak government had to agree to a shackling treaty which made Armenia a Turkish protectorate. The treaty, however, did not go into force, because by November 29, when it was to be signed, the Dashnak government had been overthrown and Soviet power proclaimed in Armenia. Claiming that the treaty was still valid, the Turkish Government held up the evacuation of Alexandropol district. Only after the Soviet Government had, in the middle of May 1921, firmly demanded the evacuation of the district, were the Turkish forces withdrawn. p. 415

145 Lenin is referring to his "Report on the Immediate Tasks of the Soviet Government" which he delivered at a session of the All-Russia Central Executive Committee on April 29, 1918 (see present edition, Vol. 27, pp. 281-305). p. 417

146 The reference is to the book *Plan for the Electrification of the R.S.F.S.R. Report of the State Commission for the Electrification of Russia to the Eighth Congress of Soviets* published in Moscow in 1920. The outcome of collective work by leading scientists and specialists, the plan was the first long-term plan for the creation of the material foundation of socialism on the basis of the country's electrification. Lenin called this plan "the Party's second programme". p. 419

147 Lenin is referring to the resolutions of the Ninth All-Russia Conference of the R.C.P.(B.) (see *VKP(B) v rezolutsiyakh i resheniyakh syezdov, konferentsii i plenumov TsK* [*the C.P.S.U.(B.) in the Resolutions and Decisions of Its Congresses, Conferences and Plenums of the Central Committee*], Part I, 1940, pp. 349-54). p. 422

148 This Conference was held in the Hall of Columns, the House of Trade Unions, on November 25, 1920, and was attended by more than 2,000 delegates. Lenin delivered a report on the international and domestic position of the Soviet Republic and the immediate tasks of the working class. p. 429

149 Held in the Hall of Columns, the House of Trade Unions, on November 26, 1920, this meeting discussed reports on the Moscow Gubernia Conference of the R.C.P.(B.) and the war situation. Lenin spoke at the meeting in connection with the publication of the decree on concessions, on November 25. p. 430

150 The *Council of People's Commissars*, with Lenin as chairman, was formed by the Second All-Russia Congress of Soviets in October 1917. It was occasionally called the great, or full, Council to distinguish it from the small, or limited, Council, which functioned under its auspices from December 1917 to 1926 as a commission dealing with minor questions and preparing various questions for consideration by the full Council of People's Commissars. p. 430

151 The *Peace Treaty of Versailles*, which concluded the First World War, was signed on June 28, 1919, by the U.S.A., the British Empire, France, Italy, Japan and other Allied Powers, on the one hand, and Germany, on the other.

Lenin wrote, "this is an unparalleled and predatory peace, which has made slaves of tens of millions of people, including the most civilised" (see p. 326 in this volume). The treaty consolidated the re-partition of the capitalist world in favour of the victors, and established a system of relationships between countries which was aimed at strangling Soviet Russia and suppressing the world revolutionary movement. p. 431

152 The imperialist government of Japan, in collusion with U.S. and British ruling circles, invaded the Far East in the spring of 1918 in an attempt to seize Soviet territory east of Lake Baikal. On April 5, Japanese troops landed in Vladivostok. Operating from their main strategic base in Vladivostok, they occupied the Maritime Province, Northern Sakhalin and the Trans-Baikal region. The rout of Kolchak at the end of 1919, the growing guerilla movement and the economic crisis in Japan in 1920-21, which was aggravated by the Japanese-American contradictions, spelled the doom of the interventionists. By the autumn of 1922 their rout was complete and on October 25 the last interventionists left Vladivostok. p. 431

153 The reference is to the talks with Bullitt (see Note 47). p. 432

154 The *Workers' Opposition* was an anti-Party anarcho-syndicalist factional group led by Shlyapnikov, Medvedev, Kollontai, Kutuzov, Lutovinov and others. Demagogically calling itself the "Workers' Opposition", the group came out into the open for the first time at the Ninth All-Russia Conference of the R.C.P.(B.) in September 1920. In November, during the Moscow Gubernia Conference of the R.C.P.(B.), the group called a special conference, thus taking the path of factional struggle and the subversion of the Party's unity. The "Workers' Opposition" group was

finally constituted during the discussion on the trade unions in 1920-21. The views of the group, as an anarcho-syndicalist deviation in the Party, were most fully set forth in the pamphlet by Kollontai entitled *Workers' Opposition*, published on the eve of the Tenth Congress of the Party. The opposition suggested that the management of the economy should be entrusted to "the All-Russia Congress of Producers" united in producers' trade unions, which were to elect their central organ to manage the economy. The opposition demanded that all economic management bodies be elected by the respective trade unions, whose candidates could not be revoked by Party or government bodies. This amounted to the denial of the Party's leading role and the dictatorship of the proletariat as the main instrument in socialist construction. The opposition set the trade unions against the Soviet state and the Communist Party, regarding trade unions, and not the Party, as the highest form of the organisation of the working class.

On inner-Party questions the platform of the Workers' Opposition amounted to slanderous accusations that the Party leadership had "lost links with the Party rank and file", "underestimated the creative power of the proletariat", and "degenerated".

There was a time when the Workers' Opposition had some support from backward sections of the workers, who more than any others succumbed to the influence of the petty-bourgeois environment. The opposition took advantage of the vacillation in this unstable section of the workers to further their ends. The opposition got support from a number of central and local Party organisations, its platform gaining 21 per cent of the votes at the Moscow Gubernia Conference of the R.C.P.(B.) in November 1920 and 30 per cent at a meeting of the Communist group of the Second All-Russia Congress of Mine Workers at the beginning of 1921. As a result of the Party's explanatory work exposing the demagogical anti-Party slogans of the opposition, the number of its supporters declined. Less than 6 per cent of the delegates to the Tenth Party Congress voted for its platform. The Congress dealt a crushing blow at the opposition's views. The resolution "On the Syndicalist and Anarchist Deviation in Our Party" tabled by Lenin pointed out that these views were incorrect theoretically and "in practice weakened the sustained guiding line of the Communist Party and served the interests of the class enemies of the proletarian revolution" (*KPSS v rezolutsiyakh i resheniyakh syezdov, konferentsii i plenumov TsK* [*The C.P.S.U. in the Resolutions and Decisions of Its Congresses, Conferences and Plenums of the Central Committee*], Part I, 1954, p. 532). The Congress recognised propaganda of the views of the Workers' Opposition to be incompatible with Party membership. The resolution on Party unity adopted by the Congress demanded the immediate dissolution of all groups without exception, which had a political platform of their own. After the Congress most of the Party rank and file broke with the Workers' Opposition and unreservedly supported the line of the Party. Under Shlyapnikov and Medvedev, the remnants of the opposition, however, retained their illegal organisation and continued their anti-Party propaganda under cover of arch-revolutionary phrases. In February 1922 they sent "a statement of 22" to the Executive Committee of the Comintern, which was nothing short of a slanderous lampoon against the Party. After a thorough study of the statement, the Executive Committee condemned the group's actions and warned them that, if continued, their actions would place the group outside the Third International. At the Eleventh Party Congress held in 1922 the group was defeated organisationally. p. 436

155 This telegram was sent in reply to greetings from the Revolutionary Military Committee of Armenia on the occasion of the establishment of Soviet power there. The Committee sent its greetings on November 30, 1920. p. 437

156 The *Far Eastern Republic* was set up in April 1920 and included the Trans-Baikal, Amur, Maritime and Kamchatka regions and Northern Sakhalin. Formally a bourgeois-democratic state, it actually pursued a Soviet policy. Its formation was in keeping with the interests of Soviet Russia, which needed a prolonged respite from war in the Far East and wanted to stave off war with Japan. At the same time, however, its creation was a step the Soviet Government had been compelled to take by the pressure of circumstances (see p. 465 in this volume).

After the interventionists and whiteguards were driven out of the Soviet Far East (except Northern Sakhalin), the People's Assembly of the Republic voted for entry into the R.S.F.S.R. on November 14, 1922. p. 445

157 This refers to the draft of a trade agreement between Great Britain and the R.S.F.S.R., which President of the Board of Trade Edward F. Wise presented to L. B. Krasin, head of the Soviet trade delegation in London, on November 29, 1920. The talks to normalise economic and political contacts, which had started in May 1920, dragged on and nearly broke down on several occasions. On March 16, 1921, they ended in the signing of a trade agreement. p. 452

158 *Narody Vostoka* (Peoples of the East)—a monthy journal, organ of the Council for Propaganda and Guiding the Activities of the Peoples of the East, published by a decision of the First Congress of the Peoples of the East, which was held in Baku from September 1 to September 7, 1920. Only one issue appeared—in October 1920. It came out in Russian, Turkish, Persian and Arabic. p. 453

159 Lenin is referring to the bill "On Measures to Strengthen and Develop Peasant Farming" which the Council of People's Commissars submitted to the Presidium of the All-Russia Central Executive Committee for consideration by the Eighth All-Russia Congress of Soviets. It was published in *Izvestia* No. 281 on December 14, 1920.

The bill combined measures for the state regulation of agricultural development and incentives for the peasants to raise output on their farms. The Eighth Congress of Soviets passed the bill by a unanimous vote. p. 458

160 The Conference met in Moscow from December 1 to 6, 1920, with over 200 women delegates participating, representing 5 republics, 65 gubernias and 5 administrative regions. The Conference discussed a report on the foreign and domestic situation of the country, a report of the C.C.'s Department on work among women, the immediate tasks of departments for work among women, and the question of mother and child protection. The Conference emphasised the need to boost production and extend production propaganda and the enrolment of working women in the trade unions and the Workers' and Peasants' Inspection.

Lenin's message of greetings, conveyed by telephone, was read at a sitting of the Conference on December 6. p. 460

161 The Congress was held in Moscow from December 22 to 29, 1920. There was a record attendance of 2,537 delegates, of whom 1,728 had full voting rights, and 809 had deliberative votes.

The Congress met at a time when the Soviet Republic had won victory over the foreign interventionists and internal counter-revolution, and the economic front, as Lenin said, had become "the main, the principal front".

The Congress was guided by Lenin, who delivered a report on the work of the All-Russia Central Executive Committee and the Council of People's Commissars, and a speech closing the debate on his report at plenary sessions of the Congress on December 22 and 23. He also took the floor six times at sittings of the Communist group of the Congress on December 21, 22, 24 and 27 to deal with the question of concessions and the bill on measures to strengthen and develop peasant farming.

After the debate on Lenin's report, the Congress passed a resolution by an overwhelming majority, approving the activities of the Soviet Government. The delegates gave a concerted rebuff to representatives of the petty-bourgeois parties who made a number of anti-Soviet declarations at the Congress and tabled a draft resolution of their own.

The Congress adopted the plan for the electrification of Russia which was drawn up on Lenin's initiative and in keeping with his directions. This was the first long-term economic plan of the Soviet state, which Lenin called "the Party's second programme". The resolution adopted on Krzhizhanovsky's report was drafted by Lenin (see p. 532 in this volume).

One of the most important questions on the agenda was the bill on measures to strengthen and develop peasant farming, passed by the Council of People's Commissars on December 14, 1920. Lenin participated in the discussion of the main clauses of the law at a private meeting of non-Party peasant delegates on

December 22 and in the Communist group of the Congress on December 24 and 27. The Congress unanimously approved the bill.

The transition to peaceful construction called for the improvement and reorganisation of the entire Soviet apparatus. The Congress passed a detailed resolution on the question, setting up proper relations between central and local administrative bodies. The Congress dealt extensively with questions relating to the reorganisation of the entire system of economic management to meet the new tasks. The delegates discussed and approved a new statute of the Council of Labour and Defence.

The Congress instituted the Order of the Red Banner of Labour to be awarded for labour heroism, initiative and organisation in solving economic tasks. p. 461

162 Lenin is referring to his speech at the meeting of activists of the Moscow organisation of the R.C.P.(B.) on December 6, 1920 (see pp. 438-59 in this volume). p. 464

163 Lenin is apparently referring to the collection *Red Calvary* put out in memory of the victims of the Japanese intervention. p. 465

164 On May 26, 1919, the Supreme Council sent a Note to Kolchak over the signatures of Wilson, Lloyd George, Clemenceau, Orlando and Saionji informing him of the Allies' readiness to recognise Kolchak and supply him with food and munitions to enable him to become ruler of all Russia. In return Kolchak was to convene a constituent assembly after he took Moscow, recognise the independence of Poland and Finland and, unless agreement could be reached on the relations between Russia, on the one hand, and Estonia, Latvia, Lithuania, the Caucasian and Trans-Caspian territories, on the other, to submit this question to the League of Nations and to recognise their autonomy pending a decision by the League, etc. In his reply Kolchak accepted a number of conditions. On July 12 Britain, France, the U.S.A. and Italy, considering Kolchak's reply satisfactory, reaffirmed their readiness to give him help. p. 466

165 The decree of the Council of People's Commissars on concessions, the accompanying maps of forest, agricultural and mining concessions and several articles by leading Soviet specialists were published in the journal *Russische Korrespondenz* No. 1-2 for 1921. p. 476

166 The reference is to a meeting of activists of the Moscow organisation of the R.C.P.(B.) on December 6, 1920. p. 481

167 "Sukharevka" was the name of a market-place near the Sukharev Tower built under Peter I in 1692. At the time of the foreign military intervention and the Civil War it became a centre and symbol of black marketeering. In December 1920 the Moscow Soviet decided to close the market.

When the New Economic Policy was introduced, the market reappeared and existed till 1932. In 1934 the Sukharev Tower was demolished as a hindrance to traffic. p. 483

[168] On August 10, 1920, the French Government officially recognised Wrangel as the ruler of South Russia. p. 488

[169] This agreement, which established friendly relations between the R.S.F.S.R. and Persia was signed in Moscow on February 26, 1921, despite opposition from British ruling circles. It was based on the principles of peaceful coexistence and co-operation—equality, respect for the sovereignty of the two countries, non-interference in internal affairs, and mutual advantage. All the treaties concluded by tsarist Russia with Persia and third parties which infringed on the sovereignty of the Persian people were revoked. Persia got back all the concessions of the tsarist government on her territory. The Soviet Government renounced claims to the loans granted to Persia by the tsarist government. Especially important were the articles pledging both parties to preclude the formation or the existence on their respective territories of organisations or groups with aims subversive to Russia or Persia. This was the first equal treaty in the history of Persia. p. 491

[170] See present edition, Vol. 27, pp. 314-17. p. 495

[171] The *All-Russia Bureau for Production Propaganda* of the All-Russia Central Council of Trade Unions was set up by a decision of the C.C. R.C.P.(B.) on December 8, 1920. It consisted of representatives of the Central Committee of the Communist Party (Bolsheviks), the All-Russia Central Council of Trade Unions, the Supreme Council of the National Economy, the Chief Committee for Political Education, the Central Board for Vocational Training, and the Commissariat of Agriculture. On January 21, 1921, the Organising Bureau of the Party's Central Committee approved the statute of the bureau which defined the aims and tasks of central and local bodies in charge of production propaganda and their structure. The bureau was instructed to work out a general plan of propaganda, and direct and supervise various organs and bodies in carrying out their production propaganda. p. 500

[172] The decree of the Council of People's Commissars on "Provisional Rules on Bonuses in Kind" was published on October 23, 1920. p. 508

[173] Order No. 1042 was issued by the Chief Department of Railways on May 22, 1920. It dealt with the repair of locomotives damaged during the First World War and the Civil War. Railway depots were ordered to lower the percentage of locomotives under repair from 60 to 20 per cent in four and a half years, beginning from July 1, 1920. p. 510

[174] The first session of the All-Russia Central Executive Committee of the seventh convocation held on February 2-7, 1920, instructed the Presidium of the Supreme Council of the National Economy and the People's Commissariat of Agriculture to work out a plan for the construction of a network of power stations. On February 21, 1920, the Supreme Council of the National Economy, by agreement with the People's Commissariat of Agriculture, appointed a State Commission for the Electrification of Russia. The Commission began its work on March 20 and by the time the Eighth Congress of Soviets met it had compiled an over-all plan for the electrification of the R.S.F.S.R. The State Commission was set up on Lenin's initiative and in keeping with his directives. p. 514

[175] On November 14, 1920, Lenin attended the ceremony of the opening of an electric power station in the village of Kashino, Yaropolets Volost, Volokolamsk Uyezd, where he had been invited by the local peasants. Lenin spoke to the latter and then gave an address on the importance of electrification for the national economy. p. 517

[176] On December 22, 1920, Lenin attended a private conference of non-Party peasant delegates to the Eighth Congress of Soviets, which was called on Lenin's request by M. I. Kalinin, then Chairman of the All-Russia Central Executive Committee. The conference discussed the bill on measures to strengthen and develop agriculture adopted by the Council of People's Commissars on December 14, and submitted for consideration by the Congress. Lenin closely followed the debate, and took notes of the speeches. p. 520

[177] The meeting of the Communist group of the Congress, called in the morning of December 24, 1920, was devoted to a discussion of the bill presented by the Council of People's Commissars on measures to promote peasant farming. p. 525

[178] Lenin is referring to the following passage in his report on work in the countryside, which he delivered at the Eighth Congress of the R.C.P.(B.) on March 23, 1919: "Coercion applied to the middle peasants would cause untold harm" (see present edition, Vol. 29, p. 210). p. 525

[179] The reference is to the law on the socialisation of the land passed on January 18 (31), 1918, by the Third All-Russia Congress of Soviets which was held on January 10-18 (23-31), 1918.

Clause 6 of the law read: "All livestock and agricultural implements in private possession shall pass, without indemnification, from the hands of the non-working farmers exploiting the labour of others into the hands of uyezd, gubernia, regional and federative Soviets, depending on the importance of the implements and livestock transferred." p. 528

[180] The reference is to the armed uprising in Moscow in December 1905, during the first Russian revolution. In December 1905 and

January 1906 the uprising spread to Nizhni-Novgorod, Rostov-on-Don, Novorossiisk, the Donets coal basin, Ekaterinoslav, Perm (Motovilikha Plant), Ufa, Krasnoyarsk, and Chita. Large-scale armed uprisings took place in the Trans-Caucasus, Poland, the Baltic provinces and Finland, which were ruthlessly suppressed by the tsarist government.

The December armed uprising was the peak of the first Russian revolution. Lenin wrote about the uprising in his article "Lessons of the Moscow Uprising" (see present edition, Vol. 11, pp. 171-78). p. 535

THE LIFE AND WORK OF

V. I. LENIN

Outstanding dates

(April-December 1920)

1920

April-May	Lenin writes *"Left-Wing" Communism—an Infantile Disorder.*
	In a letter to K. A. Timiryazev Lenin gives a high appraisal of the latter's book *Science and Democracy.*
April 29	Lenin speaks on the foreign and domestic situation of the Soviet Republic at the Fourth All-Russia Congress of glass and porcelain workers.
May 1	In the morning Lenin participates in a subbotnik in the Kremlin.
	At 2 p.m. Lenin speaks at a meeting dedicated to the laying of the foundation stone of a monument to Karl Marx in Teatralnaya Square (now Sverdlov Square).
	At 3 p.m. Lenin speaks at a meeting dedicated to the laying of the foundation stone of a monument to Liberated Labour on the Moskva River embankment, visits an exhibition of the designs for the future monument at the Museum of Fine Arts (now the Pushkin Museum of Fine Arts).
	Lenin speaks at meetings in Zamoskvorechye and Baumansky districts in Moscow, at the inauguration of the Zagorsky Workers' Palace of Blagusha-Lefortovo district and at the meeting of workers of the Prokhorov manufacture in Red Presnya district.
May 2	Lenin's article "From the First Subbotnik on the Moscow-Kazan Railway to the All-Russia May Day Subbotnik" is published in the handbill *Pervomaisky Subbotnik.*
May 4	Lenin presides over a meeting of the Council of People's Commissars; submits for approval the message of greetings to the Government of the Azerbaijan Soviet Republic, which is endorsed

by the Council. The meeting also discusses the measures to help the Western front, the composition of a commission to be appointed to prepare materials on the formation of the Tatar Autonomous Soviet Socialist Republic, and other questions.

May 4 or 5 Lenin sends a telegram to all gubernia executive committees, the Moscow and the Petrograd city executive committees and gubernia revolutionary committees, instructing them to assist the Central Statistical Board and its local branches in taking an all-Russia census of the population.

May 5 Lenin addresses a parade of troops leaving for the Polish front, in Teatralnaya Square.

Lenin speaks on the tasks in the defence of the Soviet Republic against the attack of bourgeois-landowner Poland, at a joint session of the All-Russia Central Executive Committee, the Moscow Soviet and representatives of the trade unions and factory committees of Moscow.

Lenin sends a message of greetings to the Soviet Socialist Government of Azerbaijan on the formation of an independent Soviet Republic of Azerbaijan.

In a letter to M. N. Pokrovsky, Lenin writes about the need to publish a dictionary of present-day Russian.

May 7 In a letter to the 30th Regiment of Red Communards of the Turkestan front Lenin thanks them for the macaroni and flour sent to him. The products were given to the children of Moscow.

May 10 Lenin directs an emergency session of the Council of Labour and Defence to discuss the supply of the armies on the Western front with munitions and clothing.

May 12 Lenin writes the Appendix to his *"Left-Wing" Communism—an Infantile Disorder.*

Lenin sends a directive to the Revolutionary Military Council of the Caucasus front demanding the immediate dispatch of divisions to help the Western front.

May 13 Lenin delivers a speech on the international situation at an enlarged conference of workers and Red Army men of Rogozhsko-Simonovsky district.

May 14 Lenin directs a session of the Council of Labour and Defence, which discusses the supply of armies on the Western front with clothes, the food situation in the Donets Basin, and production of cartridges, rifles and machine-guns. Lenin raises the question of building narrow-gauge railway lines for the transportation of timber.

May 18 Lenin presides over a session of the Council of People's Commissars, reports on Stalin's appointment as member of the Revolutionary Military Council of the Republic, Y. S. Hanecki's co-optation into the Central Union of Consumers' Societies and the extension of the sphere of activity of the Caucasian Soviet Labour Army to include the Don region and the whole of the Soviet Caucasus.

May 20 Lenin's reply to the Indian Revolutionary Association is published.

May 21 Lenin writes a letter to Serafimovich conveying his condolences on the death of the latter's son.

Lenin directs a session of the Council of Labour and Defence which discusses the supply of the army with cartridges, rifles and machine-guns, the shipment of motor vehicles for the army, food supplies for the workers of the Chief Leather Committee, and of the oilfields in Baku and Astrakhan, supply of fuel to Petrograd, etc.

May 23 Lenin writes his letter "To Petrograd Party Workers" containing instructions on the publication of *"Left-Wing" Communism—an Infantile Disorder*.

May 25 Lenin writes his comments on the draft decree on measures for proper distribution of housing accommodations among working people.

May 26 Lenin writes a draft decision of the Council of People's Commissars on food procurements.

Lenin talks with a delegation of British workers.

May 27 Lenin writes amendments and addenda to the draft decision of the Council of People's Commissars on higher technical educational establishments.

May 30 Lenin writes his "Letter to the British Workers".

June 1	Lenin draws up a plan of theses on the national and the colonial questions for the Second Congress of the Communist International.
June 2	Lenin sends a telegram to Stalin, member of the Revolutionary Military Council of the South-Western front, informing him of the situation on the Western and the Caucasus fronts and indicating the need of vigorously prosecuting the offensive to Kiev, and of sending reinforcements there from the Crimea.
June 4	Lenin receives Mr. Fuse, correspondent of the Japanese newspapers *Osaka Mainichi* and *Tokyo Nichi-Nichi*.
	Lenin writes a note to the State Publishing House and the Supreme Council of the National Economy asking that comrades from Kirghizia be provided with a typefoundry, a printing press and stocks of paper.
June 5	Lenin writes "Preliminary Draft Theses on the National and the Colonial Questions (For the Second Congress of the Communist International)".
Beginning of June	Lenin writes "Preliminary Draft Theses on the Agrarian Question (For the Second Congress of the Communist International)".
June 8-10	*"Left-Wing" Communism—an Infantile Disorder* is published.
June 12	Lenin writes a review of issues Nos. 1-18 of the journal *Kommunismus*, organ of the Communist International for the countries of South-Eastern Europe, published in German in Vienna
	Lenin speaks on the international situation of the Soviet Republic and the current tasks of the Party in the countryside, at the Second All-Russia Conference of organisers responsible for rural work.
June 13	Lenin writes amendments and addenda to the draft decision of the C.C. R.C.P.(B.) on the tasks of the R.C.P.(B.) in Turkestan.
June 18	Lenin directs a meeting of the Council of Labour and Defence, which discusses the defence of the country against the Polish offensive, revision of the list of militarised enterprises and other questions.

June 19	Speaking at a meeting of the Executive Committee of the Communist International, Lenin criticises the policy of the French Socialist Party and of the Right wing of the Italian Socialist Party.
June 20	Lenin instructs the Deputy People's Commissar of Education to give help to the Pulkovo Observatory.
June 29	Lenin writes a note to the Secretariat of the C.C. R.C.P.(B.) proposing to obligate the State Publishing House to arrange for the translation and publication of new economic works and a number of works by materialist philosophers of the seventeenth and eighteenth centuries.
June	Lenin writes "The Plan of the Resolution on the Content of the Concept 'Dictatorship of the Proletariat' and on the Struggle Against the 'Fashionable' Distortion of This Slogan".
July 2	Lenin writes the appeal "Aid the Wounded of the Red Army!"
July 4	Lenin writes his "Theses on the Fundamental Tasks of the Second Congress of the Communist International".
July 6	Lenin writes the preface to the French and German editions of his *Imperialism, the Latest Stage of Capitalism.*
July 8	Lenin gives directives on checking the English, French and German translations of the pamphlet *"Left-Wing" Communism—an Infantile Disorder.*
July 10	Lenin writes a letter to Chicherin concerning the text of the treaty with Lithuania.
Between July 10 and 19	Lenin prepares his report on the international situation and the fundamental tasks of the Communist International for the Second Congress of the Communist International.
Not later than July 18	In a letter to the Communist International Executive Committee, Lenin sets forth his plan of theses on the economic and political situation in the world for the Second Congress of the Third, Communist International.
July 18	Lenin leaves for Petrograd to take part in the proceedings of the Second Congress of the Communist International.

July 19-August 7	The Second Congress of the Communist International is held. Its work is directed by Lenin.
July 19	At the first session of the Congress, Lenin is elected to the Presidium; he delivers a report on the international situation and the fundamental tasks of the Communist International.
	Lenin speaks at a meeting dedicated to the laying of the foundation stone of a monument to Karl Liebknecht and Rosa Luxemburg on Uritsky Square in Petrograd. The meeting is attended by delegates to the Congress.
	Lenin and Congress delegates lay wreaths on the graves of revolutionary fighters on the Mars Field in Petrograd.
July 20	Lenin returns to Moscow.
July 23	Lenin presides over the second session of the Second Congress of the Comintern, which has moved to Moscow; he speaks on the role of the Communist Party.
July 24	The third session of the Congress elects Lenin to the commission on the international situation and the fundamental tasks of the Communist International, the commission on the national and the colonial questions, and the commission on the agrarian question.
July 25	Lenin directs the work of the commission on the national and the colonial questions and delivers a speech.
	Lenin's theses on the terms of admission into the Communist International and his proposal concerning the formation of the leading bodies of the parties applying for admission (Article 20 of the terms of admission into the Comintern) are discussed and approved at a meeting of the commission of the Congress.
	Lenin writes critical remarks on Levi's theses on the national and the colonial questions, exposing his nationalist stand.
July 26	Lenin directs the work of the Congress commissions on the agrarian question and the fundamental tasks of the Communist International. The commissions approve Lenin's theses on the questions under discussion.

Lenin addresses the fourth session of the Congress on behalf of the commission on the national and the colonial questions and submits his theses approved by the commission.

July 28 Lenin's theses on the national and the colonial questions are unanimously adopted at the fifth session of the Second Congress of the Communist International.

July 30 Lenin addresses the eighth session of the Congress during the debate on the terms of admission into the Communist International. Lenin's theses are approved by the Congress.

July Lenin writes a note to Kursky asking him if steps have been taken to establish Soviet power without delay, drive out the landowners and transfer their lands to the poor peasants and the Soviets of farm labourers in the areas liberated by the Red Army.

Lenin writes his critical comments on the French Socialist Party's declaration to the Second Congress of the Communist International.

August 2 Lenin sends a telegram to Stalin informing him of the decision of the Political Bureau of the Party C.C. to constitute a separate Southern front, in view of the increased threat from Wrangel.

Lenin addresses the tenth session of the Congress during the debate on parliamentarianism.

August 3 Lenin replies to the telegram by Stalin who expressed his dissatisfaction with the Party C.C.'s decision to constitute a separate Southern front, emphasising the correctness of the C.C. decision.

August 4 The thirteenth session of the Second Congress of the Communist International discusses and unanimously approves Lenin's theses on the agrarian question.

Lenin sends a telegram to Stalin asking for the appraisal of the situation on the South-Western and the Wrangel fronts.

August 6 Lenin addresses the sixteenth session of the Second Congress of the Communist International on the British Communist Party's affiliation to the Labour Party.

August 7	Lenin attends the first sitting of the newly elected Executive Committee of the Communist International.
	Lenin writes to the State Publishing House, indicating the need to translate the material appearing in Soviet newspapers, as well as in Communist and bourgeois newspapers of various countries and publish monthly pamphlets in foreign languages exposing the imperialist policy of the Entente.
August 11	Lenin sends a telegram to Stalin informing him of the progress of the peace talks with Poland and instructing him to intensify the offensive on the Crimean front in order to complete the rout of Wrangel and liberate the whole of the Crimea.
August 15	Lenin writes his "Letter to the Austrian Communists".
August 18	Lenin sends a telegram to the Revolutionary Military Council of the Western front instructing it to intensify the offensive against the Poles.
	Lenin forwards to the "small" Council of People's Commissars Gorky's request that the Petrograd scientists be provided with increased food rations, proposing that the request be granted.
August 19	Lenin sends a telegram to the Revolutionary Military Council of the Western front, instructing it to send without delay reinforcements of Byelorussian workers and peasants to the front.
August 20	Lenin directs a meeting of the Council of Labour and Defence which discusses the Kashira power project, special measures to be taken in the case of the retreat of the Soviet troops on the Wrangel front, the supplying of Moscow with firewood and other questions.
August 28	Lenin fills in a registration form of the all-Russia census of the population.
September 1	In a note to the Rumyantsev Museum library (now the Lenin Library) Lenin asks to be lent two best available Greek-German, Greek-French, Greek-Russian or Greek-English dictionaries, the best philosophical dictionaries, dictionaries of philosophical terms in German, French, English or Russian and books on the history of Greek philosophy.

	Lenin reports to the Second All-Russia Congress of the Union of Workers of Education and Socialist Culture on the current situation.
September 2	Lenin writes the preface to the second edition of *Materialism and Empirio-Criticism.*
September 6	Lenin sends on to the Podolsk Uyezd Food Committee an appeal by the peasants of the village of Bogdanovo to cut down the food requisitioning quotas and writes a telephone message ordering an immediate consideration of the appeal and reducing the quotas as much as possible.
September 14	Lenin directs a meeting of the Council of People's Commissars which discusses grain requisitioning, the establishment of the Turkestan Autonomous Soviet Socialist Republic, etc.
September 17	Lenin receives a peasant delegate from Siberia and in the course of the talk makes notes on the measures to improve the condition of the peasants in Siberia.
September 20	Lenin directs a plenary meeting of the Party C.C. which discusses the peace talks with Poland, the All-Russia Conference of the R.C.P.(B.) and other questions.
September 22-25	Lenin directs the work of the Ninth All-Russia Conference of the R.C.P.(B.).
September 22	Lenin opens the Conference and is elected to the Presidium; he delivers the political report of the C.C. and makes amendments to the resolution on the Polish question. At the evening session of the Conference Lenin closes the debate on the political report of the C.C.
Before September 23	Lenin edits the draft declaration of the All-Russia Central Executive Committee on the terms of peace with Poland.
September 24	Lenin writes the draft resolution "The Immediate Tasks of Party Development" for the All-Russia Conference of the R.C.P.(B.). Lenin addresses the evening session of the Conference during the debate on the report on the immediate tasks of Party development.

	Lenin writes the "Letter to the German and the French Workers. Regarding the Discussion on the Second Congress of the Communist International".
Not later than September 28	Lenin writes a letter to the Congress of the Czechoslovak Communist Party.
September 29	Lenin writes proposals for the Conference resolution "The Immediate Tasks of Party Development".
October 2	Lenin speaks on the tasks of the youth leagues, at the Third All-Russia Congress of the Russian Young Communist League.
	Lenin speaks on the foreign and domestic situation of the Soviet Republic at the Congress of leather industry workers.
	Lenin writes an appeal "To the Poor Peasants of the Ukraine".
October 8	Lenin writes a draft resolution for the *Proletcult* congress and submits it for consideration by the Party's C.C.
October 12	Lenin takes part in the funeral of Inessa Armand on Red Square.
The middle of October	Lenin receives H. G. Wells, the British writer.
October 15	Lenin reports on the foreign and domestic situation of the Soviet Republic, at a conference of chairmen of uyezd, volost and village Executive Committees of the Soviets of Moscow Gubernia.
October 16	Lenin telegraphs instructions to Frunze on preparations for capture of the Crimea.
October 19	Lenin writes notes on the immediate tasks of the Party after the termination of the war against Wrangel.
October 20	Lenin writes the article "A Contribution to the History of the Question of the Dictatorship".
October 21	In a letter to the Presidium of the Petrograd Soviet, Lenin directs that scientists would be provided with additional accommodation (for study rooms and laboratories) in the distribution of flats.

	Lenin receives a delegation of Stavropol peasants who have brought grain for Moscow children, discusses their needs and addresses a letter to the People's Commissariat of Food asking it to prepare, by the next morning, its conclusions as to the possibility of meeting the peasants' requests.
October 24	Lenin telegraphs a directive to the Revolutionary Military Council of the First Cavalry Army for steps to be taken for the speedy defeat of Wrangel.
October 27	Lenin talks to a delegation of the Party Conference of Alexandrov Uyezd, Vladimir Gubernia; after learning of abuses at the Troitsky Factory, he writes a letter to the Vladimir Gubernia Committee of the Party and directs the delegation to Dzerzhinsky, head of the Central Control Commission.
	Lenin attends a show of a film about the operation of a new hydraulic peat-suction machine designed by engineer Klasson and then calls a conference to discuss the invention.
October 28	In a telegram to Frunze, Lenin gives directives for measures to be immediately taken for the dispatch of heavy artillery to the Crimean front-line, so as to ensure the success of the operation aimed at the liberation of the Crimea.
October 29	Lenin sends a telegram to Stalin in Baku instructing him to take urgent steps to fortify the approaches to Baku from the land and the sea.
Before November 1	Lenin writes amendments and addenda to the draft decree on the centralisation of libraries in the R.S.F.S.R.
Beginning of November	Lenin writes his theses for the resolution "The Tasks of the Trade Unions, and the Methods of Their Accomplishment" and a draft resolution for the R.C.P.(B.) group of the Fifth All-Russia Conference of Trade Unions.
November 3	Lenin delivers a speech on the main tasks of the Chief Committee for Political Education and local political education departments at an All-Russia Conference of Political Education Workers of Gubernia and Uyezd Education Departments.

November 4 Lenin writes the article "On the Struggle Within the Italian Socialist Party".

November 6 Lenin writes to Krzhizhanovsky on the tasks of the State Commission for the Electrification of Russia.

Lenin delivers a speech on the third anniversary of the October Revolution, at a joint plenum of the Moscow Soviet, the Moscow Committee of the R.C.P.(B.) and the Moscow City Trade Union Council.

November 7 Lenin delivers a speech on the third anniversary of the October Revolution, at a plenary meeting of the Sokolniki District Soviet attended by representatives of factory trade union committees.

November 9 Lenin directs a plenary meeting of the Party C.C. which discusses and approves in a preliminary way the draft theses on the tasks of trade unions, drawn up by Lenin.

November 12 Lenin sends a telegram to the Revolutionary Military Council of the Southern front, in which he formulates the conditions of Wrangel's capitulation.

November 13 In a telegram to Stalin, Lenin asks about the progress of the struggle against the bands in the Caucasus and the fortification of the approaches to Baku; he also asks Stalin's opinion as to the prospects of a peaceful settlement of relations between the R.S.F.S.R., and Georgia and Armenia.

Lenin receives the chairman of the group committee of the Grozny oilfields, who has brought a message of greetings from the workers.

November 14 Lenin attends the commissioning of a power electric station in the village of Kashino in Volokolamsk Uyezd of Moscow Gubernia, talks to the peasants, and makes a speech on the importance of electrification for the country's economy; in the evening, Lenin addresses a meeting of peasants in the People's House in the village of Yaropolets.

November 16 Lenin has a talk with a peasant delegate from Mosalsk Uyezd of Kaluga Gubernia, makes notes of the peasants' needs and writes to the People's Commissariat of Food and the People's Commissariat of Agriculture, asking for information on the possibility of satisfying the peasants' needs.

November 18 Lenin writes his "Theses on Production Propaganda (Rough Draft)".

Lenin speaks at a meeting of delegates of Party organisations of Baumansky district in Moscow.

November 19 Lenin directs and addresses a meeting of delegates to the Moscow Gubernia Party Conference, which discusses nominations for the Moscow Committee of the R.C.P.(B.).

November 20 Lenin writes notes on the electrification of Yaropolets Volost, Volokolamsk Uyezd, Moscow Gubernia.

November 20-22 Lenin takes part in the Moscow Gubernia Party Conference.

November 21 Lenin delivers a speech on "Our Foreign and Domestic Position and the Tasks of the Party" at the Conference.

Lenin speaks on the elections to the Moscow Committee of the R.C.P.(B.).

November 25 Lenin speaks on the foreign and domestic situation of the Soviet Republic, at a conference of factory T.U. committees of Moscow printing and publishing enterprises.

November 26 Lenin speaks on concessions at a meeting of cells' secretaries of the Moscow organisation of the R.C.P.(B.).

November 29 Lenin writes to Lunacharsky on the reorganisation of the People's Commissariat of Education.

Lenin reports on the results of the work of the Moscow Gubernia Party Conference at a general meeting of Communists of Zamoskvorechye district and closes the debate on his report.

December 2 Lenin sends a telegram to the Chairman of the Revolutionary Military Committee of Armenia conveying greetings to Soviet Armenia on her liberation from the imperialist yoke.

December 6	Lenin speaks on concessions at a meeting of activists of the Moscow Party organisation. Lenin sends greetings to the All-Russia Conference of Gubernia Departments for Work Among Women.
December 7	Lenin directs a plenary meeting of the Party C.C. which discusses the conflict between water transport workers and the Central Committee of the Railway and Water Transport Union. The meeting approves Lenin's proposal for calling the Tenth Party Congress on February 6, 1921.
December 8	Lenin directs a plenary meeting of the Party C.C., submits his theses on production propaganda, and writes a draft decision of the C.C. "Statute of the People's Commissariat of Education".
December 11	Lenin writes the epilogue "False Talk on Freedom" to his article "On the Struggle Within the Italian Socialist Party".
December 15	Lenin reports on the foreign and domestic situation of the Soviet Republic, at a meeting of the peasants of the village of Modenovo, Bogorodsk Volost, Vereya Uyezd, Moscow Gubernia.
December 18	Lenin sends a telegram to the Vladikavkaz Revolutionary Committee instructing it to take urgent steps to provide Civil War refugees with permanent housing.
Between December 19 and 21	At Gorki Lenin works on the plan of his report on the work of the Council of People's Commissars for the Eighth All-Russia Congress of Soviets. In a letter to Krzhizhanovsky, Lenin outlines practical measures for the electrification of Russia.
December 21	Lenin reports on concessions at a meeting of the Communist group of the Eighth All-Russia Congress of Soviets. After the report, he replies to the questions from delegates.
December 22-29	The Eighth All-Russia Congress of Soviets is held. Its work is directed by Lenin.

December 22 The first session of the Congress elects Lenin to the Presidium; Lenin reports on the work of the Council of People's Commissars.

Lenin speaks on the foreign and home policy of the Soviet Government, at a meeting of the Communist group of the Congress.

Lenin attends a conference of non-Party peasant delegates to the Eighth Congress of Soviets.

December 23 Lenin closes the debate on his report on the work of the Council of People's Commissars, at the second session of the Congress.

December 24 Lenin addresses the Communist group of the Congress.

December 27 Lenin addresses the Communist group of the Congress during the debate on the draft law on measures to strengthen and develop peasant farming and replies to the questions of delegates.

December 29 The seventh session of the Congress adopts Lenin's resolution on the report on electrification.

The seventh session of the Congress elects Lenin member of the All-Russia Central Executive Committee (Eighth Convocation).

December 30 Lenin delivers a speech on the trade unions, the current situation, and Trotsky's mistakes, at a joint meeting of R.C.P.(B.) members elected delegates to the Eighth Congress of Soviets, members of the All-Russia Central Council of Trade Unions, and the Moscow City Council of Trade Unions.

December 31 The plenary meeting of the All-Russia Central Executive Committee (Eighth Convocation) elects Lenin Chairman of the Council of People's Commissars.

December Lenin writes to Krzhizhanovsky on the drawing up of a plan for supplying electricity to every house in the R.S.F.S.R.

В. И. ЛЕНИН

СОЧИНЕНИЯ

Том 31

На английском языке